SILVER BURDETT & GINN

GENERAL SCIENCE

BOOK ONE

Series Authors

Peter Alexander, Ph.D.
Professor of Biology and Computer Science
St. Peter's College
Jersey City, New Jersey

Marilyn Fiegel, Ed.D.
Educational Consultant and
Former District Science Coordinator
West Seneca Central Schools
West Seneca, New York

Steven K. Foehr
Teacher of Science
Davisville Middle School
North Kingstown, Rhode Island

Anne F. Harris
Environmental Scientist
Black and Veatch, Engineers/Architects
Kansas City, Missouri

Joseph G. Krajkovich, Ed.D.
Principal
Martin Luther King School
Edison, New Jersey

Kenneth W. May
Chairperson, Science Department and
Teacher of Chemistry
Camden Central School
Camden, New York

Nicholas D. Tzimopoulos, Ph.D.
Director of Science
Public Schools of the Tarrytowns
North Tarrytown, New York

Rita K. Voltmer, Ph.D.
Assistant Professor of Science Education
Miami University
Oxford, Ohio

SILVER BURDETT & GINN
MORRISTOWN, NJ • NEEDHAM, MA
Atlanta, GA • Cincinnati, OH • Dallas, TX • Menlo Park, CA • Deerfield, IL

Content Reviewers

Teacher Reviewers

About the cover
The front and back covers illustrate a space shuttle being used to build a proposed
NASA space station. NASA's schedule calls for the space station assembly to begin
around 1995. More information about the shuttle, the space station, and other ways in
which space is being explored can be found in Chapter 15, Section 15•5 of this book.

Contents

Chapter 1   THE MEANING OF SCIENCE *viii*
1•1   How Scientists Think:
         Investigating Dinosaurs   *viii*
1•2   Science for People   *12*
1•3   Skills of Science   *16*

UNIT ONE   DISCOVERING LIFE SCIENCE   24

Chapter 2   THE CHARACTERISTICS OF LIFE   *26*
2•1   Traits of Living Things   *28*
2•2   The Chemicals of Life   *33*
2•3   The Structure of Cells   *36*
2•4   Transport in Cells   *40*
2•5   Energy for Cells   *45*
2•6   Cell Division   *48*

Chapter 3   THE SIMPLEST ORGANISMS   *54*
3•1   Classification in the Life Sciences   *56*
3•2   Viruses   *59*
3•3   Monerans   *62*
3•4   Protists   *68*
3•5   Fungi and Their Relatives   *74*

Chapter 4   PLANTS   *82*
4•1   Traits of Nonseed Plants   *84*
4•2   Algae   *86*
4•3   Mosses and Liverworts   *91*
4•4   Club Mosses, Horsetails, and Ferns   *94*
4•5   Traits of Seed Plants   *98*
4•6   Varieties of Seed Plants   *100*

Chapter 5   VERTEBRATES   *108*
5•1   Traits of Vertebrates   *110*
5•2   Fish   *113*
5•3   Amphibians   *117*
5•4   Reptiles   *120*
5•5   Birds   *123*
5•6   Mammals   *128*

Chapter 6   THE ENVIRONMENT   *136*
6•1   The Biosphere   *138*
6•2   Populations and Communities   *141*
6•3   Energy Flow in the Biosphere   *144*
6•4   Symbiotic Relationships   *148*
6•5   Preserving the Environment   *150*

UNIT TWO   DISCOVERING MATTER AND ENERGY ▬ *160*

**Chapter 7   PROPERTIES OF
                MATTER**   *162*
   7•1 What Is Matter?   *164*
   7•2 The Four States of Matter   *166*
   7•3 Physical Properties of Matter *168*
   7•4 Density and Specific Gravity *174*
   7•5 Physical Changes and
           Chemical Changes   *179*

Chapter 8   THE ATOM   *186*
   8•1 The Structure of the Atom   *188*
   8•2 How Atoms Differ   *192*
   8•3 How Atoms Are Represented   *197*
   8•4 The Periodic Table   *201*

Chapter 9   COMPOUNDS   *210*
   9•1 What Is a Compound?   *212*
   9•2 Symbols and Formulas   *214*
   9•3 Ionic Compounds   *219*
   9•4 Covalent Compounds   *226*

Chapter 10   MIXTURES   *232*
   10•1 Kinds of Mixtures   *234*
   10•2 Making Solutions   *238*
   10•3 Properties of Solutions   *243*
   10•4 Suspensions and Colloids   *249*

**Chapter 11   FORCE, ENERGY,
                 AND WORK**   *254*
   11•1 Force   *256*
   11•2 Forces in Fluids   *261*
   11•3 Energy   *264*
   11•4 Work and Power   *267*
   11•5 Simple Machines   *271*
   11•6 Compound Machines   *277*

Chapter 12   HEAT   *282*
   12•1 Heat Energy   *284*
   12•2 Change of State   *290*
   12•3 Expansion and Gases   *294*
   12•4 Heat Transfer   *297*
   12•5 Heat Engines   *301*

**Chapter 13   WAVES AND
                 SOUND**   *306*
   13•1 Properties of Waves   *308*
   13•2 Behavior of Waves   *313*
   13•3 Sound   *316*
   13•4 Properties of Sound   *320*
   13•5 Acoustics and Noise Pollution *325*

Chapter 14 THE EARTH AND THE MOON 336
- 14•1 Describing the Earth 338
- 14•2 The Earth's Movements 342
- 14•3 The Earth's Seasons 346
- 14•4 The Moon 349
- 14•5 The Earth's Origin 353

Chapter 15 THE SOLAR SYSTEM 360
- 15•1 Members of the Solar System 362
- 15•2 The Sun 366
- 15•3 The Inner Planets 371
- 15•4 The Outer Planets 376
- 15•5 Exploring Space 380

Chapter 16 EARTH'S RESOURCES 386
- 16•1 Earth's Minerals 388
- 16•2 Identifying Minerals 392
- 16•3 Natural Resources 397
- 16•4 Mineral Resources 402
- 16•5 Energy Resources 404

Chapter 17 EARTH'S HISTORY 412
- 17•1 The Record of Rocks 414
- 17•2 Fossils 417
- 17•3 Studying the Earth's Past 421
- 17•4 The Geologic Time Scale 426
- 17•5 Paleozoic, Mesozoic, and Cenozoic Eras 430

Chapter 18 EARTH'S ATMOSPHERE 438
- 18•1 The Atmosphere 440
- 18•2 Heat Transfer in the Atmosphere 444
- 18•3 Air Pressure 447
- 18•4 Wind 450
- 18•5 Types of Wind 452

Chapter 19 THE CHANGING WEATHER 460
- 19•1 Air Masses 462
- 19•2 Weather Fronts 466
- 19•3 Thunderstorms 471
- 19•4 Tornadoes 475
- 19•5 Hurricanes 478

Chapter 20 EARTH'S FRESH WATER 484
- 20•1 Water Budget 486
- 20•2 Ground Water 488
- 20•3 The Work of Ground Water 493
- 20•4 Two Great Rivers 497
- 20•5 Lakes and Ponds 500
- 20•6 The Great Lakes 503

UNIT FOUR   DISCOVERING THE HUMAN BODY   512

Chapter 21   SUPPORT, MOVEMENT, AND BODY COVERING   514

21•1   Organization of the Human Body   516
21•2   The Skeletal System   519
21•3   Structure and Growth of Bones   523
21•4   The Muscular System   525
21•5   Body Movement and Disorders   528
21•6   Skin   531

Chapter 22   NUTRITION AND DIGESTION   536

22•1   Carbohydrates, Proteins, and Fats   538
22•2   Vitamins, Minerals, and Water   541
22•3   A Balanced Diet   544
22•4   The Digestive System   548
22•5   Digestion and Absorption   552

Chapter 23   TRANSPORT, RESPIRATION, AND EXCRETION   558

23•1   Blood   560
23•2   Blood Vessels and Lymph   564
23•3   The Heart and Circulation   567
23•4   The Respiratory System   572
23•5   The Excretory System   577

Appendix 1   Taxonomy Tree   586
Appendix 2   Periodic Table of Elements   588
Appendix 3   Properties of Minerals   590
Appendix 4   Safety   592
Glossary   593
Index   604

ACTIVITIES

Chapter 1
Now try this   15
How Is Mass Measured Using a Balance?   18

Chapter 2
How Do Animal and Plant Cells Differ?   39
How Does Temperature Affect the Spreading of Food Coloring in Water?   43

Chapter 3
What Are the Characteristics of a Paramecium?   72
What Substances Do Yeasts Need for Growth?   76

Chapter 4
What Is the Structure of a Moss?   93
How Do Monocots and Dicots Differ?   104

Chapter 5
What Is the Structure of a Frog?   119
How Do Contour and Down Feathers Differ?   124

Chapter 6
What Are Some Biotic and Abiotic Factors?   138
What Interactions Occur in a Plot of Land?   141

Chapter 7
How Is Density Determined?   177
How Do Chemical and Physical Changes Differ?   181

Chapter 8
How Can Masses Be Compared?   196
How Is the Periodic Table Arranged?   206

Chapter 9
How Do Compounds Differ? — *213*
What Compounds Conduct Electricity? — *228*

Chapter 10
How Many Substances Are in Black Ink? — *236*
How Is a Supersaturated Solution Prepared? — *246*

Chapter 11
What Is the Center of Gravity? — *259*
How Can Work Be Calculated? — *269*

Chapter 12
How Is Heat Exchanged? — *289*
What Happens During a Change of State? — *292*

Chapter 13
What Are the Properties of Waves? — *312*
How Do Vibrations Produce Sound? — *317*

Chapter 14
The Surface of the Moon — *350*
What Model Can Illustrate the Nebular Hypothesis? — *355*

Chapter 15
The Solar System to Scale — *365*
How Do Meteorites Form Craters? — *374*

Chapter 16
How Can You Distinguish Between Unknown Liquids? — *389*
How Does Halite Cleave? — *394*

Chapter 17
How Do Molds and Casts Differ? — *418*
A Model of Geologic Time — *428*

Chapter 18
How Much Oxygen Does the Air Contain? — *441*
What Is the Greenhouse Effect? — *446*

Chapter 19
How Does an Air Mass Affect Weather? — *470*
How Is Tornado Alley Determined? — *476*

Chapter 20
How Does Permeability of Soil Differ? — *490*
How Does Water Hardness Affect Sudsing Action? — *494*

Chapter 21
What Is the Structure of a Bone? — *524*
How Does a Chicken Wing Move? — *529*

Chapter 22
How Can Food Be Tested for Starch? — *539*
What Nutrition Information Is on Food Labels? — *546*

Chapter 23
How Does the Pulse Vary? — *569*
How Can You Use a Model to Show Breathing? — *575*

SPECIAL FEATURES

Science in Careers
Animal Breeder — *156*
Park Ranger — *156*
Aeronautical Engineer — *330*
Paint Analyst — *330*
Surveyor — *508*
Civil Engineer — *508*
Food Lab Technician — *582*
Respiratory Therapist — *582*

People in Science
Dr. Nam-Hai Chua — *156*
Dr. Stephen Hawking — *330*
Dr. Florence van Straten — *508*
Dr. Angella D. Ferguson — *582*

Issues and Technology
Insecticides and the Food Web: Are Humans in Danger? — *157*
Is Personal Information Confidential? — *331*
Will the Decrease of Tropical Forestland Affect the Earth? — *509*
How Healthy Is Fast Food? — *583*

THE MEANING OF SCIENCE

1·1 How Scientists Think: Investigating Dinosaurs

*O*f the many kinds of dinosaurs discovered during
the last 100 years, one of the best-known is Brontosaurus. Brontosaurus, which lived 150 million years
ago, was a huge creature. It was as long as four cars
and weighed 25–30 tons.

　　After studying fossils of Brontosaurus, scientists
concluded that the bones were like those of reptiles,
such as lizards. But it was thought that the skeleton
of a lizardlike creature could not support the weight
of Brontosaurus. Most scientists thought that Brontosaurus must have been a sluggish animal that
spent much of its time in swamps and lakes, as in the

drawing at left. The water would have helped to support Brontosaurus's weight. Recently there have been new ideas about how Brontosaurus lived. Some scientists now think that Brontosaurus was an active animal that lived in forests. The drawing below is based on these newer ideas about Brontosaurus.

How do we know that Brontosaurus fossils are 150 million years old? Did Brontosaurus live in swamps and lakes or in forests? What can scientists tell about an animal's life by looking at its bones? Were dinosaurs dull lizardlike creatures or were they active like the mammals of today's earth? All of these questions are concerned with things in nature. Finding the answers to such questions is what science is all about.

Scientists unearthing fossil dinosaur bones and reconstructing a dinosaur skeleton.

The drawing shows some of the largest and smallest known dinosaurs, mammals, and reptiles. The size range of dinosaurs is closer to the size range of modern mammals than to the size range of modern reptiles.

Science is a method of obtaining knowledge about nature. Nature includes the earth, space, living things, and nonliving things. Scientists are men and women who try to find explanations for things they observe in nature.

Science often begins with curiosity. Questions about nature that begin with how? or why? or when? often form the start of a scientific process. Ever since the first dinosaur bones were found, over a century ago, people have wondered: How did dinosaurs live? Why did they disappear? Curiosity about dinosaurs has kept many scientists working for many decades. All this scientific work has led to many ideas about the life of dinosaurs. This work has also led to a better understanding of the history of life on the earth.

After asking a question about some part of nature, a scientist forms a hypothesis. A **hypothesis** is a proposed answer to a question about nature. A hypothesis is an educated guess about the answer to a problem. Hypotheses are often based on what is already known about a subject. Consider this question: How did dinosaurs carry on their lives? One hypothesis is that dinosaurs lived much as the cold-blooded lizards of today's earth live. This hypothesis is based on the fact that some dinosaur bones seem like larger versions of lizard bones. Scientists formed this hypothesis soon after dinosaur bones were first discovered.

22   21   20   19   18   17   16   15   14   13   12

Length

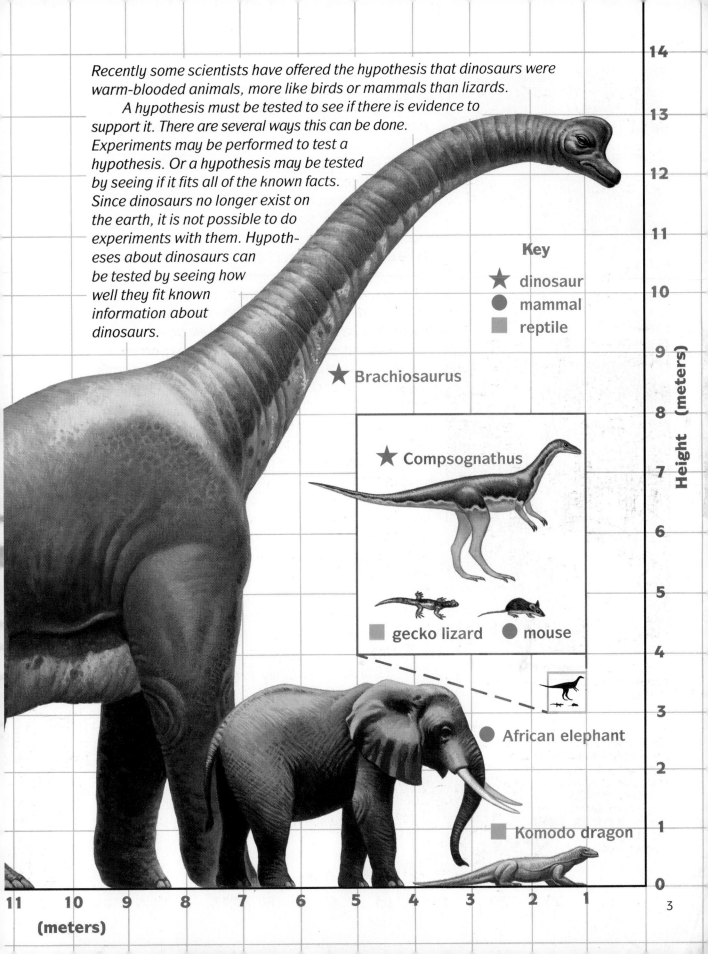

Recently some scientists have offered the hypothesis that dinosaurs were warm-blooded animals, more like birds or mammals than lizards.

A hypothesis must be tested to see if there is evidence to support it. There are several ways this can be done. Experiments may be performed to test a hypothesis. Or a hypothesis may be tested by seeing if it fits all of the known facts. Since dinosaurs no longer exist on the earth, it is not possible to do experiments with them. Hypotheses about dinosaurs can be tested by seeing how well they fit known information about dinosaurs.

Key
★ dinosaur
● mammal
■ reptile

★ Brachiosaurus

★ Compsognathus

■ gecko lizard   ● mouse

● African elephant

■ Komodo dragon

Height (meters)

14 13 12 11 10 9 8 7 6 5 4 3 2 1 0

11 10 9 8 7 6 5 4 3 2 1

(meters)

3

To consider the hypothesis that dinosaurs were like lizards, we must first learn about lizards. Lizards and other reptiles are cold-blooded animals. A lizard's body temperature rises and falls as the temperature of the environment rises and falls. A lizard spends much of its time resting, lying flat on its belly. The legs of a lizard stick out to the sides as shown in the drawing. Lizards become sluggish when the weather turns cold. They usually live as single individuals, rather than in groups. Most lizards do not care for their young. They lay eggs in a suitable place and then abandon them. Lizards have a scaly skin that offers little insulation from the cold.

How do warm-blooded animals differ from cold-blooded reptiles? Birds and mammals are warm-blooded animals. The body temperature of a bird or mammal remains fairly constant. Birds and mammals stand upright, with their legs beneath them. Notice the front legs of the wolf shown in the drawing.

Warm-blooded animals are far more active than lizards. Birds and mammals remain active even when the weather is cold. Many birds live in flocks, and mammals such as buffalo and zebra live in herds. Most birds and mammals take care of their young until the young can survive on their own. Birds have feathers, and mammals have fur. Feathers and fur help to insulate warm-blooded animals from the cold.

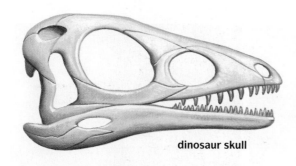

dinosaur skull

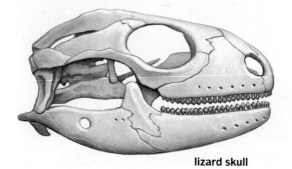

lizard skull

Were dinosaurs like lizards or were they more like warm-blooded animals? Which hypothesis best fits the facts? What can be learned from dinosaur fossils to help choose between these two hypotheses?

The skeletons of dinosaurs share several features with the skeletons of today's reptiles. Look at the drawings at left. Compare the skull of the lizard with the skull of the dinosaur. There are holes at the rear sides of the skulls of snakes, lizards, and crocodiles. As you can see, similar holes are found in the skulls of dinosaurs. This likeness was first noticed over a century ago. Each dinosaur skull that has been found since then has shared this feature. This repeated observation supports the hypothesis that dinosaurs were similar to lizards.

Dinosaur fossil skin imprint of *Scolosaurus*, an armored dinosaur.

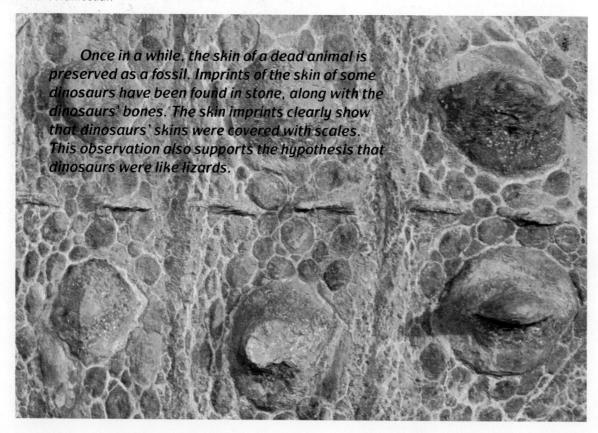

Once in a while, the skin of a dead animal is preserved as a fossil. Imprints of the skin of some dinosaurs have been found in stone, along with the dinosaurs' bones. The skin imprints clearly show that dinosaurs' skins were covered with scales. This observation also supports the hypothesis that dinosaurs were like lizards.

lizardlike
dinosaur

mammallike
dinosaur

Animals walking on damp soil leave footprints behind. A footprint can become a fossil if the soil it is in turns to stone. Fossil dinosaur footprints in stone have been found in many places. What can be learned from such footprints? In some places, rows of fossil footprints show how dinosaurs walked. Did dinosaurs walk like lizards or did they walk like warm-blooded animals? Because their elbows and knees stick out to the sides, the footprints of lizards are set wide apart. Warm-blooded animals walk with their feet closer together. Fossil dinosaur footprints show that dinosaurs walked with their legs fairly close together. Look at the picture at the top of the page. Notice that a lizardlike dinosaur could not have produced the dinosaur tracks that have been found.

These fossil tracks of *Brontosaurus* were found in Texas. Compare the size of the man with the size of the footprints.

In a few places, fossil footprints of many dinosaurs have been found together. It seems, then, that some dinosaurs traveled in herds. The smallest footprints were found in the middle of the group. Herds of elephants and some other mammals travel with their young in the center for protection. Could it be that the dinosaurs were protecting their young?

Fossil dinosaur eggs have been found many times, but several nests were found in Montana in 1978 and 1979. Some of these nests contained eggs, but one held fossil bones of 15 baby dinosaurs. Each of the baby dinosaurs was about 1 meter (3 feet) long. If baby dinosaurs stayed in the nest after hatching, how did they get food? Perhaps food was brought to them by their mother. Such actions are seen among warm-blooded birds but not among cold-blooded lizards.

Scientists have noticed a difference in the amount of food eaten by warm-blooded and cold-blooded animals. Warm-blooded animals eat much food to get the energy they need to keep their bodies warm. Cold-blooded animals eat far less. Lions, which are warm-blooded, and crocodiles, which are cold-blooded, are meat eaters. Both may feed on plant-eating animals. But, as shown above, it takes far fewer plant-eating animals to feed a crocodile than to feed a lion. Unlike a lion, a crocodile does not use food to make heat.

Another difference between the two groups of animals—warm-blooded and cold-blooded—is in the ratio of plant eaters to meat eaters. Among warm-blooded animals the ratio of meat eaters to plant eaters is low: only 1 meat eater for every 100 plant eaters. Among cold-blooded animals the ratio of meat eaters to plant eaters is much higher: 10 meat eaters for every 100 plant eaters. Fossil evidence indicates that, for dinosaurs, the ratio of meat eaters to plant eaters was low. Which hypothesis about dinosaurs does this evidence tend to support?

Two early views of dinosaurs: the engraving of an "extinct monster" (*left*) was done in the nineteenth century; the early-twentieth-century painting (*right*) shows a dinosaur called *agathaumas*, a type of *Triceratops*.

Neither of the ideas about how dinosaurs lived is accepted by all scientists. And neither idea can be accepted as a theory yet. A **theory** is a hypothesis that has been tested many times and that is supported by evidence. A theory can also be thought of as the best available explanation of some part of nature. As new information becomes available, theories change. The idea that dinosaurs were similar to cold-blooded lizards is a hypothesis. This hypothesis competes with the hypothesis that dinosaurs were warm-blooded.

The future may bring information that will support one hypothesis or show the other to be false. Or evidence may prove that both of these hypotheses are false, and they may be replaced with new hypotheses.

You will find a great deal of information in this book. The information itself is not science. Science is the methods, the activities, and the processes that produced the information in this book.

Current view of dinosaurs as active, not sluggish, animals.

1·2 Science for People

Information obtained through science often can be used in practical ways. Knowledge from science is often used to make people's lives better or easier. **Technology** is the use of scientific knowledge to improve the quality of human life. As you have learned, science is a way of getting knowledge about nature. Technology is using or applying that knowledge.

Products of technology are all around us. The paper these words are printed on is better and less costly than the paper your parent's textbooks were printed on. Better paper is a useful result of the scientific study of trees, wood, and the paper-making process. You may be wearing some products of technology. Much clothing is made from artificial fibers. The making of artificial fibers is a form of technology that resulted from the scientific study of how substances can be made to combine.

The production of artificial fibers for use in clothing is an example of technology.

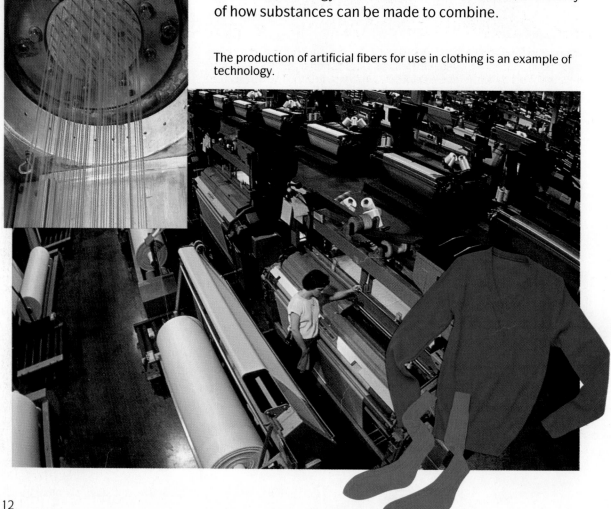

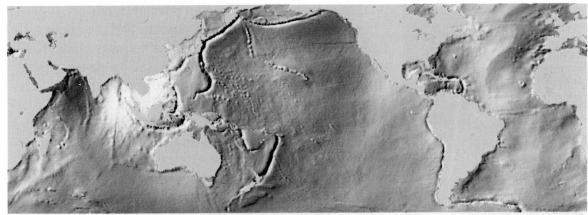

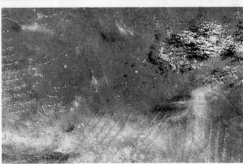

Data from Seasat produced this world view of the features of the ocean floor (*top*). Hurricane Allen (*left*) was photographed by GOES, a weather satellite. This Landsat image shows a rain forest (*right*). The blue-white areas are places where trees and other plants have been cleared.

Another example of technology is based on the scientific study of gravity and of how planets move around the sun. From these studies, scientists have learned how to keep artificial satellites in orbit around the earth. Today many such satellites orbit the earth. These satellites follow weather patterns and search for mineral deposits. Some satellites transmit information and television pictures from one continent to another. Others locate fish in the ocean or measure the health of crops.

The scientific study of living things often gives rise to new ways of improving people's health. Medicine is partly a technology that uses information that comes from the study of life. Scientists have studied the kidneys of animals. Kidneys are natural filters in an animal's body that remove wastes from the blood. Knowledge of how kidneys work has been applied to the design of kidney machines, such as the one shown. These machines can filter wastes from the blood of a person whose own kidneys are damaged or have had to be removed.

This woman is using a portable kidney machine.

13

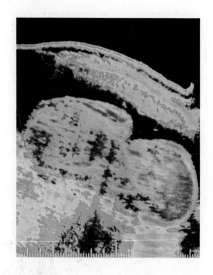

Technology has also produced many kinds of new equipment that allow doctors to find out about a person's health. The photograph at left was made by a machine that uses sound waves to see inside a person's body. Such photographs are called sonograms. Sonograms are often used to see a baby inside its mother's body. The sonogram tells about the baby's size and position. Such information allows doctors to see that a baby will be born in a normal and healthy way.

The scientific study of plants and the way they grow has many practical applications. Information about plants has been used to produce improved varieties of crops. These crops produce more food from less land. They provide more food for the ever-growing population of the world. Improved crops may contain more food value, may taste better, or may be easier to store. Which of the foods below would you prefer, the wild varieties or the improved varieties?

You have seen that technology affects many parts of our lives. Technology affects the things we wear, our health, and the things we eat. Technology is intended to improve people's lives. However, technology sometimes has unwanted side effects.

The scientific study of chemicals has resulted in new ways to make chemicals combine. This information has led to the development of many kinds of plastics. Many things are packaged in plastic wrapping or containers. However, plastic wastes can cause pollution. Many plastic containers are thrown away each day, resulting in large amounts of garbage. Getting rid of plastic waste is a growing problem in many cities.

As new technologies arise, people must be aware of problems that might result. Someday you may have to make decisions about balancing the advantages and disadvantages of a new technology. Studying science will help to prepare you to make these decisions.

Now try this

Many people are not aware of the amount of plastic waste that they discard. Do a 2-week survey of the plastic waste that the members of your household throw away. Set up a separate garbage bag or box for plastic waste, such as empty food and beverage containers. Ask the members of your household to throw plastic waste into this bag or box. At the end of the 2-week period, make a list of each plastic item. Then record the total weight of all the plastic waste.

Look at the list you have made. Next to each plastic item, suggest another type of material that might be used to make that item. Keep in mind the cost of the material you suggest and whether it might also cause pollution problems. Record this information in your list.

You may wish to discuss your findings with the other members of your household. Perhaps you can work together to find ways to reduce the amount of plastic waste you discard.

1·3 Skills of Science

Look at the two horizontal lines in the drawing shown. Are the two lines the same length? Or is one line longer than the other? Can you think of a way to find out for sure? Things are not always what they seem. Scientists must make accurate measurements to test hypotheses about nature. Many kinds of tools are used by scientists in making measurements.

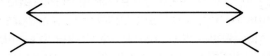

Scientists send their results to other scientists around the world. For this reason, measurements must have the same meaning in all countries. When a scientist describes the size of a dinosaur bone, that description should have a clear meaning to any other scientist.

In 1960 a modern system of measurement was adopted by most of the world's countries. It is known as the International System of Units, or *SI*. Four important units used in SI are the meter (m), kilogram (kg), liter (L), and second (s). Each unit can be made larger or smaller by multiplying or dividing by ten. Prefixes are used to show how many times the unit is multiplied or divided.

Table 1·1
Units of Measurement

Measurement	Unit	Symbol
length	meter	m
mass	kilogram	kg
volume	liter	L
temperature	degree Celsius	°C
time	second	s

Table 1·2 *Common Prefixes for SI Units*

PREFIX	MEANING	SYMBOL	EXAMPLE
kilo-	one thousand	k	1 km, or 1 kilometer, is 1000 meters.
centi-	one hundredth	c	1 cm, or 1 centimeter, is 1/100 (.01) of 1 meter.
milli-	one thousandth	m	1 mm, or 1 millimeter, is 1/1000 (.001) of 1 meter.
micro-	one millionth	μ	1 μm, or 1 micrometer, is 1/1,000,000 (.000001) of 1 meter.

The prefix is added to the name of the unit. Table 1•2 shows some of the prefixes used with SI units. How many meters are there in a kilometer? What part of a liter is a milliliter?

The **meter** (m) is the SI unit used when measuring length or distance. A meter is slightly longer than a yard. Length can be measured with a meterstick or a metric ruler. Metersticks and metric rulers are marked in centimeters (cm). Look at Table 1•2 to see what part of a meter a centimeter is. The smallest markings on a metric ruler show millimeters (mm). There are 10 mm in 1 cm. In the photograph, how wide is the stamp in mm and in cm?

The **kilogram** (kg) is the SI unit used to measure mass. *Mass* is a measure of the amount of matter in an object. Mass is different from weight. Weight is a measure of the force of gravity acting on matter. Gravity is not constant from place to place. The force of gravity is less on the moon than on the earth. Thus an object weighs less on the moon than on the earth. But the object's mass is the same in both places.

Mass is measured with a device called a balance. There are several types of balances. A double-pan balance works like a seesaw. The object to be measured is placed on one pan. Objects of known mass are added to the other pan until the pans balance. When the pans balance, the total of the known masses is equal to the mass of the unknown object.

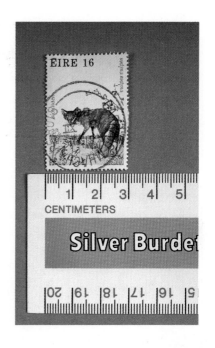

A double-pan balance is used to measure mass.

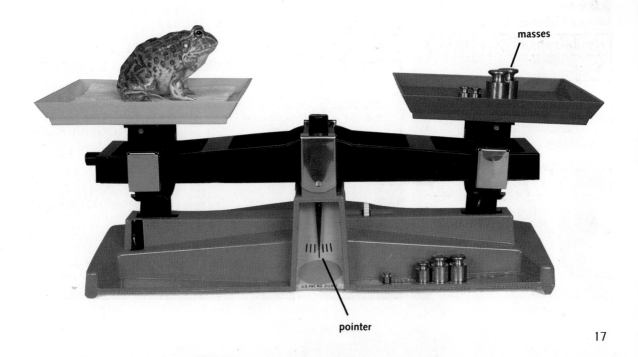

masses

pointer

How Is Mass Measured Using a Balance?

Measure the mass of various objects in metric units, using a balance.

balance and masses, small objects, forceps

A. Study the drawing that shows the labeled parts of a balance. Find these parts on your balance.

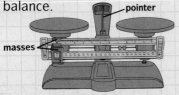

B. Notice the pointer and the scale in the center of the balance. The long line at the center of the scale is the zero point. When the pans are empty, the pointer should line up with the zero point. This means that your balance is zeroed. If your balance is not zeroed, use the adjustment knob to zero the balance.

C. Place a small object on the left pan. Use forceps to pick up and place masses on the right pan. Continue adding masses until the balance is again zeroed. When the balance is zeroed, the mass of the object is equal to the total of the masses on the right pan. Record the mass of the object.

D. Repeat step **C** to determine the masses of other objects.

1. For each object, give the mass in grams and in milligrams.
2. Would the results of this activity be affected if it were done on the moon? Explain why or why not.

The **liter** (L) is a unit of volume. *Volume* is a measure of how much space something takes up. The volume of liquids can be measured with a graduated cylinder, or graduate. A graduate is marked in milliliters (mL). Notice that the liquid curves upward at the sides of the graduate shown below. This curved surface is a *meniscus*. To read a graduate, view the liquid's surface at eye level. Read the mark that lines up with the lowest point of the meniscus. What is the volume of the liquid in the graduate shown?

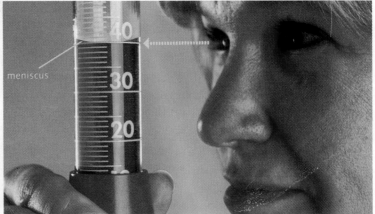

The volume of a solid can be measured in two ways. When a solid has a regular shape, its dimensions can be used. The volume of a box, for example, can be measured by multiplying its three dimensions (Volume = length x width x height). A box that is 5 cm by 4 cm by 3 cm has a volume of 60 cubic centimeters (cm³), as shown. A volume of 1 cm³ is equal to 1 mL. What is the volume of a box that is 8 cm by 4 cm by 6 cm?

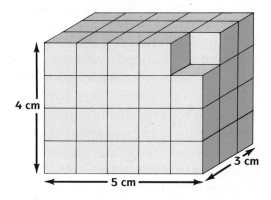

When an object does not have a regular shape, its volume can still be measured. The object is placed in a graduate that is partly filled with water. The amount of water that the object displaces is equal to its volume. What is the volume of the rock in the drawing at right?

The **degree Celsius** (°C) is a unit for measuring temperature. On the Celsius scale, water freezes at 0° and boils at 100°. Find the normal body temperature of humans on the Celsius thermometer shown.

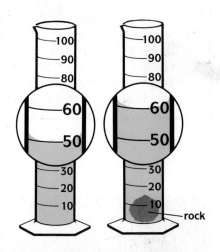

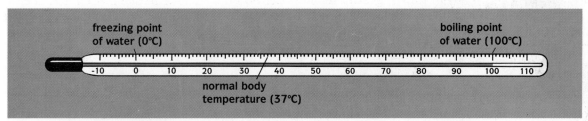

Time is the interval between two events. Measurements of time are needed to study how objects move. The SI unit of time is the *second* (s). In the present system there are 60 seconds in a minute, 60 minutes in an hour, and 24 hours in a day. This system is used everywhere on the earth. Stop watches used in laboratories and at sporting events can measure time in hundredths or thousandths of a second.

One of the most important tools of the scientist is a technique called a controlled experiment. A **controlled experiment** is a method for testing hypotheses. Recall that a hypothesis is a proposed answer to a question about nature. A controlled experiment usually has two parts or groups. One part is called the *control* or the *control group*. The other part is the *experimental group*. For some experiments the terms *control setup* and *experimental setup* are used. The experimental group differs from the control group in only one factor or condition. The factor that makes the experimental group different from the control is called a *variable*.

At the end of the experiment, the two groups are compared with each other. The scientist must then determine if the variable affected the experimental group. It is best to have only one variable in an experiment. An experiment with more than one variable may give confusing results. It may be hard to decide which one of the variables affected the experimental group.

Consider the hypothesis that tomato plants grow faster at temperatures higher than room temperature. A controlled experiment to test this hypothesis might be done in this way: A large number of tomato plants of the same size are divided into two groups. The two groups of plants are grown in the same soil and given the same amounts of water, light, and plant food. The variable in the experiment is temperature. The control group is kept at 21°C (70°F), which is room temperature. The experimental group is kept at 30°C (86°F).

control setup

experimental setup

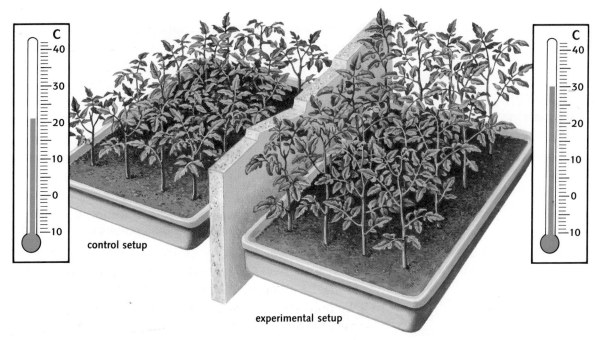

control setup

experimental setup

During the experiment the height of each plant is regularly measured and recorded. Information recorded from an experiment is called *data*. At the end of a suitable period of time, the data for the two groups of plants are compared. Based on the data, a *conclusion* will be reached as to whether the higher temperature made the plants grow faster. Any difference in the size of the plants must be due to the temperature difference, since all other factors are the same for both groups.

The results of experiments are often used to make *predictions* about the answers to other questions. If tomato plants grow faster at 30°C than at 21°C, how do you predict that they will grow at 15°C (59°F)?

A binocular light microscope (*below*) is one of the many tools scientists use to help them study nature. A microscope allows scientists to study very small things, such as these sand grains (*left*) and this tiny living thing called a diatom (*middle*).

Chapter Review

VOCABULARY

Answer the following in complete sentences.

1. Distinguish between *science* and *technology*.
2. What is a hypothesis? How does a theory differ from a hypothesis?
3. Distinguish between *mass* and *weight*.
4. Identify the two parts of a typical controlled experiment.
5. Explain what the terms *mass* and *volume* mean.
6. Distinguish between *liters* and *meters*.

CONCEPTS

1. What is a scientist?
2. Why is a hypothesis sometimes described as an educated guess?
3. Give several ways in which warm-blooded animals differ from cold-blooded animals.

4. What evidence supports the hypothesis that dinosaurs were cold-blooded animals similar to lizards?
5. What evidence supports the hypothesis that dinosaurs were warm-blooded?
6. If a theory is the best available explanation of some part of nature, why is it that theories often change?
7. Why are standard units of measurement needed?
8. List four prefixes used with SI units, and explain what each prefix means.
9. What unit would you use in measuring a person's mass? Explain why you chose that unit.
10. Describe the Celsius temperature scale.
11. What device is used to measure liquid volume? What is a meniscus, and what part of it is used when measuring liquid volume?
12. What is an experiment?
13. Explain how the two groups used in an experiment differ from each other.
14. Why is it best that there be only one variable in an experiment?

APPLICATION/ CRITICAL THINKING

1. Cars that have a streamlined shape burn less fuel than do cars of the same size and weight that are not streamlined. Suggest a hypothesis to explain this observation.
2. Design an experiment to test the hypothesis that a frog's heart beats faster as the temperature of the water that the frog is in rises.
3. If a large number of living things are used in an experiment, they must be as alike as possible. Explain why.
4. There are 2.54 cm in an inch. How many centimeters are there in a yard (36 inches)? What percent of a meter is a yard?
5. The fossils of dinosaurs believed to have been land dwellers are often found in rocks that formed at the bottom of lakes or rivers. Suggest reasons why these fossils are found in such rocks.

EXTENSION

1. Prepare a report on how scientific research for the space program has led to many new kinds of technology.
2. Microscopes are tools that are used in many branches of science. There are many types of microscopes. Research and report on the various types.
3. Many outstanding scientists have won Nobel Prizes. Find out what these prizes are and when they were first awarded.

DISCOVERING
LIFE SCIENCE

Plant life covers much of our planet. ▼

*T*here are several million kinds of living things. Life science is the study of all varieties of living things. Some living things are invisible to the unaided eye and can only be studied by using devices such as microscopes. Other living things can be studied in their environment as well as in the laboratory. In this unit you will study the characteristics of life, the structure and function of cells, and how animals are classified. You will learn about protists, plants, vertebrates and how organisms interact with their environment.

A slime mold. Slime molds grow on the floor of a damp, shady forest. ▼

▲*A fluorescent micrograph of a cell dividing.*

Seeds develop on a pine cone. ▶

◀ *Giant pandas are in danger of becoming extinct.*

CHAPTER 2

THE CHARACTERISTICS OF LIFE

Have you ever seen something and wondered whether it was alive? Look at the photograph. Flowers seem to be growing out of stones. These "stones" are actually plants. Sometimes these plants are called living stones, because they are similar in size and shape to the stones around them. However, the plants are living things, and the stones are not.

You may know that plants are green. Is being green a characteristic of living things? Notice that one of the stones is green, too. Are the flowers a sign that the plants are living? In this chapter you will learn some of the differences between things that are alive and things that are not alive.

- *What are the special characteristics that make something alive?*
- *What materials make up living things?*
- *How are new living things produced?*

2·1 Traits of Living Things

LIFE PROCESSES

Living things come in many forms. An oak tree, a zebra, and an ant do not look alike, but they are all living things. A single, complete living thing is called an **organism** (AWR guh nihz uhm). Organisms do similar things to stay alive. For example, organisms take in materials and give off wastes. The things that organisms do to stay alive are called *life processes*. The following sections explain the life processes.

● *Growth* An organism usually grows, or increases in size, during its life. An organism may also go through a series of changes called a *life cycle*. Each kind of organism has its own life cycle. An oak tree changes from acorn to seedling to tree in its life cycle.

● *Taking In Materials* An organism takes in materials such as food and gases from its surroundings. An organism needs food for two reasons. An organism uses food as building materials for growth and repair of the body. An organism also uses food as a source of energy. Pumping blood and growing are examples of activities that use energy.

Figure 2·1
Three methods of getting food.

A plant *makes* food.

A mushroom *absorbs* food.

An animal *eats* food.

Organisms differ in how they get food. Animals get food by eating other organisms or parts of other organisms. Plants use sunlight, gases, and water to make their own food. Other life forms, such as the mushroom shown in Figure 2·1, absorb food substances from the soil.

● *Releasing Energy* Several processes are involved in using food as a source of energy and building materials. These processes are part of an organism's metabolism (muh TAB uh lihz uhm). **Metabolism** is the sum of all the chemical activities that take place in an organism.

One part of metabolism is digestion (duh JEHS chuhn). *Digestion* is a process in which large, complex food substances are broken into smaller, simpler forms. Food substances are often too large to be used directly. Figure 2·2A shows how digestion breaks up food into usable pieces.

metabole (change)
-ism (act of)

Figure 2·2
Digestion breaks down complex food substances *(A)*. Synthesis joins together simple substances *(B)*.

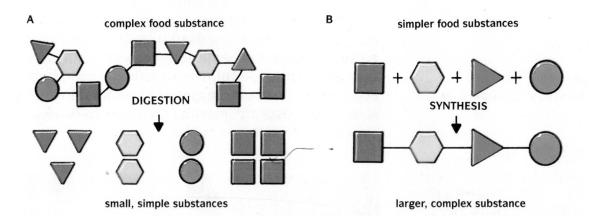

Some of the products of digestion are used as building materials. Such materials are used for growth and to replace worn-out parts. Organisms build new materials by synthesis (SIHN thuh sihs). *Synthesis* is a process in which small substances are joined to form a larger substance. You can see this process in Figure 2·2B. Why is synthesis thought of as the opposite of digestion?

Figure 2·3

Besides arching its back, what other responses might a frightened cat have to the stimulus of a dog or some other larger animal?

Many of the products of digestion are used for energy. The process of releasing energy from food is called *respiration* (rehs puh RAY shuhn). In this process, food is combined with oxygen. Water and other waste products are given off. Energy is the most important product of respiration. The energy from food is used to carry on the life processes.

● *Releasing Wastes* Some of the waste products of metabolism are poisons. An organism must have a way to get rid of such wastes. *Excretion* (ehk SKREE shuhn) is the term for the processes that remove wastes from an organism.

● *Response* Have you ever seen a cat with its back arched, as shown in Figure 2·3? Cats sometimes react this way when frightened. An event or a condition that causes an organism to react is known as a **stimulus** (STIHM yuh luhs) (pl., *stimuli*). The reaction of an organism to a stimulus is called a **response.** In the case of the dog and cat, the presence of the dog served as a stimulus. The arching of the cat's back was the response to the stimulus.

An organism responds to stimuli to survive and grow. A stimulus may mean danger. Or it may mean that something useful, such as food, is available. For example, a spider responds to the shaking of its web. This shaking may mean that an insect is caught in the web.

Figure 2·4

Two kinds of asexual reproduction. One cell can split into two new cells *(left)*. A new organism can form from part of the parent *(right)*.

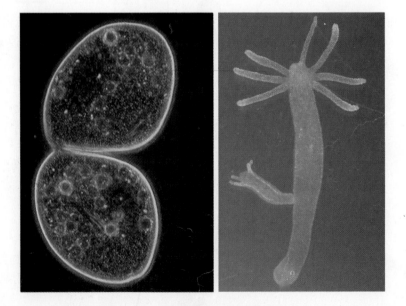

● *Producing New Organisms* The process by which organisms make others of their kind is called **reproduction** (ree pruh DUHK shuhn). The ability to reproduce is one of the most basic features of life. Reproduction allows for the survival of life. If all organisms of a kind fail to reproduce, that group of organisms will pass out of existence.

There are two very different ways in which organisms reproduce. Asexual reproduction is the simpler of the two methods. *Asexual reproduction* is a form of reproduction that involves only one parent. The organism may simply split in half to form two new organisms. New organisms produced by asexual reproduction always look like their parent. Look at the examples of asexual reproduction in Figure 2·4. Many simple organisms reproduce in this way.

Sexual reproduction involves the joining of two cells, usually from two parents. Each parent contributes a cell. The two cells join to form a new organism. Since it gets cells from each parent, the new organism usually resembles the two parents. Compare the kittens in Figure 2·5 with their parents. How are the kittens like each parent? How are they different from each parent? Many organisms can reproduce sexually. Complex animals can reproduce only by sexual reproduction.

Figure 2·5
The kittens have traits of both parents: the mother *(left)* and the father *(right)*.

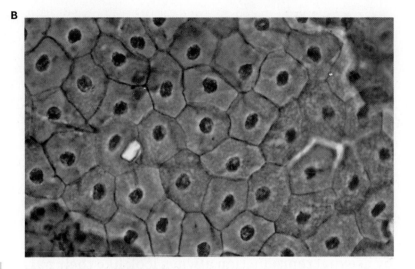

Figure 2·6

A paramecium is an organism that is made up of just one cell *(A)*. Many cells make up an organ of a complex plant or animal *(B)*. Why is the cell called the basic unit of life?

CELLS

Organisms are made of cells. A **cell** is the smallest unit in which all of the life processes are carried on. A complex organism, such as a human, may consist of trillions of cells. Some simple organisms, like the one shown in Figure 2·6A, are made of a single cell. The study of many different kinds of living things has led biologists to form the cell theory. The *cell theory* states that

- All organisms are made up of one or more cells.
- Cells are the basic unit of structure and function in organisms.
- New cells come only from other cells and not from nonliving things.

"The unit of structure" means that organisms are built from cells. "The unit of function" means that life processes go on within cells.

REVIEW

1. What are the life processes carried on by all organisms?
2. What do all the many kinds of living things have in common?
3. How do organisms differ from nonliving things?
4. Explain in your own words the cell theory.

CHALLENGE Two one-celled organisms of the same kind join together. A wall encloses the two cells. At a later time the wall breaks open and many new organisms are released. What type of reproduction is this? Explain your answer.

2·2 The Chemicals of Life

MATTER

Both living and nonliving things are made up of matter. *Matter* is anything that has mass and takes up space. Most matter on the earth exists in three states: solid, liquid, and gas. All matter is made up of tiny particles called atoms. An *atom* is the smallest unit of matter that can exist and still be recognized as a particular type of matter.

Scientists have learned that there are many types of atoms. An *element* is a substance that is made up of only one type of atom. There are 92 elements known to exist naturally on the earth. Scientists use chemical symbols to represent the elements. The symbols of 12 elements found in all living matter are listed in Table 2·1. What is the symbol for carbon? What element is represented by the symbol Fe?

Different elements can combine to form different kinds of matter. A *compound* is a substance that contains atoms of two or more elements joined. The smallest unit of many compounds is a *molecule* (MAHL uh kyool). For example, water is a compound. A molecule of water contains 2 hydrogen atoms joined with 1 oxygen atom.

Table 2·1
Elements in Living Things

ELEMENT	SYMBOL
Carbon	C
Hydrogen	H
Oxygen	O
Nitrogen	N
Phosphorus	P
Sulfur	S
Potassium	K
Magnesium	Mg
Calcium	Ca
Iron	Fe
Sodium	Na
Chlorine	Cl

Figure 2·7
Carbon, hydrogen, oxygen, nitrogen, and magnesium are the elements in the compound that makes leaves green.

33

Figure 2·8

Spaghetti contains starches, a kind of carbohydrate. What other foods contain starches?

ORGANIC COMPOUNDS

Chemists divide compounds into two groups. An *organic compound* contains the element carbon. An *inorganic compound* does not contain carbon. Organic compounds are found mainly in living things and in the remains of once-living things. Inorganic compounds are found in nonliving matter. Although water is an inorganic compound, it makes up a large part of living things.

Sugars are organic compounds found in many foods, especially fruits. There are many kinds of sugars. Glucose is a sugar that is found in most living things. *Starches* consist of many sugar molecules joined together to form chains. Figure 2·9 shows how a starch is formed. Starches are found in foods such as bread, spaghetti, and potatoes.

Sugars and starches are carbohydrates (kahr boh HĪ drayts). **Carbohydrates** are organic compounds that are the main source of energy for living things. All carbohydrates are made up of carbon, hydrogen, and oxygen atoms.

lipos (fat)

Fats, oils, and waxes are all lipids (LIHP ihdz). **Lipids** are organic compounds that store energy. They are found in meat, butter, and vegetable oils. Lipids can be used as an energy source. But they are often stored by living things for long periods of time. Like carbohydrates, lipids are made up of carbon, hydrogen, and oxygen. But the proportion of the three types of atoms is quite different in these two groups of compounds.

Figure 2·9

Starches are formed from sugar molecules joined in long chains.

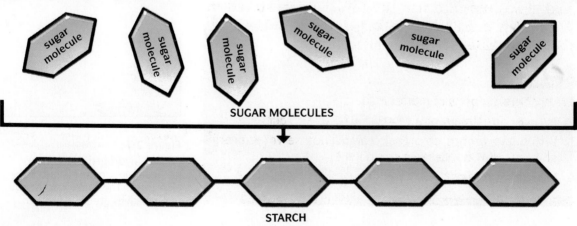

SUGAR MOLECULES

STARCH

Proteins (PROH teenz) are organic compounds that form the structure and control the function of living things. Proteins are the building materials of life. They are made up of smaller units called amino (uh MEE noh) acids. There are 20 different amino acids. Figure 2·10 shows how different amino acids can be joined to form a protein. Each amino acid is made up of the elements carbon, hydrogen, oxygen, and nitrogen. Which of these elements is not found in carbohydrates or lipids?

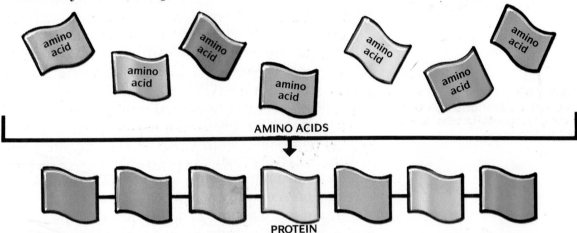

AMINO ACIDS

PROTEIN

Figure 2·10

Proteins are formed from different amino acids joined together in various arrangements.

Many proteins act as enzymes (EHN zīmz). *Enzymes* are proteins that control the activities of living things. For example, some enzymes control the release of energy from sugars.

Nucleic (noo KLEE ihk) *acids* are organic compounds that control the use of information in cells. **DNA** is a nucleic acid that stores all of the information needed for a cell to function. DNA contains instructions for making proteins. *RNA* is a nucleic acid that puts into use the information stored in DNA. DNA and RNA are abbreviations for the long, chemical names of the nucleic acids.

REVIEW

1. What are all forms of matter made of?
2. Is water an element or a compound? Explain your answer.
3. Which two groups of organic compounds serve as energy sources? How do these groups differ?
4. What are proteins? What are the functions of proteins?

CHALLENGE How are proteins and nucleic acids related?

2·3 The Structure of Cells

ANIMAL CELLS

Recall that all living things are made up of cells. Cells, too, are made up of parts. *Organelles* are cell structures that carry out the work of a cell. The animal cell shown in Figure 2·11 contains many organelles. Locate each of the organelles as you read its description below.

- If you were to look at an animal cell through a microscope, you would probably notice a large rounded structure. This structure is the nucleus (NOO klee uhs). The **nucleus** is the organelle that controls the activities of a cell. The nucleus contains DNA. Recall that DNA stores information used to control the activities of a cell. DNA is contained within structures called *chromosomes* (KROH muh sohmz). Chromosomes are found within the nucleus but can be seen only when a cell reproduces. You will learn more about chromosomes in Section 2-6.

- The **nuclear membrane** is a membrane that surrounds the nucleus and separates it from the rest of the cell. This membrane controls the movement of substances into and out of the nucleus.

Figure 2·11
A typical animal cell.

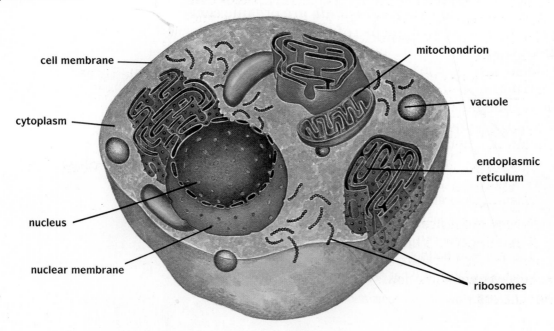

cell membrane

cytoplasm

nucleus

nuclear membrane

mitochondrion

vacuole

endoplasmic reticulum

ribosomes

- The jellylike material that surrounds the nucleus is the **cytoplasm** (SĪ tuh plaz uhm). Notice in Figure 2·11 that most of the cell is filled with cytoplasm. Other organelles are found within the cytoplasm.

cyto- (cell)
plasm (to form)

- **Mitochondria** (mī tuh KAHN dree uh) (sing., *mitochondrion*) are organelles that release energy from food. These structures supply energy to other parts of a cell. Look at the mitochondrion shown in Figure 2·12. The process of releasing energy from food takes place on the folded inner membranes of the mitochondrion. Why are mitochondria sometimes called the powerhouses of the cell?

Figure 2·12

The folded inner membranes of the mitochondrion contain enzymes used in the release of energy.

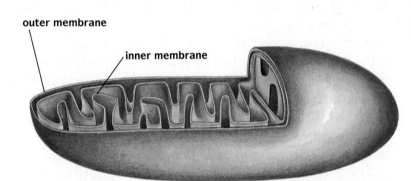

outer membrane

inner membrane

- **Ribosomes** (RĪ buh sohmz) are organelles that build the proteins needed by a cell. Ribosomes contain the nucleic acid RNA. The RNA carries instructions from DNA in the nucleus to control the making of proteins.
- The **endoplasmic reticulum** (ehn doh PLAZ mihk rih TIHK yuh luhm), or **ER,** is a network of membranes that runs throughout the cytoplasm. The ER forms tubes through which materials move to all parts of a cell.

endo- (inner)
rete (net)

- **Vacuoles** (VAK yoo ohlz) are fluid-filled sacs in a cell. Vacuoles store many different substances in liquid form.

vacuus (empty)

- Notice in Figure 2·11 that the cell is enclosed by a cell membrane. The **cell membrane** controls the flow of materials into and out of the cell. The membrane allows some materials to pass through, but not others.

PLANT CELLS

You have just read about many of the organelles in animal cells. These organelles are also found in plant cells. But some of these organelles look different in plant cells. Look at the typical plant cell shown in Figure 2·13. Notice that the vacuole is very large compared with the other organelles in this cell. As in an animal cell, the vacuole in a plant cell is used for storage.

Plant cells have some structures that are not found in animal cells. Notice that the plant cell in Figure 2·13 is enclosed by a cell wall. A **cell wall** is a nonliving structure that surrounds a plant cell. The cell wall lies outside the cell membrane and gives the cell shape and support. The cell membrane is part of the living cell, but the cell wall is not. Some cell walls, such as those in woody plants, are very strong.

Plant cells contain organelles called *plastids* (PLAS tihdz). Plastids serve as food factories or as storage places. Many plant cells store starches in plastids. Such plastids are colorless. Other plastids contain pigments, or coloring matter. For example, plastids filled with orange pigment give a carrot its orange color.

Figure 2·13
A typical plant cell.

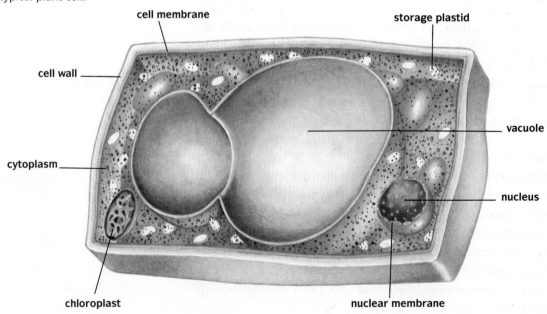

38

OBJECTIVE

Compare the organelles of an animal cell with those of a plant cell.

MATERIALS

iodine stain, 2 droppers, 2 microscope slides, toothpicks, coverslips, microscope, *Elodea*, scissors, forceps

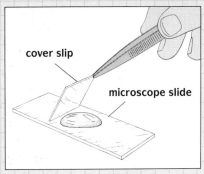

cover slip

microscope slide

PROCEDURE

A. Use a dropper to place a small drop of iodine stain on a microscope slide.
B. Use the flat side of a clean toothpick to gently scrape the inside of your cheek.
C. Place the end of the toothpick with the cells scrapings in the drop of iodine and mix thoroughly. Cover the mixture with a coverslip as shown in the figure.
D. Observe the cheek cells under low power of a microscope. Then switch to high power.
E. Make a drawing of a cheek cell as it appears under high power. Label the cell and any parts of it that you can identify.
F. Use a dropper to place a drop of water on a clean microscope slide.
G. Cut the tip off an *Elodea* leaf. Use forceps to place the leaf tip in the water on the slide. Add a coverslip.
H. Observe the *Elodea* under low power.
I. Make a drawing of an *Elodea* cell under low power. Label the cell and any structures that you can identify.

RESULTS AND CONCLUSIONS

1. What structures did you find in both cheek cells and *Elodea* cells?
2. What structures did you find only in *Elodea* cells?
3. Identify each of the structures that you observed and give its function.

Locate the oval, green chloroplasts (KLAWR uh plasts) in Figure 2·13. A **chloroplast** is an organelle in which food is made in a plant cell. These plastids contain *chlorophyll*, a green pigment that absorbs energy from sunlight. Chlorophyll is used in the process of making food in the plant cell.

REVIEW

1. What are the functions of the nucleus of a cell?
2. Why are mitochondria called the powerhouses of the cell?
3. Distinguish between a cell membrane and a cell wall.
4. What organelles are found only in plants? What are the functions of these organelles?

CHALLENGE The cells in a potato have no chloroplasts. If you saw such cells under a microscope, how could you identify them as plant cells?

2·4 Transport in Cells

THE CELL MEMBRANE

Cells get many substances from their surroundings. All cells need water, which forms a large part of the cytoplasm. Most cells need oxygen. Some cells need carbon dioxide or other gases. Many cells must take in food. Wastes and excess water pass out of cells. There is a steady movement of substances into and out of cells. The cell membrane controls this movement.

Figure 2·14

How is this mesh bag similar to a cell membrane?

Look at Figure 2·14. The mesh bag holds the oranges. But what would happen if you poured water into the bag? The water would move through the holes in the mesh. The mesh is *permeable* (PER mee uh buhl) to water. A permeable material allows materials to flow through it. However the mesh does not allow the oranges to pass through. Thus the mesh is *semipermeable;* it allows some materials to flow through, but not others.

Only some materials can pass through a cell membrane. Thus the cell membrane is semipermeable. It is permeable to oxygen and water. Molecules of oxygen and water are small. Cell membranes are not permeable to many kinds of large molecules, such as proteins.

PASSIVE TRANSPORT

Some substances can move freely through the cell membrane. Pores, or small holes, in the cell membrane allow small molecules to pass into and out of the cell. This free movement is an example of passive transport. *Passive transport* is the movement of a substance through a cell membrane without the use of energy by the cell. Water, oxygen, and other gases move through the cell membrane by passive transport.

The atoms and molecules in matter are always moving. In solids the particles vibrate in place. Particles in liquids and gases move from one place to another. They move in many directions, as you can see in Figure 2·15A.

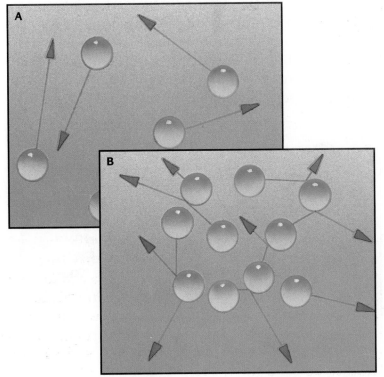

PUZZLER

A helium-filled, rubber balloon will float in air because helium is lighter than air. If you have ever had a helium-filled balloon, you have probably found it on the floor after a day or so. Can you explain what happened? How can you compare a rubber balloon to a cell?

Figure 2·15
Particles of matter move in random directions *(A)*. When particles of matter are crowded, they often bump into each other and move apart *(B)*.

41

When particles of matter are crowded together, they are likely to bump into each other. As particles bump into each other, they change direction and move apart, as shown in Figure 2·15B. As a result, the particles move from a crowded area to an area that is less crowded. The movement of particles from a crowded area to a less crowded area is called **diffusion** (dih FYOO zhuhn).

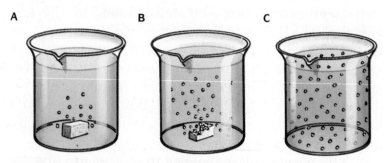

A   B   C

In part *A*, Figure 2·16, you can see a cube of sugar in a glass of water. In the cube the sugar molecules are very crowded. In part *B* you can see that some of the sugar molecules have moved away from the cube. They have spread out in the water to areas that are less crowded. Part *C* shows the sugar molecules spread evenly through the water. The sugar molecules have diffused through the water.

Recall that cell membranes are semipermeable. **Osmosis** (ahz MOH sihs) is the diffusion of water through a semipermeable membrane. Figure 2·17

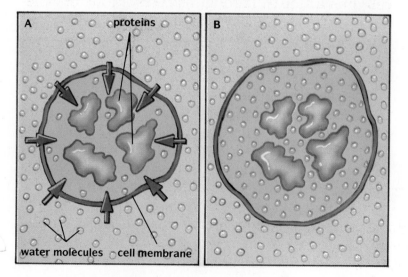

A   proteins   B

water molecules   cell membrane

How Does Temperature Affect the Spreading of Food Coloring in Water?

Identify the process by which food coloring spreads out in water.
Determine how temperature affects this process.

MATERIALS
lab apron, glass-marking pencil, two 250-mL beakers, cold water, hot water, dropper, red food coloring

PROCEDURE
A. Wear a lab apron during this activity. With a glass-marking pencil, label two beakers. Label one beaker *cold* and the other one *hot*.
B. Fill the beaker labeled *cold* with cold water.
C. Fill the beaker labeled *hot* with hot water. **Caution:** Do not splash the hot water on your skin.
D. Place both beakers where they will not be disturbed.
E. Add one drop of red food coloring to each beaker. Release the drop just above the surface of the water to avoid splashing.
F. Observe the two beakers immediately after adding the food coloring. Record your observations.
G. Observe the beakers again after 10 minutes. Record your observations.

RESULTS AND CONCLUSIONS
1. Describe what happens to the red food coloring in each beaker in step **F**.
2. Describe what happens to the food coloring in each beaker in step **G**.
3. What process did you observe in this activity?
4. How does temperature affect the rate at which this process occurs?
5. Predict what the contents of each beaker would look like after 24 hours. Explain your predictions.

shows the process of osmosis. Water molecules pass through the semipermeable membrane. Some of the molecules inside the cell are too large to pass through the membrane. In Figure 2·17A, notice that the water molecules are more crowded outside the cell than inside it. Through osmosis the water molecules move from a crowded area to a less-crowded area, as can be seen in Figure 2·17B.

ACTIVE TRANSPORT

Sometimes, molecules are more crowded inside the cell than outside the cell. When this happens, molecules do not enter the cell by passive transport. For example, root cells of plants need minerals from the soil. But the minerals are more crowded in the root cells than they are outside the roots. So the minerals cannot diffuse into the root cells. The cells must use energy to move the minerals. **Active transport** is the use of energy by a cell to move particles across the cell membrane.

Figure 2·18 shows one way in which active transport may occur. *Carrier molecules* are thought to be part of the cell membrane. These molecules can turn within the cell membrane. Notice in Figure 2·18*A* that a molecule to be carried through the membrane fits into a slot on the carrier molecule. In Figure 2·18*B* you see that the carrier molecule has turned within the membrane. The molecule being carried is now released into the cell. The carrier then rotates back to its first position. Energy is used to turn the carrier molecule.

Figure 2·18

A model of active transport. The molecule to be carried fits into the carrier molecule. The carrier molecule turns, and it then releases the molecule inside the cell.

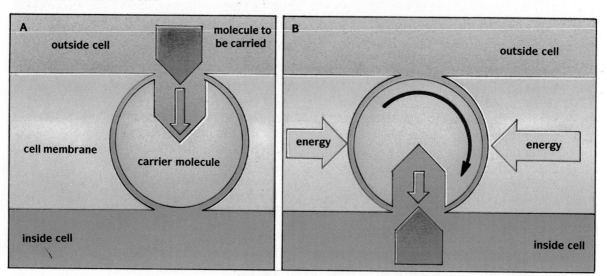

Passive transport and active transport can be compared to riding a bicycle. Imagine coasting downhill. You need not use energy to coast downhill. The downhill movement without use of energy can be likened to passive transport. Now imagine pedaling uphill. You must use energy to pedal uphill. How can pedaling uphill be compared to active transport?

REVIEW

1. What is a semipermeable membrane?
2. Distinguish between osmosis and diffusion.
3. How do passive transport and active transport differ?

CHALLENGE A smoke detector sounds an alarm when smoke fills the air. Explain why several minutes may pass between the time a fire starts and the time the alarm sounds.

2·5 Energy for Cells

You have learned that organisms get energy from food. Lipids, such as fats and oils, are one source of energy. Carbohydrates, especially sugars, are the best source of energy.

RESPIRATION

Within cells, many kinds of carbohydrates are changed to glucose. *Glucose* is a sugar that is the main source of energy for cells. But cells cannot directly use glucose to do work. The energy in glucose must be changed to a usable form. Through a complex process that takes place in cells, glucose is broken down. When glucose is broken down, energy is released. **Respiration** is the process of releasing energy from food.

Much of the energy that is given off during respiration is stored in the compound *ATP*. ATP is an abbreviation for a chemical name. ATP is a substance in cells that stores energy. The energy in ATP can be used directly to do work in cells. Respiration can be shown by this equation.

glucose + oxygen → carbon dioxide + water + ATP (energy)

This process takes place in the mitochondria of cells. Notice in Figure 2·19 that glucose and oxygen are used by a mitochondrion in respiration. Carbon dioxide and water are given off. ATP is the energy product of this process.

After completing this section, you will be able to

- **describe** the process by which cells get energy from food.
- **compare** the processes of respiration and photosynthesis.

The key terms in this section are
photosynthesis
respiration

re- (again)
spirare (breathe)

Figure 2·19
In respiration, glucose and oxygen are used by the mitochondrion. The energy product is ATP. What other products are given off?

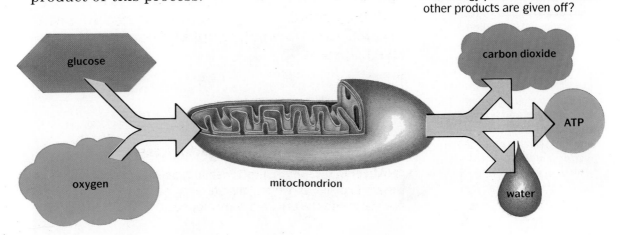

glucose

oxygen

mitochondrion

carbon dioxide

ATP

water

PHOTOSYNTHESIS

The energy in ATP comes from the energy in glucose. But where does glucose come from? Directly or indirectly, plants provide food for living things. Animals get food by eating plants or by eating other animals that have eaten plants. You know that plants make food. The food that plants make is glucose. **Photosynthesis** (foh tuh SIHN thuh sihs) is the process by which glucose is made by plants. Photosynthesis can be shown by this equation.

photo- (light)
-syn (together)
-thesis (to place)

carbon dioxide + water + light (energy) → glucose + oxygen

Recall that chlorophyll, which is found in chloroplasts, absorbs light energy from the sun. This provides the energy needed for food making to occur. Figure 2·20 shows the process of photosynthesis. What materials are used by the chloroplast? What materials are given off?

Compare the equations for respiration and photosynthesis, shown in Table 2·2. Notice that the two equations are opposites. In respiration, glucose combines with oxygen. Energy, carbon dioxide, and

DO YOU KNOW?

Special cells in a firefly use ATP for an unusual activity. These cells produce light. The giving-off of light by a living thing is called bioluminescence (bi oh loo muh NEHS-uhns).

In a firefly, these special cells are grouped together to form a structure called a lantern. Many lanterns are found on the underside of the firefly. Within the cells of the lanterns, a chemical change takes place. ATP is combined with oxygen and a substance called luciferin (loo SIHF-uhr ihn). During the change, luciferin molecules absorb energy from ATP and then release this energy as light.

There are other organisms that are bioluminescent. The processes that produce light in these organisms are basically the same as those in fireflies.

Most light-producing organisms live in the ocean.

These include some types of clams, snails, squid, and fish. At the surface of warm ocean water, there is a very common single-celled organism that is bioluminescent. The cells of this organism give off light when disturbed.

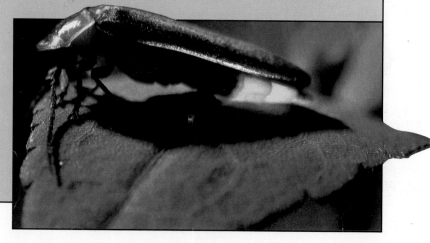

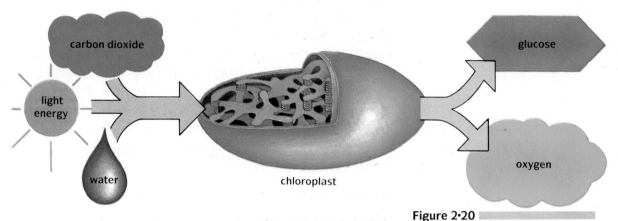

Figure 2·20
In photosynthesis the chloroplast uses carbon dioxide, water, and energy from sunlight. Glucose is made, and oxygen is given off.

water are produced. In photosynthesis, energy from sunlight is used to join carbon dioxide and water. Oxygen and glucose are produced.

Animal cells carry on respiration only. Plant cells carry on both respiration and photosynthesis. Plant cells often produce more oxygen in photosynthesis than they use in respiration. The extra oxygen is given off into the air. This oxygen can then be used in respiration by animal cells.

Table 2·2 *Respiration and Photosynthesis Compared*

RESPIRATION	PHOTOSYNTHESIS
glucose + oxygen → carbon dioxide + water + ATP (energy)	carbon dioxide + water + light (energy) → glucose + oxygen
Takes place in most cells.	Takes place only in cells that contain chlorophyll.
Glucose is broken down.	Glucose is made.
Energy in glucose is released.	Energy is stored in glucose.
Carbon dioxide is given off.	Carbon dioxide is taken in.
Water is given off.	Water is used.
Oxygen is used.	Oxygen is given off.

REVIEW

1. Why do cells need energy?
2. Describe the process of respiration.
3. Explain the process of photosynthesis.

CHALLENGE You may have heard the process of breathing referred to as respiration. In this section you have learned that respiration is a process that cells use to get energy from food. Explain why the same word is used for both processes.

2·6 Cell Division

Growth results from an increase in the number of cells in the body. New cells are formed by *cell division*. Cell division is the process by which a cell divides to form new cells. Cell division provides cells for growth and for replacing worn-out or damaged cells.

MITOSIS

When a cell divides, the two new cells are just like the one that divided. The cell that divides is called the parent cell. The two new cells that form are called daughter cells. **Mitosis** (mī TOH sihs) is cell division in which daughter cells are made that are just like the parent cell.

Recall that the information stored in DNA controls the activities of a cell. After mitosis, each daughter cell carries an exact copy of the DNA and can perform all the functions of the parent cell.

After mitosis, most cells have a period of growth. This time of growth between cell divisions is called *interphase*. All of the life processes except mitosis go on during this time. Many cell parts, including the DNA, double during interphase. Figure 2·21 shows a cell in interphase.

Mitosis may be shown as a series of four stages. Though mitosis is a continuous process, dividing it into stages makes it easier to understand. Identify the four stages shown in Figure 2·22 as you read about mitosis.

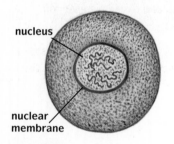

Figure 2·21
An animal cell in interphase. During interphase, the cell grows, and duplicates its DNA.

Figure 2·22
These four drawings show the process of mitosis.

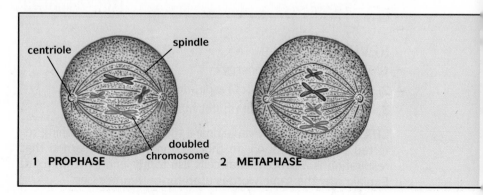

1 PROPHASE   2 METAPHASE

1. *Prophase* is the first stage of mitosis. As you have learned, chromosomes are found in the nucleus. A **chromosome** is a threadlike structure that contains DNA. The DNA molecules, which doubled during interphase, shorten during prophase. Doubled chromosomes are thick and can now be seen in the nucleus.

The nuclear membrane disappears during prophase. A structure called the *spindle* appears. The spindle is a group of fibers that guide the movement of chromosomes during mitosis. In Figure 2·22 you can see that many spindle fibers connect to the centrioles. The *centrioles* are organelles that seem to control the spindle in animal cells. Plant cells form spindles but do not have centrioles.

2. *Metaphase* is the second stage of mitosis. Locate the metaphase cell in Figure 2·22. Notice that the chromosomes are lined up in the middle of the cell.

3. *Anaphase* is the third stage of mitosis. In this stage the spindle fibers seem to pull apart the doubled chromosomes. Each doubled chromosome separates and forms two single chromosomes. Two identical sets of chromosomes move to opposite sides of the cell.

4. *Telophase* is the fourth stage of mitosis. In this stage the spindle disappears. A nuclear membrane forms around each set of chromosomes. Note that the cell membrane and cytoplasm pinch inward. Two new cells form. All of the information that was in the nucleus of the parent cell is in the nucleus of each daughter cell.

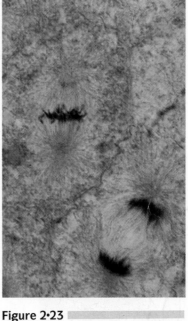

Figure 2·23

What stages of mitosis are shown in these cells?

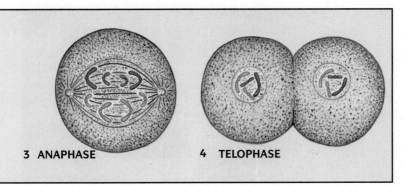

3 ANAPHASE   4 TELOPHASE

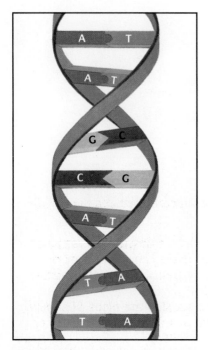

Figure 2·24

A DNA molecule has the shape of a twisted ladder.

Figure 2·25

These two daughter cells have identical DNA.

THE ROLE OF DNA

DNA has been called the master molecule of life because it controls life processes. A single molecule of DNA may contain millions of atoms. This great size allows DNA to store large amounts of information. The information in DNA is used to build proteins. The proteins then carry out the work of the cell. Thus DNA controls life processes.

Notice in Figure 2·24 that a DNA molecule has the form of a twisted ladder. The ladder is made up of two long sides that hold the DNA together. Between the sides are steps or rungs. These rungs are made of substances called *bases*. There are four different bases. The letters *A, C, G,* and *T* are symbols for these bases. Notice that the rungs of the DNA ladder are pairs of bases. You can see that there are four different base pairs: A-T, T-A, C-G, and G-C.

DNA stores information about how to make proteins. The order in which the four types of base pairs appear in the DNA molecule is a code. The order of hundreds of bases is the code for a single protein.

Scientists have found that DNA can make exact copies of itself. Exact copies of DNA molecules in the chromosomes go to each daughter cell. Thus each daughter cell shown in Figure 2·25 contains the same information.

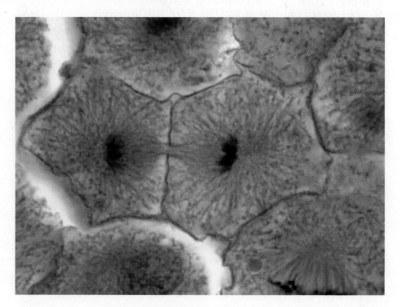

REVIEW

1. What occurs during interphase?
2. Describe what happens during each stage of mitosis.
3. What is stored within DNA molecules?

CHALLENGE What would be the result if DNA did not copy itself before mitosis?

CHAPTER SUMMARY

The main ideas in this chapter are listed below. Read these statements before you answer the Chapter Review questions.

- Life processes carried on by organisms include taking in materials, releasing energy, releasing wastes, growth, response, and producing new organisms. (2·1)
- The cell theory states that the cell is the basic unit of life. (2·1)
- Matter is made up of atoms. An atom is the smallest unit of an element. Elements combine to form a compound. A molecule is the smallest unit of many compounds. (2·2)
- Carbohydrates and lipids are organic compounds that supply organisms with energy. Proteins are organic compounds that serve as building materials and as enzymes. DNA and RNA are nucleic acids that control the activities of cells. (2·2)
- Animal cells contain a nucleus surrounded by cytoplasm. Within the cytoplasm are many organelles. The cell membrane encloses the cell. (2·3)
- Plant cells contain most of the organelles found in animal cells. In addition, chloroplasts, other plastids, and cell walls are found in plant cells. (2·3)

- Cell membranes are described as semipermeable. Substances can move through cell membranes by passive transport or active transport. (2·4)
- Diffusion and osmosis are types of passive transport and do not require the use of energy by the cell. (2·4)
- Active transport requires the use of energy by the cell. (2·4)
- Respiration is the process of releasing energy from food. The energy is stored in ATP. Photosynthesis is the process by which plants make glucose. (2·5)
- Mitosis is a type of cell division that forms two daughter cells that are just like the parent cell. The four stages of mitosis are prophase, metaphase, anaphase, and telophase. (2·6)
- Chromosomes contain DNA. DNA stores information to control cell activities. The DNA molecule is able to form identical copies of itself. (2·6)

The key terms in this chapter are listed below. Use each term in a sentence that shows the meaning of the term.

active transport	cytoplasm	mitosis	reproduction
carbohydrates	diffusion	nuclear membrane	respiration
cell	DNA	nucleus	response
cell membrane	endoplasmic reticulum (ER)	organism	ribosomes
cell wall	lipids	osmosis	stimulus
chloroplast	metabolism	photosynthesis	vacuoles
chromosomes	mitochondria	proteins	

Chapter Review

VOCABULARY

Use the key terms from the previous page to complete the following sentences correctly.

1. An event or condition that causes an organism to react is a/an _____.

2. The smallest unit in which all the life processes can be carried out is a/an _____.

3. _____ is cell division in which daughter cells that are just like the parent cell are made.

4. A single, complete living thing is called a/an _____.

5. The organelle that controls the activities of a cell is the _____.

6. The nonliving structure that surrounds a plant cell is the _____.

7. The jellylike material that surrounds the nucleus of a cell is called _____.

8. _____ are organelles that release energy from food.

9. The diffusion of water through a semipermeable membrane is called _____.

10. A/An _____ is a threadlike structure that contains DNA.

CONCEPTS

Write the correct term for each cell structure shown in the diagram.

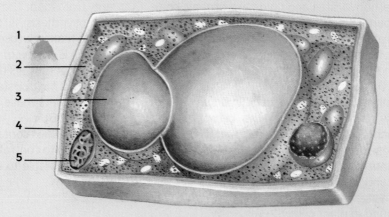

1 _____
2 _____
3 _____
4 _____
5 _____

Choose the term or phrase that best answers the question or completes the statement.

6. Which of these is made up of amino acids?
   a. carbohydrates   c. proteins
   b. lipids   d. DNA

7. Carbohydrates are mostly used in the body for
   a. energy.
   b. storing energy for long periods.
   c. building materials.
   d. controlling the use of information in cells.

8. Which of these is part of active transport?
   a. diffusion   c. passive transport
   b. osmosis   d. carrier molecules
9. Which of these is the period of growth before cell division?
   a. interphase
   b. metaphase
   c. prophase
   d. telophase
10. Which of these is found only in plant cells?
    a. nucleus
    b. mitochondrion
    c. cell wall
    d. cell membrane

Answer the following in complete sentences.

11. What life processes are carried on by all organisms?
12. What does the cell theory state?
13. Compare the processes of respiration and photosynthesis.
14. Briefly describe the changes that occur during each of the four phases of mitosis.

APPLICATION/ CRITICAL THINKING

1. Glucose is put directly into the blood of some hospital patients. What part of metabolism is by-passed by this procedure? Why might this be done?
2. Do mitochondria make energy? Explain your answer.
3. You have learned that glucose, a sugar, is used by cells in respiration. Does that mean animals need to eat a lot of foods containing sugar? Explain your answer.
4. A volume of seawater has more salt in it than the same volume of water from a cell. Suppose a shipwrecked person drank only seawater. What would happen to that person's body cells?

EXTENSION

1. Use reference books to help you write a report about the cell wall of plants. What material makes up the cell wall? What uses have been found for this material?
2. Make a three-dimensional model of a plant cell or of an animal cell. You might use a shoebox, plastic foam balls, balsa wood, clay, and paper to build the structures. Label each structure.
3. The process by which DNA makes a copy of itself is called replication. Use reference books to find out what happens during replication. How does this process make exact copies of the DNA code?

CHAPTER 3

THE SIMPLEST ORGANISMS

*Y*ou probably have seen mushrooms in a field or forest. But have you ever looked at a mushroom from this angle? Notice that the underside of a mushroom has many folds. Special cells for reproduction are found on these folds. Although this mushroom is white, other mushrooms can be orange, yellow, or pink.

A mushroom is a kind of fungus, a simple organism. Many simple organisms live in water or in damp places. These mushrooms live in forests. The shade from trees keeps the mushrooms from drying out.

- What other kinds of simple organisms are there?
- How are simple organisms classified?
- How do simple organisms get food?

3·1 Classification in the Life Sciences

After completing this section, you will be able to

- **explain** the basis for the modern classification system.
- **list** the seven major groups in the classification of organisms.
- **describe** the basis for scientific names.

The key terms in this section are
classification
scientific name

CLASSIFICATION GROUPS

There are many kinds of organisms. To be able to study them, scientists have a method of classification (klas uh fuh KAY shuhn). **Classification** is the grouping of things according to a system.

Scientists classify organisms according to how closely they are related. To see how organisms are related, scientists look at the structure of organisms and their cells. Scientists also look at fossils. Fossils are the preserved remains of once-living things. The chemical makeup of living things is also used in classification.

In the classification of living things, large groups are broken down into smaller and smaller groups. A *kingdom* is the largest unit of classification. Each living thing can be placed in one of five kingdoms. The five kingdoms are shown in Table 3·1. To which kingdom do humans belong?

Figure 3·1 shows the seven main levels of classification as a kingdom is divided into smaller and smaller groups. The top row shows only a few of the many kinds of organisms in the animal kingdom.

Table 3·1 *The Five Kingdoms*

	KINGDOM MONERA	KINGDOM PROTISTA	KINGDOM FUNGI	KINGDOM PLANTAE	KINGDOM ANIMALIA
Major traits	Single-celled; absence of nucleus; nuclear material scattered	Most are single-celled; some make own food; some cannot make own food	Most are many-celled; cannot make own food	Single-celled and many-celled; make own food; cannot move from place to place	Many-celled; cannot make own food; can move from place to place
Examples	Bacterium, blue-green bacterium	Paramecium, amoeba, euglena	Mushroom, mold, yeast	Tree, small flowering plant, fern, alga	Sponge, insect, clam, fish, bird, snake, human

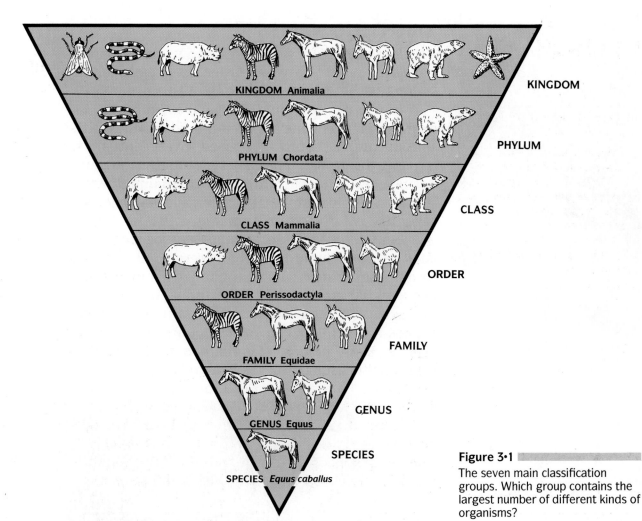

KINGDOM

PHYLUM

CLASS

ORDER

FAMILY

GENUS

SPECIES

KINGDOM Animalia

PHYLUM Chordata

CLASS Mammalia

ORDER Perissodactyla

FAMILY Equidae

GENUS Equus

SPECIES *Equus caballus*

Figure 3·1

The seven main classification groups. Which group contains the largest number of different kinds of organisms?

The level just below a kingdom is called a phylum (FĪ luhm). A *phylum* (pl., *phyla*) is a group of closely related classes. A *class* is a group of closely related orders. An *order* is a group of closely related families. A *family* is a group of closely related genera (sing., *genus*). A *genus* is a group of closely related species. A *species* (SPEE sheez) (pl., *species*) is a group of living things that can mate with each other and whose young can also mate and produce offspring.

As you look down the rows of the triangle, you see that each row has fewer members. But the animals in each lower row are more and more alike. Look at the bottom of the triangle. Notice that only one kind of organism is shown there. Only one kind of organism can be in a species.

Figure 3·2
Tiger lily. Kingdom: Plantae. Phylum: Tracheophyta. Class: Angiospermae. Order: Lilales. Family: Liliaceae. Genus: *Lilium*. Species: *Lilium tigrinium*.

SCIENTIFIC NAMES

Look at Figure 3·2, which shows the classification of a plant. To what order does the tiger lily belong? Other lilies also belong to this order.

In classifying living things, it is helpful to use names that everyone agrees upon. The names of the classification groups are used by scientists all around the world. The last two names, the genus and species, make up the **scientific name** of an organism. For example, the scientific name of the tiger lily is *Lilium tigrinium.*

Scientific names are important because common names of organisms change from one language to another. They can also change from place to place. What is the name of the animal in Figure 3·3? In some places it is called a mountain lion. In other places it is called a cougar or a puma. Scientists do not use these names. The one name that all scientists use for this animal is *Felis concolor.*

Figure 3·3
What do scientists call this animal?

REVIEW

1. What information is used in the classification of living things?
2. List the seven major classification groups. Which group is the largest?
3. What are the two parts of a scientific name?

CHALLENGE The scientific name of the house cat is *Felis domesticus.* The scientific name of the ocelot is *Felis pardalis.* What do these names tell you about whether a cat and an ocelot can mate and produce young that can also mate and produce young?

3·2 Viruses

TRAITS OF VIRUSES

Have you ever had mumps or chicken pox? If so, you have had a disease caused by a virus. A **virus** is a very small particle made up of nucleic acid with a protein covering, or protein coat. The nucleic acid in a virus contains directions for making more viruses. The protein coat protects the virus. The structure of one type of virus is shown in Figure 3·4. Some other viruses are also shown. How do the viruses in Figure 3·4 compare in size with the cell they are attached to?

Viruses seem to be on the borderline between living and nonliving things. Viruses are made of some of the substances in living cells. But viruses are not cells, nor are they made of cells. Viruses cannot reproduce unless they are inside a living cell. They cannot carry on other life processes.

When it is inside a living cell, a virus acts like a computer program for making new viruses. A virus contains the information needed to make thousands of new viruses. A virus enters a living cell and "programs" it. The cell then makes new viruses.

In general, each kind of virus infects the cells of one species. A virus that infects tobacco will not usually infect wheat or corn. Some viruses infect only certain cell types within an organism. The virus that causes rabies invades only nerve tissue.

After completing this section, you will be able to

- **compare** viruses to both living things and nonliving things.
- **explain** how viruses reproduce.
- **name** some diseases caused by viruses.

The key terms in this section are
vaccine
virus

Figure 3·4

Virus that causes hepatitis *(left)*, virus that infects bacteria *(middle)*, and the structure of a virus *(right)*.

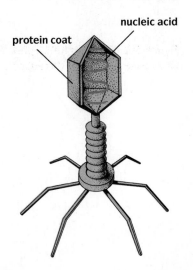

nucleic acid

protein coat

HOW VIRUSES REPRODUCE

By studying viruses that infect bacteria, scientists have learned how viruses reproduce. Look at Figure 3·5 as you read the steps in the reproduction of this kind of virus. This process can take place in less than one hour. Similar steps occur in viruses that infect animals and plants.

1. The virus attaches to the surface of a cell.

2. The nucleic acid of the virus is injected into the cell. Recall that this nucleic acid contains the information needed to make new viruses.

3. The nucleic acid of the virus directs the cell to make new virus parts.

4. The virus parts come together to form many new viruses.

5. The cell bursts open and dies. Many new viruses are released. Each new virus is able to infect another cell.

Figure 3·5

Reproduction of a virus that infects bacteria.

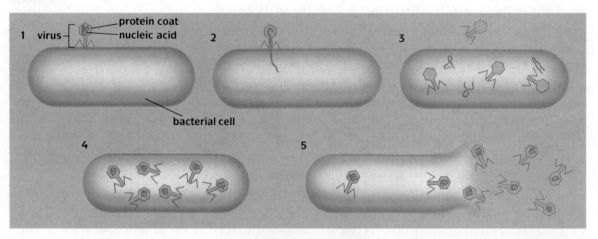

VIRUSES AND DISEASE

Disease may result when viruses destroy cells. Viruses cause disease in plants and animals and are a major cause of disease in humans. In addition to causing mumps and chicken pox, viruses cause polio, smallpox, flu, the common cold, and other diseases. Viruses have also been found to cause some types of cancer. Acquired Immune Deficiency

For the first time in history, scientists have been able to see the detailed structure of a virus that infects animals. The new technology of supercomputers has made this scientific breakthrough possible. Supercomputers process information up to 200 times faster than other types of computers. Using X rays and supercomputers, researchers have made models of one of the viruses that cause the common cold. Since a cold may be caused by one of more than a hundred related viruses, this research may not lead to an immediate cure for the common cold. However, the knowledge gained may have far-reaching benefits.

Pictures produced by the supercomputer show areas on the virus's surface that allow the virus to attach to the cell membrane of a human cell. Using this information, scientists may be able to prevent viruses from attaching to cells and beginning their reproductive cycle. Other structures on the surface of the virus show how human antibodies attach to the virus as the body fights the infection. It is hoped that

all of this information will lead to the development of effective treatments for virus-caused diseases.

Syndrome, or AIDS, is an often-fatal disease caused by a virus. The ability to fight infection is reduced or absent in a person who has AIDS.

Some virus-caused diseases can be prevented by the use of vaccines. A **vaccine** is a substance that contains viruses or other disease-causing agents that have been weakened and can no longer cause disease. A vaccine is injected into the body. It causes the body to form substances called *antibodies*. Antibodies protect against further infection by the type of virus in the vaccine. Vaccines have been made for some virus-caused diseases, including polio, measles, and some kinds of flu. You probably had to be vaccinated against some virus-caused diseases before you could start school.

REVIEW

1. What are the parts of a virus?
2. How are viruses like living things? How are they like nonliving things?
3. Describe how a virus reproduces.
4. How does a vaccine prevent infection by a virus?

CHALLENGE Viruses to be used in vaccines are often weakened by being heated. What might happen if a sample of viruses to be used in a vaccine was not heated enough?

3·3 Monerans

After completing this section, you will be able to

- **identify** the two major groups in the kingdom Monera.
- **describe** the shapes and structures of bacterial cells.
- **compare** the processes of fission and mitosis.
- **describe** how some bacteria are helpful and how some are harmful.

The key terms in this section are
bacteria
blue-green bacteria
fission
monerans
parasite

The organisms that have the simplest cell structure are the **monerans** (muh NIHR uhnz). Monerans are single-celled. The cell of a moneran is unlike any other cell. For this reason, the monerans are placed in their own kingdom—kingdom Monera. There are two major groups of monerans: the *blue-green bacteria* and the *bacteria*.

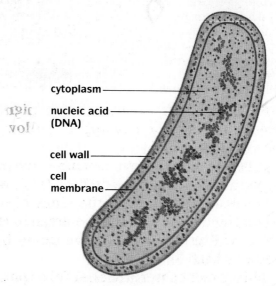

cytoplasm

nucleic acid (DNA)

cell wall

cell membrane

Figure 3·6
Structure of a typical moneran cell.

Unlike other cells, moneran cells lack a nucleus. A typical moneran cell is shown in Figure 3·6. The cell contains DNA, but it is found in the cytoplasm of the cell, not in a nucleus. Monerans lack many of the structures found in other cells. Notice that a cell wall and cell membrane surround a moneran cell.

BLUE-GREEN BACTERIA

Blue-green bacteria are monerans that can make their own food by photosynthesis. These monerans can exist alone or in colonies. A *colony* is a group of similar cells that are attached to each other. Figure 3·7 shows a colony of blue-green bacteria.

All blue-green bacteria contain chlorophyll, which is green. They also contain a bluish pigment. Despite their name, not all of these bacteria are

blue-green in color. Many contain other pigments. Thus, blue-green bacteria may appear yellow, red, brown, or violet.

Blue-green bacteria are common wherever there is moisture. They can live in both fresh water and salt water. They grow on the sides of damp rocks and on the bark of trees. Blue-green bacteria have been found growing at temperatures below freezing and as high as 80°C.

Most blue-green bacteria are useful organisms. They are a food source for many animals that live in water. In addition, blue-green bacteria can be used to determine water quality. They are among the first living things to react to the presence of sewage in water. Sewage causes these bacteria to grow rapidly. What does the presence of a large number of blue-green bacteria in water indicate?

Figure 3·7

Some blue-green bacteria grow in hot springs. Blue-green bacteria called *Nostoc* form colonies *(inset)*.

BACTERIA

The other major group of monerans are the bacteria. **Bacteria** are monerans that do not contain blue and green pigments. Unlike their blue-green relatives, most bacteria cannot make food. They must get food from other sources. Bacteria are almost everywhere. They live in and on your body. They are in air, water, and soil. They live in and on plants and animals.

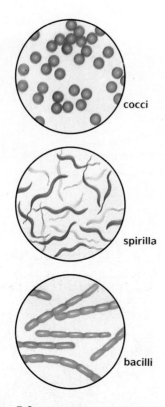

Figure 3·8

Three shapes of bacterial cells.

Figure 3·9

Structure of a typical bacterial cell.

The cells of bacteria are found in three forms, shown in Figure 3·8. *Cocci* (KAHK sī) (sing., *coccus*) are sphere-shaped bacteria. They may be found alone, or in pairs, chains, or grapelike clusters. Acne and strep throat are diseases caused by cocci. *Bacilli* (buh SIHL ī) (sing., *bacillus*) are rod-shaped bacteria. Some grow in chains. Whooping cough is caused by a bacillus. *Spirilla* (spī RIHL uh) (sing., *spirillum*) are bacteria that are shaped like spirals or corkscrews. Spirilla are always found alone. Some species of spirilla enrich the soil.

The cells of all bacteria have a similar structure. Like other monerans, bacteria lack a nucleus. Note in Figure 3·9 that the DNA is in the central part of the cell, but not enclosed in a nucleus. The cytoplasm contains ribosomes and stored food. Outside the cell membrane is a tough cell wall that gives the cell its shape. In some bacteria a jellylike layer called a capsule is found outside the cell wall. The capsule protects the cell and allows it to stick to surfaces.

Many bacteria move by means of flagella (fluh-JEHL uh) (sing., *flagellum*). *Flagella* are whiplike structures that extend from the cytoplasm. A bacterial cell may have one or many flagella. Some bacteria have none.

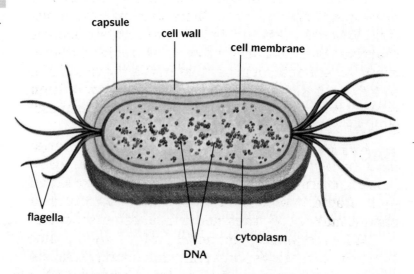

REPRODUCTION OF BACTERIA

Bacteria reproduce asexually by splitting into two cells in a process called **fission** (FIHSH uhn). Fission is simpler than mitosis. Fission does not involve a spindle, centrioles, or visible chromosomes. Bacteria sometimes reproduce very quickly. Some species can divide as often as once every 20 minutes. Refer to Figure 3·10 as you read about fission.

1. The DNA molecule makes a copy of itself.

2. The cell membrane and cell wall grow inward near the middle of the cell.

3. New cell walls form between the daughter cells. Each new cell has an identical strand of DNA.

Figure 3·10
Bacteria reproduce asexually by the process of fission. How is this process simpler than mitosis?

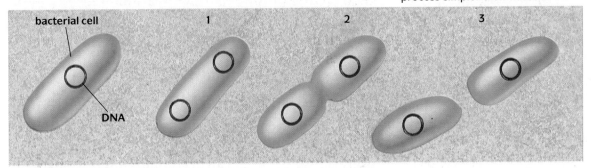

bacterial cell

DNA

1   2   3

GROWTH OF BACTERIA

Favorable conditions must exist for bacteria to grow and divide quickly. Bacteria must have moisture. When there is too little moisture, they become inactive. Bacteria only grow at suitable temperatures. Most bacteria grow best in the range of 25°C to 40°C. A few species can grow at very low or high temperatures. Most bacteria grow best in darkness. Sunlight kills many kinds of bacteria.

Oxygen is a factor in the growth of bacteria. Most bacteria can grow with or without oxygen. Some bacteria need oxygen while others are killed by it. Bacteria also need food. Since most bacteria cannot make food, they get it from other sources.

When conditions are not right for growth, some bacteria form endospores (EHN doh spawrz). An *endospore* is a structure that contains bacterial DNA and a small amount of cytoplasm surrounded by a

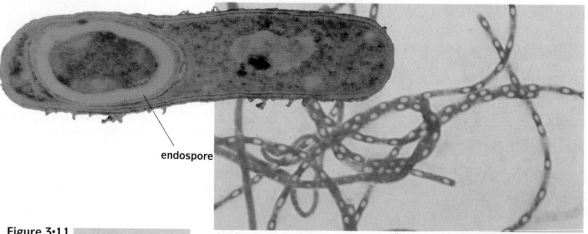

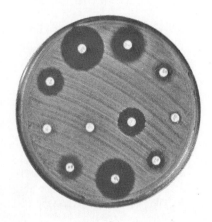

Figure 3·11

An endospore inside a bacterial cell. Under what conditions will endospores form?

Figure 3·12

Disks containing different antibiotics are placed on a bacterial culture. A clear area around a disk means that the growth of bacteria has been stopped.

tough, protective covering. An endospore forms within a bacterium, as shown in Figure 3·11. Then the bacterial cell bursts and the endospore is released. Endospores can survive harsh conditions over a long time. When conditions improve an endospore grows into a new bacterium.

HELPFUL AND HARMFUL BACTERIA

Some bacteria use the tissues of living animals or plants as food. These bacteria are parasites (PAR-uh sīts). A **parasite** is an organism that lives in or on another organism and harms it. The organism that the parasite feeds on is called the *host*. Bacterial parasites cause disease in two ways. Some directly destroy the host's tissues by feeding on them. Others produce poisons that harm the host.

Many bacterial diseases can be prevented by the use of vaccines. If a bacterial disease is caught it may be cured by the use of antibiotics (an tee bī-AHT ihks). *Antibiotics* are drugs that slow or stop the growth of bacteria. You can see the effect of antibiotics in Figure 3·12.

Some bacteria cause food to spoil. They can also cause two different kinds of food poisoning. One kind results from poisons in the food. These poisons are waste products of bacteria in the food. *Botulism* (BAHCH uh lihz uhm) is an example of this kind of food poisoning. Botulism often results from eating food that has been improperly treated during home canning.

The other kind of food poisoning is caused by eating food containing certain kinds of bacteria. These bacteria reproduce inside the body and give off poisons. *Salmonella* (sal muh NEHL uh) are bacilli that cause this type of food poisoning.

Although some bacteria cause disease, most are helpful to other living things. Many bacteria play a useful role in recycling matter. Bacteria decay, or break down, matter that was once living. Simple substances are released by this breakdown. These substances are used for new growth by plants and other organisms.

Nitrogen-fixing bacteria combine nitrogen from the air with other elements to form compounds that are useful to plants. Plants use these compounds to make proteins. Animals get their proteins by eating plants.

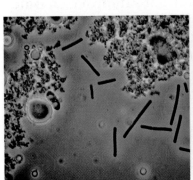 

Figure 3·13
Yogurt is made by using the action of these bacilli bacteria *(left)*. Many people enjoy the taste of yogurt *(right)*.

Bacteria also help in the making of a variety of foods. Sauerkraut is made by using bacteria to turn the sugar in cabbage leaves into a sour substance. Bacteria are also used in making yogurt and cheese.

REVIEW

1. What are the two main groups of monerans, and how do they differ?
2. Describe the structure of a bacterial cell. What shapes do bacteria have?
3. How is fission in bacteria different from mitosis in other cells?
4. Give two ways in which bacteria cause disease. Identify two ways in which bacteria are helpful.

CHALLENGE Suggest a reason for the rapid growth of blue-green bacteria in polluted water.

3·4 Protists

After completing this section, you will be able to

- **identify** traits of protists.
- **compare** the three groups of plantlike protists.
- **distinguish** between the four groups of protozoans on the basis of movement.
- **list** some ways in which each group of protists is useful and harmful.

The key terms in this section are

ciliates	flagellates
conjugation	protists
cyst	protozoan
diatom	pseudopod
dinoflagellate	sporozoan

proto- (first)

Figure 3·14

These protists are found in fresh water.

TRAITS OF PROTISTS

The second kingdom of life is made up of the protists (PROH tihsts). **Protists** are mostly single-celled microscopic organisms that live in water or in moist places. The cells of protists are much more complex than those of monerans. Unlike a moneran cell, a protist cell contains a nucleus and other cell structures, such as chloroplasts.

Both protists and monerans exist either alone or in colonies. Recall that a colony is a group of similar cells that are attached to each other. Plants and animals are multicellular. A multicellular plant or animal is made up of many different types of cells. Protists and monerans may form colonies, but they are not multicellular.

Protists can be found in both the fresh water of streams and ponds and in the salt water of oceans. A few can also be found in moist places on land, such as in damp soil. Scientists have found thousands of species of protists in all regions of the earth.

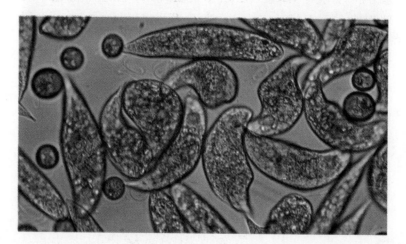

Species of protists differ from each other in several ways. One important difference is the way in which they get food. Some protists are like animals in that they eat other living things. Some protists have chloroplasts and can make their own food. These protists are like plants in that they use

68

the energy in sunlight to make sugars. Recall that this process is called photosynthesis. A protist that makes its own food is called a plantlike protist. Some protists are neither plantlike nor animallike. These protists get their food in yet other ways.

Most protists reproduce by fission. How does this compare with reproduction in monerans? Fission is a form of asexual reproduction, since just one parent is needed to make new organisms. Figure 3·15 shows a protist dividing by fission. Some protists can also reproduce by sexual means.

PLANTLIKE PROTISTS

A *euglena* (yoo GLEE nuh) is a plantlike protist that is common in fresh water and damp soil. Look at the euglena shown in Figure 3·16. How can you tell from the drawing that this is not a moneran? Notice the chloroplasts and the starch granules. Photosynthesis takes place in the chloroplasts. Sugar made by photosynthesis is stored as starch in the granules.

A euglena is a plantlike protist, but it also has some animallike traits. Like an animal, a euglena lacks a cell wall. Also, it can use its flagellum to move through the water. A euglena can also take food from the surrounding water when there is not enough light for photosynthesis.

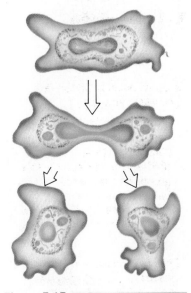

Figure 3·15
Fission in a protist.

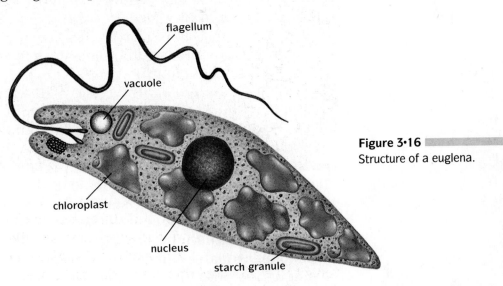

flagellum

vacuole

chloroplast

nucleus

starch granule

Figure 3·16
Structure of a euglena.

A second type of plantlike protist can be found in both fresh water and salt water. A **diatom** (DĪ uh-tahm) is a plantlike protist with a glassy cell wall. The cell wall is made of a substance like glass, and it forms a two-part shell. The two parts of the shell fit together like the two halves of a gift box. Each species has a shell with a different shape. Look at Figure 3·17. Do diatoms have flagella?

Diatoms exist in great numbers in the ocean and are food for many organisms. Diatoms carry on photosynthesis and thus release much oxygen into the water. The oxygen can be used by other organisms. As diatoms die, their shells fall to the bottom of the ocean. These shells may collect, forming a powdery substance. Because it is gritty, this substance is used in making toothpaste and scouring powder.

dino- (rotation)
flagellare (whip)

Figure 3·18

Structure of a dinoflagellate.

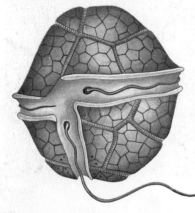

A third group of plantlike protists are the dinoflagellates (dih nuh FLAJ uh layts). A **dinoflagellate** is a plantlike protist that has two flagella. Note the two flagella in Figure 3·18. The flagellum that trails behind is used to move forward. The flagellum that circles around the middle is used to steer.

Like all plantlike protists, dinoflagellates contain chlorophyll. These protists also contain other pigments, especially red ones. Some red dinoflagellates release poisons into the water. A large number of red dinoflagellates can make the water look red, causing a "red tide." The poisons released by these protists during a red tide may kill many fish.

ANIMALLIKE PROTISTS

An animallike protist is called a **protozoan** (proh tuh ZOH uhn). Protozoans have no chloroplasts and get their food from other living things. Protozoans are placed into four groups, based on the way they move about.

Flagellates (FLAJ uh layts) are protozoans that use flagella for movement. Most flagellates live inside other organisms. Some flagellates are useful to the animals in which they live. Those in the intestines of termites help the termites digest wood. Other flagellates are harmful. The flagellates shown in Figure 3·19 are parasites. They live in the blood of insects and other animals, including humans. These flagellates cause African sleeping sickness.

A second group of protozoans are those that move by means of pseudopods (soo duh pahdz). A **pseudopod** is a fingerlike extension of the cell and is used in moving and feeding. Pseudopods stretch out ahead of the rest of the cell. The remainder of the cell flows toward the pseudopods, moving the cell forward.

An *amoeba* (uh MEE buh) is a freshwater protozoan that moves and feeds by forming pseudopods. This protist has no definite shape. Look at the amoeba in Figure 3·20. Pseudopods move toward a piece of food and surround it. The food particles are then taken into the cell, where they are digested.

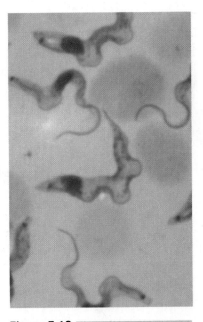

Figure 3·19
These flagellates cause African sleeping sickness.

pseudo- (false)
podium (foot)

Figure 3·20
An amoeba feeds by forming pseudopods.

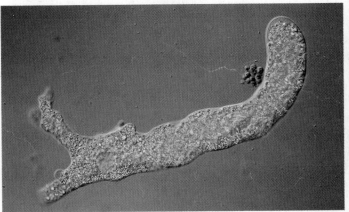
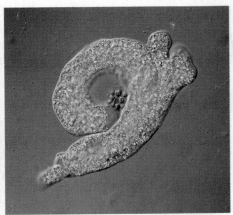

Amoebas may live in ponds that dry up when there is no rain. During a drought, an amoeba forms into a ball and makes a thick, protective cover. A protozoan in this form is called a **cyst** (sihst). Amoebas that form cysts can survive dryness or extreme temperatures. When better conditions return, the cysts open, and the amoebas become active again.

Most amoebas are harmless, but a few kinds cause disease. One disease is caused by amoebas that are parasites in human intestines. This disease is spread by water that is polluted by sewage.

A third group of protozoans use cilia (SIHL ee-uh) for movement. *Cilia* are short hairlike structures. Cilia are much shorter and more numerous than flagella. Protists that move by means of cilia

---

ACTIVITY — What Are the Characteristics of a Paramecium?

OBJECTIVE
Observe the structures, movement, and feeding of a paramecium.

MATERIALS
lab apron, 2 toothpicks, petroleum jelly, depression slide, 3 droppers, culture of paramecia, coverslip, methyl cellulose, microscope, yeast cells stained with crystal violet

PROCEDURE
A. Wear a lab apron during this activity.
B. Using a toothpick, make a thin ring of petroleum jelly around the depression of a depression slide.
C. Use a dropper to place a drop of a culture of paramecia on a coverslip. Use a clean dropper to add a drop of methyl cellulose. This substance will slow the movements of the paramecia.
D. Quickly turn the coverslip over and lower it onto the ring of petroleum jelly. Observe the slide with a microscope. Locate and study some paramecia.
E. Use the point of a clean toothpick to carefully lift the coverslip without moving it from side to side. Use a clean dropper to add a drop of stained yeast to the slide, and then replace the coverslip.
F. Place the slide on a microscope, and locate some paramecia. Observe the paramecia feeding on the yeast. Record your observations.
G. Make a drawing of a paramecium as you observe it through the microscope. Label as many structures as you can find.

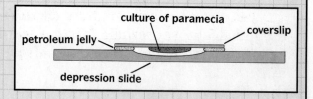

culture of paramecia — coverslip — petroleum jelly — depression slide

RESULTS AND CONCLUSIONS
1. Describe how a paramecium moves.
2. Explain how a paramecium gets its food. What do you think a paramecium might eat besides yeast?
3. In what structure or structures were the yeast cells digested?

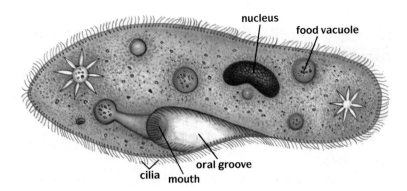

nucleus

food vacuole

cilia   mouth   oral groove

Figure 3·21
Structure of a paramecium.

are called **ciliates** (SIHL ee ayts). A *paramecium* (par uh MEE shee uhm) (pl., *paramecia*) is a slipper-shaped ciliate. Notice the many cilia on the paramecium in Figure 3·21. The cilia beat together in a rhythmic manner. This beating causes the paramecium to move through the water. Cilia also move bits of food into a groove that leads to the mouth. Once inside the cell, food is digested in vacuoles.

A paramecium can reproduce by fission. It can also reproduce sexually, through conjugation (kahn juh GAY shuhn). **Conjugation** is a form of sexual reproduction in which two cells join and then exchange nuclear material. Two paramecia join and exchange part of their nuclear material. The new cells that form have traits of both parents.

The fourth group of protozoans are those that have no means of movement. A **sporozoan** (spawr-uh ZOH uhn) is a protozoan that has no means of movement and that sometimes forms spores. A *spore* is an asexual reproductive cell with a thick, protective covering. Most sporozoans are parasites. One type causes malaria (muh LAIR ee uh), a disease of humans. The sporozoan that causes malaria is carried from person to person by mosquitos.

cilium (eyelash)

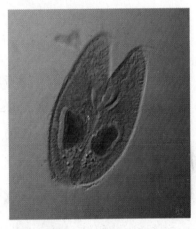

Figure 3·22
Conjugation is a form of sexual reproduction.

REVIEW

1. How are protists similar to monerans? How do protists differ from monerans?
2. How do the three groups of plantlike protists differ?
3. How do the four groups of protozoans differ?
4. List some ways in which protists are harmful. List some ways in which they are useful.

CHALLENGE Some protists move toward light, and some move away from light. Which way do you think a euglena moves? Why?

3·5 Fungi and Their Relatives

TRAITS OF FUNGI

Yeasts, mushrooms, molds, and mildews are examples of fungi (FUHN jī). A **fungus** (FUHN guhs) (pl., *fungi*) is an organism that lacks chlorophyll, absorbs food, and produces spores. Figure 3·23 shows some spores.

Fungi were once classified as plants. They have some plantlike traits: they do not move, and they have cell walls. But fungi differ from plants, too. They lack chlorophyll and cannot make their own food. The cell walls of fungi are made of different materials than are those of plants. Fungi are placed in a separate kingdom — kingdom Fungi.

Fungi grow best in places that are dark and moist. Fungi absorb their food. A fungus releases chemicals into its food source. The chemicals digest the food outside the body of the fungus. The fungus then absorbs the digested food.

Most fungi use the remains of dead organisms as food. Fungi often feed on such things as dead leaves or rotting wood. This action helps to keep dead materials from building up in nature.

Some fungi are parasites that live in the tissues of plants or animals. For example, athlete's foot is a skin disease caused by a parasitic fungus.

Figure 3·23

Spores of fungi. A spore is a reproductive cell with a thick, protective covering.

KINDS OF FUNGI

There are three main groups of fungi. In one group are fungi whose bodies are made up of masses of fine threads. Fungi of the second group form spores within sacs. Fungi of the third group form spores on tiny club-shaped stalks.

Look at the bread mold shown in Figure 3·24. This mold is an example of a fungus made up of fine threads. The threadlike structures of molds are called **hyphae** (HĪ fee). Notice in Figure 3·24 that some hyphae grow on the surface of the bread. Other hyphae grow downward into the bread. Notice the *spore cases* on the hyphae that grow upward. Each spore case contains many spores. As the spore cases ripen, they turn black, giving the fungus a black color. The ripe spore cases break open, releasing many spores into the air. Each spore can grow into a new fungus if it lands in a suitable place.

PUZZLER

Some fungi make antibiotics, chemicals that kill bacteria. Suggest at least two ways that such chemicals might be helpful to a fungus in its natural surroundings.

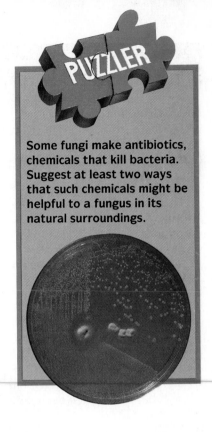

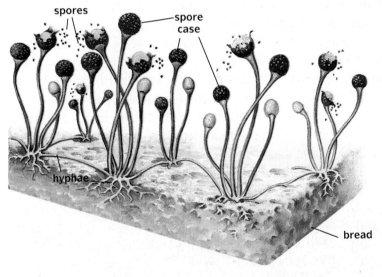

spores

spore case

hyphae

bread

Figure 3·24
Structure of a bread mold.

You may have seen a green mold growing on an orange. This fungus produces spores in sacs. The fungus damages the orange, but it also makes the useful product penicillin. This antibiotic is used to treat diseases caused by bacteria.

Yeasts also produce spores in sacs. These single-celled, microscopic fungi are very useful. Yeasts use sugar to get energy to carry on life processes.

ACTIVITY   What Substances Do Yeasts Need for Growth?

OBJECTIVES

Observe the changes in yeast mixed with a variety of substances.

Draw conclusions about the growth needs of yeasts.

MATERIALS

hand lens, dry yeast, glass-marking pencil, 4 test tubes, test-tube rack, sugar, dropper, tap water, 4 small balloons, 4 microscope slides, 4 coverslips, microscope

PROCEDURE

A. Use a hand lens to examine some dry yeast. Record what you see.

B. Use a glass-marking pencil to label each of four test tubes *A, B, C,* and *D*. Place the test tubes in a test-tube rack.

C. Put a pinch of dry yeast into each test tube. Put a pinch of sugar into test tubes *B* and *D*.

D. Use a dropper to add 10 drops of water to test tube *C* and 10 drops to test tube *D*.

E. Cover the opening of each test tube with a small balloon. Record the appearance of the contents of each test tube. Note the appearance of each of the balloons.

F. Place the test tubes in a warm, draft-free place, out of direct sunlight, for 24 hours.

G. The next day, look for changes in the contents of each of the test tubes and in the balloons. Record your observations.

H. Make a wet mount of a sample from each test tube. Observe the samples under both low power and high power of a microscope. Record what you see.

RESULTS AND CONCLUSIONS

1. Compare the appearance of the contents of each test tube in steps **C, D,** and **G**. Account for any changes you see.

2. Compare the appearance of the balloons of each test tube in steps **E** and **G**. Account for any changes you see.

3. Compare the appearance of each sample of yeast cells in step **H**. Account for any differences you observe.

4. What are some substances needed for the growth of yeasts? Explain your answer.

Figure 3·25
Budding yeast cells.

When yeasts use sugar in this way, alcohol and carbon dioxide gas are given off. The process of releasing energy, alcohol, and carbon dioxide from sugar is called **fermentation** (fer mehn TAY shuhn). When yeast is allowed to ferment grape juice, wine is produced. When yeast is mixed into bread dough, carbon dioxide bubbles from the fermentation cause the dough to rise.

Like other sac fungi, yeasts reproduce by forming spores. But yeasts also reproduce by budding. **Budding** is a form of asexual reproduction in which a new organism forms as an outgrowth of the parent. During budding, a yeast cell grows a small bud on one side of the cell. The bud later grows to the size of a mature yeast cell. Find budding yeasts in Figure 3·25.

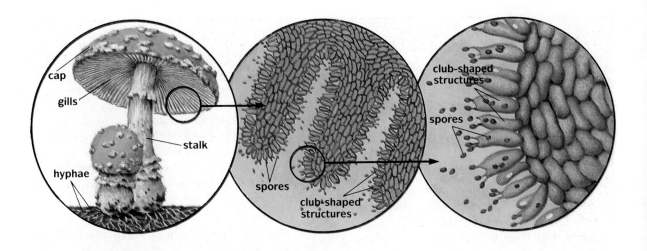

Mushrooms are examples of fungi that form spores on club-shaped stalks. The part of a mushroom seen aboveground is just part of a much larger organism. Most of a mushroom is made of hyphae that spread through a large area of soil. The part aboveground is the reproductive organ of this large fungus.

Look at the mushroom in Figure 3·26. The *stalk* is the upright part of a mushroom. The *cap* is the umbrella-shaped part. The many thin sheets on the underside of the cap are called *gills*. The enlarged view of gills in Figure 3·26C shows the club-shaped stalks that carry the spores. A single mushroom may produce hundreds of millions of spores.

RELATIVES OF FUNGI

A *slime mold* is a funguslike protist. Slime molds get their name from the fact that they often appear as slimy masses, as you can see in Figure 3·27 *(bottom)*.

Slime molds have stages in their life cycle similar to those of both protozoans and fungi. During part of its life cycle, a slime mold exists as single cells that look and act much like amoebas. At certain times the single cells come together to form large, slimy masses. At this time the slime mold reproduces by forming spores. How is this behavior like that of fungi? Spores that land on damp, shaded soil may grow into new single cells.

Figure 3·26
Structure of a mushroom *(A)*, enlargement of gills *(B)*, and enlargement of club-shaped structures that carry spores *(C)*.

Figure 3·27
Slime mold developing spore cases *(top)*. Slime mold mass *(bottom)*.

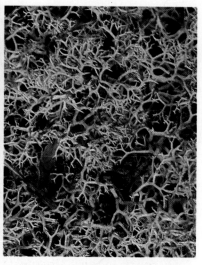

Figure 3·28
Types of lichens.

syn- (together)
bios (life)

There are many examples in nature of two different organisms living together. **Symbiosis** is the close relationship between two different kinds of organisms. A common example of symbiosis involves fungi. A *lichen* (LĪ kuhn) is made up of a fungus and an alga living together. An *alga* is a simple plant. You can see three types of lichens in Figure 3·28.

Both the alga and the fungus in a lichen benefit from the symbiosis. The alga, being a plant, can make food by using energy from the sun. The fungus cannot make its own food. The food made by the alga is used by both the alga and the fungus.

An alga lives in water or in wet places on land. A fungus can store a good deal of water. The inside of a fungus makes a good home for an alga. Because of the symbiosis of the alga and the fungus, a lichen can live almost anywhere. It can live where there is no food and very little water.

REVIEW

1. Describe the traits of fungi.
2. List two uses of fungi.
3. How is a slime mold like a fungus? How is a slime mold like a protist?
4. Explain the relationship that occurs in a lichen. What is the name of this relationship?

CHALLENGE Few organisms can grow on bare, sunny rock. Explain why lichens can grow in such places.

CHAPTER SUMMARY

The main ideas in this chapter are listed below. Read these statements before you answer the Chapter Review questions.

- A system of classification gives a way of understanding how the many life forms on the earth are related to each other. The classification of a living thing is based on structure, fossil studies, and chemical makeup. (3·1)

- The seven major classification categories in the classification system are kingdom, phylum, class, order, family, genus, species. (3·1)

- Living things are divided into five kingdoms. The five kingdoms are Monera, Protista, Fungi, Plantae, and Animalia. (3·1)

- A virus is a small particle made of nucleic acid with a protein covering. A virus can reproduce only inside a living cell. Some viruses cause disease in animals and plants. (3·2)

- Blue-green bacteria and bacteria make up kingdom Monera. Monerans are simple, one-celled organisms that have a cell wall but lack a nucleus. (3·3)

- Blue-green bacteria make their own food by photosynthesis. Most bacteria get their food from other sources. (3·3)

- Bacteria reproduce by fission and grow best in moist, dark conditions. Some bacteria cause disease, but many others perform useful functions. (3·3)

- Protists are organisms with complex cells that exist alone or in colonies. Protists include both animallike and plantlike forms. (3·4)

- Plantlike protists produce their own food by photosynthesis. Plantlike protists provide food and oxygen for other organisms. (3·4)

- Protozoans are animallike protists. Protozoans are divided into four groups, based on their method of movement. (3·4)

- A fungus is an organism that absorbs food and reproduces by spores. Fungi are divided into three groups, based on their structure and method of reproduction. (3·5)

- Slime molds are funguslike protists that reproduce by forming spores. Lichens are organisms made up of an alga and a fungus living together in a symbiotic relationship. (3·5)

The key terms in this chapter are listed below. Use each term in a sentence that shows the meaning of the term.

bacteria	dinoflagellate	protists
blue-green bacteria	fermentation	protozoan
budding	fission	pseudopod
ciliates	flagellates	scientific name
classification	fungus	sporozoan
conjugation	hyphae	symbiosis
cyst	monerans	vaccine
diatom	parasite	virus

Chapter Review

VOCABULARY

Write the letter of the term that best matches the definition. Not all the terms will be used.

1. The grouping of things according to a system
2. A plantlike protist with two flagella
3. Monerans that make food by photosynthesis
4. A plantlike protist that has a glassy cell wall
5. Threadlike structures formed by fungi
6. A protozoan that has no means of movement
7. A particle made of nucleic acid with a protein covering
8. Asexual reproduction process of splitting into two cells
9. Animallike protists
10. A close relationship between two different kinds of organisms

a. bacteria
b. blue-green bacteria
c. budding
d. ciliates
e. classification
f. diatom
g. dinoflagellate
h. flagellates
i. fission
j. hyphae
k. monerans
l. protists
m. protozoan
n. sporozoan
o. symbiosis
p. virus

CONCEPTS

Identify each statement as True or False. If a statement is false, replace the underlined term or phrase with a term or phrase that makes the statement true.

1. Bacteria and protists reproduce asexually by the process of <u>fission</u>.
2. <u>Blue-green bacteria</u> help to produce sauerkraut, yogurt, and cheese.
3. Chicken pox, polio, and mumps are diseases caused by <u>fungi</u>.
4. Bacilli, cocci, and spirilla are the three forms of cells in <u>protozoans</u>.
5. <u>Viruses</u> cannot reproduce unless they are in a living cell.

Choose the term or phrase that best answers the question or completes the statement.

6. The largest classification group is a
   a. class.
   b. kingdom.
   c. order.
   d. phylum.
7. The scientific name of an organism is its genus and
   a. class.
   b. family.
   c. order.
   d. species.
8. Which of these is a product of fermentation?
   a. carbon dioxide
   b. oxygen
   c. sugar
   d. water

9. Amoebas move by means of
   a. cilia.
   c. pseudopods.
   b. flagella.
   d. spores.
10. Lichens are made up of an alga and a
   a. bacterium.
   c. protist.
   b. fungus.
   d. virus.

Answer the following in complete sentences.

11. List the seven major groups used in classification.
12. Why are viruses described as being on the borderline between living and nonliving things?
13. How do the cells of monerans differ from the cells of other living things?
14. Identify three types of plantlike protists. Explain how they can be distinguished from each other.
15. Explain how a slime mold resembles both protists and fungi.

APPLICATION/
CRITICAL
THINKING

1. An organism is found in moist soil. This single-celled creature has a cell wall but lacks a nucleus and flagella. What kingdom does this organism belong to? What additional information would you need to decide whether it is a bacterium or a blue-green bacterium?
2. Milk is pasteurized to prevent spoilage by bacteria. In this process the milk is heated briefly and then cooled quickly. Why is it important to cool the milk quickly?
3. Suppose you find a protist in pond water. The protist has no cilia or flagella but is able to move around. What type of protist might it be?
4. Since dinoflagellates have flagella, they might be grouped with the flagellate protozoans. Why would this grouping be incorrect?
5. Fungi were once thought to be plants. Why, do you think, did scientists think this? Why is this idea incorrect?

EXTENSION

1. The scientific name for dogs is *Canis familiaris.* Use a reference book to find the complete classification of the dog.
2. Use reference books to find out how to grow a hay infusion. Make drawings of the organisms you observe with a microscope. Ask your parents' permission before you try this activity.
3. How was penicillin discovered? How is it produced today? Use reference books and write a report on your findings.
4. Yeasts are used for many purposes in addition to brewing and baking. Research the uses of yeasts, and report to your class.

CHAPTER 4

PLANTS

What are the structures shown in the photograph? Would you be surprised to learn that they are part of a moss? You probably have seen mosses before. Mosses are simple plants that form spongy, green mats on damp soil and on rocks. But you may not have noticed these structures, which are only a few centimeters tall. What might be their function?

These structures contain spores, which are special cells that are used for reproduction. Some mosses produce green spore cases, like these. Others produce brown spore cases.

- What kinds of plants reproduce by forming spores?
- How are mosses different from other kinds of plants?
- In what other ways do plants reproduce?

4·1 Traits of Nonseed Plants

Look at the plants in Figure 4·1. Although they look different from one another, these plants share one trait. They all reproduce without forming seeds. Because of the way they reproduce, these plants can be referred to as nonseed plants.

There are three main groups of nonseed plants. The first group is algae (AL jee) (sing., *alga*). An alga (AL guh) is a plant that lacks roots, stems, and leaves. The second group includes mosses and liverworts (LIHV uhr werts). Club mosses, horsetails, and ferns make up the third group.

Like all plants, nonseed plants carry on photosynthesis. Recall that photosynthesis is a process by which plants use energy from the sun to make their own food. This process takes place in the chloroplasts of plant cells. During photosynthesis, light energy is changed into chemical energy. The energy is stored in the form of a sugar called glucose.

Figure 4·1

Kinds of nonseed plants: green alga *(A)*, brown alga *(B)*, moss *(C)*, and fern *(D)*.

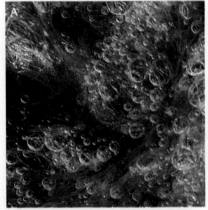

The classification of nonseed plants is based on the presence or absence of vascular tissue. A *tissue* is a group of similar cells that performs a certain function. **Vascular tissue** is a group of tubelike cells that carries food and water from one part of a plant to another. Vascular tissue also provides support for a plant. Some plants with vascular tissue

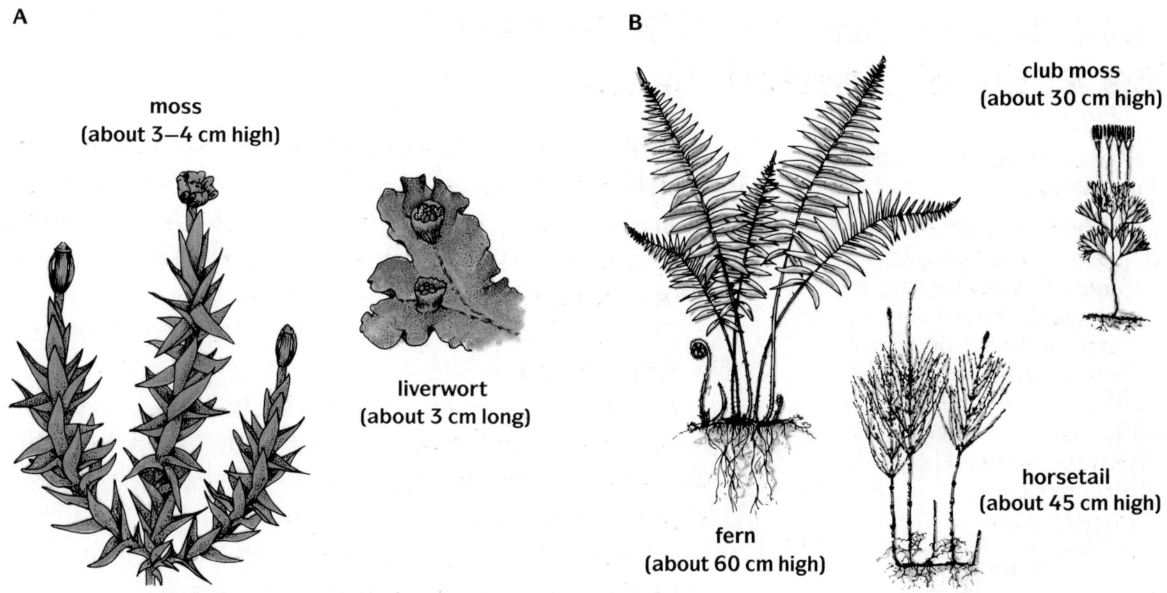

moss
(about 3—4 cm high)

liverwort
(about 3 cm long)

B

club moss
(about 30 cm high)

horsetail
(about 45 cm high)

fern
(about 60 cm high)

Figure 4·2
Nonvascular plants *(A)* and
vascular plants *(B)*.

can grow to great heights. Plants that have vascular tissue are called **vascular plants**. Nonseed plants such as club mosses, horsetails, and ferns are vascular plants.

Plants that lack vascular tissue are called **nonvascular plants**. Algae, mosses, and liverworts are nonvascular plants. These plants are very small. Look at Figure 4·2. How tall are moss plants?

Most nonvascular plants live in water. They are either very small or very thin. Some green algae consist of only a single cell. Some brown algae grow to be many meters long but are only a few cells thick. Such an alga can grow large because it floats in water. The water surrounds the plant and supports its mass. Almost all cells of the alga are in contact with water. Therefore, needed materials can be taken in directly from the water.

vasculum (vessel)
non- (lack of)

REVIEW

1. What features do all nonseed plants have in common?
2. What are the three main groups of nonseed plants? Which of these groups includes vascular plants?
3. What are the functions of vascular tissue?

CHALLENGE You have learned that some vascular plants grow to be very tall. Would you expect nonvascular land plants to grow tall? Explain your answer.

4·2 Algae

After completing this section, you will be able to

- **compare** the three main groups of green algae.
- **give examples** of ways in which green algae are important in their environment.
- **explain** how green algae, brown algae, and red algae are alike and different.
- **list** some uses of brown algae and red algae.

The key terms in this section are

alga	plankton
brown algae	red algae
green algae	

A nonseed plant that lacks roots, stems, and leaves is called an **alga**. There are three kinds of algae, classified according to the pigments they contain. The three groups of algae are green algae, brown algae, and red algae.

GREEN ALGAE

The most common of the algae are the green algae. **Green algae** are simple plants with cells that contain chloroplasts and a rigid cell wall. Recall that chloroplasts are cell structures that contain chlorophyll and carry on photosynthesis. Most green algae live in water—either fresh water or salt water. Some live in damp soil. *Protococcus*, shown in Figure 4·3*B*, grows on tree bark.

Green algae can be grouped according to their structure. One group of green algae consists of single-celled plants. A second group is made up of colonies. A *colony* is a group of similar cells attached to each other. A third group of green algae consists of multicellular plants.

The cells of some multicellular green algae form long threadlike structures called *filaments* (FIHL-uh muhnts). Other green algae are tube-shaped. Look at Figure 4·3*A*. *Ulva*, or sea lettuce, has a flat bladelike body that floats on the water. Although some algae have leaflike parts, none have true roots, stems, or leaves.

Figure 4·3

Ulva, or sea lettuce *(A)*; *Protococcus* on tree bark, with inset of cells *(B)*; *Volvox (C)*.

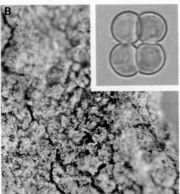
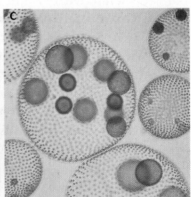

Chlorella (kluh REHL uh) is a single-celled green alga. Each *Chlorella* cell has a nucleus and a cup-shaped chloroplast. *Chlorella* is easy to grow and has been used by scientists to study the process of photosynthesis.

Volvox is a green alga that forms colonies. A *Volvox* colony, shown in Figure 4·3C, is a hollow ball made of hundreds of cells. The cells are held together by a sticky substance. Each *Volvox* cell has two flagella. What is the function of the flagella?

Spirogyra (spī ruh JĪ ruh) is a green alga that forms filaments. In part *A* of Figure 4·4, you can see a single filament of this alga. *Spirogyra* reproduces by both sexual and asexual means. Asexual reproduction is by mitosis. A cell divides to form two cells, which increases the number of cells in the filament.

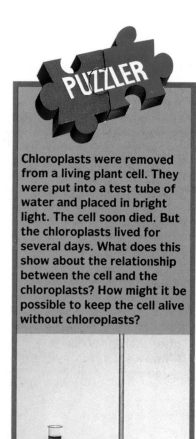
Figure 4·4
Conjugation in *Spirogyra*. In part *D*, what will each cell become?

Spirogyra reproduces sexually by conjugation. Recall that conjugation is a process in which two cells exchange nuclear material. Figure 4·4 shows the process of conjugation in *Spirogyra*. Two filaments line up side by side, as shown in part *B*. A tube is formed between cells that are opposite each other. The contents of one cell flow into the opposite cell, as shown in part *C*. You can see in part *D* that the nuclei of the two cells unite. Each cell that forms will grow into a new filament.

planktos (drifting)

Green algae perform several important functions. Green algae are a major source of food for animals that live in water. Green algae make up an important part of plankton. **Plankton** consists of small organisms that float near the surface of a body of water. Many animals, such as fish, feed on plankton. Green algae also release oxygen during photosynthesis. Some scientists think that half of the oxygen in the atmosphere is released by green algae.

BROWN ALGAE

Many of the plants called seaweed are brown algae. **Brown algae** are many-celled algae that live in water and that contain both a green pigment and a brown pigment. These pigments give the algae a brown or olive-green color. Most brown algae live in salt water and are common along coasts of the Pacific and North Atlantic oceans.

Figure 4·5

Kelp *(left)* and *Fucus (right)* are kinds of brown algae.

Fucus (FYOO kuhs), also known as rockweed, is a common brown alga that grows in shallow ocean water. The base of this alga attaches to rocks in the water. *Fucus* is shown in Figure 4·5 *(right)*. Notice the air-filled chambers at the top of the plant. What is the function of these air chambers?

Researchers have found red algae growing at a greater depth than anyone believed possible. The scientists found the algae near the Bahama Islands, in water 268 m deep. Before this discovery, scientists thought that no marine plants could live in water deeper than 160 m because there would not be enough light for photosynthesis to occur. The discovery was made possible through the use of a new submarine. This submarine, called the Johnson Sea Link I, is shown in the photograph.

These deep-sea red algae can carry on the food-making process for two reasons. First, unlike algae growing at lesser depths, these red algae contain certain pigments that can capture the tiny amounts of light energy that reach great depths. These pigments then pass the energy on to chlorophyll *a*, the pigment that most plants contain. Second, the cell walls of the red algae are very thin. The thin walls allow light to pass through the cells and reach the pigments easily.

The discovery of these deep-sea red algae has raised new questions for scientists. They now wonder what the lowest level of light is that would keep plants alive.

Brown algae called *kelps* are among the largest of plants. Kelps may grow to a length of over 50 m. Figure 4·5 *(left)* shows some kelp that has washed up on the shore. In the ocean, kelps like this provide homes for animals such as otters.

Some kelps contain large amounts of minerals, such as iodine and iron. These plants are harvested and used as fertilizer and to feed livestock. Kelps also make a gummy substance that is used to give ice cream, toothpaste, and other products a smooth texture.

RED ALGAE

Red algae are many-celled algae that live in water and that contain green, blue, and red pigments. They are usually red, purple, or green in color. Most red algae live in salt water and are common in tropical oceans. Red algae live at greater depths than do other algae.

Figure 4·6
Red algae.

Figure 4·7
Agar is made from red algae. The streaks on the agar show the growth of bacteria.

Chondrus (KAHN druhs), or Irish moss, is a red alga that grows along the Atlantic coast. As you can see in Figure 4·6, Irish moss grows attached to rocks. A jellylike substance from this alga is used to thicken some salad dressings, puddings, toothpastes, and lotions.

Other species of red algae produce agar. *Agar* is a jellylike substance used to grow bacteria and fungi in the laboratory. A food source, such as sugar, is added to the agar. In Figure 4·7 you can see bacteria growing on a plate of agar.

Red algae are used as food in some parts of the world. One kind of red alga is grown as a crop in Japan. This alga is harvested from shallow waters and then dried. Red algae are valuable as food because they contain protein, vitamins, and minerals.

REVIEW

1. Describe and give examples of the three types of green algae.
2. Why are green algae important to their environment?
3. How are green, brown, and red algae alike? How are they different?
4. Describe some commercial uses of red and brown algae.

CHALLENGE Suppose all the green algae growing in a pond were destroyed. How would this affect the pond?

4·3 Mosses and Liverworts

TRAITS OF MOSSES AND LIVERWORTS

Mosses and liverworts are small, green nonvascular plants that live on land. A **moss** is a small nonvascular plant that often grows in moist areas in woods or near stream banks. Mosses have stemlike parts and small leaflike parts.

A **liverwort** is a small nonvascular plant that grows flat along a surface. Liverworts grow in wet places or on rocks near water. You can see the leaflike parts of a liverwort in Figure 4·8.

The lack of vascular tissue in mosses and liverworts limits their size. In plants without vascular tissue, water and food can move from one part of the plant to another only by diffusion. Substances moving by diffusion move too slowly to supply all parts of a large plant.

Mosses and liverworts conserve water. Because they grow close together, very little surface is exposed to the air. Thus, little water is lost to the air. In some of these plants, the surface of the plant is coated with a waxy substance. This coating cuts down on the amount of water lost by evaporation.

Mosses and liverworts have rootlike rhizoids (RĪ zoidz). A **rhizoid** anchors a moss or liverwort to the soil and absorbs water and minerals. Water moves from the rhizoids to the rest of the plant.

After completing this section, you will be able to

- **compare** the structure of mosses and liverworts.
- **describe** the stages in the life cycle of a moss.

The key terms in this section are
liverwort
moss
rhizoid

rhiza (root)
-oid (like)

Figure 4·8
Mosses *(left)* and liverworts *(right)*.

Figure 4·9

Close-up of a moss plant. In which structure are spores found?

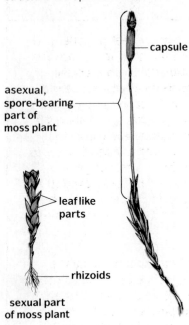

- capsule

asexual, spore-bearing part of moss plant

leaflike parts

rhizoids

sexual part of moss plant

Compared with a familiar plant, such as a rose-bush, a moss has a simple structure. Look at the moss plant shown in Figure 4·9. At the base of the moss are the rhizoids. What is their function?

During part of its life cycle, a moss plant makes *spores*. The spores are in a structure called a *capsule*. Find the capsule at the tip of the long stalk shown in Figure 4·9.

REPRODUCTION IN MOSSES

Mosses have two stages in their life cycle. Spores are produced in the asexual stage. A spore is an asexual reproductive cell with a hard covering. A spore can survive harsh conditions, such as dryness. Why are spores important to land plants?

Sexual reproduction occurs in the other stage in the life cycle. A male reproductive cell is a *sperm cell*. A female reproductive cell is an *egg cell*.

The life cycle of a moss is shown in Figure 4·10. The life cycle of a liverwort is similar. Refer to the figure as you read about the life cycle.

1. The mature moss plant is the sexual stage. Sperm and egg cells are produced at the tips of the plant.

2. Sperm cells swim through water to an egg cell. The source of water is rain or dew that covers the moss. A sperm and an egg join, in a process called *fertilization* (fer tuh luh ZAY shuhn). The fertilized egg is called a *zygote* (ZĪ goht).

Figure 4·10

Life cycle of a moss. Where are the eggs and sperm found in the moss?

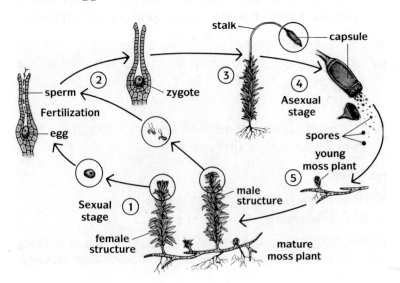

stalk

capsule

2 zygote

3

4 Asexual stage

sperm

Fertilization

egg

spores

young moss plant

5

male structure

Sexual 1 stage

female structure

mature moss plant

What Is the Structure of a Moss?

OBJECTIVE
Observe the structure of a moss.

MATERIALS
moss plants with and without spore capsules, toothpick, hand lens, microscope, microscope slide, coverslip, dropper

PROCEDURE
A. Use a toothpick to separate from a clump of moss plants a single moss plant that lacks a stalk and capsule.

B. Examine the plant with a hand lens. Make a drawing of the moss. Label the rhizoids and leaflike structures. Draw a circle around the part of the plant where the zygote would be formed.

C. Use the same toothpick to separate a moss plant that has a stalk and a capsule. Examine the parts of the plant with a hand lens. Make a drawing of the moss with the stalk and capsule. Label the rhizoids, leaflike structures, stalk, and capsule. Draw an arrow to the part of the plant where the spores are located.

D. Place a capsule on a sheet of paper and examine it with the hand lens. Look for a small lidlike structure on the capsule.

E. Place the capsule on a microscope slide. Use a pencil eraser to press down on the capsule until it splits open and spores fall onto the slide. Discard the capsule.

F. Use a dropper to add a drop of water to the spores on the microscope slide. Cover with a coverslip. Look at the spores under low and high power of a microscope. Make a drawing of several spores.

RESULTS AND CONCLUSIONS
1. Which parts of the plant make up the sexual stage in the life cycle? Which parts of the plant make up the asexual stage?

2. Which parts of the moss plant can carry on photosynthesis? Which parts are unable to photosynthesize? How can you distinguish between the parts that can photosynthesize and those that cannot?

3. What might be the function of the lidlike structure on the capsule?

---

3. The zygote develops into a stalk that grows up from the top of the moss plant. The stalk is the asexual stage. Hundreds of spores form in a capsule at the tip of the stalk.

4. The capsule ripens and breaks open, releasing the spores. They may be carried long distances by wind.

5. If a spore lands in a suitable environment, it will grow into a new moss plant.

REVIEW
1. How is a moss different from a liverwort?
2. Briefly describe the life cycle of a moss.

CHALLENGE The capsule of a moss is usually at the end of a long stalk. What advantage does this long stalk provide for mosses?

4·4 Club Mosses, Horsetails, and Ferns

Club mosses, horsetails, and ferns are nonseed plants that live on land. Unlike mosses and liverworts, these plants have vascular tissue. Thus club mosses, horsetails, and ferns grow much larger than mosses or liverworts.

CLUB MOSSES

A **club moss** is a small, evergreen vascular nonseed plant with tiny, pointed leaves. Most club mosses grow in shady, damp woods and along rocky mountain slopes. The leaves of club mosses grow in overlapping rows along the stem. Some club mosses look like small evergreen trees, as you can see in Figure 4·11. This club moss is sometimes called ground pine. But it is not related to pine trees. The pine is a more complex plant.

Figure 4·11
Club mosses.

HORSETAILS

A **horsetail** is a vascular nonseed plant with hollow stems. Most horsetails grow in wet, swampy areas. The hollow stems of horsetails have joints. At each joint is a ring of small, toothlike leaves. These leaves are not green. Only the stems of horsetails are green.

Branches grow from between the leaves at some joints on the stem. Look for the leaves and branches in Figure 4·12. How do you think horsetails got their name?

The outer covering of a horsetail stem contains a glassy substance and has a rough texture. Because of their rough texture, horsetails were used by pioneers in America to clean pots. Because of this use, horsetails are sometimes called scouring rushes.

In addition to their aboveground stems, horsetails have underground stems. An underground stem is called a **rhizome** (RĪ zohm). The parts of the plant aboveground may shrivel up during periods of cold or drought. When better conditions return, new stems and leaves grow from the rhizome.

FERNS

A **fern** is a vascular nonseed plant with roots, stems, and leaves. Ferns are the most common vascular nonseed plant. They grow in moist, shady areas. Like horsetails, ferns form a rhizome that grows just below the surface of the soil. Notice that the fern in Figure 4·13 has roots that grow from the rhizome. These roots take in water and minerals. The mature leaf of a fern is called a **frond**. As you can see in Figure 4·13, the developing fronds of a fern are tightly coiled. Because of the way they look, these coiled fern leaves are called *fiddleheads*. Each fiddlehead slowly uncoils and grows into a mature frond.

Figure 4·12
Horsetail in the spring (*left*) and in the summer (*right*).

frondis (leaf)

Figure 4·13
Structure of a fern. What does a fiddlehead develop into?

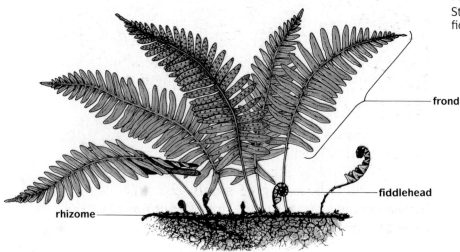

frond

fiddlehead

rhizome

95

The life cycle of a fern is like that of a moss. There is a sexual stage with sperm and egg cells, and an asexual stage with spores. The roots, rhizome, and fronds are the asexual stage. Spores are formed inside spore cases, which usually grow on the underside of a frond. Clusters of these spore cases may look like brown spots on the underside of a frond. Find the spore cases in Figure 4·14. When the spore cases split open, the spores are released into the wind. Refer to Figure 4·14 as you read about the life cycle of a fern.

Figure 4·14
Life cycle of a fern.

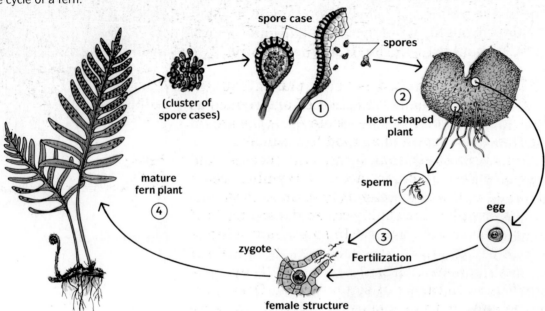

1. Spores are released from a spore case.

2. A spore grows into a flat, green, heart-shaped plant that is smaller than a dime. The heart-shaped plant grows close to the soil. Sperm and egg cells are produced by this small plant. The heart-shaped plant is the sexual stage.

3. Sperm swim to the egg cell in rain water or dew that collects on the plant. The sperm and egg join to form a zygote, or a fertilized egg. When the zygote is formed, the asexual stage begins.

4. The zygote grows into a mature fern plant, with roots, rhizome, and fronds.

Figure 4·15
An ancient forest of vascular plants, with inset of a fossil fern.

Ferns are often used as house plants. The tender, young fiddleheads are collected and cooked as a vegetable by some people. Some ferns are grown as a crop and harvested as food for animals.

Scientists think that ferns, club mosses, and horsetails were abundant about 300 million years ago. The earth was warmer at that time. Large forests of these plants probably covered many parts of the earth's surface. Figure 4·15 shows how a forest of these plants might have looked. As the climate of the earth changed, these plants died. They were buried beneath layers of soil and rock. Over time, the remains of these plants decayed. They were changed to coal, oil, and natural gas.

Scientists have found traces of these early ferns in rock. Many of the early ferns were the size of trees and grew to a height of 30 m. Most of the ferns of today are less than one meter tall.

REVIEW

1. How are club mosses different from mosses?
2. How would you distinguish a horsetail from a club moss?
3. Describe the sexual stage in the life cycle of a fern.
4. Where are spores produced in a fern?

CHALLENGE Club mosses, horsetails, and ferns need water for sperm to reach the egg cell. Why? How is this need for water a disadvantage to these plants?

4·5 Traits of Seed Plants

angeion (container)
sperma (seed)

gymnos (naked)

Recall that a vascular plant is a plant with vascular tissue that carries water and food. A **seed plant** is a vascular plant that reproduces by forming seeds. There are two main groups of seed plants: gymnosperms (JIHM nuh spermz) and angiosperms (AN jee uh spermz).

An **angiosperm** is a seed plant that produces flowers and that forms seeds within a fruit. Grasses, oak trees, dandelions, and corn are examples of angiosperms. The word *angiosperm* means "seed in a container." Angiosperm seeds are completely enclosed by a structure called a fruit. There are many kinds of fruits. The pod in which peas grow is a fruit that encloses the seeds, or peas. Tomatoes, corn kernels, cucumbers, and cherries are fruits that people eat.

A **gymnosperm** is a seed plant whose seeds do not form within a fruit. Trees such as pines, spruces, and ginkgoes are gymnosperms. Many of the shrubs that are used to decorate the land around buildings are also gymnosperms. Examples include junipers and yews.

The word *gymnosperm* means "naked seed." The seeds are said to be naked because they are not enclosed in a fruit. In many gymnosperms, such as in pines, the seeds grow on the woody scales of a cone. Such trees have two kinds of cones—male

Figure 4·16

Structure of a female cone. Where are the seeds located?

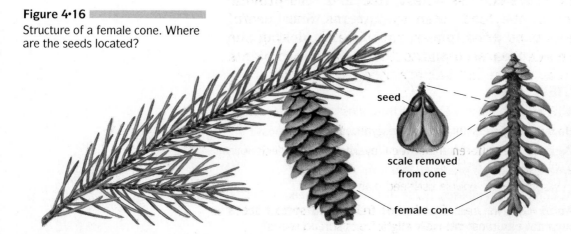

seed

scale removed
from cone

female cone

Figure 4·17
Blue spruce *(A)*, larch *(B)*, and sugar maple *(C)*.

and female. Male cones contain pollen. Female cones hold the seeds. Locate the seeds in the cone on the right in Figure 4·16.

Most gymnosperms are evergreens. An *evergreen* is a plant that is green all year because it does not shed all of its leaves at once. Most evergreens shed only their oldest leaves and keep their newer leaves. Many angiosperms and a few gymnosperms are deciduous (dih SIHJ yoo uhs). A *deciduous plant* is one that sheds all of its leaves at one time. In Figure 4·17, which trees are deciduous? Which trees are evergreens?

People use seed plants in many different ways. Seed plants such as wheat, rice, and corn provide much of the food eaten by humans. Such useful products as wood, paper, rubber, and cooking oils are made from seed plants. Fibers from seed plants such as cotton and flax are used to make cloth.

REVIEW

1. How do angiosperms differ from gymnosperms?
2. What is the difference between evergreen and deciduous plants?
3. In what ways do people use seed plants?

CHALLENGE The main function of fruits is to spread seeds through the environment. How might fruits spread seeds?

4·6 Varieties of Seed Plants

GYMNOSPERMS

Conifers are the largest group of gymnosperms. A **conifer** (KOH nuh fuhr) is a tree or shrub that bears its seeds in cones. Recall that a cone is a woody structure on which naked seeds form. The leaves of most conifers are thin and needlelike. Conifers make up a large part of the forests in the cooler regions of North America and northern Europe.

Most conifers are evergreens. Evergreen conifers include pines, hemlocks, firs, and spruces. Some evergreen conifers are shown in Figure 4·18. A few conifers, such as the larch, are deciduous. How do the larches differ from pines and firs?

Both the oldest and the largest living things on the earth are conifers. Some bristlecone pine trees are over 4000 years old. Some giant redwood trees in California and Oregon are about as tall as a 30-story building.

Other groups of gymnosperms are not as well known as the conifers. *Cycads* (sī kadz) are cone-bearing plants with a single trunk and a circle of

Figure 4·18

Kinds of conifers: Sequoia *(A)*, Scotch pine *(B)*, and bristlecone pine *(C)*.

palmlike leaves at the top. These gymnosperms were common during the age of dinosaurs. Today there are only a few species growing in warm regions. Figure 4·19 shows a cycad that grows in Florida. People often mistake cycads for palm trees, but palm trees are angiosperms.

Ginkgoes (GIHNG kohz) are deciduous trees with fan-shaped leaves. Ginkgoes belong to a group of gymnosperms that was common millions of years ago. Today there is only one living species. There are both male and female ginkgo trees. The male trees produce pollen in conelike structures. The female trees produce pairs of seeds with thick coats. Is the ginkgo shown in Figure 4·20 a male or a female? Ginkgoes are often planted as shade trees in yards and along city streets. They are hardy plants that resist air pollution, insects, and many diseases.

Figure 4·19

Zamia, a kind of cycad. Why is this plant considered to be a gymnosperm?

Figure 4·20
Ginkgo leaves and seeds.

ANGIOSPERMS

Most land plants on the earth today are angiosperms. All angiosperms have two traits in common. They form some type of flower, and their seeds are enclosed within a fruit. Angiosperm seeds are better protected than gymnosperm seeds.

You are probably familiar with the flowers of angiosperms such as roses and dandelions. Most of the best-known plants—daisies, lilies, marigolds, and sunflowers—are angiosperms. However, you may not know that grasses and trees such as oaks and ashes also form flowers. Look at the flowers of the oak and the ash in Figure 4·21. How do these flowers differ from those of roses or daisies?

Angiosperms are found in many kinds of places. Water lilies and water hyacinths are freshwater angiosperms. Eelgrass is a saltwater angiosperm. Cactuses are angiosperms that grow in deserts. Some angiosperms, such as mistletoe, are parasites. Recall that a parasite lives in or on another organism and harms it. Other angiosperms, such as the Indian pipe shown in Figure 4·21, feed on the remains of dead plants. How does the Indian pipe differ from other plants?

KINDS OF ANGIOSPERMS

The seed of an angiosperm contains either one or two cotyledons (kaht uh LEE duhnz). A **cotyledon** is a food-storing part of a seed. The food in a cotyledon is used by a sprouting plant until the plant can make its own food. The food stored in seeds makes them a useful food for humans. The seeds of wheat and rye are ground to make flour. What seeds do people eat?

Figure 4·21

Flowers of Indian pipe *(left)*, mountain ash *(middle)*, and red oak *(right)*.

102

Table 4·1 *Comparison of Monocots and Dicots*

	VEINS	VASCULAR BUNDLES	FLOWER PARTS	COTYLEDONS
MONOCOTS	parallel	vascular bundles — scattered bundles	parts in 3's or multiples of 3	1 cotyledon
DICOTS	netlike	vascular bundles — bundles in rings	parts in 4's or 5's or multiples of 4 or 5	2 cotyledons

Angiosperms are divided into two groups based on the number of cotyledons in the seed. An angiosperm with one cotyledon is called a **monocot** (MAHN uh kaht). Lilies, tulips, onions, and grasses are examples of monocots. Almost one third of all angiosperm species are monocots. An angiosperm with two cotyledons is called a **dicot** (DĪ kaht). Peanuts, beans, daisies, and maple trees are dicots.

mono- (one)

di- (two)

Table 4·1 shows four traits in which monocots and dicots differ. Refer to the table as you read about each trait. Notice that monocots have leaves with parallel veins. Dicots have leaves with a branching network of veins.

Inside a monocot stem the vascular tissue is found in scattered bundles. Inside a dicot stem the vascular tissue forms rings. The stem shown in Table 4·1 has vascular tissue in bundles that form a ring. Other dicot stems have a series of rings.

Monocots have flower parts, such as petals, in threes or multiples of three. Dicots have flower parts in fours or fives or multiples of four or five. How many petals are shown on the dicot flower in the table? Monocot seeds have one cotyledon. How many cotyledons do dicot seeds have?

How Do Monocots and Dicots Differ?

OBJECTIVE

Describe differences in structure between monocots and dicots.

MATERIALS

hand lens, 2 monocot leaves, 2 dicot leaves, 2 monocot flowers, 2 dicot flowers, soaked corn kernel, soaked lima bean, prepared slides of monocot and dicot stem cross sections, microscope

PROCEDURE

A. Use a hand lens to examine two monocot leaves and two dicot leaves. Observe the pattern of the veins.

B. Count the parts of two monocot flowers and two dicot flowers. Record the name of each flower and the number of flower parts you counted.

C. Compare the structure of a corn kernel with that of a lima bean seed. Note the location of stored food in each.

D. Examine a cross section of a monocot stem under low power of a microscope. Make a drawing of the stem, and label some of the vascular bundles. Repeat this procedure with a dicot stem cross section.

RESULTS AND CONCLUSIONS

1. Compare the pattern of the veins in the monocot leaves with that in the dicot leaves.

2. Compare the number of flower parts in the monocot flowers with the number of flower parts in the dicot flowers.

3. Compare the structure of the corn kernel with the structure of the lima bean.

4. Describe the location of the vascular bundles in the cross section of the monocot stem. How does the location of the vascular bundles in the dicot stem compare?

LIFE PATTERNS OF ANGIOSPERMS

Flowering plants may be grouped according to their life patterns. *Annuals* (AN yoo uhlz) are plants that live for only one growing season. They sprout from seeds, mature, make new seeds, and die in a single season. Annuals like the zinnias shown in Figure 4·22 are often used in flower gardens.

Biennials (bī EHN ee uhlz) are plants that live for two growing seasons. During the first year, the roots, stems, and leaves grow from the seed. In the second growing season, flowers, fruits, and seeds are formed, and then the plant dies. Beets, radishes, and carrots are all biennials.

Perennials (puh REHN ee uhlz) are plants that continue to grow year after year. The roots, stems, and leaves form in the first growing season. Flowers, fruits, and seeds are usually produced during the second or later growing season. Roses, tulips, and all trees are perennials.

Figure 4·22

Zinnia is an annual.

REVIEW

1. What are the three groups of gymnosperms?
2. How do monocots differ from dicots? Give an example of each.
3. What are two traits shared by all angiosperms?
4. Describe the life pattern of a biennial.

CHALLENGE Suppose that the flowers of a plant have six petals. What type of veins would this plant have?

CHAPTER SUMMARY

The main ideas in this chapter are listed below. Read these statements before you answer the Chapter Review questions.

- Nonseed plants reproduce without forming seeds. Algae, mosses, liverworts, club mosses, horsetails, and ferns are all nonseed plants. (4•1)
- Vascular plants have tissue of tubelike cells that carries water and food and that supports the plant. Nonvascular plants lack this tissue. (4•1)
- Algae are simple nonvascular plants that live mostly in water. Some algae are single-celled, some are colonial, and many are multicellular. (4•2)
- Green algae, brown algae, and red algae are distinguished by the pigments they contain, although they all contain chlorophyll. Some algae are used as food and for other products used by people. (4•2)
- Mosses and liverworts are small, green nonvascular plants that live on land. These plants have a life cycle with an asexual stage and a sexual stage. (4•3)

- Club mosses, horsetails, and ferns are nonseed plants with vascular tissue. These plants have a life cycle with alternating sexual and asexual stages. (4•4)
- There are two main groups of seed plants: gymnosperms, which have naked seeds, and angiosperms, which have seeds enclosed in a fruit. (4•5)
- The largest group of gymnosperms, the conifers, are trees or shrubs with needlelike leaves and seeds in cones. Other gymnosperms include cycads and ginkgoes. (4•6)
- Angiosperms are the most abundant land plants. They are flowering plants that produce seeds enclosed in a fruit. Angiosperms are divided into two groups—monocots and dicots. (4•6)

The key terms in this chapter are listed below. Use each term in a sentence that shows the meaning of the term.

alga	frond	plankton
angiosperm	green algae	red algae
brown algae	gymnosperm	rhizoid
club moss	horsetail	rhizome
conifer	liverwort	seed plant
cotyledon	monocot	vascular plants
dicot	moss	vascular tissue
fern	nonvascular plants	

Chapter Review

Use the key terms from the previous page to complete the following sentences correctly.

1. A tissue of tubelike cells that carries food and water in a plant is called _____.
2. Many-celled plants that live in water and contain red, blue, and green pigments are _____.
3. A rootlike structure that anchors a moss to the soil is a/an _____.
4. An underground stem of a fern is called a/an _____.
5. The mature leaf of a fern is called a/an _____.
6. _____ is made up of small organisms that float near the surface of a body of water.
7. A/An _____ is a food-storing part of a seed.
8. A seed plant that forms seeds enclosed in a fruit is called a/an

   _____.
9. A/An _____ is a small, evergreen vascular nonseed plant with tiny, pointed leaves.
10. A _____ is a vascular nonseed plant with roots, stem, and leaves.

CONCEPTS

Make a table like the one shown. Write the correct information under each heading.

TYPE OF ANGIOSPERM	TYPE OF VEINS	NUMBER OF FLOWER PARTS	NUMBER OF COTYLEDONS	EXAMPLE
Monocots				
Dicots				

Choose the term or phrase that best answers the question.

1. Which of these plants lives in fresh water?
   a. brown alga
   b. fern
   c. green alga
   d. club moss
2. Which of these plants is a vascular plant?
   a. fern
   b. liverwort
   c. moss
   d. red alga
3. Which of these plants has rhizomes?
   a. horsetail   c. liverwort
   b. gymnosperm   d. moss

4. Which of these plants forms seeds?
   a. club moss   **c.** gymnosperm
   b. fern   **d.** horsetail
5. Which of these plants forms flowers?
   a. angiosperm
   b. club moss
   c. gymnosperm
   d. liverwort

Answer the following in complete sentences.

6. Compare the size of vascular and nonvascular land plants. Account for their differences in size.
7. Describe some ways in which green algae are important to the environment.
8. Describe the two main stages in the life cycle of a moss.
9. What is the major difference between angiosperms and gymnosperms?

1. Algae are much more abundant in water than on land. Why, do you think, are algae not able to grow well on land?
2. The spores of which plant—a moss or a fern—are more likely to be carried by the wind? Explain your answer.
3. Suppose a plant in your yard grows many leaves but no flowers during its first year. It forms flowers, fruits, and seeds the next year and each year from then on. Is the plant an annual, a biennial, or a perennial? Explain your answer.

APPLICATION/
CRITICAL
THINKING

1. Scientists have sent along green algae, especially *Chlorella,* on space flights. The scientists want to find out if these plants can be successfully grown to be used as food on space flights. Do research on the findings.
2. Find out if algae are available in any food store in your community. If they are available, find out what types they are and how they can be prepared.
3. Seeds may be carried away from their parent plant by wind, water, or animals. Do research to find examples of seeds carried by each of these methods. Why, do you think, is it advantageous for a seed to be carried away from its parent?
4. Visit a florist's shop, and make a list of all the plants and flowers available. Check each plant to see if it is a dicot or a monocot. Mark your list accordingly.

EXTENSION

CHAPTER 5

VERTEBRATES

*T*he animal shown in the photograph is a bird called an
egret. Egrets live in marshes and ponds. An egret's long
legs are useful for wading. The long bill is useful for catching
fish and other organisms in the water.

Notice this bird's neck. When flying, the egret folds
its neck into an S shape. When standing the egret can
straighten its neck and hold its head up high. As it is in
other animals with a backbone, the backbone in the egret is
made up of many small bones. As a result, the bird's neck
is very flexible. Imagine how stiff the backbone would be if it
were one long bone. The bird could not turn its head to look
around or lower its head to catch food.

- What are some advantages of having a backbone?
- What other kinds of animals have a backbone?
- How do birds vary from other animals with a backbone?

5·1 Traits of Vertebrates

What do a frog, a fish, and a snake have in common? Figure 5·1 shows that each has a back-bone. An animal that has a backbone is called a **vertebrate** (VER tuh briht).

All vertebrates are chordates (KAWR dayts). *Chordates* are animals in phylum Chordata. Chor-dates share three traits. A flexible, rodlike struc-ture called a *notochord* (NOH tuh kawrd) is one trait of chordates. The notochord gives support to the animal's body and is present at some time in the animal's life cycle. In more-complex chordates the notochord is present only before birth.

Figure 5·1

The rainbow trout *(A)*, the tree frog *(B)*, and the sand boa *(C)* are all vertebrates.

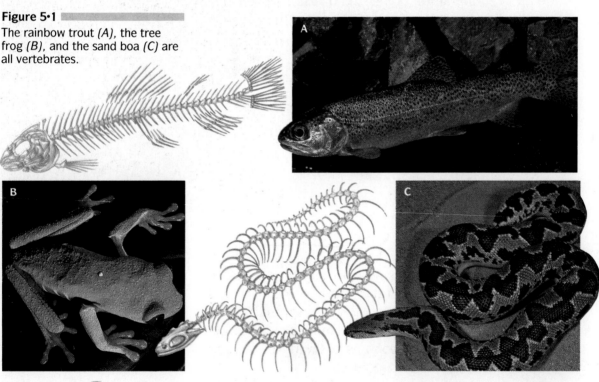

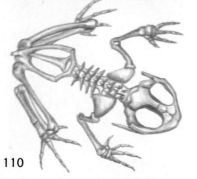

Another chordate trait is a tubelike *nerve cord* that extends the length of the body, just above the notochord. Chordates also have pairs of *gill slits*. Gill slits are openings that water-dwelling animals use in breathing. In many animals, gill slits are present before birth only.

The chordate phylum is divided into three groups. The sea squirt, shown in Figure 5·2, belongs to the first of these groups. The sea squirt gets its name from the way it expels water and wastes from its lower opening. Sea squirts lack a backbone.

The lancelet (LANS liht), also shown in Figure 5·2, is a member of the second group of chordates. Lancelets lack a backbone. Lancelets feed by filtering algae and other tiny organisms from the water.

Vertebrates are the third and largest group of chordates. The five main groups of vertebrates are fish, amphibians (am FIHB ee uhnz), reptiles (REHP-tīlz), birds, and mammals.

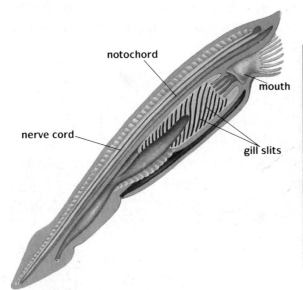

notochord

mouth

nerve cord

gill slits

The backbone of a vertebrate is part of an endoskeleton (ehn doh SKEHL uh tuhn). An **endoskeleton** is a skeleton that is inside an animal's body. This internal skeleton gives support to the animal's body and works with muscles to cause movement. An endoskeleton is a living structure and can grow as an animal grows.

In most vertebrates the endoskeleton is made of bone and cartilage (KAHR tuh lihj). *Bone* is the hard tissue that makes up most of the skeleton. *Cartilage* is a tough but flexible tissue. If you feel your ears, you will discover how flexible cartilage is. In some vertebrates, such as in sharks, the skeleton is made only of cartilage.

Figure 5·2
The sea squirt *(top)* and the lancelet *(left* and *right)* are chordates that lack a backbone.

endo- (inner)

Figure 5·3

Frogs and lizards are cold-blooded. Birds and foxes are warm-blooded.

The circulatory system of vertebrates includes a well-developed heart. The heart pumps blood through blood vessels to all parts of the body. The nervous system of vertebrates is more complex than that of other animals. Vertebrates have a brain that controls many body functions. The nerve cord of vertebrates is protected by the backbone, which replaces the notochord early in life.

Most vertebrates are cold-blooded. The temperature of a *cold-blooded animal* changes as the temperature of its surroundings changes. The body temperature of most fish is about the same as the temperature of the water in which they swim. Birds, humans, and horses are warm-blooded. A *warm-blooded animal* keeps the same body temperature, regardless of the outside temperature.

REVIEW

1. What is a vertebrate? Give two examples of vertebrates.
2. What is an endoskeleton? What tissues make up an endoskeleton?
3. How do warm-blooded vertebrates and cold-blooded vertebrates differ?

CHALLENGE Form a hypothesis about whether cold-blooded vertebrates perspire. Explain the reasoning you used in forming this hypothesis.

5·2 Fish

TRAITS OF FISH

A **fish** is a cold-blooded vertebrate that lives in water and has gills that are used for breathing. **Gills** are organs that absorb oxygen that is dissolved in water. Although fish vary in many ways, there are some traits that most fish have in common. The bodies of most fish are sleek and streamlined in shape. This shape helps a fish move easily through the water.

Fins are another trait of most fish. **Fins** are winglike structures used for balance and steering when swimming. Some fins occur in pairs, while others are single. The single tail fin is used for movement. The body muscles of a fish move its tail fin from side to side as it swims. This motion propels the fish through the water.

Most fish also have scales. **Scales** are overlapping, flat plates that cover a fish's body and give protection. Scales grow larger as the fish grows.

After completing this section, you will be able to

- **describe** the traits of fish.
- **compare** the three classes of fish.
- **describe** the sense organs of bony fish.

The key terms in this section are
bony fish
cartilage fish
external fertilization
fins
fish
gills
jawless fish
scales

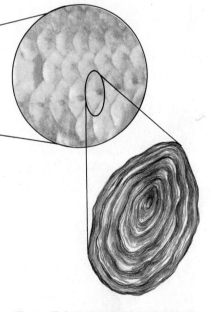

In most fish, reproduction begins with the release of eggs into the water by the female fish. The male then releases sperm over the eggs. Some of the sperm join with the eggs. This joining of egg and sperm outside the body of the female is called **external fertilization**. Female fish release many thousands of eggs, some of which will grow into new fish. How does the great number of eggs produced help to ensure the survival of fish?

Figure 5·4
Some kinds of fish scales have yearly growth rings.

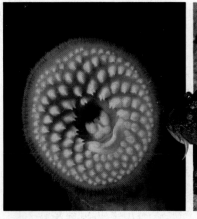

Figure 5·5

Mouth of a lamprey *(left)*. Three lampreys attached to a carp *(right)*. How can you tell lampreys are parasites?

Figure 5·6

A lemon shark *(top)* is a meat eater. A basking shark *(bottom)* feeds on microscopic organisms.

JAWLESS FISH

Scientists have grouped fish into three classes: *jawless fish, cartilage fish,* and *bony fish.* The simplest of the three classes are the jawless fish. **Jawless fish** are wormlike fish that have no jaws. These fish also lack the scales and paired fins that most other kinds of fish have. The endoskeleton of a jawless fish is made only of cartilage.

Lampreys are the most common type of jawless fish. Lampreys are found in both fresh water and salt water. In the adult stage, most lampreys are parasites. Recall that a parasite is an organism that lives in or on another living thing and harms it. The lamprey attaches itself to another fish, as shown in Figure 5·5 *(right)*. A lamprey has a round mouth with many toothlike structures. Figure 5·5 *(left)* shows a lamprey's mouth. The toothlike parts you see are used to cut into the other fish, whose body fluids are sucked out by the lamprey.

CARTILAGE FISH

Cartilage fish are fish that have jaws and a skeleton made of cartilage. There are two groups of cartilage fish: sharks and rays. Unlike jawless fish, sharks and rays have scales and paired fins.

A shark has many rows of sharp, pointy teeth. Notice in Figure 5·6 that the teeth slant backward. How does this feature help a meat-eating shark hold its prey? Although many sharks eat meat, some sharks eat microscopic plants and animals.

PUZZLER

These photographs show the same porcupine fish under different conditions. Photograph *A* shows how the fish looks under normal conditions. Hypothesize about what caused the change shown in photograph *B*. How might this change aid the porcupine fish in its survival?

Rays look very different from sharks. The paired fins of the ray look like large, flat wings. Rays swim by moving their fins in a wavelike motion. Most rays live at the ocean floor, where they feed on small fish, mollusks, and crustaceans. Rays have a long, narrow tail. A poison spine in the tail may be used for defense.

BONY FISH

Bony fish are the largest class of fish. A **bony fish** is a fish that has an endoskeleton made up mostly of bone. Most bony fish also have scales and paired fins. There are about 20,000 species of bony fish. Bony fish are found in both fresh water and salt water throughout the world. Figure 5·8, on the next page, shows a common freshwater fish called a perch. Notice the perch's fins. How are these fins used by the fish?

Figure 5·7

Examples of bony fish include lionfish *(A)*, stonefish *(B)*, and surgeonfish *(C)*.

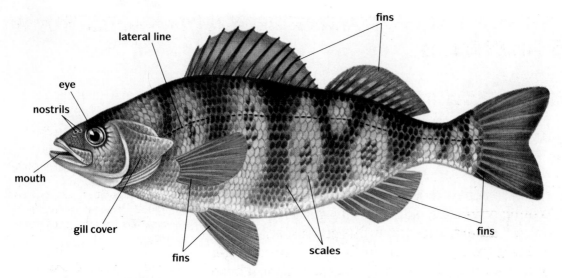

fins

lateral line

eye

nostrils

mouth

gill cover

fins

scales

fins

Figure 5·8

The structure of a perch.

Look again at Figure 5·8 to see another trait of bony fish. Each gill is covered by a bony flap called a *gill cover*. The gill cover aids in gas exchange, or breathing. Water is taken into the body through the mouth. The opening and closing of the gill covers helps to move water over the gills and out of the body. As the water passes over the gills, oxygen is absorbed from the water.

Find the *lateral line* in Figure 5·8. The lateral line is a row of cells that detect vibrations in the water. How is detecting vibrations in the water helpful to fish? Notice the nostrils of the perch. Bony fish have a sharp sense of smell. The sense of sight is not as well developed as is the sense of smell.

Within the center of the perch's body is a long sac called an *air bladder*. The air bladder contains gas and helps the fish stay at a certain depth in the water. As the fish swims to different depths, the amount of gas in the air bladder changes.

REVIEW

1. Describe the traits of fish.
2. How are cartilage fish and bony fish similar? How are they different?
3. What is the function of the lateral line?

CHALLENGE As a fish swims from a greater depth to a lesser depth, does the amount of gas in the air bladder increase or decrease? Explain your answer.

5·3 Amphibians

TRAITS OF AMPHIBIANS

Amphibians can be said to lead a double life. An **amphibian** is a cold-blooded vertebrate that lives in water when young but can live on land as an adult. Most amphibians have thin, moist skin. As adults, they usually have two pairs of limbs.

Young amphibians use gills to get oxygen from water. As adults, most amphibians breathe with lungs. *Lungs* are organs through which animals get oxygen from air. Gases can also pass through an amphibian's skin. Although adult amphibians can live on land, most live near water. Amphibians must return to water to reproduce. The eggs are laid in water, and fertilization is external.

TAILLESS AMPHIBIANS

There are two major groups of amphibians: tailed and tailless. The *tailless amphibians* include frogs and toads. As adults, frogs and toads have a short body, no neck, and no tail. The front legs are short. The large hind legs are used for jumping.

Frogs have smooth, moist skin, and usually live near water. Toads, such as the one shown in Figure 5·9, have rough, dry skin. A toad can live in moist places far from water and might not return to water until it is ready to reproduce.

After completing this section, you will be able to
- **describe** the traits of amphibians.
- **give examples** of amphibians from the two major groups.
- **describe** metamorphosis of a frog.

The key terms in this section are
amphibian
hibernation
metamorphosis

amphi- (double)
bios (life)

Figure 5·9
A black-spotted toad that is found in Asia. Toads have drier, rougher skin than do most frogs.

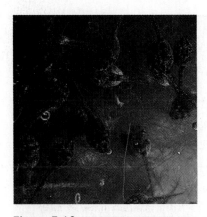

Figure 5·10
Leopard frog tadpoles.

Figure 5·10 shows what leopard frogs look like one week after hatching from eggs. These young amphibians are called *tadpoles*. They will grow and change into adult leopard frogs in about 3 months. **Metamorphosis** (meht uh MAWR fuh sihs) is a series of distinct changes in form through which an organism passes as it grows from egg to adult. Refer to Figure 5·11 as you read about metamorphosis.

1. An adult female frog releases a mass of eggs into the water. An adult male releases sperm. The sperm fertilize the eggs in the water.

2. Legless tadpoles hatch from the eggs.

3. Tadpoles have gills and look like fish.

4. Hind legs form, and then front legs form. The tail shrinks, and lungs form.

5. Lungs replace gills as the frog moves onto land.

During the cold winter months, frogs and toads become inactive. Like all cold-blooded animals, an amphibian has a body temperature that changes with the outside temperature. In winter, frogs bury themselves in the mud at the bottom of a lake or pond. Toads burrow into soft, moist soil. Body temperature falls, and life processes slow down. This period of inactivity of animals during winter months is called **hibernation**.

Figure 5·11
The metamorphosis of a leopard frog.

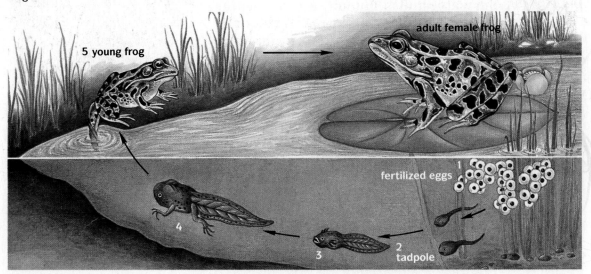

OBJECTIVES
Identify external features of a frog.
Hypothesize about the function of certain features of a frog.

MATERIALS
preserved frog, dissecting pan, probe, hand lens

PROCEDURE
A. Examine the skin of a preserved frog. Note differences between the skin on the top and on the underside of the frog.
B. Use a probe to help you open the frog's mouth. Observe how the tongue is attached.
   1. Hypothesize about the relationship between the way a frog's tongue is attached to its mouth and the way a frog gets its food.

C. Observe the oval-shaped membrane just behind each eye of the frog. This is the tympanic (tihm PAN ihk) membrane.
   2. Using the location of this structure as a clue, hypothesize about the function of the tympanic membrane.
D. Compare the front and hind legs of the frog. Record the differences in structures and size. Observe the toes.
   3. What structures on the feet suggest that the frog spends time in water?

RESULTS AND CONCLUSIONS
1. Make a drawing of the frog. Label the following parts: head, front legs, hind legs, tympanic membranes, eyes, mouth, and nostrils.
2. Explain how the features of the frog are helpful in living on land and in the water.

TAILED AMPHIBIANS

The *tailed amphibians* are commonly called salamanders. As adults, these amphibians have a long body, a neck between the head and body, short legs, and a long tail. The adults can breathe with lungs or through their smooth, moist skin. Most salamanders are less than 20 cm long.

Salamanders are usually found near water or in damp places. The mud puppy and a few other salamanders spend their entire life underwater. Figure 5·12 shows a young salamander living in water. What structures does this animal have that allow it to live in water?

REVIEW

1. What are the traits of amphibians?
2. What are the two major groups of amphibians? Give an example of each.
3. Describe the metamorphosis of a frog.

CHALLENGE During hibernation, a frog is completely buried in mud. How do you think a frog breathes during this time?

Figure 5·12
A young tiger salamander.

5·4 Reptiles

After completing this section,
you will be able to

- **describe** the traits of reptiles.
- **compare** reptiles and amphibians.
- **distinguish** between the
  major groups of reptiles.

The key terms in this section are
internal fertilization
reptile

TRAITS OF REPTILES

Reptiles live mostly on land. A **reptile** is a cold-blooded vertebrate with a dry, scaly skin. There are three main groups of reptiles. Turtles form one group; alligators and crocodiles form a second group; lizards and snakes form the third group.

Reptiles have adaptations for living on land. An *adaptation* (ad ap TAY shuhn) is a trait that makes an organism better able to survive in its environment. The scaly skin of reptiles protects the animal from drying. Except for snakes, reptiles have four limbs. The limbs usually have claws for digging or climbing. Reptiles use lungs to breathe air.

Fertilization is internal in reptiles. **Internal fertilization** is the joining of egg and sperm cells inside the body of the female. This trait is another adaptation of reptiles to life on land. Because the sperm and egg cells join within the body, they are protected. The fertilized egg of a reptile has a leathery shell that keeps moisture in but allows gases to pass in and out. The egg contains stored food used by the young reptile as it grows within the egg.

Reptiles are very different from amphibians. Reptiles have dry, leathery skin. Amphibians have thin, moist skin. Unlike amphibians, reptiles never have gills. Amphibians must return to water to reproduce, but reptiles can reproduce on land. Newly hatched reptiles look like small adults.

Figure 5·13
A king snake hatching from its leathery-shelled egg.

120

TURTLES

A turtle is a reptile with two hard, bony shells that cover and protect its body. A dome-shaped shell covers the top of the body, and a flat shell covers the bottom. Many turtles can pull their head and legs inside their shells for more protection.

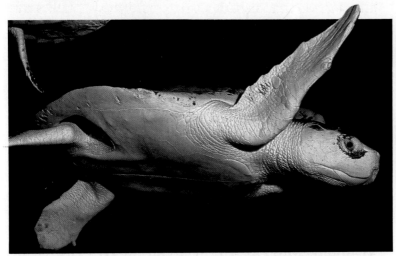

Figure 5·14
A sea turtle *(left)* and a land turtle *(right)*. Land turtles are also called tortoises.

Although turtles breathe air, many can live in water. But even water-dwelling turtles must return to land to lay their eggs. Turtles that live on land are often called tortoises (TAWR tehs ehz). Compare the leg structure of the land turtle and sea turtle in Figure 5·14. Land turtles have short, strong, clawed legs that are used for walking and digging. How does the sea turtle use its clawless flippers?

CROCODILES AND ALLIGATORS

Crocodiles and alligators live in tropical streams, rivers, and swamps. These reptiles can reach lengths of over 6 m. Their long, muscular bodies are covered with thick, tough scales. They have strong jaws with very sharp teeth. Both crocodiles and alligators have a large tail that is used in swimming. These reptiles are able to float in the water with only their eyes and nostrils above the water's surface. Crocodiles and alligators can be distinguished by the shape of the snout. As you can see in Figure 5·15, an alligator has a blunt snout. A crocodile has a narrower, pointed snout.

Figure 5·15
An alligator *(top)* has a rounded snout. A crocodile *(bottom)* has a more pointed snout.

Figure 5·16
A snake molts as it grows *(left)*. The unhinging of the lower jaw allows this snake to eat a large rat *(right)*.

Figure 5·17
A Komodo dragon is a kind of lizard.

SNAKES AND LIZARDS

Snakes and lizards have scaly skin that is shed from time to time as the animal grows. This periodic shedding of skin is called *molting*. Most lizards have four legs, movable eyelids, and ear openings. Snakes lack all three of these traits.

Snakes and lizards both can eat prey that seems larger than their mouth. The lower jaw is loosely joined to the skull and can unhinge. This allows the mouth to open very wide. This trait allows the snake shown in Figure 5·16 to swallow a large animal in one piece.

Snakes are meat eaters. Many snakes are helpful because they eat insect and rodent pests. Most snakes are not poisonous. Poisonous snakes kill their prey by injecting a poison. The poison flows through pointed, hollow teeth called *fangs*.

Most lizards live in hot, dry places, although some live in forests. Some lizards eat plants, but most feed on insects and worms. Large lizards also eat eggs, birds, and other lizards.

REVIEW

1. What traits of reptiles are adaptations to life on land?
2. Describe the differences between reptiles and amphibians.
3. What are the three groups of reptiles? How do they differ from each other?

CHALLENGE Salamanders and lizards have a similar body form. Suppose you found one of these animals. What traits would you check to determine if it was a salamander or a lizard?

5·5 Birds

TRAITS OF BIRDS

A **bird** is a warm-blooded vertebrate that has a body covering of feathers. There are over 8500 species of birds. They are found on all continents and in a variety of environments. Since birds are warm-blooded, they are able to live in places where temperatures are extreme. Some penguins live in the cold, ice-covered Antarctic. Other birds live in hot, humid jungles or in hot, dry deserts.

Most birds can fly. Flight requires a light body and a great amount of energy. All birds have feathers, and most have adaptations for flight. The front limbs of birds are wings, and the back limbs are legs. Most birds use their wings for flying. The legs are used for walking and perching.

Birds have several traits that result in a low body weight. The skeleton of birds is very light. Many of the bones are filled with air spaces. Look at the bird bone shown in Figure 5·18. This structure makes the bone strong but adds little weight.

Large amounts of oxygen are needed for flight. Look at Figure 5·19. Birds have a well-developed system for getting oxygen. This system includes

After completing this section, you will be able to

- **describe** the traits of birds.
- **relate** the structure of beaks, feet, and feather types to their functions.
- **describe** the structure of a bird egg.

The key terms in this section are

bird	incubation
contour feather	migration
down feather	

Figure 5·18

The crisscross structure of a bird bone makes it strong but light.

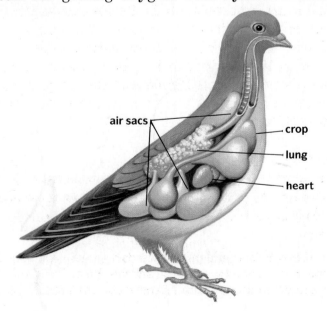

air sacs — crop — lung — heart

Figure 5·19

The structure of a pigeon.

123

lungs and air sacs. An *air sac* is a sac that is connected to the lungs of a bird and that helps to move air through the lungs. When a bird inhales, air enters the lungs and the air sacs. When a bird exhales, air goes out of its lungs. At the same time, air also moves from the air sacs to the lungs. Thus the lungs are filled with air both when the bird inhales and when it exhales.

Birds are able to eat large amounts of food at one time. After the food is eaten, it is stored in the crop. The *crop* is an organ in which food is stored before digestion. Locate the crop in Figure 5·19.

FEATHERS

Birds are aided in flight by the streamlined shape of their body. Overlapping feathers cover a bird's body and help to give it this shape. There are two main types of feathers: contour (KAHN tur) feathers and down feathers. A **contour feather** is one of the large feathers that give a bird's body its streamlined shape. Contour feathers also cover the wings. Notice in Figure 5·20 that a contour feather has a main stem called a *shaft*. The flat part of the feather attached to the shaft is the *vane*.

Figure 5·20
Contour feather and down feather.

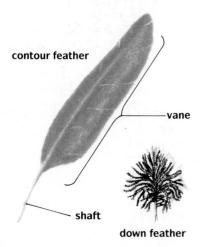

contour feather

vane

shaft

down feather

ACTIVITY   How Do Contour and Down Feathers Differ?

OBJECTIVE
Compare contour and down feathers.

MATERIALS
contour feather, scissors, hand lens, down feather

PROCEDURE
A. Examine a contour feather, and locate the long central shaft.
B. Feel the vane along either side of the central shaft. Use scissors to cut about 2 cm off the end of the shaft. Look at the cut end. Record your observations.
C. Notice that the vane is soft yet firm. Hold the feather by the shaft, and fan yourself. Describe what you feel.

D. Examine a down feather. Note the shape of the feather and how it feels. Hold the feather by the shaft, and fan yourself. Describe what you feel.

RESULTS AND CONCLUSIONS
1. How is the shaft of the contour feather an adaptation for flight?
2. Did the down feather fan the air in the same way as the contour feather? Explain any differences you observed in the way the feathers fanned the air.
3. As you have learned, down feathers function in insulation. How does the structure of a down feather serve this function?

Figure 5·21

Notice the differences among the beaks and feet of the hawk, woodpecker, duck, and cardinal.

A **down feather** is a short, fluffy feather. Down feathers are the main covering of young birds. In adult birds the down feathers are found under the contour feathers, close to the body. Down feathers trap air, which is warmed by the bird's body. This layer of air helps to keep the bird warm.

ADAPTATIONS OF BIRDS

Birds lack teeth but have a strong beak. The structure of a bird's beak is adapted to the kind of food the bird eats. Look at Figure 5·21. Notice the long, pointed beak of the woodpecker. This beak is used to bore into trees as the woodpecker searches for insects. The cardinal breaks open seeds with its strong, thick beak. How does the meat-eating hawk use its sharp, hooked beak?

Different types of bird feet also can be seen in Figure 5·21. The shape of the cardinal's feet allows this bird to grasp tree branches. The hawk's sharp claws are used to strike at and hold prey. How does the duck use its paddle-shaped, webbed feet?

MIGRATION

Many birds cannot stay in the same place throughout the year. In some areas the weather gets very cold and the food supply becomes scarce. As winter nears, many birds fly to warmer areas. The seasonal movement of animals from one area to another is called **migration**. In the Northern Hemisphere, many birds migrate south in the fall and north in the spring. For example, the bobolink breeds in North America in the late spring. In the fall the bobolink flies to South America.

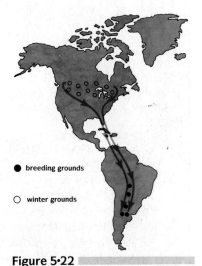

● breeding grounds

○ winter grounds

Figure 5·22

The bobolink's migration route covers a distance of 11,000 km.

REPRODUCTION IN BIRDS

In some ways, reproduction in birds is similar to that in reptiles. In both groups, fertilization is internal. The developing animal grows in an egg that is covered by a shell. But unlike a reptile egg, which has a soft, leathery shell, a bird egg has a hard, brittle shell.

Refer to Figure 5·23 as you read about the structure of a bird egg. At the center of the egg is the *yolk*, which serves as food for the growing bird. On the surface of the yolk is the embryo (EHM bree oh). An *embryo* is an organism in the early stages of its growth. The yolk and embryo are surrounded by *albumen* (al BYOO muhn), also called egg white. Albumen is a watery substance that acts as a cushion, protecting the embryo from injury.

A tough *shell membrane* surrounds the albumen. The hard *shell* protects the embryo from injury. The shell and the shell membrane both help to protect the egg from drying out. Both structures have pores through which gases can pass. Thus, oxygen can pass into the egg, and carbon dioxide can pass out of the egg.

Bird eggs are usually protected by the parents. Either the male parent or female parent sits on the eggs until they hatch. Sitting on the eggs protects

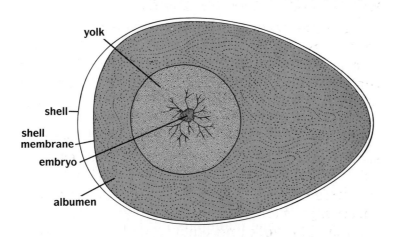

yolk

shell

shell membrane

embryo

albumen

them and warms them. **Incubation** (ihn kyuh BAY-shuhn) is the warming of an egg to body temperature over a period of time while the embryo grows. A bird embryo can grow only if the egg is incubated.

Most birds incubate their eggs in a nest. Nests vary in size and shape. The materials used to build nests include twigs, grasses, and mud. Some birds that do not build nests lay their eggs on the ground. Often the color of such eggs matches the color of the surroundings.

The length of incubation varies with the species of bird. Small birds, such as sparrows, wood thrushes, and robins, incubate their eggs for 10–20 days. Figure 5·24A shows newly hatched wood thrush chicks. These chicks are weak and blind, and they have few feathers. Larger birds, such as ducks and geese, incubate their eggs for 21–28 days. These birds are strong and independent soon after they hatch. They can feed themselves, walk, and swim. How do the ducklings and the wood thrush chicks shown in Figure 5·24 differ?

Figure 5·24
Wood thrush chicks in their nest (A). One-day-old ducklings and their mother (B).

REVIEW

1. Describe three ways in which birds are adapted for flight.
2. Describe the functions of contour feathers and down feathers.
3. Give an example of how a bird's beak is related to the kind of food it eats. Give an example of how a bird's feet are related to how it lives.
4. Describe the structure of a bird egg.

CHALLENGE How does having a streamlined body help birds fly?

5·6 Mammals

TRAITS OF MAMMALS

What do a dog, a bat, a monkey, and a whale have in common? They are all mammals. A **mammal** is a warm-blooded vertebrate that has hair and that feeds milk to its young. Mammals live in many places. Look at Figure 5·25. Where are mammals found?

Mammals are the only animals with hair or fur. Though some mammals have little or no hair, most are covered with hair. Hair insulates mammals in the same way that feathers insulate birds.

Fertilization is internal in mammals. The young of nearly all mammals develop inside the mother's body. The amount of care given to the young is greater in mammals than in any other class of animal. The mammary (MAM uhr ee) gland is found only in mammals and is used in the care of their young. A **mammary gland** is a structure in female mammals that secretes milk. The milk is food for the young.

Another important trait of mammals is a well-developed nervous system with a complex brain. In general, mammals are more intelligent than other vertebrates and have more complex behavior. Some of the behavior of mammals is *inborn behavior*. For example, a newborn animal finds its mother's mammary gland and feeds on milk without being taught.

Figure 5·25

The mountain lion *(left)*, the insect-eating bat *(middle)*, and the dolphin *(right)* are mammals found in three different environments.

Migration during a set season is another inborn behavior. Other behaviors of mammals are *learned behavior*. For example, young mammals learn to hunt for their food.

There are about 4000 species of mammals. They are divided into three groups based on how the young develop.

Figure 5·26
The duckbilled platypus *(left)* and the spiny anteater *(right)* are the only two living species of monotremes.

EGG-LAYING MAMMALS

A **monotreme** (MAHN uh treem) is an egg-laying mammal. Like other mammals, monotremes have hair and mammary glands. But unlike other mammals, monotremes lay eggs. Only two species of monotremes exist: the spiny anteater and the duckbilled platypus. Compare these two monotremes, shown in Figure 5·26. How do their body coverings differ? These two species also differ in how they live. The anteater burrows in dry places. The duckbilled platypus lives along the banks of lakes or streams.

POUCHED MAMMALS

A **marsupial** (mahr soo pee uhl) is a mammal whose young complete their development in a pouch on the female's body. Marsupials spend only a short time growing within the mother's body. A marsupial is tiny and not well developed at birth. The tiny marsupial crawls into its mother's pouch, where it feeds from the mammary glands.

Kangaroos and koalas are marsupials. Most marsupials live in Australia. Only one marsupial — the opossum — is found in North America.

Figure 5·27
Like most marsupials, the kangaroo lives in Australia.

PLACENTAL MAMMALS

Most of the mammals with which you are familiar are placentals (pluh SEHN tuhlz). A **placental mammal** is a mammal whose young are nourished through a placenta as they grow inside the female's body. A *placenta* is a structure through which a mammal embryo gets food and oxygen and gives off wastes. In placentals the embryos complete most of their development within the mother's body. Placentals are more fully formed at birth than are other mammals. Placentals are found in all kinds of habitats. The most common groups of placentals are shown in the photographs below and on the following pages.

● *Bats*   These flying mammals have wings formed from long arm and finger bones that are joined by a thin, smooth skin. Although bats cannot see well in the dark, most hunt at night. They use sound to sense objects around them. Many bats eat insects. This hammerhead bat eats fruit.

● *Insect Eaters*   Shrews, moles, hedgehogs, and other small placentals belong to this group. Many insect-eating mammals, like this shrew, live in underground burrows and use the sense of smell to search for insects and worms.

● *Meat Eaters*   Mammals in this group have sharp teeth for tearing and cutting meat. Though they are called meat eaters, some members of this group, such as bears, also eat fruits and plants. This group includes dogs, wolves, raccoons, seals, walruses, and all types of cats.

● **Aquatic Mammals**   These are large mammals with a streamlined body that is adapted to life in the water. Whales and porpoises belong to this group. These mammals live in water, but they swim to the surface to breathe. At the surface, they breathe air through one or two nostrils found on top of the head. The whale shown is exhaling through its nostril, or blowhole.

● **Rodentlike Mammals**   These are small, plant-eating mammals such as rabbits, hares, and the pika, shown here. Rodentlike mammals have twice as many front teeth as rodents have.

● **Rodents**   Rats, mice, squirrels, and beavers are members of this largest group of mammals. The chisel-shaped teeth are used for gnawing and cutting. The front teeth keep growing throughout life. What advantage might there be in having front teeth that continue to grow?

● **Elephants**   These plant-eating mammals have a long trunk. The males, like the one shown, have tusks that are actually long teeth.

● **Hoofed Mammals**   These plant-eating mammals have hoofs formed from their toes and nails. Examples of hoofed mammals include horses, giraffes, deer, pigs, and cattle.

● **Primates**   Mammals in this group have a well-developed brain and an *opposable thumb*. An opposable thumb can touch each of the other fingers. With this arrangement of fingers, a primate is able to grasp objects. Apes, monkeys, and humans are primates. What human activities are possible because of opposable thumbs?

REVIEW

1. Describe three traits of mammals.
2. Name the three major types of mammals, and explain how the development of the young differs in the three groups.
3. Identify five groups of placental mammals, and give examples of each.

CHALLENGE What disadvantages do the embryos of egg-laying mammals have compared to embryos of pouched mammals?

CHAPTER SUMMARY

The main ideas in this chapter are listed below. Read these statements before you answer the Chapter Review questions.

- Chordates are animals that have a nerve cord and have a notochord and gill slits at some time in their life cycle. (5•1)
- Vertebrates are a group of chordates that have an endoskeleton and a complex nervous system. Some vertebrates are cold-blooded; others are warm-blooded. (5•1)
- Fish are cold-blooded vertebrates that live in water and breathe with gills. (5•2)
- The three major groups of fish are jawless fish, cartilage fish, and bony fish. (5•2)
- Amphibians are cold-blooded vertebrates. They usually live in water and breathe with gills when young. As adults, most have lungs and live on land. (5•3)
- Frogs and toads are tailless amphibians. Salamanders are tailed amphibians. (5•3)
- Reptiles are cold-blooded vertebrates. They have lungs and dry, scaly skin, and they lay eggs with a leathery shell. (5•4)
- The three major groups of reptiles are turtles, crocodiles and alligators, and snakes and lizards. (5•4)

- Birds are warm-blooded vertebrates that have a body covering of feathers. Birds have adaptations that result in the low body weight needed for flight. Feathers insulate a bird and streamline the body for flight. (5•5)
- Fertilization in birds is internal. The embryo develops within a hard shell, outside the female's body. (5•5)
- Mammals are warm-blooded vertebrates that have hair and that feed milk to their young. Mammals have a complex brain. Behavior may be inborn or learned. (5•6)
- Monotremes are egg-laying mammals. Marsupials are mammals that have a pouch in which the young complete their development. (5•6)
- Placental mammals nourish their young through a placenta inside the female's body. The most common groups of placentals include insect eaters, bats, rodents, rodentlike mammals, aquatic mammals, meat eaters, hoofed mammals, elephants, and primates. (5•6)

The key terms in this chapter are listed below. Use each term in a sentence that shows the meaning of the term.

amphibian	external fertilization	jawless fish	placental mammal
bird	fins	mammal	reptile
bony fish	fish	mammary gland	scales
cartilage fish	gills	marsupial	vertebrate
contour feather	hibernation	metamorphosis	
down feather	incubation	migration	
endoskeleton	internal fertilization	monotreme	

Chapter Review

VOCABULARY

Write the letter of the term that best matches the definition. Not all the terms will be used.

1. An animal that has a backbone
2. A skeleton that is inside an animal's body
3. The joining of egg and sperm cells inside the body of the female
4. A period of inactivity of some animals during winter
5. Organs used by fish and young amphibians to get oxygen from water
6. A large feather that helps to give a bird its streamlined shape
7. The seasonal movement of animals from one area to another
8. An egg-laying mammal
9. A cold-blooded vertebrate that has dry, scaly skin
10. A type of mammal whose young complete their development in a pouch

a. amphibian
b. contour feather
c. down feather
d. endoskeleton
e. external fertilization
f. gills
g. hibernation
h. incubation
i. internal fertilization
j. marsupial
k. metamorphosis
l. migration
m. monotreme
n. reptile
o. vertebrate

CONCEPTS

Look at the drawings below, and identify the major vertebrate group to which each animal belongs. Then list two traits of each group.

Choose the term or phrase that best answers the question or completes the statement.

6. Which of the following is not a trait of all chordates?
   a. notochord
   b. backbone
   c. paired gill slits
   d. tubelike nerve cord.

7. Warm-blooded animals
    a. all have hair.
    b. have a body temperature that is the same as the temperature of the surroundings.
    c. have a constant body temperature.
    d. live only in warm climates.
8. An adult frog breathes through its
    a. gills.
    b. lungs.
    c. skin and gills.
    d. lungs and skin.
9. A trait shared by all mammals is
    a. a placenta.
    b. hair.
    c. external fertilization.
    d. a pouch in which the young develop.
10. A mammal that eats plants is likely to have
    a. flat teeth.
    b. pointy teeth.
    c. square teeth.
    d. no teeth.

Answer the following in complete sentences.

11. Explain how blood circulates in a fish and how a fish gets oxygen.
12. Describe metamorphosis in a frog.
13. What trait of snakes allows them to swallow their prey whole?
14. Explain how the beaks of birds are adapted to the types of food the birds eat.
15. Describe the major differences between monotremes, marsupials, and placentals.

1. Animals in which fertilization is external produce many more eggs than do animals in which fertilization is internal. Explain why.
2. How does respiration occur in a frog swimming underwater? Why does a frog need to come to the surface from time to time?
3. The opposable thumb is an important trait of primates. Explain the role that this trait has played in making human society as it is today.
4. Hoofed mammals tend to feed in herds. How might this behavior aid the survival of these mammals?

APPLICATION/ CRITICAL THINKING

1. Find out which, if any, poisonous snakes live in your state. How can these snakes be identified?
2. Porpoises are aquatic mammals that have a complex brain. They use sounds to communicate with each other. Do research to find out what scientists have learned about porpoise communication. Write a brief report on your findings.

EXTENSION

CHAPTER 6

THE ENVIRONMENT

A pond forms a little world within itself. All the animals and plants that live in or near the pond interact with each other and with their surroundings.

There are many ways in which organisms interact with each other. Most animals must compete with each other for food, water, and space. Plants must compete for water, sunlight, and space. There is also an exchange of gases between animals, plants, and the air.

The birds in this photograph are visiting the pond. They are eating fish, insects, and plants and are drinking water. The birds are taking in oxygen and giving off carbon dioxide to the air. They are giving off wastes, and the birds' bodies will decay after they die. All of these things affect the pond.

- *How do living and nonliving things interact with their environment?*

- *What happens to a group of animals when the environment changes?*

- *What needs to be done to preserve natural environments?*

6·1 The Biosphere

Organisms live in and interact with an *environment* (ehn VĪ ruhn muhnt). The **environment** includes all of the living things and nonliving things that affect the life of an organism. A fish in a pond is an example of an organism in its environment. The pond contains such living things as fish and plants. The pond also contains such nonliving things as water. The study of the interactions between living things and their environment is called **ecology** (ee KAHL uh jee).

FACTORS IN THE ENVIRONMENT

bio- (life)

a- (without)

The living things in an environment are called **biotic** (bī AHT ihk) **factors**. Plants, animals, and fungi are biotic factors. The nonliving things in an environment are called **abiotic factors**. Light, temperature, and wind are abiotic factors.

ACTIVITY   What Are Some Biotic and Abiotic Factors?

OBJECTIVE
Determine which factors in different environments are biotic and which are abiotic.

MATERIALS
none

PROCEDURE
A. Examine the area around your school. Note those factors that are biotic and those that are abiotic.
B. Make a data table like the one shown. In the table, list at least ten biotic factors and ten abiotic factors found around your school. If you are not sure if a factor is biotic or abiotic, list it in the column marked *Uncertain*.
C. Examine the area inside your science classroom. In the table, list at least ten biotic factors and ten abiotic factors found in the classroom.

ENVIRONMENT	BIOTIC FACTORS	ABIOTIC FACTORS	UNCERTAIN
School area			
Science classroom			

RESULTS AND CONCLUSIONS
1. How would you describe the environment around your school?
2. In what ways does the environment around your school differ from that inside your science classroom?
3. In each of the environments that you examined, state how the biotic factors and the abiotic factors interact.
4. If your school did not exist, what biotic factors might be present in the area?
5. What biotic factors can be found as a direct result of the school being built there?

Many kinds of environments exist all over the earth. Think about the birds in the nest shown in Figure 6·1. The nest is a small environment that contains both biotic factors and abiotic factors. For example, organisms such as fungi and insects often live in bird nests. But the nests themselves are made of nonliving materials, such as twigs, mud, and pieces of dried grass. What other abiotic factors might there be in the nest?

THE BIOSPHERE AND ECOSYSTEMS

Life on the earth is found in a zone called the **biosphere** (BĪ uh sfihr). The biosphere is made up of the land, the ocean, and part of the atmosphere. Notice in Figure 6·2 that the biosphere extends from the deepest parts of the ocean to several kilometers into the air. How deep is the biosphere?

The biosphere is made up of smaller units called ecosystems (EE kuh sihs tuhmz). An **ecosystem** is an area in which living things interact, exchanging energy and materials. The word *ecosystem* is a short form of the term *ecological system*. An ecosystem is the basic unit of ecology. Ecosystems can be large, like a forest, or small, like a leaf or a drop of water.

A tree and the space around it can be thought of as an ecosystem. Leaves fall from the tree and make hiding places for small animals. Acorns also fall to the ground and may be used as food by squirrels. Other acorns may be used by insects as places in which to lay eggs.

Figure 6·1
A bird's nest contains both biotic factors and abiotic factors.

Figure 6·2
The biosphere.

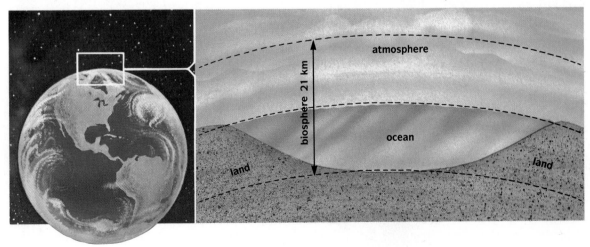

atmosphere

biosphere 21 km

ocean

land

land

If humans ever go to the moon or Mars to live, they will have to live in a contained environment similar to the earth. An idea, by scientists, to build an experimental contained environment here on the earth has been approved. Scientists call this environment Biosphere II because the first biosphere is the earth. Biosphere II is being built near Tucson, Arizona. Biosphere II will give scientists an opportunity to study the earth's environment. A model of Biosphere II is shown in the photograph.

Biosphere II will include five ecosystems: desert, savanna, rain forest, marine, and estuary. Each ecosystem will include a variety of plants and animals. Making the species selections is not a simple task. The trees cannot grow too tall, or they will break through the roof. There must also be a balance between plants and animals in order for them all to thrive.

Biosphere II will be completed in 1989. At that time, eight people will begin an experiment there. They will move into Biosphere II and live there for 2 years without any contact with the outside world. The people working on the project will give equal weight to two main objectives: to develop technology for settlements on the moon and Mars, and to find ways to improve our management of the earth's environment.

A stream running through a forest is also an ecosystem. The stream has specific biotic factors and abiotic factors. Notice that these factors, such as fish and water, are different from those in the forest floor ecosystem. The stream and the forest floor are examples of small ecosystems. These small ecosystems are part of a larger ecosystem—the forest. The forest ecosystem includes all the biotic factors and abiotic factors within the forest.

REVIEW

1. How do biotic factors and abiotic factors differ? Give an example of each type of factor.
2. What parts of the earth make up the biosphere?
3. What is an ecosystem? Give two examples of ecosystems.

CHALLENGE Describe the changes that would occur in an ecosystem that has been flooded. How would the biotic factors and abiotic factors change? Explain your answer.

6·2 Populations and Communities

HABITATS AND NICHES

Ecosystems can be divided into habitats. A **habitat** (HAB uh tat) is the kind of place in which an organism lives. Think of an ecosystem as an organism's neighborhood. Think of the organism's habitat as its address. The habitat must supply all the biotic factors that the organism needs for survival.

Different species of organisms live in different habitats. Earthworms live in the soil. Starfish live on the ocean floor. But different species can live in the same habitat. Insects and plants live in the soil habitat with earthworms. Clams and oysters live on the ocean floor with the starfish. What organisms live in your habitat?

After completing this section, you will be able to

- **compare** a habitat and a niche.
- **distinguish** between a population and a community.

The key terms in this section are
community   niche
habitat   population

ACTIVITY   What Interactions Occur in a Plot of Land?

OBJECTIVE
Identify the interactions of organisms in a small plot of land.

MATERIALS
meterstick, 4 wood stakes, 4.5 m of string, garden trowel, plastic bag, white paper towel, hand lens, probe

PROCEDURE
A. Work with a partner or in teams of three. Use a meterstick to measure a square plot of ground that is 1 m long on each side. Push a stake into the ground to mark each corner of the plot. **Caution:** Do not touch any plants that have not been identified as safe. Some plants may irritate your skin.
B. Connect the stakes with a piece of string to form a square.
C. List the kinds of plants and animals found within the square. Count each kind of organism. Record your results.

D. Identify and record the kinds of nonliving things found in the plot.
E. With a garden trowel, take a small amount of soil from the plot, and place it in a plastic bag. Take this sample to your classroom.
F. In the classroom, spread the soil sample out on a paper towel on your desk. Use a hand lens and a probe to examine the soil for living things and nonliving things. Note if decaying matter is present.
G. After 2 weeks, repeat steps C through F. Note any changes that may have occurred.

RESULTS AND CONCLUSIONS
1. Describe the plot of land in your study.
2. Describe the soil sample that you obtained.
3. List any interactions that you think may occur between organisms in the plot.
4. List any changes you noted in the plot after the 2-week period.
5. Describe the ecosystem in which the plot is located.

The organisms in an ecosystem interact with each other in many ways. Each kind of organism has a specific role. The role of an organism in an ecosystem is called its **niche** (nihch). Recall that an organism's habitat is where it lives. An organism's niche can be thought of as what the organism does. The niche of an organism includes all of the ways it interacts with biotic factors and abiotic factors. Look at the vultures in Figure 6·3A. Eating dead animals, giving off carbon dioxide to the air, and nesting in certain kinds of trees are all part of the niche of a vulture. The niche of the orchid shown in Figure 6·3B includes rooting in the bark of a tree, getting energy from sunlight, and giving off oxygen to the air. What is the niche of a wolf?

Figure 6·3

The niche of vultures involves eating a dead animal (A). The niche of an orchid includes growing on the bark of a tree (B).

Different types of organisms can have the same habitat. But in a balanced ecosystem, no two species have the same niche. Each species has its own role. When two species try to have the same niche, they are said to *compete* with each other. In time, the species that is better suited to the environment will fill the niche. The other species will disappear or move away.

142

COMMUNITIES AND POPULATIONS

All the organisms living together in an area make up a **community**. A community is the living part of an ecosystem. Nonliving things, such as soil and water, are part of the ecosystem but not part of the community. A desert community, as shown in Figure 6·4A, might include cactuses, shrubs, rabbits, snakes, scorpions, and other organisms. A tidal pool community, as shown in Figure 6·4B, might include starfish, worms, clams, and algae. What organisms might be found in a forest community?

Figure 6·4
A desert community *(A)* and a tidal pool community *(B)*.

Each community is made up of several populations. A **population** is a group of organisms of one species that lives in a given area. All of the jack rabbits in a desert community make up a population. All of the starfish in a tidal pool community make up a population.

REVIEW

1. How does a habitat differ from a niche?
2. What is the habitat of a squirrel? Give an example of part of a squirrel's niche.
3. What is the difference between a population and a community?
4. What is the difference between a community and an ecosystem?

CHALLENGE Explain how a frog and a tadpole occupy the same habitat but different niches.

6·3 Energy Flow in the Biosphere

herba- (plant)
carnis (flesh)

PRODUCERS AND CONSUMERS

All living things need energy to survive. The main source of energy for most living things is the sun. Green plants use sunlight to make food, in a process called photosynthesis. Green plants are producers. A **producer** is an organism that makes its own food. Plantlike protists and some monerans are also producers.

Living things get food by eating other organisms. An organism that eats other organisms is called a **consumer**. All animals are consumers. Look at Figure 6·5. Which of these organisms are consumers?

There are several kinds of consumers. A consumer that eats plants is called a **herbivore** (HER-buh vawr). Mice, deer, horses, and cows are examples of herbivores.

A consumer that eats animals is a **carnivore** (KAHR nuh vawr). Lions, dogs, and cats are exam-

Figure 6·5
Producers and consumers.

ples of carnivores. Some carnivores, such as the cougar, are *predators*. A predator is an animal that hunts and kills other animals for food. The *prey* is the animal that is hunted. A raccoon may be the prey of a cougar. What might be the prey of a shark? Other carnivores, such as vultures, are *scavengers*. A scavenger is an animal that feeds on dead or dying organisms.

A third kind of consumer eats both plants and animals. A consumer that eats both plants and animals is an **omnivore** (AHM nuh vawr). Bears and raccoons are omnivores. Which are humans—herbivores, carnivores, or omnivores?

In addition to having producers and consumers, a community has organisms called decomposers. A **decomposer** (dee kuhm POH zuhr) is an organism that breaks down the remains of dead plants and animals into simpler substances. Fungi and most bacteria are decomposers. They release nutrients from dead organisms into the environment. These nutrients can then be reused.

Figure 6·6

Fungi are decomposers. What material is being decomposed?

FOOD CHAINS AND FOOD WEBS

When one organism eats another, energy is transferred. Consider a field mouse eating grain. Energy is passed from the grain to the mouse. In fact, this energy can be passed from one organism to another more than once. If the mouse is then eaten by an owl, some of the energy from the grain is passed to the owl.

Figure 6·7

A food chain can consist of grain, a mouse, and an owl.

The transfer of energy in the form of food from one organism to another is called a **food chain**. In the food chain in Figure 6·7, the energy is passed from the grain to the mouse to the owl. The first energy source for almost all food chains is the sun. How is the sun the first energy source in the grain-mouse-owl food chain? What consumers are shown in Figure 6·7?

Most consumers have more than one food source. Owls, for example, may eat mice, snakes, and rabbits. Thus, organisms may be involved in many overlapping food chains. A **food web** is an overlapping of food chains in a community. Study the food web shown in Figure 6·8. Which organisms are producers? Which are consumers?

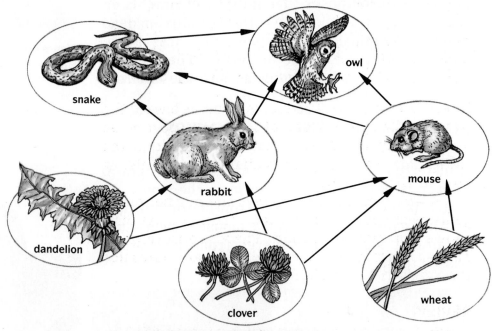

Figure 6·8

Many organisms make up a food web.

ECOLOGICAL PYRAMIDS

Most of the energy from sunlight that is used by producers goes into carrying on life processes. Just a small part of the energy is stored as food. When a plant is eaten by an animal, most of the food energy is used for the animal's life processes.

At each level of a food chain, some energy is passed on, but most energy is lost. Figure 6·9A shows an energy pyramid. An *energy pyramid* is a drawing that shows the amount of energy at each

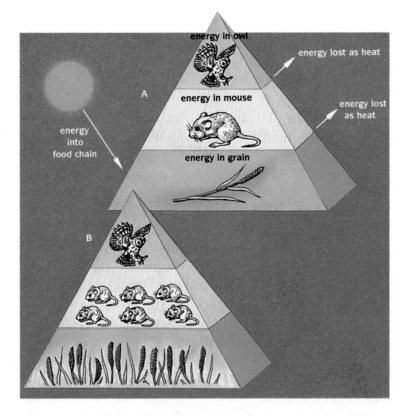

Figure 6·9
An energy pyramid *(A)* and a numbers pyramid *(B)*.

level of a food chain. Producers form the base of the pyramid. The upper levels of the pyramid are made up of consumers. Notice that the pyramid shape shows that less energy is available at each higher level of the food chain.

A *numbers pyramid* shows the number of organisms at each level of a food chain. Figure 6·9*B* shows a numbers pyramid. There are more grain plants than mice in a food chain. The are more mice than owls in a food chain.

REVIEW

1. How do producers, consumers, and decomposers differ?
2. What are the different types of consumers?
3. How is a food chain different from a food web?
4. Explain why there is less energy at each higher level of a food chain.

CHALLENGE Think about a food chain in the ocean. Suppose that the producers get 1000 units of energy a day from photosynthesis. The small fish that eat the producers get only 1 percent of that energy. The large fish that eat the small fish get 10 percent of the energy available at that level. How many units of energy do the large fish get each day?

6·4 Symbiotic Relationships

mutuus (exchanged)

Organisms in an ecosystem depend on each other for food. Organisms may also depend on each other for protection, transportation, or shelter. A close, long-term relationship between two organisms is called *symbiosis* (sihm bī OH sihs). There are several kinds of symbiosis.

Mutualism (MYOO chu uh lihz uhm) is a kind of symbiosis in which both organisms benefit. Figure 6·10*A* shows an example of mutualism. The oxpecker bird spends a lot of time on the back of the wart hog. The bird eats ticks and other organisms that live on the skin of the wart hog. Both the bird and the wart hog benefit from this relationship.

Look at the sea anemones living on the shell of a hermit crab in Figure 6·10*B*. This is another example of mutualism. The sea anemones hide the crab, helping to protect it from predators. A sea anemone cannot move from place to place on its own. When the hermit crab moves, it carries the sea anemones with it. How does this benefit the anemones?

Commensalism (kuh MEHN suh lihz uhm) is another kind of symbiosis. This kind of symbiosis is when one organism is helped and the other is neither helped nor harmed. A blue jay living in a tree is one example of commensalism. The blue jay gains

Figure 6·10

Examples of mutualism: oxpecker birds on a wart hog *(A)*; sea anemones on the shell of a hermit crab *(B)*.

Figure 6·11
The relationship between a remora and a shark is an example of commensalism.

protection and a place to live. The tree is not affected. Figure 6·11 shows a shark, and a fish called a remora. Notice that the remora is attached to the shark. The remora feeds on scraps of the shark's food and the shark is not affected.

Parasitism (PAR uh sī tihz uhm) is a form of symbiosis in which one organism is helped and the other is harmed. The organism that benefits from the relationship is called a *parasite*. The organism that is harmed is called the *host*. A parasite lives in or on the body of its host. A tick, on a dog, is an example of parasitism. The tick feeds on the dog's blood which causes the dog to be weakened.

Many diseases are caused by parasites that are microscopic. Athlete's foot is a skin infection caused by a parasitic fungus. Malaria, a serious blood disease, is caused by a parasitic protist. What are other diseases that are caused by parasites?

Plants may be parasites of other plants. Mistletoe is a plant that attaches itself to trees, as shown in Figure 6·12. Being a plant, mistletoe can make its own food. But this plant also takes food and moisture from the tree.

Figure 6·12
An example of parasitism is mistletoe growing into the branch of a tree.

REVIEW

1. What is symbiosis?
2. Compare mutualism and commensalism.
3. What is parasitism? Give an example of a parasitic relationship.

CHALLENGE Termites cannot digest the wood they eat. The wood is digested by protists that live in the termites' intestines. Both the termites and the protists get food from the digested wood. What kind of symbiosis is this? Explain your answer.

6·5 Preserving the Environment

After completing this section, you will be able to

- **compare** the causes of water, air, and land pollution.
- **give examples** of conservation methods that protect wildlife.

The key terms in this section are
acid rain
endangered species
pollution
smog

Organisms need clean water, air, and land. In some areas the supplies of these resources have already become limited because of pollution (puh-LOO shuhn). **Pollution** is the release of unwanted, usually harmful materials into the environment. A *pollutant* (puh LOO tuhnt) is a substance that is released by human activity and that harms the environment.

WATER POLLUTION

Water pollution is the presence of harmful materials in water. Pollution makes water unsafe for drinking, washing, and recreation. Water pollution is caused by the improper disposal of substances.

Some major causes of water pollution are improperly treated sewage, industrial wastes, and oil spills. *Sewage* is wastewater from sinks, showers, and toilets. When untreated sewage is dumped into water, the sewage is broken down by bacteria. The bacteria use oxygen. As a result, living things in the water may die from lack of oxygen. Industries often pollute water supplies with poisonous metals, such as lead or mercury. Oil spills in the ocean are another source of water pollution. Oil spills kill fish and other organisms. Oil washing up on shore can damage beaches, as shown in Figure 6·13.

Figure 6·13

Oil spills pollute water and kill wildlife.

150

AIR POLLUTION

The presence of harmful materials, such as smog, in the air is called *air pollution*. **Smog** is a mixture of smoke and fog. A common type of smog forms when sunlight reacts with car exhaust.

Burning fossil fuels in factories is another source of air pollution. These fuels contain sulfur. When sulfur dioxide gas combines with oxygen and water in the air, sulfuric acid is formed. The mixture of acid and rain water is called **acid rain**.

Acid rain adds acid to lakes, ponds and the land. Acid rain kills fish and trees. Acid rain can be reduced by using fuels that have low amounts of sulfur. It is also possible to limit sulfur gases by controlling the burning process at factories.

LAND POLLUTION

Wastes that are disposed of on land cause *land pollution*. Land pollutants include litter, organic materials, and hazardous wastes. *Litter* includes glass, plastic, metal, and paper. Most litter can be recycled. Organic materials such as food remains can be buried in *landfills*. These organic materials will be broken down over time by the action of bacteria. *Hazardous wastes* are wastes that are poisonous, that burn easily, or that react dangerously with other substances. Some landfills have been polluted with hazardous wastes.

PUZZLER

A chemical called DDT was widely used in the 1950s and 1960s to kill insect pests on crops. Its use was stopped in the early 1970s. The DDT caused the shells of osprey eggs to be much thinner than normal. Ospreys are birds that eat fish. The osprey eggs were crushed when the parent birds sat on them. How do you think the use of DDT affected the number of ospreys? Describe a food chain through which the DDT could have reached the ospreys.

151

PROTECTING WILDLIFE

Have you ever seen any of the living things in Figure 6·15? Once there were many of each of these kinds of organisms. One kind, the passenger pigeon, is now *extinct* (ehk STIHNGKT). When an organism is extinct, it means that there are no members of the species left alive. If a species becomes extinct, the food chains of which it is a part may be changed.

Look at the other animals shown in Figure 6·15. These and many other species of wildlife are endangered. An **endangered species** is a species that is in danger of becoming extinct. The California condor and the Florida panther are other endangered animals. The Tennessee purple coneflower and the green pitcher plant are endangered plants. More plants than animals are endangered. If action is not taken to preserve these species, they are likely to become extinct in your lifetime.

Loss of habitat is the main cause of extinction. Most habitat loss is caused by human activities. The clearing of land to plant crops and to build roads destroys many habitats. Chemicals and other wastes that people release into the environment also can destroy habitats.

Figure 6·15

The passenger pigeon is an extinct animal *(A)*. The Tennessee purple coneflower *(B)* and the green pitcher plant *(C)* are endangered plants. The California condor *(D)* is an endangered animal.

REVIEW

1. Give at least two ways in which each of these resources can be polluted: water, air, and land.
2. What are some ways endangered species are protected?

CHALLENGE Sometimes swamplands are filled in so that people can build houses or other buildings. What kinds of organisms might be threatened by this action?

CHAPTER SUMMARY

The main ideas in this chapter are listed below. Read these statements before you answer the Chapter Review questions.

- The biosphere is the zone in which living things are found on the earth. The biosphere is formed of smaller units called ecosystems. (6•1)
- Living things and nonliving things in an ecosystem interact, exchanging energy and materials. (6•1)
- A habitat is the place in which an organism lives. The role of an organism in its habitat is called its niche. (6•2)
- A population is a group of organisms of one species that lives together in an area. All of the populations that live together in an area form a community. (6•2)
- Depending on how they get food, organisms can be grouped as producers, consumers, or decomposers. (6•3)
- The transfer of energy in the form of food is called a food chain. Overlapping food chains form a food web. (6•3)
- An energy pyramid shows the amount of energy at each level in a food chain. A numbers pyramid shows the number of organisms at each level. (6•3)
- Symbiosis is a close, long-term relationship between two organisms. There are three kinds of symbiosis: mutualism, commensalism, and parasitism. (6•4)
- Pollution is the release of unwanted, usually harmful materials into the environment. (6•5)
- There are three general types of pollution — water, air, and land. (6•5)
- Smog and acid rain are two of the results of air pollution. (6•5)
- An endangered species is a species that is in danger of becoming extinct. (6•5)

The key terms in this chapter are listed below. Use each term in a sentence that shows the meaning of the term.

abiotic factors	ecology	niche
acid rain	ecosystem	omnivore
biosphere	endangered species	parasitism
biotic factors	environment	pollution
carnivore	food chain	population
commensalism	food web	producer
community	habitat	smog
consumer	herbivore	
decomposer	mutualism	

Chapter Review

VOCABULARY

Identify each statement as True or False. If a statement is false, replace the underlined term or phrase with the term or phrase that makes the statement true.

1. A form of symbiosis in which both partners benefit is called <u>commensalism</u>.
2. A form of symbiosis in which one partner is harmed while the other benefits is called <u>mutualism</u>.
3. The zone in which all living things are found on the earth is called the <u>biosphere</u>.
4. <u>Ecology</u> is the study of the relationships between living things and their environment.
5. A <u>niche</u> is an area in which living things and nonliving things interact, exchanging materials and energy.
6. All of the living things in an area make up a <u>population</u>.
7. The transfer of energy in the form of food from one organism to another is called a <u>pyramid</u>.
8. An organism that eats both plants and animals is an <u>omnivore</u>.
9. The role of an organism in its environment is called its <u>ecosystem</u>.
10. <u>Acid rain</u> is a mixture of smoke and fog.

CONCEPTS

Choose the letter for the organism in the food web that best matches each of the following terms.

1. producer
2. carnivore
3. omnivore
4. herbivore
5. scavenger
6. decomposer

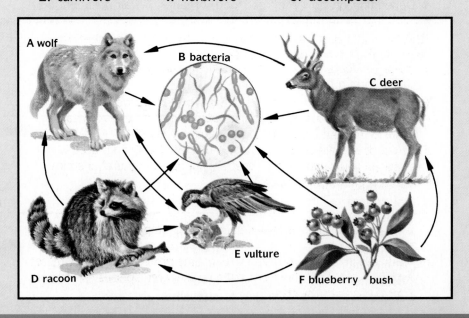

A wolf
B bacteria
C deer
D racoon
E vulture
F blueberry bush

Choose the term or phrase that best answers the question or completes the statement.

7. An abiotic factor that affects many organisms is.
   a. predators.   **c.** decomposers.
   b. oxygen.   **d.** producers.
8. A community may contain:
   a. several populations.   **c.** several different habitats.
   b. many abiotic factors.   **d.** two or more ecosystems.
9. Eating insects is part of a frog's
   a. habitat.   **c.** population.
   b. community.   **d.** niche.
10. Which of the following does *not* describe the habitat of a cactus?
    a. lives in a dry climate   **c.** uses sunlight for photosynthesis
    b. lives in sandy soil   **d.** lives in a very sunny area
11. The largest part of a numbers pyramid is formed by the
    a. producers.   **c.** predators.
    b. consumers.   **d.** herbivores.

Answer the following in complete sentences.

12. How does an organism's habitat differ from its niche?
13. What is the role of decomposers in an ecosystem?
14. Describe how sewage harms water supplies.
15. How is acid rain formed? What are its effects?
16. Why is it important that a species not become extinct?

APPLICATION/ CRITICAL THINKING

1. What might happen to an ecosystem in which the number of predators was greatly reduced?
2. Explain why there are always more herbivores than carnivores in a community.
3. What is the largest ecosystem? Explain your answer.
4. Is more energy lost from an ecosystem when a herbivore eats a plant or when a carnivore eats an animal? Why?
5. Suppose an animal species not normally found in your area is released where you live. If that animal has no natural enemies there, what might happen?

EXTENSION

1. Observe organisms in your neighborhood. Report on a food chain that you observe.
2. Study the laws that your state has for the protection of endangered wildlife. Find out if there is a state endangered species list. Report your findings to the class.

Science in Careers

Have you ever seen photographs of wild oxen? Through years of breeding, certain modern species of cows were developed from this older species. Animal breeders have developed several types of farm animals by studying the traits of many oxen and then carefully selecting which animals to breed.

Animal breeders work to improve animal breeds. Such work has produced cattle that yield more meat and less fat, cows that give more milk, chickens that lay more eggs, and animals that are resistant to some types of diseases.

Animal breeders work on farms and ranches. Some work on special farms run by the government. Others work at universities. Some animal breeders are trained on farms. Others receive a college degree and an advanced degree. If you are interested in this career, you should take biology and chemistry courses in high school.

ANIMAL BREEDER

Have you ever gone camping in a state or national park? If so, you may have noticed the presence of park rangers. Park rangers ensure the safety of the people who use the park.

Park rangers also answer questions about park use. Some park rangers conduct tours describing the wildlife. They explain what animals reside in the park and what kind of habitats these animals live in. They make sure that the wildlife is not harmed as people use the park for recreation. Park rangers also check that habitats are not being damaged.

Park rangers usually have a 4-year college degree in biology or natural resource management. Often, candidates must pass an additional examination before they can work in a park. If you like being outdoors, and are interested in a career as a park ranger, you should take courses in biology and earth science in high school.

PARK RANGER

People in Science

Scientists know that light affects plants in special ways. Without light, plants cannot make food. Dr. Nam-Hai Chua has a special interest in understanding photosynthesis and the functioning of the chloroplast. Dr. Chua and members of his research team want to learn what is actually occurring in the chloroplast of plant cells when the cells are exposed to light.

In his work, Dr. Chua removes parts of chromosomes from the cells of pea plants. He moves the parts of these chromo- somes to cells of petunia plants. He has found that the petunias react to light in much the same way as the pea plants do. In this way he has been able to tell the function of the parts of chromosomes that he has moved.

Today, Dr. Chua's work is helping farming. His work with other scientists is improving crop plants. One possible outcome of Dr. Chua's research might be the development of crop plants that can resist heat. Dr. Chua works at Rockefeller University in New York City.

Dr. Nam-Hai Chua
CELL BIOLOGIST

Issues and Technology

Insecticides and the Food Web: Are Humans in Danger?

Although many kinds of insects are useful to humans, some insects cause serious problems. For centuries, people have tried to find ways to control the insects that spread diseases and destroy crops.

Insecticides are chemicals that are used to kill insects. One of the best-known insecticides is DDT. This chemical was first used to control the mosquitoes that carry malaria. The DDT was so effective that it was soon being used to kill other insects that carry disease. By the 1950s, DDT was also widely used on farmland.

Some insects sprayed with DDT were not affected by it. These insects survived to breed more insects with the same resistance. To overcome this new problem, people increased the amount of DDT they used.

Insecticides like DDT are poisons. They can kill many species of animals in addition to insects. As more and more DDT was used, the chemical began to pollute waterways. Plants in rivers, lakes, and marshes took in the chemical. Some animals fed on the plants and took in DDT as they fed. These animals were food for larger animals and they in turn were food for even larger animals. These food relationships among organisms make up a *food web*.

Figure 1 shows a food web in a marsh that had been sprayed with DDT for many years. The arrows show the transfer of DDT as the animals feed. The numbers show the level of DDT in each animal.

APPLYING CRITICAL THINKING SKILLS

1. What kinds of organisms have the lowest levels of DDT?
2. What is the DDT level in minnows? How did DDT get into these fish?
3. What kinds of organisms in the figure show the highest levels of DDT? Suggest a reason for these high levels of insecticide.
4. Blowfish eat clams and snails, yet the DDT level of blowfish is less than that of either of these other animals. Suggest a reason for this.
5. Do you think it would be hard to avoid getting insecticides in your body once they are in the food web? Explain your answer, and suggest some ways to avoid taking in insecticides.
6. To control mosquitoes, the marsh was sprayed with DDT. Suggest another method that might have been used to control the mosquitoes. Discuss some advantages and disadvantages of your suggestion.

Figure 1

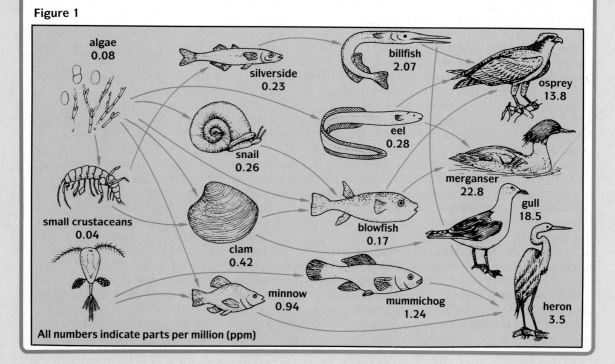

algae 0.08
silverside 0.23
billfish 2.07
osprey 13.8
snail 0.26
eel 0.28
merganser 22.8
gull 18.5
small crustaceans 0.04
clam 0.42
blowfish 0.17
minnow 0.94
mummichog 1.24
heron 3.5

All numbers indicate parts per million (ppm)

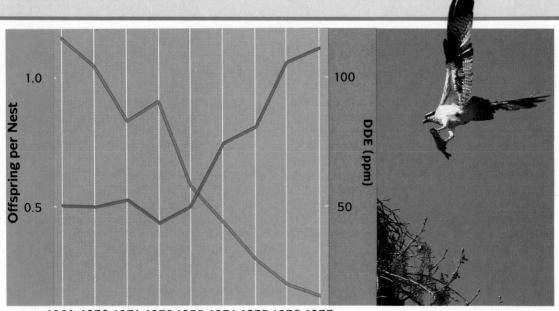

Figure 2

As scientists studied the DDT problem, they began to see some surprising effects. Large birds of prey, such as eagles and ospreys, were decreasing in population. Adults were alive and breeding, but very few offspring were being raised. What was happening to the eggs of these birds?

Because DDT is poisonous, you might think that the baby birds were poisoned. This was one of the early hypotheses. However, when scientists looked at the nests of many broken eggs were found. The baby birds were not poisoned. They had died because their eggs were crushed.

The DDT interferes with the proper development of the eggshell. As a result, the eggshells were very thin. When the parents sat on the eggs, the weight of the parent birds broke the eggs. So many eggs were broken that only one of out every two or three nests was producing one living offspring.

In 1972 the use of DDT was banned in the United States. However, an increase in the population of eagles and ospreys was not seen right away, because DDT remains in the soil, in the water, and in organisms for many years.

Figure 2 shows the offspring production of ospreys over 9 years. It also shows the amount of DDE found in the eggs that failed to hatch. This DDE is a chemical formed when DDT is broken down. A measurement of DDE levels in the eggs indicates the amount of DDT taken in by the parent birds.

APPLYING CRITICAL THINKING SKILLS

1. During which year was the amount of DDE highest? During which year was it lowest?
2. During which year was offspring production lowest? During which year was it highest?
3. Does the graph show a relationship between DDE levels and offspring production? If so, what is the relationship?
4. Eventually the increase in offspring production will level off, although the amounts of DDE found will probably continue to decrease. Why won't offspring production continue to increase as DDE levels decrease?
5. After DDT was banned, what do you think happened to the mosquito population in this marsh?

The chemical DDT is one of many insecticides that have been developed. Some, like DDT, are banned in the United States. Others are still in use. Scientists are trying to find safer insecticides. The scientists have rated insecticides on the basis of how poisonous they are to organisms other than insects and how long insecticides take to break down after they are used.

Figure 3 shows the ratings of some insecticides. On a scale of 0 to 4, the rating for the most poisonous pesticide is 4, and the rating for the least poisonous is 0. On a scale of 0 to 4, the rating for the chemicals that last the longest is 4, and the rating for chemicals that break down fast is 0.

Insecticides are probably the fastest way to control insect pests, but they are not the only method available. Another way to control insects is to find a natural enemy of that insect and bring that enemy into the area. This method is good because it does not pollute the environment and kill organisms other than the ones that are causing problems. But there are some drawbacks to using natural enemies. Sometimes the organism that is introduced to control a pest cannot survive in the area. Sometimes the organism that is introduced eats other insects or harms other animals, instead of the pest. A natural enemy should not be introduced into an area until the natural enemy's effects on the environment can be determined.

Scientists are trying to find viruses and other disease-causing organisms that will control insect populations. Like the natural-enemy method, control methods that use diseases must be tested very carefully before they are used.

Natural enemies and diseases will not completely destroy an insect population. They will only keep the insect population from becoming too large. Although these methods are slow to get started, once they are used they remain effective for a long time. In contrast, insecticides have to be reapplied every year.

APPLYING CRITICAL THINKING SKILLS

1. The chemical makeup of DDT, dieldrin, and lindane are similar. How else are these three insecticides similar?
2. Which insecticide shown in Figure 3 is the least poisonous to mammals? To fish?
3. Several of the insecticides that are banned in the United States are still made here and exported to other countries. Some of these countries are in Central America. Coffee and other foods are imported to the United States from these countries. What risks are there in importing these foods? What should we do to protect ourselves against these risks?
4. Insecticides produced in the United States are also exported to many countries where lack of food is a serious problem. Should insecticides that are known to be poisonous be used in these countries? Explain your answer.
5. Do you think control by natural enemies is better than control by insecticides? Compare the advantages and disadvantages of each.
6. Suppose you wanted to use a disease to control an insect population in a farming region. What reaction do you think there would be to your idea? How would you convince people that this is a good control method?

Figure 3

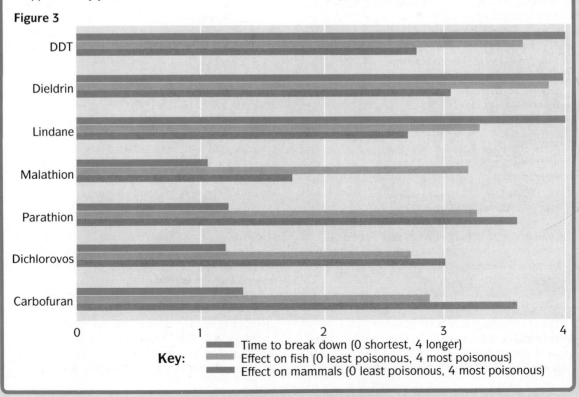

Key:
Time to break down (0 shortest, 4 longer)
Effect on fish (0 least poisonous, 4 most poisonous)
Effect on mammals (0 least poisonous, 4 most poisonous)

DISCOVERING
MATTER
AND ENERGY

*O**n the earth, matter can exist as either a solid, liquid, or a gas. Physical science is the study of matter and energy, and their interactions. In this unit you will learn about the atomic structure of some elements and how they form compounds. You will study the varieties of forces and how machines work. You will also study heat, waves, and sound.*

▼ *Crystals of butyl benzoic acid.*

The ▶ *mechanisms inside a watch illustrate how simple machines work.*

▲ *Medieval alchemy symbols for copper* (left), *potassium nitrate* (middle), *and ammonium chloride* (right).

Wind energy helps Stars and *Stripes* win the America's Cup. ▶

A special technique was used to photograph this model of the space shuttle producing shock waves. ▼

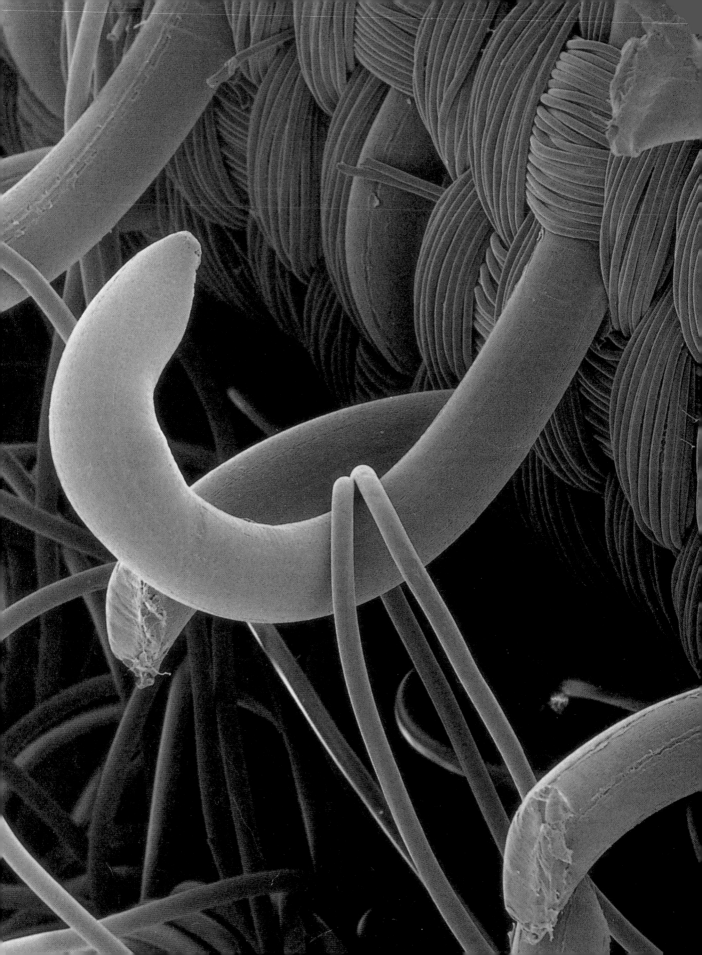

CHAPTER 7

PROPERTIES OF MATTER

Do you recognize the material shown in this photograph? You probably have seen it before. It is used as fasteners of shoes, jackets, and wallets, among other things. It is Velcro, a two-part fastening material made of nylon. One part, or surface, is covered with tiny loops. The other surface is covered with hooks. When these surfaces touch, the hooks slip through the loops. The surfaces stay together until they are peeled apart.

To be able to make a product like Velcro, scientists must understand the behavior of the matter that will be used. This photograph was taken with an electron microscope. The color was added by computer. Microscopes and computers are two of the devices that scientists use to study matter.

- *What are some of the ways that scientists study matter and its properties?*
- *Can the same kind of matter that is used to make Velcro be used to make other products?*

7·1 What Is Matter?

com- (together)
ponere (to put)

Figure 7·1

How are mixtures different from
compounds?

Matter makes up all objects. You and all of the things around you are made of matter. **Matter** is anything that has mass and takes up space. *Mass* is a measure of the amount of matter in an object.

Each of the many kinds of matter has properties that help to identify it. Some examples of properties are color, odor, and the temperature at which a substance melts or boils. Other properties describe the way kinds of matter can combine.

Any sample of matter may be classified as either a substance or a mixture. A *substance* is a particular kind of matter. Gold, silver, water, salt, and sugar are examples of substances. All particles in a substance are the same. As you can see in Figure 7·1, there are two kinds of substances: elements and compounds. An **element** is a substance that cannot be changed into simpler substances by ordinary means, such as heating, cooling, or crushing. Gold and silver are examples of elements.

A **compound** is a substance that is made up of two or more elements chemically combined. Water, salt, and sugar are all compounds. Each compound has its own properties. Compounds can be made into their elements. Water can be broken down into its parts, hydrogen and oxygen.

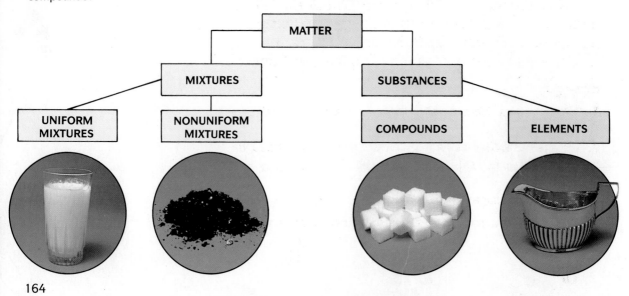

Figure 7·2

Granite *(left)* is a mixture that contains mica *(top)*, feldspar *(middle)*, and quartz *(bottom)*. Is this mixture uniform?

Air, brass, and salt water are all examples of mixtures. A **mixture** is a combination of two or more kinds of matter that can be separated by physical means. Each kind of matter in a mixture can be found in any amount. The different kinds of matter keep their own properties.

Some mixtures have the same makeup throughout the sample. For example, brass is a uniform mixture of the elements copper and zinc. The amount of copper and zinc in brass is the same at any point in a brass object. The skim milk shown in Figure 7·1 is a uniform mixture.

Not all mixtures are uniform. An example of a mixture that is not uniform is the rock called granite. Look at Figure 7·2. The sample of granite is a mixture that contains quartz, feldspar, and mica.

REVIEW

1. What characteristics do all samples of matter have in common?
2. What is the difference between an element and a compound?
3. Label each of the following as an element, a compound, or a mixture.
   a. air   **b.** sugar   **c.** silver   **d.** brass   **e.** water

CHALLENGE How might you separate a mixture of iron filings and salt?

7·2 The Four States of Matter

After completing this section, you will be able to

- **list** and **compare** the four states of matter.
- **describe** the events that take place during a change of state.

The key terms in this section are

gas   plasma
liquid   solid

Matter is found in four forms, or states: solid, liquid, gas, and plasma. Each state of matter has certain properties. A **solid** has a definite shape and takes up a definite volume. As shown in Figure 7·3, the particles in a solid are very close together. They are held together by strong forces. The particles in matter are always in motion. In a solid the particles vibrate but do not move around.

Solids are divided into two main groups — crystals and amorphous (uh MAWR fuhs) solids. A *crystal* is a solid whose particles are arranged in a regular, repeating, three-dimensional pattern. Salt and sugar form crystals. An *amorphous solid* is a solid whose particles lack a regular, repeating order. In an amorphous solid the particles are jumbled together. Butter and wax are amorphous solids. What kind of a solid is a diamond?

A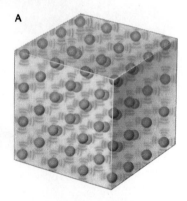

B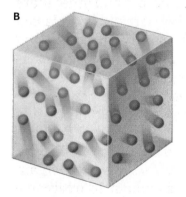

C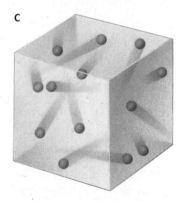

Figure 7·3

Most matter on the earth exists as a solid *(A)*, a liquid *(B)*, or a gas *(C)*.

A **liquid** has a definite volume but not a definite shape. As in a solid, forces hold together the particles in a liquid. But the forces between the particles in a liquid are not strong enough to hold the liquid in a definite shape. Thus a liquid flows and takes the shape of its container.

A **gas** does not have a definite shape or volume. Notice in Figure 7·3 that the particles in a gas are very far apart compared with those in a liquid and a solid. The forces between gas particles are very weak. As a result, a gas expands to fill and take the shape of its container.

Most of the matter in the universe is in the plasma state. Stars, including the sun, are glowing masses of plasma. The sun sends out clouds of plasma.

When these clouds of plasma reach the earth, they collide with air particles in the upper atmosphere. This causes the formation of colored lights called auroras. Auroras at the North Pole are called the Northern Lights.

Matter in the plasma state may be used to produce energy in the future. Plasma is very difficult to study in a laboratory. The Northern Lights are giving scientists a chance to learn more about plasma. If scientists can learn more about the behavior of plasma in nature, they may be able to learn how to better control plasma under laboratory conditions.

Matter is not usually found in the plasma state on the earth, although plasma may exist under some laboratory conditions. The sun and other stars are in the plasma state. The particles of plasma shake violently at very high temperatures, making **plasma** a hot gas of electrically charged particles.

Substances can be changed from one state to another. Recall that particles in matter are held together by forces. These forces give a solid its definite shape. When you heat a solid, you add energy to its particles. This energy causes the particles to move faster and farther apart. As the particles gain more energy, they move fast enough to overcome the forces that hold them in place. Thus the solid melts, losing its shape. If enough heat is added to a liquid, the liquid will change to the gas state. What happens to a liquid as it changes to a solid?

REVIEW

1. Name the four states of matter.
2. Which states of matter have no definite shape?
3. How does the space between particles of a solid change when it becomes a liquid?

CHALLENGE Suggest an explanation for the fact that matter is not usually found in the plasma state on the earth.

7·3 Physical Properties of Matter

After completing this section, you will be able to

- **list** examples of physical properties.
- **describe** practical uses of physical properties.

The key terms in this section are
boiling point
condensation point
freezing point
melting point
physical properties

Physical properties are characteristics of matter that can be studied without changing the makeup of a substance. Color, taste, odor, and melting temperature are physical properties. The physical properties of a kind of matter stay the same regardless of the shape or amount of that matter. For example, think of an iron nail. Its mass is 12 g, and it is rod-shaped. If the nail is cut into two pieces, each piece has a mass of less than 12 g. However, the nail is still the same kind of matter — iron.

When talking about physical properties of matter the conditions under which the properties are determined should be stated. For example, iron could be described as a gray solid. This description is correct for iron at room temperature. But it is not correct for iron at the temperature in a blast furnace. The physical properties of matter often vary with temperature, pressure, and state.

PROPERTIES OF LIQUIDS

Because liquids do not have a definite shape, they can flow. Some liquids resist flow more than do others. A liquid's resistance to flow is called *viscosity* (vihs KAHS uh tee). Liquids such as water flow

Figure 7·4

The viscosity of oil changes as the temperature changes.

Figure 7·5
The attraction of the particles in the water causes the property of surface tension.

easily and have low viscosities. Some liquids, such as heavy oils, have high viscosities. These liquids flow slowly. Motor oil, which lubricates the moving parts of an engine, is rated according to viscosity. The viscosity of oil changes with temperature. Look at Figure 7·4. The sample of oil on the left has been heated. As you can see, viscosity becomes lower and the oil flows more freely as the temperature rises. A driver must use an oil with a viscosity that is high enough to lubricate but low enough to flow through the engine.

Figure 7·5 shows an insect standing on the surface of a pond. Why doesn't the insect fall into the water? Recall that there are forces of attraction between the particles in a sample of matter. These forces exist in all directions within a liquid. But at the surface of the liquid, forces do not exist in all directions. As you can see in Figure 7·5, surface particles are acted on by forces of attraction from below but not from above. The surface particles also attract each other. As a result, the surface particles are pulled inward and close together, forming a "skin" on the surface of the liquid. The tendency of a liquid to form a skin at the surface is called *surface tension*. The surface tension of water makes it possible for certain insects to stand on top of water.

PUZZLER

The liquid in the graduate is mercury. Notice that the meniscus formed by mercury is highest at the center. Most liquids form a meniscus that is lowest at the center. Use the terms *adhesion* and *cohesion* to explain the difference in the way meniscuses form.

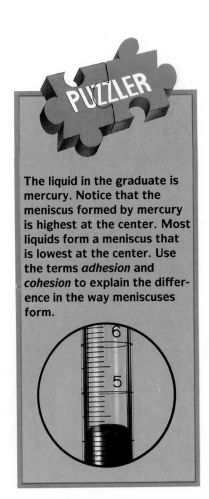

The cohesion of the particles in water contributes to surface tension. *Cohesion* (koh HEE zhuhn) is the attraction between particles of the same substance. If you add soap to water, particles of the soap get between particles of water. Some of the soap particles are attracted to the water particles. This attraction between particles of different substances is called *adhesion* (ad HEE zhuhn). The soap particles break up the cohesion in the water, and the surface tension decreases. Could an insect stand on the surface of soapy water?

PROPERTIES OF SOLIDS

Solids show a variety of properties. A rubber band can be stretched by pulling. When the pulling stops, the rubber band goes back to its original shape. A solid that can stretch and then return to its original shape shows the property of *elasticity* (ih-las TIHS uh tee). Elasticity gives the balls shown in Figure 7·6 the ability to bounce.

Some solids are *malleable* (MAL ee uh buhl). This means they can be hammered into very thin sheets. Copper and gold, for example, are malleable.

Figure 7·6

Compare the elasticity of golf balls *(white)*, tennis balls *(yellow)*, and rubber balls *(pink)*.

Substances such as sulfur cannot be hammered into thin sheets. Sulfur shows the property of *brittleness*. It breaks if it is hammered. Many solids show a physical property known as hardness. Hardness is the ability to resist being scratched. Diamond is the hardest substance in nature.

Some solids can be drawn into wire. The ability of a solid to be drawn into wire is known as *ductility*. Copper and steel have the property of ductility. The physical property called *tensile* (TEHN-suhl) *strength* describes how well a solid resists breaking under tension. If a copper wire and a steel wire of the same thickness are pulled with great force, the copper wire will break first. The steel wire has a higher tensile strength than the copper wire.

Knowledge of physical properties helps people choose ways to use matter. The hardness of diamonds makes them useful in drill bits like the ones shown in Figure 7·7B. Figure 7·7C shows steel wires supporting the weight of a bridge. What property is useful in these wires?

Figure 7·7

Matter can be used in many objects, including steel saw blades *(A)*, diamond drill tips *(B)*, and steel bridge cables *(C)*.

CHANGE OF STATE

The temperatures at which changes of state take place are physical properties. The temperature at which a solid becomes a liquid is called the **melting point.** If a melted substance is cooled, it will change back into the solid state. This reverse change is called freezing. The temperature at which a liquid freezes is called the **freezing point.** The freezing point and the melting point of a substance are the same. For water, this temperature at sea level is 0°C. Look at the icicles shown in Figure 7·8. When ice is warmed to 0°C it begins to melt. As more heat is added to ice at 0°C more and more of the ice melts. But the temperature remains at 0°C until all of the ice melts. Both the solid and liquid states of water exist at this temperature. The temperature begins to rise only after all of the ice has melted.

The melting point and freezing point of a substance are physical properties that help to identify the substance. Table 7·1 shows the melting and freezing points of some substances. The strength of the forces between particles determines the melting and freezing points of different kinds of matter. Oxygen has a low melting point because the forces between the particles of oxygen are weak. Iron has a high melting point. The forces between iron particles are very strong. The high melting point of iron makes it a good material for cooking utensils.

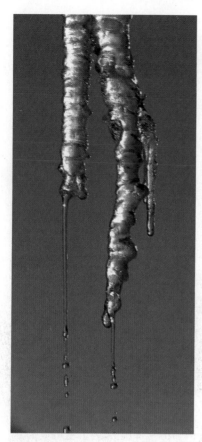

Figure 7·8

Water can exist as both a solid and a liquid at 0°C.

Table 7·1 *Change of State*

SUBSTANCE	MELTING/FREEZING POINTS (°C)	BOILING/CONDENSATION POINTS (°C)
Water	0	100
Aluminum	658	2467
Copper	1080	2595
Iron	1530	3000
Lead	328	1740
Helium	−272	−269
Mercury	−39	357
Oxygen	−219	−184
Hydrogen	−259	−252
Sulfur dioxide	−73	−10

A liquid can change to a gas state by evaporation or by boiling. Evaporation takes place at the surface of a liquid. Boiling takes place all through a liquid. The temperature at which a liquid boils at sea level is the **boiling point** for that liquid. Table 7·1 shows the boiling points of several substances. Water, which melts at 0°C, is a liquid between 0°C and 100°C. The temperature of boiling water is 100°C.

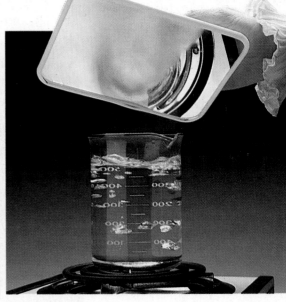

Figure 7·9
Condensation is the reverse of boiling.

Condensation is the reverse of boiling. The temperature at which a gas condenses, or changes to a liquid, is called the **condensation point.** The boiling point and the condensation point of a substance are the same. Water vapor can be condensed into liquid water. What is the temperature of the water vapor when it condenses?

REVIEW

1. List four physical properties of matter.
2. What is surface tension?
3. Compare a substance's melting point and freezing point.
4. What properties are important in selecting the kind of matter to be used for fire doors?

CHALLENGE Look at Table 7·1 on page 172. At 20°C what is the state of matter of each substance listed in the table?

7·4 Density and Specific Gravity

After completing this section, you will be able to

- **calculate** the density of a substance.
- **compare** densities of different substances.

The key terms in this section are
density
specific gravity

densus (thick)

Which has more mass, one kilogram of bricks or one kilogram of feathers? They both have the same mass. Which has the greater volume? One kilogram of feathers has a much larger volume than does one kilogram of bricks. The feathers are less dense than the bricks.

Density (DEHN suh tee) is a measure of how closely the mass of a substance is packed into a given volume. **Density** is the mass per unit volume of a substance. It is a ratio, and it does not depend on sample size. As volume increases, mass increases. The ratio is always the same. The density of a substance can be used to help identify that substance. Figure 7·10 shows two different kinds of wood. Notice that these blocks of wood have the same mass. However, one block of wood has a larger volume. Which block of wood is more dense?

Figure 7·10
Samples of matter that have the same mass but different volumes have different densities.

The density of a sample of matter is found by measuring its mass and volume and then dividing the mass by the volume. The formula to find the density of a substance is written as follows.

$$D = \frac{M}{V}$$

In the formula, D stands for density, M stands for mass, and V stands for volume.

Sample Problem

Find the density of a sample of a substance. The sample has a volume of 2.0 cm³ and a mass of 38.6 g.

1. Write the formula.

$$D = \frac{M}{V}$$

2. Substitute the numbers in the problem for the symbols in the formula.

$$D = \frac{38.6 \text{ g}}{2.0 \text{ cm}^3}$$

3. Determine the unit that will be part of the answer. In this case the unit is g/cm³.

$$D = \frac{38.6}{2.0} \text{ g/cm}^3$$

4. Complete the calculations that are required. In this example, 38.6 divided by 2.0 equals 19.3.

$$D = 19.3 \text{ g/cm}^3$$

The unit used to express density is g/cm³. For example, the density of water is written as 1.0 g/cm³. Table 7·2 shows the densities of some common materials. Which material has the same density as does the substance in the sample problem?

Figure 7·11
A cork and a rubber stopper. Which object has more mass?

NOTE Throughout this book there are sample problems like the one shown here. The lines printed in blue show how to solve the problem.

Table 7·2 Densities of Some Common Materials at 20°C

MATERIAL	DENSITY (g/cm³)	MATERIAL	DENSITY (g/cm³)
Platinum	21.4	Seawater	1.025
Gold	19.3	Water	1.00
Mercury	13.6	Ice	0.92
Lead	11.3	Oil	0.90
Silver	10.5	Paraffin	0.87
Copper	8.9	Gasoline	0.7
Brass	8.5	Oak (wood)	0.7
Iron	7.9	Pine (wood)	0.4
Steel	7.8	Cork	0.24
Aluminum	2.7	Oxygen	0.0014
Marble	2.7	Air	0.0013
Rubber	1.1	Helium	0.0002

Figure 7·12

The density of the iceberg is less than the density of the seawater.

Notice that Table 7·2 lists densities at 20°C. Most kinds of matter expand when their temperatures rise, and contract when their temperatures drop. Thus the density changes with temperature. Would density increase or decrease as temperature increases?

Gases are less dense than are liquids and solids. The solid states of matter generally have higher densities than do liquids. One exception to this pattern is water. Unlike other liquids, water expands as it freezes. How does Figure 7·12 demonstrate that ice is less dense than liquid water?

It can be useful to understand density. For example, wearing a life jacket decreases a person's overall density. This is because the life jacket increases the body's volume but adds very little mass. The decreased density makes it easier for a person to stay afloat.

A submarine changes depth as water is removed or added to its ballast tanks. When water is removed from the tanks, the submarine loses mass. Thus it floats higher in the water. When water is added to the tanks, the submarine gains mass. Then it sinks lower in the water because its density is greater.

It is useful to compare the density of a substance with the density of water. **Specific gravity** is the ratio between the density of a substance and the density of water. The formula for calculating specific gravity is as follows.

$$\text{specific gravity} = \frac{\text{density of substance}}{\text{density of water}}$$

Consider a problem to find the specific gravity of steel. The densities of steel and water are found in Table 7·2. Substituting these values into the formula shows the following.

$$\text{specific gravity} = \frac{7.8 \text{ g/cm}^3}{1.0 \text{ g/cm}^3}$$

The same unit is in the numerator and the denominator of the equation. The units therefore cancel each other. Thus specific gravity is not represented with a unit, and the specific gravity of steel is 7.8. What is the specific gravity of platinum?

ACTIVITY　How Is Density Determined?

OBJECTIVE
Calculate the densities of several objects.

MATERIALS
several solid objects, balance and masses, metric ruler, 100-mL graduate, water

PROCEDURE
A. Draw a data table like the one shown.
B. Measure the mass of each object. Record this information in the data table.
C. Measure the length, width, and height of the regular objects. Record this data.
D. Calculate the volume of each regular object by multiplying length x width x height.
E. Find the volume of each irregular object by using water displacement.
F. Compute the density of each object, using the following formula.

$$D = \frac{M}{V}$$

G. Record the densities in the data table.

RESULTS AND CONCLUSIONS
1. What was the densest sample you tested?
2. What was the least dense sample?
3. Did more than one sample have the same density? If so, do you think they are the same kind of matter?

OBJECT	MASS (g)	LENGTH (cm)	WIDTH (cm)	HEIGHT (cm)	VOLUME (cm³)	DENSITY (g/cm³)
Regular Object						
Irregular Object		—	—	—		

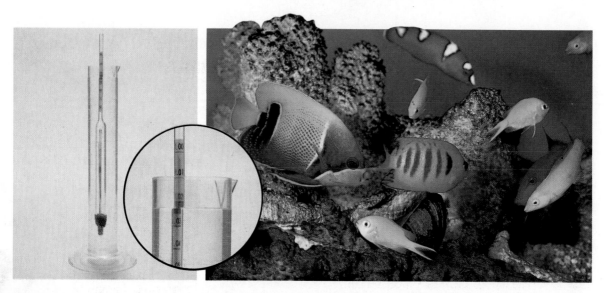

Figure 7·13

A hydrometer is used to measure the density of a liquid.

Specific gravity is often used to describe liquids. The specific gravity of a liquid can be measured with a device called a hydrometer. A *hydrometer* (hī DRAHM uh tuhr) is a sealed tube with a weight in the bottom and markings along its side. The hydrometer is floated in a liquid. It floats high in a dense liquid and lower in a less dense liquid. The specific gravity is determined by the mark at the surface of the liquid. Figure 7·13 shows a hydrometer being used to test a sample of water from an aquarium. Is this salt water or fresh water?

REVIEW

1. What is density?

2. Find the density of each substance shown in the table.

SUBSTANCE	MASS (g)	VOLUME (cm³)	DENSITY
A	84	30	
B	204	24	
C	28	31	
D	757	67	

3. Explain why a 2-kg sample of lead is denser than a 10-kg sample of iron.

CHALLENGE A piece of glass is 4.5 cm long, 2.0 cm wide, and 0.2 cm thick. Its mass is 4.5 g. What is the density of the glass? Suppose the piece of glass is cut exactly in half. What is the density of each piece?

7·5 Physical Changes and Chemical Changes

The evaporation of water, the melting of wax, the dissolving of salt in water, and the breaking of glass are physical changes. In each case, no new matter is formed. Matter is changed from one state to another in evaporation and melting. Two kinds of matter are mixed when salt is dissolved in water. Matter is changed in size and shape when glass is broken. A **physical change** is one in which the appearance of matter changes but its chemical properties and makeup remain the same.

Although water and ice look different, they are the same kind of matter. The water can be frozen and then melted again. Melting is a physical change. Boiling also is a physical change.

Most solids melt when heated. However, some solids change directly to a gas without melting. The direct change from solid to gas is known as *sublimation* (suhb luh MAY shuhn). Moth balls and solid carbon dioxide sublime. Ice and snow sublime when the temperature is less than 0°C.

Figure 7·14 shows the results of two different kinds of changes. Both the bat and the ashes started as a piece of wood. The bat is the result of a physical

Figure 7·14
Wood can be changed physically *(left)* or chemically *(right)*.

change. But how were the ashes produced? New substances are produced when wood burns. There are ashes, which were not there before. Smoke is given off. Odors that were not present before are now present.

Burning causes chemical changes in matter. A **chemical change** is a change that produces one or more kinds of matter that are different from those present before the change. Iron rust is made of oxygen and iron. Rust is not the same as the matter from which it formed. Thus the formation of iron rust is a chemical change.

Every time you cook an egg, you cause changes. Look at Figure 7·15. Breaking the egg is a physical change. If you scramble the egg, you cause another physical change. As the egg cooks, a chemical change takes place.

When you eat the egg, another series of physical and chemical changes begins. The egg is broken down by grinding and cutting, which are physical changes. Then it is changed chemically by enzymes in digestive juices.

Figure 7·15
Which of these changes are physical changes?

ACTIVITY How Do Chemical and Physical Changes Differ?

OBJECTIVE
Classify changes as chemical or physical.

MATERIALS
safety goggles, lab apron, 4 test tubes, water, test-tube holder, Bunsen burner, striker, glass plate, steel wool, tongs, glass-marking pencil, test-tube rack, wood splint, salt, dilute HCl, mossy zinc, solutions A and B, 2 droppers

PROCEDURE
A. Wear safety goggles and a lab apron during this activity.
B. Draw a data table like the one shown.
C. Read each direction carefully. Make observations before, during, and after the change. Record all observations.
D. Add water to a depth of 2 cm to a test tube. Gently heat the tube over the flame of a Bunsen burner. After the water has been heated for a few minutes, hold a glass plate near the mouth of the test tube.
E. Hold a small piece of steel wool with tongs. Place the steel wool into the flame. Remove the steel wool from the flame. Set it aside to cool.
F. Label three test tubes *1* through *3*. Place the test tubes in a test-tube rack.
G. Add water to a depth of about 1 cm to test tube *1*. Using a wood splint, add a small amount of salt.

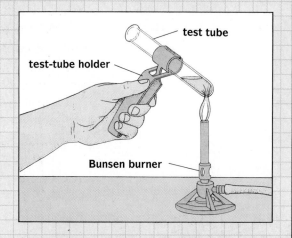

H. Add dilute HCl to a depth of about 1 cm to test tube *2*. Add a small piece of mossy zinc.
I. In test tube *3*, mix five drops of solution A and two drops of solution B. Use a different dropper for each solution.

RESULTS AND CONCLUSIONS
1. Which procedure(s) produced a physical change?
2. What observation(s) indicate that a physical change took place?
3. Which procedure(s) produced a chemical change?
4. What observation(s) indicate that a chemical change took place?

PROCEDURE	OBSERVATION BEFORE CHANGE	OBSERVATION DURING CHANGE	OBSERVATION AFTER CHANGE	TYPE OF CHANGE
Heating water				
Heating steel wool				
Combining water and salt				
Combining HCl and mossy zinc				
Combining solutions A and B				

Figure 7·16
Restoring the Statue of Liberty.

The ability of a substance to undergo or resist chemical changes is called a **chemical property.** When iron is placed in some acids, a chemical change causes hydrogen gas to be released. The ability to undergo this change is a chemical property of iron. When gold is placed in acid, no chemical change takes place. Thus iron and gold differ in this property.

Knowledge of chemical properties is important in using materials. For example, the rusting of iron is a kind of corrosion. *Corrosion* (kuh ROH zhuhn) is a chemical change that takes place when a metal combines with a substance around it, such as oxygen. Iron rust flakes off after it forms. As a result, rusting continues on the newly exposed surface. Buildings, bridges, and cars made of iron must be painted or protected in some other way to prevent rusting.

Metal structures that have not been protected may become corroded. Pollution can cause corrosion. Millions of dollars were spent to restore the Statue of Liberty after corrosion had damaged it.

REVIEW

1. Describe two physical changes.
2. Describe two chemical changes.
3. How do physical and chemical changes differ?

CHALLENGE Identify one physical change and one chemical change that take place as a candle burns.

CHAPTER SUMMARY

The main ideas in this chapter are listed below. Read these statements before you answer the Chapter Review questions.

- Matter is anything that has mass and takes up space. (7·1)

- An element is a substance that cannot be changed into simpler substances by ordinary means. (7·1)

- A compound is a substance made up of two or more elements chemically combined. (7·1)

- A mixture is made of two or more kinds of matter, each keeping its own properties. (7·1)

- Matter is found in four states: solid, liquid, gas, and plasma. (7·2)

- Solids are classified as crystals or amorphous solids. (7·2)

- Matter in the plasma state is a hot, electrically charged gas. (7·2)

- Physical properties are characteristics of matter that can be studied without changing the makeup of a substance. (7·3)

- Physical properties include color, odor, melting point, and boiling point. (7·3)

- Density is the mass per unit volume of a substance. The unit used to express density is g/cm^3. (7·4)

- The specific gravity of a substance is the ratio between the density of a substance and the density of water. There is no unit for specific gravity. (7·4)

- A physical change may change the appearance of matter but not its chemical properties and makeup. Physical changes include melting and boiling. (7·5)

- A chemical change produces new kinds of matter that are different from those present before the change. (7·5)

- The ability of a substance to undergo or resist chemical changes is called a chemical property. (7·5)

The key terms in this chapter are listed below. Use each in a sentence that shows the meaning of the term.

boiling point	element	mixture
chemical change	freezing point	physical change
chemical property	gas	physical properties
compound	liquid	plasma
condensation point	matter	solid
density	melting point	specific gravity

Chapter Review

VOCABULARY

Use the key terms from the previous page to complete the following sentences correctly.

1. The temperature at which a solid becomes a liquid is called the _____ .
2. A substance that cannot be changed into simpler substances by ordinary means is called a/an _____ .
3. A/An _____ results when new substances are formed from the combination of two or more elements.
4. The _____ of a substance is the mass per unit volume of that substance.
5. A/An _____ is the combination of two or more substances, each keeping its own properties.
6. The ratio between the density of a substance and the density of water is called _____ .
7. A new substance that differs in appearance and makeup from the original substance is produced in a/an _____ .
8. Anything that has mass and takes up space is called _____ .
9. Matter in the _____ state has a definite shape and takes up a definite volume.
10. The _____ state of matter is a hot, electrically charged gas.

CONCEPTS

Identify each statement as True or False. If a statement is false, replace the underlined term or phrase with a term or phrase that makes the statement true.

1. Gold, silver, and oxygen are examples of <u>compounds</u>.
2. Matter is not usually found in the <u>gas</u> state on the earth.
3. Maple syrup and other liquids that do not flow easily have high <u>viscosities</u>.
4. Solids that show the property of <u>ductility</u> break if they are hammered.
5. The boiling point and the <u>condensation point</u> of a substance are the same.

Identify each of the following as a physical change or a chemical change.

6. Burning wood
7. Breaking a window
8. Grinding a salt crystal into a powder
9. Exploding fireworks
10. Boiling water

Answer the following.

11. What is the relationship between elements and compounds?
12. What are the three states of matter that normally exist on the earth? Give one example of each.

SUBSTANCE (AT 20°C)	MASS (g)	VOLUME (cm³)	DENSITY
A	386	20	
B	84	8	
C	12	50	
D	2	10,000	

13. Copy and complete the table above by finding the density of each of the substances.
14. Use Table 7·2 to identify each substance in question 13.

APPLICATION/ CRITICAL THINKING

1. Suppose you have been given two samples of matter. These two substances have the same melting and boiling points. You want more evidence to determine whether the two substances are the same. What other properties would you investigate?
2. A student has two blocks with the same volume. One block is made of wood, and the other of cork. The density of the wood is 0.70 g/cm³. The density of the cork is 0.24 g/cm³. How many times heavier than the cork block is the wood block?
3. Crystals are usually harder than amorphous solids. Suggest a reason for this difference.
4. Baking a cake involves both chemical changes and physical changes. Describe some of the changes that take place as a cake bakes. Classify these changes as chemical or physical.

EXTENSION

1. Do research on the Brenell test. Find out how it is used in the laboratory.
2. The tensile strength of a fiber in a spider's web is as great as that of some metals. Find out how tensile strength is measured and what units are used to express it.

CHAPTER 8

THE ATOM

*T*he streaks of light in this photograph are the images produced by the lights of moving cars. These streaks of light show you where the cars were going when the photograph was taken. Look more closely at the photograph. You cannot see the cars. But the streaks of light provide evidence that the cars were there. The white streaks show that some cars were moving toward the person taking the photograph. The red streaks show that some cars were moving away. Notice the short yellow streaks. What might they indicate?

Scientists cannot see the tiny particles that make up matter, but they have evidence that these particles exist. Like the lights of cars, these particles can make images on film. Scientists use these images to study the behavior of matter.

- *What are the particles that make up matter?*

- *Are these particles the same in all kinds of matter?*

- *How do scientists organize their information about kinds of matter?*

8·1 The Structure of the Atom

Imagine taking a pure sample of an element, such as gold, and cutting it in half. Suppose you cut it in half again and again. You would finally have a piece so tiny that it could not be divided further and still be gold. That piece is called an atom. An **atom** is the smallest particle of an element that has the properties of that element.

MODELS IN SCIENCE

The concept of the atom is an example of a scientific model. In science a *model* is a means by which scientists try to explain something they cannot see or understand by relating it to something that they do see or understand. Scientists use models to describe things that they cannot observe directly. There are models for very small things, like the atom. There are also models for huge things, like the solar system.

Figure 8·1 shows three kinds of models used in science. The scale model of the space shuttle shows a three-dimensional replica. The diagram is a model that shows how the shuttle is built. The equation is a mental model that tells the speed needed for the shuttle to escape the earth's gravity.

Figure 8·1

Scientists use many kinds of models, including a scale replica *(A)*, a diagram *(B)*, and an equation *(C)*.

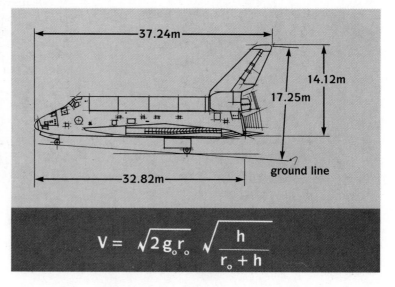

$$V = \sqrt{2 g_o r_o} \ \sqrt{\frac{h}{r_o + h}}$$

MODELS OF THE ATOM

Most models of an atom show a tiny nucleus at the center. The **nucleus** is the part of the atom that has most of the mass of the atom and that has a positive charge. The nucleus is made up of two kinds of particles. The **proton** is a positively charged particle in the nucleus of an atom. The **neutron** is a particle with no charge, also found in the atom's nucleus.

protos (first)

The model of the atom also shows negatively charged particles moving around the nucleus. A negatively charged particle in the atom is called the **electron.**

electr- (electric)
-on (particle)

Figure 8·2

If an atom were as large as a football stadium, its nucleus would be the size of a marble.

A mental model can help you compare the sizes of the parts of an atom. Imagine an atom the size of a large football stadium, like the one shown in Figure 8·2. Its nucleus would have the volume of a small marble in the center of the field. The electrons would be like tiny insects buzzing around in the stands.

But of course, atoms are not the size of stadiums. In fact, it is difficult to imagine the size of an atom. The period at the end of this sentence might hold one hundred billion atoms.

SCIENCE & TECHNOLOGY

You know that all matter is made of atoms and that atoms are made of protons, neutrons, and electrons. But are these particles made up of still smaller particles?

Scientists think that a few kinds of basic particles make up protons, neutrons, and electrons. One basic particle is a quark. Scientists believe that an atom's neutrons and protons are made of different kinds of quarks.

Studying objects as tiny as these particles requires massive equipment. A particle accelerator, like the one shown in the photograph, is used to study subatomic particles. Particles travel through a circular path and gain speed. From here the particles follow a straight path until they collide with atomic nuclei. These collisions break apart the nuclei into subatomic particles.

As you can see in Table 8·1, protons and electrons have opposite charges. Notice that the electron has very little mass. Protons and neutrons have the same mass, about 1836 times the mass of an electron. Thus, nearly all the mass of an atom is in the nucleus.

Table 8·1 *The Three Particles in Atoms*

PARTICLE	RELATIVE MASS	CHARGE	LOCATION
Proton	1	1+	Nucleus
Neutron	1	0	Nucleus
Electron	1/1836	1−	Outside nucleus

In 1913 a young Danish physicist, Niels Bohr, suggested a model of the atom. According to the Bohr model, the electrons in an atom move in paths around the nucleus. As you can see in Figure 8·3A, each path is a certain distance from the nucleus. The paths in which electrons circle the nucleus are called energy levels. Electrons are found in energy levels, not between them.

In 1926 an Austrian physicist, Erwin Schrodinger, proposed a new model of the atom. His model is shown in Figure 8·3B. It is often called the electron cloud model. According to this model, electrons move very rapidly in regions of space around the nucleus. These regions of space are called electron clouds. An *electron cloud* is a region of space in which there is a good chance of finding a particular electron in an atom.

Remember that a model is a tool. Many times, scientists use either the Bohr model or the electron cloud model. Each model is a useful tool.

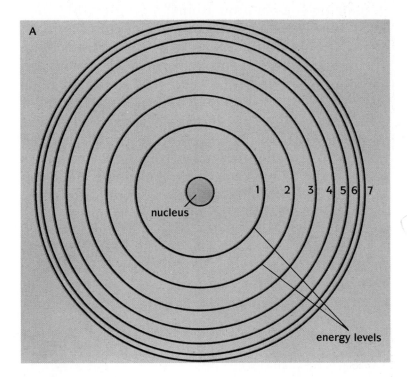

Figure 8·3

How does the Bohr model *(A)* differ from the electron cloud model *(B)*?

REVIEW

1. Define the term *atom*.
2. Why do scientists use models?
3. Describe the electron cloud model.
4. Name the three particles found in an atom. Give the charge, mass, and location of each particle.

CHALLENGE Assume some positively charged particles called alpha particles are shot at a piece of gold foil. Most of the alpha particles will pass through. Why do some of the particles bounce back, away from the gold foil?

8·2 How Atoms Differ

ATOMIC NUMBER

The number of protons in the nucleus of an atom of an element is the **atomic number** of the element. Every element has its own atomic number. For example, the element hydrogen has an atomic number of 1. All atoms of hydrogen have one proton, and any atom that has just one proton is a hydrogen atom. The atomic number of the element helium is 2. Are all atoms that have only two protons in their nucleus helium atoms?

When you know the number of protons in an atom, you also know the number of electrons in an uncharged atom. If an atom has no charge, the number of protons equals the number of electrons. Each element has its own number of protons and number of electrons. Figure 8·4 shows electron cloud models of the elements sulfur and chlorine. Notice that sulfur has 16 protons and 16 electrons. Chlorine has 17 protons and 17 electrons. These elements have different properties under the same conditions. Chlorine is a greenish-yellow gas. How would you describe sulfur?

Figure 8·4

How do atoms of chlorine and atoms of sulfur differ?

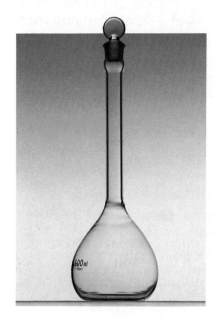

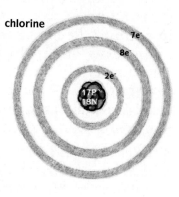

chlorine

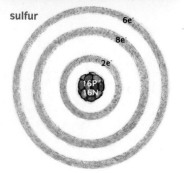

sulfur

MASS NUMBER

Another term used to describe atoms is mass number. **Mass number** is the sum of the protons and neutrons in an atom. The number of neutrons in an atom can be found by subtracting the atomic number from the mass number.

number of neutrons = mass number — atomic number

For example, the mass number of chlorine is 35. The atomic number of chlorine is 17. Thus the number of neutrons in an atom of chlorine is 18.

Figure 8·5
There are three isotopes of the element hydrogen.

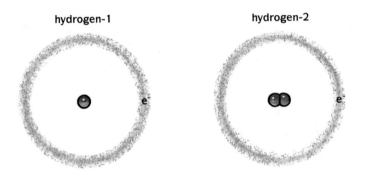

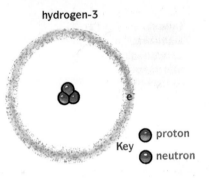

All atoms of the same element have the same number of protons, but they may have different mass numbers. Atoms of the same element have different mass numbers if they have different numbers of neutrons. Atoms of the same element with different numbers of neutrons are called **isotopes** (Ī suh tohps). Three isotopes of hydrogen are found in nature. They are sometimes called hydrogen-1, hydrogen-2, and hydrogen-3. Each has one proton. The numbers 1, 2, and 3 refer to the mass number of each isotope. As you can see in Figure 8·5, hydrogen-1 has one proton and no neutrons. Hydrogen-2 has one proton and one neutron. Hydrogen-3 has one proton and two neutrons. How many electrons does each isotope have?

All isotopes of any element have the same chemical properties of that element. There are seven isotopes of the element carbon. All atoms of these isotopes have six protons and six electrons. But each isotope has a different number of neu-

iso- (same)
-topos (place)

Figure 8·6

This pile of coal contains seven isotopes of carbon.

trons. The properties of an element are determined by the number of protons and electrons in the atoms of that element. Thus all of the carbon in the coal shown in Figure 8·6 would have the same chemical properties.

ATOMIC MASS

The actual mass of a single atom is very small. Such small numbers are not easy to work with. So scientists use an atomic mass scale. This scale compares all atomic masses with that of one atom. This atom is the most common isotope of carbon, carbon-12. Each atom of carbon-12 has been assigned a mass of exactly 12 atomic mass units. One **atomic mass unit** (amu) is defined as one-twelfth the mass of a carbon-12 atom.

The mass of an atom in relation to the carbon-12 atom is called the **atomic mass** of the atom. An atom of hydrogen-1 has a mass of about one-twelfth the mass of a carbon-12 atom. Thus the atomic mass of hydrogen-1 is about 1.0 amu. The exact value of the atomic mass of hydrogen-1 is 1.007825 amu.

The atomic mass of any isotope can be measured by comparing it with the mass of a carbon-12 atom. For example, the atomic mass of an atom of magnesium-24 is nearly twice that of an atom of carbon-12. The exact atomic mass of magnesium-24 is 23.98504 amu.

Table 8·2 *Isotopes of the Elements Hydrogen, Carbon, and Oxygen*

ISOTOPE	NATURAL ABUNDANCE (PERCENT)	ATOMIC MASS (AMU)	ATOMIC NUMBER	NUMBER OF NEUTRONS	MASS NUMBER
Hydrogen-1	99.985	1.007825	1	0	1
Hydrogen-2	0.0015	2.001410	1	1	2
Hydrogen-3	Trace	?	1	2	3
Carbon-12	98.89	12.00000	6	6	12
Carbon-13	1.11	13.003	6	7	13
Carbon-14	Trace	?	6	8	14
Oxygen-16	99.759	15.995	8	8	16
Oxygen-17	0.037	16.999	8	9	17
Oxygen-18	0.204	17.999	8	10	18

Most elements are found as mixtures of different isotopes. The atomic mass of an element is the mass of the mixture of isotopes that occurs in nature. The mixture of isotopes is the same in all samples that are found.

The atomic mass of the element carbon is given as 12.011. This number is an average. Table 8·2 shows some of the isotopes of carbon. Notice that most carbon atoms have an atomic mass of 12. There are very few carbon atoms with a mass of 13. No carbon atom has a mass of 12.011. But all carbon atoms taken together and averaged give the element an atomic mass of 12.011.

ENERGY LEVELS OF ELECTRONS

According to the Bohr model of the atom, electrons are found in paths called energy levels. Think of the energy levels as rings around the nucleus. The levels are referred to by numbers. Level 1 is the level closest to the nucleus. Figure 8·7 shows the first four energy levels.

Each energy level of an atom can hold a certain number of electrons. The first energy level can hold up to 2 electrons. The second energy level can hold up to 8 electrons. The third energy level can hold up to 18 electrons, and the fourth, 32 electrons.

The wire shown contains copper. The stainless steel spoon contains nickel. Some isotopes of these elements are listed below. Which of these atoms belong in the wire? Which belong in the spoon? Do any of these atoms not belong in either object?

ATOM	ATOMIC NUMBER	MASS NUMBER
A	27	59
B	28	59
C	29	59
D	28	63
E	29	63

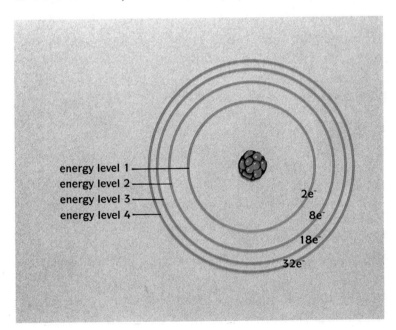

energy level 1
energy level 2
energy level 3
energy level 4

2e⁻
8e⁻
18e⁻
32e⁻

Figure 8·7

Each of the first four energy levels of an atom holds a different number of electrons.

How Can Masses Be Compared?

OBJECTIVE
Determine a relative mass unit.
Use your relative mass unit to measure masses of objects.

MATERIALS
balance, nickel, glass beads, penny, quarter

PROCEDURE
A. Prepare a data table like the one shown.
B. Place a nickel on the left pan of a balance. Add enough glass beads to the right pan to balance the nickel.
C. Record the number of beads whose mass equals that of the nickel.
D. Repeat step **B**, using a penny. Record the number of beads whose mass equals that of the penny.
E. Repeat step **B**, using a quarter. Record the number of beads whose mass equals that of the quarter.
F. Make the coin whose mass is neither the heaviest nor the lightest your standard. Give your standard a whole-number value.

G. Calculate in standard units the relative mass of each of the other coins using the following expression.

$$\frac{\text{beads equal to mass of coin}}{\text{beads equal to mass of standard}} \times \text{standard value}$$

COIN	NUMBER OF BEADS	RELATIVE MASS
Nickel		
Penny		
Quarter		

RESULTS AND CONCLUSIONS
1. Which coin was your standard?
2. What would happen to the value of the relative mass of the heaviest coin if you doubled the value assigned to the standard coin?
3. How does this model compare with the atomic mass scale?

The electrons that have the most effect on the properties of an element are those found in the outer energy level. The outer energy level is the one farthest from the nucleus. No atom has more than 8 electrons in its outer energy level.

REVIEW
1. Define each of the following terms: atomic number, mass number, atomic mass.
2. The atomic number of sodium is 11. The mass number of sodium is 23. How many neutrons are there in an atom of sodium?
3. How is the atomic mass unit defined?
4. Compare the number of electrons in the first and second energy levels.

CHALLENGE Predict how the densities of the three isotopes of hydrogen compare.

8·3 How Atoms Are Represented

CHEMICAL SYMBOLS

Scientists have developed a set of symbols to stand for the elements. A **chemical symbol** is a notation of one or more letters that represents an element. As you can see in Table 8·3, the first letter of each symbol is a capital letter. If a second letter is used, it is always a lower-case letter. A symbol may be the first letter of the name of the element. For example, the letter *C* stands for carbon. Calcium also begins with the letter *C*, so a second letter is added to make its symbol. Find the chemical symbol for calcium in Table 8·3.

The symbol of an element also represents the atoms of the element. When you write B, the symbol for boron, it stands for both the element boron and one atom of boron. Thus 2B represents two atoms of boron. What does 3K stand for?

Scientists all around the world use the same chemical symbols. This is important because the names of some elements are different in different languages. For example, iron is named *fer* in French and *hierro* in Spanish. But all scientists use the symbol Fe to stand for the the element iron. This symbol comes from *ferrum*, the Latin word for iron.

After completing this section, you will be able to
- **list** the symbols of some of the elements.
- **sketch** the electron arrangement of an atom, given its atomic number.

The key term in this section is **chemical symbol**

Table 8·3 *Symbols of Elements with Atomic Numbers 1 – 20*

ELEMENT	SYMBOL	ATOMIC NUMBER	ELEMENT	SYMBOL	ATOMIC NUMBER
Hydrogen	H	1	Sodium	Na	11
Helium	He	2	Magnesium	Mg	12
Lithium	Li	3	Aluminum	Al	13
Beryllium	Be	4	Silicon	Si	14
Boron	B	5	Phosphorus	P	15
Carbon	C	6	Sulfur	S	16
Nitrogen	N	7	Chlorine	Cl	17
Oxygen	O	8	Argon	Ar	18
Fluorine	F	9	Potassium	K	19
Neon	Ne	10	Calcium	Ca	20

The names of the elements have many different origins. Some are named after scientists. Einsteinium (īn STĪ nee uhm) is named after Albert Einstein. Curium is named after Marie Curie.

Some elements are named after places. Californium (kal uh FAWR nee uhm) is named after the state of California. Polonium is named after the country of Poland. What name would be used for an element named after the planet Pluto?

The names of some elements come from mythology. Prometheus is a mythological character who stole fire from the gods. Scientists first found the element promethium (pruh MEE thee uhm) in the wastes of a nuclear reactor. Because this element was made in the nuclear "fire," scientists named the element after Prometheus.

So far scientists have discovered 109 elements. Official names have not yet been given to elements 104 to 109. To provide temporary names and symbols for these elements, and ones that still might be discovered, a special system has been devised.

The names of the six new elements begin with the prefix *unnil-*. Each name ends with *-ium*. *Quad* stands for "four," and *pent* stands for "five." So element 104 is called *unnilquadium*. Element 105 is *unnilpentium*. The root *hex* is used for element 106, *unnilhexium*. *Sept* stands for seven, *oct* stands for eight, and *en* is the root for nine. What are the names for elements 107 to 109?

Recall that isotopes are atoms of a given element that differ in mass number. Scientists show isotopes with the symbol of the element, a superscript, and a subscript. As you can see in Figure 8·9, the superscript is a small, raised number that shows the mass number. The subscript is a small, lowered number that shows the atomic number. For example, $^{12}_{6}C$ stands for carbon-12, an isotope of carbon. This isotope of carbon has an atomic number of 6 and a mass number of 12. Another isotope of carbon is $^{13}_{6}C$. This isotope also has an atomic number of 6, but its mass number is 13. Look at the isotope of zinc shown in Figure 8·9. What is the atomic number? What is the mass number?

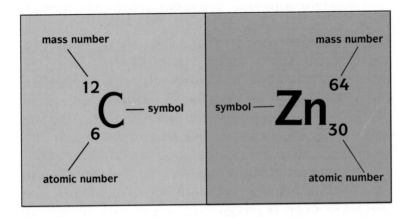

DRAWING MODELS OF ATOMS

All electrons are the same. They have the same mass and charge. But the number of electrons and the way in which they are arranged in an atom are important. One way to draw a model of an atom is shown in Figure 8·10 on the next page. The small circle stands for the nucleus. The P+ stands for protons, and the N, neutrons. The circles around the nucleus show these energy levels. The e⁻ stands for electrons. To draw a model of hydrogen, you would place one proton in the nucleus. Then you would place one electron in the first energy level.

In the model of helium in Figure 8·10, there are two protons and two neutrons in the nucleus. The two electrons are in the first energy level. An atom of lithium has three protons, four neutrons, and

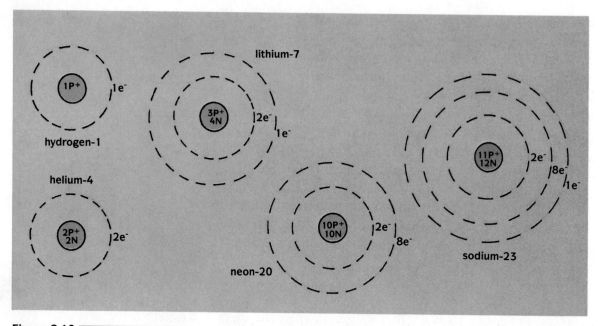

Figure 8·10

These models show how atoms differ.

three electrons. The first two electrons are placed in the first energy level, and the third electron is placed in the second energy level. Recall that the first energy level can hold up to two electrons. The second energy level can hold up to eight electrons.

If you were to continue adding one proton, one electron, and the correct number of neutrons, the second energy level would soon hold eight electrons. This occurs with the element neon, as shown in Figure 8·10. Two of neon's ten electrons are in the first energy level, and eight are in the second. You would add another proton, another electron, and two neutrons to make the sodium atom. Notice that the additional electron would go into the third energy level.

REVIEW

1. Name the element that each of the following symbols represents: Na, N, Al, P, K.
2. What does 2Ca mean?
3. Explain the meaning of $^{16}_{8}O$.
4. Sketch the energy levels of the atoms with atomic numbers 10 and 12.

CHALLENGE How many protons, neutrons, and electrons are there in the isotope $^{238}_{92}U$?

8·4 The Periodic Table

HISTORY OF THE PERIODIC TABLE

As scientists learned about the elements, they noticed that certain elements have similar properties. For example, sodium, lithium, and potassium all conduct electricity and react strongly with water. Fluorine and chlorine are gases that combine with sodium and other elements.

As more and more elements were discovered, scientists needed to organize the information they had about elements. A Russian chemist, Dmitri Mendeleev (mehn duh LAY uhf), arranged the elements in rows according to atomic mass. He also grouped the elements into columns based on similar chemical and physical properties. When the elements are arranged in this manner, the properties of the elements repeat in a pattern. In 1869, Dmitri Mendeleev published a Periodic Table of the 63 elements known at the time.

In 1871, Mendeleev used his Periodic Table to predict the existence and properties of some elements. For example, he predicted that one day scientists would discover element 32. This element, identified in 1886, is called germanium. Look at Table 8·4. How do the predicted properties compare with the real properties?

After completing this section, you will be able to

- **describe** the organization of the Periodic Table.
- **locate** an element in the Periodic Table, given its atomic number.
- **distinguish** between periods and groups of elements in the Periodic Table.

The key terms in this section are
group
period
periodic law
Periodic Table

Figure 8·11
Mendeleev predicted that germanium would be discovered.

Table 8·4 *Properties of Germanium*

PROPERTY	PREDICTION	OBSERVATION
Atomic mass	72	72.6
Density (g/mL)	5.5	5.47
Color	Dirty gray	Grayish white
Compound formed with oxygen	EsO_2	GeO_2
Density of oxygen compound	4.7	4.703
Compound formed with chlorine	$EsCl_4$	$GeCl_4$
Density of chlorine compound	1.9	1.887
Boiling point of chlorine compound	Below 100°C	86°C

Figure 8·12

Which element is more like chlorine and bromine, iodine or tellurium?

A Periodic Table based on atomic mass was not perfect. For example, the atomic mass of tellurium is greater than that of iodine. Thus, listed by increasing atomic mass, iodine would be placed ahead of tellurium. But iodine resembles the elements bromine and chlorine, and tellurium does not. Mendeleev broke his "rule" of listing by increasing atomic mass, positioning these elements by their properties. Thus he placed tellurium before iodine.

When Mendeleev did his work, protons had not yet been discovered. In 1913, a young British physicist named Henry Moseley (MOHZ lee) discovered a way to find the number of protons in the nucleus of an atom. Recall that the number of protons in the nucleus determines the atomic number of an atom. As a result of Moseley's work, a Periodic Table was arranged according to atomic number. The properties of elements repeat in a pattern when the elements are arranged by increasing atomic number.

THE MODERN PERIODIC TABLE

For most elements, their order by increasing atomic mass is the same as their order by increasing atomic number. In the modern **Periodic Table,** elements are arranged in order of increasing atomic number. The **periodic law** states that the properties of the elements form a pattern if the elements are arranged by increasing atomic number.

Different forms of the Periodic Table have been proposed over the years. The form shown on pages 204–205 is the form used most often. The vertical columns are called groups or families. A **group** is made up of elements that have similar chemical properties. The elements in any one group behave alike chemically because they have the same number of electrons in their outer energy levels.

The groups on the left side of the Periodic Table are metals. Metals have three or fewer outer electrons. Metals usually are shiny and are good conductors of heat. All elements in Groups 1 through 12 and some in Groups 13, 14, and 15 are metals.

Groups on the right side of the Periodic Table are nonmetals. These elements have five or more outer electrons. Nonmetals usually are dull and do not conduct heat well. Their solids are brittle. All elements in Groups 17 and 18 and some in Groups 13 through 16 are nonmetals.

Figure 8·13 shows some examples of metals and nonmetals. Metals usually have high melting points and are solids at room temperature. Nonmetals usually have lower melting and boiling points. Use the color key on the Periodic Table to identify the nonmetal that is a liquid at room temperature. How many elements are gases at room temperature?

Figure 8·13
Platinum *(A)* and tin *(C)* are metals. Carbon *(B)* and sulfur *(D)* are nonmetals.

Periodic Table of Elements

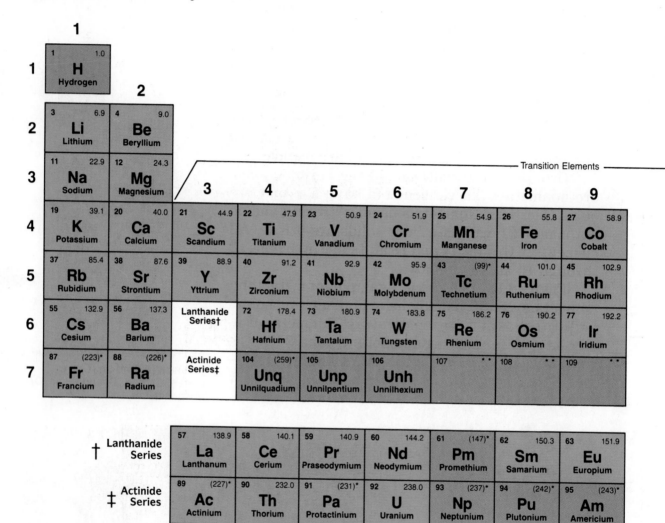

*Atomic masses appearing in parentheses are those of the most stable known isotopes.

☐ These elements occur in nature, and are solids at room temperature (20°C).

☐ These elements occur in nature, and are liquids at room temperature (20°C).

☐ These elements occur in nature, and are gases at room temperature (20°C).

☐ These elements do not occur in nature, and have been produced in laboratories.

			13	**14**	**15**	**16**	**17**	**18**
								2 4.0 **He** Helium
			5 10.8 **B** Boron	6 12.0 **C** Carbon	7 14.0 **N** Nitrogen	8 15.9 **O** Oxygen	9 18.9 **F** Fluorine	10 20.1 **Ne** Neon
10	**11**	**12**	13 26.9 **Al** Aluminum	14 28.0 **Si** Silicon	15 30.9 **P** Phosphorus	16 32.0 **S** Sulfur	17 35.4 **Cl** Chlorine	18 39.9 **Ar** Argon
28 58.7 **Ni** Nickel	29 63.5 **Cu** Copper	30 65.3 **Zn** Zinc	31 69.7 **Ga** Gallium	32 72.5 **Ge** Germanium	33 74.9 **As** Arsenic	34 78.9 **Se** Selenium	35 79.9 **Br** Bromine	36 83.8 **Kr** Krypton
46 106.4 **Pd** Palladium	47 107.8 **Ag** Silver	48 112.4 **Cd** Cadmium	49 114.8 **In** Indium	50 118.6 **Sn** Tin	51 121.7 **Sb** Antimony	52 127.6 **Te** Tellurium	53 126.9 **I** Iodine	54 131.3 **Xe** Xenon
78 195.0 **Pt** Platinum	79 196.9 **Au** Gold	80 200.5 **Hg** Mercury	81 204.3 **Tl** Thallium	82 207.1 **Pb** Lead	83 208.9 **Bi** Bismuth	84 (210)* **Po** Polonium	85 (210)* **At** Astatine	86 (222)* **Rn** Radon

64 157.2 **Gd** Gadolinium	65 158.9 **Tb** Terbium	66 162.5 **Dy** Dysprosium	67 164.9 **Ho** Holmium	68 167.2 **Er** Erbium	69 168.9 **Tm** Thulium	70 173.0 **Yb** Ytterbium	71 174.9 **Lu** Lutetium
96 (247)* **Cm** Curium	97 (247)* **Bk** Berkelium	98 (251)* **Cf** Californium	99 (254)* **Es** Einsteinium	100 (257)* **Fm** Fermium	101 (258)* **Md** Mendelevium	102 (255)* **No** Nobelium	103 (256)* **Lr** Lawrencium

* *No names have been given and no mass data is available.

Atomic masses based on C-12 = 12.0000

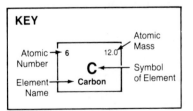

KEY

Atomic Number → 6   12.0 ← Atomic Mass

C ← Symbol of Element

Element Name → Carbon

ACTIVITY   How Is the Periodic Table Arranged?

OBJECTIVE

Construct atomic model drawings and use them to make a Periodic Table.

MATERIALS

unlined paper, metric ruler, scissors, drawing compass, posterboard, tape

PROCEDURE

A. Cut out eighteen 8-cm squares of paper.

B. On each square of paper, make a drawing to serve as a model of an atom. Follow the style in Figure 8·10 to draw each of the atoms listed in the table to the right.

C. For each model, represent the nucleus as a circle 1.0 cm in diameter. Use the atomic number and the mass number to determine the number of protons and neutrons in the nucleus of each atom. Indicate these numbers on each drawing.

D. Show the correct number of electrons in each atom by placing them in the proper energy levels. Make the first energy level a dashed circle 3.0 cm in diameter.

E. Make the second energy level a dashed circle 5.0 cm in diameter. Make the third level a dashed circle 6.0 cm in diameter.

F. Arrange the models in order of increasing atomic number on your desk.

G. Look at the drawings. Arrange them in a table so that each column contains atoms with similar features. Mount the squares in this arrangement on the posterboard.

ATOMIC NUMBER	MASS NUMBER	ATOMIC NUMBER	MASS NUMBER
1	1	10	20
2	4	11	23
3	7	12	24
4	9	13	27
5	11	14	28
6	12	15	31
7	14	16	32
8	16	17	35
9	19	18	40

RESULTS AND CONCLUSIONS

1. How many groups does your Periodic Table have?

2. How many periods does your Periodic Table have?

3. Where would you place an atom with an atomic number of 19 and a mass number of 39? Explain your answer.

Notice the heavy, dark zigzag line in the Periodic Table. Elements that border this line are metalloids. Metalloids show some properties of metals and some properties of nonmetals.

Each horizontal row in the Periodic Table is called a **period.** Elements in a period are not alike. They have different properties because each has a different number of outer electrons. But elements in a period have the same number of energy levels.

The Periodic Table is a useful tool. It helps chemists predict how elements may react with each other. It shows information about each element. Look at the key shown in Figure 8·14. Then use the Periodic Table to find the atomic number and the atomic mass of boron.

Figure 8·14

This key will help you use the Periodic Table.

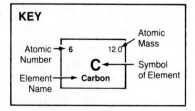

KEY

Atomic Number → 6   12.0 ← Atomic Mass

C ← Symbol of Element

Element → **Carbon**
Name

REVIEW

1. How are elements arranged in the Periodic Table?

2. Name the elements represented by each of the following atomic numbers: 6, 7, 12, 17, 30.

3. How are members of a group similar? How are members of a period similar?

CHALLENGE Give the symbols and names of the elements that occupy the following positions in the Periodic Table: Period 3, Group 15; Period 2, Group 16; Period 5, Group 16.

CHAPTER SUMMARY

The main ideas in this chapter are listed below. Read these statements before you answer the Chapter Review questions.

- Matter is made of atoms. An atom is the smallest particle of an element that has the properties of that element. (8·1)

- Scientists use models to try to explain something they cannot see or understand by relating it to something that they do see or understand. (8·1)

- An atom has a tiny positive core called the nucleus. Electrons are negatively charged particles outside the nucleus. (8·1)

- Electrons move in regions of space called electron clouds. (8·1)

- The proton is a positively charged particle found in the nucleus of an atom. The neutron is a particle with no charge, also found in the nucleus of an atom. (8·1)

- The atomic number of an element is the number of protons in its nucleus. The mass number is the sum of the protons and neutrons in an atom. (8·2)

- Atoms of the same element with different numbers of neutrons have different mass numbers, and are called isotopes. (8·2)

- One atomic mass unit (amu) is defined as one-twelfth the mass of a carbon-12 atom. The atomic mass is the mass of an atom in relation to the carbon-12 atom. (8·2)

- A chemical symbol is a notation of one or two letters that stands for the name of an element. (8·3)

- The modern Periodic Table is an arrangement of the elements by increasing atomic number. (8·4)

- Vertical columns of the Periodic Table are called groups. Elements in a group have similar chemical properties. (8·4)

- Horizontal rows in the Periodic Table are called periods. Elements in a period have the same number of energy levels. (8·4)

The key terms in this chapter are listed below. Use each term in a sentence that shows the meaning of the term.

atom	electron	nucleus
atomic mass	group	period
atomic mass unit	isotopes	periodic law
atomic number	mass number	Periodic Table
chemical symbol	neutron	proton

Chapter Review

VOCABULARY

Identify each statement as True or False. If a statement is false, replace the underlined term with a term that makes the statement true.

1. The <u>nucleus</u> is the part of an atom that has most of the mass of the atom.
2. The orderly arrangement of the elements according to their atomic numbers makes up the <u>Periodic Table</u>.
3. A <u>period</u> is made up of elements that have similar chemical properties.
4. The <u>atomic number</u> of an element is equal to the number of protons.
5. Atoms of the same element that have different numbers of neutrons are called <u>isotopes</u>.
6. The smallest particle of an element that has the properties of that element is called an <u>atom</u>.
7. <u>Electrons</u> are particles that have an electric charge of zero.
8. The <u>neutron</u> is a negatively charged particle that is located outside the nucleus.
9. The mass of an atom in relation to the carbon-12 atom is called the <u>mass number</u>.
10. A <u>model</u> is a scientist's way of explaining something that cannot be seen or understood by relating it to something that can be seen or understood.

CONCEPTS

Make a table like the one shown. Write the correct information under each heading.

ELEMENT	ATOMIC NUMBER	MASS NUMBER	NUMBER OF PROTONS	NUMBER OF NEUTRONS	NUMBER OF ELECTRONS
Carbon		12	6		
Copper	29			35	
Beryllium		9		5	
Oxygen				8	8
Xenon	54	131			

Write the letter of the particle that best matches the description on the left.

1. Particle with a charge of 1+
2. Particle found outside the nucleus
3. Particle with the same mass as a neutron
4. Particle with the least mass
5. Particle with no charge

a. electron
b. neutron
c. proton

Answer the following in complete sentences.

6. What is the function of a model in science?
7. Describe the electron cloud model of the atom.
8. Compare the three isotopes of hydrogen.
9. Give an example of an element that is named for a person and an element that is named for a location.
10. How are the elements arranged into groups and periods in the Periodic Table?

APPLICATION/ CRITICAL THINKING

1. Would it be possible for someone to discover a new element that would be placed between carbon and nitrogen on the Periodic Table? Explain your answer.
2. Elements are arranged in the Periodic Table according to increasing atomic number. If elements were arranged according to atomic mass, iodine would be placed ahead of tellurium. Find two other pairs of elements that would be reversed if the order were based on atomic mass.
3. How many neutrons are there in each of the following isotopes?
   a. $_1^3H$ d. $_{11}^{23}Na$
   b. $_2^4He$ e. $_{35}^{80}Br$
   c. $_{15}^{31}P$
4. How does a scientific model differ from models such as toy airplanes used by children?

EXTENSION

1. Democritus and Aristotle had different hypotheses about the nature of matter and elements. Research these hypotheses. Which hypothesis is in agreement with the current atomic theory?
2. Do library research on Rutherford's gold foil experiment.
3. The hydrogen isotopes have the same chemical properties. Do research to find out if they have the same physical properties.
4. Use wires and plastic foam spheres to construct a model of an atom.

CHAPTER 9

COMPOUNDS

*T*he object shown in the photograph is called a spinneret. It is named after structures in the body of a spider. The spider uses its spinnerets to make the fibers of a web. The fibers being produced here are made of rayon, a complex compound first made in the late 1800s.

Rayon is a synthetic compound made from wood. When wood is treated with lye and other compounds, a syrupy substance forms. This substance is forced through tiny holes in the spinneret. The thin streams that come out of the holes are pulled upward through a liquid that contains acid. The acid causes the compound to solidify into fibers. These fibers can be made into yarn or fabric for clothing.

- *What other synthetic compounds are used in clothing?*
- *How do scientists find new compounds?*

9·1 What Is a Compound?

com- (together)
ponere (to put)

The 109 known elements are the basic building blocks of all matter. These elements are usually not found alone. Instead, most matter in the earth's crust exists as elements in combinations known as compounds. Water, salt, and sugar are examples of compounds.

A **compound** is a pure substance made up of two or more elements that are combined chemically. The properties of a compound do not change. For example, the makeup and the properties of the compound water are always the same, whether the water is found in oceans, rivers, or clouds.

A compound contains elements in definite proportions. For example, water consists of two atoms of hydrogen and one atom of oxygen. The proportion of atoms in water is always the same.

If the proportion of elements in a compound is changed, a new compound is formed. Both water and hydrogen peroxide are made of hydrogen and oxygen atoms. In water each unit contains two hydrogen atoms and one oxygen atom. In hydrogen peroxide each unit contains two hydrogen atoms and two oxygen atoms. Hydrogen peroxide is not like water. The two compounds have different properties. For example, hydrogen peroxide can be used as a bleach, but water can not.

Figure 9·1
A compound, such as sugar, can be broken into its elements.

ACTIVITY   How Do Compounds Differ?

OBJECTIVE
Compare the properties of two compounds of the same elements.

MATERIALS
safety goggles, lab apron, 2 test tubes, glass-marking pencil, test-tube rack, 10-mL graduate, water, hydrogen peroxide, spatula, manganese dioxide, matches, wood splints

PROCEDURE
A. Wear safety goggles and a lab apron during this activity.
B. Draw a data table like the one shown.
C. Label two test tubes A and B. Add 5 mL of water to test tube A. Add 5 mL of hydrogen peroxide to test tube B.
D. Record the physical properties of each liquid in the data table.
E. Use a spatula to add 0.5 g of manganese dioxide to test tube A.
F. Use a match to light a wood splint. Blow out the flame so that the splint glows.

Insert the glowing splint into the mouth of test tube A. **Caution:** Be careful not to point the test tube toward another student or yourself.
  1. Describe the results of the splint test.
G. Use a spatula to add about 0.5 g of manganese dioxide to test tube B.
H. Repeat the splint test.
  2. Describe the results of the splint test.

COMPOUND	STATE OF MATTER	COLOR	BEHAVIOR WITH MANGANESE DIOXIDE
Water			
Hydrogen peroxide			

RESULTS AND CONCLUSIONS
1. Can you distinguish between water and hydrogen peroxide by looking at them?
2. Can you distinguish between water and hydrogen peroxide on the basis of their behavior? Explain your answer.

Compounds do not look like or act like the elements that form them. Sucrose, or table sugar, contains the elements hydrogen, oxygen, and carbon. Hydrogen and oxygen are gases at room temperature. Carbon is a black solid. The compound sucrose is white crystals. Notice in Figure 9·1 what happens to sugar when it is heated. The black, solid carbon is all that is left. What happened to the hydrogen and the oxygen?

REVIEW
1. What is a compound?
2. Compare the properties of sucrose with those of the individual elements hydrogen, oxygen, and carbon.
3. How are elements different from compounds?

CHALLENGE As a reddish powder is heated, it produces a gas and a silvery substance. Is the powder an element or a compound? Explain your answer.

9·2 Symbols and Formulas

After completing this section, you will be able to

- **define** the term *chemical formula*.
- **interpret** chemical formulas.
- **identify** several compounds when given their formulas.

The key term in this section is **chemical formula**

WRITING CHEMICAL FORMULAS

A **chemical formula** is a group of symbols that shows the makeup of a compound. Recall that the symbol Na stands for sodium, and the symbol Cl stands for chlorine. Look at Figure 9·2. The formula NaCl stands for the compound sodium chloride, which is table salt. This formula shows that the elements sodium and chlorine make up sodium chloride. The formula also shows that there is an equal number of sodium particles and chlorine particles in the compound.

$C_{12}H_{22}O_{11}$ NaCl $NaHCO_3$

Figure 9·2

Some common substances are made up of a single compound.

Most compounds are made up of elements that are not present in equal amounts. Water has two atoms of hydrogen for each atom of oxygen. The formula for water is H_2O. The number 2 here is called a subscript. A subscript is a small number lowered to the right of a chemical symbol of an element. The subscript shows the number of atoms of that element in one unit of a compound. The subscript 2 in the formula H_2O shows that there are two atoms of hydrogen present. Notice in the formula that there is no subscript after the symbol for oxygen. When only one atom of an element is present, the subscript 1 is not used. It is understood to be 1.

Most compounds are made of more than two elements. Recall that table sugar is made up of the elements carbon, hydrogen, and oxygen. Each unit of sugar contains 12 atoms of carbon, 22 atoms of hydrogen, and 11 atoms of oxygen. Sugar is shown by the formula $C_{12}H_{22}O_{11}$. Figure 9·2 shows the formulas of three compounds. How many atoms of each element are there in one unit of salt? Of baking soda? Figure 9·3 shows a model of the compound methane. What is the formula for methane?

Some formulas contain groups of symbols enclosed in parentheses that are followed by a subscript. For example, the formula for calcium hydroxide is $Ca(OH)_2$. The group of symbols shown in parentheses stands for one oxygen atom and one hydrogen atom. The subscript outside the parentheses tells how many of these groups there are. The number of each atom in the parentheses is multiplied by the subscript after the parentheses. Thus each unit of $Ca(OH)_2$ contains one calcium atom, two oxygen atoms, and two hydrogen atoms.

The formula for aluminum sulfate, a compound used in fire extinguishers, is $Al_2(SO_4)_3$. The group of symbols shown in the parentheses stands for one sulfur atom and four oxygen atoms. The subscript outside the parentheses shows that there are three of these groups in the formula. How many atoms of aluminum, sulfur, and oxygen are in aluminum sulfate, $Al_2(SO_4)_3$?

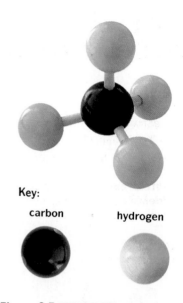

Key:

carbon   hydrogen

Figure 9·3
A model of the compound methane.

NOTE The ball-and-stick models shown in this book represent the arrangement of atoms in compounds.

Figure 9·4
The compound aluminum sulfate, $Al_2(SO_4)_3$, is used in some kinds of fire extinguishers.

NAMING COMPOUNDS

The name of a compound is a combination of the names of the elements in the compound. You may have read about preservatives added to foods. If you read food labels, like the ones shown in Figure 9·5, you will see the names of compounds. The names of compounds give clues about their makeup.

Figure 9·5

Foods contain many different compounds.

INGREDIENTS:
Enriched unbleached flour* (enriched with iron and the vitamins: niacin, thiamine mononitrate, riboflavin), sugar,* blueberries packed in water, vegetable shortening* (partially hydrogenated soybean and/or palm oils), leavening (baking soda and sodium aluminum phosphate) to make muffins rise, dextrose,* salt, natural flavors,* xanthan gum (for easy depanning).

*Part or all of these in topping packet.

INGREDIENTS: FLOUR, RAISINS, WATER, CORN SYRUP, MAY CONTAIN 2% OR LESS OF THE FOLLOWING: YEAST, SALT, SOY FLOUR, SOYBEAN OIL, SPICES, DRY HONEY, DEXTROSE, SUGAR, CALCIUM CARBONATE, MONO AND DIGLYCERIDES, LECITHIN, ETHOXYLATED MONO AND DIGLYCERIDES, AMMONIUM CHLORIDE, CALCIUM SULFATE, AMMONIUM SULFATE, BARLEY MALT, ASCORBIC ACID (VITAMIN C), NIACIN, FERROUS SULFATE, POTASSIUM BROMATE, THIAMINE HYDROCHLORIDE, RIBOFLAVIN.

Compounds made up of two elements, usually one metal and one nonmetal, are the easiest to name. The element whose symbol appears first in a formula also appears first in the name. The name of the second element follows, but with the ending changed to *-ide*. For example, the name for a compound of sodium and chlorine is sodium chloride. The formula for this compound is NaCl. Notice that the name for the first element has not been changed. But the name for the second element has been changed from chlorine to chloride. The name for a compound of copper and sulfur, CuS, is copper sulfide. What are the names for the compounds shown in Figure 9·6?

Sometimes, two or more compounds may result from the same two elements. These compounds are named in the way that other compounds of metals and nonmetals are named, but with one difference. A Roman numeral is written in parentheses after

Figure 9·6
Each of these compounds contains a metal and chlorine, a nonmetal.

the name of the metal. For example, two different compounds may be formed from copper and chlorine. The formulas for these compounds are $CuCl$ and $CuCl_2$. The name of the compound $CuCl$ is copper (I) chloride. It is pronounced "copper one chloride." The name of the compound $CuCl_2$ is copper (II) chloride. This is pronounced "copper two chloride."

Naming compounds made up of two nonmetals requires the use of prefixes. Some prefixes are shown in Table 9·1. For example, both CO and CO_2 are made of carbon and oxygen. In naming the compound, prefixes are used before the name of the second element to show the number of atoms of that element. Thus, CO is named carbon monoxide, and CO_2 is named carbon dioxide. What would be the name for SiO_2? For CCl_4?

Many compounds are made up of three or more elements. These compounds usually contain groups of elements that behave like a single atom. Each of these groups has a special name, as shown in Table 9·2. Notice that the names of these groups of atoms end with -*ate* or -*ite*. For example, the name for the compound with the formula KNO_3 is potassium nitrate. The first part of the name, potassium, is the name of the element whose symbol is K. The second part of the name is nitrate, the name for the group

Table 9·1 *Common Prefixes*

PREFIX	MEANING
mono-	1
di-	2
tri-	3
tetra-	4
penta-	5
hexa-	6

Table 9·2
Special Groups of Elements

GROUP	NAME
(CO_3)	Carbonate
(ClO_3)	Chlorate
(ClO_2)	Chlorite
(NO_3)	Nitrate
(NO_2)	Nitrite
(PO_4)	Phosphate
(SiO_3)	Silicate
(SO_4)	Sulfate
(SO_3)	Sulfite

The automotive industry is trying to make engines more durable by using ceramic parts. Ceramics are made of material from the earth's crust. Pottery made from clay is the oldest kind of ceramic. Most modern ceramics are compounds of silicon, carbon, oxygen, and nitrogen in combination with other elements. Ceramics are hard and are not affected by acids, salts, or heat.

A new type of ceramic made from the compound silicon nitride is so tough that it is replacing some metals in engine parts. Not only is the ceramic hard and light, it can be shaped into any form needed. Though many ceramics are extremely hard, few can be molded so easily.

The special properties of this new ceramic have made it valuable in many components of car engines, especially those exposed to wear and heat.

Some car manufacturers are already using ceramic parts in their car engines. One

maker of diesel-powered cars uses ceramic glow-plugs. A glow-plug is a kind of heating element that helps to start a diesel engine. In the engine the plug is exposed to intense heat. The ceramic glow-plugs can withstand heat better than can metal ones.

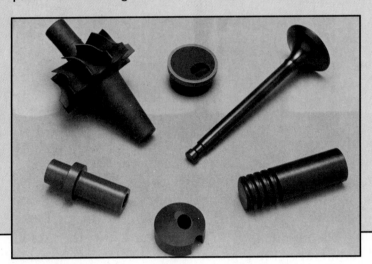

of atoms shown by NO_3. The name for the compound with the formula KNO_2 is potassium nitrite. The second part of the name, nitrite, stands for the group of atoms shown by NO_2. What is the name for $CaCO_3$? For $MgSO_4$?

REVIEW

1. How many atoms does each of the following represent?
   a. He   **b.** P_4 **c.** S_8 **d.** H_2

2. What is a chemical formula?

3. How many atoms of each element are present in the following compounds?
   a. NaCl   **b.** H_2O **c.** CCl_4 **d.** Na_2CO_3
   e. $NaHCO_3$ **f.** SO_2

4. Name each of the following compounds.
   a. CO_2 **b.** KCl   **c.** CaF_2 **d.** Na_2O
   e. $NaClO_3$ **f.** KOH

CHALLENGE Write the chemical formulas for the compounds with the following names: silicon dioxide, lithium chloride, selenium trioxide, barium hydroxide.

9·3 Ionic Compounds

A **chemical bond** is a force that holds particles of matter together. The atoms of hydrogen and oxygen in water are held together by bonds.

To understand how bonds form, look at the elements that rarely form bonds. The elements in Group 18 of the Periodic Table are called the noble gases. These elements are very stable — that is, under normal conditions they do not form chemical bonds. All noble gases have a complete outer energy level, as shown in Figure 9·7. They are stable because of this electron arrangement.

The elements that are not noble gases do not have a complete outer energy level. These atoms share, lose, or gain electrons to have a stable arrangement like that of the noble gases. In the process of changing their electron arrangement, atoms form chemical bonds.

After completing this section, you will be able to

- **explain** how ions form.
- **explain** how an ionic bond forms.
- **describe** the properties of ionic compounds.

The key terms in this section are
chemical bond
formula unit
ion
ionic bond
ionic compound

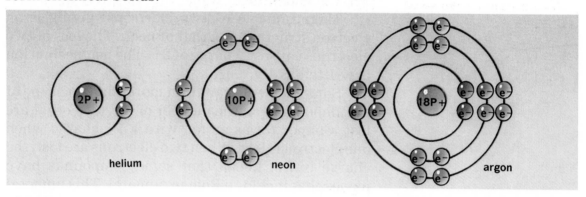

IONS

Many atoms gain or lose electrons and end up with the same number of outer electrons as a noble gas. When a neutral atom loses or gains electrons, it becomes a charged particle. A charged particle is called an **ion** (ī ahn). In an ion the number of protons and the number of electrons are not equal. Recall that protons have a positive charge and electrons have a negative charge. If there are more electrons than protons, the ion has a negative charge. If there are fewer electrons than protons, the ion has a positive charge.

Figure 9·7

All noble gases have a complete outer energy level.

Figure 9·8

A neutral sodium atom loses one electron to become a sodium ion, Na^+.

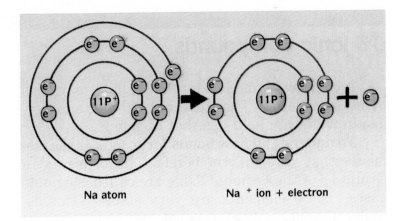

Na atom   Na $^+$ ion + electron

Usually, metals lose electrons and nonmetals gain electrons. When a neutral sodium atom loses one electron, it becomes a positive sodium ion. As you can see in Figure 9·8, the new ion still has 11 protons in the nucleus but now has only 10 electrons. The sodium ion has a charge of 1+. It is written as Na^+. When the charge of an ion is 1+ or 1−, only the positive or negative sign is used. The number 1 is understood.

Magnesium loses two electrons, giving it an electron structure like that of neon. The loss of two electrons causes a charge of 2+. The magnesium ion is written as Mg^{2+}.

Some elements can form more than one type of ion, depending on the number of electrons that are lost. Copper forms an ion with a 1+ charge when one electron is lost. When two electrons are lost, the charge is 2+. Recall that some compounds have names that include a Roman numeral. This numeral shows the charge of the ion in the compound. Look at Table 9·3. What are the charges on the two kinds of iron ions?

Table 9·3 *Common Positive Ions*

1+ IONS	2+ IONS	3+ IONS
Cesium Cs^+	Barium Ba^{2+}	Aluminum Al^{3+}
Copper (I) Cu^+	Cadmium Cd^{2+}	Iron (III) Fe^{3+}
Lithium Li^+	Calcium Ca^{2+}	—
Sodium Na^+	Copper (II) Cu^{2+}	—
Potassium K^+	Iron (II) Fe^{2+}	—

When a neutral atom gains an electron, the atom becomes a negative ion. For example, a chlorine atom can gain one electron and become an ion. The ion of chlorine has an outer electron structure like that of an atom of argon, a noble gas. The ion has 17 protons, like the neutral chlorine atom. But as you can see in Figure 9·9, this ion has 18 electrons. Its charge is 1−. This ion is called the chloride ion and is written as Cl^-.

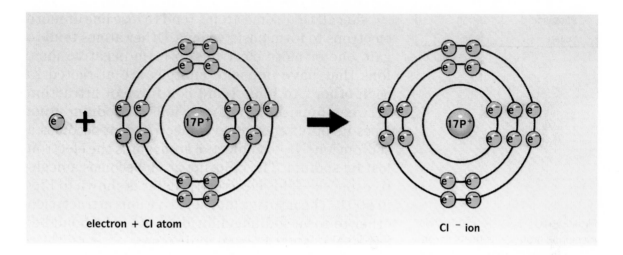

electron + Cl atom

Cl⁻ ion

Figure 9·9
A neutral chlorine atom gains one electron to become a chloride ion, Cl^-.

Table 9·4 lists some negative ions. Notice that the ending for the name of a negative ion is different from that of the neutral atom. The name of a negative ion ends in *-ide*.

Some atoms of nonmetals gain more than one electron when they become ions. Sulfur gains two electrons. This ion, called sulfide, is written as S^{2-}. Look at Table 9·4 and find the ion of nitrogen. How many electrons does it gain?

Table 9·4 *Common Negative Ions*

1− IONS	2− IONS	3− IONS
Bromide Br⁻	Oxide O²⁻	Nitride N³⁻
Chloride Cl⁻	Sulfide S²⁻	Phosphide P³⁻
Fluoride F⁻	—	—
Iodide I⁻	—	—
Astatide At⁻	—	—

Table 9·5 *Polyatomic Ions*

NAME	ION
Acetate	CH_3COO^-
Ammonium	NH_4^+
Bicarbonate	HCO_3^-
Carbonate	CO_3^{2-}
Chlorate	ClO_3^-
Hydroxide	OH^-
Nitrate	NO_3^{2-}
Phosphate	PO_4^{3-}
Sulfate	SO_4^{2-}

There are some atoms that are joined together in a group and have a charge. These atoms stay together as a group and behave like one charged atom. Groups of atoms that have a charge are called *polyatomic* (pahl ee uh TAHM ihk) *ions*. In Section 9·2, you learned the names of some of these groups. Find the sulfate ion and the chlorate ion in Table 9.5. What is the charge of each?

IONIC BONDS

Recall that some atoms tend to lose one or more electrons to form positive ions. Other atoms tend to gain one or more electrons to form negative ions. Ions that have opposite charges are attracted to each other. An **ionic bond** is a force of attraction between oppositely charged ions. A sodium atom loses its outer energy level electron and becomes a sodium ion, Na^+. A chlorine atom gains the electron lost by sodium. The chlorine atom becomes a negative ion, Cl^-. This electron transfer is shown in Figure 9·10. The positive and negative ions attract each other to form sodium chloride, NaCl. The bond between Na^+ and Cl^- is an ionic bond.

Figure 9·10

A chlorine atom gains the electron lost by a sodium atom.

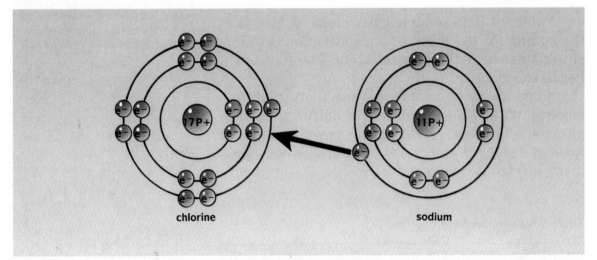

chlorine   sodium

Figure 9·11 shows the formation of ionic bonds between calcium and fluorine. Each calcium atom loses two electrons. Each fluorine atom can gain only one electron. It takes two fluorine atoms to accept the two electrons from the calcium atom. The

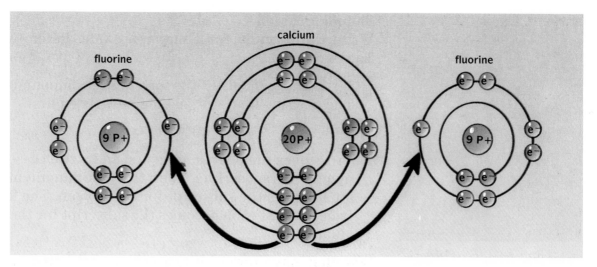

calcium ion and the two fluoride ions form calcium fluoride, CaF_2. What effect does the 2+ charge of the calcium ion have on the two negative charges of the fluoride ions?

Figure 9·11

A calcium atom loses two electrons, forming a Ca^{2+} ion. Each fluorine atom gains an electron, forming a F^- ion.

IONIC COMPOUNDS

An **ionic compound** is a compound that contains ionic bonds. The charges on the ions determine the ratio of ions in the compound. The formula shows this ratio.

If two ions have equal but opposite charges, no subscripts are needed. The ions are present in a one-to-one ratio, as in NaCl. If the charges are not equal, the formula for the ionic compound must contain subscripts. Determining the correct formula for an ionic compound involves these steps.

1. Write the symbols of the ions in the compound next to each other. Write the positive ion first. Write the charge on each ion.

2. Cross over the numbers but not the + and − signs of the charges, and write the numbers as subscripts. The charge number of the positive ion will be the subscript of the negative ion. The charge number of the negative ion will be the subscript of the positive ion.

3. Write the formula for the compound, showing the subscripts but not the charges. If any subscript is 1, you do not need to write it.

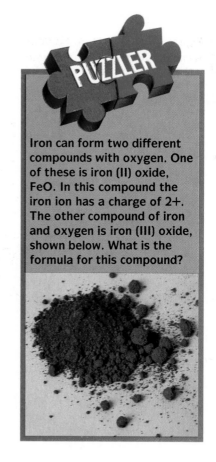

Iron can form two different compounds with oxygen. One of these is iron (II) oxide, FeO. In this compound the iron ion has a charge of 2+. The other compound of iron and oxygen is iron (III) oxide, shown below. What is the formula for this compound?

Figure 9·12

Although a ruby is red and a sapphire is blue, both contain the compound aluminum oxide.

Figure 9·13

In the crystals of an ionic compound, such as sodium chloride, the ions are arranged in a lattice structure.

Key:

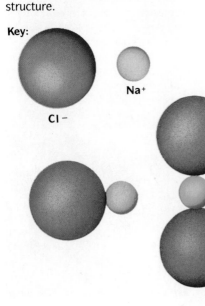

Na^+

Cl^-

Sample Problem

Write the formula for aluminum oxide. Refer to Tables 9·3 and 9·4.

1. Write the symbols of the ions in the compound. The positive ion, Al^{3+}, should be written first.

$$Al^{3+}O^{2-}$$

2. Cross over the charge numbers, and write these numbers as subscripts. The 3 from the aluminum ion becomes the subscript for the oxygen. The 2 from the oxide ion becomes the subscript for the aluminum.

$$Al^{3+}_2O^{2-}_3$$

3. Write the formula for the compound, showing the subscripts but not the charges.

$$Al_2O_3$$

Check the formula. Multiply the charge on each ion by its subscript. Two Al^{3+} ions have a charge of 6+. Three O^{2-} ions have a charge of 6−. These charges cancel. The formula is correct.

The smallest repeating group of atoms in an ionic compound is called the **formula unit**. The formula unit is made up of two or more oppositely charged ions. As you can see in Figure 9·13, ionic compounds are more than just simple pairs of ions. First a sodium ion, Na^+, and a chloride ion, Cl^-, attract each other and form the formula unit Na^+Cl^-. Then more Na^+Cl^- units join. The compound continues to build up in a repeating pattern

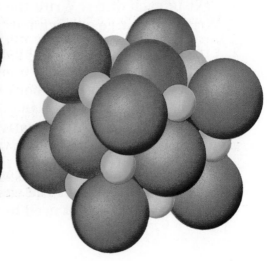

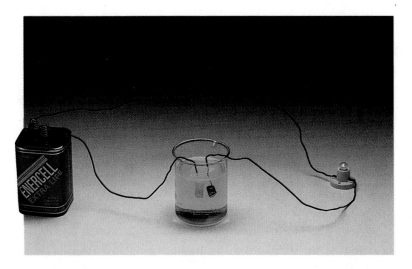

Figure 9·14
These crystals are potassium chromate, $K_2Cr_2O_7$. When they dissolve, they release potassium ions, K^+, and dichromate ions, $Cr_2O_7^{2-}$. These dissolved ions conduct electricity.

in all directions. Thus a three-dimensional crystal of sodium chloride is formed. This orderly, repeating pattern of units is known as *lattice*. All ionic compounds form some kind of lattice structure.

Ionic bonds are very strong. Because of these bonds, ionic compounds have high melting points and high boiling points. Ionic compounds are usually brittle. Their crystals can be broken apart along smooth, flat surfaces.

As solids, ionic compounds do not conduct electricity. However, if they are melted or dissolved in water, ionic compounds do conduct electricity. When an ionic compound is melted or dissolved in water, its ions are able to flow and to carry a charge.

REVIEW

1. How is an ion different from the neutral atom that forms it?
2. What is an ionic bond?
3. What are some of the properties of ionic compounds?
4. Write the correct formula for each of the following compounds.
    a. magnesium chloride   d. copper (II) acetate
    b. lithium bromide   e. calcium phosphate
    c. barium hydroxide   f. ammonium sulfate

CHALLENGE Lithium (Li), sodium (Na), potassium (K), and rubidium (Rb) all have one electron in the outer energy level. Rubidium gives up its electron to form a positive ion much more easily than do any of the others. Potassium gives up its one electron more easily than does sodium or lithium. Sodium gives up its one electron more easily than does lithium. Suggest an explanation for these differences.

9·4 Covalent Compounds

After completing this section, you will be able to

- **explain** how a covalent bond forms.
- **describe** properties of covalent compounds.
- **compare** properties of covalent compounds and ionic compounds.

The key terms in this section are
covalent bond
covalent compounds
molecule

Sometimes, atoms form bonds by sharing electrons. A bond in which electrons are shared between atoms is called a **covalent** (koh VAY luhnt) **bond**. By forming covalent bonds, atoms form a stable outer electron level.

The simplest substance in which atoms form a covalent bond is hydrogen gas, H_2. A hydrogen atom has one electron and must gain an electron to have the stable structure of the noble gas helium. Each of two hydrogen atoms shares its one electron with the other hydrogen atom, as shown in Figure 9·15. A covalent bond is formed in this manner. The shared pair of electrons gives each hydrogen atom two electrons.

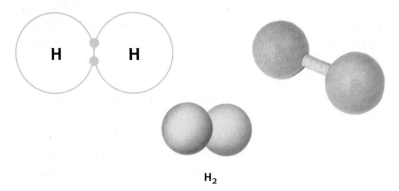

H_2

Figure 9·15

These three models represent a molecule of hydrogen.

A **molecule** is the smallest unit of any covalent substance that can exist alone and still show the properties of that substance. A molecule may be formed by two or more atoms of the same element. A molecule of the element phosphorus is made up of four atoms of phosphorus. The formula for a molecule of phosphorus is P_4. The formula for sulfur is S_8. How many sulfur atoms are there in a sulfur molecule?

A molecule may also be formed from two or more atoms of different elements. One example is water, H_2O. How does a water molecule form? An oxygen atom has six electrons in its outer energy level. Thus, it needs two electrons to have a com-

hydrogen atoms + oxygen atom ⟶ water molecule

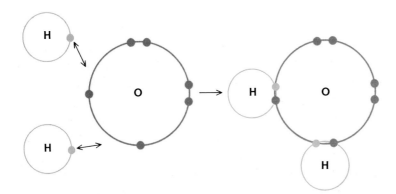

Figure 9·16
The formation of a molecule of water.

plete outer energy level and a stable electron structure. As you can see in Figure 9·16, the oxygen atom shares one electron with one hydrogen atom and another electron with the other hydrogen atom. Each hydrogen atom shares its electron with the oxygen atom. This sharing gives the oxygen atom eight outer electrons. Each hydrogen atom has two outer electrons in its outer energy level. The resulting molecule has two covalent bonds. Compounds that contain covalent bonds are called **covalent compounds**.

In a water molecule, each covalent bond involves the sharing of one pair of electrons. Such bonds are called single covalent bonds. Look back at Figure 9·15. The bond in a hydrogen molecule is also a single covalent bond.

Look at the diagram of carbon dioxide shown in Figure 9·17. The carbon atom shares two pairs of electrons with each oxygen atom. Such a bond is known as a double covalent bond. Count all the electrons around the carbon atom in carbon dioxide. You can see that by forming a double covalent bond with each oxygen atom, the carbon atom has an outer energy level with eight electrons. This gives it a stable electron structure. Count the electrons around each of the oxygen atoms. How many electrons are there around each oxygen atom? Does each of these atoms have a stable electron structure?

Figure 9·17
A molecule of carbon dioxide, CO_2. What kind of bond is shown?

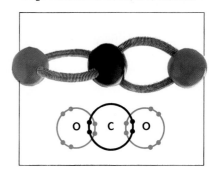

What Compounds Conduct Electricity?

OBJECTIVE

Classify compounds, based on their ability to conduct electricity.

MATERIALS

safety goggles, lab apron, dry cell, insulated wire, wire stripper, light bulb and socket, six 250-mL beakers, glass-marking pencil, table salt, sugar, baking soda, distilled water, hydrogen peroxide, rubbing alcohol

PROCEDURE

A. Wear safety goggles and a lab apron during this activity.

B. Set up the equipment as shown in the figure. The ends of the wires should have 2 cm of insulation removed. **Caution:** Do not touch the ends of the wires.

C. Label six beakers *A – F*.

D. Place table salt to a depth of about 0.5 cm in beaker *A*.

E. Hold an insulated part of the wires, and touch the ends of the wires to the salt. If the light bulb lights, the compound conducts electricity. If the light bulb does not light, the compound does not conduct electricity. Record all observations.

F. Place sugar to a depth of about 0.5 cm in beaker *B*. Repeat the test for conducting electricity.

G. Place baking soda to a depth of about 0.5 cm in beaker *C*. Repeat the test for conducting electricity.

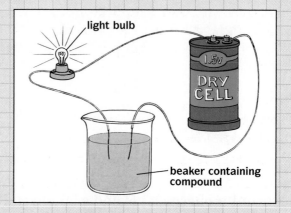

light bulb

DRY CELL 1.5v

beaker containing compound

H. Add enough distilled water to beakers *A*, *B*, and *C* to half fill them. Swirl each gently to mix. Half fill beaker *D* with distilled water.

I. Test the distilled water and each mixture for ability to conduct electricity. Rinse the ends of the wires in distilled water after each test.

J. Half fill beaker *E* with hydrogen peroxide. Repeat the test for conducting electricity. Rinse the ends of the wires.

K. Half fill beaker *F* with rubbing alcohol. Repeat the test for conducting electricity. Rinse the ends of the wires.

RESULTS AND CONCLUSIONS

1. Which substances conducted electricity?
2. Which substances are ionic compounds?
3. Which substances are covalent compounds?

Nitrogen gas is found in air. Its formula is N_2. A molecule of nitrogen is shown in Figure 9·18. How many pairs of electrons do the atoms in each nitrogen molecule share? The bond between the nitrogen atoms is called a triple covalent bond.

Covalent substances are different from ionic substances. Covalent compounds do not form a lattice structure. As a rule, covalent compounds have low melting points and low boiling points. Also, most covalent compounds do not conduct electricity. Ionic compounds form ions when they dissolve, but covalent compounds do not. When a covalent compound dissolves, its molecules remain bonded. Thus there are no charged particles to carry electricity.

Figure 9·18
A molecule of nitrogen, N_2.

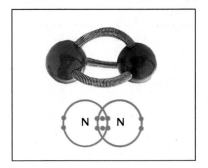

REVIEW

1. How does a covalent bond form?

2. Define the term *molecule.*

3. How do covalent bonds differ from ionic bonds?

CHALLENGE Predict how two chlorine atoms bond to form a chlorine molecule, Cl_2.

CHAPTER SUMMARY

The main ideas in this chapter are listed below. Read these statements before you answer the Chapter Review questions.

- A compound is a pure substance made up of two or more elements that are combined chemically. (9·1)

- The proportion of elements in a compound does not change. (9·1)

- If the proportion of elements in a compound is changed, a new compound is formed. (9·1)

- A chemical formula is a group of symbols that shows the makeup of a compound. (9·2)

- A subscript is a small number lowered to the right of a chemical symbol of an element in a compound. (9·2)

- Chemical bonds are forces that hold particles of matter together. (9·3)

- When a neutral atom gains or loses an electron, the atom becomes a charged particle called an ion. (9·3)

- An ionic bond is a force of attraction between oppositely charged ions. (9·3)

- Ionic bonds form when atoms gain or lose electrons. (9·3)

- Covalent bonds form when atoms share electrons. (9·4)

- A molecule is the smallest unit of any covalent substance that can exist alone and still show the properties of that substance. (9·4)

The key terms in this chapter are listed below. Use each term in a sentence that shows the meaning of the term.

chemical bond
chemical formula
compound
covalent bond

covalent compounds
formula unit
ion
ionic bond

ionic compound
molecule

Chapter Review

VOCABULARY

Use the key terms from the previous page to complete the following sentences correctly.

1. A neutral atom becomes a charged particle called a/an _____ when an electron is gained or lost.

2. A/An _____ is a compound that contains ionic bonds.

3. A/An _____ is the force that holds particles of matter together.

4. A/An _____ is a group of symbols that shows the makeup of a compound.

5. Compounds that contain covalent bonds are called _____.

6. A pure substance made of two or more elements that are combined chemically is called a/an _____.

7. A/An _____ is the smallest repeating group of atoms in an ionic compound.

8. A/An _____ is the smallest part of a covalent substance that has the properties of that substance.

9. A/An _____ is the force of attraction between oppositely charged ions.

10. The bond formed by the sharing of electrons between two atoms is called a/an _____.

CONCEPTS

Answer the following.

1. How many atoms of each element are present in one unit of each of these compounds?
   a. CO_2
   b. H_2CO_3
   c. $C_{12}H_{22}O_{11}$
   d. KBr
   e. $CuCl_2$

2. Name each of the following compounds.
   a. PCl_3
   b. $KClO_3$
   c. CaO
   d. $BaCl_2$
   e. $Al_2(SO_4)_3$

3. Write the formula for each of the following compounds.
   a. sodium iodide
   b. potassium phosphate
   c. barium chloride
   d. calcium carbonate
   e. copper (II) fluoride

Answer the following in complete sentences.
   4. How are elements and compounds related?
   5. Describe how the ionic bond in potassium bromide is formed.
   6. What is the difference between a sodium ion and a sodium atom?
   7. A white solid has a high melting point and a high boiling point. When it is melted, this compound conducts electricity. What kind of bond is found in this compound? Explain your answer.
   8. Explain why ionic compounds can conduct electricity when they are melted but not when they are solids.
   9. What is the difference between a covalent bond and an ionic bond?
   10. What is the difference between a hydrogen atom and a hydrogen molecule?

---

1. A bottle of hydrogen peroxide, H_2O_2, was left open for a few weeks. Then the material in the bottle was tested. The tests showed that the material in the bottle was water, not hydrogen peroxide. Explain what happened.
2. Why does a calcium ion have a smaller radius than a calcium atom?
3. Compare oxygen atoms, ions, and molecules.

APPLICATION/ CRITICAL THINKING

---

1. Some of the noble gases have been made to react and form new compounds. Do library research to find out what these compounds are and how they form.
2. In addition to the type of bonds in a molecule, the shape of a molecule determines the properties of a substance. Find out how scientists have determined the shapes of molecules.
3. Look up the term *electronegativity*. Explain how electronegativity can help to determine the type of chemical bond that exists in a molecule.

EXTENSION

CHAPTER 10

MIXTURES

*W*hat caused the color patterns shown in the photograph? You probably have seen patterns like this before. The photograph shows a mixture of soap and water. A thin film of soapy water actually is a layer of soap over a layer of water. Some light is reflected by the soap layer. Some light is reflected by the water layer. When these rays of light meet, they produce a variety of colors. The shapes and colors that you see depend on the thickness of the soap layer.

Not all mixtures produce color patterns. To get this effect, a mixture must form layers, and each layer must reflect light.

- *What are some properties of mixtures?*
- *What are some common mixtures?*
- *How are mixtures used?*

10·1 Kinds of Mixtures

Any sample of matter can be classed as a pure substance or as a mixture. A pure substance is either an element or a compound. A **mixture** is made up of two or more substances that can be separated by physical means. Air is a mixture of oxygen, nitrogen, and other gases. Gasoline is a mixture that may contain from a few to 200 substances.

The properties of a mixture depend upon the properties of its parts. Brass is a mixture of copper and zinc. Copper is a yellow-red metal, and zinc is a silvery-white metal. Brass made from mostly copper is red-gold. Brass that has at least 50 percent zinc is white.

The properties of mixtures can vary from sample to sample. For example, a mixture made of half a spoonful of sugar in one cup of water has different properties than does a mixture of two spoonfuls of sugar in one cup of water. Each drop of mixture from the second cup contains more sugar than each drop of mixture from the first cup. Which sugar mixture is sweeter?

Figure 10·1

Each of these mixtures contains more than one substance.

234

In some mixtures the different substances can be seen easily. One example is a mixture of sand and water. A mixture of sand and water does not have the same makeup throughout the mixture. Instead it differs from one point to another. A mixture whose makeup differs from point to point is called a **heterogeneous** (heht uhr uh JEE nee uhs) **mixture**.

Some mixtures do not differ from point to point. A mixture whose makeup is the same throughout is called a **homogeneous** (hoh muh JEE-nee uhs) **mixture**. Seawater and brass are homogeneous mixtures. Homogeneous mixtures are also called *solutions*. Which of the samples in Figure 10·1 are homogeneous mixtures?

hetero- (another)
genos (kind)

homo- (same)

Each substance in a mixture keeps its own physical properties. Therefore the parts of a mixture can be separated by physical means. For example, sand can be separated from water by a filter. Look at Figure 10·2. How is a magnet being used to separate this mixture?

To separate mixtures of liquids, scientists use a method called *distillation* (dihs tuh LAY shuhn). In distillation, liquids are separated by differences in their boiling points. A mixture of methyl alcohol and water can be distilled. Methyl alcohol boils at 64.5°C. Water boils at 100°C. When the mixture is heated to 64.5°C the alcohol boils but the water does not. The alcohol can be collected as it boils out of the mixture. The water is left behind.

Figure 10·2
A magnet can be used to separate steel objects from brass objects.

ACTIVITY — How Many Substances Are in Black Ink?

OBJECTIVE
Compare the substances in ink.

MATERIALS
chromatography paper, forceps, ruler, capillary tube, black ink, test tube, cork stopper, thumbtack, graduate, distilled water, 3 small test tubes, test-tube rack, dropper, stirring rod

PROCEDURE

A. Place a small pencil mark about 3 cm from the pointed end of a strip of chromatography paper. Do not touch the paper with your fingers; use forceps to handle the paper.

B. Use a capillary tube to apply black ink to the chromatography paper. Place one end of the capillary tube in the ink, and let some ink rise in the tube. Put your finger on top of the tube, and transfer a small drop of ink to the pencil mark on the paper. Let the ink dry. Repeat the application once or twice.

C. Assemble the apparatus as shown in the figure. Fold the top of the paper strip over about 1 cm, and attach the strip to the bottom of a cork stopper with a thumbtack. Place the strip in the test tube, and adjust the stopper so that the point of the strip is about 2 cm above the bottom of the test tube. Remove the stopper and paper strip. Carefully pour 10 mL of distilled water into the test tube. Make sure that the walls of the test tube remain dry.

D. Place the stopper into the tube so that the point of the paper strip extends into the water. The ink mark should be about 1 cm above the water.

E. Place the test tube in the test-tube rack. Be careful not to disturb the test tube. Allow the water column to rise to within 3 cm of the top of the strip. Remove the stopper, and hang the strip to dry.

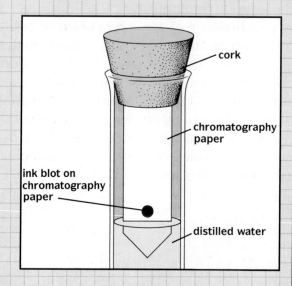

cork

chromatography paper

ink blot on chromatography paper

distilled water

F. Examine the dry strip, and record your observations.

G. Cut one color section from the strip. Cut the section into small pieces, and place them in a small test tube. Add 10 drops of distilled water, and then mash the paper in the water with a stirring rod. Record your observations.

H. Repeat step **G** with each color section. Combine the liquids obtained. Compare them with the original ink.

RESULTS AND CONCLUSIONS

1. How many different colors did the separation procedure produce?
2. What might each color represent?
3. What resulted when you mixed the separate colors? How does the material produced in step **H** compare with the original ink? How could you make it more like the original ink?
4. Develop a model to explain how chromatography paper separated the parts of the ink. Base your model on your observations.

Many plant oils used in perfumes, flavorings, and medicines are purified by distillation. Peppermint oil, which is used in toothpaste, is obtained in this way. The juices of the plant are distilled, and the oil is collected.

In hospitals, modern tools are used to separate mixtures such as blood. Blood is a mixture of proteins, sugar, oxygen, carbon dioxide, and other substances. The substances in blood can be separated according to their densities. Tubes of blood are spun at very high speeds in a machine called a centrifuge (SEHN truh fyooj). Figure 10·3 shows two tubes of blood. The tube on the right has been spun in a centrifuge. The densest parts of the mixture are at the bottom of the tube. The least dense substances are at the top of the tube. Hospital workers can then test the different parts of the blood.

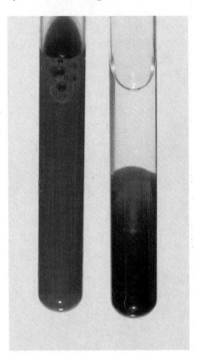

Figure 10·3
Which test tube of blood has been spun in a centrifuge?

REVIEW

1. State two ways in which mixtures are different from pure substances.
2. Identify each of the following mixtures as homogeneous or heterogeneous: muddy water, brewed coffee, orange juice, cough medicine, soft drink.
3. Describe a method to separate a mixture of sawdust and sand.

CHALLENGE Describe how you would separate a mixture of marble chips, water, wax, and salt.

10·2 Making Solutions

After completing this section, you will be able to

- **distinguish** between a solute and a solvent.
- **describe** how solutions form.
- **list** the factors that affect the rate of solution.

The key terms in this section are
solute
solution
solvent

solvere (to dissolve)

THE NATURE OF SOLUTIONS

Many of the materials that you come in contact with each day are solutions. For example, the gasoline used in cars is a solution. Dental fillings are solutions of mercury in silver.

A **solution** is a homogeneous mixture of two or more substances. Recall that a homogeneous mixture has the same makeup throughout. Solutions can be made by mixing solids, liquids, or gases. For example, a soft drink contains a solution of carbon dioxide in water—a gas in a liquid.

The **solvent** in a solution is the substance that is present in the greater amount. The solvent usually determines the state of the solution. The substance present in the smaller amount is called the **solute**. When a solute enters a solution, the solute is said to *dissolve*. In the solution shown in Figure 10·4, water is the solvent. The compound copper sulfate is the solute. The copper sulfate has dissolved in the water. The solution is in the liquid state, like the solvent. Some solutions have more than one solute. Seawater is a solution that contains many solutes dissolved in water.

Figure 10·4

In an aqueous solution, water is the solvent.

238

In a solution the solute particles are not visible. They will not settle to the bottom, no matter how long the solution is allowed to stand. The parts of a solution cannot be separated by filtering.

In most solutions the solvent is a liquid and the solute is a solid, liquid, or gas. The most common liquid solvent is water. Solutions in which water is the solvent are called *aqueous* (AI kwee uhs) *solutions*. Is the solution shown in Figure 10·4 an aqueous solution?

In solid solutions, both the solvent and the solute are solids. Such solutions are called *alloys*. Bronze, an alloy of copper and tin, is used to make statues like the one shown in Figure 10·5. Pewter, stainless steel, and sterling silver are also alloys.

Some solutions conduct electricity. An electric current is carried in a solution by ions. Fluids in the human body contain ions such as sodium, Na^+, and potassium, K^+. These ions allow body fluids to conduct electricity. In the human nervous system, information moves as electrical signals. The passage of these signals can be studied with machines like the one shown in Figure 10·6.

Notice the paste on the boy's chest. This paste is a solution that contains many ions. The ions carry electrical signals from the body to the wires of the machine.

Figure 10·5
This statue is made of bronze. What metals make up this alloy?

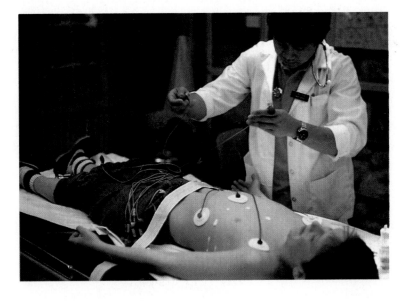

Figure 10·6
This machine is an electrocardiograph. It shows the electrical pattern produced by the heart.

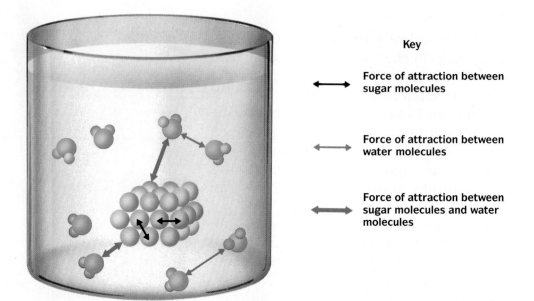

Key

→ Force of attraction between sugar molecules

→ Force of attraction between water molecules

→ Force of attraction between sugar molecules and water molecules

Figure 10·7

As sugar dissolves, its molecules spread out through the water.

Figure 10·8

This instant cold pack absorbs heat as the substances in it dissolve.

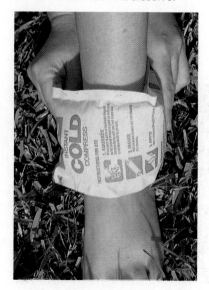

HOW SUBSTANCES DISSOLVE

Solutions form when particles of the solute spread out evenly in the solvent. Figure 10·7 shows what happens when sugar, a covalent compound, dissolves in water. The sugar molecules are held together by attractive forces.

Notice that when sugar is placed in water, there is a strong attraction between the sugar molecules and the water molecules. This attraction is greater than the attraction between the sugar molecules alone. Thus the sugar molecules are pulled away from each other and can mix with the water molecules.

Forces of attraction between the solvent and the solute also cause ionic compounds to dissolve. But when ionic compounds dissolve, they separate into ions. Figure 10·9 shows sodium chloride dissolving in water. What ions are formed?

In most cases, heat energy is either given off or absorbed when a solute dissolves. Dissolving some substances involves large amounts of energy. For example, when ammonium nitrate, NH_4NO_3, dissolves in water, the solution becomes very cold. Other substances, like calcium chloride, $CaCl_2$, produce heat when they dissolve. Their solutions are very hot. These properties are used in the instant cold or hot packs used to treat injuries.

Key

Cl⁻

H₂O

Na⁺

RATE OF SOLUTION

How quickly a solute dissolves is called the rate of solution. The rate of solution depends on three factors. The first factor is particle size. The smaller the solute particles are, the faster they dissolve. Many small crystals dissolve faster than does a single large crystal. As you can see in Figure 10·10, breaking, crushing, or grinding a solid into smaller pieces increases the surface area of the crystals. A solid dissolves only at the surface of its crystals. Thus, making the surface area of the solute greater will increase the rate of solution.

Movement is the second factor that affects the rate of solution. Stirring or shaking the mixture increases the rate of solution. This action increases

Figure 10·9
As sodium chloride dissolves, it separates into ions.

Figure 10·10
Cutting a crystal into smaller pieces increases the surface area on which reactions can take place.

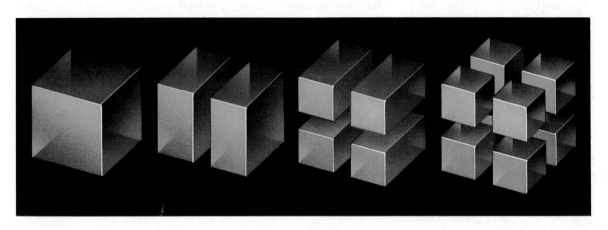

Under intense temperatures and pressures, matter can be converted into a form that seems to be a cross between a liquid and a gas. This form of matter is called a supercritical fluid. Supercritical fluids were discovered in 1822 by a French scientist, Charles Cagniard de la Tour. However, only recently have scientists found a way to make use of supercritical fluids.

Supercritical fluids can be used as solvents that can dissolve one substance in a solid object without dissolving the rest of the solid. This procedure is already being used to produce caffeine-free coffee. One advantage of using this new procedure is that the flavor of the coffee

is not changed. Another advantage is that none of the solvent is left in the coffee. The problem with the procedure is that the temperature

and pressure must be carefully controlled.

High-pressure chambers that can withstand high temperatures and pressures are needed to control supercritical fluids. Dr. Erdogan Kiran of the University of Maine has built a special high-pressure chamber. His chamber has a window that is made of half-inch-thick synthetic sapphire, one of the hardest materials known. Now Dr. Kiran can watch the progress of his experiments.

Soon, supercritical fluids may be useful in the production of medicines and foods. One idea is to extract the oil from potato chips so that they remain crispy without being high in fats and calories.

the rate of contact between the solute and the solvent. Stirring or shaking also moves dissolved solute particles away from the solute crystals. Thus a fresh surface is exposed to the solvent.

The third factor that affects the rate of solution is temperature. Heating can increase the rate of solution by increasing the motion of the particles. The solvent molecules pass more quickly over the surface of the solute. Heat also causes the solute particles to come off a solid more easily. Thus the solid dissolves faster. However, heating has the opposite effect on gases in solution. Gases dissolve faster in cold solutions than in warm ones.

REVIEW

1. How does a solute differ from a solvent? Give two examples of each.
2. Describe how sugar dissolves in water.
3. List the three factors that affect the rate of solution.

CHALLENGE Give two reasons why the rate of solution in boiling water is so much greater than in water at 95°C.

10·3 Properties of Solutions

Have you ever made lemonade or another flavored drink? If so, you know that differences in the amount of sugar used can affect the taste. Some drinks may be sweeter than others. A solution can be made with different amounts of solute in a given amount of solvent.

SOLUBILITY

If the amount of solute is small compared with the amount of solvent, the solution is said to be *dilute*. If the amount of solute is large compared with the amount of solvent, the solution is said to be *concentrated*. For example, if 10 g of sodium nitrate are dissolved in 100 g of water, the solution is dilute. If the solution contains 70 g of sodium nitrate in 100 g of water, the solution is concentrated.

After completing this section, you will be able to

- **list** factors that affect solubility.
- **compare** saturated, unsaturated, and supersaturated solutions.
- **describe** how solute particles affect the boiling point and freezing point of a solution.

The key terms in this section are
saturated solution
solubility
supersaturated solution
unsaturated solution

Figure 10·11
Which beaker contains the more concentrated solution?

The amount of solute that will dissolve in a given amount of solvent at a given temperature is called **solubility**. For example, the solubility of sucrose at 1°C is 180 g per 100 g of water. Less than 1 g of silver chloride will dissolve in 100 g of water at that same temperature. Thus, compared with the solubility of silver chloride, the solubility of sucrose is high.

243

Notice that the temperature is stated when the solubility of a substance is given. This is because solubility changes with temperature. Look at Figure 10·12. The red line shows how much potassium nitrate, KNO_3, dissolves in 100 g of water. These amounts are given for a range of temperatures. Such a graph is called a solubility curve. The graph shows that at 0°C the solubility of this compound is about 12 g per 100 g of water. At 80°C it is about 170 g per 100 g of water. What is the solubility of potassium nitrate at 60°C?

Figure 10·12
Solubility curves of several substances.

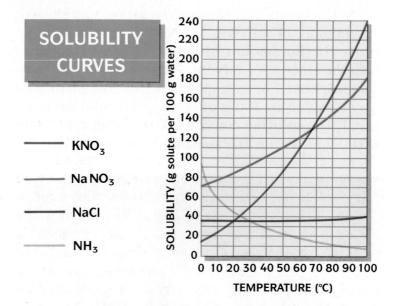

SOLUBILITY CURVES

KNO₃

NaNO₃

NaCl

NH₃

The solubility of most solids and liquids increases as temperature increases. However, temperature has a different effect on the solubility of gases. The solubility of a gas decreases as temperature rises. When the temperature of a solution rises, the dissolved gas leaves the solution in the form of bubbles.

Pressure affects the solubility of gases, but not that of solids and liquids. More gas dissolves in a liquid when pressure over the liquid increases. If the pressure over a liquid is decreased less gas dissolves. In a container of a soft drink, there is pressure over the liquid. When you open the container, you release this pressure. What happens to gases dissolved in the liquid?

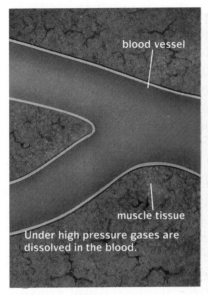
blood vessel

muscle tissue

Under high pressure gases are dissolved in the blood.

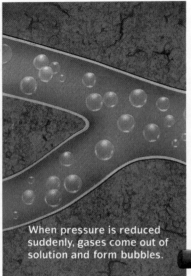
When pressure is reduced suddenly, gases come out of solution and form bubbles.

Figure 10·13
The diver must rise to the surface slowly so that gases in solution will not form bubbles.

Gases such as oxygen and nitrogen are dissolved in blood. The amount of gas in solution depends partly on pressure. Deep-sea divers, like the one shown in Figure 10·13, go through pressure changes that affect the amount of gases dissolved in the blood. The greater the depth, the greater the pressure on the diver's body. If the pressure is great, the blood absorbs more gases. The pressure may be quickly reduced if the diver swims up quickly from the deep sea. A rapid loss of pressure causes the blood gases to come out of solution as many tiny bubbles. These bubbles clog small blood vessels and cause severe pain. This condition is called the bends. The bends can be avoided if pressure is reduced slowly. To reduce pressure slowly, a diver must rise to the surface slowly.

SATURATED SOLUTIONS

Look again at Figure 10·12. At 20°C, about 85 g of sodium nitrate will dissolve in 100 g of water. If you add more sodium nitrate, it will not dissolve. The extra solid will settle to the bottom of the beaker. Such a solution is said to be saturated. A **saturated solution** contains all the solute that will dissolve at a given temperature. If you add more solute, it will not dissolve.

satur- (full)

Suppose you have a solution of 50 g of sodium nitrate in 100 g of water at 80°C. You can see from Figure 10·12 that the solubility of sodium nitrate at this temperature is about 145 g per 100 g of water. Therefore this solution can dissolve another 95 g of solid. A solution in which more solute can be dissolved is an **unsaturated solution**.

un- (not)
satur- (full)

SUPERSATURATED SOLUTIONS

Some solutions can be made to contain more solute than is normal for a given temperature. This can be done by making a saturated solution at a high temperature and then letting it cool slowly. As the solution cools, all of the solute stays in solution. A **supersaturated solution** is a solution that has more dissolved solute than is normal for a given temperature. Such solutions are not stable. The extra solute may not stay dissolved for long.

super- (to excess)

ACTIVITY   How Is a Supersaturated Solution Prepared?

OBJECTIVE
Prepare a supersaturated solution.

MATERIALS
safety goggles, lab apron, 2 test tubes, hypo (sodium thiosulfate), 10-mL graduate, distilled water, Bunsen burner, striker, test-tube holder, wash bottle, rubber stopper, test-tube rack

PROCEDURE
A. Wear safety goggles and a lab apron during this activity.
B. Thoroughly clean two test tubes. Dry one of the test tubes.
C. Fill the dry test tube with hypo. Place 2 mL of distilled water in the other test tube.
D. Pour one fourth of the hypo into the test tube containing water. Heat the mixture gently until all of the solid material dissolves.
E. Repeat step **D** three more times. All the hypo should now be dissolved. If any undissolved hypo remains near the top of the test tube containing the solution, use the wash bottle and a small amount of distilled water to flush the solid into the solution.
F. Allow the solution to cool for 5–10 minutes and then stopper the test tube.
G. Place the test tube in a test-tube rack, and leave it in a safe place overnight.
H. The next day, examine the test tube. Drop one crystal, sometimes called a seed crystal, of hypo into the solution.
   1. Describe what happens.
   2. Touch the test tube. Does it feel warm or cool?

RESULTS AND CONCLUSIONS
1. Why is it necessary to heat the mixture to dissolve all of the hypo?
2. Explain what happened when you dropped the seed crystal of hypo into the cooled solution.
3. Was heat given off or absorbed when the seed crystal was added? Why?

Figure 10·14

When one crystal was added to this supersaturated solution, the extra solute formed crystals.

Figure 10·14 shows a supersaturated solution before *(left)* and after *(right)* a single solute crystal was added. As you can see, the added crystal causes the excess solute to crystallize. How could adding solute help you find out whether a solution is unsaturated, saturated, or supersaturated?

BOILING POINT AND FREEZING POINT

Have you ever seen an overheated car parked along the road? A car overheats when water from its cooling system has reached the boiling point. By adding antifreeze to the radiator, you can keep a car's cooling system from boiling over in the summer and from freezing in the winter. Antifreeze contains ethylene glycol. This solute changes the boiling point and freezing point of water.

For a liquid to boil, the liquid particles must gain enough energy to leave the liquid and form a gas. In a pure substance there is only one kind of particle. However, there are two kinds of particles in a solution — solute and solvent. The solute particles make it difficult for the solvent particles to break away from the liquid. More energy is needed for the solvent particles to break free. Thus the solution boils at a higher temperature than does the pure solvent. The increase in boiling point caused by adding solute is called *boiling point elevation*.

Adding solute to a solvent can also change the freezing point of the liquid. For a liquid to freeze, energy must be removed. Because of the solute par-

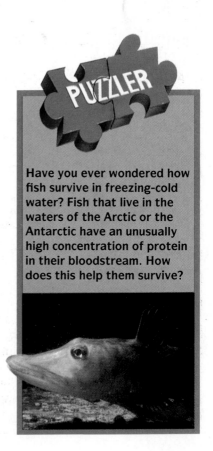

Have you ever wondered how fish survive in freezing-cold water? Fish that live in the waters of the Arctic or the Antarctic have an unusually high concentration of protein in their bloodstream. How does this help them survive?

ticles, more energy must be removed to form a solid.
Thus a solution freezes at a lower temperature than
does a pure substance. Adding salt to icy roads and
sidewalks lowers the freezing point of ice. The decrease in freezing point is called *freezing point depression.*

These changes in boiling point and freezing
point depend only on the number of solute particles.
They do not depend upon the nature, mass, or size of
the solute particles. As the number of particles in
solution increases, the boiling point increases and
the freezing point decreases.

REVIEW

1. What factor has the greatest effect on the solubility of a solid in
   a liquid?
2. Compare the effects that temperature and pressure have on
   the solubility of a gas in a liquid.
3. How does a saturated solution differ from a supersaturated
   solution? What is an unsaturated solution?
4. Why is the boiling point of a water solution different from that
   of pure water?
5. How is the freezing point of a water solution affected when
   sugar is dissolved in it?

CHALLENGE Would fish in a stream be more likely to suffer from
a lack of oxygen when the water is cold or when it is hot? Explain
your answer.

10·4 Suspensions and Colloids

If you shake a bottle of salad dressing, the substances from which it is made seem to be evenly mixed. But if the bottle is left standing, the mixture separates, as shown in Figure 10·16. Many particles settle to the bottom of the bottle. Salad dressing is an example of a suspension. A **suspension** is a heterogeneous mixture in which particles are temporarily mixed in a liquid.

A suspension differs from a solution. The particles in a suspension are found in large clusters. These clusters can be seen with the unaided eye or with a magnifier. They can be separated from the liquid by filtering. Recall that the dissolved particles in a solution are atoms, ions, and molecules. These particles are small. They cannot be seen, and they cannot be filtered.

Heavy particles settle from a suspension faster than do lighter particles. When a river floods, it picks up many rocks and soil particles, forming a suspension. As the suspension of muddy water flows downstream, it loses some of the particles. Large particles settle out first. The finest silt stays suspended longer, and these particles are carried farther downstream.

Figure 10·16
Salad dressing is a suspension. If it is left standing, the oil and vinegar will gradually separate.

Table 10·1 *Properties of Solutions, Colloids, and Suspensions*

PROPERTY	SOLUTION	COLLOID	SUSPENSION
Particle type	Atoms, ions, molecules	Large particles, clusters of small particles	Large clusters of particles
Particles visible with microscope	No	No	Yes
Particles settle on standing	No	No	Yes
Particles separate by filtering	No	No	Yes
Particles scatter light	No	Yes	Yes
Example	Seawater	Soot in air	Muddy water

Another kind of mixture contains particles that are larger than the particles in solutions but smaller than the particles in suspensions. Such mixtures are called colloids (KAHL oidz). A **colloid** is a mixture whose properties are between those of a solution and a suspension. Smoke, fog, mayonnaise, gelatin, and egg white are examples of colloids.

Colloids are similar to solutions in many ways. Table 10·1 compares the properties of solutions, colloids, and suspensions. Notice that like solutions, colloids do not separate upon standing. Can colloids be separated by filtering?

Figure 10·17
Because of the Tyndall effect, beams of light are visible in the fog.

250

Like suspensions, colloids scatter light. The scattering of light by colloid particles is known as the *Tyndall effect*. Because of the Tyndall effect, you can see light beams from a lighthouse in a fog.

REVIEW

1. What is a suspension? Give two examples.

2. What is a colloid? Give two examples.

3. How do solutions, suspensions, and colloids differ?

CHALLENGE Describe how you would determine whether an unknown liquid mixture is a solution or a colloid.

CHAPTER SUMMARY
The main ideas in this chapter are listed below. Read these statements before you answer the Chapter Review questions.

- Mixtures are made up of two or more substances that can be separated by physical means. Homogeneous mixtures are the same throughout. Heterogeneous mixtures vary from one point to another. (10·1)

- In a solution the solute dissolves in the solvent. (10·2)

- The rate at which a solution forms depends on the size of the particles, movement, and the temperature of the mixture. (10·2)

- Solubility is the amount of solute that will dissolve in a given amount of solvent at a given temperature. (10·3)

- The solubility of solids increases with increasing temperature. The solubility of gases decreases with increasing temperature. The solubility of gases increases with increasing pressure. (10·3)

- A saturated solution has the maximum amount of solute that will dissolve at a given temperature. An unsaturated solution can dissolve more solute. A supersaturated solution contains more dissolved solute than is normal for a given temperature. (10·3)

- The addition of solute raises the boiling point and lowers the freezing point of a solution. (10·3)

- A suspension is a mixture in which particles are temporarily mixed in a liquid. The particles in a suspension will settle if the mixture is left standing (10·4)

- A colloid is a mixture whose properties are between those of a solution and a suspension. The particles of a colloid will not settle if the mixture is left standing. (10·4)

The key terms in this chapter are listed below. Use each term in a sentence that shows the meaning of the term.

colloid	saturated solution	solvent
heterogeneous mixture	solubility	supersaturated solution
homogeneous mixture	solute	suspension
mixture	solution	unsaturated solution

Chapter Review

Use the key terms from the previous page to complete the following sentences correctly.

1. A solution that can dissolve more solute at a given temperature is a/an _____.
2. Two or more substances that can be separated by physical means make up a/an _____ .
3. A homogeneous mixture of two or more substances is a/an _____.
4. A mixture in which particles remain suspended and cannot be filtered out is called a/an _____ .
5. A solution in which the maximum amount of solute has been dissolved in the solvent is called a/an _____ .
6. A solution that contains more dissolved solute than it can normally hold at a given temperature is a/an _____ .
7. A heterogeneous mixture that has solid particles temporarily mixed in a liquid is a/an _____ .
8. A mixture whose makeup differs from point to point is called a/an _____ .
9. The amount of solute that will dissolve in a given amount of solvent at a given temperature is called _____ .
10. In a solution the substance present in the greater amount is the _____ .

CONCEPTS

Make a table like the one shown. Write the correct information under each heading.

PROPERTY	SOLUTION	SUSPENSION
Particles visible with microscope		
Particles separate by filtering		
Particles settle on standing		
Particles scatter light		
Particle type		

Choose the term or phrase that best answers the question or completes the statement.

1. Air is an example of
   a. a pure substance.
   b. an element.
   c. a compound.
   d. a mixture.
2. Which of these is an example of a heterogeneous mixture?
   a. salad dressing
   b. bronze
   c. seawater
   d. a soft drink

3. Ten grams of iodine are dissolved in 100 mL of alcohol. The alcohol is
   a. a mixture.   c. the solvent.
   b. the solute.   d. aqueous.
4. To increase the rate of solution of a solid in water,
   a. increase the pressure over the water.
   b. decrease the pressure over the water.
   c. crush the particles of the solid.
   d. chill the water.
5. A solvent is capable of dissolving 50 g of solute per 100 g of water at a given temperature. If 70 g of solute are dissolved under the same conditions, the solution is
   a. supersaturated.   c. unsaturated.
   b. saturated.   d. dilute.

Answer the following in complete sentences.

6. How are mixtures different from pure substances?
7. How can differences in densities be used to separate mixtures?
8. What factors affect the rate of solution?
9. How does a dilute solution differ from a concentrated solution?
10. Why does a solution boil at a higher temperature than does a pure solvent?

---

1. What tests can be used to find out if a liquid is a pure solvent or a solution?
2. Explain why warm water has a stale taste.
3. Why does an uncovered soft drink "go flat"?
4. If you dissolve the same number of formula units of NaCl and $CaCl_2$ in equal volumes of water, the $CaCl_2$ solution will have a higher boiling point. Explain why.
5. At times, highway departments report that it is too cold to spread salt on icy roads. What is the basis for this statement?

APPLICATION/ CRITICAL THINKING

---

1. An estuary is an area where fresh water from a river mixes with salt water from the sea. Prepare a report on the ways in which living things in an estuary are affected by the mixing of these two solutions.
2. Find out what an emulsifier is. Present to your class a report on the uses of emulsifiers.
3. Hemodialysis is a technique used to cleanse the blood. Do library research on hemodialysis. Write a report that explains how hemodialysis makes use of the properties of liquid mixtures.

EXTENSION

CHAPTER 11

FORCE, ENERGY, AND WORK

*W*hat happens when you break a balloon? Probably what you notice most is the sound. The balloon breaks so quickly that you cannot see exactly what happens. This photograph shows what a balloon looks like a fraction of a second after it is popped with a pin.

When you inflate a balloon, you push a large amount of air into it. The air in the balloon exerts a force against the balloon. When the balloon is popped, the force of the air rushing out through the newly formed opening tears the balloon apart.

- *What forces exist in an inflated balloon?*
- *What other kinds of forces are there?*
- *How do forces act on matter?*

11·1 Force

After completing this section, you will be able to

- **identify** different kinds of forces.
- **describe** the effect of forces on an object.
- **describe** an object's center of gravity.

The key term in this section is
force

KINDS OF FORCES

A **force** is a push or a pull. Forces cause objects to move, change speed, or stop moving. What are some examples of forces in daily life? Some forces act when one object is in contact with another. If you use a force to push a book across a desk, there is contact between your hand and the book. Other forces can act between objects that are not in contact. For example, there is a force of attraction between all objects in the universe. Several forces are described below.

- *Gravitational force*, or gravity, is the force of attraction between two objects that have mass. As mass increases, the attraction increases. The earth's gravity causes objects to fall toward the earth. How does gravity affect the divers shown in Figure 11·1A?

- *Electrical force* is a force between electric charges. Objects that have opposite charges attract each other. Thus they pull toward each other. Look at Figure 11·1B. The girl's hair is attracted to the brush because the hair and the brush have opposite charges. Objects with the same charge repel, or push away from, each other.

Figure 11·1

What kind of force is at work in each of these examples?

256

● *Magnetic force* is a force caused by moving electric charges. Moving charges in atoms make some substances, such as iron, magnetic. Magnets attract or repel each other because of this force.

Figure 11·2
Friction stops the baseball player from sliding past the base.

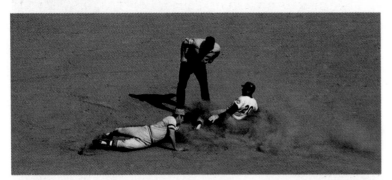

● *Friction* is a force that opposes motion. There is friction whenever two objects are in contact. When two objects rub together, the friction causes wear. Automobile tires become worn because of the friction between the tires and the road. But friction is also useful. If there were no friction between the tires and the road, a moving car would skid. The driver would not be able to control the car's motion.

● *Nuclear* (NOO klee uhr) *force* is a force of attraction that holds the nucleus of an atom together. Compared with other forces, nuclear force is very strong. However, this force acts over very short distances. Gravity is a weaker force, but it acts over much longer distances.

● *Weak interactions* are forces thought to cause the nuclei of some atoms to break apart. Scientists have not learned much about weak interactions.

COMBINED FORCES

An object may be acted upon by more than one force at a time. Figure 11·3 shows two opposing forces. A magnetic force is pulling the truck upward. At the same time, gravity is pullng the truck down toward the earth. In which direction is the force on the truck greater? When the forces acting on an object are not equal, the forces are said to be *unbalanced*. Unbalanced forces acting on an object at rest cause the object to move.

Figure 11·3
A crane equipped with an electro-magnet can lift a heavy object, such as this truck.

257

Figure 11·4

Two forces can combine to move an object.

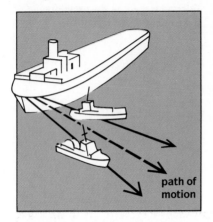

path of motion

Combined forces can act together instead of against each other. Lifting a piano would be a difficult task for one person. However, many people lifting together could move the piano easily. In many cases, combined forces act in directions that are at an angle. Look at Figure 11·4. The tugboats are pulling in different directions. The ship moves along a path that is between the two forces.

When the forces acting on a mass are equal and opposite, the forces are said to be *balanced*. Balanced forces acting on an object at rest do not cause motion. Imagine two teams having a tug of war. Suppose each team has the same number of people and everyone is pulling equally hard. Are the forces balanced or unbalanced? What would happen if one team added an extra member?

MEASURING FORCES

The amount of force acting on an object can be measured. The SI unit of force is a *newton* (N). One force that can be measured is gravity. The amount of gravitational force between two objects is called *weight*. Weight is different from mass. Recall that mass is a measure of the amount of matter in an object. The mass of an object stays the same, no matter how much force acts on it. However, weight varies with the distance between two objects.

On the earth the weight of an object is a measure of the gravity between the object and the earth. On the moon the weight of an object is a measure of the gravity between the object and the moon. The gravity on the moon is less than the gravity on the earth. Therefore an object weighs less on the moon than on the earth. But the mass of the object is the same on the moon as it is on the earth.

ACTIVITY   What Is the Center of Gravity?

OBJECTIVES
Predict and **locate** the center of gravity of an object.

MATERIALS
unweighted box, lead sinker, string, dissecting needle, metric ruler, weighted box

PROCEDURE
A. Examine an unweighted box.
   1. Predict where the center of gravity is.
B. Attach a lead sinker to a 30-cm long piece of string. Tie the string to a dissecting needle. Stick the needle into the broad surface of the box at any point near the edge of the box. With a pencil, mark this point.
C. Let the box and the weighted line hang freely from the needle, as shown in the figure. Mark the position of the weighted line at the edge of the box.
D. Remove the dissecting needle. Use a metric ruler to draw a line between the two points that you marked.
E. Repeat this procedure for three more points on the surface of the box. Remember to mark each point near the edge of the box. The point at which the four lines cross shows the center of gravity of the box.

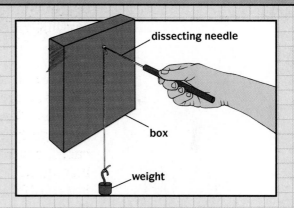

F. Examine a weighted box.
   2. Predict where the center of gravity is.
G. Repeat steps **B** through **E** with the weighted box.
H. Extend your index finger, and try to balance each box on your finger.
I. Place each box, with the marked side up, on a flat surface. Spin each box.

RESULTS AND CONCLUSIONS
1. How do your predictions compare with the actual location of the center of gravity of each box?
2. How is the center of gravity related to the way each box balances?
3. How is the center of gravity related to the way each box spins?

CENTER OF GRAVITY

Figure 11·5A shows a meterstick balanced at the 50-cm mark. The gravitational force acting on the whole stick seems to be focused in one place. In other words, the weight of the meterstick seems to be at one point. This point is called the center of gravity. The *center of gravity* of an object is the point at which all of an object's mass seems to be located. An object is balanced if its center of gravity is supported. If the center of gravity of an object is not supported, the object falls. Look at Figure 11·5B. Why is the center of gravity of the bat closer to its larger end?

The earth is nearly a perfect sphere. Thus the earth's center of gravity is near the planet's center. When an object is weighed on the earth, the weight of the object depends on its distance from the earth's center of gravity.

Figure 11·5

The center of gravity of an object affects how the object will balance.

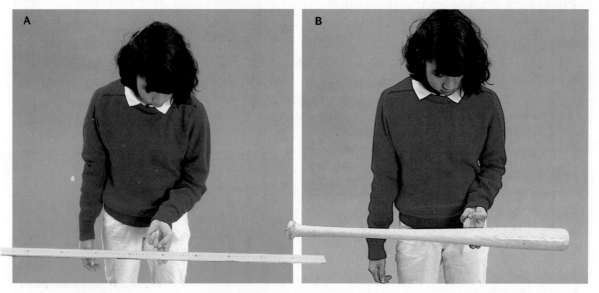

REVIEW
1. What is a force? Name six types of forces.
2. Why would it be impossible to walk if there were no friction?
3. How do mass and weight differ?
4. What is the center of gravity of an object?

CHALLENGE Identify the forces that act on a sled being pulled across a snow-covered field. Draw a diagram to show the direction of the forces.

11·2 Forces in Fluids

Liquids and gases are fluids. Fluids are materials that flow. They do not have a definite shape. Thus they take the shape of a container. Liquids have a definite volume, but gases do not. A gas expands to fill a container. Because they are not rigid like solids, fluids can exert special kinds of forces.

ARCHIMEDES' PRINCIPLE

Look at the rock shown in Figure 11·6. It weighs 4.0 N in air. What force is being measured? When the rock is put into water and weighed, the scale reads 3.0 N. The rock seems to have lost weight in the water. The water exerts an upward force on the rock. Therefore the upward force of the water makes the rock seem lighter.

The upward force exerted on an object by a fluid in which the object is placed is called **buoyant** (BOY uhnt) **force**. When an object is placed into a fluid, the object takes the place of, or displaces, some of the fluid. The volume of the fluid displaced is equal to the volume of the object. The buoyant force is equal to the weight of the displaced fluid.

About 2000 years ago a Greek scientist named Archimedes (ar kuh MEE deez) observed the behavior of buoyant forces. He concluded that an object in a fluid is supported by a force equal to the weight of the fluid displaced by the object. His conclusion is known as *Archimedes' principle.*

After completing this section, you will be able to

- **distinguish** between force and pressure.
- **explain** and **give examples** of forces in fluids.

The key terms in this section are
buoyant force
pressure

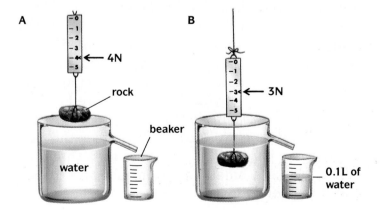

Figure 11·6
An object placed in water appears to lose weight.

Figure 11·7
Because a ship displaces a large amount of water, the buoyant force on the ship is large.

Archimedes' principle can help to explain why some objects sink and some float. An object floats if its weight is equal to or less than the weight of the fluid it displaces. An object sinks if its weight is greater than the weight of the fluid it displaces. A ship floats because it is hollow. The open spaces in the ship increase its volume. Thus the ship will displace a large amount of water.

PASCAL'S LAW

A fluid in a container pushes against the walls of the container — that is, the fluid exerts a force on the container. Force acting on a unit area is called **pressure**. The amount of pressure depends on the size of the force and the size of the area on which the force acts. The SI unit of pressure is called a pascal (Pa). A pascal is equal to one newton of force acting on an area of one square meter.

In a closed container the pressure of a fluid is the same at all points. This property of fluids is called *Pascal's law*. Pascal's law is applied in devices such as automobile lifts, dentists' chairs, and the brake systems in cars. Notice in Figure 11·8 that the two pistons are supported by a fluid. According to Pascal's law, the pressure of the fluid is the same at all points. Piston B has a smaller area than does piston A. Thus a small force on piston A causes piston B to exert a larger force.

Figure 11·8
Pascal's law explains how a hydraulic lift works.

BERNOULLI'S PRINCIPLE

Look at Figure 11·9. An airplane stays in flight because the air pressure under the wings is greater than the air pressure over the wings. The air moving over the top of the wing travels farther than the air moving under the wing. To do so, the air moving over the wing must move faster than the air moving under the wing. When the air moves faster, air pressure decreases. The resulting difference in air pressure holds the airplane up. This illustrates a property of fluids known as Bernoulli's (ber NOO-leez) principle. *Bernoulli's principle* states that pressure in a moving fluid decreases as the speed of the fluid increases.

Figure 11·9
Bernoulli's principle explains how an airplane is able to fly.

REVIEW

1. How do force and pressure differ?
2. What is Pascal's law? How is it applied?
3. What is Bernoulli's principle? Give an example of its use.

CHALLENGE A block weighs 4.0 N. It floats in water. What will the block's weight seem to be when it is floating?

11·3 Energy

After completing this section,
you will be able to

- **compare** potential energy and
  kinetic energy.
- **describe** some forms of
  energy.
- **state** the Law of Conservation
  of Energy.

The key terms in this section are
energy
kinetic energy
Law of Conservation of Energy
potential energy

en- (in)
ergon (work)

Energy is the ability to do work. The energy from the burning of a car's fuel moves the car on a road. The energy in a dry-cell battery causes a flashlight to light.

POTENTIAL AND KINETIC ENERGY

There are two types of energy. They are potential energy and kinetic energy. **Potential energy** is stored energy. **Kinetic energy** is energy of motion.

A lump of coal has potential energy. The energy will be released as the coal burns. The water at the top of a dam has potential energy. The amount of potential energy in the water depends on the mass of the water and the height of the dam. As the water falls, its potential energy is changed to kinetic energy. The amount of kinetic energy in the water depends on the mass of the water and its speed at which it moves.

A roller coaster changes potential energy to kinetic energy. Look at Figure 11·10. The car of a roller coaster has the most potential energy at the high points. It has the least potential energy at the low points. The car has the most kinetic energy at the low points, where it moves the fastest.

Figure 11·10

As a roller coaster car moves downward, it converts potential energy into kinetic energy. As the car moves upward, it converts kinetic energy into potential energy.

264

FORMS OF ENERGY

All energy can be classed as potential or kinetic. However, there are several forms of energy. Some of these forms are listed below.

● *Chemical energy* is given off in chemical changes. This energy comes from the chemical bonds that are broken during a change. When fuels such as wood burn, bonds are broken, and energy is given off.

● *Mechanical energy* is the energy in moving objects. The energy of the windmill shown in Figure 11·11 is used to pump water out of the ground. The turning windmill and the running water are moving. Thus, they have mechanical energy.

Figure 11·11

Lightning is a form of electrical energy *(left)*. A turning windmill has mechanical energy *(right)*.

● *Electrical energy* is produced by moving charges. Lightning is a form of electrical energy found in nature. Televisions, radios, and many appliances are powered by electrical energy. What other household uses of electrical energy can you name?

● *Heat energy* is the energy of colliding particles. When you rub your hands together friction causes the particles in your skin to move faster. Thus they collide more often. You feel the energy of these collisions as heat. Heat energy can also be produced from electrical energy or chemical energy.

● *Sound energy* is produced by vibrating particles. The sound energy of thunder can make a house shake. The sound energy that comes from the speakers of a rock band can make a room vibrate.

• *Nuclear energy* is released when the force that holds together the nucleus of an atom is overcome. Nuclear reactions on the sun produce large amounts of heat and light. Many power companies use nuclear energy to produce electricity. And some submarines are driven by nuclear energy.

Energy can be changed from one form to another. Look at Figure 11·12. Electrical energy is changed to the mechanical energy that moves power tools like the one shown. Although energy can be changed from one form to another, the total amount of energy stays the same. The **Law of Conservation of Energy** states that energy cannot be created or destroyed but can be changed from one form to another.

Figure 11·12
The chemical energy in fuel is changed into electrical energy *(A)*. This energy is carried to many places *(B)*. Electrical energy is changed into mechanical energy *(C)*.

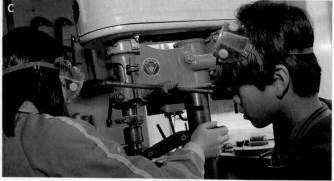

REVIEW

1. What is the difference between potential and kinetic energy?
2. Describe chemical energy, nuclear energy, and sound energy.
3. What is the Law of Conservation of Energy?

CHALLENGE Explain how water at the bottom of a waterfall can have both potential energy and kinetic energy.

11·4 Work and Power

FORCE AND WORK

You may think of work as a job to earn money. Or you may think of work as a task that is difficult. To a scientist the word *work* has a special meaning. **Work** is the use of a force to move an object through a distance.

Suppose you have to move a desk. If you try to push the desk, you are using force. The force that is applied to do work is called the **effort force**. If you cannot push against the desk with enough force, the desk will not move. Thus, no work will be done. The force of friction between the desk and the carpet is greater than your effort force. A force that opposes an effort force is called a **resistance force**.

To move an object, you must use an effort force that is greater than the resistance force. If you can push with an effort force greater than the force of friction the desk will move. Work will be done.

Now suppose you lift the desk and carry it across the room. Lifting the desk is work. Carrying the desk is not work. Why is this so? For work to be done, an effort force must overcome a resistance force. When you lift the desk, your effort force overcomes the gravitational force. However, there is no resistance to carrying the desk. The lift force does no work in moving the desk horizontally.

Figure 11·13
To move an object, you must apply an effort force that is greater than the resistance force.

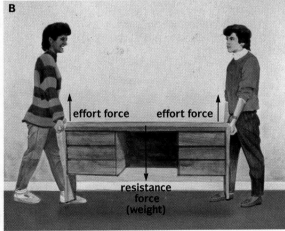

The formula that is shown below is used to calculate work.

$$W = Fd$$

In the formula, W stands for the work done, F stands for the force, and d stands for the distance through which the force moves.

Sample Problem

A person uses a force of 200 N to move a box a distance of 5 m. How much work is done?

1. Write the formula.

$$W = Fd$$

2. Substitute the amounts given in the problem for the symbols in the formula.

$$W = 200\ N \times 5\ m$$

3. Determine the unit that will be part of the answer. The unit will be newton-meters (N·m).

$$W = 200 \times 5\ N \cdot m$$

4. Complete the calculations that are required.

$$W = 1000\ N \cdot m$$

The amount of work done is 1000 N·m. Work is also measured in units called joules (joolz). A *joule* (J) is a unit of work and is equal to one newton-meter. Thus the amount of work done is 1000 J.

Figure 11·14

It takes 1000 J of work to push this crate a distance of 5 m. How much work is needed to push the crate 8 m?

effort force   200 N

How Can Work Be Calculated?

MATERIALS
2 blocks of wood, string, spring scale, meterstick

PROCEDURE
A. Draw a data table like the one shown.
B. Obtain two blocks of wood. Tie a piece of string around each block so that you can pick up the blocks by the string.
C. Use a spring scale to weigh each block. Record the weights in the data table.
D. Using the spring scale and a steady pull, lift block *A* 0.5 m high. Record the force needed to lift the block.
E. Using the spring scale and a steady pull, slide block *A* 0.5 m along the floor. Be sure the spring scale is held parallel to the floor. Record the force needed to slide the block.

F. Repeat step **D**, using block *B*.
G. Repeat step **E**, using block *B*.

BLOCK	WEIGHT (N)	FORCE NEEDED TO LIFT (N)	FORCE NEEDED TO SLIDE (N)
A			
B			

RESULTS AND CONCLUSIONS
1. Calculate the work done in lifting each block.
2. Calculate the work done in sliding each block.
3. Is there a difference between the amount of work done to slide a block and that done to lift the same block? Explain your answer.
4. Is there a difference in the amount of work done lifting block *A* compared with lifting block *B*? Explain your answer.

POWER

Like the term *work*, the term *power* has a special meaning in science. **Power** is the amount of work done in a period of time. Power can be calculated by using the formula shown below.

$$P = \frac{W}{t}$$

In the formula, P stands for power, W stands for work, and t stands for time.

Sample Problem
A person who weighs 600 N gets on an elevator. The elevator lifts the person 6 m in 10 seconds. How much power is used to lift the person?

1. Write the formula.

$$P = \frac{W}{t}$$

2. Substitute the amounts given in the problem for the symbols in the formula. Recall that work is equal to force times distance.

$$P = \frac{600 \text{ N} \times 6 \text{ m}}{10 \text{ s}}$$

3. Determine the unit that will be part of the answer. In this case the unit will be newton-meters per second, or joules per second (J/s).

$$P = \frac{600 \times 6}{10} \text{ J/s}$$

4. Complete the calculations that are required.

$$P = 360 \text{ J/s}$$

The elevator uses 360 J/s of power. The unit of power is also called a watt. A *watt* (W) is a unit of power equal to one joule per second.

Figure 11·15

Power is the amount of work done in a period of time. The faster these elevators move, the more power they use.

REVIEW

1. What is the scientific meaning of the term *work*?
2. What is an effort force? What is a resistance force?
3. How is a newton-meter related to a joule?
4. Calculate the amount of work done in each of the following.
   a. You use a force of 50 N to push a chair 10 m.
   b. A box that weighs 20 N is lifted 0.20 m.
   c. A force of 6.0 N is used to pull a cart 50 m.

CHALLENGE It takes 8.0 N of force to push a box that weighs 24.0 N. If the box is pushed a distance of 15.0 m and then lifted to a table 0.8 m high, how much work is done?

11·5 Simple Machines

A **simple machine** is a device used to change the size, direction, or speed of a force being used to do work. Simple machines do work with a single movement. There are six classes of simple machines: inclined plane, wedge, screw, lever, pulley, and wheel and axle.

Many machines make work easier by reducing the amount of effort force needed. They are said to multiply the effort force. Some machines change the direction in which a force is applied. Others multiply the distance through which an effort force moves. Some machines multiply speed.

MECHANICAL ADVANTAGE

The number of times a machine multiplies an effort force is called the **mechanical advantage** of that machine. The mechanical advantage of a machine may be calculated by using this formula.

$$MA = \frac{R}{E}$$

In the formula, MA stands for mechanical advantage, R stands for resistance force, and E stands for effort force. Look at Figure 11·16. How large is the resistance force?

After completing this section, you will be able to

- **name** and **give examples** of the six classes of simple machines.
- **calculate** mechanical advantage.
- **describe** factors that affect the efficiency of a machine.

The key terms in this section are
efficiency
inclined plane
lever
mechanical advantage
pulley
screw
simple machine
wedge
wheel and axle

machina (a device)

Figure 11·16
With this simple machine an effort force of 200 N can be used to move a resistance force of 2000 N.

resistance force
2000 N

effort
force
200 N

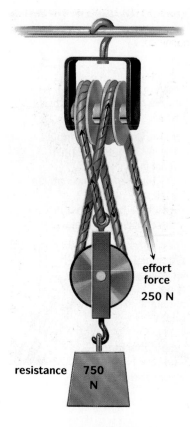

Figure 11·17

This block and tackle is a pulley system with a mechanical advantage of 3. How great a resistance force can be lifted with an effort force of 600 N?

effort force 250 N

resistance 750 N

Sample Problem

A pulley uses a force of 250 N to lift an object that weighs 750 N. Find the mechanical advantage.

1. Write the formula.

$$MA = \frac{R}{E}$$

2. Substitute the amounts given in the problem for the symbols in the formula.

$$MA = \frac{750 \text{ N}}{250 \text{ N}}$$

3. Find the unit that will be part of the answer. Both the effort and the resistance are in newtons, so the units cancel. There will be no unit.

$$MA = \frac{750}{250}$$

4. Complete the calculations that are required.

$$MA = 3$$

The mechanical advantage is 3. This means the effort force is multiplied three times.

EFFICIENCY

Efficiency compares the amount of work a machine does with the amount of work put into the machine. No machine is 100 percent efficient. Some of the work put into a machine must be used to overcome friction. Recall that friction is a force that opposes motion.

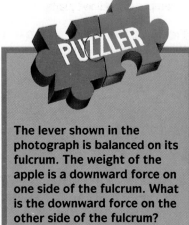

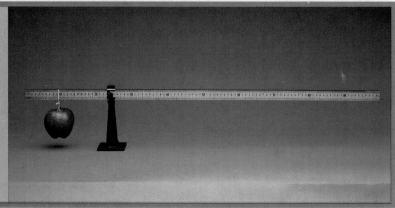

The lever shown in the photograph is balanced on its fulcrum. The weight of the apple is a downward force on one side of the fulcrum. What is the downward force on the other side of the fulcrum? Where is this force located?

Look at Figure 11·18. If someone puts 60 J of work into the jack and produces 36 J of work, the jack is 60 percent efficient. This means 40 percent of the work put into the jack is used to overcome friction. If you could touch the jack, you would feel the heat that the friction produces. The moving parts in many machines are oiled to reduce friction. This improves the efficiency of the machine. What other benefit is there in oiling a machine?

INCLINED PLANES

Have you ever used a ramp? A ramp is an **inclined plane**, a simple machine that consists of a sloping surface. An inclined plane is often used to raise a heavy object to a higher position.

Figure 11·18
An automobile jack contains simple machines.

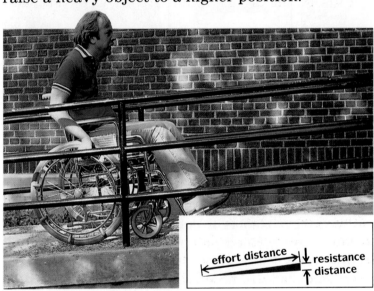

effort distance → ↓ resistance distance ↑

Figure 11·19
A ramp is an inclined plane.

Look at Figure 11·19. The effort distance is the length of the ramp. The resistance distance is the height of the ramp. The force needed to lift an object by using an inclined plane is much less than that needed to lift the object straight up. Although the effort force is smaller, it is applied for a greater distance because the length of the inclined plane is greater than its height.

The mechanical advantage of an inclined plane can be found by dividing its length by its height. It is easier to do a job with a long inclined plane than with a short one.

Figure 11·20

An ax is an example of a wedge *(A)*. A screw is an inclined plane wrapped around a cylinder *(B)*.

A **wedge** is a modified inclined plane that has a thick end and a thinner or sharper end. Knives and other cutting tools are wedges. Look at Figure 11·20*A*. This wedge is two inclined planes placed back to back. When you use an ax to split wood, a downward effort force is changed to a force that pushes apart the fibers of the wood. The longer and thinner the wedge, the smaller the effort force needed.

A screw also is a modified inclined plane. A **screw** is an inclined plane that is wound around a cylinder. Look at Figure 11·20*B*. With each turn, the screw moves up or down a certain distance. A small effort force is applied through a large distance.

LEVERS

A **lever** is a rigid bar that moves around a fixed point. The fixed point is called the *fulcrum*. The distance from the effort force to the fulcrum is the *effort arm* of the lever. The distance from the resistance force to the fulcrum is the *resistance arm*.

There are three classes of levers. They are grouped by the positions of the fulcrum, effort force, and resistance force. In a first class lever, the fulcrum is located between the effort force and the resistance force. Look at Figure 11·21*C*. Depending on how it is used, a first class lever may multiply effort force or speed, but not both at once. Crowbars and seesaws are first class levers.

In a second class lever, the resistance force is between the effort force and the fulcrum. Look at Figure 11·21A. The effort arm is longer than the resistance arm. A second class lever multiplies effort force and decreases speed. Wheelbarrows and bottle openers are other second class levers.

In a third class lever, the effort force is between the resistance force and the fulcrum. A small resistance force requires a larger effort force. Third-class levers multiply speed and distance. Rakes, fishing rods, and shovels are third-class levers.

PULLEYS

A **pulley** is a machine made up of a rope that turns around a wheel. There are two kinds of pulleys. A fixed pulley does not move. Figure 11·22B on the next page shows a single fixed pulley. It changes the direction of a force.

Figure 11·21
A nutcracker is a second class lever (A). A rake is a third class lever (B). A seesaw is a first class lever (C).

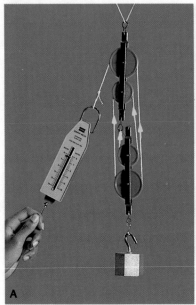

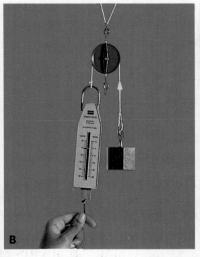

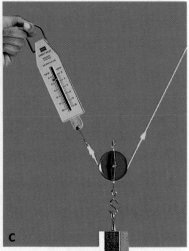

Figure 11·22

A combination of fixed pulleys and movable pulleys *(A)*. A single fixed pulley *(B)*. A single movable pulley *(C)*.

A pulley that moves with the resistance is a movable pulley. Look at Figure 11·22*C*. Two strands of rope support the resistance in the movable pulley. The force needed to lift an object with a movable pulley is half that needed with a fixed pulley.

Pulleys may be combined as in Figure 11·22*A*. The mechanical advantage of all pulleys can be found by counting the number of strands that support the resistance. What is the mechanical advantage of the pulley combination in Figure 11·22*A*?

WHEEL AND AXLE

A **wheel and axle** is a simple machine made up of two wheels that turn around a pivot. Examples include doorknobs, screwdrivers, and steering wheels. The larger wheel is usually the effort wheel. The smaller wheel, or the axle, is usually the resistance wheel. A small effort force applied to the larger wheel results in a large force at the axle.

REVIEW

1. What is a simple machine?
2. List the six classes of simple machines.
3. A machine can be used to move a 500-N object with a force of 20 N. What is the machine's mechanical advantage?
4. What is meant by the efficiency of a machine?

CHALLENGE How many simple machines are there in a pair of scissors? Name them.

11·6 Compound Machines

Many devices contain more than one simple machine. A machine that is made up of two or more simple machines is called a **compound machine**.

A hand lawn mower is made up of several machines. The handle is a lever. The blade is a wedge. There are also wheels connected to an axle, as well as many screws and bolts. The mechanical advantage of a lawn mower would be difficult to find. You would have to know the mechanical advantage of each simple machine in it. The mechanical advantage of the lawn mower could then be found by multiplying all of the mechanical advantages together. The mechanical advantage of any compound machine is the product of the mechanical advantages of its simple machines.

A bicycle is a compound machine. The wheels are wheel and axle systems. The pedals make up another wheel and axle system. Look at Figure 11·23 on the next page. Each pedal moves in a circle,

SCIENCE & TECHNOLOGY

Someday a tunnel beneath the English Channel will connect Folkestone, England, with Calais, France. Construction of the tunnel has been planned for many decades. But the machines that will make it possible have only recently been developed.

Tunnel-boring machines are called TBMs. These machines vary, depending on the type of soil they must bore through. The type of TBM that will start from the English side of the Channel has 49 steel disks and 236 picks. The disks will slice through rock, and the picks will chop off chunks and fling them backward onto a

conveyor belt. The conveyor belt will bring the fist-sized chunks to cars that will roll on tracks and take the chunks out of the tunnel.

If all goes well the TBMs will progress at an average speed of 1.5 m per hour. Machines will start at each side and meet in the middle of the tunnel. Only the middle 50 m will be drilled by hand. The tunnel should be completed in the early 1990s.

277

like a wheel. The rod around which the pedals turn is an axle. A bicycle also contains several levers. What are some levers in a bicycle?

A bicycle is a machine that multiplies speed, not effort force. You can adjust the mechanical advantage of a bicycle by using gears. *Gears* are toothed wheels. The pedals turn a gear that is connected by a chain to gears on the rear wheel. Each of the gears on the rear wheel is a different size.

Each rear gear is smaller than the front gear. Thus the wheel turns more times than do the pedals. The ratio of the number of teeth on the front gear to the number of teeth on the rear gear tells how many times the wheel turns for one turn of the pedals.

A ten-speed bicycle has two gears in front and five gears in back. Thus, ten combinations of gears are possible. In the lowest gear the ratio of gear teeth is the lowest. In this gear it is easy to pedal the bicycle. A small effort force is needed. However, the bicycle moves slowly. For one turn of the pedals, the wheel goes through about 1.4 turns.

In the highest gear the ratio of gear teeth is the highest. One turn of the pedals causes more than 3.5 turns of the wheel. The bicycle moves quickly, but a larger effort force is needed to turn the pedals.

Figure 11·23

A bicycle contains many simple machines.

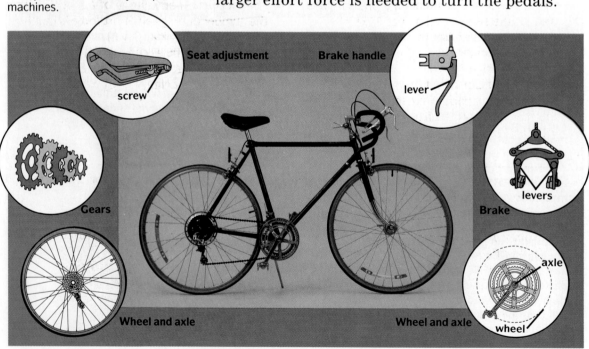

Seat adjustment screw

Brake handle lever

Gears

Brake levers

Wheel and axle

Wheel and axle axle wheel

REVIEW

1. Name two compound machines.

2. What are two simple machines in a bicycle?

CHALLENGE The mechanical advantage of a lever is 6. The mechanical advantage of a pulley system is 5. What is the combined mechanical advantage of a compound machine made up of the lever and the pulley system?

CHAPTER SUMMARY

The main ideas in this chapter are listed below. Read these statements before you answer the Chapter Review questions.

- A force is a push or a pull. Several kinds of forces exist. They are gravitational force, electrical force, magnetic force, friction, nuclear force, and weak interactions. (11·1)
- The amount of force acting on an object is measured in newtons. Weight is a measure of the amount of gravity between two objects. (11·1)
- A buoyant force is an upward force exerted on an object by a fluid. The amount of force exerted on the object depends on the amount of water displaced by the object. (11·2)
- Pressure is a force acting on a unit of surface area. In a closed container the pressure of a fluid is the same at all points. (11·2)
- Energy is the ability to do work. The two types of energy are potential energy and kinetic energy. (11·3)
- The Law of Conservation of Energy states that energy cannot be created or destroyed but can be changed from one form to another. (11·3)

- Work is done when an object is moved through a distance because of a force acting on the object. A joule is a unit of work. (11·4)
- An effort force is a force that is applied to an object to do work. A resistance force is a force that opposes an effort force. (11·4)
- Power is the rate at which work is done. A watt is a unit of power. (11·4)
- A simple machine changes the size, direction, or speed of a force that is being used to do work. The six classes of simple machines are inclined plane, wedge, screw, lever, pulley, and wheel and axle. (11·5)
- The mechanical advantage of a machine is the number of times an effort force is multiplied by the machine. (11·5)
- Compound machines consist of two or more simple machines. A bicycle is an example of a compound machine. (11·6)

The key terms in this chapter are listed below. Use each term in a sentence that shows the meaning of the term.

buoyant force	kinetic energy	pulley
compound machine	Law of Conservation of Energy	resistance force
efficiency	lever	screw
effort force	mechanical advantage	simple machine
energy	potential energy	wedge
force	power	wheel and axle
inclined plane	pressure	work

Chapter Review

VOCABULARY

Use the key terms from the previous page to complete the following sentences correctly.

1. _____ is energy of motion.
2. A/an _____ is a push or a pull.
3. An upward force exerted on an object by a fluid is called a/an _____.
4. The _____ states that energy cannot be created or destroyed.
5. Force acting on a unit area is called _____.
6. The number of times an effort force is multiplied by a machine is called the _____ of the machine.
7. A combination of two or more simple machines is called a/an _____.
8. A/an _____ is a machine that consists of a long sloping surface.
9. The amount of work done in a period of time is called _____.
10. A/an _____ is an inclined plane wound around a cylinder.

CONCEPTS

Look at the drawing below, and answer the questions.

1. What class of lever is shown?
2. Where is the fulcrum of the lever?
3. If person B will be the effort force, where is the resistance force?
4. What kind of energy does person B have before he jumps from the platform?
5. When person B jumps from the platform, what force will cause him to move downward, toward the lever?

Write the letter of the word or phrase that best completes the sentence on the left.

6. If the force acting on an object increases, the mass of the object will _____ .

7. If an object is placed into water, the weight of the object appears to _____ .

8. According to Bernoulli's principle, as the speed of a fluid increases, the pressure in a moving fluid will _____ .

9. As the speed of a moving object increases, its kinetic energy will _____ .

10. According to the Law of Conservation of Energy, as one form of energy is changed into another form, the total amount of energy will _____ .

a. increase
b. decrease
c. stay the same

Answer the following.

11. What is a simple machine? Name the classes of simple machines.
12. What causes the efficiency of machines to be less than 100 percent?
13. A person uses a force of 50 N to push a table a distance of 8 m. How much work is done?
14. A person carries a 300-N box up a flight of stairs that is 4 m high. How much work is done in carrying the box? If this work is done in 6 seconds, how much power is used?
15. Using pulleys and a 12-N effort force, a person can move a 60-N resistance force. What is the mechanical advantage of this system?

APPLICATION/ CRITICAL THINKING

1. Explain why electrical energy can be made from chemical energy, heat energy, or mechanical energy.
2. Explain why a force can sometimes be applied to an object without causing the object to move.
3. List the machines, simple or compound, that you use in a day.
4. Why is it easier to pull down on a rope over a pulley than to pull down on a rope thrown over a wood beam?
5. The pyramids of Egypt were built by workers who had to drag heavy stone blocks over long distances. Name two machines that would have made their work easier. Explain your choices.

EXTENSION

1. Find out how Bernoulli's principle is used in the carburetor of a car.
2. Find diagrams of water wheels and windmills. How do they use simple machines to turn grinding stones in a grist mill?

CHAPTER 12

HEAT

*T*his photograph is a thermogram of a boy and a dog. The thermogram was made with a heat-sensitive scanner. The scanner identified areas of different temperatures. The colors of the thermogram show which areas were warm and which areas were cold. White shows the warmest area, with orange, yellow, green, blue, magenta, and purple showing decreasing temperature. Black shows the coldest area.

You can interpret the thermogram by looking at the colors. The boy's face was very warm, but his hair and his clothing were cooler. Look at the dog's face. Like most dogs, this one had a very cold nose!

- *What causes some areas to be warmer than other areas?*
- *What other ways are there for measuring temperature?*
- *In what other ways could thermograms be useful?*

12·1 Heat Energy

After completing this section,
you will be able to

- **state** the kinetic theory.
- **distinguish** between heat and
  temperature.
- **calculate** changes in heat
  energy.

The key terms in this section are
heat   specific heat
kinetic theory   temperature

kinetikos (to move)

KINETIC THEORY

Have you ever walked past a bakery and smelled bread baking? Why do you smell flowers the instant you walk into a flower shop? Odors are caused by tiny moving particles. When these particles reach your nose, they trigger your sense of smell.

All matter is made of particles that are always moving. Observations about moving particles led scientists to develop the kinetic theory. The **kinetic theory** states that all matter is made of particles that are in constant motion. The theory also states that there are forces of attraction between particles. Without these forces, the particles in matter would drift apart.

Figure 12·1

You smell flowers when tiny moving particles from the flowers reach your nose.

The motion of the particles in matter is a form of *kinetic energy*. The faster the particles move, the more kinetic energy they have. **Temperature** is the measure of the average kinetic energy of the particles in a sample of matter. An object that has a high average kinetic energy has a high temperature. An object with a low average kinetic energy has a low temperature. If you increase the kinetic energy of an object, its temperature will rise. If you decrease the kinetic energy, the temperature will fall.

Temperature is measured with a thermometer. One type of thermometer is a long, sealed glass tube, which contains a liquid—either mercury or alcohol. As the temperature rises, the liquid rises in the tube. As the temperature falls, the liquid sinks.

You probably have seen thermometers like the one shown in Figure 12·2A. Changes in temperature affect a metal coil, which moves the pointer.

Another type of thermometer is called a digital thermometer. Look at Figure 12·2B. The digital thermometer uses electric circuits to measure temperature. The numbers on the screen show the temperature reading.

Figure 12·2

Changes in a metal coil can be used to measure temperature (A). Electric circuits can be used to measure temperature (B).

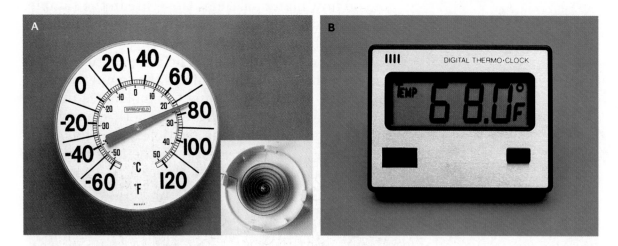

Look at Figure 12·3. On the Celsius scale the freezing point of water is 0° and the boiling point is 100°. How many degrees are there between the freezing point and boiling point of water on this scale? The Celsius degree is one hundredth of the distance between the freezing point and boiling point of water on the Celsius scale.

Figure 12·3

Notice that the units on a Celsius thermometer and the units on a Kelvin thermometer are the same size.

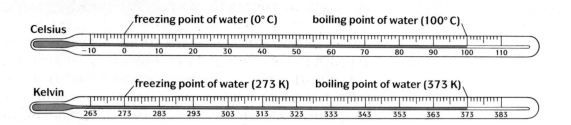

The SI temperature scale is the Kelvin scale. The units are Kelvins (K), not degrees Kelvin. One Kelvin equals one degree on the Celsius scale. On the Kelvin scale the lowest possible temperature is *absolute zero*. It is written 0 K. Absolute zero on the Kelvin scale is equal to $-273\,°C$.

CHANGES IN HEAT ENERGY

Temperature and heat are not the same. Temperature is the average kinetic energy of the particles in a sample of matter. **Heat** is the total energy of all the particles in a sample of matter. Heat depends on the average kinetic energy of the particles and on how many particles there are in the sample.

To understand the difference between temperature and heat, look at Figure 12·4. The pail is filled with water from the lake. The temperature of the water in the pail is the same as the temperature of the water in the lake. Thus the molecules in both samples have the same average kinetic energy. But the lake has more moving particles, so it has more total energy. Thus the water in the lake has more heat than does the water in the pail.

Figure 12·4

The lake has more energy than does the pail of water removed from the lake.

It is difficult to find the total energy of an object. Therefore, heat energy is measured in terms of the energy that is added to or removed from an object. Adding heat to an object gives it more energy. Different substances need different amounts of heat to cause the same change in temperature.

Heating a copper pot would cause its temperature to rise. Suppose you heated an aluminum pot that has the same mass. The same amount of heat energy would not cause the same temperature change in both pots. Look at Figure 12·5. Which pot shows the greater temperature change?

Figure 12·5
When objects, like these pots, are heated, their temperatures increase.

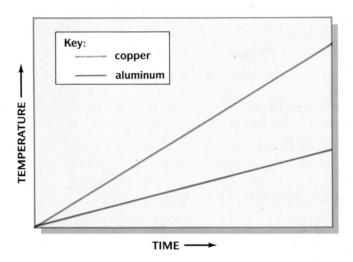

Each of the pots seems to have a different capacity for absorbing heat. The amount of heat energy needed to raise the temperature of 1.0 g of a substance by 1°C is called the specific heat capacity, or the **specific heat**. Specific heat is a measure of the ability of a substance to absorb heat. Look at Table 12·1. It shows the specific heat of several substances. Which of the substances listed in the table has the highest specific heat?

To find the amount of heat needed to raise the temperature of a sample of matter, use the following formula.

$$H = mC_p\Delta t$$

In this formula, H stands for the amount of heat, m stands for the mass of the sample, and C_p stands for the specific heat. The symbol Δt, read as "delta tee," stands for the change in temperature. The SI unit of heat energy is the joule (J). One joule is the amount of energy needed to raise the temperature of 0.24 g of water by 1°C.

Table 12·1 *Specific Heat*

SUBSTANCE	SPECIFIC HEAT (J/g°C)
Aluminum	0.90
Copper	0.38
Gold	0.13
Ice	2.06
Iron	0.45
Lead	0.13
Steam	2.06
Water	4.18

Sample Problem

How much heat is needed to raise the temperature of 10 g of iron from 20°C to 30°C?

1. Write the formula.

$$H = mC_p\Delta t$$

2. Substitute the amounts given in the problem for the symbols in the formula. The specific heat of iron can be found in Table 12·1 on page 287.

$$H = 10 \text{ g} \times 0.45 \text{ J/g°C} \times 10°C$$

3. Determine the unit that will be part of the answer. The units g and °C will cancel, leaving J as the unit.

$$H = 10 \times 0.45 \times 10 \text{ J}$$

4. Complete the calculations.

$$H = 45 \text{ J}$$

It takes 45 J of heat energy to cause the temperature of the iron to rise 10°C.

Heat transfer can be measured in the laboratory by using a tool called a *calorimeter*. One kind of calorimeter is shown in Figure 12·6. The inner chamber holds water. The thermometer is used to

Figure 12·6

A laboratory calorimeter.

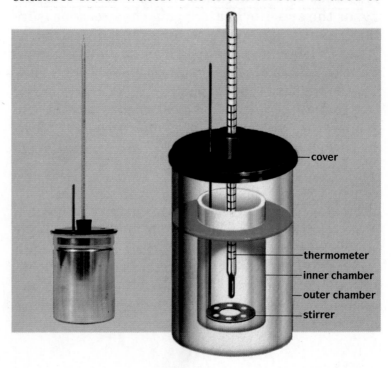

cover

thermometer

inner chamber

outer chamber

stirrer

OBJECTIVE

Measure heat exchange between samples of hot water and cold water.

MATERIALS

100-mL graduate, 2 plastic foam cups, 2 thermometers

PROCEDURE

A. Draw a data table like the one shown.
B. Add 50 mL of cold water to a cup. Add 50 mL of hot water to a second cup.
C. Measure and record the temperatures of the two samples of water.
D. Immediately pour the cold water into the cup containing the hot water. As soon as the temperature remains steady, record this temperature in the data table.
E. The mass of 50 mL of water is 50 g. The specific heat of water is 4.18 J/g°C.
   1. Calculate the heat lost by the hot water.
   2. Calculate the heat gained by the cold water.
F. Repeat steps **B, C,** and **D,** but use 25 mL of cold water and 75 mL of hot water.
   3. Calculate the heat lost by the hot water.
   4. Calculate the heat gained by the cold water.
G. Repeat steps **B, C,** and **D,** but use 75 mL of cold water and 25 mL of hot water.
   5. Calculate the heat lost by the hot water.
   6. Calculate the heat gained by the cold water.

RESULTS AND CONCLUSIONS

1. How do the calculations of heat loss and heat gain from step **E** compare?
2. How do the calculations of heat loss and heat gain from step **F** compare?
3. How do the calculations of heat loss and heat gain from step **G** compare?
4. Does this experiment support the Law of Conservation of Energy? Explain your answer.

MASS OF HOT WATER (g)	TEMPERATURE OF HOT WATER (°C)	MASS OF COLD WATER (g)	TEMPERATURE OF COLD WATER (°C)	TEMPERATURE OF MIXTURE (°C)
50		50		
75		25		
25		75		

measure changes in the water temperature when an object is placed in the water. This data can be used to calculate the amount of heat lost or gained by the water.

REVIEW

1. What is the kinetic theory?
2. How does heat differ from temperature?
3. How much heat energy must be taken away from 24 g of water to lower its temperature by 7°C?

CHALLENGE How much will the temperature of 250 g of ice change if 845 J of energy is removed?

12·2 Change of State

After completing this section, you will be able to

• **describe** how adding or removing heat causes matter to change state.

The key terms in this section are
heat of fusion
heat of vaporization

Figure 12·7 shows snow on the ground on a warm day. Even though the air temperature rose above 0°C, much of the snow did not melt. Why does it take so long for snow to melt? This question can be answered by studying what happens when matter changes from one state to another.

Figure 12·7
The air temperature is above 0°C, but some snow remains on the ground.

STATES OF MATTER

Recall that most matter on the earth exists in one of three states—solid, liquid, or gas. In the solid state, particles of matter are held together tightly. These particles cannot move around very much. In the liquid state, particles are held together loosely. Particles in a liquid move around more than do those in a solid. Thus, particles in a liquid have more energy than do those in a solid.

Particles in a gas are not held together. These particles are free to spread out. Particles in a gas move more rapidly and have more energy than do particles in either a solid or a liquid. Thus the heat energy of a gas is greater than the heat energy of a solid or liquid.

When matter changes from one state to another, the amount of heat energy in the sample of matter also changes. To change a solid to a liquid, heat must be added. To change a liquid to a gas, heat must also be added. To change a gas to a liquid or a liquid to a solid, heat must be removed.

ADDING HEAT

Figure 12·8 shows the temperature changes as a sample of ice is heated. As the ice is heated, the water molecules move faster. The temperature of the ice rises to 0°C. Then it stops rising. As more heat is added, the motion of the molecules in the ice does not increase. Instead, the molecules overcome the forces that hold them together in a solid. The molecules move farther apart, and the ice melts. The temperature at which this change takes place is called the melting point. Both the solid state and the liquid state exist at the melting point.

The amount of heat energy that will change a solid at its melting point to a liquid at the same temperature is called the **heat of fusion** (FYOO-zhuhn). Each substance has a characteristic heat of fusion. For example, it takes 334 J of energy to melt 1.0 g of ice at 0°C. Table 12·2 on page 293 shows the heat of fusion of several substances. The amount of heat energy needed to change a substance from a solid to a liquid is equal to the heat of fusion times the mass.

Figure 12·8

Heating a sample of matter causes a change in temperature or a change in state.

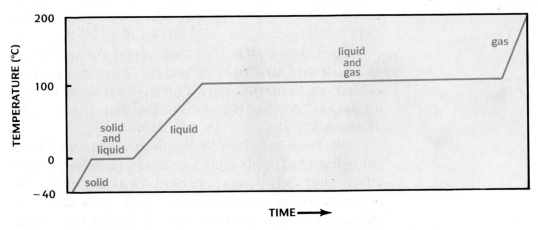

ACTIVITY What Happens During a Change of State?

OBJECTIVE
Measure the temperature of a substance as it changes from a liquid to a solid.

MATERIALS
safety goggles, lab apron, 250-mL beaker, hot plate, paradichlorobenzene, test tube, thermometer, test-tube rack, clock or watch with second hand

PROCEDURE

A. Wear safety goggles and a lab apron during this activity.
B. Draw a data table to record the time, temperature, and state of matter for at least 20 minutes.
C. Half fill a 250-mL beaker with water. On a hot plate, heat the water but do not boil it.
D. Place paradichlorobenzene in a test tube to a depth of about 2 cm. Place the test tube in the beaker of hot water.
E. After the substance has melted, put a thermometer in the test tube. When the temperature is above 65°C, remove the test tube from the beaker of hot water. Place the test tube in a test-tube rack.
F. Allow the material to cool. During this time, read the thermometer every 30 seconds. Record the time and the temperature in the data table. The first

time reading should be *0 minutes*. Also record with each reading the state of the material in the test tube. Continue until the temperature reaches 45°C.

TIME (min)	TEMPERATURE (°C)	STATE OF MATTER
0.0		
0.5		
1.0		
1.5		
2.0		
...		
20.0		

RESULTS AND CONCLUSIONS
1. Make a graph of the results. Put time on the x-axis and temperature on the y-axis.
2. On the graph, mark the point at which crystals first formed. Label this point *A*. What was the temperature at this point?
3. On the graph, mark the point at which the last of the paradichlorobenzene solidified. Label this point *B*. What was this temperature?
4. What is the freezing point of paradichlorobenzene?

Look again at Figure 12·8. After the ice melts, the temperature of the water rises. As heat is added, the kinetic energy of the water molecules increases. The temperature of the water rises until it reaches 100°C.

At 100°C the water begins to boil. Any heat added at this point does not raise the temperature of the water. However, as energy is added, the molecules overcome the forces that hold the liquid together. The water then changes from the liquid state to the gas state. Water in the gas state is called water vapor or steam. During the change of state, both liquid water and water vapor exist at the same temperature—the boiling point.

The amount of heat energy that will change a liquid at its boiling point to a gas at the same temperature is called the **heat of vaporization** (vay puhr uh ZAY shuhn). Each substance has a characteristic heat of vaporization. The heat of vaporization of water is 2260 J/g. Thus it requires 2260 J of energy to change 1.0 g of water to steam. How does this number compare with the heat of fusion of water? The heat energy needed to change a material from a liquid to a gas is equal to the heat of vaporization times the mass.

Table 12.2 *Heat of Fusion and Heat of Vaporization*

SUBSTANCE	HEAT OF FUSION (J/g)	HEAT OF VAPORIZATION (J/g)
Aluminum	376	11,370
Gold	64	1,576
Iron	276	6,290
Lead	25	861
Mercury	12	293
Silver	88	2,332
Water	334	2,260

REMOVING HEAT

It takes energy to change a liquid to a gas or to change a solid to a liquid. To reverse these changes, heat energy must be removed from the sample of matter. For example, as water vapor changes to water in the liquid state, energy is given off. If 10 g of water vapor is condensed, 22,600 J of energy is given off. What happens to the energy given off by the condensing steam in Figure 12·9?

Figure 12·9
Steam coming from the kettle is condensing on the metal surface nearby.

REVIEW

1. Explain how adding heat energy to a substance causes it to change from a solid to a liquid.

2. How does removing heat energy from a substance cause it to change from a gas to a liquid?

CHALLENGE Give two reasons why a burn caused by steam is likely to be more serious than a burn caused by boiling water.

12·3 Expansion and Gases

EXPANSION AND CONTRACTION

Most substances expand when they are heated. *Expansion* is an increase in the space between the particles in an object. Recall that when an object is heated, its particles gain energy. As these particles move faster, they collide more often. They also collide with more force. The force of the collisions pushes the particles apart. Thus the object expands, and its volume becomes larger.

A metal bridge expands on a hot day. Bridges are built with devices called expansion joints. Look at Figure 12·10. As the bridge expands, the spaces in the joints become smaller.

When an object cools, it loses energy. The particles move more slowly, and the space between them decreases. Thus the object contracts, and its volume becomes smaller. *Contraction* is a decrease in the space between the particles in an object.

Each substance expands and contracts at its own rate. You can loosen a jar's lid by using hot water. The lid becomes loose because it expands more than the jar does. The steel rods used to reinforce concrete expand at the same rate as the concrete. What would happen if they expanded at different rates?

Figure 12·10

Expansion joints in a bridge *(left)*, and reinforcing rods in concrete *(right)*.

When a gas is heated it expands. If the gas is heated in a closed container, the particles are confined by the walls of the container. As the gas particles move around, they strike the walls of the container. The force of the gas particles striking the inside of the container causes pressure. **Pressure** is force acting on a unit area. Two laws describe the relationships between the volume, pressure, and temperature of a gas. They are Boyle's law and Charles's law.

pressura (to press)

BOYLE'S LAW

According to **Boyle's law**, the volume of a gas decreases as its pressure increases if the temperature stays the same. Increasing the pressure on the gas forces the particles closer together. Thus the gas takes up less space. Decreasing the pressure on the gas allows the particles to move farther apart. Thus the gas takes up more space.

Figure 12·11

These balloons have been filled with helium from the tank.

Helium gas from tanks is sometimes used to fill balloons. The gas in the tank is under pressure. Therefore a large amount of helium can be held in a small tank. Look at Figure 12·11. The tank of helium shown was used to fill all of these balloons. The total volume of the balloons is much greater than the volume of the tank. Where is the helium under more pressure, in the tank or in the balloons?

CHARLES'S LAW

According to **Charles's law**, the volume of a gas increases as its temperature increases if the pressure stays the same. If the temperature of a gas decreases while the pressure stays the same, the volume of the gas decreases. If you blow up a balloon indoors and then take it outdoors on a cold day, the balloon will get smaller. What would happen if you took the balloon indoors again?

You can use Charles's law to explain why a hot-air balloon rises. Figure 12·12 shows the gas burner used to heat the air in the balloon. The air expands and takes up more space. Although the volume of the balloon increases, the mass does not. The density of the balloon is now less than the density of the air around it. The balloon floats in the air just as a cork floats in water.

Figure 12·12

Heating the air in a balloon causes the balloon to rise.

REVIEW

1. How is expansion different from contraction?
2. What will happen to the volume of a gas if its pressure increases and its temperature stays the same?
3. What will happen to the volume of a gas if its temperature decreases and its pressure stays the same?

CHALLENGE As a tank of helium, like the one shown in Figure 12·11, is being emptied, its temperature decreases. Explain why.

12·4 Heat Transfer

HOW HEAT MOVES

Heat moves from an area of higher temperature to an area of lower temperature. This transfer takes place by conduction, convection, or radiation.

Conduction is the transfer of heat by direct contact between particles. When particles with a large amount of kinetic energy strike particles with less kinetic energy, energy is transferred to the lower-energy particles. This transfer continues until all of the particles have the same kinetic energy. Most metals are good conductors. Wood, plastic, glass, and all gases are poor conductors. Why do some pots and pans have plastic handles?

Convection is heat transfer that takes place in fluids. When a fluid is heated, it expands and becomes less dense. Less-dense materials rise above denser materials. Hot liquids and gases rise. Cold liquids and gases fall. These movements create currents that carry heat energy.

How does heat from the sun reach the earth through space? In space there is no matter to carry the energy. The sun's energy travels in the form of waves through space. The transfer of energy by waves is called **radiation**. No particles are needed to transfer energy by radiation.

After completing this section, you will be able to

- **compare** the ways in which heat is transferred.
- **describe** how heat transfer is used to control temperature.

The key terms in this section are
conduction
convection
radiation

radians (beam)

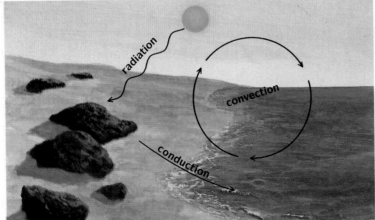

Figure 12·13
Transfer of heat can occur by conduction, convection, or radiation.

When waves of heat energy strike the earth, some are absorbed and some are reflected. Dark colors absorb more energy than do light colors. Dark-colored rocks on a beach would absorb energy faster than would the light-colored sand. If you touched the rocks and the sand on a sunny day, the rocks would feel warmer than the sand.

HEATING AND COOLING SYSTEMS

Heat transfer is used to control the air temperature in houses and other buildings. Heating systems transfer heat by conduction, by convection, by radiation, or by a combination of these. Fireplaces heat a room mainly by radiation. Hot-water and steam heating systems use all three types of heat transfer. The hot water or steam transfers heat to the radiator by conduction. The air near the radiator is heated by radiation. Convection currents carry warm air through the room.

SCIENCE & TECHNOLOGY

This photograph is a thermogram, a picture that shows heat. All objects give off heat, which can be detected by a special camera. The camera changes the pattern of heat into a picture. The differences in temperatures are shown as colors. Usually the warmest temperatures show up as white, red, and yellow. The cooler temperatures show up as green, blue, and black.

One town in Michigan used thermograms to show where its residents were losing heat from their homes during the winter. Windows and doors released most of the heat that was lost. Roofs that were not well insulated also released heat. Many homeowners responded to the thermograms by insulating attics, plugging leaks in doors and windows, and closing in porches.

Thermograms taken of entire cities show what kinds of buildings lose the most heat. By pinpointing heat losses, architects and engineers learn how to design buildings to conserve more energy.

298

Look at Figure 12·14. In a steam heating system, heat from the furnace boils water to form steam. The steam rises into radiators. There the steam condenses, giving off heat to the room. The water flows back to the boiler, where it is heated again. In a hot-water heating system, the water is heated but not boiled. A pump forces the hot water through radiators and then back to the furnace.

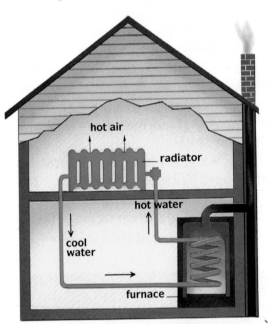

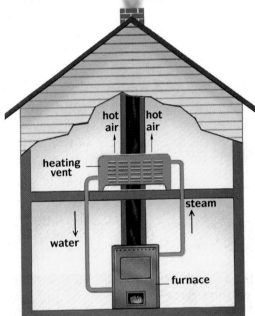

Hot-water heating system

Steam heating system

Figure 12·14

Hot-water heating system *(left)*, and steam heating system *(right)*.

Heat transfer is also used in cooling systems. Refrigerators and air conditioners are cooling systems. They use the process of evaporation to absorb heat. In cooling systems a liquid flows through metal tubing. As the liquid evaporates in the tubing, heat is absorbed from the air in the refrigerator or from the air in the room. Freon (FREE ahn) is the liquid most often used in cooling systems.

The Freon gas then flows to a compressor. The compressor increases the pressure of the gas and thus changes it back to a liquid. As the Freon gas condenses, heat is given off. The liquid Freon then flows back into the tubing, and the cycle is repeated. Why does the back of a refrigerator or the exhaust from an air conditioner feel warm?

INSULATION

The heating and cooling systems in a building have to work against natural heat transfer processes. When the weather is cold and a building is being heated, the building is warmer than the air around it. The building loses heat. When the weather is warm or hot and a building is being cooled, the air around the building is warmer than the building. Thus the building absorbs heat.

Most of this heat exchange takes place by conduction. So many buildings are insulated. Insulation does not stop heat transfer, but it slows the process. Materials that are poor conductors are good insulators. Most insulation is made of fluffy materials. The air spaces in these materials slow the rate of heat conduction through them.

Figure 12·15A shows the fiberglass insulation that is used in buildings. Notice the air spaces between the fibers. Down jackets and quilts work on the same principle. Down is made up of tiny, fluffy feathers like the one shown in Figure 12·15B.

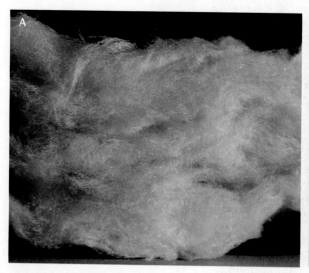

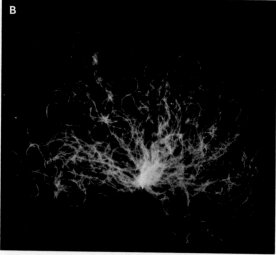

Figure 12·15
Fiberglass building insulation (A). Down feather (B).

REVIEW

1. Compare and contrast conduction and convection.
2. Define and give an example of radiation.
3. How does a refrigerator lower the temperature of food?

CHALLENGE What is the name given to the amount of heat absorbed by Freon as it evaporates?

12·5 Heat Engines

Heat energy can be changed into mechanical energy and be used to do work. A **heat engine** is a device that changes the heat energy from burning fuel into mechanical energy.

A steam engine is a kind of heat engine called an external combustion engine. In an *external combustion engine*, fuel is burned outside the engine. Look at the locomotive shown in Figure 12·16. A fuel such as coal is burned to boil water to steam. Steam under high pressure pushes a piston. The energy of the moving piston is transferred to the wheels.

After completing this section, you will be able to

- **describe** how a heat engine works.
- **give examples** of heat engines.

The key term in this section is **heat engine**

Figure 12·16
The steam engine in this locomotive is an external combustion engine.

The gasoline engines and diesel engines in cars and trucks are internal combustion engines. In an *internal combustion engine*, fuel is burned inside the engine. The engines in most cars have four, six, or eight cylinders. Each cylinder is a container with two openings. The openings are controlled by valves. As the fuel burns, pistons move up and down in the cylinders. The motion of the pistons turns a rod called the crankshaft.

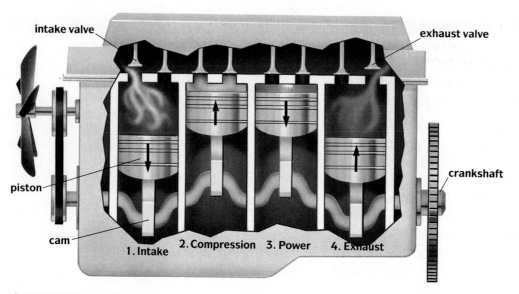

intake valve

exhaust valve

piston

crankshaft

cam

1. Intake   2. Compression   3. Power   4. Exhaust

Figure 12·17
A four-stroke engine.

Figure 12·17 shows a four-stroke engine. Each upward or downward motion of a piston is a stroke. Look at the figure as you read about this engine.

1. During the *intake stroke*, the piston moves downward. This causes a mixture of fuel and air to enter the cylinder through the intake valve.

2. During the *compression stroke*, the intake valve closes and the piston moves upward. The fuel-air mixture is compressed into a smaller space.

3. During the *power stroke*, a spark plug creates a spark that ignites the gases in the cylinder. As the gases ignite and expand, they force the piston downward. This is the only stroke in which burning takes place.

4. During the *exhaust stroke*, the exhaust valve opens to let out the waste products of the burning reaction. This stroke is followed by the intake stroke of the next cycle.

A diesel engine works differently. It has no spark plugs. A diesel engine compresses the fuel more than does a gasoline engine. As a result, the compressed gases become very hot—so hot that they burn spontaneously. However, the rest of the cycle is the same as for other four-stroke engines.

Jet engines are also internal combustion engines. But there are no pistons. Instead, hot gases produced by burning fuel are forced out of the engine. The escaping gases cause the jet to move forward. Rocket engines work in a similar way.

REVIEW

1. What is a heat engine? Give two examples of heat engines.
2. Describe how a four-stroke gasoline engine works.

CHALLENGE Sometimes fuel in a cylinder in a car's engine will continue to ignite after the engine has been turned off and the spark plugs are no longer firing. This process is called dieseling. Why is this name appropriate?

CHAPTER SUMMARY

The main ideas in this chapter are listed below. Read these statements before you answer the Chapter Review questions.

- The kinetic theory states that particles of matter are always in motion. Forces of attraction prevent the particles from drifting apart. (12·1)
- Temperature is the measure of the average kinetic energy of the particles in a substance. Heat is the total kinetic energy of all the particles in a sample of matter. (12·1)
- Specific heat is the amount of heat energy needed to raise the temperature of 1.0 g of a substance by 1°C. (12·1)
- Matter will change from one state to another if heat is added to or removed from the sample of matter. (12·2)
- The amount of heat energy needed to change a solid to a liquid is called the heat of fusion. The amount of heat energy needed to change a liquid to a gas is called the heat of vaporization. (12·2)

- Most substances expand when heated and contract when cooled. (12·3)
- Boyle's law states that if the temperature of a gas stays the same and the pressure increases, the volume of the gas will decrease. (12·3)
- Charles's law states that if pressure of a gas remains the same and the temperature increases, the volume of the gas will increase. (12·3)
- Conduction, convection, and radiation are the three different ways in which heat energy is transferred from one sample of matter to another. (12·4)
- Heat engines convert heat energy to mechanical energy. (12·5)

The key terms in this chapter are listed below. Use each term in a sentence that shows the meaning of the term.

Boyle's law	convection	heat of fusion	pressure	temperature
Charles's law	heat	heat of vaporization	radiation	
conduction	heat engine	kinetic theory	specific heat	

Chapter Review

Identify each statement as True or False. If a statement is false, replace the underlined term with a term that makes the statement true.

1. Heat is transferred in moving fluids by the process of <u>conduction</u>.
2. The <u>kinetic theory</u> states that all matter is made of tiny particles in constant motion.
3. Force per unit area is called <u>heat</u>.
4. <u>Temperature</u> is the measure of the average kinetic energy of a sample of matter.
5. The amount of heat energy that will change a liquid to a gas is called the <u>specific heat</u>.
6. The amount of heat energy needed to raise the temperature of 1.0 g of a substance by 1 °C is called the <u>heat of vaporization</u>.
7. A <u>heat engine</u> is a device that changes heat energy into mechanical energy.
8. The transfer of heat energy by direct contact between particles is called <u>radiation</u>.
9. <u>Heat of fusion</u> is the amount of heat energy that will change a solid to a liquid.
10. The total energy of the particles in a sample of matter is called <u>pressure</u>.

CONCEPTS

Write the letter of the term that best matches the statement on the left.

1. The intake valve closes, and the piston moves upward.
2. This follows the exhaust stroke.
3. A spark ignites the gases in the cylinder.
4. A mixture of fuel and air is drawn into the cylinder.
5. The waste products of the burning reaction are released from the cylinder.

a. intake stroke
b. compression stroke
c. power stroke
d. exhaust stroke

Complete the following sentences.

6. Particles of matter in _____ state move around the least freely.
7. The lowest possible temperature, 0 K, is called _____.
8. As a solid is heated, its temperature rises and then levels off. When the temperature levels off, the solid is _____.

9. If the pressure on a gas decreases and the temperature stays the same, the volume will _____ .
10. If the temperature of a gas increases and the pressure stays the same, the volume will _____ .

Answer the following.
11. Compare the movements of the particles found in gases, liquids, and solids.
12. How much heat is needed to raise the temperature of 100 g of iron from 50°C to 70°C?
13. How much heat is needed to raise the temperature of 20 g of water from 10°C to 40°C?
14. List and explain the three ways in which heat can be transferred from one sample of matter to another.
15. Where do heat engines get their energy? What kind of energy do they produce?

1. Explain why winter clothes are usually dark colored and summer clothes are usually light colored.
2. The radiators used in steam and hot-water heating systems are usually built to have a large surface area. What advantange is there in this design?
3. Water in the liquid state expands when heated and contracts when cooled. Why isn't water used to make thermometers?
4. Explain why the Great Lakes usually remain unfrozen in the winter while other lakes at the same latitude freeze.

1. The diesel engine is used in many trucks and is sometimes used in automobiles. Do some research to find advantages and disadvantages of the diesel engine.
2. The insulation used in buildings is rated for its R-value. Find out how these ratings are determined and what R-value is recommended for the area in which you live.
3. Although James Watt did not make the first steam engine, his name is often associated with the invention of the steam engine. Where were steam engines first used? What were they used for?

CHAPTER 13

WAVES AND SOUND

*T*his photograph was made by using a Scanning Laser Acoustic Micrograph, or SLAM. This device uses sound to make an image of an object. The object shown is a computer microchip.

The SLAM produces sound waves. These sound waves pass through the object and strike a gold mirror. The sound waves make the mirror vibrate. A laser scans the surface of the mirror and detects its movement. A computer attached to the laser produces an image and adds color to it. The color makes it possible to identify separate areas of the object.

- *How are sounds made?*
- *How do sounds travel through matter?*
- *How are sounds used?*

13·1 Properties of Waves

After completing this section, you will be able to

- **compare** transverse waves with compressional waves.
- **identify** the parts of a wave.

The key terms in this section are
amplitude
compression
compressional wave
frequency
rarefaction
transverse wave
wavelength

ENERGY AND WAVES

If you drop a pebble into a still pond, a ripple will spread out in all directions across the water. What causes this ripple to form? The falling pebble has kinetic energy. When the pebble hits the water, this energy is transferred to water molecules. These molecules then transfer energy to the molecules near them. Thus the energy moves through the water in the form of a wave. A *wave* is a disturbance that travels through space and matter.

The energy carried by the wave causes water molecules to move from their original positions. In a water wave the molecules move in an up-and-down pattern. If a piece of wood were floating in the water, it would bob up and down as the wave passed. However, the wood would not move along with the wave. After the wave passed, the wood would be in its original position. The water molecules do not move with the wave either. The water molecules move up and down. Only the wave of energy moves outward.

Figure 13·1

These ripples are waves that carry energy through the water.

308

The wave in the pond is caused by the disturbance of the falling pebble. Waves also can be caused by repeated disturbances. If you drop one pebble into the pond each second, you will cause one wave each second. The waves will move outward in a series of rings, one for each pebble you drop.

KINDS OF WAVES

Sound waves and water waves are mechanical waves. *Mechanical waves* are waves that transfer energy through matter. The matter through which mechanical waves travel is called the *medium*. Sound waves carry energy through gases, like air, and through some liquids and solids. Water waves carry energy through water. Some waves, such as radio waves, X rays, and light waves, do not need matter to transfer energy.

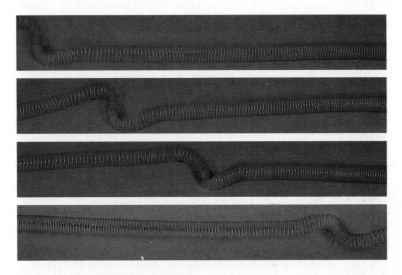

Figure 13·2
In a transverse wave, matter vibrates at right angles to the direction in which the wave travels.

There are two kinds of mechanical waves: transverse waves and compressional waves. Water waves are transverse waves. In a **transverse wave**, particles of matter vibrate up and down at right angles to the direction in which the wave travels. Figure 13·2 shows a transverse wave moving along a spring. After the wave passed through the spring, the spring returned to its original position. Energy moved from one end of the spring to the other. Did any matter move from one end of the spring to the other?

tranversus (to turn across)

compressare (to press together)

Sound waves are compressional waves. In a **compressional wave**, particles of matter move back and forth parallel to the direction of the wave. Compressional waves are also called longitudinal waves. Figure 13·3 shows a compressional wave on a spring. The movement that starts this wave pushes parts of the spring closer together and then returns the spring to its original position. The section of the spring that is pushed together is said to be compressed. As one section of the spring is compressed, it pushes on the section of the spring in front of it. Thus the compression moves along the spring. A **compression** is the part of a compressional wave where particles of matter are pushed close together. Look again at Figure 13·3. Behind the compression is an area in which the spring is stretched. The part of a compressional wave where particles of matter are spread apart is called a **rarefaction** (rair uh FAK shuhn).

Figure 13·3

In a compressional wave, matter vibrates parallel to the direction in which the wave travels.

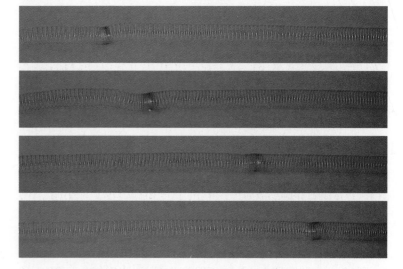

CHARACTERISTICS OF WAVES

If you were to graph the amount of compression in a series of compressional waves on a spring, you would get a graph that looks like a series of transverse waves. Look at Figure 13·4. The straight line represents the condition of the spring when no waves move along it. As you read about the characteristics of waves, refer to Figure 13·4. Compare the graph with the drawings of waves.

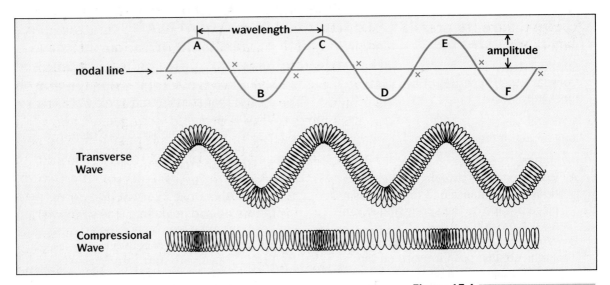

Notice in Figure 13·4 that several points on the graph are labeled. Points *A*, *C*, and *E* are crests. A *crest* shows the top of a transverse wave. It can also show the point of greatest compression in a compressional wave. Points *B*, *D*, and *F* are troughs (trawfs). A *trough* is the bottom of a transverse wave. It can also show the point of greatest rarefaction. The points marked *X* are called nodes. A *node* is a point halfway between a crest and a trough. The line that connects the nodes is the nodal line. The *nodal line* shows the original position of the matter that carries the wave.

The distance from point *A* to point *C* is a wavelength. The **wavelength** is the distance from any point on a wave to the same point on the next wave.

Another characteristic of waves is amplitude (AM pluh tood). The **amplitude** of a wave is a measure of the greatest movement of matter from its normal resting position. Amplitude can be measured from a crest to the nodal line or from a trough to the nodal line. The greater the amplitude of a wave, the greater the amount of energy in the wave. Compare the waves shown in Figure 13·5. Which wave has the greater amplitude?

Waves can be also described in terms of frequency. **Frequency** is the number of waves that pass a given point each second. Frequency depends

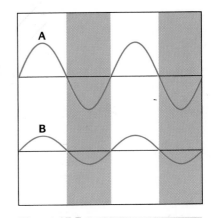

Figure 13·5
These two waves have different amplitudes. How do the wavelengths compare?

What Are the Properties of Waves?

OBJECTIVE
Compare the properties of two kinds of mechanical waves.

MATERIALS
long spring, meterstick, tape

PROCEDURE
A. With a partner, stretch a spring along the floor for a distance of 3 m. Place a small piece of tape on the spring about 1 m away from you.

B. While your partner holds one end of the spring steady, push forward on the spring to produce a compression. Adjust the tension of the spring by gathering some of the coils until you can produce a compressional wave that is easy to see.

C. With a forward and backward motion, produce a single compression.
  1. Describe what happens to the spring.
  2. Describe the motion of the tape.

D. Now use a greater force to produce a single compression on the spring.
  3. How does this wave compare with the wave produced in step **C**?

E. While your partner holds one end of the spring, use a flick of the wrist to produce a pulse that starts a transverse wave in the spring.
  4. Describe the motion of the tape.

F. Now produce a stronger transverse pulse.
  5. How does this wave compare with the wave produced in step **E**?

G. Gather about one fourth of the coils of the spring and hold them. The spring will be under more tension but should cover the same distance as before.

H. Produce a pulse to start a transverse wave.
  6. How does this wave compare with the waves produced in steps **E** and **F**?

RESULTS AND CONCLUSIONS
1. Compare the motions of the tape in steps **C** and **E**.
2. Does the force of the wave affect its speed? What evidence do you have for your answer?
3. Does the tension of the spring affect the speed of the wave? What evidence do you have for your answer?

on the source of the wave. Frequency can be written as waves per second or cycles per second. The SI unit for frequency is the hertz (Hz). One hertz is equal to one wave per second.

A high-frequency wave will not travel faster than a low-frequency wave in the same medium. The speed of a wave depends mostly on the nature of the substance through which it travels.

REVIEW
1. What is a mechanical wave?
2. How do transverse waves and compressional waves differ?
3. What are the parts of a wave?

CHALLENGE Suppose you are making waves in a pool of water by throwing stones into the water. How might you vary the frequency of the waves? How might you vary the amplitude?

13·2 Behavior of Waves

REFLECTION

Water waves can be studied in a ripple tank. A ripple tank is a shallow container with a glass bottom. A light shines on the water in the tank. When waves are made in the water, their pattern can be seen in the water and below the tank. Look at Figure 13·6. It shows the reflection of waves. **Reflection** is the bouncing back of waves that strike a surface. A wave that strikes a surface is called an *incident wave*. A wave that bounces off is called a *reflected wave*. When an incident wave reaches the side of the ripple tank, some of the wave's energy is absorbed by the tank. But most of the wave's energy is reflected back into the water.

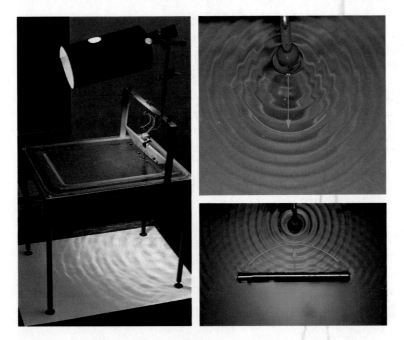

Figure 13·6
A ripple tank *(left)*. Reflection is the bouncing back of waves that strike a surface *(right)*.

DIFFRACTION

As you have seen, waves that strike a barrier are reflected. What happens when a barrier does not completely block waves? Waves that miss the barrier continue on their path. Waves that hit the edge of the barrier seem to change.

313

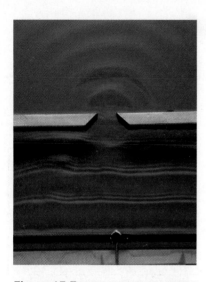

Figure 13·7

When a wave reaches a slit in a barrier, a new wave spreads out from the slit.

Figure 13·8

The speed of the waves changes as they pass into shallow water. This change causes refraction.

Waves that hit the edge of a barrier seem to move around the corner. When a wave hits the edge of a barrier, a new wave spreads out from that point. The spreading out of waves past the edge of a barrier is called **diffraction** (dih FRAK shuhn). Diffraction also occurs at a hole or slit in a barrier. Look at Figure 13·7. When a wave reaches a hole in a barrier, it starts a new wave. This wave spreads out in all directions.

REFRACTION

The frequency of a wave depends on the frequency of the source of the wave. As a wave passes from one medium to another, the frequency of the wave does not change. However, the speed of the wave and the wavelength change.

Suppose the speed of a wave decreases as the wave crosses the boundary from one medium to another. As the speed of the wave decreases, its wavelength decreases. The crests are closer together. If the path of the waves is at a right angle to the boundary, the waves continue in the same direction.

Figure 13·8 shows waves that do not reach a boundary on a right angle path. Notice that these waves change direction as they cross the boundary. The change in direction of a wave as it passes from one medium to another is called **refraction** (rih-FRAK shuhn).

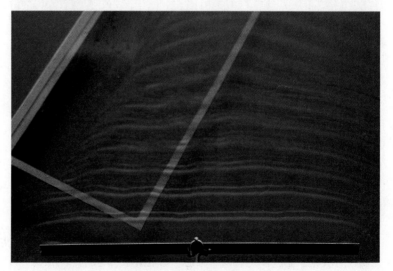

INTERFERENCE

Two or more waves can pass through the same medium at the same time. When two such waves meet, they have an effect on each other. The effects caused by two or more waves passing through a medium at the same time are called **interference**.

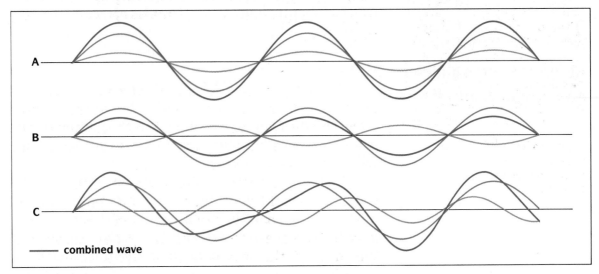

combined wave

Figure 13·9

Constructive interference occurs when two crests or two troughs meet *(A)*. Destructive interference occurs when a crest meets a trough *(B)*. When waves of different wavelengths meet, the interference is irregular *(C)*.

Look at Figure 13·9. Where two crests meet, they produce a higher crest. Where two troughs meet, they produce a lower trough. The two waves are said to reinforce each other. The amplitude of the combined wave is greater than that of either wave alone. This kind of interference is called *constructive interference*. When the crest of one wave meets the trough of another wave, these waves "cancel" each other. This kind of interference is called *destructive interference*.

If two waves have different wavelengths, their interference pattern is irregular. Look at Figure 13·9C. In some places, one crest reinforces another. In other places a crest cancels a trough.

REVIEW

1. Describe what happens when a wave strikes a surface.
2. How is refraction different from diffraction?
3. How do constructive and destructive interference differ?

CHALLENGE If a barrier has two slits in it, diffraction will take place at each slit. What will happen to the new sets of waves?

13·3 Sound

After completing this section, you will be able to

- **identify** the parts of a sound wave.
- **compare** the speed of sound in different mediums.

The key term in this section is **resonance**

Sound is produced by vibrating objects. Hard solids, such as a bell or a tuning fork, vibrate when struck. Flexible solids, such as rubber bands, vibrate when plucked. Gases, such as air, can be made to vibrate. When you blow a whistle, the sound is produced by a vibrating air column.

HOW SOUND WAVES TRAVEL

When you strike a bell with a hammer, the bell vibrates and produces sound waves. You hear the sound as the waves travel through the air, from the bell to your ears. Suppose you place the bell in a jar attached to a vacuum pump. Then suppose the pump draws all the air out of the jar. Will you still hear a sound when the hammer strikes the bell? The bell will vibrate. But without air or some other medium to carry the wave, no sound will be heard.

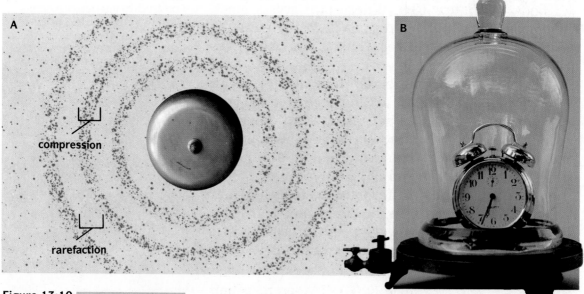

Figure 13·10

Sound waves are compressional waves that can travel through air (A). Sound waves cannot travel through a vacuum (B).

Look at Figure 13·10. It shows how a sound wave is produced by a bell. As the bell vibrates, it expands and contracts. As the bell expands, particles in the air are pushed together. Thus, a compression is formed. When the bell contracts, particles in

316

OBJECTIVE

Demonstrate that sounds come from a vibrating object.

MATERIALS

20 cm of thread, ring stand, ring, thumbtack, small cork, 3 different tuning forks, rubber mallet

PROCEDURE

A. Attach one end of a piece of thread to a ring on a ring stand. Using a thumbtack, fasten the other end of the thread to a cork.

B. Strike the smallest tuning fork with a mallet, and touch the cork with the tuning fork.

C. Repeat step **B** two times.

D. Repeat steps **B** and **C**, using the middle-size tuning fork.

E. Repeat steps **B** and **C**, using the largest tuning fork.

RESULTS AND CONCLUSIONS

1. What happened when a tuning fork was hit with a mallet?
2. What happened to the cork when it was touched with a tuning fork?
3. What evidence was there that each tuning fork made a sound?
4. What evidence was there that each tuning fork was vibrating?

the air are spread apart. Thus, a rarefaction is formed. This rarefaction will be followed by another compression. Each sound wave is made up of one compression and one rarefaction.

Sound waves can be passed between objects. A vibrating tuning fork makes the air around it vibrate. If you hold the base of the vibrating tuning fork against a table, the table will vibrate, too. The energy of the tuning fork makes the table vibrate.

If you hold the vibrating tuning fork near the table, the table will not vibrate. Yet if you hold the vibrating tuning fork near a glass of the right size, the glass will vibrate. Why is it that one object picks up vibrations but another does not?

Any object that can be made to vibrate has a natural frequency. This frequency depends on the shape and nature of the object. If two objects with the same natural frequency are vibrating at the same time, their sound waves will match. When only one of these objects is caused to vibrate, the other will begin to vibrate. The sound waves produced will reinforce each other. The response that an object has to vibrations that match its natural frequency is called **resonance** (REHZ uh nuhns).

The vibrations caused by resonance can have a large amount of energy. Resonance caused vibrations in the glass shown in Figure 13·11A. A singer can break a glass in this way if he or she can make a loud sound at the natural frequency of the glass. The bridge shown in Figure 13·11B collapsed because it vibrated in the wind.

Resonance does not take place between objects with different natural frequencies. Direct contact or very strong vibrations are needed to transfer wave energy between two objects that do not have the same natural frequency.

Figure 13·11
Resonance can shatter a glass *(A)* or tear apart a bridge *(B)*.

SPEED OF SOUND

The speed of a sound wave depends on the medium through which the wave travels. Table 13·1 shows the speed of sound in different mediums. Sound generally moves faster in solids and liquids than in gases. In air at 20°C, sound moves at a rate of 334 m/s. How fast does sound move in silver?

Temperature has been shown to affect the speed of a sound wave. The speed of sound in air increases slightly as the air temperature rises.

The speed of sound can be used to estimate distances. You probably have noticed that you usually see a flash of lightning before you hear the thunder

Table 13·1 *Speed of Sound*

MEDIUM	SPEED (m/s) AT 20°C
Air	334
Aluminum	5104
Glass	5000
Lead	1227
Nickel	4973
Seawater	1490
Silver	2610
Steel	5000
Water	1461

The H.M.S. *Titanic* sank on April 14, 1912, about 600 km off the coast of Newfoundland. It took 73 years to develop the technology that enabled scientists and oceanographers to find the *Titanic*. In a joint effort the French and Americans mapped out a 160-km² search area. With the use of side-scan sonar, the location of the *Titanic* was pinpointed.

The side-scan sonar equipment is usually mounted on the side of a ship or towed underwater alongside the ship. Sound waves are transmitted out from the side of the source rather than straight down. This way, a larger area can be mapped.

The side-scan sonar transmits its data to a computer. As the ship moves, the computer makes a map of the sea floor. Side-scan sonar is so sensitive that the map will show pipelines, oyster beds, and shipwrecks. The image shown was produced by side-scan sonar.

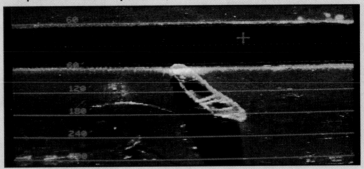

it causes. This time difference occurs because light waves travel faster than do sound waves. For every second that passes between seeing the lightning and hearing the thunder, the sound travels 334 m. If the time difference is 2 seconds, the lightning is 668 m away. How far away is the lightning if you hear the thunder 5 seconds after you see the lightning flash?

Another way that sound is used to measure distances uses echoes. An echo is a sound wave that reflects off a surface. If you direct a loud sound at a hard surface, the sound will bounce back to you. This behavior of sound is used in a technology called sonar. *Sonar* stands for <u>so</u>und <u>na</u>vigation <u>r</u>anging. In sonar, sound waves are sent out from a ship. A receiver analyzes the reflections of these waves. This data can be used to find fish and other objects below the water. It can also be used to map the ocean floor.

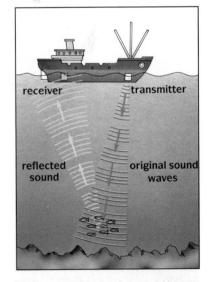

Figure 13·12
Sonar can be used to locate objects underwater.

REVIEW

1. Name the two parts of a sound wave.

2. How does air temperature affect the speed of sound?

CHALLENGE Soldiers marching over a footbridge purposely march out of step. Why is this a good safety practice?

13·4 Properties of Sound

After completing this section, you will be able to

- **distinguish between** pitch and intensity.
- **describe** the Doppler effect.
- **explain** how musical instruments produce sounds.

The key terms in this section are

decibel   intensity
Doppler effect   pitch

INTENSITY AND PITCH

Recall that amplitude is a measure of the amount of energy in a wave. The greater the compression in a compressional wave, the greater the amplitude of the wave. The amplitude of a sound wave determines the **intensity** of the sound. The intensity of a sound is heard as loudness.

The unit used to measure sound intensity is the **decibel** (dB). A loud sound has a higher intensity than does a quiet sound. Table 13·2 shows the intensity of some sounds. Sounds over 100 dB can cause hearing loss. Look at Figure 13·13. People who work around loud sounds should wear earplugs or some other device to protect their hearing.

Table 13·2 *Intensity of Sounds*

INTENSITY (dB)	EXAMPLES
10	Rustle of leaves, soft whisper
20	Quiet room
30	Quiet office, soft music
40	Quiet talking, average home
50	Common talking voice
60	Loud talking
70	Loud radio music, heavy traffic noise
80	Moving subway, very loud radio music
90	Air hammer
100	Riveter, full symphony orchestra
110	Loud thunder

Figure 13·13
How is this airport worker protecting his hearing?

The intensity of sounds can be compared by using a device called an oscilloscope (uh SIHL uh-skohp). An oscilloscope shows wave patterns on a screen. Look at the patterns shown in Figure 13·14. Some waves have higher amplitudes than do others. The lengths of the waves also vary. Waves that are shorter show more crests on the screen. These waves have high frequencies. Waves that are longer show fewer crests and have low frequencies. Which wave has the lower frequency?

A person hears the frequency of a sound as its pitch. The **pitch** is how high or low a sound is. High-pitched sounds have high frequencies. Low-pitched sounds have low frequencies.

The range of human hearing is between 20 Hz and 20,000 Hz. Sounds above 20,000 Hz are called *ultrasonic* (uhl truh SAHN ihk) *sounds*. Some animals can hear ultrasonic sounds. Dogs, for example, can be trained to respond to ultrasonic whistles. Bats make ultrasonic sounds. As bats fly, they use the echoes of these sounds to find food in the dark.

Ultrasonic sounds are also called ultrasound. It is used in medicine. Ultrasonic sound waves are reflected off body tissues or organs. The echoes are used to study organs such as the heart.

DOPPLER EFFECT

Suppose you are standing on a street corner when a car drives by with its horn blowing. As the car approaches, the pitch you hear is higher than the actual pitch of the horn. As the car passes, the pitch of the sound decreases.

Figure 13·15 shows why the pitch of a sound seems to change. A car's horn sends out sound waves in all directions. When the car is not moving, these sound waves all have the same frequency. But when the car moves forward, the sound waves in front of the car are closer together. Thus the frequency of the waves increases. Someone at point *A* hears a pitch higher than the pitch that the horn

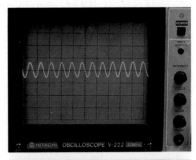
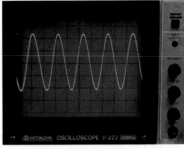

Figure 13·14
These wave patterns represent sound waves.

Figure 13·15
The Doppler effect.

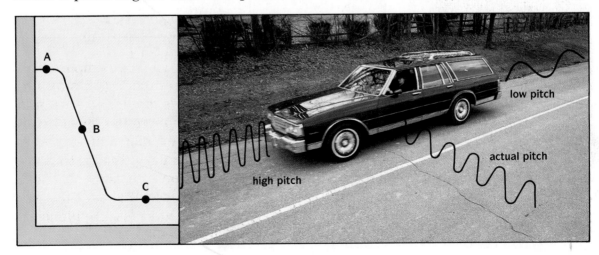

A

B

C

high pitch

low pitch

actual pitch

really produces. At the same time the sound waves behind the car are spread apart. The frequency decreases. Someone at point *B* hears a pitch lower than the pitch that the horn really produces.

The pitch of the sound would also change if the car stayed in one place and the listener moved. The change in pitch that occurs when the source of a sound and the listener are moving in relation to each other is called the **Doppler effect**. The Doppler effect only happens when the listener is almost directly in front of or behind the source of the sound. Someone next to the car or off to one side of its path would hear the actual pitch of the horn.

QUALITY

Musical sounds, or tones, have three properties that can be distinguished by the human ear — pitch, loudness, and quality. Recall that the pitch depends on the frequency of the wave. Loudness depends on the amplitude of the wave, or how much energy it carries. The *quality* of a tone is its distinct sound. Quality allows you to tell a note played on a piano from the same note played on a flute.

Compare the wave patterns shown in Figure 13·16. All three patterns have the same frequency and the same amplitude. Only their shapes differ. The differences in the shapes of these waves are heard as the quality of each tone.

Figure 13·16

Wave patterns of musical tones. Which instrument produces the smoothest wave pattern?

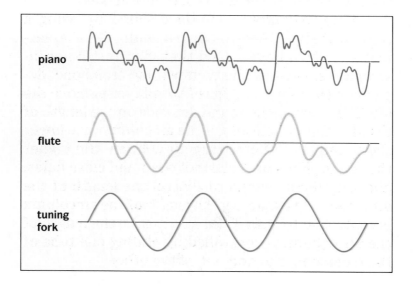

MUSICAL INSTRUMENTS

There are four classes of musical instruments: string, wind, percussion, and electronic. They all produce vibrations in regular patterns. Electronic instruments get the energy to produce sound from electricity. The other classes of instruments get the energy to produce sounds from the people who play the instruments.

Figure 13·17

The saxophone *(left)* is a wind instrument. The french horn, tuba, and trombone *(middle)* are also wind instruments. The violin *(right)* is a string instrument.

The violin, viola, cello, and guitar are some string instruments. Musical tones are produced when the strings of these instruments are made to vibrate. The shorter, thinner, or tighter the string, the higher the pitch of the sound it makes.

Wind instruments produce sound by using a column of air. Some wind instruments, like the clarinet and oboe, have a reed that vibrates. Other instruments, such as the trumpet and trombone, depend on the vibrating lips of the player to move the air. The pitch of the sound depends on the length of the air column. The longer the air column, the lower the sound. The shorter the air column, the higher the sound. Keys on a clarinet open and close holes, allowing the musician to control the length of the air column. In a trumpet the length of the air column is controlled by valves. In a trombone the length of the air column is controlled by sliding one tube of the trombone into and out of the other.

Figure 13·18

Xylophones may be large *(right)* or small *(left)*.

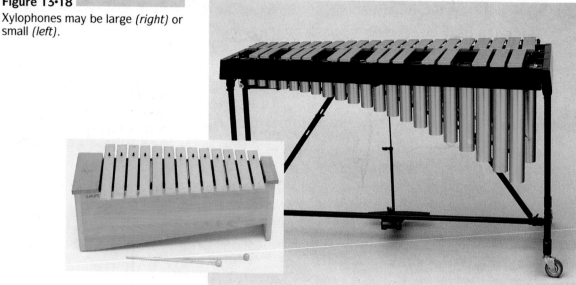

Figure 13·19

A synthesizer electronically produces the sounds of many different musical instruments.

The sounds of percussion instruments are made by striking membranes, bells, or metal plates with a hammer or stick. The tone produced is determined by the shape of the instrument and the material from which the instrument is made. To get more than one note from a percussion instrument, more than one shape must be used. Look at the xylophones shown in Figure 13·18. Each bar is a different size and produces a different tone. Which bars would you expect to make the highest notes?

Electronic instruments are the newest class of instruments. They were invented in the twentieth century. The most common kind of electronic instrument is the keyboard synthesizer. The synthesizer changes electrical signals into sound waves. The synthesizer is able to duplicate the sounds of many instruments.

REVIEW

1. How does pitch differ from intensity?
2. What is the Doppler effect?
3. How is sound produced by each of the four classes of musical instruments?

CHALLENGE A bottle nearly full of water will make a low-pitched sound when you tap it. But when you blow across the top of the bottle, a high-pitched sound is made. Explain this difference.

13·5 Acoustics and Noise Pollution

Have you ever heard music played in a concert hall where the sound echoed? The music made by the players may have bounced around the room. If the walls of the hall reflected sound strongly, then the echoes may have bounced around several times before fading away. Such multiple echoes are called reverberations (rih ver buh RAY shuhnz). A *reverberation* is a mixture of repeating echoes. When sound reverberates, it seems to come from different places at different times. When the waves of the repeating sounds combine, they produce irregular wave patterns that sound like noise. Figure 13·20 shows wave patterns of noise. Notice that the wave on the left has a smaller amplitude. Which wave stands for a louder noise?

After completing this section, you will be able to

- **describe** reverberation and how it can be controlled.
- **give examples** of the effects of noise pollution.

The key term in this section is **acoustics**

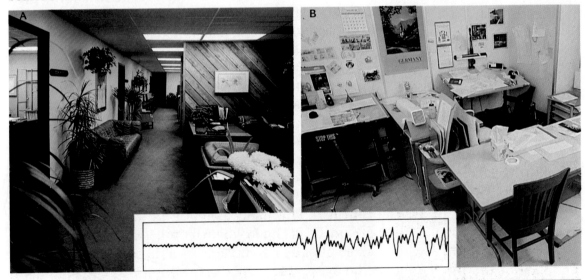

Figure 13·20

Irregular wave patterns sound like noise *(inset)*. Soft materials reduce noise levels.

Rooms and buildings can be designed to control echoes and other unwanted noise. Hard surfaces, like wood, stone, and plaster, reflect sound waves. Soft materials, like draperies and carpet, absorb sound waves. Specially designed tiles also absorb sound waves. Thus the walls, floors, and ceilings of many rooms are covered with sound-absorbing materials. Look at Figure 13·20. Which office would be quieter?

The office in Figure 13·20A was designed using the principles of acoustics (uh KOOS tihks). **Acoustics** is the study of sound. Scientists and acoustic engineers study sound to reduce noise and to improve the environment. Some concert halls, for example, have sloping ceilings and uneven walls. This kind of design uses the reflection of sound waves to improve the sound of the music. The design also reduces the amount of reverberation.

Noise has been found to affect health and to cause other problems. *Noise pollution* is the term used to describe unwanted noise and its effects. Stress and hearing loss can be caused by noise pollution. Noise pollution has also been found to cause high blood pressure, headaches, and fatigue.

Noise can damage buildings and other objects. High-frequency sounds can shatter glass. The sonic boom from a jet can damage windows and weaken plaster walls. A *sonic boom* is a loud sound produced as an airplane flies at the speed of sound. Loud trucks driving past a house that is close to the road can also cause damage.

Noise pollution can be controlled. New jet engines are designed to produce less noise. Most jets are not allowed to fly over land at the speed of sound. When highways are built near homes, walls like the one shown in Figure 13·21 are put up to keep road noise from reaching the homes.

Figure 13·21

Noise barriers reduce the amount of noise that reaches homes near the highway.

REVIEW

1. What is reverberation?
2. What kinds of materials reflect sound waves? What kinds absorb sound waves?
3. Describe two effects of noise pollution.

CHALLENGE Why does a concert rehearsal in an empty auditorium sound different from a performance in an auditorium that is full of people?

CHAPTER SUMMARY

The main ideas in this chapter are listed below. Read these statements before you answer the Chapter Review questions.

- A wave is a disturbance that travels through space and matter. A transverse wave vibrates at a right angle to the direction in which the wave travels. A compressional wave moves particles back and forth parallel to the direction in which the wave travels. (13·1)
- The wavelength is the distance from any point on a wave to the corresponding point on the next wave. The frequency is the number of waves that pass a given point each second. (13·1)
- Reflection is the bouncing of waves off a surface. Refraction is the change in direction of a wave as it passes from one medium to another. (13·2)
- Interference occurs when two or more waves pass through a medium at the same time. (13·2)
- Sound waves are compressional waves. A sound wave is made up of a compression and a rarefaction. (13·3)

- Resonance occurs when an object vibrates in response to vibrations that match its natural frequency. (13·3)
- Intensity is the loudness of a sound. Intensity is measured in decibels. (13·4)
- The pitch of a sound is determined by the frequency of the wave. The greater the frequency, the higher the pitch. (13·4)
- The Doppler effect is a change in the pitch heard when the listener and the source of the sound are moving in relation to each other. (13·4)
- The quality of a tone is its distinctive sound. (13·4)
- Sounds that produce irregular patterns are called noise. (13·5)
- Acoustics is the study of sound. The principles of acoustics can be used to reduce noise pollution. (13·5)

The key terms in this chapter are listed below. Use each term in a sentence that shows the meaning of the term.

acoustics	Doppler effect	reflection
amplitude	frequency	refraction
compression	intensity	resonance
compressional wave	interference	transverse wave
decibel	pitch	wavelength
diffraction	rarefaction	

Chapter Review

VOCABULARY

Write the letter of the term that best matches the definition. Not all the terms will be used.

1. A wave that vibrates up and down at right angles to its direction of travel
2. The distance from one point on a wave to the same point on the next wave
3. How high or low a sound is
4. The study of sound
5. The part of a compressional wave where the particles of matter are spread apart
6. The spreading of waves around the edge of a barrier
7. The change in direction of a wave as it passes from one medium to another
8. The effect caused by two or more waves passing through a medium at the same time
9. The number of waves that pass a given point each second
10. The unit used to measure sound intensity

a. acoustics
b. amplitude
c. compressional wave
d. decibel
e. diffraction
f. frequency
g. interference
h. pitch
i. rarefaction
j. refraction
k. resonance
l. transverse wave
m. wavelength

CONCEPTS

The drawings below show two different waves on a spring. Look at the drawings and answer the questions.

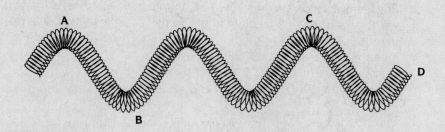

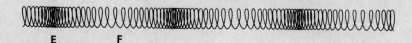

1. What is point *A* called?
2. What is point *B* called?
3. How many wavelengths are there between points *A* and *C*?
4. What is the distance from point *C* to line *D* called?
5. What is line *D*?
6. What is point *E* called?
7. What is point *F* called?
8. Points *A – C* are on what kind of wave?
9. Points *E* and *F* are on what kind of wave?

Answer the following in complete sentences.

10. What causes a wave to be reflected? What causes a wave to be diffracted?
11. What characteristic of sound is determined by its amplitude? What characteristic of sound is determined by its frequency?
12. Compare the speeds of sound in solids, liquids, and gases.
13. Why do you hear a change in pitch when a source of sound moves toward you?
14. How are wind instruments different from string instruments?
15. Why do some rooms seem loud, and others quiet?

APPLICATION/
CRITICAL
THINKING

1. Why does sound travel faster in steel than in air?
2. How could the Doppler effect be used to measure the speed of an approaching car?
3. An astronaut claimed to hear an explosion while on the surface of the moon. Since the moon has no air to carry the sound, how could this be true?
4. At what position does a slide trombone produce the lowest note? Why does a piccolo produce higher tones than does a flute?

EXTENSION

1. Research the term *sound barrier*. Find out who the first person to break this barrier was and what importance this event had. Report back to the class on your findings.
2. Ask a hospital official or a doctor for information about sonograms. Prepare a report for the class.
3. If you play a musical instrument, demonstrate to the class how that instrument makes and varies sound.

Science in Careers

Have you ever noticed that the wings of an airplane are curved on the upper surface and flat on the bottom? The shape of the wings gives lift, or upward movement, to the airplane.

It is the job of aeronautical engineers to design airplanes so that their shape serves their function. Aeronautical engineers may begin with a drawing and then use mathematical and engineering principles to refine the airplane design. Based on the drawing, a small model is built.

Aeronautical engineers also use computers and computer graphics to design and study airplanes. Supercomputers are now being used to show how airplanes will perform in flight.

Aeronautical engineers may work for private industry or for the government. They must have a college degree in engineering. To prepare for a career in engineering, you should take courses in physics and mathematics in high school.

AERONAUTICAL ENGINEER

Have you ever looked at the hundreds of color chips in a paint or hardware store? Color chips are small samples of the various colors of paint that are available at the store.

Workers in the store prepare the colors that the customers choose. The directions for mixing each color of paint are provided by a paint analyst.

Paint analysts work for companies that manufacture paint. Their job is to mix basic colors together to produce new colors. These new colors must be easily reproducible by the people who sell paint in the local stores.

Paint analysts receive on-the-job training. Some have college degrees, and most have artistic talent. If you are interested in this field, you will benefit from taking courses in art and chemistry in high school.

PAINT ANALYST

People in Science

Dr. Stephen Hawking is a theoretical physicist. He is famous for having proposed the existence of black holes before they were found by astronomers.

Dr. Hawking had theorized that a black hole forms when a large star grows old and stops producing energy. Its gravity causes the star to shrink and compress. As the star compresses, the gravitational pull increases. Finally, nothing, not even light can escape from the black hole.

Like other theoretical physicists, Dr. Hawking makes his predictions by using his imagi-nation and mathematical calcu-lations. But, in some ways, Dr. Hawking is different from the other scientists. He is almost com-pletely paralyzed by a progressive nerve disorder. Dr. Hawking is unable to write, and his speech is so weak that he needs an interpreter to translate what he says. Dr. Hawking does most of his work in his head and then dictates his ideas to assistants.

Dr. Hawking prefers not to concentrate on his physical limita-tions. Instead he sees his illness as something that forces him to focus on basic physics, freeing him from other distractions.

Dr. Stephen Hawking
THEORETICAL PHYSICIST

Issues and Technology

Is Personal Information Confidential?

Most people do not give much thought to the amount of personal information that is held in computers. Schools keep computer files on grades and school activities. State motor vehicle agencies collect information on everyone who has a driver's license. Credit card companies even keep records of what individuals buy, where they buy it, and how much they spend.

Generally, people do not worry about giving out information. They feel that government agencies and businesses keep their information confidential. Most people also expect that the information will be used only for the purpose for which it was collected.

It now appears that information may not always be kept confidential. More and more cases have been revealed in which personal information collected by one business or government agency is shared with others. Computers are simplifying this widespread use of personal information.

Some people feel that this sharing of information is an invasion of privacy. They say that people have the right to control information about themselves or to at least know how the information will be used.

Figure 1 shows a number of organizations that keep computerized records on Americans. People in several job categories were asked if they thought that the release of information by these organizations would be an invasion of privacy.

APPLYING CRITICAL THINKING SKILLS

1. A release of information by which agency was thought to be the greatest invasion of privacy?
2. Which organization's sharing of information would you consider to be the greatest invasion of privacy? Why?
3. Which group has the lowest percentage of people who objected to selling credit information? Why, do you think, this group is different?
4. Some people think that a business or government agency should only be able to get information about an individual from that individual. What do you think?

Figure 1

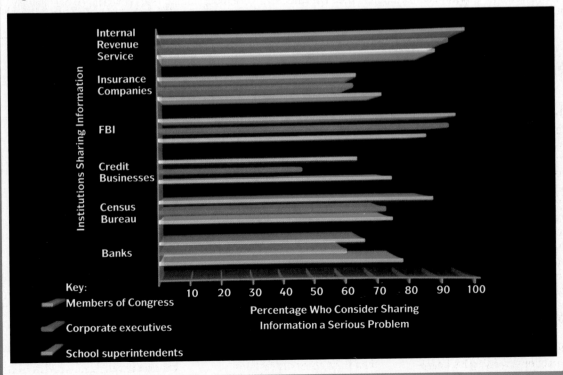

Key:
- Members of Congress
- Corporate executives
- School superintendents

Percentage Who Consider Sharing Information a Serious Problem

Institutions Sharing Information: Internal Revenue Service, Insurance Companies, FBI, Credit Businesses, Census Bureau, Banks

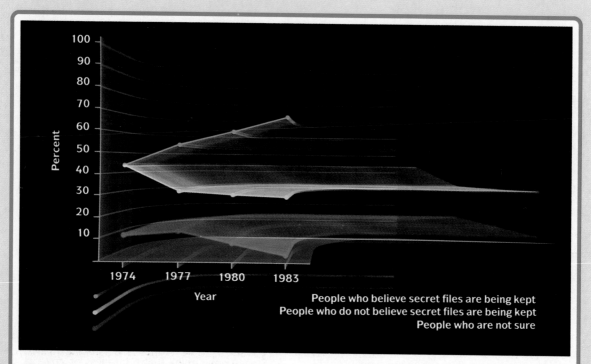

Figure 2

Privacy is a right that Americans cherish. It is protected by many laws, including the Fourth Amendment to the Constitution. The Fourth Amendment, which protects Americans against unreasonable search and seizure, was strengthened in 1974 by the Privacy Act. This act gives people control over information collected by the federal government. The act provides that there should be no secret record systems, that individuals are allowed to see and correct records about themselves, and that information collected for one purpose cannot be used for another.

The federal government alone keeps an average of 15 separate files on each American. These files include employment information kept by the Social Security Administration, financial data from the Internal Revenue Service, and personal data from the Census Bureau. Now it is known that some of these agencies share and compare information in ways that were never intended when the information was collected. And though the practice is known, it is still very hard to control.

One way of sharing information involves computer matches. In a computer match, two sets of data are compared to find people whose names are on both sets. The matches can be used to find people who should not be on two lists. For ex-

ample, lists of people earning above a certain income level can be matched with lists of people receiving food stamps, thus revealing those illegally receiving food stamps.

Matches are also used to find people who should be on two lists. By matching lists, the Selective Service can find males who have registered their cars but have not registered for the draft.

Perhaps doing computer matches to find fraud does not bother people. But is it right to examine an individual's purchases, even when there is no reason to suspect that the person has done anything wrong? Where should the line be drawn? Has the computer made it impossible to draw the line at all? Figure 2 shows the percentage of people polled who thought that secret files were kept on them.

APPLYING CRITICAL THINKING SKILLS

1. Has the percentage of people who think that secret files are kept gone up or down? Describe the trend.
2. If you were polled, how would you answer?
3. If you think that secret files are kept on you or others, who would keep these files, and why?
4. Do you see a problem with secret files about individuals? Are these files justified? Explain your answers.

Another problem involves people who break into computers. In 1982 a man left a computer company after not getting a pay raise. He used a home computer and telephone link-up to access his former employer's computer to steal information. This man was caught, but many others are not.

In 1983 a group of Milwaukee teenagers made a game of using their home computers to break into a number of corporate and government computers. One of these computers was at the Los Alamos National Laboratory, a facility that develops nuclear weapons. The teens said it was easy. They just kept guessing passwords that would access the computer. Once they typed in the right word, they could look at all the top-secret information in the files. Many people feel that more security is needed to keep computerized information out of the hands of the nosy, the mischievous, and the criminal.

Some security measures have been developed. Encryption is a security measure that codes information. A device that scrambles information into a code is put into the computer. The code can only be read by authorized individuals.

Another security measure is the call-back system. When a computer is contacted by telephone, the computer calls back an authorized number. The computer will not give out information if an unauthorized person is requesting it. In this way, only authorized users can access the computer by telephone. Figure 3 shows some links among computer systems.

APPLYING CRITICAL THINKING SKILLS

1. What are some of the organizations from which credit bureaus collect computerized information about people?
2. Often, credit bureaus collect information without the knowledge of the individual. Do you think this is a problem? Explain your answer.
3. If some of these linkages were not by computer but were just exchanges of typewritten information, do you think that there would be less of a problem? Why or why not?
4. Schools share information about students. Do you see a problem with schools sharing an individual's personal record?

Figure 3

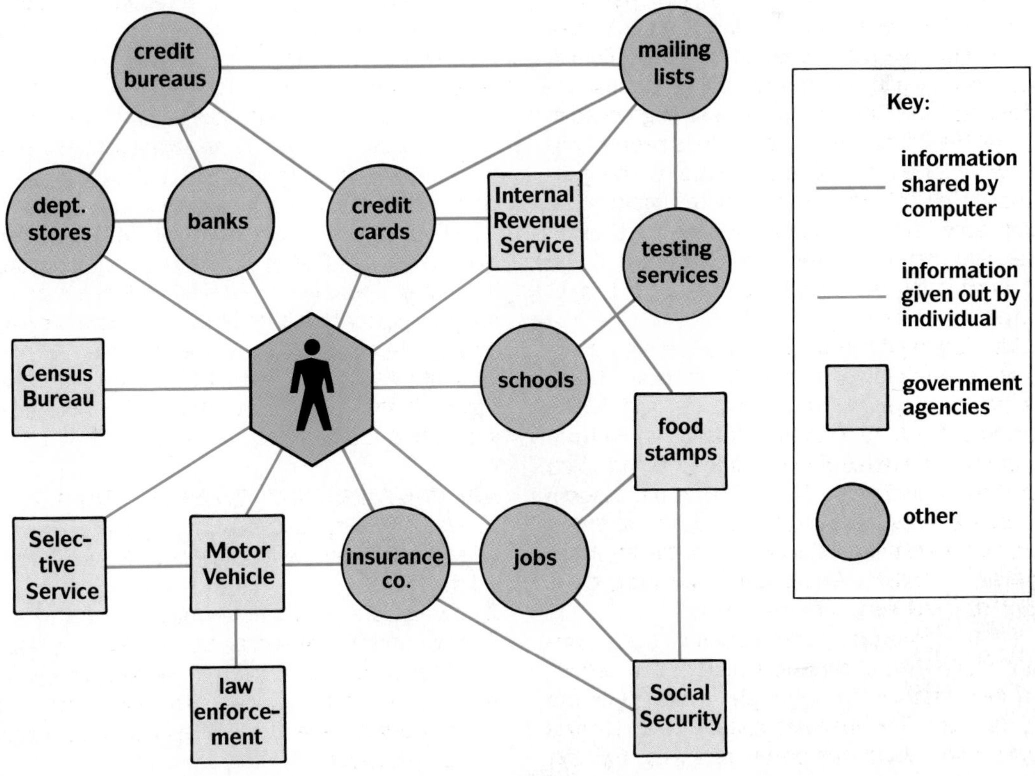

Key:

information shared by computer

information given out by individual

government agencies

other

DISCOVERING
THE EARTH AND SPACE

Humans have always been intrigued by the history of the earth. Even the ancient Greeks wondered how marine shells could be found on mountaintops. In this unit you will learn about the earth and the solar system. You will also study the earth's resources, history, and weather.

Lake Powell, in Utah, is one example of the various structures on the earth's surface.▼

◀ *Saturn and some of its moons.*

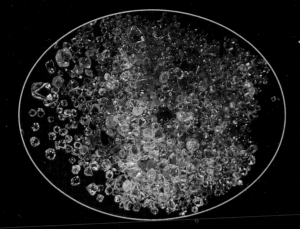

◀ *Materials from the earth include diamonds.*

This frog, fossilized in amber, is nearly 40 million years old. ▼

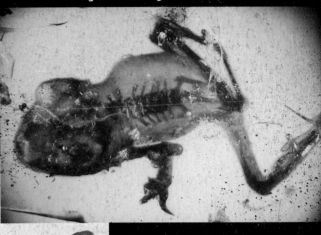

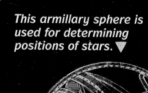

This armillary sphere is used for determining positions of stars. ▼

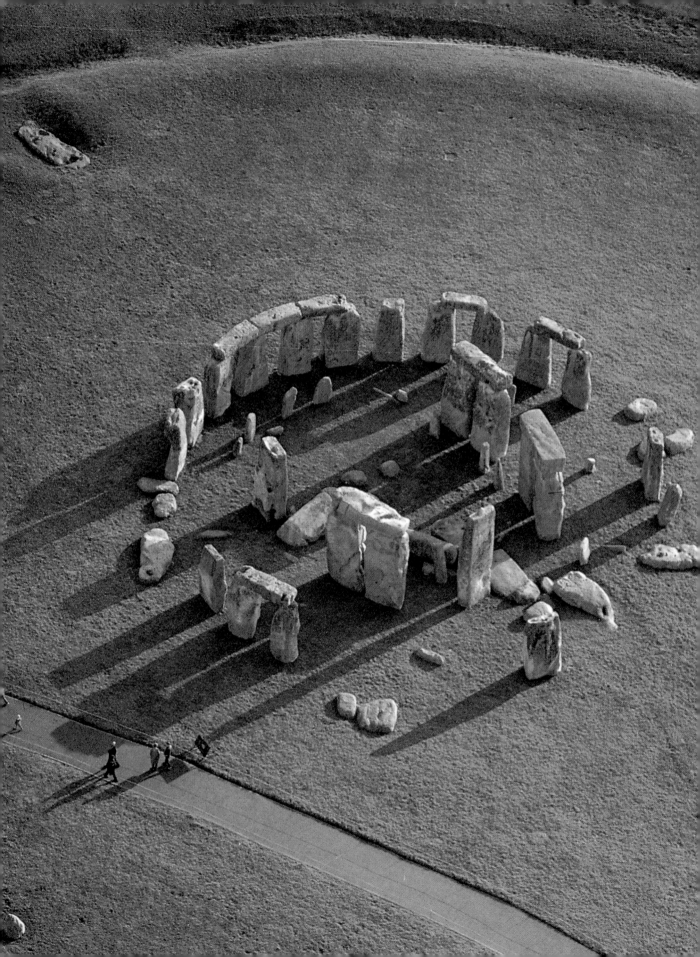

CHAPTER 14

THE EARTH AND THE MOON

*T*hese 4-m-high stones rest on Salisbury Plain in England. They stand in a circle that is about 30 m in diameter. The exact purpose of the monument they form is a mystery. Clues have been uncovered slowly. In the 1950s, scientists used carbon dating to estimate the age of the monument to be around 3500 years.

In the 1960s a scientist using a computer hypothesized that the stones could have been used to predict the seasons. The monument was, in that scientist's opinion, a calendar. Certain stones mark the sun's position on the first day of summer. Other stones mark the sun's position on the first day of winter.

- *Why is it useful to predict the changes in seasons?*

- *Besides the seasons, what other events involving the earth, moon, and sun can be predicted to occur on a regular basis?*

- *Why do these events occur on a regular basis?*

14·1 Describing the Earth

THE EARTH'S LOCATION

The earth is located in a solar system. Our solar system consists of the star we call the sun, nine planets, more than 50 moons, and thousands of smaller objects that circle the sun. Figure 14·1 shows the planets of the solar system. The sizes of the planets are to scale, but the distances between the planets are not. The earth is the third planet from the sun.

Our solar system is located in a galaxy called the Milky Way galaxy. A galaxy is made up of dust, gas, and billions of stars. The Milky Way galaxy is 100,000 light-years in diameter. A *light-year* (ly) is the distance light travels in one year, about 9.5 trillion km. The Milky Way galaxy contains over 100 billion stars. Find our solar system in Figure 14·1. Our sun is an average-sized star located near the outer edge of the Milky Way galaxy.

Figure 14·1

The solar system *(A)*. The Milky Way galaxy *(B)*.

Astronomers (uh STRAH nuh muhrz) have observed that many galaxies are in clusters. The Milky Way galaxy is located in a cluster of about 20 galaxies called the local group. The local group is just one of countless clusters in the universe.

It can be difficult to understand how far apart objects are in outer space. A long trip on the earth might cover a few thousand kilometers. A trip across the solar system would cover more than 12 billion km. To measure such large distances, scientists use the astronomical (as truh NAHM uh kuhl) unit. An *astronomical unit* (AU) is a unit of length that equals the average distance from the sun to the earth. This distance is about 150 million km. Table 14·1 shows the average distance from the sun to each planet. What is the average distance from the sun to Neptune? How much greater is this distance than the distance from the sun to the earth?

THE SHAPE AND SIZE OF THE EARTH

Through most of recorded history, people thought the earth was flat. It is easy to understand why. While traveling from one place to another, you do not sense the earth's curving surface. When you stand on the top of a mountain or tall building, the earth's surface seems to stretch out endlessly in all directions.

Today we know that the earth is round. This was proved in 1522, when one of Ferdinand Magellan's ships circled the earth. The distance around the earth is about 40,000 km. Precise measurements have shown that the earth is not a perfect sphere. The earth is slightly flattened at the poles and it bulges at the equator, as shown in Figure 14·2. Thus, the distance around the equator is greater than the distance around the poles.

Table 14·1 *Distances from Sun*

| PLANET | DISTANCES FROM SUN | |
	IN MILLIONS OF km	IN AU
Mercury	57.9	0.4
Venus	108.2	0.7
Earth	149.6	1.0
Mars	228.0	1.5
Jupiter	778.4	5.2
Saturn	1424.6	9.5
Uranus	2866.9	19.2
Neptune	4486.0	30.0
Pluto	5889.7	39.4

Figure 14·2
The earth is not perfectly round.

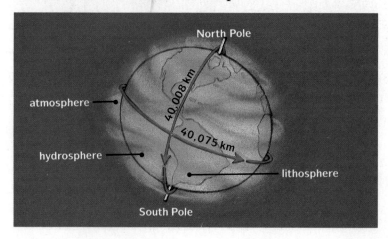

339

LAYERS OF THE EARTH

atmos (vapor)

hydro (water)

litho (stone)

The earth can be divided into three spheres. The **atmosphere** (AT muh sfihr) is the layer of air that surrounds the earth. The atmosphere extends from the earth's surface to more than 10,000 km into space. However, most of the air is concentrated in the first 10 km above the earth. The **hydrosphere** (hī druh sfihr) is the layer of water that covers the earth. This layer includes water on the surface — such as rivers, lakes, and oceans — and water that is found beneath the ground. The **lithosphere** (LIHTH uh sfihr) is the solid surface of the earth. It consists of the continents, the ocean floor, and solid materials such as rocks and minerals.

THE EARTH'S MAGNETISM

The earth behaves as if it had a bar magnet inside it. Look at Figure 14·3. One pole of this imaginary magnet is located near the geographic North Pole. The other pole is located near the geographic South Pole. A free-hanging magnet is attracted to these magnetic poles. A compass contains a magnet that indicates the directions of the poles.

Figure 14·3

The magnetic field of the earth is similar to the magnetic field of a bar magnet.

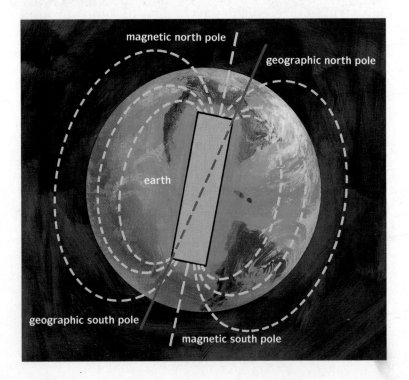

magnetic north pole

geographic north pole

earth

geographic south pole

magnetic south pole

An invisible magnetic field surrounds every magnet. Lines of force can be drawn to show the size and shape of the field. The *magnetosphere* (mag-NEE tuh sfihr) is the magnetic field of the earth.

Charged particles stream from the sun and affect the shape of the magnetosphere. Notice in Figure 14·4 that the magnetosphere is pushed outward by these particles. It may reach millions of kilometers into space.

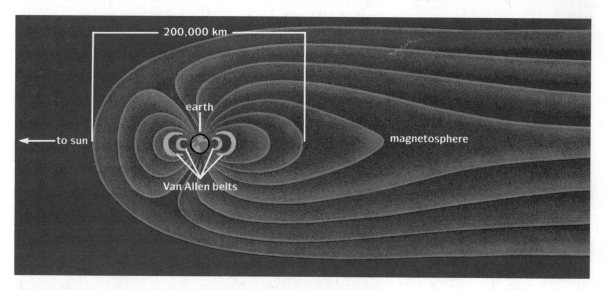

The *Van Allen belts* are two doughnut-shaped regions in which charged particles from the sun are collected by the magnetosphere. The charged particles are held in place by the magnetosphere. One belt is found about 4000 km above the equator. The other belt is about 16,000 km above the equator. You can see the locations of these belts in Figure 14·4. The Van Allen belts help to protect living things on the earth by trapping charged particles that would otherwise reach the earth's surface.

REVIEW

1. Where is the earth located in the universe?
2. Describe the shape and size of the earth.
3. Identify the atmosphere, hydrosphere, lithosphere, and magnetosphere.

CHALLENGE Why does a compass needle usually not point to the geographic North Pole?

341

14·2 The Earth's Movements

roto- (wheel)

ROTATION AND REVOLUTION

Even if you are sitting still, you are actually moving extremely fast because the earth is moving extremely fast. The earth rotates, or spins, on an imaginary line called an axis. As you can see in Figure 14·5, the earth's axis extends from the geographic North Pole to the geographic South Pole. **Rotation** is the turning of an object on its axis. The earth rotates on its axis once each day, or every 24 hours. Since the distance around the earth is about 40,000 km, an object at the equator travels 40,000 km in 24 hours, or about 1670 km/h.

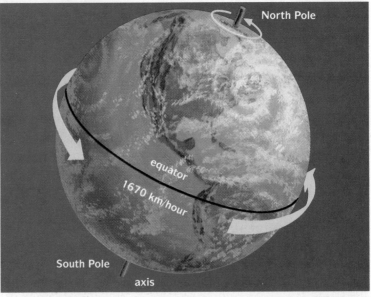

North Pole

equator

1670 km/hour

South Pole

axis

Figure 14·5

The earth is rotating on its axis. Where would you be moving faster, at the equator or at the poles?

re- (back)
volvere (to roll)

While the earth is rotating, it is also revolving, or moving around the sun, at a tremendous rate. **Revolution** is the movement of an object along an orbit, or path, around another body. The orbit of the earth is an ellipse, or a slightly flattened circle. From above the North Pole, the earth appears to revolve around the sun in a counterclockwise direction. It takes 365.24 days for the earth to revolve once. In that time the earth travels about 942 million km. Thus the earth is moving faster than 107,000 km/h.

TIME ON THE EARTH

The movement of the sun, changes in the appearance of the moon, and changes in the positions of stars have all been used to measure time. Of these, the movement of the sun across the sky is the easiest to observe. The time from one sunrise to the next is one day. What movement of the earth takes place in this time period?

Noon originally was the time the sun reached its highest point in the sky. Then people became aware that noon occurs at different times in different places. For example, noon occurs later as you move west. Because of this difference, clocks were set at slightly different times from one city to another. By the late 1800s, travelers crossing the United States by train went through 53 different local times.

In 1883 an international system was set up to solve this problem. This system, which is still used today, is shown in Figure 14·6. Notice that the earth is divided into 24 equal segments called **time zones.** Clocks in a time zone are set to the local time at the center of the zone. The boundaries of the time zones vary according to local boundaries so that cities or towns are not split into different zones. The time zone to the east of your time zone is one hour later. The time zone to the west is one hour earlier.

This photograph was made by pointing a camera at the night sky and leaving the shutter open for a period of time. The circular pattern of stars that formed in the picture was caused by the rotation of the earth. By looking at the pattern carefully, you can see that the stars form arcs, or parts of circles. Using the length of the arcs, find the amount of time the shutter of the camera was left open.

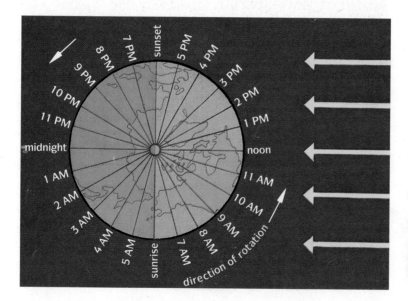

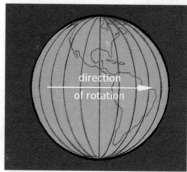

Figure 14·6
The earth is divided into 24 time zones. The lines in these figures mark the centers of time zones.

Figure 14·7

What time zone do you live in?

The time zones for North America are shown in Figure 14·7. When it is 2:00 P.M. in Atlanta, what time is it in Phoenix? What time is it in Montreal? Imagine leaving home at 3:00 P.M., traveling west for one hour, and arriving in the next time zone. What time would it be there?

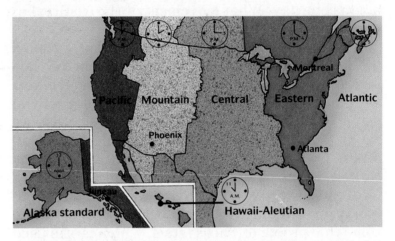

Suppose you go on a one-day trip around the world and a friend remains at home. You leave on Friday, November 20, at 9:00 A.M. You travel west, pass through all 24 time zones in 24 hours, and return home. You have set your watch back one hour for each time zone. So according to your watch, it is still 9:00 A.M. on Friday, November 20, when you return. But by your friend's watch, it is 9:00 A.M. on Saturday, November 21.

The creation of the International Date Line eliminated problems such as this. The International Date Line is the place where one calendar day ends and the next begins. Notice in Figure 14·8 that the *International Date Line* passes through the Pacific Ocean. A traveler crossing this line finds that the time on a clock remains the same. However, the date changes when you cross the line. When you go west across the line, the date changes to the next day. When you go east across the line, the date changes to the previous day.

In addition to being measured in days, time is also measured in years and months. A year is based on the time it takes for the earth to complete one revolution around the sun. One revolution of the

Figure 14·8

When people travel west from North America to Japan, they lose a day. They regain it when they return to North America.

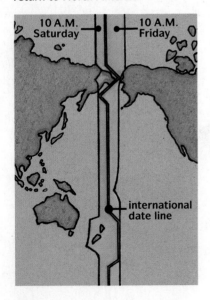

The earth does more than revolve around the sun and rotate on its axis—it also wobbles. Think of a spinning top. As the spinning slows, the top begins to wobble. The earth wobbles, or moves in a slow circle, as it spins on its axis. The movement of the earth's axis in a slow circle is called precession.

Precession will cause different stars to become the polestar, the star above the North Pole. Right now the polestar is Polaris, in the Little Dipper. It takes the earth's axis 26,000 years to complete one wobble. In half that time, 13,000 years, the axis will be tilted in the opposite direction. Our polestar will then be Vega, a star in the constellation Lyra. At that time, Vega will be the North Star. Polaris will again become the North Star 13,000 years after that.

Precession will also change the time of the seasons. The first day of spring occurs around March 21, and the first day of autumn occurs around September 23. In 13,000 years the seasons will be reversed.

Precession is one of four motions that the earth undergoes. The earth takes 24 hours to rotate on its axis, a bit more than a year to revolve around the sun, 26,000 years to complete one precession, and 200 million years to revolve around the galaxy.

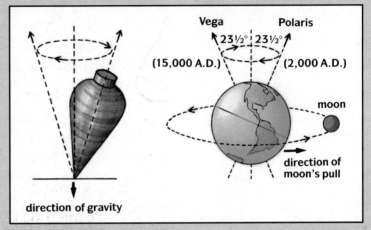

earth takes 365.24 days. A calendar year is usually 365 days. An extra day is added to February of every fourth year to account for the extra 0.24 days per year. This fourth year is called a leap year.

A year is divided into 12 months. A month is based on the time it takes for the moon to change from one full moon to the next. This lunar month is 29.5 days. However, calendar months have been set to 28, 30, or 31 days.

REVIEW

1. Describe the rotation and revolution of the earth.

2. How is time related to the earth's rotation and revolution?

3. Explain why the earth is divided into time zones.

CHALLENGE A year is 365.24 days long. For 3 years the calendar year is 365 days long. In the fourth year an extra day is added to make up for the additional 0.24 days per year. However, adding a whole day every 4 years adds too much time. Calculate how many leap years pass before one day too many has been added and a leap year must be skipped.

14·3 The Earth's Seasons

THE TILT OF THE EARTH'S AXIS

In addition to days and years, seasons can be used to measure time. The change of seasons is caused by the tilt of the earth's axis and by the earth's revolution around the sun. As you can see in Figure 14·9, the earth's axis is not vertical. It is tilted at an angle of 23.5°.

As the earth revolves around the sun, its axis always points in the same direction. As the earth revolves, the relationship between the tilt of its axis and the sun changes. When the earth's axis points toward the sun, the region of the earth that leans toward the sun receives the sun's rays more directly, as shown in Figure 14·9. That region is also in sunlight for a longer period of time each day as the earth rotates. This combination of more-direct rays and longer periods of daylight causes this part of the earth to be warm. When the earth is in the position shown in Figure 14·10, it is summer in the Northern Hemisphere. Notice that the Southern Hemisphere leans away from the sun. There the sun's rays are less direct, the daylight hours are shorter, and this part of the earth is cool. What season is it in the Southern Hemisphere?

Figure 14·9
The tilt of the earth's axis causes part of the earth to lean toward the sun.

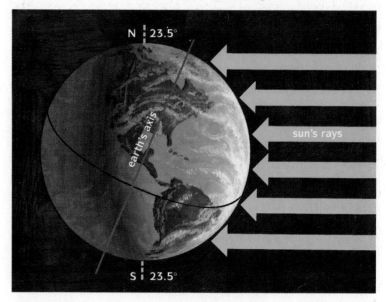

346

THE CHANGING SEASONS

The tilt of the earth's axis and the earth's position in its orbit determine the season. As you read about the changing seasons in the following paragraphs, refer to Figure 14·10.

Figure 14·10
This diagram shows the earth's position at the start of each season.

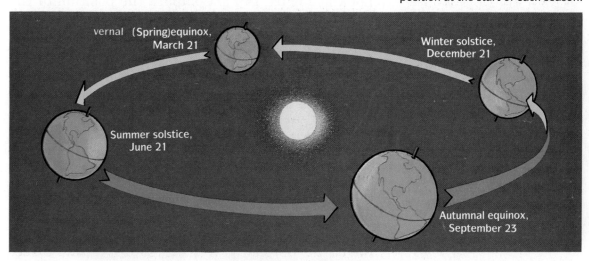

vernal (Spring)equinox, March 21

Winter solstice, December 21

Summer solstice, June 21

Autumnal equinox, September 23

The **summer solstice** (SAHL stihs) is a point in the sky through which the sun passes on the first day of summer in the Northern Hemisphere. The sun passes through the summer solstice around June 21. At this time, the North Pole axis tilts toward the sun. On this day the Northern Hemisphere receives its longest period of daylight and its most direct rays. At noon the sun appears at its highest point in the sky. Each day after that, the noon sun appears lower and lower in the sky and the period of daylight grows shorter.

The **autumnal equinox** (aw TUHM nuhl EE-kwih nahks) is a point in the sky through which the sun passes on the first day of fall in the Northern Hemisphere. The sun passes through the autumnal equinox around September 23. On this day, neither pole points toward the sun. There are 12 hours of daylight and 12 hours of darkness. As the earth continues to revolve, daylight hours in the Northern Hemisphere continue to grow shorter and the sun's rays become less direct.

The **winter solstice** is a point in the sky through which the sun passes on the first day of

sol (sun)
sistere (to stand still)

aequus (equal)
nox (night)

winter in the Northern Hemisphere. The sun passes through the winter solstice around December 21. At this time, the North Pole points away from the sun. On this day the Northern Hemisphere receives its shortest period of daylight and its least direct rays. Look at Figure 14·11. Compare the position of the sun at noon on this day with the position of the sun at the summer solstice. As the earth continues to revolve, the period of daylight in the Northern Hemisphere grows longer.

Figure 14·11
Winter solstice *(left)* and summer solstice *(right)*.

vernus (spring)

The **vernal equinox** (VER nuhl EE kwuh nahks) is a point in the sky through which the sun passes on the first day of spring in the Northern Hemisphere. The sun passes through the vernal equinox around March 21. On this day there are 12 hours of daylight and 12 hours of darkness. As the earth continues in its orbit, the North Pole tilts more and more toward the sun. In the Northern Hemisphere the daylight hours increase and the sun's rays become more direct. Each day at noon the sun appears higher in the sky.

REVIEW

1. Describe the tilt of the earth's axis.
2. How does the angle of the sun's rays on a surface relate to the amount of energy that surface receives?
3. What causes the earth's seasons?

CHALLENGE If you could be at the North Pole on the first day of summer you would see the sun at midnight. What would be happening at the South Pole? Explain your answer.

14·4 The Moon

WHAT IS THE MOON LIKE?

The moon is the earth's only natural satellite. Its average distance from the earth is 384,400 km. The moon rotates once every 27.3 days, the same length of time as its period of revolution. Thus the same side of the moon always faces the earth.

The moon's diameter, 3476 km, is about one fourth of the earth's diameter. The moon's mass is about one eightieth of the mass of the earth. The force of gravity on the moon is one sixth of that on the earth. This weak force holds only a very thin atmosphere. A thicker atmosphere, like that of the earth, helps to insulate a planet. On the moon the temperature in sunlight reaches 130°C, but in the shade the temperature can drop to −170°C.

The same elements that make up the earth make up the moon. But the elements are found in different amounts on the moon. The moon is thought to have layers. The crust, or top layer, is made up of rock material similar to that found on the earth. Below the crust is a layer called the mantle. It also is thought to be made of rock material. Beneath the mantle, the moon probably has a small core. This core may contain iron and other metals.

> After completing this section, you will be able to
> - **compare** the moon and the earth.
> - **illustrate** the phases of the moon.
> - **distinguish** between a solar eclipse and a lunar eclipse.
>
> *The key terms in this section are*
> **lunar eclipse**
> **phases**
> **solar eclipse**

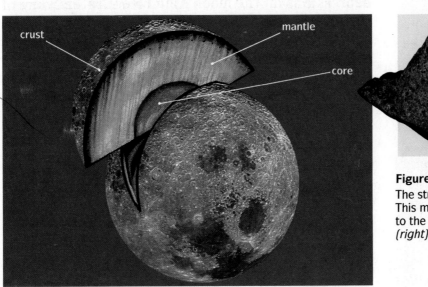

Figure 14·12
The structure of the moon *(left).* This moon rock was brought back to the earth by Apollo astronauts *(right).*

OBJECTIVES
Sketch the surface of the moon.
Identify some of the features on the moon's surface.

MATERIALS
binoculars, lunar map

PROCEDURE
A. Use a calendar to determine when the next full moon will occur.
B. On the night of the full moon — or the night before or the night after — go outdoors and observe the moon.
C. Make a sketch of the moon. Label the sketch *Moon — Naked-Eye View.*
D. Observe the moon with a pair of binoculars.

E. Make a sketch of the moon as it appears in the binoculars. Label the sketch *Moon — Through Binoculars.*
F. Using a map of the lunar surface, identify and label as many features as you can in each sketch.

RESULTS AND CONCLUSIONS
1. Which of your sketches is more detailed?
2. List the features that could be identified with the naked eye.
3. List the features that could be identified when using the binoculars.

EXTENSION
Observe the moon through a small telescope. Make a sketch of the moon. Identify the features in your sketch by using a lunar map.

Figure 14·13

This large crater probably formed when a meteorite struck the moon.

Scientists believe that after the moon formed, its surface was a hot liquid. Very light gases overcame the moon's gravity and escaped into space. In time the moon's surface cooled and formed a solid crust.

Rocks from space formed craters as they crashed into the moon's surface. *Craters* are round depressions on the moon's surface. Craters vary in size from small pits in boulders to depressions over 200 km in diameter. Sometimes, molten material from below the surface leaked over the floor of a huge crater. When this happened, a mare (MAHR ee) was formed. A mare is a flat area on the moon's surface. A soil made of broken rock and dust covers the moon's surface.

PHASES OF THE MOON

The moon does not produce its own light. The moon is seen from the earth because sunlight reflects from its surface. The sun lights the half of the moon that faces it. The moon seems to have different shapes, depending on how much of its lighted side we can see. The different shapes that the moon appears to have are called **phases.** As you read about the phases of the moon, look at Figure 14·14.

The *new-moon phase* occurs when the moon is between the earth and the sun. At this time, the side of the moon that faces the earth is dark. As the moon revolves around the earth, more of the side facing the earth is lighted each evening. During this time, the moon is said to be waxing, or growing larger. This first visible phase is a *crescent phase.*

After about a week, half of the side that faces the earth is lighted. This phase is the *first-quarter phase.* The moon has now traveled one quarter of the way around the earth. Following the first-quarter phase is a *gibbous* (GIHB uhs) *phase.* At this time, more than half of the side that faces the earth is lighted. Near the end of the second week, the moon enters the *full-moon phase.* How much of the surface that we see is lighted during a full moon?

After the full-moon phase, the moon begins to wane, or grow smaller. By the end of about 3 weeks, the moon has gone through another gibbous phase and has reached the *last-quarter phase.* As in the first-quarter phase, only half of the side of the moon that faces the earth is now lighted. During the final week of its revolution around the earth, the moon goes through another crescent phase. Then it becomes a new moon again.

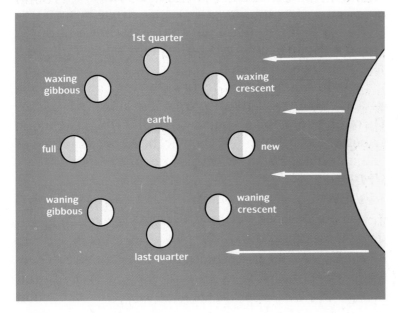

Figure 14·14
The phases of the moon.

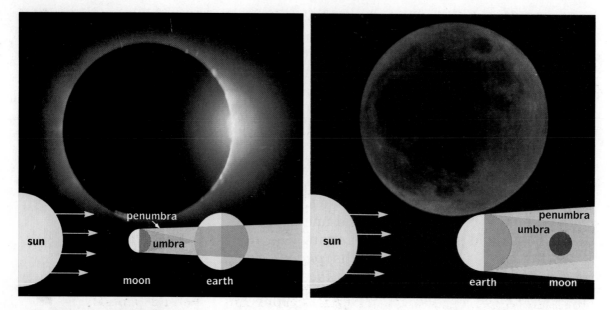

Figure 14·15

A total solar eclipse *(left)* and a
lunar eclipse *(right)*.

ECLIPSES

Shadows have two parts. The part directly behind an object is a cone-shaped area called the
umbra (UHM bruh). Light is completely blocked in
the umbra. A larger cone-shaped area called the
penumbra (pih NUHM bruh) surrounds the umbra.
Only some light is blocked in the penumbra.

An *eclipse* occurs when one object is in the
shadow of another. A total eclipse is seen in a region
covered by the umbra. A partial eclipse is seen in a
region when the penumbra covers that region. A
lunar eclipse occurs when the moon passes through
the shadow of the earth.

A lunar eclipse occurs during a full-moon
phase. A **solar eclipse** occurs when the earth passes
through the moon's shadow. At this time, the moon
is between the sun and the earth. At what phase of
the moon does a solar eclipse occur?

REVIEW

1. How are the moon and the earth similar?

2. Draw the phases of the moon.

3. What is the difference between solar and lunar eclipses?

CHALLENGE How much of the moon's surface would be seen
during a year if the moon did not rotate on its axis?

14·5 The Earth's Origin

THE NEBULAR HYPOTHESIS

Figure 14·16 shows a nebula in the constellation Orion. A *nebula* is a cloud of gas and dust. It is thought that stars are forming in this nebula.

One hypothesis of the origin of the earth and the solar system says that the solar system formed from such a cloud. According to the **nebular hypothesis,** the solar system formed from a dust cloud that contracted, or came together.

The nebular hypothesis is shown in Figure 14·17 on the next page. The dust cloud is shown in step 1. Notice in step 2 how the spinning cloud contracted. The spinning motion of the cloud caused it to flatten into a disk. Most of the matter in the cloud was pulled by gravity to the center of the cloud, as you can see in step 3. This matter formed a *protostar* that became the sun.

As the cloud continued to spin, small whirlpools formed within it. Matter collected in the whirlpools. These whirlpools of matter, which were the beginning of the bodies of the solar sys-

After completing this section, you will be able to

- **describe** the nebular hypothesis for the origin of the earth.
- **explain** how the earth's oceans and atmosphere may have formed.

The key terms in this section are
nebular hypothesis
protoplanets

nebula (cloud)

Figure 14·16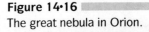

The great nebula in Orion.

353

proto (first) tem, are called **protoplanets.** It is thought that it took 10 million to 100 million years for the dust cloud to form the protoplanets shown in step 4.

The protoplanets were probably much larger than the planets today. Each probably had a thick atmosphere. Inside the protoplanets, solid particles combined to form large chunks. The heavier matter settled near the centers of the protoplanets. In time the planets that are known today formed. Steps 5 and 6 show the final stages in the formation of the solar system.

The nebular hypothesis explains many things about the solar system. For example, the spinning motion of the cloud explains why the planets revolve in the same direction around the sun.

Figure 14·17

The nebular hypothesis.

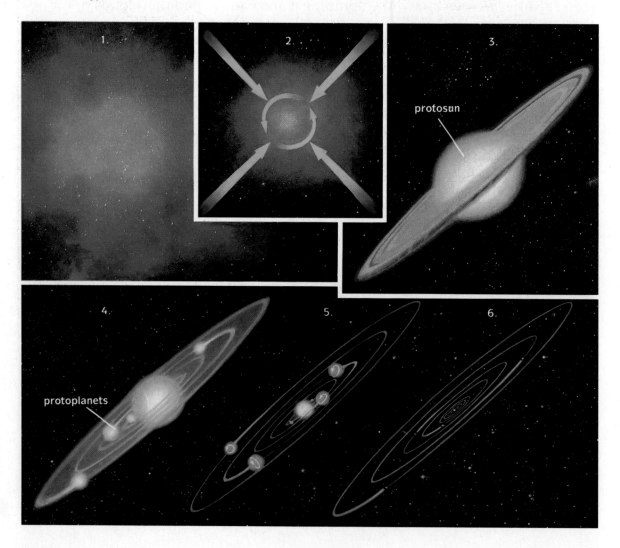

What Model Can Illustrate the Nebular Hypothesis?

OBJECTIVES

Construct and **analyze** a model of the nebular hypothesis.

MATERIALS

safety goggles, round pot or pan, hot plate, water, beaker, 2 eggs, 2 culture dishes, slotted spoon, spoon

PROCEDURE

A. Wear safety goggles during this activity.
B. Place a round pot or pan on a hot plate. Pour water from the beaker into the pan. Make sure the water is at least 8 cm deep. Plug in the hot plate.
C. Crack an egg on the edge of a culture dish and empty the egg into the dish.
D. When the water is almost boiling, unplug the hot plate. Slowly slide the egg into the hot water. Place it in the center of the pan. As the egg cooks observe its shape.
E. Remove the cooked egg with the slotted spoon, and place it back in its dish.
F. Repeat steps **B** and **C**.
G. Using a spoon, slowly begin to stir the water after it almost comes to a boil. **Caution:** Be very careful that you do not spill or splash the hot water.
   1. If you were to place an egg into this moving water, what do you predict would happen?
H. While you continue to stir the water, have your partner carefully slide the egg into the center of the pan.
   2. What do you observe?

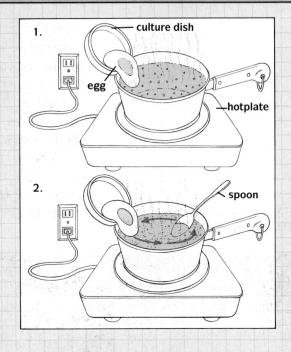

1.
culture dish
egg
hotplate

2.
spoon

3. What shape does this egg have?
I. After the egg has stopped cooking, stop stirring and remove the egg with the slotted spoon. Return the egg to its dish.

RESULTS AND CONCLUSIONS

1. Compare the cooked eggs. How are their shapes different?
2. Was your prediction about what would happen to the second egg correct?
3. In what way does this model represent the nebular hypothesis?
4. In what way does this model differ from the nebular hypothesis?

The nebular hypothesis also explains why the planets near the sun are different from the planets farther from the sun. The heat of the early sun drove off the lighter elements from the proto-planets near the sun. For this reason, the planets near the sun became solid and rocklike. The planets farther away kept the lighter gases.

carbon dioxide
sulfur gases
methane
water vapor
ammonia

Figure 14·18

Volcanoes helped to form the earth's early atmosphere.

ORIGIN OF OCEANS AND ATMOSPHERE

Water makes up a large part of the earth's surface. How can the origin of the oceans be explained? Water is made up of hydrogen and oxygen. Hydrogen is abundant in dust clouds in space. Oxygen is also found in such clouds. Since the earth probably formed from a dust cloud, water probably formed on the early earth.

The earth's water was probably trapped inside minerals within the earth. Such minerals would have been found within the earth shortly after it formed. The water may have escaped from the earth's interior through volcanoes. It would then have collected in the atmosphere as steam and vapor. As the earth cooled, rain would have fallen. The water would have collected on the surface, forming shallow pools. These shallow pools were the earth's first oceans.

The earth's first atmosphere was probably quite different from the atmosphere today. The primitive atmosphere was probably produced by volcanic activity on the early earth. Figure 14·20 shows what conditions may have been like at that time. According to the figure, what gases made up the primitive atmosphere? What gas is missing?

Oxygen was probably added to the atmosphere by early living things. Like today's plants, such organisms may have produced oxygen during food-making activities.

REVIEW

1. How does the nebular hypothesis explain the origin of the earth?
2. Explain how the earth's oceans and atmosphere may have formed.

CHALLENGE Unlike the earth, the moon has almost no atmosphere. How can you account for the lack of an atmosphere on the moon?

CHAPTER SUMMARY

The main ideas in this chapter are listed below. Read these statements before you answer the Chapter Review questions.

- The earth is the third planet from the sun in a solar system in the Milky Way galaxy. The Milky Way is located in a cluster of galaxies called the local group, which is one of countless clusters in the universe. (14•1)
- The earth is sphere-shaped. It can be divided into three spheres—the atmosphere, the hydrosphere, and the lithosphere—and is surrounded by a magnetic field. (14•1)
- The earth rotates on its axis and revolves around the sun. (14•2)
- Time on the earth is measured according to the movements of the earth, moon, and sun. (14•2)
- Time zones have been set up around the world to standardize time measurement. (14•2)
- The tilt of the earth's axis and the earth's position in its orbit cause the change in the seasons. (14•3)

- The moon is about one-fourth the size of the earth and has a force of gravity that is one sixth of that on the earth. (14•4)
- As seen from the earth, the moon changes from a full moon to a new moon and back to a full moon each month. (14•4)
- Eclipses occur either when the earth passes through the moon's shadow or when the moon passes through the earth's shadow. (14•4)
- The nebular hypothesis states that the solar system formed from a spinning cloud of gas and dust. The sun formed from matter in the center and the planets formed from whirlpools of matter surrounding the sun. (14•5)
- Volcanic activity may have been involved in the production of the earth's atmosphere and in the production of the earth's oceans. (14•5)

The key terms in this chapter are listed below. Use each term in a sentence that shows the meaning of the term.

atmosphere	lunar eclipse	revolution	time zones
autumnal equinox	nebular hypothesis	rotation	vernal equinox
hydrosphere	phases	solar eclipse	winter solstice
lithosphere	protoplanets	summer solstice	

Chapter Review

Vocabulary

Use the key terms from the previous page to complete the following sentences correctly.

1. The first day of spring in the Northern Hemisphere occurs when the sun passes through the _____.
2. The earth is divided into 24 equal segments called _____.
3. When the earth passes through the moon's shadow, a/an _____ occurs.
4. The turning of an object on its axis is _____.
5. The layer of water that covers the earth is called the _____.
6. The movement of an object along an orbit around another body is _____.
7. That the solar system formed from a cloud of dust and gas is proposed by the _____.
8. Whirlpools of matter that were the beginning of the bodies of the solar system are called _____.
9. The different shapes that the moon appears to have are called _____.
10. The layer of gases that surrounds the earth is called the _____.

CONCEPTS

Choose the term or phrase that best answers the question or completes the statement.

1. The Van Allen belts are part of the earth's
   a. atmosphere.
   b. hydrosphere
   c. lithosphere.
   d. magnetosphere.
2. One rotation of the earth is completed in
   a. one hour.
   b. one day.
   c. one month.
   d. one year.
3. If it is 9:00 A.M. in your time zone, what time is it in the next time zone to the east?
   a. 8:00 A.M.
   b. 9:00 A.M.
   c. 10:00 A.M.
   d. 11:00 A.M.
4. The longest daylight period of the year occurs when the sun passes through the
   a. summer solstice.
   b. winter solstice.
   c. vernal equinox.
   d. autumnal equinox.
5. Oxygen was probably added to the earth's first atmosphere by
   a. minerals.
   b. volcanoes.
   c. living things.
   d. steam.

Look at the drawing and answer the questions.

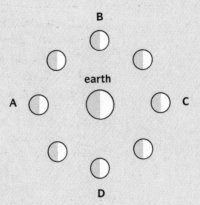

6. What phase of the moon is seen when the moon is in position *A*?
7. What phase of the moon is seen when the moon is in position *B*?
8. What phase of the moon is seen when the moon is in position *C*?
9. What phase of the moon is seen when the moon is in position *D*?
10. What kind of eclipse could occur when the moon is in position *A*?

Answer the following in complete sentences.

11. Describe the movement of the earth around the sun.
12. Describe two factors that help to determine how much energy a region of the earth receives from the sun.
13. Describe the surface of the moon.
14. How does the nebular hypothesis explain why the planets closer to the sun are different from the planets that are farther away from the sun?

---

1. Explain why there is little seasonal change in the region between the Tropic of Cancer and the Tropic of Capricorn.
2. How would the weather and seasons be different if the earth were not tilted?
3. Is the surface of the moon likely to change in the next 100 years? In the next 500 years? Explain your answers.
4. What changes would you observe if
   a. the earth rotated in the opposite direction?
   b. the earth rotated faster?
   c. the earth rotated slower?

APPLICATION/ CRITICAL THINKING

---

1. Design an experiment to prove that the earth rotates. If you need help, find out about a pendulum designed by the French scientist named Jean Foucault (1819–1868).
2. Make a scale model of the earth and sun, showing their relative sizes and their distance apart.
3. Find out why we see the planet Venus in phases.

EXTENSION

CHAPTER 15

THE SOLAR SYSTEM

*T*his photograph of the great red spot of Jupiter was taken by the Voyager 2 spacecraft. The great red spot was first seen through a telescope on the earth in 1665. Since then, scientists have been trying to find out more about the spot. The spot is believed to be like a giant swirling hurricane over 40,000 km long. Data collected by Voyager 2 indicate that wind speeds around the spot may be as high as 280 km/h.

Voyager 2 continues to collect information about the planets. It was launched in 1977 and passed Jupiter in July 1979. Voyager 2 went on to pass Saturn in 1981 and Uranus in 1986. Voyager 2 is expected to pass Neptune in 1989.

- *What other information has been collected by spacecraft?*
- *In what other ways do scientists collect information about the planets?*

15·1 Members of the Solar System

You may have noticed that stars form patterns in the sky. These patterns do not change, although different star groups are visible at different times. A few objects, however, seem to wander among the stars. Some race across the sky and disappear within seconds. Others grow tails as they slowly move across the heavens. These objects that move against the background of the stars are members of the solar system. The **solar system** is the sun and the objects that move around it. The solar system includes the planets and their moons, asteroids (AS-tuh roidz), meteoroids (MEE tee uh roidz), and comets. The members of the solar system are much closer to the sun than are the stars.

THE PLANETS

Scientists divide the planets into two groups: the **inner planets** and the outer planets. The inner planets are Mercury, Venus, the earth, and Mars, the four planets closest to the sun. These planets are very dense. It is thought that they each have a metal core and a rocky mantle. The earth, Venus, and Mars all have atmospheres.

The **outer planets** are Jupiter, Saturn, Uranus (yu RAY nuhs), Neptune, and Pluto. Each of these

Figure 15·1
The solar system.

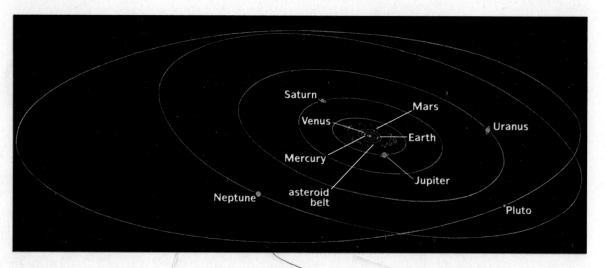

planets is thought to have a rocky core. Jupiter, Saturn, Uranus, and Neptune are surrounded by a layer of liquid hydrogen and a thick atmosphere.

Pluto is different from the other planets. Table 15·1 shows information about the planets. Notice that compared with the other outer planets, Pluto is not very big. Compared with the inner planets, Pluto is not very dense. How does the temperature of Pluto compare with the temperatures of the other planets?

Table 15·1 *The Planets*

PLANET	DIAMETER (in km)	MASS (EARTH = 1.0)	DENSITY (H₂O = 1g/cm³)	DISTANCE FROM SUN (in millions of km)	REVOLUTION	ROTATION	TILT OF AXIS	GRAVITY (EARTH = 1)	TEMPERATURE	KNOWN SATELLITES
Mercury	4,878	0.055	5.4	57.9	88.0 d	59.0 d	0.0°	0.38	430°C daylight −180°C dark	0
Venus	12,100	0.8	5.2	108.2	225.0 d	243.0 d	3.0°	0.90	475°C	0
Earth	12,756	1.0	5.5	149.6	365.25 d	23.93 h	23.5°	1	15°C Average	1
Mars	6,787	0.1	3.9	227.9	687.0 d	24.6 h	25.2°	0.38	−50°C Average	2
Jupiter	142,800	318.0	1.3	778.3	11.86 y	9.9 h	3.1°	2.54	−130°C cloud tops	16
Saturn	120,000	95.0	0.7	1,427.0	29.46 y	10.7 h	26.7°	1.07	−185°C cloud tops	20
Uranus	50,800	15.0	1.3	2,870.0	84.0 y	16.0 h	97.9°	0.9 (?)	−215°C cloud tops	15
Neptune	48,600	17.0	1.8	4,497.0	165.0 y	18.0 h	29.6°	1.15(?)	−200°C cloud tops	2
Pluto	3,000(?)	0.002	1.0	5,900.0	248.0 y	6.4 d	60.0°(?)	0.03(?)	−230°C	1

ASTEROIDS

Between Mars and Jupiter, thousands — perhaps millions — of pieces of rock and metal orbit around the sun. The largest of these objects are called *asteroids*. Some asteroids are several hundred kilometers wide, but most are small. The region where most asteroids are found is the asteroid belt.

How did the asteroids come to occupy this region of space? Some scientists think that the asteroids may be pieces of a planet that once existed but was torn apart millions of years ago. Other scientists have suggested that the asteroids are materials that never came together to form a planet.

In June 1908 an explosion occurred in Siberia in the Soviet Union. Trees were scorched and flattened. Scientists suspect that an object from space caused the explosion. What do you think it was? What evidence might you look for to test your hypothesis?

METEOROIDS

Small bodies of rock or metal that move through the solar system are called *meteoroids*. Meteoroids sometimes strike the earth. They enter the atmosphere at speeds ranging from 15 km/s to 70 km/s. At such speeds, friction between air particles and a meteoroid causes the meteoroid to burn white-hot. This burning meteoroid is called a meteor (MEE tee uhr), or a "shooting star."

Sometimes a piece of a large meteoroid does not burn up completely, and it reaches the earth's surface. A piece of a meteoroid that strikes the surface is called a meteorite (MEE tee uh rīt). Large meteorites produce craters in the earth's surface.

COMETS

Comets are large chunks of ice, frozen gases, dust, and rock that orbit the sun. They are often described as dirty snowballs. Comets are perhaps the most unusual objects in the solar system. They appear to move slowly across the sky. A comet usually grows a tail as it approaches the sun. Charged particles that stream from the sun cause a comet's tail to always point away from the sun. Notice in Figure 15·2 that when a comet is approaching the sun, the tail lags behind the comet head. Where is the tail when the comet is moving away from the sun?

Figure 15·2

The tail of a comet always points away from the sun *(left)*. Computer-enhanced photograph of a comet *(right)*.

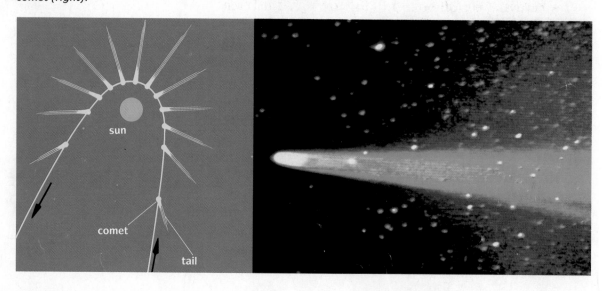

ACTIVITY The Solar System to Scale

OBJECTIVE
Construct a scale model of the solar system.

MATERIALS
large piece of white cardboard or paper, metric ruler, drawing compass, local map

PROCEDURE

A. Scale models are useful because they help you understand the relationships among the parts of a system. The scale for this model will be 1 mm = 1000 km. Set up a data table. It should list the diameter of each planet in kilometers, and the scale diameter. The table should also list the distance of each planet from the sun, and the scale distance. (See Table 5·1 for diameters and distances from the sun.)

B. On a piece of cardboard, draw a circle to represent each planet according to your scale measurements. Label each circle with the name of the planet that it represents.

C. Find the location of your school on a local map. The school will represent the sun. Draw a line on the map in any direction from your school through the town. Using your scale and the map scale, mark and label where on the line the planets you have drawn would be placed. For example, if Jupiter was 1 km from the school according to your scale, you would find on your line the point that is 1 km from the school according to the map scale and then mark it.

RESULTS AND CONCLUSIONS
1. Which planets are clearly larger than the others?
2. The diameter of the sun is 1.4 million km. How large is it according to your scale?
3. Where are the distances greater, between the inner planets or between the outer planets?
4. Proxima Centauri, the nearest star to the solar system, is 38.7 trillion km from the sun. According to your scale, how far away is Proxima Centauri? Where would you place it on the map?
5. What are the advantages of making a scale model such as this? What are the disadvantages of this model?

A comet gives off no light of its own. Light from the sun reflects off the comet and its tail. The brightness of a comet depends mostly on its distance from the sun and the earth. The brightness is also affected by the size of the comet. Halley's comet is a large comet that passes the sun every 76 years. It usually can be seen without a telescope.

REVIEW
1. What objects does the solar system include?
2. How are the inner planets different from the outer planets?
3. Distinguish between an asteroid, a meteoroid, and a comet.

CHALLENGE Sunlight reaches the earth in 8⅓ minutes. The speed of light is about 300,000 km/s. How long does it take sunlight to reach Pluto?

15·2 The Sun

After completing this section,
you will be able to

- **explain** how the sun produces
  energy and how this energy
  reaches the earth.
- **describe** the composition and
  structure of the sun.
- **identify** the features of the
  sun.

The key terms in this section are
chromosphere
core
corona
photosphere
solar wind
sunspots

THE SUN PRODUCES ENERGY

The sun is the source of the earth's light and heat. Fusion in the sun produces the sun's energy. Fusion is a kind of nuclear reaction. In fusion, hydrogen nuclei join under high temperature and pressure to form helium nuclei. In this process a small amount of mass is changed into a large amount of energy.

The fusion process is shown in Figure 15·3. Six hydrogen nuclei join to form one helium nucleus and two hydrogen nuclei. Notice that the nuclei have less mass after this process. The missing mass has been changed into energy.

The energy given off by the sun is called *solar radiation*. Solar radiation moves through space at a speed of 300,000 km/s. At this speed the sun's energy reaches the earth in about 8 minutes.

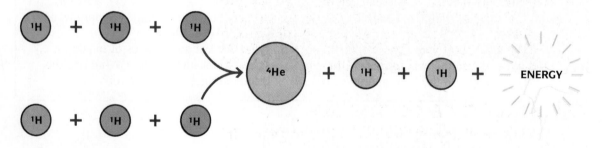

6.048 total atomic mass   6.019 total atomic mass

Figure 15·3
Nuclear reactions in the sun produce energy.

Almost all of the solar radiation that reaches the earth's surface is in the form of *visible light* and *infrared rays*. These types of radiation are harmless to life. The sun also gives off forms of radiation that are harmful. These include *gamma rays, X rays*, and *ultraviolet rays*. However, the earth's atmosphere absorbs most of these harmful waves before they reach the earth's surface. For example, a gas called ozone absorbs ultraviolet rays in the atmosphere. As a result, only small amounts of ultraviolet rays reach the earth's surface.

The sun also gives off a steady stream of electrically charged particles called the **solar wind**. The solar wind moves at speeds from 300 km/s to 700 km/s and reaches beyond the orbit of Saturn.

Living things on the earth are protected from the solar wind by the earth's magnetic field. The earth's magnetic field deflects many of the charged particles away from the earth. Figure 15·4 shows how the solar wind is steered away. Notice that the magnetic field on the side of the earth away from the sun is pulled away from the earth.

sol (sun)

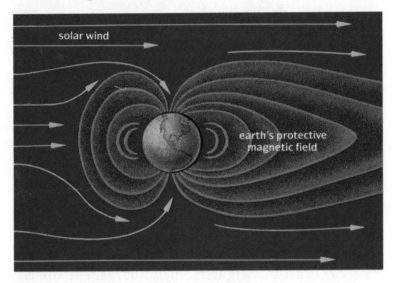

solar wind

earth's protective magnetic field

Figure 15·4
The earth's magnetic field protects the planet from the solar wind.

THE STRUCTURE OF THE SUN

The sun is a large sphere of very hot gases. Its diameter is 1.392 million km. It is so large that all the planets and moons of the solar system could easily fit inside the sun. Nearly 99.8 percent of all the matter in the solar system is in the sun.

The sun contains at least 80 of the elements that are found on the earth. Hydrogen makes up 92.1 percent of the atoms in the sun and helium makes up 7.8 percent. The remaining 0.1 percent is a combination of other elements. All of these elements are in a form of matter called plasma. *Plasma* is matter in which atoms have lost their electrons because of very high temperatures. Particles in plasma are electrically charged, and they shake violently.

367

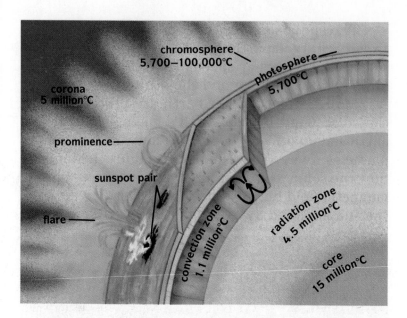

Figure 15·5
The structure of the sun.

The sun is believed to have layers. But because the sun is made up of plasma, which behaves like a gas, there are no definite boundaries between the layers. Instead the layers blend into each other.

At the center of the sun is the **core.** As you can see in Figure 15·5, the core is small compared with the rest of the sun. But the core contains almost half of the sun's matter. The pressure in the core is about 200 billion times the pressure on the earth's surface. According to Figure 15·5, what is the temperature of the core? How would conditions in the core make the process of fusion possible?

Scientists believe that the fusion reaction that produces the sun's energy takes place in the core. It may take as much as 10 million years for energy to reach the surface from the core. As energy from the core moves outward, it passes through two layers. The first layer is the *radiation zone,* the thickest layer of the sun. Energy is passed from particle to particle through this layer. Each particle absorbs energy and then releases it to the next particle.

The next layer of the sun is the *convection zone.* Notice in Figure 15·5 the curved arrows that show the flow of plasma in this layer. Energy is carried through the convection zone in currents of hot plasma. What is the temperature in the convection zone?

The **photosphere** (FOH tuh sfihr) is the visible surface of the sun. Much of the energy that reaches the photosphere is changed into visible light. The temperature of the photosphere is about 5700°C. How does this compare with the temperature of the layer below it?

Notice in Figure 15·6 that the photosphere is granular. Bright areas appear where hot plasma breaks through the photosphere. These bright areas are called granules. Granules are too small to be seen without a telescope, but they average 2000 km across.

Above the photosphere are the two layers of the sun's atmosphere. These layers are usually not visible because the photosphere is so bright. Both layers can be seen during solar eclipses and with special telescopes. The first layer of the sun's atmosphere is called the **chromosphere** (KROH muh-sfihr). The name *chromosphere*, meaning "colored sphere," is used because of the faint red light of this layer. The temperature of the chromosphere rises from 5700°C at its bottom to 100,000°C at its top.

The outer layer of the sun's atmosphere is called the **corona.** This layer is less dense than the chromosphere. During a solar eclipse, the corona can be seen as a halo around the sun. Identify the corona in Figure 15·7. Temperatures reaching almost 3 million°C have been measured in the corona.

Figure 15·6
The surface of the sun is granular.

chromo- (color)

corona (crown)

Figure 15·7
The corona of the sun is visible during a solar eclipse. This is a computer-enhanced photograph.

FEATURES OF THE SUN

Dark areas on the surface of the sun are called **sunspots.** They are often found in pairs. Figure 15·8 shows a sunspot pair. Sunspots mark areas of strong magnetic fields. Sunspots look dark because they are cooler than the rest of the sun's surface. They may last a few days or several weeks. Sunspots near the sun's equator cross the surface of the sun faster than those closer to its poles. This is because not all places on the sun rotate at the same speed.

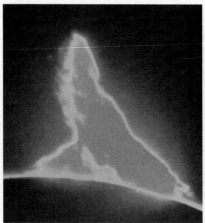
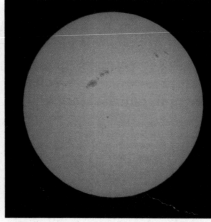
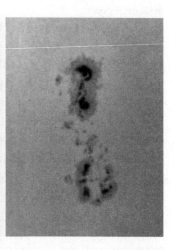

Figure 15·8
Solar prominence *(left)*. Sunspots *(middle, right)*.

Magnetic fields seem to be responsible for forming solar prominences and flares. A *prominence* is a loop or cloud of plasma. It shoots from the photosphere but is held in the corona by a magnetic field. The temperature within a prominence can reach 10,000°C. These loops or clouds of plasma can last from a few hours to several months. A *solar flare* is a sudden, violent eruption of plasma from the chromosphere. The temperature within a flare may reach 100 million°C.

REVIEW

1. How does energy from the sun travel to the earth?
2. What substances make up the sun?
3. How is a solar flare different from a prominence?

CHALLENGE If you could see a prominence in the corona, would the corona appear dark or appear bright, based on its estimated temperature? Why?

15·3 The Inner Planets

Mercury, Venus, the earth, and Mars are the inner planets. They each seem to have a metal core surrounded by a rocky mantle. The inner planets are very different from the giant outer planets. Figure 15·9 shows the four inner planets. Notice that the diameter of each of these planets is given. Which planet has the smallest diameter? Which has the largest?

Why do the inner planets differ from the outer planets? According to the nebular hypothesis, the solar system formed from a cloud of gas and dust. As matter collected to form the planets, each planet was large and made of the same materials. When the sun began to produce energy, the solar wind removed lighter elements from the bodies closest to the sun. These lighter elements were carried to the outer part of the nebula. These lighter elements became part of the outer planets.

In time, only the dense materials that the solar wind could not remove remained close to the sun. These dense materials formed the inner planets. In this way the inner planets became smaller and denser than the outer planets.

Figure 15·9
The inner planets.

Mercury	Venus	Earth	Mars
Diameter (km) 4,878	12,100	12,756	6,787

Figure 15·10
This mosaic of the planet Mercury
was taken by Mariner 10.

MERCURY

Mercury is the planet closest to the sun. For this reason, Mercury is difficult to see from the earth. At times, Mercury is seen in the sky just before the sun rises. At other times, it is seen just after the sun sets. Mercury is always close to the horizon when it is visible.

In the spring of 1974, a United States spacecraft, Mariner 10, gave astronomers their first good look at Mercury. Figure 15·10 shows Mercury's surface as photographed by that spacecraft. This kind of photograph is called a mosaic because it is made of photographs of areas of the planet. Notice that Mercury is covered with craters much like the earth's moon. How might these craters have been formed? Mercury also has long, steep cliffs that stretch across its surface.

Mercury is different from the earth in many ways. For example, Mercury is much smaller than the earth. Also, there is no water on Mercury. And the force of gravity there is about one-third that on the earth. How much would you weigh on Mercury?

There is a big difference in temperature between the sunlit side and the dark side of Mercury. The temperature on the sunlit side can be more than 400°C. On the dark side the temperature can drop to less than −180°C.

VENUS

Venus is the second planet from the sun. It is the brightest object in the sky except for the sun and the moon. Like Mercury, Venus also appears in the sky shortly before sunrise or shortly after sunset. Venus comes closer to the earth than does any other planet.

As shown in Figure 15·11, Venus is wrapped in thick layers of clouds. No sign of the planet's surface can be seen from the earth. How do the thick clouds that cover Venus help to account for its brightness?

Several spacecraft have studied Venus. The studies have shown that the clouds in the upper atmosphere of Venus contain sulfuric acid. These clouds are swept along by winds that travel at 360 km/h. Beneath the acid clouds, the wind speed is slower, and the atmosphere is mostly carbon dioxide.

The thick clouds around the planet trap heat from the sun, making Venus warmer than Mercury. At the surface of Venus, the temperature is around 470°C and the pressure is 91 times greater than that of the earth's atmosphere.

Figure 15·11
Venus has a thick pattern of cloud cover *(inset)*. This is an artist's conception, based on measurements taken by spacecraft, of the large mountain ranges on Venus.

How Do Meteorites Form Craters?

OBJECTIVE
Demonstrate how meteorite impacts could form craters on the surface of a planet.

MATERIALS
20 cm x 20 cm baking pan, sifted flour, metric ruler, paprika, different-sized pebbles, forceps

PROCEDURE
A. Draw a data table with headings like the one shown.

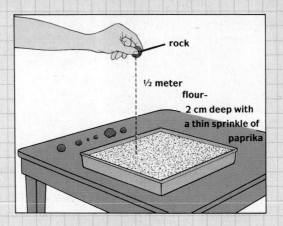

rock

½ meter

flour-
2 cm deep with a thin sprinkle of paprika

PEBBLE NUMBER	HEIGHT	DIAMETER OF CRATER
1		

B. Cover the bottom of a baking pan with a layer of flour about 2 cm deep. Gently shake the pan to smooth the layer of flour. Lightly sprinkle a thin layer of paprika over the flour. These layers represent the surface of a planet or the moon.

C. The pebbles represent meteorites that strike the surface. Hold one of the pebbles 0.5 m above the pan, and drop the pebble into the pan.
   1. What does the crater look like?
   2. What is the distance across the top of the crater? Record the data.
   3. What do you see outside the rim of the crater?

D. Use forceps to remove the pebble.

E. Repeat steps **C** and **D** several times with the same pebble but from different heights and over different parts of the pan. Record the results.
   4. How does changing the height from which the pebble falls change the crater?

F. Repeat steps **C** through **E** several times with different pebbles. Record the results.
   5. How does the size of the pebble affect the size of the crater?
   6. How does the shape of the pebble affect the crater?

RESULTS AND CONCLUSIONS
1. How does the material in the pan now resemble the surface of Mercury or Mars?
2. How might the craters of the moons and planets have been formed?
3. Why are few craters found on the earth?

MARS

Mars, the fourth planet from the sun, is often called the red planet. Reddish-brown sand and rocks on its surface and dust in its atmosphere give Mars a reddish look.

Mars is similar to the earth in some ways. For example, Mars rotates on its axis in just over 24 hours. Mars is tilted on its axis. Its tilt is almost the same as the tilt of the earth. As a result, Mars has seasons, as does the earth. The north and south

Figure 15·12

The surface of Mars as photographed by Viking 2. Mars as seen through a telescope on earth *(inset)*.

poles of Mars are covered by icecaps. They are probably made of frozen carbon dioxide and water.

The atmosphere of Mars is thin. It does not trap heat as do the atmospheres of Venus and the earth. As a result, the surface of Mars is always cold. A high temperature at Mars's equator is 0°C.

Spacecraft that have visited Mars have found huge volcanoes, large craters, areas of lava flow, and deep canyons. When the two Viking spacecraft landed on Mars in 1976, they probed the surface for any sign of life. They took photographs, like the one shown in Figure 15·12. The spacecraft studied soil samples and conducted other tests. But they found no evidence of life on Mars.

Mars has two small moons: *Phobos* (FOH buhs) and *Deimos* (DĪ mohs). Both moons are irregularly shaped. Phobos, the larger of the two, is only 25 km wide. Deimos is only 15 km across. They look more like asteroids than like moons.

REVIEW

1. How do scientists explain the lack of lighter elements in the inner planets?

2. Describe the main features of Mercury. How does Mercury differ from Venus?

3. Compare Mars with the earth. How are they similar? How are they different?

CHALLENGE Like the moon, Venus appears to go through phases. When Venus is full, it looks circular. Sketch the relative positions of the sun, the earth, and Venus when Venus is full.

15·4 The Outer Planets

With the exception of Pluto, the outer planets are much larger and less dense than the inner planets. Jupiter, Saturn, Uranus, and Neptune are known as the gas giants. Although each of the gas giants has a rocky core, they are made mostly of the light elements hydrogen and helium. The outer planets are shown in Figure 15·13. Which three planets have rings?

Recall that some scientists think the solar wind drove the lighter elements to the outer regions of the nebula. The outer planets collected the lighter elements and grew to great size.

Jupiter	Saturn	Uranus	Neptune	Pluto

| Diameter (km) | 142,800 | 120,000 | 50,800 | 48,600 | 3,000 (?) |

Figure 15·13
The outer planets.

JUPITER

Jupiter, the fifth planet from the sun, is by far the largest planet in the solar system. Jupiter's total mass is more than twice that of all the other objects in the solar system except the sun.

Jupiter turns on its axis about every 9 hours and 50 minutes. This rapid rate of rotation causes the planet to bulge at the equator and flatten at the poles.

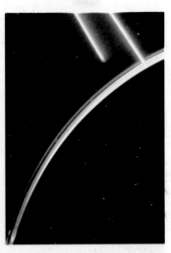

Figure 15·14
A photograph of the planet Jupiter, taken by Pioneer 10 *(left)*. The red spot, photographed by Voyager 1 *(middle)*. A color composite of Jupiter's rings, photographed by Voyager 2 *(right)*.

Jupiter's atmosphere is 88 percent hydrogen and 11 percent helium. Pressure within Jupiter's atmosphere increases with depth. The gases become thicker and denser until, finally, they become liquid. An ocean of liquid hydrogen surrounds the core. Deep within the planet, increased pressure produces metallic hydrogen. This metallic hydrogen, along with the planet's rapid rotation, creates a strong magnetic field.

Jupiter gives off more energy than it receives from the sun. The temperature at Jupiter's core is around 30,000°C. Heat from the planet causes some parts of the atmosphere to be warmer and less dense than other parts. As a result, Jupiter's atmosphere is in constant motion. Storms appear as colored spots in the atmosphere. The most striking of these is the great red spot, shown in Figure 15·14.

Jupiter has a ring and 16 known moons. The 4 largest were first seen by Galileo. Each Galilean moon is larger than Pluto.

SATURN

Saturn, the sixth planet from the sun, is the second largest planet. Saturn is well known for its system of rings, shown in Figure 15·15. The rings of Saturn can be seen from the earth by using a small telescope.

Saturn's rings are probably made of flecks of frozen gases and tiny chunks of matter covered with ice. Sunlight bouncing off these materials

Figure 15·15

Saturn, as viewed with a telescope on the earth *(left)*. A Voyager 2 photograph of Saturn *(right)*.

Figure 15·16

Uranus and its moons.

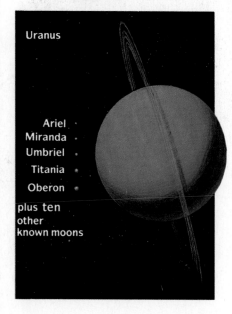

makes the rings appear more solid than they actually are. The Pioneer 11 spacecraft passed through the rings without serious damage.

Saturn is similar to Jupiter in many ways. Saturn is made mostly of hydrogen. The planet is thought to have a dense, hot core surrounded by metallic hydrogen, and a strong magnetic field. Like Jupiter, Saturn gives off more energy than it takes in and has a stormy atmosphere. Saturn turns on its axis in 10 hours and 40 minutes. How would this rapid rotation rate affect the shape of Saturn?

URANUS AND NEPTUNE

Uranus is the seventh planet from the sun and **Neptune** is the eighth planet from the sun. These planets are often called twin planets because they are much alike. Each has a diameter about four times that of the earth. Each is composed mostly of hydrogen and helium. And each appears to be bluish-green with shaded bands.

Uranus is more tilted on its axis than is any other planet. As shown in Figure 15·16, Uranus is almost lying on its side. As a result of this tilt, at certain places in its orbit, the north pole of Uranus points almost directly at the sun. On the other side of its orbit, the north pole points away from the sun.

A system of dark rings encircles Uranus. Some scientists think that the dark rings contain pieces of rock. In fact the rings may be moons in the making. Besides having dark rings, Uranus has a number of moons. No rings have been found around far-off Neptune. But scientists think there may also be dark rings there. Neptune is known to have two moons, and it may have a third.

PLUTO

Pluto was the ninth planet to be discovered in the solar system. Most of the time, it is the ninth planet from the sun. Refer back to Figure 15·1. Notice that Pluto's orbit crosses inside that of Neptune. So at times, Pluto is closer to the sun than is Neptune. This is the case now.

Pluto is very different from all other planets. It is the smallest planet. Pluto does not have large mass like the other outer planets. Nor does it have high density like the inner planets. It is so small and far away that little is known about it. Pluto has one moon, named Charon (KAIR uhn).

Figure 15·17
Neptune and its moons, Triton and Nereid.

Figure 15·18
This is what Charon and the sun would look like if you were on Pluto.

REVIEW

1. How do scientists explain the large amount of light elements in the outer planets?

2. Compare the features of Jupiter and Saturn.

3. How are Uranus and Neptune similar?

CHALLENGE Some scientists have suggested that Pluto is an escaped moon of Neptune. What evidence would support this hypothesis?

15·5 Exploring Space

A **satellite** is any object that revolves around another object. Moons are natural satellites of planets. In space exploration the term *satellite* usually refers to an artificial satellite.

More than a thousand satellites have been placed in orbit around the earth. There are many different kinds of satellites. Weather satellites have improved the accuracy and speed of weather forecasting. Other satellites allow messages, including television broadcasts, to be sent around the world faster than ever before. Landsat satellites study the earth's surface. They keep track of resources, such as croplands, forests, and water supplies. Seasat photographs, like the one shown in Figure 15·19, have been used to study oceans.

Exploration of other parts of the solar system has been going on since the 1960s. Spacecraft sent to study the moon and other planets are called **space probes.** Much of the information you have

Figure 15·19

A photograph of the earth, taken by the Seasat satellite.

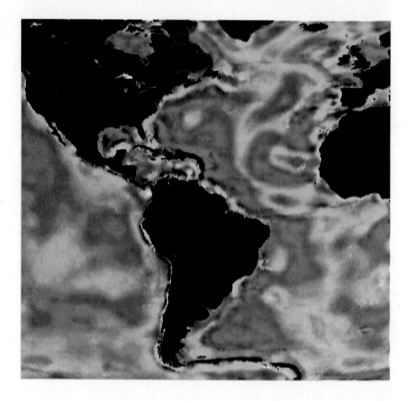

already read about the planets was gathered by space probes. For example, the United States has sent Mariner missions to Mercury and Venus. The Soviet Union's Venera probes have also studied Venus. The Viking spacecraft from the United States have landed on Mars.

Figure 15·20
Edwin E. Aldrin, Jr., setting up an experiment on the moon *(left)*. Recovery of an Apollo spacecraft *(middle)*. Apollo mission liftoff *(right)*.

Exploration of the outer planets of the solar system began in the 1970s. A great deal of knowledge about the outer planets has been provided by the Voyager missions. Voyager 2 was launched on August 20, 1977, and Voyager 1 followed on September 5. These two spacecraft have taken thousands of photographs of Jupiter and Saturn. Voyager 2 has also visited Uranus.

Of course, the exploration of space has not been left to machines alone. Since 1961, people have also been going into space. A high point of the United States effort was the Apollo program to put a person on the moon. Before the Apollo program ended, 24 Americans viewed the moon's surface from close-up and 12 walked on the moon. Apollo astronauts completed 60 experiments on the moon's surface, and 30 in orbit around the moon. More than 30,000 photographs and many samples of moon rocks were brought back to the earth.

The space shuttle has allowed astronauts to remain in space for only a short time. Now there are plans for a permanent space station in orbit around the earth.

The space shuttle will be used to carry into orbit the materials needed to build the space station. The space station will be big enough for a crew of eight. Crews will be flown between the earth and the station aboard the shuttle. The space station should be ready by 1996.

The space station will have a living section, or crew section, and a laboratory section. The crew section will have a kitchen with micro-wave ovens and a bathroom with showers. The laboratory section will include areas for conducting experiments, and doing research.

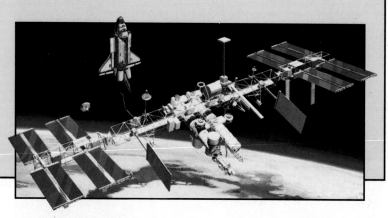

The *space shuttle* program began in the 1980s. The space shuttle is a reusable craft. It is launched like a rocket, it orbits like a satellite, and it returns like a glider. The shuttle has been used to launch, retrieve, and repair satellites. It has also been used for various experiments in orbit. A space shuttle may be used to build a space station in orbit. The crews of the space shuttles are no longer all astronauts. Scientists, engineers, technicians, and doctors have gone into space aboard the shuttle.

The space shuttle *Challenger* was destroyed in 1986 when the rocket that was launching it exploded. The seven people aboard were killed. Changes had to be made in the design of the rocket.

Several future space programs are being planned or considered. They include the Galileo program to put an artificial satellite in orbit around Jupiter. The satellite would then send probes to Jupiter's surface and to some of Jupiter's moons.

The construction of a permanent space station in orbit around the earth is also being considered. The station would serve as an observatory and a launching point for deep-space probes. It would be supplied and serviced by space shuttles.

Some scientists believe that an outpost could be established on the moon. They say there are enough valuable materials on the moon to make such a project worth the cost.

REVIEW

1. Describe some uses of satellites and space probes.
2. What was the Apollo program?
3. What future space programs are being considered?

CHALLENGE Look back at Section 15•3 at the description of conditions on Mars. What needs would have to be met to have a team of astronauts spend time on Mars?

CHAPTER SUMMARY

The main ideas in this chapter are listed below. Read these statements before you answer the Chapter Review questions.

- The solar system includes the sun, the planets and their moons, asteroids, meteoroids, and comets. (15•1)
- The sun is the largest body in the solar system. It contains more than 99.8 percent of the solar system's matter. (15•2)
- The sun produces energy in a process called fusion and gives off many different forms of solar radiation. (15•2)
- Features of the sun include sunspots, prominences, and solar flares. (15•2)
- It is thought that as the inner planets formed, the lighter elements were driven away by the solar wind. These planets contain a metal core surrounded by a rocky mantle. (15•3)
- Mercury and Venus are closer to the sun than is the earth. Mercury resembles the earth's moon in appearance. Venus has a very thick atmosphere and extremely high temperatures. (15•3)
- Mars, the fourth planet from the sun, is smaller than the earth and has a very thin atmosphere. (15•3)
- The outer planets are made mostly of hydrogen and helium. (15•4)
- Jupiter, the largest planet, gives off more energy than it receives from the sun. (15•4)
- Saturn is the sixth planet from the sun. It is the only planet with rings visible through a small telescope. (15•4)
- Uranus and Neptune are respectively the seventh and eighth planets from the sun. They are similar in both size and composition. (15•4)
- Pluto was the ninth planet discovered in the solar system and is the smallest planet. (15•4)
- Spacecraft have gathered information about the solar system. They have tested the ability of technology and people to withstand the conditions of space. (15•5)

The key terms in this chapter are listed below. Use each term in a sentence that shows the meaning of the term.

chromosphere	Jupiter	outer planets	Saturn	sunspots
core	Mars	photosphere	solar system	Uranus
corona	Mercury	Pluto	solar wind	Venus
inner planets	Neptune	satellite	space probes	

Chapter Review

VOCABULARY

Use the key terms from the previous page to complete the following sentences correctly.

1. The sun and the objects that move around it make up the _____.
2. The closest planet to the sun is _____.
3. The fifth planet from the sun is _____.
4. The sixth planet from the sun is _____.
5. The eighth planet from the sun is _____.
6. Any object that revolves around another is called a _____.
7. Dark areas on the sun's surface are called _____.
8. The visible surface of the sun is the _____.
9. The outer layer of the sun's atmosphere is the _____.
10. The sun gives off a stream of charged particles called the _____.

CONCEPTS

Identify each statement as True or False. If a statement is false, replace the underlined term or phrase with a term or phrase that makes the statement true.

1. One characteristic of the inner planets is that they are very dense.
2. A meteor is a large chunk of ice, dust, and frozen gases that orbits the sun.
3. In the sun the process of fusion combines hydrogen nuclei to form helium nuclei.
4. The hottest layer of the sun is the radiation zone.
5. Sunspots, prominences, and solar flares all seem to be related to magnetic fields on the sun.

Write the letter for the planet that best matches the description on the left. Not all choices will be used.

6. Planet surrounded by thick clouds that contain acid
7. Planet that has polar icecaps probably made of frozen carbon dioxide and water
8. Planet with rings that can be seen from the earth by using a small telescope
9. Planet that is more tilted on its axis than is any other planet
10. Largest planet in the solar system

a. Mercury
b. Venus
c. Mars
d. Jupiter
e. Saturn
f. Uranus
g. Neptune

Answer the following in complete sentences.

11. Describe how energy is transferred from the sun's core to its surface.
12. Why do the inner planets contain small amounts of the lighter elements?
13. How are Mars and the earth similar? How are those two planets different?
14. Why do astronomers believe that the outer planets are made mostly of the lighter elements?
15. What are some of the benefits of satellites to scientists and to other people?

---

1. From observations of the sky, you could separate the members of the solar system from the rest of the universe. What kinds of observations would you need to make?
2. Some astronomers have suggested that if Jupiter were larger, it would begin to give off light, like a star. How might a star found where Jupiter is found affect life on the earth?
3. There will be a time in the future when Pluto and Neptune come very close to each other because of Pluto's intersecting orbit. What could possibly happen when this occurs?
4. What do you think are the advantages of occupied spacecraft over unoccupied spacecraft?
5. If an astronaut landed on the surface of Jupiter, what problems would he or she encounter concerning movement? Why?

---

1. What object in the solar system would you most like to visit? Why?
2. Suppose you were going to place on a spacecraft a plaque to describe the earth and its people to anyone who finds it. What would you include on the plaque?
3. What provisions must be made for the people aboard an occupied mission to Mars?
4. Sometimes as many as 50 meteors can be seen in an hour. Such a display is called a meteor shower. Find out when some of the major meteor showers take place.
5. Halley's comet was first seen in 240 B.C. It returns every 76 years. Go to the library and do research to learn about some of the sightings of this comet.

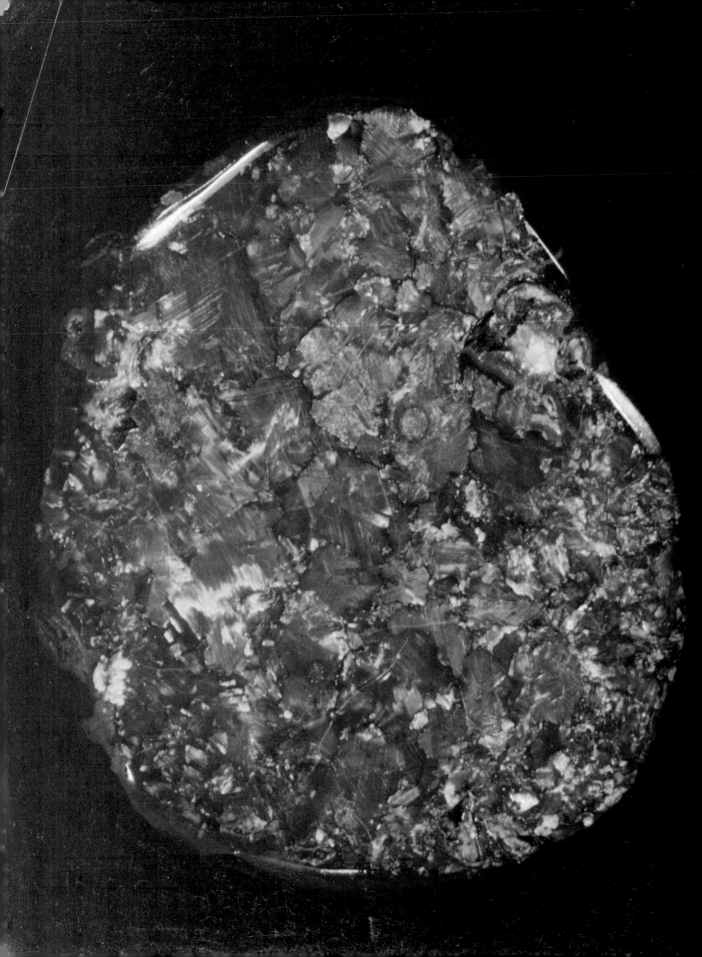

CHAPTER 16

EARTH'S RESOURCES

Materials from the earth have been important to humans for thousands of years. The photograph shows a mineral made up mostly of silicon and oxygen. It is called a pinfire black opal and it was found in Australia. Black opals are precious gems prized for their brilliant colors. Opals have a unique ability to reflect light within the stone. Notice that this sample shows nearly every color of the spectrum.

Precious opals are gem-quality opals used for jewelry. They are found in Hungary, Mexico, Honduras, New South Wales, and Australia. Opals have also been found in Nevada and Idaho.

- *What other materials from the earth are valuable?*

- *How can materials from the earth be identified?*

- *What materials from the earth will be useful in the future?*

16·1 Earth's Minerals

After completing this section, you will be able to

* **describe** the properties of minerals.
* **compare** the different crystal shapes of minerals.
* **give examples** of silicate and nonsilicate minerals.

The key terms in this section are
crystal   mineral

minera (a mine)

krystallos (clear ice)

A **mineral** (MIHN uhr uhl) is a solid that has a definite makeup and crystalline structure. Some minerals, such as gold, are single elements. Other minerals, such as salt, are compounds. Compounds are made of two or more elements that are combined chemically.

CRYSTALS

Each mineral has its own set of properties that makes it different from other minerals. One of these properties is the shape of its crystals. A **crystal** is a solid with a regular shape and flat sides. The shape of a crystal depends on the arrangement of its atoms. How are the minerals in Figure 16·1 alike?

Crystals form when a substance changes from a liquid to a solid. As a liquid changes to a solid the atoms move into an orderly pattern. Crystals may also form when liquids evaporate. For example, salt crystals are formed when seawater evaporates.

Figure 16·1
Crystals of pyrite *(A)*, copper sulfate *(B)*, azurite *(C)*, and sulfur *(D)*.

ACTIVITY How Can You Distinguish Between Unknown Liquids?

OBJECTIVES

Observe three sets of crystals.
Distinguish between three unknown liquids by comparing their crystals.

MATERIALS

5 mL of liquid X, 5 mL of liquid Y, 5 mL of liquid Z, 3 microscope slides, microscope, 3 droppers, 3 toothpicks

PROCEDURE

A. Observe liquids X, Y, and Z.
   1. Describe liquid X.
   2. Describe liquid Y.
   3. Describe liquid Z.

B. Put one to two drops of liquid X in the center of a microscope slide. Use a toothpick to spread the drop evenly on the slide.

C. Look at the slide with a microscope. Observe it for several minutes, noting any changes that may occur. Record your observations. Make sketches of what you see.

D. Repeat steps **B** and **C**, first with liquid Y, then with liquid Z. Be sure to record your observations.

RESULTS AND CONCLUSIONS

1. Compare the colors of liquids X, Y, and Z. Do you think the liquids contain the same chemicals? Explain.
2. Compare the sketches of the crystals you observed. Were the crystals of the same mineral? How do you know?
3. Can the crystal shapes be used to distinguish between these liquids?

SHAPES OF CRYSTALS

There are six basic crystal shapes, as shown in Figure 16•2. Inside each of the shapes are imaginary lines called axes (AK seez). The axes of each crystal shape have their own pattern of position, length, and number. For example, a cubic crystal has three axes of equal size. How are the axes of a cubic crystal different from those of a tetragonal crystal? The atoms that make up a mineral are lined up along the axes, giving each mineral its own crystal shape.

Figure 16•2
The six basic crystal shapes.

cubic	tetragonal	hexagonal	orthorhombic	monoclinic	triclinic
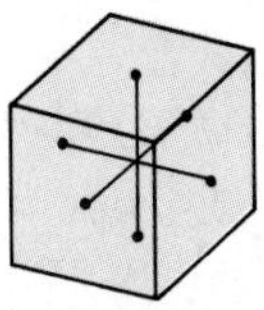	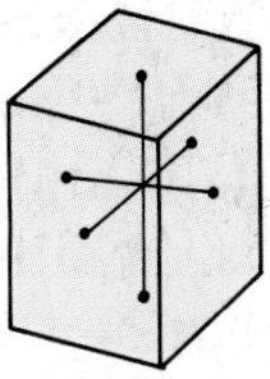	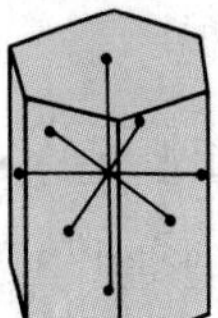	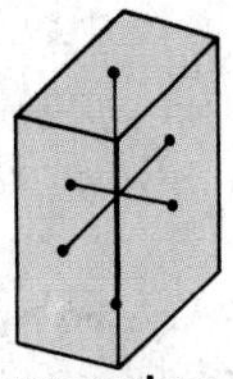	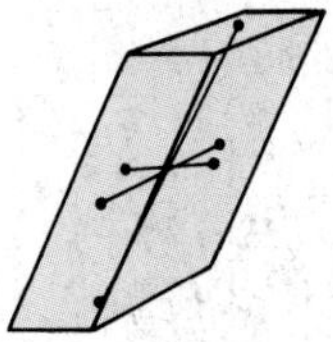	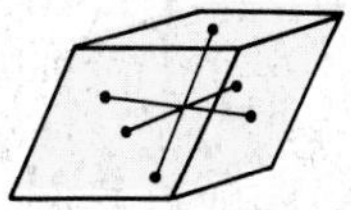
examples: **halite** **galena**	**examples:** **zircon** **chalcopyrite**	**examples:** **quartz** **calcite**	**examples:** **sulfur** **staurolite**	**examples:** **mica** **gypsum**	**examples:** **feldspar** **rhodonite**

Halite, a salt, is a mineral with a cubic crystal, as shown in Figure 16·3A. Halite is a compound made of the elements sodium and chlorine. Quartz is another mineral that is a compound. Quartz is formed from two of the most common elements in the earth's crust, silicon and oxygen. A quartz crystal is shown in Figure 16·3B. What is the crystal shape of quartz? Check your answer by referring back to Figure 16·2.

Other minerals, such as mica and feldspar, also contain silicon and oxygen. Crystals of mica are shown in Figure 16·3C. Although quartz and mica contain the same elements, these two minerals are not alike. How do mica crystals differ from quartz crystals? Mica splits into thin sheets because its crystals are in sheets.

Figure 16·3

Halite *(A)*, quartz crystals *(B)*, and mica *(C)*.

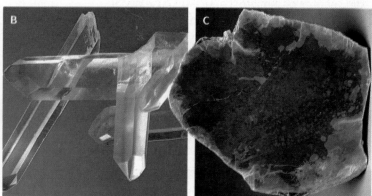

Table 16·1
Elements in the Earth's Crust

ELEMENT	PERCENT OF ELEMENT BY WEIGHT
Oxygen	46.60
Silicon	27.72
Aluminum	8.13
Iron	5.00
Calcium	3.63
Sodium	2.83
Potassium	2.59
Magnesium	2.09

GROUPS OF MINERALS

Of all the elements in the earth's crust, eight elements are found most often. These elements are oxygen, silicon, aluminum, iron, calcium, sodium, potassium, and magnesium. Look at Table 16·1. Which two of these elements are found in the greatest amounts?

Minerals that have oxygen and silicon in them are called *silicate minerals* or silicates (SIHL uh-kihts). More than 92 percent of the earth's crust consists of silicates. Examples of silicates are feldspar, quartz, mica, olivine, garnet, and talc. Three silicates are shown in Figure 16·4.

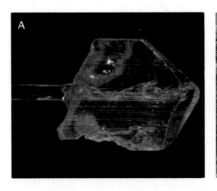

Feldspars, the most common silicates, make up about 50 percent of the earth's crust. In addition to silicon and oxygen, feldspars may contain other elements such as aluminum.

The second most common silicate is quartz. Quartz is made of only silicon and oxygen. Quartz may be colorless, white, pink, purple, or brown. Most sand consists of quartz grains.

Not all minerals are silicates. Minerals that do not contain both silicon and oxygen are called *nonsilicate minerals*. There are several families of nonsilicate minerals as shown in Table 16·2. Notice that both magnetite and hematite contain the same elements. How do you think they differ?

Figure 16·4
Olivine *(A)*, garnet *(B)*, and rose quartz *(C)* are three examples of silicates.

Table 16·2 *Nonsilicate Families*

FAMILY	EXAMPLE	MAIN ELEMENTS
Sulfides	Pyrite	Sulfur and metal
Carbonates	Calcite	Carbon and oxygen
Sulfates	Gypsum	Sulfur and oxygen
Oxides	Magnetite Hematite	Iron and oxygen Iron and oxygen
Halides	Fluorite Halite	Fluorine and calcium Chlorine and sodium

REVIEW

1. Describe the properties of a mineral.
2. How do the shapes of the six basic crystals differ?
3. List two silicate minerals and two nonsilicate minerals.

CHALLENGE Some diamonds are much larger than others. What factors might determine the size of a diamond crystal?

16·2 Identifying Minerals

PROPERTIES OF MINERALS

Figure 16·5 shows objects that are minerals. Both look like gold. However, only one of these minerals is gold. The other is pyrite, also called fool's gold. How could you tell which of these minerals is the gold and which is the pyrite?

To identify a mineral, you must look at its properties. Crystal shape, hardness, and color are some of the physical properties that can be used to identify minerals. You must look at more than one property to identify a mineral.

Figure 16·5
Gold *(left)* and pyrite *(right)*.

Hardness is the resistance a mineral shows to being scratched. Ten common minerals are used as references in a hardness test. They are arranged on a number scale in their order of hardness.

The number scale for rating the hardness of minerals is called the *Mohs scale.* Each of the reference minerals in the Mohs scale is given a number between 1 and 10. Notice in Table 16·3 that talc, the softest mineral, is given the number 1. Talc can be scratched by every other mineral. Diamond is the hardest mineral; it is given the number 10. Diamond scratches all other minerals.

The hardness of a mineral is found by learning which minerals on the Mohs scale it can and cannot scratch. For example, suppose a mineral scratches talc but it cannot scratch calcite. The unknown min-

Table 16·3 *Mohs Scale*

MINERAL	HARDNESS
Talc	1
Gypsum	2
Calcite	3
Fluorite	4
Apatite	5
Orthoclase	6
Quartz	7
Topaz	8
Corundum	9
Diamond	10

eral is harder than talc but softer than calcite. Since talc has a hardness of 1 and calcite has a hardness of 3, the unknown must have a hardness of 2. The unknown might be gypsum. Look at Table 16·3. Which minerals on the Mohs scale could be scratched by a mineral with a hardness of 3? What minerals on the scale could scratch this mineral?

Table 16·4 lists some common materials that you can use to estimate the hardness of an unknown mineral. In doing the hardness test, check the scratch to see whether it is a scratch or a mark that can be rubbed off. Soft minerals can leave marks on harder materials. A true scratch cannot be removed. Test the unknown mineral on the known material, and then reverse the test.

An easy but often misleading clue to the identity of a mineral is color. Some minerals are always the same color. Sulfur is always bright yellow. But the color of some minerals may vary, depending on the elements in the minerals. A streak test is more useful than is color. A **streak** is the color of a powder mark made by a mineral as it is rubbed against a porcelain tile. For example, the mineral hematite makes a red streak. Iron pyrite makes a black streak.

Table 16·4
Hardness of Objects

OBJECT	HARDNESS
Fingernail	2.5
Copper penny	3.0
Nail	4.5
Knife blade	5.5
Glass	5.5
Steel file	6.5

Figure 16·6
The color of the mark that a mineral makes on a porcelain tile may differ from the color of the mineral.

ACTIVITY — How Does Halite Cleave?

Luster is a physical property that describes the way the surface of a mineral reflects light. Luster can be either metallic or nonmetallic. A mineral with a metallic luster shines like a metal. Pyrite, shown in Figure 16·7, has a metallic luster. A mineral that does not shine like a metal is said to have a nonmetallic luster. Talc has a type of nonmetallic luster that is called greasy. Other types of nonmetallic lusters are pearly, waxy, glassy, and dull.

Figure 16·7

Pyrite has a metallic luster *(left)*, and talc has a nonmetallic luster *(right)*.

Cleavage and fracture are two other physical properties that are useful in identifying minerals. **Cleavage** is a property that describes how a mineral cleaves or splits apart along one or more smooth surfaces. Cleavage can take place in one or more directions. Mica cleaves in one direction, forming sheets. Galena cleaves in three directions, forming cubes as shown in Figure 16·8B.

Figure 16·8

Mica cleaves in one direction (A), and galena cleaves in three directions (B). Obsidian is a kind of mineral that fractures like glass fractures (C).

Some minerals break unevenly or along curved surfaces. A **fracture** is a break along an uneven surface. Iron pyrite is a mineral that fractures. The surface of this mineral is rough and uneven. There are also minerals that break along curved surfaces. Notice in Figure 16·8C that obsidian looks like broken glass.

Specific gravity is another way to identify minerals. The *specific gravity* of a mineral is found by comparing the mass of the mineral with the mass of an equal volume of water. The mass of 1 cm^3 of water is 1 g. The mass of 1 cm^3 of gold is 19.3 g. Thus the specific gravity of gold is 19.3 g/1.0 g, or 19.3. Each mineral has its own specific gravity. For example, sulfur has a specific gravity of 2.07.

SPECIAL MINERAL PROPERTIES

All minerals have the properties of color, hardness, luster, and streak. Some minerals have other special properties. These special properties can also be used to identify minerals. For example, light can pass through some minerals, such as calcite.

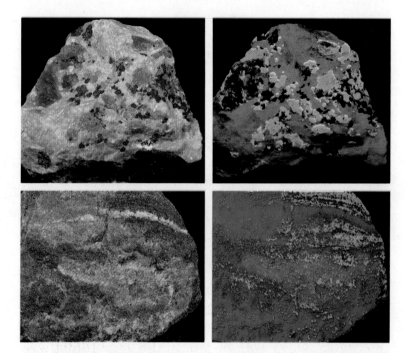

Magnetism is another special property that helps identify a few minerals. Minerals with this property are attracted to a magnet. Magnetite is a magnetic mineral.

Fluorescence (floo uh REHS uhns) is the glowing of a mineral while it is under ultraviolet (UV) light. Fluorescent minerals absorb ultraviolet light rays and give off visible light rays. Such minerals look dull in white light, as shown in Figure 16·9.

Some minerals will continue to give off visible light after the source of ultraviolet light has been removed. The minerals may continue to glow for several minutes. This property is called phosphorescence (fahs fuh REHS uhns). *Phosphorescence* is the release of visible light after the source of ultraviolet light has been removed. Sphalerite (SFAL uh-rīt) is a phosphorescent mineral.

REVIEW

1. Explain how minerals can be identified.

2. What are three special properties of minerals?

CHALLENGE Sometimes the specific gravity may vary as much as 25 percent from one sample to another of the same mineral type. Why, do you think, is this so?

16·3 Natural Resources

The earth supplies living things with air, water, and food. These materials are needed for survival. The earth also supplies minerals, including metals such as iron and copper, and energy sources such as petroleum and coal. Air, water, food, minerals, and energy sources all are examples of natural resources. A **natural resource** is any material found on the earth that is necessary for life or useful to humans.

USE OF RESOURCES

The use of the earth's natural resources has grown rapidly. One reason for this increased use is the rise in world population. In the year 1650 there were about 500 million people on the earth. In 1850 the number of people on the earth had doubled, reaching 1 billion. By 1930 the earth's population had doubled again, reaching 2 billion. The time needed for the earth's population to double had decreased from 200 years to 80 years. The earth's population now is over 5 billion, and it is expected to double in 33 years. Using the graph in Figure 16·10, predict what the earth's population will be in the year 2000. As the earth's population increases, the demand for resources, including minerals, also increases.

After completing this section, you will be able to

- **explain** how an increased population affects the supply of natural resources.
- **compare** renewable resources and nonrenewable resources.
- **give examples** of renewable resources.
- **give examples** of nonrenewable resources.

The key terms in this section are
natural resource
nonrenewable resource
renewable resource

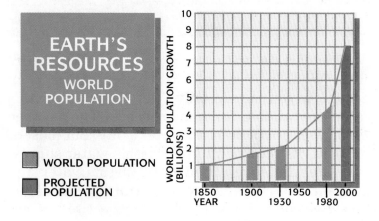

Figure 16·10
The increasing world population.

397

There are two kinds of natural resources: renewable resources and nonrenewable resources. A **renewable resource** is a resource that can be replaced. For example, trees are a renewable natural resource. They can be cut down, and new trees can be planted in the same place.

A **nonrenewable resource** is a resource that cannot be replaced once it has been used. Minerals are nonrenewable resources because they cannot be replaced. Nonrenewable resources must be used very carefully.

RENEWABLE RESOURCES

Figure 16·11 shows new trees that have been planted in an area where large trees had been cut down. This process of replacing trees is called *reforestation*. Trees are not the only natural resources that can be renewed. Water, soil, and air are also renewable resources.

Figure 16·11
Trees are renewable resources.

The earth's water supply is shown in Figure 16·12. What percent of the earth's water is in oceans? As you can see, only 1 percent of the earth's water is available for human needs. The average person uses about 266 L of water a day. But most of this water is returned to the earth's water supply.

Water that is returned to the earth's water supply is made pure again by a natural process called the *water cycle*. Look again at Figure 16·12. What causes liquid water on the earth to evaporate?

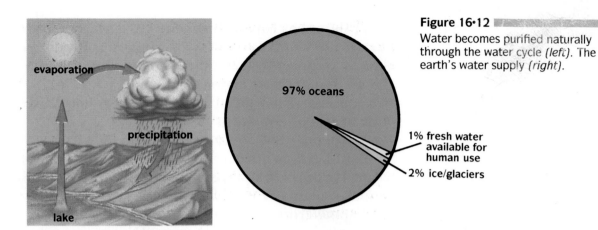

Figure 16·12
Water becomes purified naturally through the water cycle *(left)*. The earth's water supply *(right)*.

evaporation

precipitation

lake

97% oceans

1% fresh water available for human use

2% ice/glaciers

When water evaporates, it leaves behind any impurities it may have had. Therefore, when the water returns to the earth as rain or snow, it is free of impurities.

Air is a mixture of gases and solid particles. Some of the gases come from natural processes. For example, photosynthesis in plants produces oxygen gas. And volcanoes release many materials, including water vapor and dust, into the air. Other gases and particles in air come from human activities. The burning of fuels gives off smoke particles and a gas called sulfur dioxide. Smoke and sulfur dioxide can be harmful to human health.

Figure 16·13 *(right)* shows what happens when harmful gases and particles build up in the air

Figure 16·13
An area can have clean air one day *(left)* and unhealthful air the next day *(right)*.

faster than they can be removed. Air can be purified by rain and wind. Without wind to carry away dirty air and to bring in fresh air, people would not be able to live in many major cities.

Soil is another natural resource. The most important use of soil is for growing food to feed the world's people. Soil contains nutrients that are used by plants. Nutrients can be returned to the soil by natural processes, such as by the decay of plant and animal remains. Thus soil can be renewed. However, some crops may be planted in soil too often. The nutrients are then used faster than they can be replaced.

Another problem caused by planting crops too often is soil erosion. Soil erosion is the carrying away of soil by wind or water. Before crops are planted, soil must be tilled, or turned over. This uncovers the soil. Soil can also become uncovered if many grazing animals eat all of the grassy covering. The uncovered soil can be blown away by wind or washed away by water. Notice the condition of the land in Figure 16·14 *(left)*. In 1934 a layer of soil more than a meter thick was blown off the "dust bowl" region of the American Midwest. Each day, over 300 million metric tons of topsoil was removed. How do you think the modern farming method shown in Figure 16·14 *(right)* helps to reduce erosion?

Figure 16·14
The "dust bowl" disaster during the 1930s *(left)*. A modern farming method to reduce erosion *(right)*.

NONRENEWABLE RESOURCES

Recall that nonrenewable resources cannot be replaced. Minerals are a nonrenewable resource that must be used carefully. Many mineral resources, including metals, are found in very small amounts in the earth's crust. Once they have been used, they are gone forever. New sources will not likely be found.

Figure 16·15
Copper is one mineral that forms in veins and that can be mined.

Valuable minerals make up only a small part of the earth's crust. But certain natural processes can concentrate these minerals. For example, hot water moving through rock dissolves and carries minerals from the rock. The hot water may enter openings or cracks in cooler rock. As the water cools, the minerals settle out of the water and fill the cracks. A deposit of minerals that has formed in cracks in rock is called a *vein*. Copper, silver, and gold can be found in veins.

REVIEW

1. When the population increases, what happens to the demand for natural resources?
2. What is the difference between a renewable resource and a nonrenewable resource?
3. Give two examples of renewable resources.
4. Give two examples of nonrenewable resources.

CHALLENGE Aluminum makes up over 8 percent of the earth's crust. If there is so much aluminum, why should people recycle aluminum cans?

16·4 Mineral Resources

After completing this section, you will be able to

- **explain** why minerals are a natural resource.
- **give examples** of minerals that are found as ores.
- **give examples** of gems.

The key terms in this section are
gem
ore

ORES

Minerals are important natural resources. Minerals add nutrients to the soil. They form the salts in the oceans and are useful as metals and gems. Rocks that contain a large amount of a mineral are called *mineral deposits*. A mineral deposit in the earth that can be mined for profit is called an **ore**. Not all mineral deposits are ores, because the value of minerals varies. A small amount of gold might be worth mining. But a large amount of a common mineral might not be worth mining.

Ores containing minerals that are metals are called *metallic ores*. Metals obtained from metallic ores have many uses. The metal copper is used in wire because it is a good conductor of electricity. Silver and gold are metals that are used in many ways. Gold is used in jewelry and dentistry. Silver is used in photographic film.

Nonmetallic ores are materials containing minerals that are nonmetals. These minerals are used to make fertilizers and chemicals. Limestone, sand, and gravel are nonmetallic minerals that are used in construction materials. Sulfur is a nonmetallic mineral that is used in medicines and rubber. Nonmetallic minerals, such as potash, nitrates, and phosphates, are used in fertilizers to help crops grow.

Figure 16·16

Silver ore *(left)*, gold ore *(middle)*, and asbestos ore *(right)*.

PUZZLER

Like many ores, gold may form in underground cracks called veins. Gold can be obtained by digging a mine into a vein, or by panning. Panning involves swirling stream water and gravel in a pan until any gold in the gravel is separated.

If gold forms in veins, how does it end up in streams? What properties of gold enable it to be separated from gravel by panning?

GEMS

What do you think of when you see the word *gem*? Do rubies and diamonds come to mind? Like ores, gems are minerals. A **gem** is a mineral that is colorful and that reflects much light. There are many factors that determine the value of gems. Some of these factors are color, luster, hardness, size, lack of imperfections, and availability.

Gems may be thought of as either precious stones or semiprecious stones. The difference between the two groups is based mostly on the value of the gem. Precious stones are valuable because they have desirable physical properties and are uncommon. Semiprecious stones are more common and less valuable than precious stones.

Figure 16·17
Tanzanite—a blue, semiprecious gem—is grouped with diamonds and emeralds in this jewelry.

REVIEW

1. How can a mineral be a natural resource? Are minerals renewable resources or nonrenewable resources?
2. List three minerals found as ores.
3. List three examples of gems.

CHALLENGE Cutting precious gems such as diamonds is a difficult job. A gem cutter must have both skill and knowledge. What mineral properties should a gem cutter know about a diamond before it is cut?

16·5 Energy Resources

About 90 percent of the energy used in the world today comes from fossil fuels. *Fossil fuels* are energy sources that form from the remains of ancient plants and animals. The fossil fuels are petroleum, natural gas, and coal. They form over millions of years, and once they are used, they cannot be replaced. They are nonrenewable resources.

FOSSIL FUELS

Almost half of the fuels used today come from petroleum. **Petroleum,** also called oil, is a liquid that forms from the remains of sea life. These remains are buried by layers of mud and other materials on the ocean floor. Over centuries the remains decay into petroleum. The weight of the layers forces the petroleum, along with water, into rocks such as sandstone and limestone. These rocks have many tiny open spaces that petroleum and water can pass through. Eventually the petroleum and water are stopped by layers of solid rock. To reach the oil, drills must dig down into the rock, as shown in Figure 16·18.

Figure 16·18

Water, natural gas, and oil are trapped in porous rock between layers of solid rock.

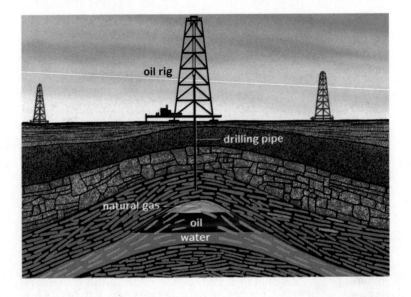

404

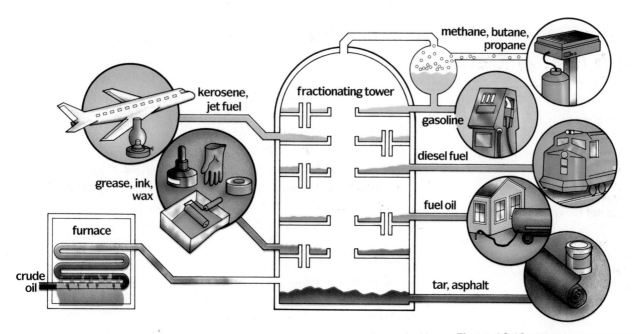

Figure 16·19
Some products of oil.

Petroleum is a mixture of many substances. They must be separated before they can be used. Look at Figure 16·19. What substances is petroleum separated into?

A fossil fuel that is often found with petroleum is natural gas. **Natural gas** is made mostly of the gas methane. When found with petroleum, natural gas is trapped between the petroleum and the layer of solid rock. Natural gas can also be found by itself in porous rock. Natural gas forms by the same processes that form petroleum.

As Figure 16·20 shows, almost three fourths of the world's reserves of fossil fuels is coal. **Coal** is a solid, black mineral formed from the remains of plants. The plants lived millions of years ago. When the plants died, their remains were buried by water and mud for millions of years, forming coal.

Coal is found in layers called seams. It can be removed from the earth by two methods: strip mining and underground mining. In strip mining, the land surface above a coal seam is removed. In underground mining a tunnel is dug to reach the coal seam. One factor in deciding which method to use is the depth of the coal seam. If the coal seam is deep, too much rock may have to be removed to use strip mining. Thus, underground mining would be used.

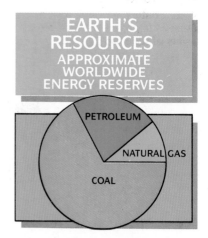

EARTH'S RESOURCES
APPROXIMATE WORLDWIDE ENERGY RESERVES

PETROLEUM

NATURAL GAS

COAL

Figure 16·20
Approximate worldwide energy reserves.

OTHER ENERGY SOURCES

One way that the United States has changed in the last 200 years is in the amount of energy it uses. In addition to heating homes and cooking food, energy is used to run cars, lights, and electric appliances. Almost all of this energy comes from fossil fuels, which cannot be replaced.

At the present rate of use, the supplies of petroleum and natural gas will be used up in the next century. The supply of coal should last longer, into the twenty-second century. But mining and using coal creates some health problems. Burning coal can also harm the environment. New ways of producing energy will be needed to meet the world's energy needs. Are there any energy sources that will not run out?

One such energy source is *solar energy,* energy from the sun. Solar energy can be used to heat homes and to make electricity. One way of heating a home with solar energy is to build the home with windows facing the sun to let sunlight in. A solar collector can be used in a home to absorb the sun's energy. A *solar collector* is a device for collecting solar energy and converting it to heat. Where is the solar collector on the house in Figure 16·21? Sunlight can produce electricity. Solar cells that can change sunlight into electricity are used in small electronic devices and in spacecraft.

Figure 16·21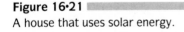

A house that uses solar energy.

Solar energy is a renewable energy source. In addition, it does not harm the environment. The amount of solar energy that reaches the earth's surface, however, is not constant. It can vary from day to day, depending on the weather.

There are many other kinds of renewable energy sources. *Geothermal energy* comes from heat produced within the earth. Hydroelectric energy produces electricity from flowing water. The flowing water runs generators that produce electricity. *Tidal energy* is produced by the rise and fall of water due to the tides. How might a dam be used to collect water at high tide and produce electricity? Finally, windmills can also be used to run generators and produce electricity.

Figure 16·22
A nuclear power plant with a large tower used to cool water.

Nuclear energy is produced from changes in the nucleus of an atom. This energy is produced when the nucleus is split into two or more smaller nuclei, in a process called fission. Uranium atoms are used in the fission process. A piece of uranium the size of the end of your thumb can produce as much heat as can a metric ton of coal.

The waste produced by nuclear power plants is radioactive and dangerous. This waste will release radiation for hundreds or thousands of years. Some radioactive waste has been stored in underground salt mines. People are questioning whether these places are good disposal sites.

Japan is reusing garbage in a new way—by building on it. Tokyo, Japan's capital city, stretches across Tokyo Bay on 18 artificial islands. These islands reach about 3 km out from the shoreline into the open bay, adding several thousand hectares to the city. The islands are being built to help solve Japan's population problem. Though slightly smaller than California, Japan has a population that is half that of the whole United States. The country is very hilly, with few flat areas on which to build.

City planners in Tokyo say that some of the garbage islands could be filled in with sand and rubble to make them more solid. Power plants and other industrial facilities that now take up valuable flat space inland could be built on these islands. Some of the islands could be used for parks.

The Japanese do have problems to overcome before the idea works. For example, garbage islands are not very firm. Even if packed with sand, they will not stand up to intensive city development.

The islands are also increasing water pollution. They have blocked the natural flow of tides that helps to cleanse the water in Tokyo Bay.

With careful planning, though, these problems are being solved. Japan is making steady progress in creating land for its growing population.

CONSERVATION

Conservation can make energy resources last longer. *Conservation* is a way to save resources by controlling how they are used. One way of conserving energy is by using less. If people find ways to use less energy, the supply of oil and coal will last longer. This would give the time needed to find other energy sources.

Another way of conserving energy is by recycling materials. *Recycling* is a process in which materials are reused or wastes are changed into usable products. It takes much less energy to recycle paper than to make new paper. Recycling also saves resources. For example, recycling a metric ton of waste paper would save about 17 trees. The recycling of natural resources that are in short supply, such as some mineral resources, may be the only way to extend the supply.

Figure 16·23

Recycling will conserve the supply of natural resources.

REVIEW

1. Name three fossil fuels and explain their origins.
2. Describe energy sources that do not come from fossil fuels.
3. Why is it important to conserve the earth's natural resources?

CHALLENGE Solar collectors on roofs are positioned to face the sun. However, the sun moves during the day, and its path across the sky is higher in the summer than in the winter. What would be the best direction for a solar collector to face?

CHAPTER SUMMARY

The main ideas in this chapter are listed below. Read these statements before you answer the Chapter Review questions.

- Minerals have special crystalline structures. There are six basic crystal shapes. (16·1)
- Minerals can be placed into one of two groups. Minerals that contain oxygen and silicon are called silicates, and those that do not are called nonsilicates. (16·1)
- A mineral can be identified by its properties. Hardness, color, streak, luster, cleavage, fracture, and specific gravity are physical properties of minerals. (16·2)
- Magnetism, fluorescence, and phosphorescence are special properties that can be used to identify some minerals. (16·2)
- Natural resources are any materials found on the earth that are necessary for life or useful to humans. (16·3)
- As the human population increases, greater demands are placed on the earth's natural resources. (16·3)
- Renewable resources are resources that can be replaced. Water, soil, and air are natural resources that can be replaced. (16·3)
- Nonrenewable resources are resources that cannot be replaced once they have been used. (16·3)
- Minerals are used in wire, jewelry, medicines, fertilizers, chemicals, and construction materials. (16·4)
- Almost all of the energy used today comes from fossil fuels. Petroleum, natural gas, and coal are fossil fuels. (16·5)
- Renewable energy resources will have to be used as the supply of fossil fuels runs out. Solar energy, hydroelectric energy, geothermal energy, tidal energy, wind energy, and nuclear energy could be used in the future. (16·5)
- Conservation can save energy and natural resources. (16·5)

The key terms in this chapter are listed below. Use each term in a sentence that shows the meaning of the term.

cleavage	hardness	nonrenewable resource
coal	luster	ore
crystal	mineral	petroleum
fracture	natural gas	renewable resource
gem	natural resource	streak

Chapter Review

VOCABULARY

Use the key terms from the previous page to complete the following sentences correctly.

1. A property that describes how light reflects from the surface of a mineral is called _____ .
2. A solid element or compound with a definite composition and crystalline structure is a/an _____ .
3. A property that describes the color of a powder mark made by a mineral on a porcelain tile is _____ .
4. A solid with a regular shape and flat sides is a/an _____ .
5. A property that describes how a mineral splits apart along a smooth surface is _____ .
6. Any material found on the earth that is necessary for life or useful to humans is a/an _____ .
7. Water, air, and soil are examples of _____ .
8. Any mineral that can be mined for a profit is called a/an _____ .
9. A fuel that forms from the remains of plants buried in swamps is called _____ .
10. A fuel made mostly of methane is called _____ .

CONCEPTS

Choose the term or phrase that best answers the question or completes the statement.

1. Silicate minerals contain oxygen and
   a. carbon.   **b.** iron.   **c.** silicon.   **d.** sulfur.
2. Which of the following is a nonsilicate mineral?
   a. pyrite   **b.** garnet   **c.** quartz   **d.** mica
3. The most common silicate mineral is
   a. feldspar.   **b.** garnet.   **c.** olivine.   **d.** talc.
4. A mineral with a hardness of 9 will not scratch
   a. quartz.   **b.** diamond.   **c.** talc.   **d.** calcite.
5. Which of the following is a nonrenewable resource?
   a. water   **b.** soil   **c.** sunlight   **d.** minerals

Identify each statement as True or False. If a statement is false, replace the underlined term or phrase with a term or phrase that makes the statement true.

6. An <u>environment</u> is all the living and nonliving things that surround an organism.
7. The continuous glowing of a mineral after the ultraviolet light has been removed is called <u>fluorescence</u>.

8. Ores containing minerals that are metals are called <u>silicate minerals</u>.
9. <u>Solar energy</u> is energy produced from changes in the nucleus, or center, of an atom.
10. Water is made pure again by a natural process called the <u>water cycle</u>.

Answer the following in complete sentences.

11. How do crystal shapes differ?
12. Explain how you would use the Mohs scale to determine the hardness of an unknown mineral.
13. Explain five ways to identify a mineral.
14. Give an example of a renewable resource and a nonrenewable resource. Explain how they differ.
15. How does the increase in the world's population affect the supply of natural resources?

APPLICATION/ CRITICAL THINKING

1. A snowflake has a regular crystalline pattern. Is a snowflake a mineral? Explain your answer.
2. In what ways could a mineral as hard as a diamond be useful?
3. Explain why fossil fuels are an indirect source of solar energy.
4. Humans have increased the amount of carbon dioxide in the atmosphere by using fossil fuels. Carbon dioxide traps the sun's heat. What effect might this have on the earth's climate?
5. During the water cycle, a drop of water may remain in the ocean for 3000 years and up to 10,000 years in the ground. Does this mean the water cycle is not balanced? Explain your answer.

EXTENSION

1. Certain minerals have been designated as birthstones for different months. Find out about your birthstone. Write a short essay about your birthstone, including the properties and uses of the stone.
2. Find out about the ores obtained in your state or province. In what ways is each of these ores used?
3. Make paper models of crystal shapes. Display your models with pictures of minerals that have these crystal shapes.
4. Collect the trash that you would ordinarily throw away in one day and weigh it. Record the weight, and dispose of the trash properly. Then multiply the weight by 365 to obtain the weight of trash you might throw away in one year.
5. Compare how far you can coast on a bicycle that has tires inflated to the recommended pressure with how far you can coast when the tires are at half the recommended pressure. How would driving a car with underinflated tires affect gas mileage?

CHAPTER 17

EARTH'S HISTORY

*T*he photograph shows a fossil of an ammonite, an extinct mollusk, or shelled animal. Ammonites were common 150 million years ago. The ammonite was similar to the chambered nautilus, a modern mollusk. Like the nautilus, the ammonite lived in the sea. The shell of this animal was coiled and divided into sections. The animal lived in the outermost section. As the animal outgrew its section, a newer and larger section was added to the coil.

Because the body of a mollusk is soft, remains of the actual animals are not often found. However, the hard shells made many fossils. As the fossils formed, each section of the shells filled in with minerals. Most ammonite fossils are between 2 cm and 12 cm across. However, a few are over a meter in diameter.

- *How are fossils formed?*
- *What kinds of clues do fossils give about living things of the past?*
- *How do scientists determine the age of fossils?*

17·1 The Record of Rocks

After completing this section, you will be able to

- **explain** the principle of uniformitarianism.
- **compare** the relative ages of rocks based on their positions.

The key term in this section is **relative age**

What happened before written history? How long has the earth existed? There are many clues in the earth's rocks. Patterns in the rocks provide a record that can be read like a reference book.

In reading this record, scientists make use of an idea put forth in 1795 by James Hutton, a Scottish geologist. Hutton observed such processes as the erosion, or wearing away, of rocks. He had the idea that the same processes must have occurred in the past. This idea is called the principle of *uniformitarianism* (yoo nuh fawr muh TAIR ee uh nihz uhm). This principle states that the processes at work today are the same processes that have been at work throughout the earth's history. This idea is stated as "The present is the key to the past."

According to the principle of uniformitarianism, rocks formed in the past in the same way they form today. For example, sedimentary (sehd uh-MEHN tuh ree) rock forms as sediments carried by wind, water, or ice are laid down in a process called deposition. Slowly the layers of sediments turn into layers of rock. Each type of sediment produces a different kind of rock. The rock layers shown in Figure 17·1 formed in this way.

Figure 17·1
Rock layers along a highway.

414

How do the layers of sedimentary rock compare in age? To answer this question, scientists try to determine the order in which the layers were deposited. Suppose you were looking at a slice of a layer cake. Which layer of the cake would have been laid down first? How would you know?

Like the bottom layer of a cake, the bottom layer in a section of sedimentary rock was deposited first. Rock layers near the top were formed later. The law of superposition states that each layer in an undisturbed section of sedimentary rock is older than those above it and younger than those below it. In Figure 17·1, where is the oldest rock layer in the formation?

Geologists use the law of superposition to compare the ages of rock layers. **Relative age** is the age of something compared with the age of something else. For example, you might describe your relative age as older than a fifth grader but younger than an eleventh grader. The relative age of a rock can be described in the same way — older or younger than some other rock.

Figure 17·2
An unconformity is a break or change in the rock record.

If rock layers were never disturbed, comparing the ages of rocks would be easy. But disturbances occur, causing a piece of the rock record to be missing or changed. A buried surface that represents a break in the rock record is called an *unconformity* (uhn kahn FAWR muh tee). Figure 17·2 shows two unconformities.

Sometimes forces within the earth can cause rock layers to change position. Figure 17·3A shows sedimentary rock in flat layers. Notice that the layers shown in Figure 17·3B have been tilted and then eroded. Then suppose more layers were deposited. The surface below layer 4 would be an unconformity, because the layers of sediment that first formed there would have been removed.

Figure 17·3
The formation of unconformities.

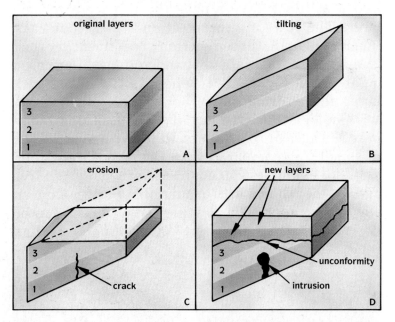

Newer features in rock formations can cut across older features. Folds and cracks in rock layers are younger than the layers they cut across. The crack shown in Figure 17·3C formed after the rock layers were deposited. Sometimes, molten rock may come up through a crack in rock layers. The rock that is deposited is an intrusion, as shown in Figure 17·3D. How does the age of this intrusion compare with the age of the rock around it?

REVIEW

1. What is the principle of uniformitarianism?
2. In undisturbed layers of sedimentary rock, which layer is the oldest layer? Which layer is the youngest?

CHALLENGE Suppose a layer of granite, which forms from molten rock, is seen below layers of sedimentary rock. Using only the law of superposition, can you tell whether the granite is older or younger than the sedimentary rock? Explain your answer.

17·2 Fossils

The bone in Figure 17·4A is being examined by a paleontologist (pay lee ohn TAHL uh jihst). *Paleontologists* are scientists who study life of the earth's past. They try to understand ancient organisms and their environments by studying fossils. **Fossils** are the preserved remains or traces of once-living things that are found in the earth's crust.

PETRIFIED REMAINS

When a plant or animal dies, its remains are usually eaten or they decay completely. But if the organism is quickly buried in mud, sand, or volcanic ash, it may become a fossil. Even then, the soft parts usually decay. But the hard parts—bone, shell, wood—can be petrified, or turned into rock.

Figure 17·4

A paleontologist is carefully chipping away rock from this dinosaur bone *(A)*. Petrified wood *(B)*. Petrified *Stegosaurus* bones 140 million years old *(C)*.

The hard parts of once-living things become petrified when minerals dissolved in water enter openings in these remains. Slowly, the minerals replace the materials that made up the parts. When the minerals harden, a fossil forms. The mineral silica may replace wood, forming petrified wood. Fine details can be preserved as rock. Notice the growth rings in the petrified wood in Figure 17·4B.

FILMS AND IMPRINTS

The carbon in living things can produce fossils. Plant and animal remains contain compounds of carbon and other elements. After an organism is buried, pressure within the earth may squeeze out the other elements, leaving a thin film of carbon. This process is called *carbonization*. The carbon film that remains may show the organism in fine detail. Figure 17·5*A* shows a carbon film fossil of a fern. In some cases the carbon itself disappears, leaving only an imprint.

ACTIVITY   How Do Molds and Casts Differ?

OBJECTIVE
Construct models of a fossil mold and a fossil cast.

MATERIALS
small seashell, petroleum jelly, modeling clay, hand lens, 12 g of plaster of Paris, 5 mL of water, plastic dish, plastic spoon

PROCEDURE
A. Coat a small seashell with a thin layer of petroleum jelly.
B. Roll a piece of modeling clay into a ball about twice the size of the shell. Press the outer side of the shell into the clay ball. Remove the shell. Use a hand lens to observe the imprint of the shell in the clay. Record what you observe.
C. Roll another piece of modeling clay into a ball about twice the size of the shell. Press the same shell into the center of the clay ball. Remove the shell.
D. Mix 12 g of plaster of Paris with 5 mL of water in a plastic dish. With a plastic spoon stir the mixture until it is smooth.
E. Pour the plaster into the imprint made by the shell in the clay in step **C**. Let it dry 30 minutes or overnight.
F. Remove the hardened plaster from the clay. Use the hand lens to observe the plaster. Record what you observe.

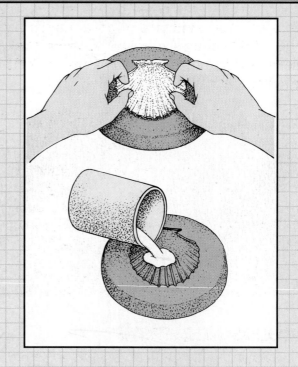

RESULTS AND CONCLUSIONS
1. Compare the imprint of the shell in the clay with the hardened plaster shape. Which model is a mold? Which model is a cast?
2. How are your models of a fossil mold and fossil cast like real fossils? How are your models different from real fossils?

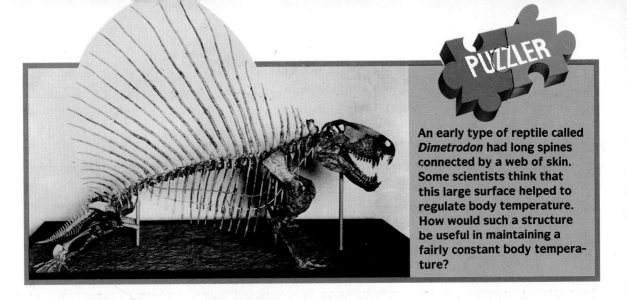

PUZZLER

An early type of reptile called *Dimetrodon* had long spines connected by a web of skin. Some scientists think that this large surface helped to regulate body temperature. How would such a structure be useful in maintaining a fairly constant body temperature?

Footprints, trails, and burrows leave imprints of another type. These imprints are traces, rather than actual remains, of living things. A trace fossil is preserved evidence of an animal's activity. Figure 17·5*B* shows dinosaur tracks that were preserved as soft mud hardened into rock. These tracks are trace fossils.

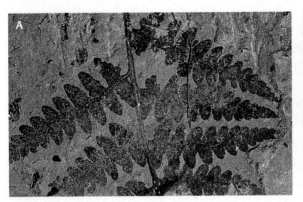
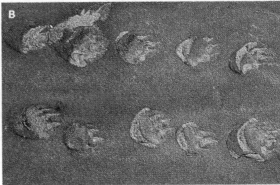

MOLDS AND CASTS

Suppose a shell is buried in mud. The mud hardens into rock. Then the shell dissolves, leaving its imprint in the rock. This kind of imprint is called a mold. A **mold** is a hollow space left in a rock by an object that has dissolved.

If a mold later fills with minerals, the filling can harden into a cast. A **cast** is a fossil that has the same outer shape as the original object. A cast of a shell looks like the shell itself, not like an imprint.

Figure 17·5
A carbon film fossil *(A)* and fossil reptile tracks *(B)*.

419

Figure 17·6
A beetle in amber *(left)* and a woolly mammoth that was discovered frozen *(right)*.

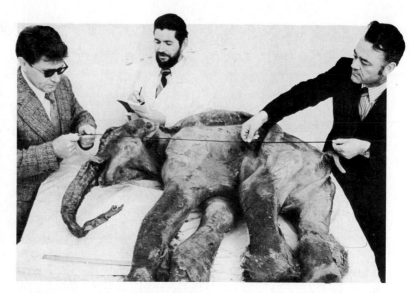

UNCHANGED REMAINS

Some fossils are the unchanged remains of once-living organisms. Actual teeth and bones of dinosaurs have been found in many parts of the United States. These hard parts of dinosaurs remained after the soft parts decayed.

Rarely is a whole animal, including the soft tissues, found preserved as a fossil. However, in Poland an entire woolly rhinoceros was found preserved in asphalt. Woolly mammoths that lived nearly 17,000 years ago have been found in ice and frozen soil in Siberia and Alaska. Hair, skin, and stomach contents were preserved. A preserved baby mammoth is shown in Figure 17·6. Why, do you think, was its body so well preserved?

The fossilized insect in Figure 17·6 was preserved inside hardened tree sap, called amber. The insect was trapped when the sap was a sticky liquid. Pieces of amber often contain insects. Recently, a frog was found preserved in amber.

REVIEW

1. What do paleontologists do?
2. Describe four ways fossils form.
3. What is the difference between a mold and a cast?

CHALLENGE If you found a fossil bone, tooth, or shell, how could you tell if it was unchanged, petrified, or a cast?

17·3 Studying the Earth's Past

FOSSILS AND TIME

Most fossils of water animals are found on land. How did they get there? Fossils provide many clues to past environments. The fossils of clams and fish found on land are evidence that the land was once underwater. Further studies may show whether the water was shallow or deep, warm or cold, fresh or salty.

The remains of living things that lived only in an unchanging environment are called *facies* (FAY-shee eez) *fossils*. Such fossils show that a certain kind of environment existed. For example, corals live only in shallow, warm seas today. Thus when fossil coral reefs are found somewhere, scientists believe that warm, shallow seas once existed there.

Some fossils are more important than others in telling the relative age of the rock in which they are found. Such fossils are called *index fossils*. Organisms that lived for a certain time span and in many different places are used as index fossils. Small organisms that lived in great numbers make good index fossils. So do organisms that are easy to identify. The trilobite (TRĪ luh bīt) is an example of an index fossil. What are some features that help in identifying the trilobites shown in Figure 17·7?

After completing this section, you will be able to

- **explain** how fossils give clues about the earth's past.
- **describe** a geologic column.
- **explain** how radioactive elements are used to find the age of rocks.

The key terms in this section are
geologic column
radiometric dating

Figure 17·7
Trilobites are used as index fossils.

421

column A   column B   column C

Figure 17·8
Fossils can be used to match up layers of rock from different areas.

Index fossils provide a way of matching rocks of the same age found in different places. The same kinds of trilobites have been found both in the Grand Canyon and in Wales. These fossils show that the rocks in which they were found formed at about the same time. This process of matching rocks of the same age from different places is called *correlation*. Look at Figure 17·8. Which fossil is found in all three columns?

The first person to use fossils to match rock layers was William Smith. In the late 1790s, Smith was building a canal in England. He noticed that each rock layer contained fossils found only in that layer. He also saw that the same sequence of layers was found in different places. Smith realized that the rock layers formed a time scale. Similar work was done by scientists in other countries. The result was the first geologic column.

A **geologic column** is a diagram of the sequence of rock layers in an area according to age. Such a diagram, like the one shown in Figure 17·9, is made by piecing together layers from separate areas. There is no place where the entire history of the earth is represented in its rocks.

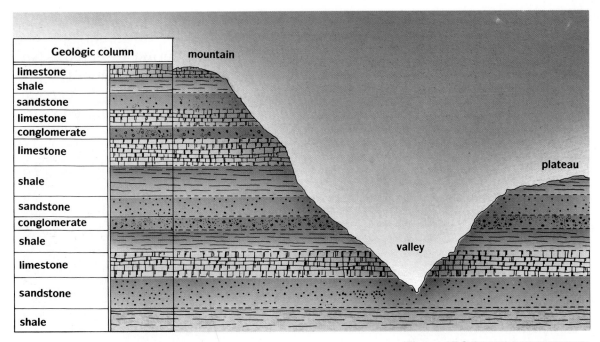

Figure 17·9
The geologic column is a record of rock formations from all over the earth.

The following labels appear in the geologic column within the figure:

Geologic column — mountain, plateau, valley

limestone
shale
sandstone
limestone
conglomerate
limestone
shale
sandstone
conglomerate
shale
limestone
sandstone
shale

RADIOMETRIC DATING

Geologic columns made during the 1800s could show only the relative age of rocks. In the late 1800s, scientists found a way to measure the actual age of rocks. Scientists discovered that some elements are radioactive. A *radioactive element* is one that decays, or breaks down, to form other elements. For example, uranium-238 changes into lead-206, in the process called radioactive decay. During *radioactive decay*, particles and energy that are forms of radiation are given off.

Radioactive elements gave scientists a better way to measure the age of rocks. **Radiometric dating** is a process that finds the age of rocks and other objects by measuring the decay of radioactive elements in the rocks and objects. Radioactive elements have a property called half-life. The *half-life* of an element is the length of time it takes for one half of its atoms to decay. For example, the half-life of uranium-238 is 4.5 billion years. After one half-life, half of the atoms in a sample of uranium-238 have changed into lead-206. This rate of decay does not change. Changes in pressure and temperature do not affect the half-life.

423

Figure 17·10 shows the decay of uranium-238 over time. The amounts of uranium-238 and lead-206 after each half-life period are given as percentages. After one half-life, 50 percent of the uranium-238 remains. In Figure 17·10, find the percentage of uranium-238 atoms left after 9 billion years. How many half-lives is this?

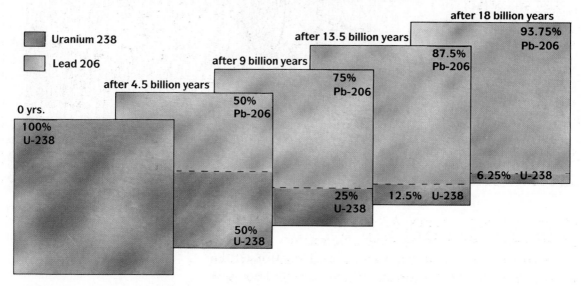

Figure 17·10

Radioactive decay of uranium-238.

Scientists use uranium-238 to measure time. Suppose uranium-238 is part of a newly formed rock. No more uranium-238 can become part of the rock. But as the rock ages, the uranium-238 will decay into lead-206. From the half-life of uranium-238 and the ratio of uranium-238 to lead-206, the rock's age can then be calculated. The oldest earth rock dated so far was formed 3.9 billion years ago. Some meteorites and moon soil dated by radiometric methods are 4.6 billion years old. Most scientists believe the earth's age to be the same — about 4.6 billion years.

Different radioactive elements are used to date objects of different ages. Table 17·1 lists some of these elements. For what is carbon-14 used?

All living things take in carbon while they are alive. Most of this carbon is carbon-12, which is not radioactive. But a small amount of the carbon in living things is carbon-14, which is radioactive. The percentage of carbon-14 in a living thing stays the

Not long ago, water from a creek in eastern Arkansas washed away the last few millimeters of sediments covering part of the creek's bank. The sediments had covered an ancient oyster reef. Using special techniques, paleontologists unearthed fossils from the ancient reef.

The fossils were those of animals that lived about 40 million years ago. Among the fossils were teeth from four kinds of sharks. These ancient sharks resembled today's tiger shark, lemon shark, and cat shark. Bones from fish and reptiles, including those of a 7-m-long snake, were also found. These types of animals indicate that the climate of eastern Arkansas 40 million years ago was warmer than it is today.

Paleontologists continue to search for evidence of oceans that existed in past geologic times. They hope to uncover more about life and climate in prehistoric America.

same until death occurs. After death the percentage of carbon-14 slowly decreases. Scientists can compare the amounts of carbon-14 and carbon-12 in fossils. The older the material, the smaller its percentage of carbon-14. By measuring the amount of carbon-14, scientists can figure out the age of the material. However, this method does not work for items older than about 50,000 years.

Table 17·1 *Half-lives of Radioactive Elements*

ELEMENT	HALF-LIFE (YEARS)	USED FOR DATING
Carbon-14	5730	Wood, shells, bone
Potassium-40	1.3 billion	Rocks
Rubidium-87	47 billion	Rocks
Uranium-235	713 million	Rocks
Uranium-238	4.5 billion	Rocks

REVIEW

1. How do fossils give clues about the earth's past?
2. What is a geologic column?
3. How can radioactive elements be used to find the age of rocks?

CHALLENGE Suppose scientists knew for sure that there were no earth rocks older than 3.9 billion years. Why might the scientists still believe that the earth itself is older than that?

17·4 The Geologic Time Scale

After completing this section, you will be able to

- **explain** how the geologic time scale is divided into units.
- **describe** the types of life forms that existed during the Precambrian Era.

The key terms in this section are
era
geologic time scale
Precambrian Era

The record of life can be seen in the rock layers of the geologic column. Many forms of life seen in lower, older layers do not appear in higher, younger layers. Other forms of life appear suddenly in the younger layers. And some forms of life are found throughout the column.

Scientists believe changes that have taken place on the earth throughout history have affected living things. For example, when the sea level rises, areas of low land become covered with water. Life forms on the land are then replaced by sea life.

Figure 17·11
Fossil of a ginkgo leaf. This fossil formed in the Mesozoic Era. When did this era begin?

Changes in rock layers and fossils can be used to divide the earth's history into units of time. The division of the earth's history into units of time based on changes in the earth's crust and sudden changes in the forms of life is called the **geologic time scale**.

The geologic time scale, shown in Table 17·2, is divided into four major parts called eras. An **era** is a major unit of time based on changes in the earth's crust and on the stages of development in certain life forms. The oldest and longest era is the **Precambrian** (pree KAM bree uhn) **Era**. It began when the earth came into existence about 4.6 billion years ago. According to Table 17·2, when did the Precambrian Era end?

Table 17·2 *The Geologic Time Scale*

ERA	PERIOD	EPOCH	BEGINNING (millions of years ago)	IMPORTANT EVENTS
	Quaternary	Holocene	less than .01	modern humans appear
	Quaternary	Pleistocene	2.5	ice age
Cenozoic	Tertiary	Pliocene	6	
Cenozoic	Tertiary	Miocene	25	mammals dominant
Cenozoic	Tertiary	Oligocene	38	
Cenozoic	Tertiary	Eocene	55	
Cenozoic	Tertiary	Paleocene	65	small mammals
Mesozoic	Cretaceous		140	mass extinction of dinosaurs; flowering plants
Mesozoic	Jurassic		195	first birds appear; dinosaurs dominant
Mesozoic	Triassic		230	first dinosaurs and first mammals appear; conifers, reptiles, shellfish, grasshoppers abundant
Paleozoic	Permian		290	most sea life disappears; mammallike reptiles dominant
Paleozoic	Carboniferous		345	first reptiles and first insects appear; club mosses and horsetails abundant; forests and swamps
Paleozoic	Devonian		400	fish abundant; first amphibians appear
Paleozoic	Silurian		440	land plants appear; jawed fish appear
Paleozoic	Ordovician		500	shelled organisms abundant; jawless fish appear
Paleozoic	Cambrian		600	trilobites, brachiopods, sponges, snails, jellyfishes, worms abundant
Precambrian			1500	first jellyfish
Precambrian			4600	bacteria, algae

427

Precambrian rock is usually covered by younger rock. However, Precambrian rock can be seen in the Grand Canyon, where erosion has cut through the younger layers. The largest area of exposed Precambrian rock is in the Canadian Shield.

Few fossils are found in Precambrian rock. Life forms during this era did not have the hard body parts that could form good fossils. Some Precambrian rock is rich in carbon, which may be the remains of this past life. Impressions of some soft-bo-

ACTIVITY   A Model of Geologic Time

OBJECTIVE
Relate events that occurred in the earth's history to the geologic time scale.

MATERIALS
adding machine tape 5 m long, meterstick

PROCEDURE
A. Your time line on adding machine tape will use a scale on which 1 m represents 1 billion (1,000,000,000) years.
   1. How many years would be represented on this scale by 1 cm? By 1 mm?
B. Make a table similar to the one below. Based on the scale of 1 m representing 1 billion years, change each number of years shown to the number of centimeters that will represent it.
C. Draw a vertical line across the tape near the left end. Label the line *Present time.*
D. Starting at this line, measure the distances on the tape that will represent the events in the table. Draw a line down the tape to mark each event. Label each event.

RESULTS AND CONCLUSIONS
1. Which is the longest geological era?
2. Which is the shortest geological era?
3. During which era do we live?
4. Compare the time span during which modern humans have been on the earth with the entire span of geologic time.

EVENT	YEARS BEFORE THE PRESENT (APPROX.)	cm
First landing of humans on the moon	10	
Beginning of Egyptian civilization	5000	
Beginning of last ice age	20,000	
Appearance of first modern human	50,000	
Appearance of earliest human	2,000,000	
Beginning of Cenozoic Era	65,000,000	
Appearance of first birds	150,000,000	
Beginning of Mesozoic Era	230,000,000	
Appearance of first insects	345,000,000	
Appearance of first land plants	440,000,000	
Beginning of Paleozoic Era	600,000,000	
Beginning of Precambrian Era	4,500,000,000	

died animals, such as jellyfish and starfish, have been found in late Precambrian rock. Figure 17·13 shows some of the forms of life that may have lived during the Precambrian Era.

Following the Precambrian Era is the *Paleozoic* (pay lee uh ᴢoʜ ihk) *Era*. Many forms of primitive life existed in this era. *Paleozoic* means "ancient life." The third large division of geologic time is the *Mesozoic* (mehs uh ᴢoʜ ihk) *Era*. *Mesozoic* means "middle life." During this era, reptiles became the dominant life form. The most recent era is the *Cenozoic* (see nuh ᴢoʜ ihk) *Era*. *Cenozoic* means "recent life." This era was and is dominated by warm-blooded animals.

Eras are divided into smaller time units called periods. These divisions are based on the fossils found in the rock layers of the different periods. According to Table 17·2, how many periods are there in the Paleozoic Era?

The two periods of the Cenozoic Era are divided into smaller units of time called epochs (ᴇʜᴘ uhks). Rocks of the Cenozoic Era contain many fossils. Thus there is enough evidence to divide these periods into smaller units of time.

Figure 17·12
The Canadian Shield contains exposed Precambrian rocks.

Key:

Canadian Shield

Other exposed Precambrian rock

Figure 17·13
Life forms of the Precambrian Era.

REVIEW

1. How is the geologic time scale divided into units?
2. What kind of living things existed during the Precambrian Era?

CHALLENGE Why isn't the Precambrian Era divided into periods?

17·5 Paleozoic, Mesozoic, and Cenozoic Eras

paleo- (old)
zoe (life)

THE PALEOZOIC ERA

The **Paleozoic Era**, an era in which abundant life forms first appeared, followed the Precambrian Era. At the beginning of the Paleozoic Era, much of the continental areas were covered by shallow seas. But later in the era, the shallow seas dried up. How might this have affected living things in the seas?

The Paleozoic Era is sometimes called the Age of Invertebrates. An *invertebrate* is an animal that does not have an internal bony skeleton. However, an invertebrate can have some hard parts, such as a shell.

The first period in the Paleozoic Era is the Cambrian (KAM bree uhn) Period. The most common form of life was the trilobite. No evidence of land animals or plants existing during the Cambrian Period has been found. Figure 17·14 shows some organisms that lived during the Cambrian Period.

The Cambrian Period is followed by the Ordovician (awr duh VIHSH uhn) Period. During this period, living things similar to squid and octopuses became the most common life forms. The first vertebrates—animals with a backbone—appeared during this period. They were fish covered with bony plates.

Figure 17·14

Trilobites and brachiopods were common during the Cambrian Period.

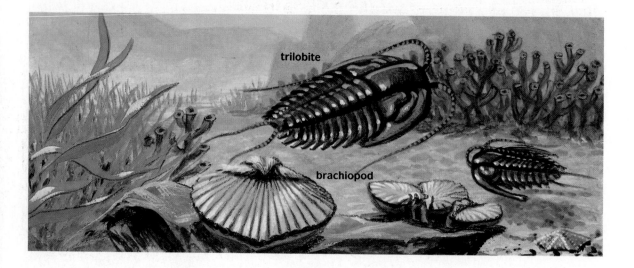

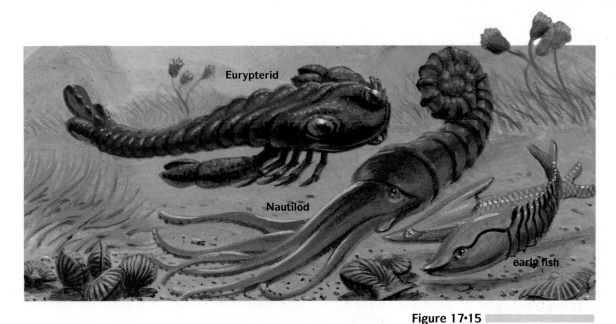

Eurypterid

Nautilod

early fish

Figure 17•15
Life forms of the Ordovician Period.

The Silurian (suh LUR ee un) Period follows the Ordovician Period. The first land plants, such as lichens and mosses, appeared during this period. And some forms of animal life, such as scorpions, moved to the land.

The next period is the Devonian (duh VOH nee-uhn) Period. By this period, fish had become abundant. The first amphibians appeared. Amphibians are animals that live in water when they are young but live on land when they are adults. Large land plants, such as giant tree ferns and evergreens, also appeared during this time.

The Devonian Period is followed by the Carboniferous (kahr buh NIHF uhr uhs) Period. At this time, forests and swamps covered the land. Many insects developed. One of the insects was a giant dragonfly with a 76-cm wingspan. A new group of vertebrates called reptiles also appeared at this time. These animals could live their whole life out of the water.

The last period of the Paleozoic Era is the Permian (PER mee uhn) Period. During this period the climate became much colder. Many living things could not survive the cold climate. Up to 90 percent of the sea life that was common during the Paleozoic Era disappeared. But reptiles and insects adapted to the change, and they survived. Conifers developed in this period.

Figure 17•16
Dimetrodon, a Permian reptile.

431

MESOZOIC ERA

meso- (middle)
zoe (life)

The third large division of geologic time, the **Mesozoic Era**, lasted 165 million years. During this time the land that is now North America took shape. The environment was warm and wet. The Mesozoic Era is often called the Age of Reptiles.

There are three periods during the Mesozoic Era. The first period is the Triassic (trī AS ihk) Period. During this period, conifers and reptiles were common, and mammals appeared. Oysters and lobsters were found in the ocean. Grasshoppers and flies were found on the land.

The next period is the Jurassic (ju RAS ihk) Period. During this period, reptiles called dinosaurs dominated. The word *dinosaur* comes from the Greek and means "terrible lizard." Both large dinosaurs and small dinosaurs existed during the Jurassic Period. The plant-eating dinosaur called the *Brontosaurus* was one of the largest animals that has ever lived on land. In contrast, some dinosaurs were about the size of a chicken. Toward the end of the Jurassic period, the first birds appeared.

The last period of the Mesozoic Era is called the Cretaceous (krih TAY shuhs) Period. Flowering plants appeared at this time. The dinosaur *Tyrannosaurus* appeared. It was a two-legged, meat-eating animal that was over 13 m long and weighed

Figure 17·17

During the Mesozoic Era, dinosaurs dominated the earth.

Brontosaurus

Allosaurus

Stegosaurus

about 8 t. But by the end of the Cretaceous Period, the dinosaurs and about half of all other life forms had disappeared from existence. Only small animals survived.

Scientists do not know why the dinosaurs suddenly died. One hypothesis suggests that worldwide volcanic activity could have put huge amounts of dust and smoke into the air. The dust and smoke would have blocked out sunlight. This may have caused the earth's climate to cool and many living things to die.

Another hypothesis, the *meteorite impact hypothesis*, suggests that a meteorite hit the earth. Upon striking the earth, the meteorite would have exploded, throwing huge amounts of dust into the air. Thus the earth's climate would have cooled.

Figure 17·18

A meteorite striking the earth could have led to the extinction of the dinosaurs.

CENOZOIC ERA

The most recent era is the **Cenozoic Era**. It is the era in which we live and in which mammals have become dominant. The Cenozoic Era is divided into two periods. The first period is the Tertiary (TER shee ehr ee) Period. During this period the Grand Canyon was carved out of rock layers by the Colorado River. Some of the great mountain ranges, including the Alps, Rockies, and Andes, also formed. The other period is the Quaternary (kwuh-TER nuhr ee) Period. During this period the climate became much colder and ice sheets advanced.

ceno- (new)
zoe (life)

Figure 17·19
Some mammals from the Oligocene Epoch.

Because there are many fossils from the Cenozoic Era, the periods can be divided into epochs. The Tertiary Period is divided into five epochs. The first is the Paleocene (PAY lee uh seen) Epoch. During this epoch the mammals were small. The plants resembled tropical plants of today.

In the next epoch, the Eocene (EE uh seen) Epoch, mammals became larger. Ancestors of modern mammals, such as the whale and the horse, appeared. During the Oligocene (AHL uh goh seen) Epoch the climate cooled. Tropical plants were replaced by grasses and pine trees. Apes, elephants, and members of the cat and dog families existed. There were many kinds of rhinoceroses, including the long-necked one shown in Figure 17·19.

During the Miocene (MĪ uh seen) Epoch, herds of horses that ate grasses roamed the plains of North America. Mastodons may have crossed a land bridge between Siberia and Alaska. In the Pliocene (PLĪ uh seen) Epoch, glaciers began to form in the Northern Hemisphere. The sea level fell. Animals crossed land that was no longer covered by water.

The Quaternary Period follows the Pliocene Epoch and has two epochs. The first is called the Pleistocene (PLĪs tuh seen) Epoch. The Pleistocene Epoch is often called the Ice Age. Glaciers advanced at least four different times during this epoch. Because of the cold climate, animals had to either develop protective coverings or move to warmer regions. Animals that could not adapt became extinct. Mammals of the Ice Age included mastodons from Asia, saber-toothed tigers, and mammoths. As this epoch ended, these large mammals became extinct.

The most recent epoch is called the Holocene (HOL uh seen) Epoch. During this epoch the earth's climate has become warmer, causing almost all of the glaciers to disappear. It is in the Holocene Epoch that human civilization arose.

REVIEW

1. How do the life forms of the Paleozoic Era compare with those of the Precambrian Era?
2. What living things existed during the Mesozoic Era?
3. What living things existed during the Cenozoic Era?

CHALLENGE Explain why some land areas became dry during the ice ages.

CHAPTER SUMMARY

The main ideas in this chapter are listed below. Read these statements before you answer the Chapter Review questions.

- According to the principle of uniformitarianism, the processes at work on the earth today were also at work in the past. (17•1)
- The law of superposition and the study of unconformities help geologists determine the relative age of rocks. (17•1)
- Fossils are the remains or traces of once-living things that are found in the earth's crust. Fossils are preserved in many different ways. (17•2)
- Index fossils and facies fossils are used in the correlation of rocks from different areas. (17•3)
- A geologic column shows the sequence, by age, of rocks in an area. (17•3)

- Radiometric dating uses the half-lives of radioactive elements to determine the age of materials. (17•3)
- The earth's history can be divided into units of time based on changes in the earth's crust and changes in life forms. (17•4)
- Little evidence of life forms is found in rock of the Precambrian Era. (17•4)
- An abundance of invertebrates appeared during the Paleozoic Era. (17•5)
- Reptiles, including the dinosaurs, dominated the Mesozoic Era. (17•5)
- The era we live in is called the Cenozoic Era. Mammals have become dominant during the era. (17•5)

The key terms in this chapter are listed below. Use each term in a sentence that shows the meaning of the term.

cast	fossils	Mesozoic Era	Precambrian Era
Cenozoic Era	geologic column	mold	radiometric dating
era	geologic time scale	Paleozoic Era	relative age

Chapter Review

VOCABULARY

Use the key terms from the previous page to complete the following sentences correctly.

1. The preserved remains or traces of once-living things found in the earth's crust are called _____.
2. A fossil that has the same outer shape as the original object is a/an _____.
3. A diagram of the sequence of rock layers in an area is a/an _____.
4. The age of one thing compared with the age of something else is the _____.
5. The age of rocks is found using the decay of radioactive elements, in a process called _____.
6. A major unit of time based on changes in the earth's crust and the development of certain life forms is a/an _____.
7. The division of the earth's history into units of time based on changes in the earth and its living things is called the _____.
8. The oldest and longest era is the _____.
9. The third era in geologic time is the _____.
10. The most recent era is the _____.

CONCEPTS

Look at the drawing below, and answer the questions.

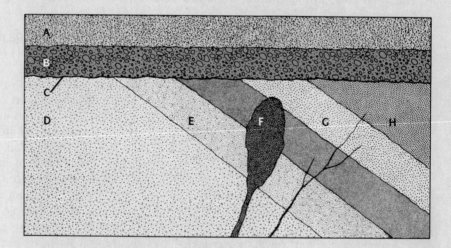

1. Which rock layer is the oldest?
2. Which rock layer is the newest?
3. Where is the unconformity?
4. Which rock layers have changed position since they were deposited?
5. Where is the intrusion?
6. Is the crack older than or younger than layer H? How can you tell?

Write the letter of the era that best matches the statement on the left.

7. The first jellyfish appear.
8. Mammals dominate.
9. Reptiles dominate.
10. Humans appear.
11. Fish appear and become abundant.
12. Mass extinction of dinosaurs occurs.

a. Cenozoic Era
b. Mesozoic Era
c. Paleozoic Era
d. Precambrian Era

Answer the following in complete sentences.

13. Give an example of how scientists use the principle of uniformitarianism to study the earth's history.
14. Describe three ways that fossils form.
15. Explain how correlation is used to make a geologic column.
16. On what evidence is the geologic time scale divided into eras, periods, and epochs?
17. What kinds of changes in the environment might have caused great changes in the kinds of living things on the earth?

1. Name some animals and plants now living on the earth that would make good facies fossils for future geologists. Give reasons for your choices.
2. Why do geologists use the age of meteorites to help determine the earth's age?
3. Suppose a piece of wood is found to contain one fourth of its original amount of carbon-14. How old is that wood?
4. How could you estimate the size of a dog from the imprint of its feet?

APPLICATION/ CRITICAL THINKING

1. Collect fossils in your area. Try to decide which of the organisms lived in an ocean environment and which did not. Give reasons for your decisions.
2. Use library resources to prepare a paper on the extinction of the dinosaurs. What are some explanations that have been suggested? What do you think caused the extinction? Why do you think so?
3. Work with a partner to build a model of oceans, continents, and prominent features for a particular period of geologic time. The model could be made of salt-and-flour paste or papier-mâché.
4. A fish called coelacanth was caught alive in the Indian Ocean in 1938. Scientists thought this fish had been extinct for over 70 million years. Find out more about the coelacanth and its special characteristics.

EXTENSION

CHAPTER 18

EARTH'S ATMOSPHERE

Have you ever been in a parade? Imagine what it would be like to be in a ticker-tape parade. Cities have ticker-tape parades to welcome famous people or to celebrate special achievements. There have been ticker-tape parades for returning astronauts and victorious sports teams.

Notice in the photograph that ticker tape and other paper streamers thrown from buildings fall down onto the parade. The paper drifts and flutters to the ground. Air resistance keeps the paper from falling straight down. Wind may blow a piece of paper blocks away from where it was thrown.

- *Do other objects fall through the air the way paper falls?*
- *What matter makes up the air?*
- *What causes wind to form?*

18·1 The Atmosphere

COMPOSITION OF THE ATMOSPHERE

You live at the bottom of an ocean of air. This ocean of air that surrounds the earth is an invisible mixture of gases called the **atmosphere**. Suppose you were to study a sample of dry air collected within 80 km of the ground. You would find that it is made up of the gases listed in Table 18·1. Which two gases make up most of the atmosphere?

As altitude increases, the air becomes thinner, or less dense. If you were to take a sample from higher in the atmosphere, you would find that heavier gases, like nitrogen and oxygen, are not found there. Air in the upper part of the atmosphere contains mostly hydrogen, the lightest gas.

In addition to the gases shown in Table 18·1, other materials can be found in the atmosphere. The amount of these materials varies from place to place and from time to time. For example, air over a desert has almost no water vapor in it. But 4 percent of the air over a rain forest may be water vapor. The amount of water vapor in the air also varies from day to day. On a wet, rainy day, there could be two to three times more water vapor in the air than there is in the same area on a dry day.

Figure 18·1

There is less water in the air over a desert *(left)* than in the air over a rain forest *(right).*

ACTIVITY   How Much Oxygen Does the Air Contain?

OBJECTIVE
Determine the amount of oxygen in air.

MATERIALS
steel wool, 2 large test tubes, deep pan, water, 2 test-tube clamps, ring stand, glass-marking pencil, metric ruler

PROCEDURE
A. Wet a piece of steel wool, and place it in the bottom of a large test tube.
B. Turn the test tube upside down in a deep pan of water so that the open end of the test tube is just under the water. Clamp the test tube to a ring stand.
C. Repeat step **B** with an empty test tube.
D. Every day, mark the level of the water in each test tube with a glass-marking pencil. After the water level has not risen in either test tube for 2 straight days, remove the test tubes from the water.
E. Use a metric ruler to measure the length of the first test tube. Record this length. Then measure the distance from the top of the test tube to the water line closest to the bottom. Record this distance.

Divide the second number by the first. Multiply the result by 100. This will tell you what percentage of the test tube had water in it. Record this percentage.
F. Repeat step **E**, using the second test tube.

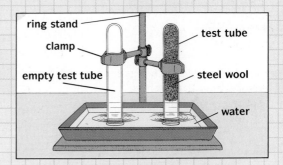

RESULTS AND CONCLUSIONS
1. Compare the percentages of water in the two test tubes. Explain the result.
2. The reaction in the first test tube used oxygen from the air in the test tube. As the oxygen was used up, water took its place. The reaction ended when there was no more oxygen in the test tube. What percentage of your first test tube had water in it? Explain this result.

The amount of solid materials in the air also varies. For example, salt is found in the air along a seashore. There the breaking waves add salt particles to the air. Rock particles and dust may be thrown into the air by an erupting volcano or by wind. Some of these solid materials may stay in the air for many years.

STRUCTURE OF THE ATMOSPHERE

The atmosphere is divided into layers. This division is based on temperature changes that occur at different levels of the atmosphere. As you read about the layers of the atmosphere, identify them in Figure 18·2 on the next page.

Table 18·1
Gases in the Atmosphere

GAS	PERCENT BY VOLUME
Nitrogen	78.08
Oxygen	20.95
Argon	0.93
Carbon dioxide	0.03
Neon	trace
Helium	trace
Methane	trace
Krypton	trace
Hydrogen	trace
Xenon	trace
Ozone	trace

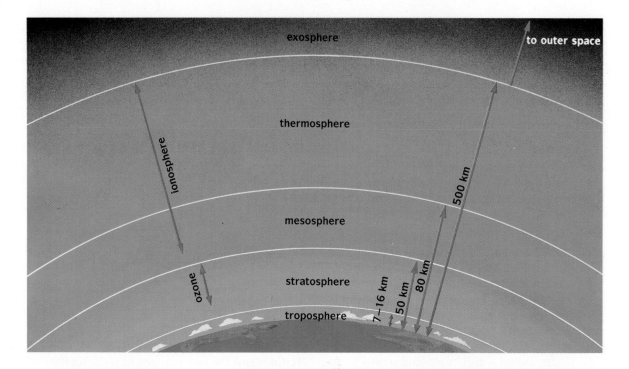

exosphere

to outer space

thermosphere

ionosphere

500 km

mesosphere

stratosphere

80 km

50 km

ozone

7–16 km

troposphere

Figure 18·2
The layers of the atmosphere.

stratus (spreading out)

meso- (middle)

● The **troposphere** (TROH puh sfihr) extends from the surface of the earth to a height of between 7 km and 16 km. The temperature drops as altitude increases. At the top of the troposphere, the temperature is about −55°C.

● The **stratosphere** (STRAT uh sfihr), the second layer of the atmosphere, extends to a height of 50 km above the earth. The temperature remains around −55°C in the lower region of this layer. The upper region contains a form of oxygen called ozone (OH zohn). Ozone absorbs ultraviolet radiation from the sun and releases heat into the atmosphere. As a result, the temperature at the top of the stratosphere is near 0°C. The ozone layer also prevents ultraviolet radiation from reaching the earth's surface. Some scientists are concerned that chemicals may be destroying the ozone layer.

● The **mesosphere** (MEHS uh sfihr), the third layer of the atmosphere, extends from the stratosphere to a height of 80 km. The gases here do not absorb much of the sun's radiation. Therefore, this layer is cold, with temperatures near −100°C. Many shooting stars, or meteors, burn up in this layer.

- The **thermosphere** (THER muh sfihr), the fourth layer of the atmosphere, extends to a height of about 500 km. This is the warmest layer of the atmosphere. Gases in the thermosphere absorb a large amount of radiation. The temperature may reach 1000°C. Radiation here causes some particles to become electrically charged, forming ions. These ions are held in place by the earth's magnetic field. The region of the thermosphere where these ions are found is called the *ionosphere* (ī AHN uh sfihr). Radio signals can be reflected off the ionosphere and relayed around the earth.

thermo- (heat)

- The **exosphere** (EHK suh sfihr), the last layer of the atmosphere, extends into outer space. There is no exact end to this layer. The molecules here are very far apart, and some escape the earth's gravity and drift into space. Many satellites orbit in this layer around the earth.

exo- (outer)

Figure 18·3
Satellites like these orbit in the exosphere.

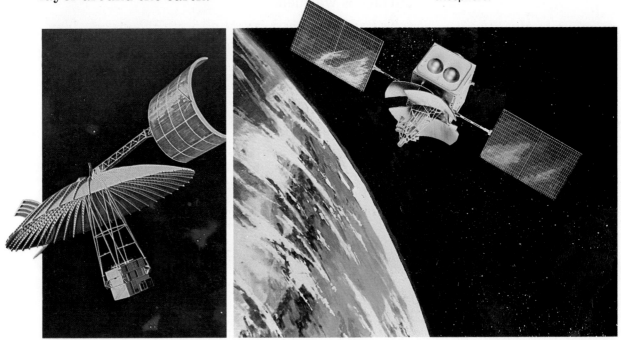

REVIEW

1. What gases make up the atmosphere?
2. In which layers of the atmosphere is the temperature rising, and in which is it falling?

CHALLENGE Why is it practical to have satellites orbit in the exosphere rather than in the mesosphere?

18·2 Heat Transfer in the Atmosphere

The source of the energy that warms the earth is the sun. The sun gives off radiant energy. **Radiant energy** is energy that travels in the form of waves. This energy is also called *radiation*. Examples of the sun's radiation include X rays, ultraviolet rays, visible light, infrared rays, and radio waves. When these waves of radiation strike matter, they are either absorbed or reflected.

Figure 18·4 shows what happens to the energy that reaches the earth. How much of this energy is reflected back into space? The atmosphere absorbs 20 percent of the energy. The remaining 50 percent passes through the atmosphere. This energy is absorbed by the surface of the earth, and the earth's surface is warmed.

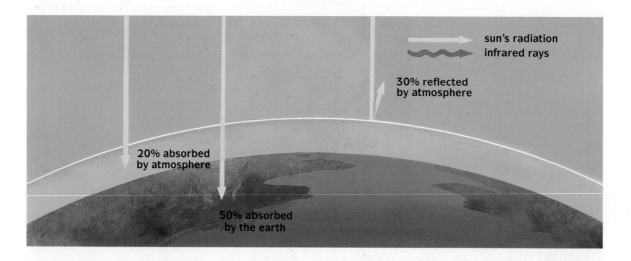

sun's radiation
infrared rays

30% reflected
by atmosphere

20% absorbed
by atmosphere

50% absorbed
by the earth

Figure 18·4

Some of the sun's radiant energy does not reach the earth's surface.

When the surface of the earth cools, it gives off energy in the form of infrared rays. These rays are absorbed by carbon dioxide and other gases in the atmosphere. Thus the atmosphere is warmed. The warming of the atmosphere due to the absorption of waves of heat energy from the earth is called the **greenhouse effect**. Because of the greenhouse effect, the atmosphere acts like a blanket keeping the earth warm.

You may have noticed that the air temperature drops more on clear nights than on cloudy nights. This difference occurs because on cloudy nights there is more water vapor in the air. The water vapor absorbs more of the heat energy radiated by the earth.

There are two other ways in which the atmosphere is heated. One way is by conduction. *Conduction* is a process by which heat energy moves from one object to another when the two objects touch. Air that touches a warm surface, like a hot road, receives warmth from that surface by conduction.

The other way that the atmosphere is heated is called convection. *Convection* is a process by which heat energy is moved by flowing matter. When air is heated, it expands and becomes less dense. Cooler, denser air sinks and pushes the warm air upward. The moving air carries heat by convection. This continuing movement of air, shown in Figure 18·5, is called a convection current. In a convection current, moving air carries heat energy.

You have learned that there are three processes involved in heating the earth and its atmosphere: radiation, conduction, and convection. These processes bring warmth to the entire earth, but the earth is not evenly heated. Different materials on

PUZZLER

Hawks, like the one shown, can spread their wings and glide, or soar, for a long distance. They can also glide in a circle and gain height without flapping their wings. Explain how this upward glide happens. What kinds of areas would provide conditions that make this action possible?

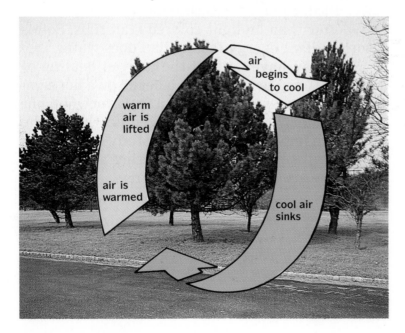

air begins to cool

warm air is lifted

air is warmed

cool air sinks

Figure 18·5

As air over the road is heated, convection currents are created.

What Is the Greenhouse Effect?

OBJECTIVE
Compare the ability of different materials to trap radiant energy.

MATERIALS
4 thermometers, 4 shoeboxes, cellophane tape, piece of wax paper, piece of clear plexiglass, piece of plastic wrap

PROCEDURE
A. Tape a thermometer in the center of the bottom of a shoebox. Repeat this with three other thermometers and shoeboxes.
B. Cover one box with a piece of wax paper, a second box with a piece of clear plexiglass, and a third box with a piece of plastic wrap. Leave the fourth box uncovered.
C. Set each shoebox in a sunlit area suggested by your teacher.
D. Check the temperature in each shoebox every minute for 20 minutes. Record the temperatures in a table.

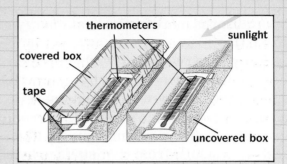

RESULTS AND CONCLUSIONS
1. Make a graph that shows the results of your experiment. Put time on the x-axis and temperature on the y-axis.
2. In which box did the temperature increase the fastest?
3. In which box did the temperature increase the slowest?
4. Which material most readily traps radiant energy?

the earth's surface absorb radiant energy differently. Dark-colored materials absorb radiant energy better than do light-colored materials. Solids absorb radiant energy faster than does water.

You may have noticed the uneven heating of the earth if you have been on a beach on a hot summer day. On such a day the sand feels very hot, but the water feels cooler. The uneven heating of the earth is an important idea in the study of weather. As you will see, this uneven heating affects both wind patterns and weather patterns.

REVIEW
1. What happens to radiant energy that reaches the earth?
2. How does the greenhouse effect help to keep the earth warm?
3. What are the three ways in which the atmosphere is warmed?

CHALLENGE What would happen to the temperature over a 24-hour period on the earth if the earth did not have an atmosphere?

18·3 Air Pressure

MEASURING AIR PRESSURE

Like all matter, air is affected by gravity and has weight. **Air pressure** is the force caused by the weight of air. The greater the amount of air above an area, the greater the air pressure on that area. Think of a square column of air 1.0 cm on each side, extending through the exosphere. This column of air weighs 10.1 N. Thus the pressure of the air at the bottom of this column is 10.1 N/cm², or 101,000 N/m². Meteorologists often use a unit called the millibar (mb) to measure air pressure. Since 1 mb equals 100 N/m², the air pressure at sea level equals 1010 mb.

A **barometer** is an instrument that is used to measure air pressure. Two kinds of barometers are shown in Figure 18·6. One kind of barometer consists of a mercury-filled tube held in a small pool of mercury. When air pressure increases, the height of the mercury in the tube increases. What happens to the mercury when the pressure decreases?

Since mercury is a toxic substance, the other kind of barometer is used more often. This barometer contains a sealed can with a spring inside. As air pressure increases, the sides of the can are pushed in. A decrease in pressure allows the spring to push the sides back out.

After completing this section, you will be able to

- **explain** what causes air pressure.
- **describe** how air pressure is measured.
- **compare** air movement in a high-pressure area with that in a low-pressure area.

The key terms in this section are
air pressure   barometer

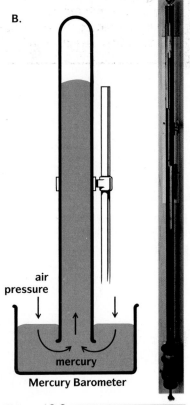

A.

scale

33

32

31

lever

30

air pressure

29

28

Aneroid Barometer

B.

air pressure

mercury

Mercury Barometer

Figure 18·6
Barometers measure air pressure.

HIGHS AND LOWS

Air pressure varies from day to day and from place to place. Measurements of pressure are recorded on weather maps. Lines called *isobars* (ī suhbahrz) are drawn on the maps to connect places that have the same air pressure. Figure 18·8 shows a weather map with isobars drawn on it. There is a difference of 4 mb between one isobar and the next on a weather map. Isobars that are far apart indicate a slow change in pressure. What do isobars that are close together indicate?

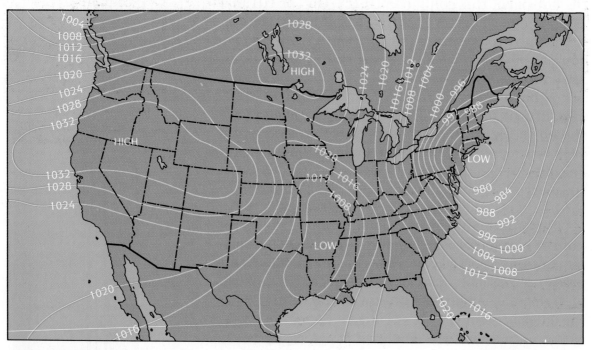

Figure 18·7

Isobars indicate places where air pressure is the same.

Look at the areas that are completely circled by isobars in Figure 18·7. Some of these areas have higher air pressure than do the surrounding areas and are called high-pressure areas, or *highs*. Other areas on the map have lower air pressure than do the surrounding areas and are called low-pressure areas, or *lows*. Air moves from areas of higher pressure to areas of lower pressure.

Air in the center of a high is heavier and exerts more pressure than the air around it. This heavy air sinks toward the earth. As the air moves away from

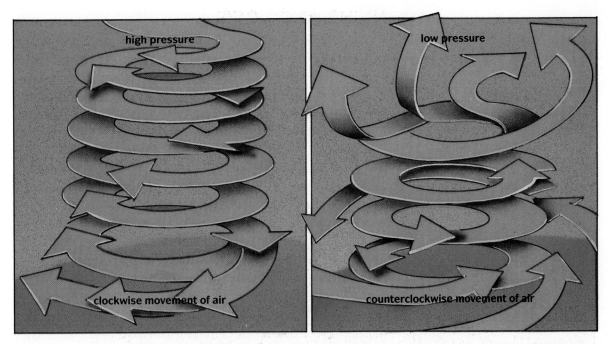

high pressure

clockwise movement of air

low pressure

counterclockwise movement of air

the center of a high in the Northern Hemisphere, the air turns in a clockwise direction. Air in the center of a low is lighter and exerts less pressure than the air around it. Unlike air in a high, the air in a low is pushed upward by denser air moving in from around the low. Look at Figure 18·8. In what direction does the rising air turn?

The change in air pressure from one place to another is called the *pressure gradient*. The closer together the isobars, the greater the pressure gradient. The greater the pressure gradient, the faster the air movement. Therefore, one indication of the wind speed and intensity of a storm is how close together the isobars are on a weather map. Which storm would have stronger winds—a storm in which the isobars are close together or a storm in which the isobars are far apart?

REVIEW

1. What causes air pressure?
2. How does a barometer measure air pressure?
3. Describe the movement of air in an area of high pressure. How is this movement different from that in a low-pressure area?

CHALLENGE How might a barometer be used to measure the altitude of an airplane?

18·4 Wind

After completing this section, you will be able to

- **explain** what causes wind.
- **give examples** of devices used to measure wind.

The key terms in this section are
anemometer
wind
wind vane

anemos (wind)
-meter (to measure)

Wind is moving air. Wind is caused by differences in air pressure. These differences in air pressure are usually caused by the uneven heating of the earth. The uneven heating of the earth causes an uneven heating of the air directly above the earth. And this uneven heating of the air starts convection currents. Cooler, denser air sinks under warm, less dense air, lifting the warm air upward. The warm air cools as it rises. As the air cools, it becomes denser and sinks back toward the earth.

The terms *warm* and *cool* are relative terms. The exact air temperature is not as important as the difference in air temperature from one place to another. This difference in temperature creates the pressure difference that causes air to move. Wind continues as long as pressure differences continue. The greater the difference in temperature, the greater the difference in pressure, and the faster the wind.

An **anemometer** (an uh MAHM uh tuhr) is an instrument that measures wind speed. An anemometer has three or four cup-shaped arms attached to an axle. The faster the wind moves, the faster the

Figure 18·9
When the differences in air pressure are great, winds can be strong. Strong winds can damage trees and buildings.

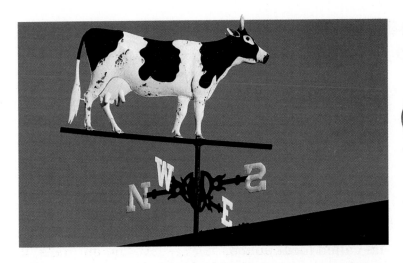

anemometer spins. This spinning produces an electric current that moves a needle on a gauge. The stronger the wind, the greater the electric current, and the farther the needle moves.

An instrument that measures the direction of the wind is called a **wind vane** or weather vane. One end of a wind vane is larger than the other end. When wind strikes the wind vane, there is more force on the large end than on the small end. As a result, the large end is pushed away. The small end acts like a pointer showing the direction from which the wind is coming. A wind is named according to the direction from which it comes. Where does a "north wind" come from?

Winds in the upper atmosphere are measured with weather balloons. These balloons are released from the earth's surface and are tracked by meteorologists with telescopes and radar. The speed and direction of the balloons indicate the speed and direction of the winds. Winds in the upper atmosphere move at high speeds. These winds have fewer changes in direction and speed than do winds near the earth's surface.

Figure 18·10

A wind vane *(left)* and an anemometer *(right)*.

REVIEW

1. What is wind? What causes wind?

2. How are the speed and direction of wind measured?

CHALLENGE Wind vanes are often designed in the shape of animals, ships, or other objects. What must be true about the design of any wind vane if it is to work correctly?

18·5 Types of Wind

LOCAL WINDS

Winds are caused by the uneven heating of the earth's surface. In some places on the earth, the temperature varies little from day to day. The air in these places moves in the same direction most of the time. In other places, however, there are large daily or seasonal changes in temperature that cause special winds to occur. These daily or seasonal winds are called *local winds*.

As you can see in Figure 18·11, a cycle of local winds occurs daily at the shore of a lake or ocean. During the day the land warms much more quickly than does the water. The air over the land also warms more quickly. The cooler, denser air over the water sinks under the air on the land and lifts the warm air upward. This cool breeze that moves from a body of water to the land during the day is called a sea breeze. During the evening the land cools off faster than does the water. The air over the land becomes cooler than the air over the water. The cool air from the land then moves over the water, creating a land breeze.

Figure 18·11
A sea breeze usually occurs during the day *(left)*. A land breeze usually occurs during the night *(right)*.

sea breeze

cool sea

warm land

land breeze

warm sea

cool land

Another example of a local wind takes place in a mountain valley. During the day the mountainside receives sunlight and warms quickly. Air along the mountain surface becomes warm. The cool air over the valley sinks, pushing the warm air up the mountain and creating a valley breeze. At some point during the evening, however, the mountainside cools off while the valley stays warm. Then the breeze changes direction. The cool mountain air moves down along the mountain surface, pushing the warm valley air upward and creating a mountain breeze.

GLOBAL WINDS

For many years, meteorologists have recorded air pressure readings from around the earth. By averaging the readings from each weather station, these scientists have shown that there is a general pattern of pressure zones on the earth's surface. These zones are called pressure belts. A *pressure belt* is an area of constant high or low pressure encircling the earth. Figure 18·12 shows the major pressure belts of the earth. Notice that high-pressure belts alternate with low-pressure belts.

Figure 18·12
Belts of high pressure and low pressure circle the earth.

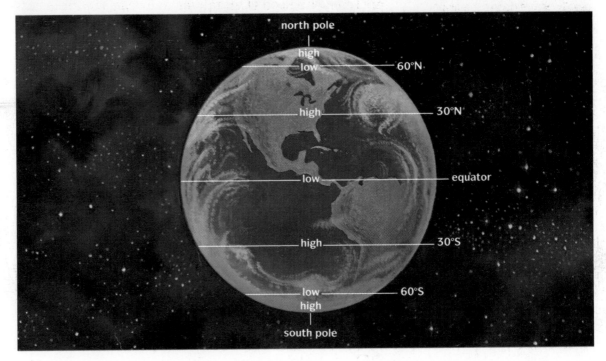

At the equator the air is warmed more than air to the north and south. The additional heat makes the air at the equator less dense than the air around it. Thus a belt of low pressure is formed. The air here is lifted, and as it reaches the top of the troposphere, the air spreads north and south. By the time it reaches latitudes 30° north and 30° south, the air has cooled. The air is now denser, and it begins to sink back toward the earth. This dense air forms a belt of high pressure around latitudes 30° north and 30° south. When the high-pressure air reaches the surface of the earth, it spreads both north and south. Figure 18·13 shows these patterns of air movement. Notice that the arrows do not point directly north or south. What is the reason for this change in direction?

If the earth were not spinning, the air traveling back to the equator from 30° north would move directly south. In the time it takes for the air to make the trip back to the equator, however, the earth has spun a distance on its axis. As a result, the air seems to curve to the west. This apparent

Figure 18·13

Global wind patterns are determined by the pressure belts of the earth.

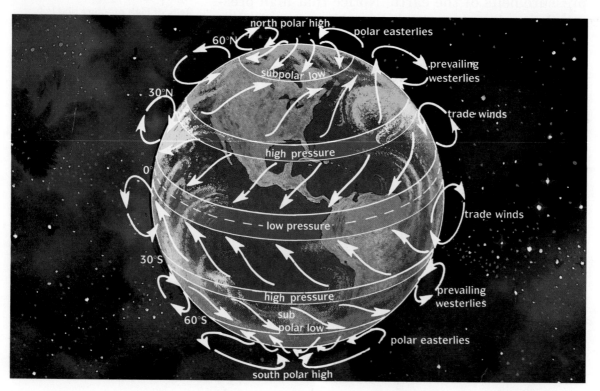

The photograph shows windmills at Altamont Pass, just east of San Francisco in California. This is the world's largest collection of windmills. Row after row of 90-m-high windmills with blades up to 20 m across capture the energy of the wind. Generators turn the wind energy into electricity sold to local power companies. The project began in 1981 with just a few windmills. By 1983 some 2500 windmills were producing enough electricity to meet the needs of 50,000 households.

The success of the Altamont wind farm shows that wind energy can be an important renewable resource. Energy developers in other states are increasing efforts to use wind power.

Other countries are also showing interest in wind energy. In island countries, energy costs are high. Experimental projects there have shown the economy of wind power.

Producing electricity from wind requires constant winds and open spaces. Such conditions occur in many places in the United States. If interest in wind power continues, wind energy could supply 14 percent of the nation's electricity by the year 2000.

change in wind direction, caused by the rotation of the earth, is called the **Coriolis** (kawr ee OH lihs) **effect**. The Coriolis effect explains why winds in the Northern Hemisphere are deflected to the right. In the Southern Hemisphere, winds are deflected to the left by the Coriolis effect.

The air at the equator is generally rising because of the constant low pressure. Therefore the equator is an area of light, shifting winds. Early sailors feared crossing here because there was always the possibility of being stranded for long periods with no wind.

Latitudes 30° north and 30° south are also areas of unstable winds. These latitudes are areas of constantly high pressure. The air here is generally sinking toward the earth, and again, there is no steady wind.

Some of the air returning to the surface of the earth at latitudes 30° north and 30° south travels back to the equator along the earth's surface. This movement of air creates winds called *trade winds*. In the Northern Hemisphere, they deflect to the right of their path because of the Coriolis effect. Northern Hemisphere trade winds are steady northeasterly winds between 30° north and the equator. During the days of large sailing vessels, these trade winds created a reliable route for trade with the New World.

The rest of the air that sinks at latitudes 30° north and 30° south travels away from the equator. In the Northern Hemisphere the winds that form also deflect to the right of their path because of the Coriolis effect. These southwesterly winds between 30° and 60° north are called *prevailing westerlies*. Much of the weather that moves across North America is carried by prevailing westerlies.

The air above the poles is cold and dense, and it sinks toward the earth. In the Northern Hemisphere this cold air spreads away from the pole and deflects to the right of its path, as shown in Figure 18·13. This movement forms the *polar easterlies*.

JET STREAMS

At latitudes 30° north and 30° south near the top of the troposphere are high-speed bands of wind called **jet streams**. These narrow bands of wind move like waves from west to east through the atmosphere. The speed, size, position, and shape of the jet streams vary from day to day and from sea-

Figure 18·14

Jet streams can affect the travel time of airplanes. In which direction of travel would a plane be slowed by the jet stream?

son to season. During the summer in the Northern Hemisphere, for example, the jet streams tend to be weaker and farther north. Jet stream winds travel as fast as 370 km/h. They seem to control the movement of weather systems across the earth. Knowing the position of the jet streams can be very useful to people who prepare weather forecasts.

REVIEW

1. What can cause the wind to shift direction along a shoreline during the day?

2. What causes winds to change direction as they move across the earth?

3. How do the jet streams influence weather?

CHALLENGE Based on what you have learned in this section, predict the direction from which the air moves in the region where you live. Does the air always move from that direction? Explain why or why not.

CHAPTER SUMMARY

The main ideas in this chapter are listed below. Read these statements before you answer the Chapter Review questions.

- The atmosphere is a mixture of gases. (18·1)
- The atmosphere consists of layers, each having its own characteristics. (18·1)
- Radiant energy from the sun heats the earth and its atmosphere. (18·2)
- Heat energy travels by the processes of radiation, conduction, and convection. (18·2)
- Air pressure can be measured with a device called a barometer. (18·3)
- Lines on a map that connect places having the same air pressure are called isobars. (18·3)
- Air moves from areas of higher air pressure to areas of lower air pressure. (18·3)
- Wind is caused by differences in air pressure. (18·4)
- Convection currents at a shore produce land breezes and sea breezes. Convection currents on mountains produce mountain breezes and valley breezes. (18·5)
- Major zones of constant high or low pressure, called pressure belts, encircle the earth. (18·5)
- The pressure belts of the earth cause global wind patterns. (18·5)

The key terms in this chapter are listed below. Use each term in a sentence that shows the meaning of the term.

air pressure	exosphere	stratosphere
anemometer	greenhouse effect	thermosphere
atmosphere	jet streams	troposphere
barometer	mesosphere	wind
Coriolis effect	radiant energy	wind vane

Chapter Review

VOCABULARY

Write the letter of the term that best matches the definition. Not all the terms will be used.

1. The ocean of air that surrounds the earth
2. The layer of the atmosphere that extends from the surface of the earth to between 7 km and 16 km
3. The fourth layer of the atmosphere
4. Energy that travels in the form of waves
5. The warming of the atmosphere due to the absorption of heat energy from the earth
6. An instrument used to measure air pressure
7. An instrument used to measure wind speed
8. An instrument used to measure wind direction
9. A change in wind direction caused by the rotation of the earth
10. High-speed bands of wind near the top of the troposphere

a. anemometer
b. atmosphere
c. barometer
d. Coriolis effect
e. exosphere
f. greenhouse effect
g. jet streams
h. radiant energy
i. thermosphere
j. troposphere
k. wind
l. wind vane

CONCEPTS

Choose the term or phrase that best answers the question or completes the statement.

1. The atmosphere is divided into different layers according to changes in the air's
   a. density.
   b. temperature.
   c. pressure.
   d. color.
2. By which process does the atmosphere receive heat?
   a. radiation
   b. conduction
   c. convection
   d. all of the above
3. The air in the center of a low is
   a. sinking.
   b. rising.
   c. turning clockwise.
   d. not moving.
4. Isobars on a map indicate areas that have the same
   a. wind speed.
   b. wind direction.
   c. air pressure.
   d. air temperature.
5. Which winds seem to direct the movement of weather systems?
   a. jet streams
   b. prevailing westerlies
   c. trade winds
   d. sea breezes

Write the correct term for each layer of the atmosphere in the diagram.

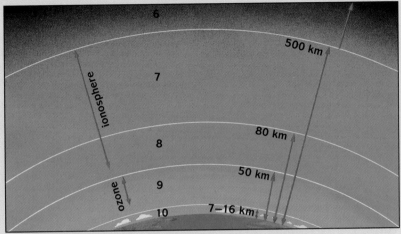

Answer the following in complete sentences.

11. Describe the materials that make up the atmosphere.
12. How does radiant energy from the sun warm the earth's atmosphere?
13. Compare the movement of air in highs and lows.
14. How does uneven heating of the earth cause wind?
15. How does the Coriolis effect affect global winds?

APPLICATION/ CRITICAL THINKING

1. Scientists are concerned about the amount of carbon dioxide in the atmosphere. What might happen to the earth if there were more carbon dioxide in the air? What might happen if there were less carbon dioxide?
2. Could a hot-air balloon travel to the top of the atmosphere? Explain why or why not.
3. How would the jet streams affect air travel between New York, New York, and Miami, Florida? How would they affect air travel between New York and Los Angeles, California?

EXTENSION

1. Use reference materials to find out about such local winds as monsoons, chinooks, harmattans, foehns, mistrals, simooms, and siroccos.
2. Use a barometer to measure the air pressure each day for 2 weeks. Record each reading. Also make notes about the type of weather you have each day. What types of weather follow a rising barometer? What types of weather follow a falling barometer? What types of weather occur when the barometer remains unchanged?

CHAPTER 19

THE CHANGING WEATHER

*D*ark clouds moving quickly with strong winds indicate that a storm is approaching. When water evaporates into the air, the water condenses into clouds. The clouds thicken, and evenutally, rain occurs.

More than 10,000 thunderstorms occur every day on the earth. An average-sized thunderstorm releases a large amount of energy into the air. Most of the energy is in the form of lightning.

- *What conditions lead to the formation of thunder-storms?*
- *What other types of storms occur over the earth?*
- *What are some signs that indicate a change in the weather?*

19·1 Air Masses

After completing this section, you will be able to

- **describe** how an air mass forms.
- **compare** four types of air masses.
- **explain** how air masses affect the temperature and humidity of an area.

The key terms in this section are
air mass
humidity
weather

AIR MASSES

Changes in the weather occur in the troposphere. Recall that the troposphere extends from the surface of the earth to a height of between 7 km and 16 km. **Weather** is the condition of the atmosphere in a particular place at a particular time. Temperature, air pressure, and wind are all factors of weather.

Large bodies of air are always moving through the atmosphere. These bodies of air are called air masses. An **air mass** is a large body of air that has about the same temperature and humidity throughout it. **Humidity** is water vapor in the air. The weather within an air mass is nearly the same everywhere in that air mass.

Air masses can be warm or cold. They can be high-pressure systems or low-pressure systems. Air masses can cover millions of square kilometers of land or water. Figure 19·1 shows two air masses. Notice the shape of the air mass shown at line AB. How deep is this air mass?

Figure 19·1

Air masses move across the earth and carry their weather with them.

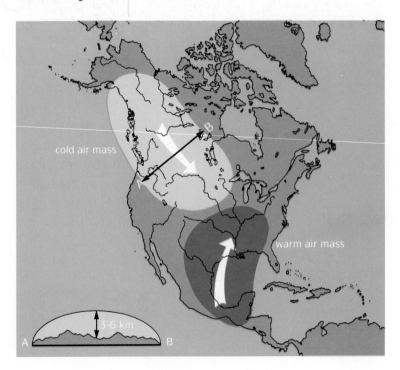

462

Air masses form when air stays over a region for a period of time. It may take a week or more for an air mass to form. The air mass takes on the temperature and humidity of the region. A region where an air mass forms is called a *source region*.

Source regions have large uniform surfaces. A uniform surface is one that is nearly the same everywhere. For example, a large land area that is not broken up by mountains or divided by a large body of water would be a good source region.

Figure 19·2
Which area would be a good source region?

Source regions are found along the pressure belts of the earth. As the air moves across the surface, the type of surface determines the properties of the air mass. An air mass in which the temperature of the air is warm is called a warm air mass. An air mass in which the temperature of the air is cold is called a cold air mass. Would you expect an air mass over Canada to be warm or cold?

Air masses tend to move from west to east across North America. As an air mass moves, its temperature and humidity slowly change. Changes occur because an air mass is affected by the surfaces it covers. For example, a cold air mass will slowly warm as it moves over a warm surface.

CLASSIFYING AIR MASSES

Air masses are classified according to the properties of their source region. An air mass that forms over an ocean is called a maritime (MAR uh tīm) air mass. Maritime air masses tend to be humid. An air mass that forms over land is called a continental (kahn tuh NEHN tuhl) air mass. Continental air masses tend to be dry. An air mass that forms near the poles is called a polar air mass. Polar air masses tend to be cold. An air mass that forms near latitudes 30° north and 30° south is called a tropical air mass. Tropical air masses tend to be warm.

Figure 19·3 shows the four major source regions that influence the weather in North America. Notice that each air mass is classified by describing two factors — humidity and temperature. For example, an air mass that forms over the northern Pacific Ocean is called a maritime polar air mass. What kind of air mass forms over Mexico?

Each kind of air mass brings its own kind of weather. A *maritime tropical air mass* is warm and humid. This air mass brings hot, humid weather in the summer. A *maritime polar air mass* is cold and

Figure 19·3

An air mass is named for the type of source region in which it forms.

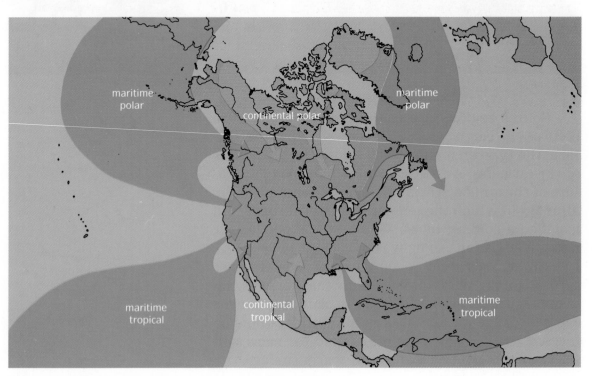

PUZZLER

A special type of snow-storm called a lake effect storm occurs south and east of the Great Lakes in the United States. Lake effect storms involve the movement of low-pressure, cold air. What is the probable source region of the air in such storms? Why do they occur south and east of the Great Lakes?

humid. Maritime polar air masses carry the water that falls as snow on the Rocky Mountains. A *continental tropical air mass* is warm and dry. Continental tropical air masses bring warm, dry weather to the southwestern United States. A *continental polar air mass* is cold and dry. These air masses cause the cold spells that grip North America during the winter.

The movement of air masses is closely related to the position of the jet streams. During the summer, when the jet streams are near the United States–Canadian border, tropical air masses push farther north. These air masses warm the United States and southern Canada. In the winter the jet streams move to the south. Cold polar air moves south with the jet streams. This cold air can reach places as far south as Florida. Meteorologists watch the position of the jet streams to help predict the direction in which an air mass will move.

REVIEW

1. How does an air mass form?
2. Describe the four kinds of air masses and how they affect weather in North America.
3. How are the temperature and humidity of an area affected by an air mass?

CHALLENGE Suppose the position of the jet streams in a particular winter stayed near the United States–Canadian border. Predict the general weather pattern for that winter in each country.

19·2 Weather Fronts

After completing this section, you will be able to

- **explain** how a front forms.
- **compare** four types of fronts.
- **give examples** of weather changes associated with fronts.

The key terms in this section are
cold front
front
occluded front
stationary front
warm front

HOW DO FRONTS FORM?

Different air masses have different densities. Warm air masses are less dense than cold air masses. Humid air masses are less dense than dry air masses. Like oil and water, one air mass does not mix or blend with another. Where two air masses meet, a distinct boundary forms between them. The boundary between two air masses is called a **front**. At a front the less dense air mass is lifted by the more dense air mass.

The shape of a front depends on the densities and speeds of the air masses. Figure 19·4 shows a front between two air masses. The warm air mass is pushing the cold air mass. Along the entire front, the less dense warmer air is slowly lifted by the more dense colder air. As the warmer air rises into the troposphere, the air cools. When the temperature of the rising air cools to the dew point, clouds begin to form. The *dew point* is the temperature at which water in the air condenses. A line of clouds will be seen. Such a line of clouds marks a front. Satellite photographs, such as the one in Figure 19·4, are helpful in locating fronts on the earth. Is the front moving ahead of the cloudy area, or behind it?

Figure 19·4

A warm front and a satellite photograph of a warm front.

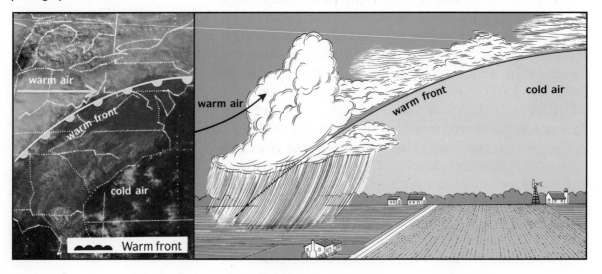

Changes on the ground indicate that a front is passing. One change that indicates a passing front is a decrease in air pressure. Another change that occurs as a front passes is a change in wind direction. Winds generally blow from the south as an air mass leaves but shift to blow from the north as a new air mass approaches. Other changes that are often measured as a front passes are temperature and humidity changes. Each air mass has its own properties. As a new air mass moves in, it brings with it different properties, including different temperature and humidity.

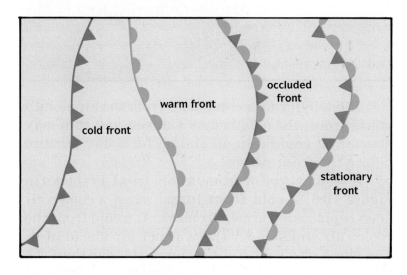

Figure 19·5
These symbols are used on weather maps to mark fronts. How does the symbol for an occluded front differ from the symbol for a stationary front?

KINDS OF FRONTS

Fronts are classified by determining whether the advancing air is warmer or colder than the retreating air. Meteorologists use symbols to mark the fronts on weather maps. Figure 19·5 shows the symbols for each front. These symbols may also be used to mark fronts on satellite photographs.

Figure 19·4 shows a warm front. A **warm front** forms when a warmer air mass replaces a cooler air mass. The warmer air is slowly lifted far over the cooler air. The clouds that form as the warm air slowly rises may extend hundreds of kilometers ahead of the place where the front meets the ground. The clouds are thin and wispy, and they are spread over a large area. It may take a day or more for the clouds to pass when a warm front moves by.

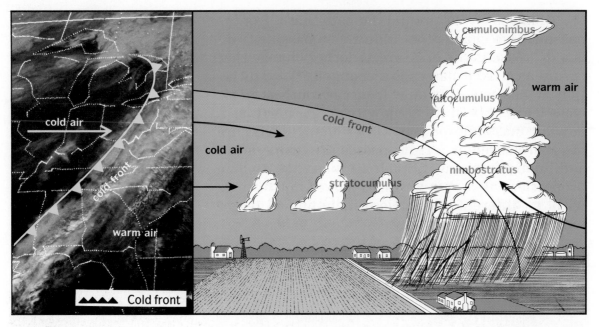

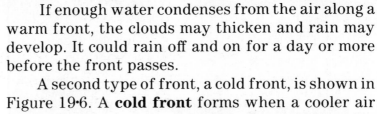

Cold front

Figure 19·6

A cold front and a satellite photograph of a cold front.

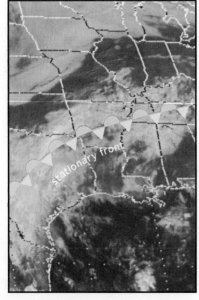

Figure 19·7

A satellite photograph of a stationary front.

If enough water condenses from the air along a warm front, the clouds may thicken and rain may develop. It could rain off and on for a day or more before the front passes.

A second type of front, a cold front, is shown in Figure 19·6. A **cold front** forms when a cooler air mass replaces a warmer air mass. At a cold front the cooler air sinks under the warmer air ahead of it. The slope of a cold front is much steeper than the slope of a warm front. This is because a cold front moves more rapidly than a warm front. The cooler air causes the warmer air mass to rise. The lifting of warmer air ahead of the front forms high clouds, and, sometimes, thunderheads. When a cold front passes by, heavy rains or thunderstorms can occur. These storms generally last for a much shorter time than do storms produced along warm fronts. A cold front is often followed by cooler, clearer weather.

A third kind of front is called a stationary front. The word *stationary* means "standing still." A **stationary front** is a front that does not move for a time. This front forms when two air masses stop moving or move sideways, so that the front between them does not move. Figure 19·7 shows a satellite photograph of a stationary front. A stationary front behaves like a warm front. The warmer air is gently lifted by the cooler air, forming thin clouds. A stationary front brings overcast skies and steady rain until the front finally moves.

As you have read, cold fronts move more rapidly than warm fronts. Sometimes a cold front catches up with a warm front that is ahead of it. When a cold front catches up with a warm front, an **occluded** (uh KLOO dihd) **front** forms. As you can see in Figure 19·8, a mass of warm air is trapped between the two fronts. This mass of warm air is lifted completely off the ground. Occluded fronts can bring very stormy weather. The light, steady rain of the warm front is followed by the heavy downpours of the cold front.

occludere (to close up)

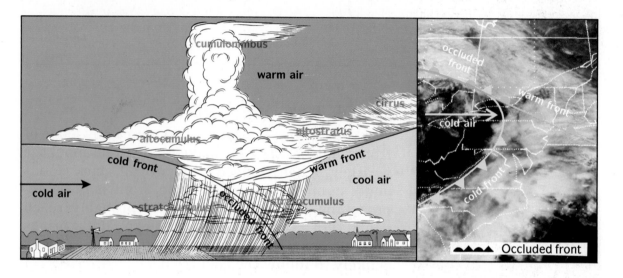

Figure 19·8

An occluded front and a satellite photograph of an occluded front.

HIGHS AND LOWS

Areas of high pressure and areas of low pressure occur along fronts. An area of high pressure, often called a *high*, occurs on one side of a front. In a high, dense air falls and circulates in a clockwise direction. The air on the other side of the front is less dense. Sometimes a section of this light air is forced upward, and the incoming air begins to swirl in a counterclockwise direction. This rising air that swirls in a counterclockwise direction along a front is called a *low*. The weather in a low can be stormy. The weather in a high is often clear.

OBJECTIVE
Determine the relationship between the movement of an air mass and weather changes.

MATERIALS
5 newspaper weather maps with national statistics for 5 consecutive days

PROCEDURE

A. Obtain five weather maps. Arrange the five maps in chronological order in front of you.

B. Select a front that you can follow across the country on the five maps. Find listed in the statistics table a city that the front moves by on the second day.

C. List the high temperature, low temperature, and weather for that city for each of the 5 days.

RESULTS AND CONCLUSIONS

1. How did the temperatures change as the front went by? What type of weather was reported as the front went by?

2. Where do you think the air mass originated? How would you classify it?

3. How did the temperatures change each day as the air mass behind the front continued to move? Explain these changes.

4. Did precipitation occur? Why or why not?

5. How was the weather in the city that you chose determined by the air mass?

PREDICTING WEATHER

You can use the clouds and your knowledge of fronts and air masses to make predictions about the weather. When you see a line of tall, dark clouds building on the horizon, a cold front may be approaching. The cold front would probably reach you within a few hours, but the storm that it brings probably would not last long. What kind of weather is likely to follow the cold front?

High, thin clouds are often seen along a warm front. When these clouds are followed by thin clouds that are spread out and that appear to be getting lower, a warm front is on the way. The rain from the warm front may not start until 24 hours or more after the first clouds have passed. The warm front will probably bring overcast skies and rain.

REVIEW

1. What changes occur at the boundary between air masses?

2. Compare the motions of four types of fronts.

3. What weather changes are associated with each of the four fronts?

CHALLENGE How might a low develop into an occluded front?

19·3 Thunderstorms

Meteorologists have estimated that at any moment, about 2000 thunderstorms are taking place on the earth. Each year, hundreds of millions of dollars in property damage is caused by thunderstorms. How do such storms form?

STAGES OF A THUNDERSTORM

A **thunderstorm** is a violent weather system that produces tall clouds, strong winds, heavy rain, lightning and thunder. A thunderstorm may also cause hail and tornadoes. The tall, dark clouds that form are called thunderheads. Notice in Figure 19·9 that a thunderhead rises higher than other clouds near it.

Thunderstorms form along cold fronts. In the first stage of a thunderstorm, warm air is quickly pushed up by an advancing cold air mass. When the temperature of the rising warm air reaches the dew point, water in the air condenses. This process forms clouds and also gives off heat into the atmosphere. The heat lowers the density of the air and causes the air to be pushed even higher. Then more warm air is forced upward, more water vapor condenses, and more heat is given off.

After completing this section, you will be able to

* **describe** the properties of a thunderstorm.
* **explain** how a thunderstorm forms.
* **list** thunderstorm safety precautions.

The key terms in this section are
lightning
thunder
thunderstorm

Figure 19·9
A thunderhead rises higher than the clouds that are near it.

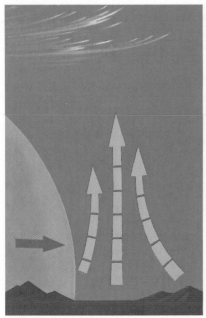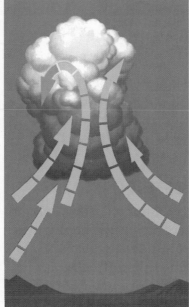

Figure 19·10

A thunderstorm begins as warm air is lifted by cooler air *(left)*. Then a thunderhead forms *(middle)*. Precipitation occurs in the mature stage of a thunderstorm *(right)*.

As the storm moves into the second stage, the growth of the cloud and the speed of the winds increase. A thunderhead is formed. Thunderheads can reach a height of more than 12 km. At that altitude the high-speed winds of the upper troposphere push the top of the cloud forward, forming the anvil-shaped top you see in Figure 19·10. When the storm matures, the cloud is filled with raindrops, snowflakes, and possibly, hail.

The start of precipitation begins the third, or mature, stage in the life of a thunderstorm. Types of precipitation include rain, snow, sleet, and hail. As shown in Figure 19·10, the falling precipitation causes the air to move downward. Storm cells form within the cloud. A *storm cell* is a system of rising and falling air within a storm. A thunderstorm generally contains more than one storm cell. A storm cell lasts about 20 minutes but may be replaced by other storm cells. Thunder and lightning accompany heavy rains in a thunderstorm. If the air moving upward in a storm cell is strong enough, hail may form. The air moving downward in a storm cell, however, slows the movement of air up through the cloud. As the upward movement of air slows down, the air starts to dry. The storm then dies out.

LIGHTNING AND THUNDER

Thunderstorms are very active electrically. Meteorologists disagree on exactly how the charges in a thunderhead are created. But it is clear that the top of a thunderhead has a positive charge, and its base is part negative and part positive. The charges in the base of the thunderhead cause the ground to become charged. Look at Figure 19·11. How does the charge on the ground under the cloud compare with the charge at the base of the cloud?

The charge on the ground gets stronger as the cloud's charge increases. When the difference between the charge on the base of the cloud and the charge on the ground or on another cloud becomes large, lightning occurs. **Lightning** is a large electrical discharge that occurs between clouds or between a cloud and the earth.

Figure 19·11
Different regions of a thunderhead have different charges. When there is a big difference in charge between cloud regions or between the cloud and the ground, lightning occurs.

The loud crash that accompanies a flash of lightning is called **thunder**. Thunder occurs because the air around a lightning bolt is heated. The temperature of the air may reach between 8000°C and 33,000°C. This heat causes the air to expand rapidly. This expansion of the air creates a sound wave.

473

Figure 19·12

Lightning is a large electrical discharge.

THUNDERSTORM SAFETY

Thunderstorms can be very dangerous, and there are certain precautions that you should take when such a storm approaches. Do not stand near a tall object, such as a tree, during a thunderstorm. Lightning tends to strike the tallest object in an area. For this same reason, you should not stand in an open field. The best place to be during a thunderstorm is inside a building and away from outside walls, windows, and electric appliances.

If you are in an open area when a thunderstorm approaches, stay low and move away from any other people you are with. It is also safe to stay inside a closed car. Do not go in or near open water during a thunderstorm, because the water can conduct electricity. Also, do not talk on the telephone during a thunderstorm. People have been killed when a telephone pole has been struck by lightning and the wires have carried the charge to the phone.

REVIEW

1. What is a thunderstorm?
2. Describe the three stages in the development of a thunderstorm.
3. What should you do if a thunderstorm approaches?

CHALLENGE Why are lightning rods often attached to tall buildings, and sometimes to old, valuable trees? How do lightning rods work?

19·4 Tornadoes

The most violent storm on the earth is a tornado. A **tornado** is a small funnel-shaped whirlwind that spins in a counterclockwise direction around an area of low pressure. Notice the funnel shape in Figure 19·13. Tornadoes occur with thunderstorms and may produce wind speeds greater than 500 km/h. More tornadoes develop in the United States than in any other country in the world. As many as 1000 tornadoes have taken place in the United States in a year.

HOW TORNADOES FORM

Meteorologists do not yet fully understand the causes of tornadoes. However, the conditions needed for a tornado to form are a layer of warm, moist air with cooler, drier air above it. The warm air begins to rise, breaking through the cooler air. How the rising air begins to rotate is not understood. One hypothesis is that lightning may help to cause tornadoes. Another hypothesis is that extreme differences in temperature between the air on the ground and the air in the upper troposphere may start the rapid rise of air.

Figure 19·13
The funnel of a tornado.

Table 19·1 *Average Number of Tornadoes per Year*

State	Value	State	Value	State	Value	State	Value
Alabama	19	Indiana	22.9	Nebraska	34.0	Rhode Island	0.04
Alaska	0	Iowa	25.5	Nevada	0.6	South Carolina	8.9
Arizona	3.8	Kansas	46.6	New Hampshire	2.5	South Dakota	22.6
Arkansas	18.4	Kentucky	7.8	New Jersey	1.6	Tennessee	11.0
California	2.9	Louisiana	18.8	New Mexico	8.5	Texas	124.2
Colorado	14.2	Maine	2.8	New York	3.4	Utah	1.36
Connecticut	1.7	Maryland	2.3	North Carolina	10.3	Vermont	1.0
Delaware	0.85	Massachusetts	4.5	North Dakota	14.6	Virginia	5.24
Florida	36.3	Michigan	14.7	Ohio	13.0	Washington	1.0
Georgia	21.1	Minnesota	17.3	Oklahoma	55.3	West Virginia	1.9
Hawaii	0.62	Mississippi	21.8	Oregon	0.9	Wisconsin	17.3
Idaho	1.3	Missouri	29.5	Pennsylvania	6.6	Wyoming	6.7
Illinois	28.0	Montana	3.5				

ACTIVITY   How Is Tornado Alley Determined?

OBJECTIVES

Analyze data on the states' average annual number of tornadoes.

Draw conclusions about the location of Tornado Alley.

MATERIALS

4 different-colored pencils

PROCEDURE

A. Trace the map on this page or obtain one like it from your teacher.

B. Using the data in Table 19·1, copy the average number of tornadoes per year for each state onto the map.

C. Obtain four different-colored pencils. Color the boxes in the key.

D. Color the states that correspond to the key. For instance, all of the states that have 25 or more tornadoes per year might be colored red.

RESULTS AND CONCLUSIONS

1. Tornado Alley is the name given to an area that has a large number of tornadoes. Where is Tornado Alley?

2. Which states in Tornado Alley have the greatest number of tornadoes per year?

3. Which state has a high occurrence of tornadoes but is not part of Tornado Alley?

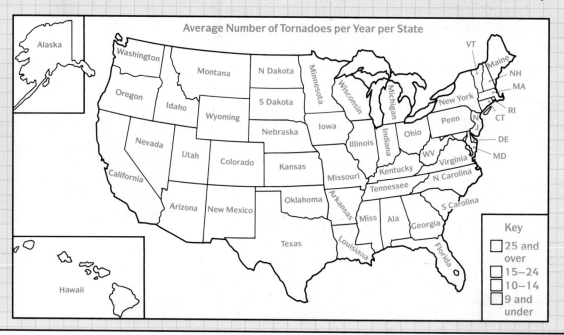

Average Number of Tornadoes per Year per State

Key
- ☐ 25 and over
- ☐ 15–24
- ☐ 10–14
- ☐ 9 and under

Tornadoes most often form during spring and early summer in the central United States. These storms can be anywhere from 50 m to 1500 m wide. They travel at speeds of from 30 km/h to 60 km/h, sometimes lifting off the earth's surface for a short time and then returning to it. A tornado seldom lasts more than a few minutes. But it may travel dozens of kilometers in this short time.

A tornado that occurs over a body of water is called a **waterspout**. A waterspout is shown in Figure 19·14. Waterspouts have been known to pick up fish and drop them over land, as if it were raining fish. Waterspouts may develop over water or they may start over land and then move over water.

Figure 19·14
A waterspout is a tornado that occurs over water.

TORNADO SAFETY

The National Weather Service issues a *tornado watch* for an area when the conditions there are right for tornadoes to form. You should listen for weather bulletins and observe the clouds around you when a watch is issued. When a tornado has been seen in an area, a *tornado warning* is issued.

A good place to be when a tornado is nearby is under a stairway or under a strong table in a basement. If your home does not have a basement, a closet or small room at the center of the first floor is the next safest place to be. Kneel on the floor and cover your head. In a public building, such as a school or a shopping center, you should move to a corridor in the middle of the first floor or go into a small room on the first floor.

REVIEW
1. Describe a tornado. How does a tornado form?
2. What should you do if a tornado approaches?

CHALLENGE Tornadoes form within thunderheads. But not all thunderstorms produce tornadoes. Scientists have found that winds in the environment play a role in producing tornadoes. How might winds affect a thunderhead to produce a tornado?

19·5 Hurricanes

After completing this section,
you will be able to

- **explain** how a hurricane forms.
- **describe** the properties of a hurricane.
- **list** hurricane safety precautions.

The key term in this section is
hurricane

A **hurricane** is a large tropical storm that usually develops during late summer near the equator. The wavy line in Figure 19·15 shows the region where hurricanes form. These tropical storms go by different names in different parts of the world. In the western Pacific Ocean, for example, they are called typhoons. In India they are called cyclones.

Hurricanes are low-pressure systems. Like other lows, hurricanes form when warm, moist air is forced upward through the atmosphere. Unlike other lows, hurricanes do not form along fronts but form in areas where air is gently rising. Hurricanes also cover a smaller area than do other lows. However, hurricanes are more powerful storms.

Figure 19·15
The wavy line shows the regions where hurricanes form. Over what type of surface do hurricanes form?

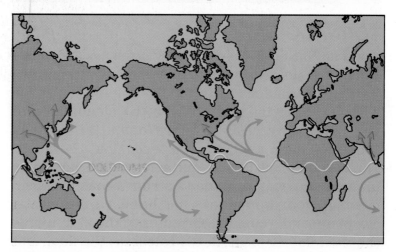

HOW HURRICANES FORM

Seventy percent of the hurricanes in the Atlantic Ocean form along the western coast of Africa during the late summer. At this time of the year, the ocean temperature is near 27°C, and the air over the ocean is very warm and wet. Warm, wet air is very light. Therefore, denser air from surrounding areas can push in across the water. The Coriolis effect causes the air to spin counterclockwise, as shown in Figure 19·16. This spinning air is the beginning of a hurricane.

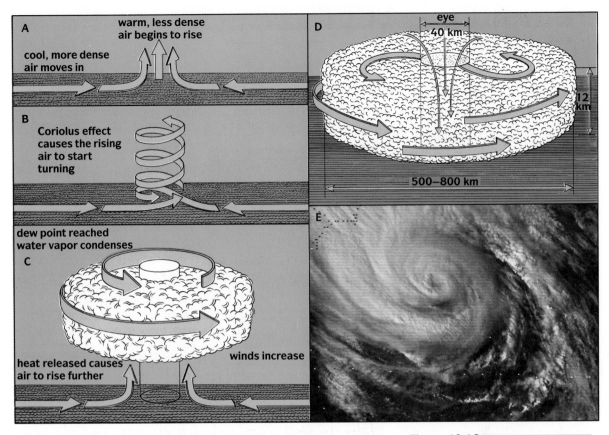

Figure 19·16

The formation of a hurricane, and a satellite photograph of a hurricane.

Notice in Figure 19·16*C* that the temperature of the rising air reaches the dew point. When water vapor condenses, heat is released. Thus the air becomes even less dense. As the air in the center becomes lighter, the surrounding air moves in faster. The faster the air moves over the ocean, the greater the amount of water vapor the air picks up. Finally, more water vapor in the air releases more heat into the atmosphere, increasing the winds further. The longer the storm stays over water, the stronger the storm becomes. The storm becomes a tropical storm when its winds reach 63 km/h. It becomes a hurricane when its winds reach 119 km/h.

A hurricane can reach a diameter of 800 km. At the center of a hurricane is an area of calm called the eye. The eye is usually about 40 km in diameter. In the eye the air is slowly sinking and the sky is clear. As air in a hurricane moves toward the eye, the air accelerates. The fastest winds in a hurricane are found in a ring around the eye.

A violent storm hit a recreation area a little north of Denver, Colorado. The storm was over in just 15 minutes, but it killed 139 people. Storms like this develop quickly and move too fast to allow accurate predictions to be made about them.

But recently a new approach has been developed to help predict how violent, short-lived storms will behave. The approach includes an updated radar system. This computer-controlled radar system collects data on such characteristics of a storm as wind speed, wind direction, and precipita-

tion. The system will detect the circular wind patterns that produce tornadoes.

In addition, a computer system is being developed to

put together many kinds of data on such storms. The data include satellite images, cloud cover, locations of lightning strikes, and temperature and moisture readings at different altitudes. All of the data can be updated every 5 minutes. Such data may allow meteorologists to precisely pinpoint the locations and movements of small storms. For example, it may become possible to predict that a certain storm will hit the southwestern area of a city in 30 minutes. Early warnings can save property and, more importantly, they can save lives.

The hurricane is the earth's most powerful storm. Its winds can exceed 300 km/h, and its heavy rains are sometimes accompanied by lightning, thunder, and tornadoes. Even more dangerous than the heavy rain and wind, however, is the tidal surge than can occur with a hurricance, as shown in Figure 19·17. The tidal surge is a bulge in the ocean under the light air of the storm. This bulge is topped by large wind-driven waves. The surge may raise the level of the ocean by 8 m. Nine out of ten people who have lost their lives in hurricanes in this century have drowned in high waters that flooded the coastal areas during the storms.

HURRICANE SAFETY

If you live along an ocean, special precautions must be taken when a hurricane is approaching. Objects outdoors should be tied down so that winds will not blow them around. Boards can be placed over windows so that they will not be broken by flying objects. It is important to remember that most deaths caused by hurricanes are caused by

Figure 19·17
A tidal surge like this can occur with a hurricane.

water, not wind. Thus, once your home and yard are secured, it is important that you go inland until the storm is over.

If you live away from the ocean, the tidal surge will not reach your home. But there are still some precautions that you should take when a hurricane is approaching. Candles or flashlights will be helpful if your home loses electricity during the storm. Also, a battery-powered radio can keep you in touch with the progress of the storm and tell you where to find help.

REVIEW

1. How does a hurricane form?
2. What is a hurricane like?
3. What should you do if a hurricane is predicted?

CHALLENGE How will a hurricane change as it moves over water and then passes over a large island?

CHAPTER SUMMARY

The main ideas in this chapter are listed below. Read these statements before you answer the Chapter Review questions.

- Large bodies of air moving through the atmosphere and having the same temperature and humidity throughout are called air masses. (19·1)
- Air masses take on the properties of their source region. (19·1)
- The boundary between two air masses is called a front. The four kinds of fronts are warm fronts, cold fronts, stationary fronts, and occluded fronts. (19·2)
- The rising air that moves in a counterclockwise direction along a front is a low. (19·2)
- A violent weather system that produces tall clouds, lightning, thunder, and heavy rains is called a thunderstorm. (19·3)

- Lightning is an electrical discharge. Thunder is the rapid expansion of air, caused by the heat of lightning. (19·3)
- A tornado is a small funnel-shaped whirlwind that spins counterclockwise around an area of low pressure. (19·4)
- A tornado that forms or moves over water is called a waterspout. (19·4)
- A low that develops near the equator in late summer can become a hurricane. (19·5)
- The most dangerous features of a hurricane are high winds and the tidal surge that may occur. (19·5)

The key terms in this chapter are listed below. Use each term in a sentence that shows the meaning of the term.

air mass	hurricane	thunder	waterspout
cold front	lightning	thunderstorm	weather
front	occluded front	tornado	
humidity	stationary front	warm front	

Chapter Review

VOCABULARY

Use the key terms from the previous page to complete the following sentences correctly.

1. The condition of the atmosphere at a particular time and place is the _____ .
2. Water vapor in the air is called _____ .
3. A large body of air that has the same temperature and humidity throughout is a/an _____ .
4. The boundary between two air masses is called a/an _____ .
5. When a cooler air mass replaces a warmer air mass, a/an _____ forms.
6. When a cold front catches up with a warm front, a/an _____ forms.
7. A large tropical low with winds faster than 119 km/h that forms over the ocean is a/an _____ .
8. A violent weather system with tall clouds, thunder, lightning, strong winds, heavy rain, and sometimes, hail is a/an _____ .
9. A small funnel-shaped whirlwind that spins in a counterclockwise direction is a/an _____ .
10. An electrical discharge that occurs between clouds or between a cloud and the earth is _____ .

CONCEPTS

Identify each statement as True or False. If a statement is false, replace the underlined term or phrase with a term or phrase that makes the statement true.

1. An air mass is classified by describing its <u>temperature and pressure</u>.
2. At a cold front the warmer air is <u>lifted upward</u> by the cooler air.
3. A <u>thunderhead</u> is so tall that high-speed winds at the top of the troposphere push the top of the cloud forward.
4. Tornadoes are most likely to form along <u>warm fronts</u>.
5. A <u>storm cell</u> is a system of rising and falling air within a storm.

Choose the term or phrase that best answers the question or completes the statement.

6. When meteorologists predict the direction in which an air mass will move, they watch the position of the
   a. clouds.
   b. sun.
   c. jet streams.
   d. troposphere.

7. What weather would you expect if you saw a line of tall, dark clouds approaching?
   a. a long-lasting rainstorm
   b. a short, heavy rainstorm
   c. a light shower
   d. no rain

8. When the updrafts within a thunderhead are strong enough, the storm will produce
   a. snow.
   b. thunder.
   c. sleet.
   d. hail.

9. Which is a safe place to be during a tornado?
   a. in a basement
   b. in a first-floor closet
   c. in an interior corridor
   d. all of the above

10. The most dangerous part of a hurricane is the
    a. eye.
    b. high water level.
    c. heavy rain.
    d. lightning.

Answer the following in complete sentences.

11. What is the relationship between an air mass and its source region?
12. Compare what happens when a warm front approaches with what happens when a cold front approaches.
13. What happens to a thunderstorm after precipitation begins?
14. Describe how a waterspout forms.
15. Describe a hurricane and how it develops.

---

1. Describe what weather conditions would occur as a front approaches an area, and as it leaves.
2. List at least five factors that meteorologists analyze to determine any changes in weather.
3. Why do highs tend to have clear weather and lows tend to be cloudy?
4. Why might it be dangerous to walk on a beach after a hurricane appears to have passed and the skies have cleared?
5. Compare the conditions needed for the development of a thunderstorm, a tornado, and a hurricane.

APPLICATION/ CRITICAL THINKING

---

1. Set up your own weather station, and using what you have learned, try to predict the weather. You will need a thermometer, an anemometer, a wind vane, and a barometer.
2. Collect a series of weather maps from a newspaper for one week. Make observations about how the fronts moved and relate them to the kind of weather that your area had.

EXTENSION

CHAPTER 20

EARTH'S FRESH WATER

Water is one of the earth's most valuable resources. All living things need water to survive. People use water for drinking, for bathing, and for washing clothes. Farms use water for irrigating crops. Industries use water in a variety of ways.

Each drop of water shown contains millions of water molecules. These molecules may have been around the world many times. Water in clouds is carried great distances. Water is found in rain, fog, and snow. Water is also found in streams, rivers, and lakes. It can be trapped beneath the earth's surface or frozen in polar icecaps.

- *What is the source of fresh water where you live?*
- *What other sources of fresh water are available?*
- *How can sources of fresh water be protected?*

20·1 Water Budget

The earth's water supply constantly circulates in a process called the *water cycle*. Water evaporates from the ocean and land and is moved around the earth by wind. Water returns to the earth as rain, snow, sleet, or hail. Precipitation does not fall evenly on the earth. The state of Arizona receives only about 20 cm of rain each year. In contrast, Florida receives about 140 cm. In addition, rain that falls in Arizona evaporates more qucikly than does rain that falls in Florida.

The amounts of precipitation and evaporation in an area determine the area's water supply. A **water budget** is a record of the amounts of precipitation and evaporation for an area. The amount of precipitation is called the *income*. The amount of evaporation is called the *outgo*.

The 1983 water budget for Yuma, Arizona, is shown in Figure 20·1. The area around Yuma is dry. When the amount of evaporation, or outgo, is greater than the amount of precipitation, or income, there is a **deficit** in an area. When the amount of precipitation is greater than the amount of evaporation in an area, there is a **surplus**. In what months does a surplus occur?

Figure 20·1

The 1983 water budget for Yuma, Arizona. Many months of deficit cause the area to be dry.

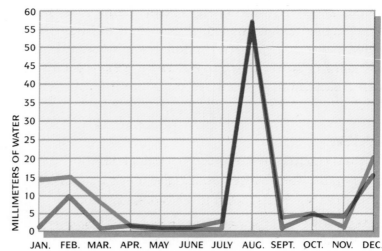

Figure 20·2 shows the 1983 water budget for New Orleans, Louisiana. Notice that a surplus occurs in every month except two. Which months do not show a surplus? When a surplus occurs for many months, the ground often becomes saturated with water. Then precipitation does not enter the ground but instead becomes surface runoff.

Figure 20·2

The 1983 water budget for New Orleans, Louisiana. When a surplus occurs, extra water flows into the Mississippi River.

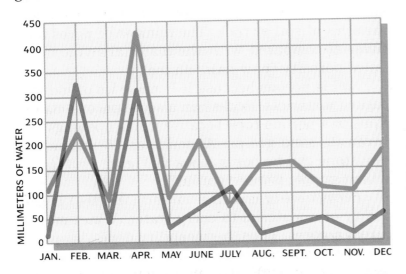

MILLIMETERS OF WATER

JAN. FEB. MAR. APR. MAY JUNE JULY AUG. SEPT. OCT. NOV. DEC

Areas of surplus can often supply water for areas of deficit. Areas in the southwestern United States, for example, often show a deficit. But in the spring and early summer, these areas receive surface runoff from melting snow in mountains located in the northwestern United States.

Surplus areas cannot supply all the water needed in deficit areas. Water can be supplied to deficit areas by diverting water from rivers. In some areas along coasts, seawater is changed to fresh water by a process called *desalination*. In desalination, salt is removed from seawater. The water can then be used for drinking or for irrigation.

REVIEW

1. What two factors are recorded in a water budget?
2. How is the water budget related to an area's water supply?
3. How can water be supplied to areas of water deficit?

CHALLENGE Explain why an area need not have a large amount of precipitation to be classified as humid.

20·2 Ground Water

POROSITY AND PERMEABILITY

Most of the world's fresh water is beneath the surface of the earth. Water enters the earth's surface through pores. Pores are open spaces between particles of soil or rock. The number of pores in a material compared with the material's volume is called porosity (paw RAHS uh tee).

Soil is porous because it is made up of loosely packed materials. Rocks can also be porous. Sandstone is a porous rock because it has openings between its sand grains. As much as 25 percent of sandstone can be pores. Look at Figure 20·3 (*left*). Which sample is more porous?

Permeability (per mee uh BIHL uh tee) is the ability of a material to carry water. Water moves through pores. Thus, permeability depends on the size of the material's pores and how the pores are connected. Materials with high permeabilities, such as sand, have large pores that are connected. A material such as clay has a low permeability because it has small pores that are not well connected. Some materials carry no water. Such materials are described as impermeable.

Figure 20·3

Loosely packed particles have a higher porosity than do tightly packed particles *(left)*. Water flows easily through permeable materials, not through impermeable materials *(right)*.

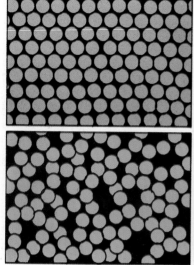

permeable — impermeable

Some rocks have a low porosity but are still permeable. As you can see in Figure 20·4, water can pass through a low-porosity rock if the rock has cracks running through it. Limestone is a low-porosity rock that is permeable.

THE WATER TABLE

When rain falls on the earth's surface, some of this water evaporates, some runs off, and some sinks into the ground. When rainfall is steady on a gentle slope, the land acts like a huge sponge, soaking up water. Some of the water may be held by soil and used by plants. But most of the water seeps downward until it is stopped by a layer of impermeable rock. The water then fills the pores above the impermeable rock. The area below the earth's surface that is filled with water is called the *zone of saturation*. The water in the zone of saturation is called **ground water**.

The area above the zone of saturation and below the surface is called the *zone of aeration* (air AY shuhn). The pores in this zone contain mostly air and some water. Most water used by plants comes from the zone of aeration.

The boundary between the zone of aeration and the zone of saturation is called the **water table**. Notice in Figure 20·5 that the water table tends to follow the shape of the land surface.

Figure 20·4

A low-porosity rock can be permeable if its pores are well connected.

low-porosity rock

Figure 20·5

How does the water table compare with the shape of the land surface?

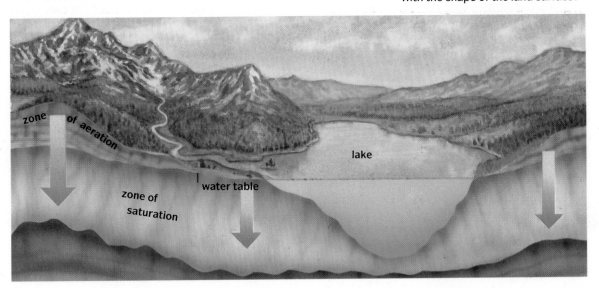

zone of aeration

zone of saturation

water table

lake

The depth of the water table below the surface varies with rainfall and climate. In areas with a large amount of rain, the water table may be only a meter under the ground. In desert areas it may be hundreds of meters down.

ACTIVITY   How Does Permeability of Soil Differ?

OBJECTIVE
Determine how different types of soils affect the movement of water.

MATERIALS
3 large plastic foam cups, 3 squares of cheesecloth large enough to cover bottoms of cups, 3 rubber bands, 3 coffee cans with plastic lids, sand, clay, gravel, 100-mL graduate, water, clock or watch with second hand

PROCEDURE

A. Draw a data table like the one shown.
B. Punch several holes in the bottoms and around the lower parts of three plastic foam cups. Be sure to punch the same size and number of holes in each cup.
C. Place a square of cheesecloth over the bottom of each cup. Be sure the cheese-cloth squares cover all the holes. Secure the squares with rubber bands.
D. Cut a hole in each of three plastic lids of coffee cans so that the lower half of a cup fits inside the lid. Place the lids on the cans, and fit the cups in the lids. Label the cups and cans A, B, and C.
E. Fill cup A half full of dry sand, cup B half full of clay, and cup C half full of a mixture of sand, clay, and gravel.
F. Using a graduate, measure 100 mL of water. Slowly pour the water into cup A, noting the time. Record the time.
G. Note and record the time when water first drips out of the cup.
H. Repeat steps F and G for cups B and C.
I. Allow the water to drip in all three cans until it stops. Using the graduate, measure the amount of water in each can. Record each amount in your table.

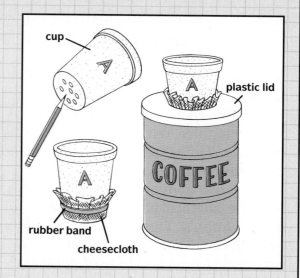

| CUP | TIME | | | AMOUNT OF WATER IN CAN |
	WATER IN	WATER OUT	DIFFERENCE	
A				
B				
C				

RESULTS AND CONCLUSIONS
1. According to the data in your table, which soil sample is the most permeable? Which soil sample is the least permeable?
2. Which kind of soil retained the most water? The least water?
3. Which kind of soil would allow ground water to build up quickly?
4. Which kind of soil would result in the most runoff?

AQUIFERS

Ground water flows slowly in a rock layer called an aquifer (AK wuh fuhr). An **aquifer** is a layer of rock or rock material that holds water. Most aquifers are made made up of sandstone, limestone, or gravel.

Aquifers are important sources of water for drinking and for irrigation. Water can be pumped from wells drilled into an aquifer. Sometimes water does not have to be pumped from a well. A well in which ground water rises naturally is called an *artesian* (ahr TEE zhuhn) *well*. Pressure caused by water flowing downward in an aquifer causes water to rise in an artesian well.

aqua (water)
ferre (to carry)

Figure 20·6

Ground water flows in porous rock layers called aquifers. How does the height of the artesian well compare with the highest point in the aquifer?

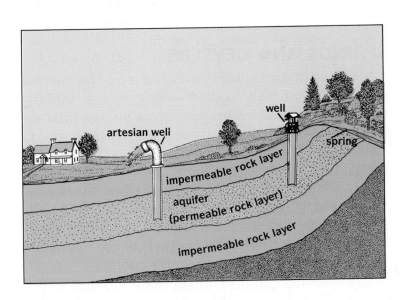

When ground water is used faster than it can be replaced, the water table becomes lower. Wells must be made deeper to reach the water. The water table may become even lower, and many wells may become dry. This overuse of ground water can leave many people without a source of water. Removing too much ground water can also cause subsidence (suhb sī duhns), or the sinking of land. In California's San Joaquin Valley, the removal of too much well water for irrigation has caused the land to sink about 10 m since 1925. The sinking has caused the land to flood during heavy rains.

Aquifer supplies around the country are dwindling because people are using more water than can be replaced by precipitation. One of the states being affected by low water supplies in aquifers is Texas. Texas obtains a lot of its water from the Ogallala Aquifer. This huge underground lake stretches from the edge of South Dakota through parts of Oklahoma, New Mexico, Kansas, Colorado, Nebraska, Wyoming, and northern Texas. Much of the water from the Ogallala is used to irrigate land in Texas.

The high use of water in Texas is quickly draining the Ogallala. Some experts say that parts of the Ogallala will be dry by the next century.

Texans are looking for other water sources. Diverting water from the Mississippi River would be expensive. Water conservation practices might be a better solution. These practices could include better irrigation methods and the use of new varieties of crops that flourish in a dry climate.

SPRINGS AND GEYSERS

Water in an aquifer flows out onto the surface if the top of the aquifer—the water table—reaches the surface. This may occur along a hillside. Water that comes naturally to the surface is called a *spring*. Springs can form swamps, streams, and lakes.

In some places where ground water moves deep in the earth, this water becomes heated. If the heated water reaches the surface, the water flows out as a hot spring. Often, minerals are deposited around a hot spring as the water cools.

Hot springs that erupt periodically are called *geysers*. Geysers form when ground water is heated to very high temperatures in underground chambers. The heating causes the water to expand and to flow up to the surface. When the water reaches the surface, it shoots out as hot water and steam, as shown in Figure 20·7.

REVIEW

1. How does water enter the earth's surface?
2. What factors affect the level of a water table?
3. What problems can result from the overuse of ground water?

CHALLENGE Explain why the water table may not follow the shape of the land near wells.

Figure 20·7
Old Faithful is a geyser that erupts about once every hour.

20·3 The Work of Ground Water

SINKHOLES

Ground water is not pure water. Minerals and carbon dioxide are dissolved in ground water. The mixture of water and carbon dioxide forms carbonic acid. Carbonic acid can dissolve limestone, a rock made of calcium carbonate. When large deposits of limestone are dissolved, caves form underground. Water in such an area has a high mineral content and is described as hard water. Hard water can affect the sudsing action of soap.

Ground water below the surface of central Florida has carved out many large caves. On May 8, 1981, in Winter Park, Florida, the earth over one such cave collapsed. A home, part of a highway, and part of a swimming pool fell into the resulting hole.

After completing this section, you will be able to

- **explain** how ground water causes erosion.
- **explain** how caverns form.
- **describe** features caused by ground water erosion.

The key terms in this section are
cavern
stalactite
stalagmite

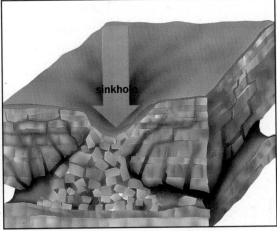

Figure 20·8

A sinkhole forms when the roof of a cave falls in. What supported the cave before it fell in?

As long as ground water remained in the caves below Winter Park, the ground was supported. But as more and more ground water was pumped out for use by a growing population, the water table dropped. In addition, the area had a drought. The drought caused the water table to drop farther. Without ground water to support it, the ground sank almost 30 m. A land depression caused by the collapse of a cave roof is called a *sinkhole*.

CAVERNS

A **cavern** is a large underground chamber formed by the action of ground water. The caves, or caverns, below central Florida formed because the rock below that surface is mostly limestone. Figure 20·9 shows how ground water can erode, or wear away, rock to form a cavern. This process takes a long time.

The erosion process begins when water enters small cracks in limestone. As the water dissolves the rock, the cracks grow wider and longer. As you can see in Figure 20·9B the cracks eventually reach the water table. Thus the acidic ground water enters the water table.

The acidic ground water moves along the water table toward a body of water such as a lake or river. As the water moves, it dissolves a horizontal channel in the limestone. Over time the water enlarges the channel and forms a cavern.

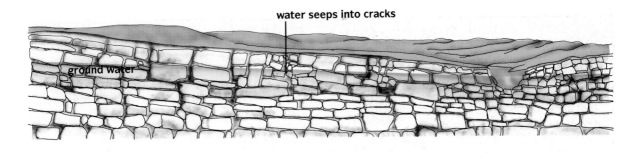

water seeps into cracks

ground water

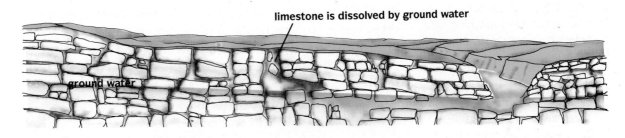

limestone is dissolved by ground water

ground water

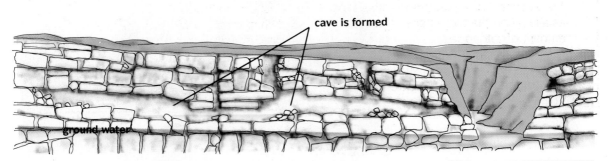

cave is formed

ground water

A cavern forms at or below the water table, in the zone of saturation. Notice in Figure 20·9C that erosion has caused the river to become lower. As the water table in a cavern lowers, ground water seeps into lower cracks. In time the lower cracks are also enlarged and a new horizontal channel is carved out. The new channel then grows to become a new cavern.

An area that contains many caverns and sinkholes is called a *karst region*. Karst regions have little surface water because most of it falls through sinkholes and enters underground rivers. One well-known karst region is Mammoth Cave, in Kentucky. This karst region extends for about 245 km. Its many underground rivers include Echo River, which flows 100 m below the earth's surface. Karst regions can also be found in central Florida, southern Indiana, and Tennessee.

Figure 20·9
Water enters limestone through cracks and flows horizontally toward a river (A). The ground water moving through limestone carves out a channel (B). As the river erodes its bed, both the river and the water table become lower. The lowered water table leaves an empty cavern (C).

495

stalaktos (dripping)

Features called stalactites (stuh LAK tīts) and stalagmites (stuh LAG mīts) form in caverns above the water table. These structures are made of calcite, a form of calcium carbonate. A **stalactite** is a formation of calcite that extends downward from the roof of a cave. A stalactite forms when water dripping from the roof of a limestone cave evaporates, leaving a deposit of calcite. Such deposits grow over many years, forming long fingers of calcite. Water dripping onto the floor of a cave forms a similar structure called a stalagmite. A **stalagmite** is a calcite structure that extends upward from the floor of a cave. Stalactites and stalagmites sometimes meet, forming columns.

Figure 20·10
Notice the stalactites, stalagmites, and columns in this cavern.

Most of the world's caverns formed over hundreds of thousands of years by the dissolving of limestone by ground water. It is believed that the Carlsbad Caverns in New Mexico began to form about 60 million years ago. About a million years ago, the first stalactites and stalagmites probably began to form in these caverns. These structures are still growing today.

REVIEW

1. In what ways can ground water cause erosion?
2. How are caverns formed?
3. Describe several features created by ground water erosion.

CHALLENGE What effect does the burning of fuels, such as that in factories and cars, have on erosion by ground water?

20·4 Two Great Rivers

A river and its tributaries, or the streams that flow into it, are called a **river system**. Every river or river system has a watershed—an area that the river or system drains. Watersheds are separated from each other by a divide. A **divide** is an area of high elevation that separates watersheds.

A divide called the *Continental Divide* runs north and south through the Rocky Mountains. The Continental Divide separates the waters that flow toward the Pacific Ocean from those that flow toward the Atlantic Ocean or the Gulf of Mexico. The Mississippi River drains much of the area east of the Continental Divide, and the Colorado River drains much of the area west of the divide.

THE MISSISSIPPI RIVER

The Mississippi River is the longest river in the United States. This huge river flows 3780 km from its source in Minnesota to its mouths in the Gulf of Mexico. The Mississippi and its tributaries have the largest watershed of any river system in North America. This watershed covers an area of more than 3 million square km. It collects water from 31 states and two Canadian provinces.

Figure 20·11

The delta of the Mississippi River *(left)*. Concrete slabs are placed along the banks of the Mississippi River to prevent flooding *(right)*.

Originating from Lake Itasca in Minnesota, the Mississippi River flows south. It is joined by such large tributaries as the Minnesota, Illinois, Missouri, and Ohio rivers. Below the Ohio River the Mississippi flows through broad plains that are between 60 and 110 km wide. The river winds back and forth through many swamps. The river carries sediments. At the Gulf of Mexico, the Mississippi deposits its sediments, building a huge delta. The delta grows and changes constantly.

Along the river there are flat areas called *flood plains*. Each spring, melting snow and rain raise the water level, often causing the river to flood. The floods deposit silt on the flood plain. The silt fertilizes farmland on the plain. But some of the floods have also caused deaths and property damage.

Pollution is a serious problem that affects the Mississippi River. Parts of the river have been polluted by chemicals from factories. Other areas have been polluted by sewage from towns and cities and by erosion from farmland.

THE COLORADO RIVER

The Colorado River is the largest river in the southwestern United States. The river originates in the Rocky Mountains of northern Colorado. The river flows about 2250 km toward the Gulf of Cali-

Figure 20•12

The Colorado River begins in the Rockies *(inset)* and flows through the Grand Canyon.

fornia. The Colorado's watershed covers more than 600,000 km². This is about one-fifth the size of the Mississippi River system's watershed. Look at Figure 20·13. What rivers join the Colorado River in Utah? The Colorado River cuts through narrow valleys with steep cliffs.

The Colorado River is very important to the western United States. It supplies water for drinking and for irrigation. It also serves as a source of electricity. Notice in Figure 20·13 that dams have been built along the Colorado. The dams block the river's flow of water. The water backs up into reservoirs for storage. Some of the water is then released to run generators in hydroelectric power plants.

Figure 20·13
The Colorado River system.

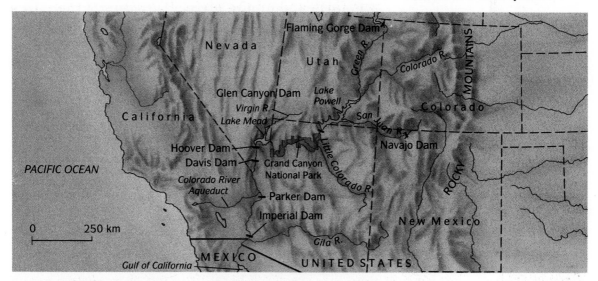

California, Arizona, and six other western states presently draw water from the Colorado River. Because of this, the river no longer reaches the Gulf of California. The Colorado River, which begins powerfully at its headwaters in the Rockies, is reduced to a trickle before it reaches the gulf.

REVIEW

1. Compare the Mississippi River system with the Colorado River system.
2. Why are the Mississippi River and the Colorado River so important?

CHALLENGE Why is it difficult for mapmakers to chart the course of the Mississippi in its flood plain region?

20·5 Lakes and Ponds

Lakes and ponds are found in all parts of the world. They are fed by rain, rivers, and springs. A **lake** is a large water-filled depression in the earth's surface. Most lakes contain fresh water. But some, like the Great Salt Lake in Utah, have salt water. A **pond** is a smaller, shallower depression that fills with water. Unlike lakes, all areas of a pond are penetrated by sunlight and have plant growth.

Lakes and ponds form in many ways. A lake or pond can form when a river is blocked. For example, a landslide can dam a river, creating a lake. In a karst region a sinkhole can fill with water, producing a lake or pond. When people build a dam, a reservoir — an artificial lake — forms. Reservoirs serve as vital sources of drinking water.

Many lakes and ponds were formed by glaciers, or ice sheets. Glaciers covered a large part of North America thousands of years ago. Glaciers widened and deepened river valleys and then left deposits that plugged both ends of the valleys. Figure 20·14 shows the Finger Lakes of New York, which were formed in this way.

Figure 20·14
The Finger Lakes in New York were formed by glaciers.

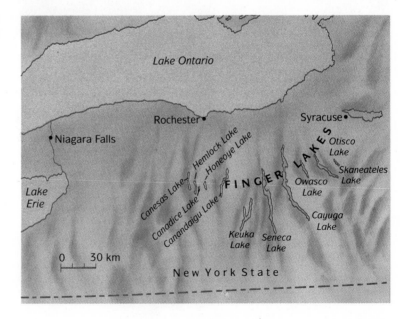

500

LIFE CYCLE OF LAKES AND PONDS

Water that flows into a lake may carry nutrients into the lake. Normally the growth of plants such as algae is limited by the small amount of nutrients dissolved in the water. But when the amount of nutrients increases—either naturally or from pollution—algae grow rapidly. As the algae die, they become food for bacteria. The bacteria use up oxygen. A lack of oxygen causes fish to die and results in a lake covered by organic wastes. The addition of nutrients to a body of water that causes the quality of the water to change is called *eutrophication* (yoo truh fuh KAY shuhn).

Figure 20·15
Is this lake in its youth, its middle age, or its old age?

Eutrophication is a natural process that slowly changes a lake. These changes can be described as a life cycle. The three stages in the life cycle of a lake are youth, middle age, and old age. In its youth a lake is rich in oxygen but poor in nutrients. Its water is clear, and it contains little plant and animal life. In its middle age a lake has more nutrients in it. Plant life and large fish, such as trout and bass, are found in the lake.

In its old age a lake has abundant nutrients in it. Large amounts of algae and other plants grow. The surface becomes covered with decaying plant matter. As the oxygen is used up, trout and bass die. They are replaced by fish such as catfish. Silt, sand, and decaying plant matter slowly fill the lake. Eventually the lake is filled with solid material.

The lake shown in the photograph formed when a dam was built. Before the area was flooded, workers removed as many trees and shrubs as possible. How would the lake be different if this vegetation had not been removed?

Human activities can affect eutrophication. Pollution may cause this process to take place faster. For example, the nitrates in fertilizers and the phosphates in detergents are nutrients that may be washed into lakes by streams.

Lakes can also be damaged by pollution from the atmosphere. The pollution often comes from the burning of fossil fuels. The burning of fossil fuels produces such gases as nitrogen oxides and sulfur dioxide, which mix with rain to form **acid rain**. Acid rain can cause a lake to become so acidic that many kinds of fish cannot survive in it. More than 200 lakes in the Adirondack Mountains of New York have been contaminated by acid rain. Fossil fuels burned in the Midwest produce gases that are carried eastward by the wind. Eventually the gases reach the Northeast and form acid rain or snow over lakes and ponds. Figure 20·16 shows a lake that has been damaged by acid rain. Lakes like this look blue and clear because they contain so few living things.

Figure 20·16
Why does this lake look so clear?

REVIEW

1. How do lakes and ponds form?
2. How does a lake change as it ages?
3. How can acid rain affect a lake?

CHALLENGE In areas where strip mining has exposed coal seams, lakes and ponds have become polluted with acid. Explain why.

20·6 The Great Lakes

The **Great Lakes** make up the largest region of fresh water in the world. They cover an area of more than 256,000 km^2. From east to west this region includes Lake Ontario, Lake Erie, Lake Huron, Lake Michigan, and Lake Superior. The water in these lakes is supplied by numerous small rivers and streams that form a huge watershed.

The Great Lakes were formed by large glaciers. As you can see in Figure 20·17, glaciers once covered much of North America. At one time the Great Lakes drained southward through rivers that eventually ran into the Mississippi River. But as the glaciers melted, they left behind rock material that plugged outlets to the south. The Great Lakes began to drain eastward through new outlets—the Susquehanna, Mohawk, Hudson, and St. Lawrence rivers. Eventually the Great Lakes began to drain into the St. Lawrence River.

After completing this section, you will be able to

- **describe** how the Great Lakes formed.
- **explain** how the Great Lakes affect climate.

The key term in this section is **Great Lakes**

Figure 20·17
The Great Lakes were formed by glaciers that once covered North America.

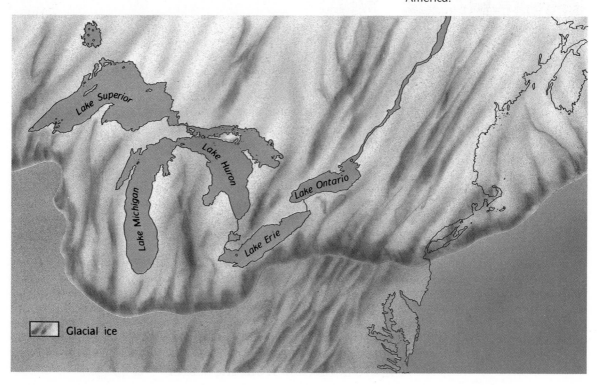

Glacial ice

Figure 20·18

Chicago *(left)* is on the shore of Lake Michigan. Split Rock Lighthouse *(right)* is on Lake Superior. This ship is near Duluth, Minnesota, which is on Lake Superior.

For centuries the Great Lakes have served as a major commercial waterway for the interior of the North American continent. Today, ocean-going ships enter the lakes from the St. Lawrence River. Other vessels, like the one shown in Figure 20·18 *(inset)*, travel between the various ports along the lakes, carrying iron ore, agricultural products, and oil products.

The Great Lakes greatly influence local weather conditions. The lakes cause heavy snowfall on the eastern shore of Lake Erie. This shore receives an average of 216 cm of snow per year. Like other large bodies of water, the lakes change temperature more slowly than do land areas. This property often means that summers and winters are milder in areas around the Great Lakes than in areas farther from the water.

The Great Lakes have suffered from a problem that affects many bodies of water: pollution. Lake Michigan and Lake Superior have been polluted by industrial wastes. Lake Erie has become a dumping site for sewage from many cities. Pollution has brought a decline in the fishing industry on the lakes. Drinking-water supplies from the Great Lakes have also been contaminated.

In recent years, Canada and the United States have undertaken a joint effort to clean up the Great Lakes. The water quality has greatly improved, but much work still remains to be done.

REVIEW

1. How did the Great Lakes form?
2. In what ways do the Great Lakes influence climate?

CHALLENGE Why does eutrophication take a longer time to occur in the Great Lakes than in smaller lakes?

CHAPTER SUMMARY

The main ideas in this chapter are listed below. Read these statements before you answer the Chapter Review questions.

- A water budget is a record of the amounts of precipitation and evaporation for an area. (20•1)
- The amount of water that can enter the ground depends on the porosity and permeability of the materials that make up the surface. (20•2)
- Ground water causes erosion in areas where limestone exists under the surface. This action can produce caverns or sinkholes. (20•3)
- The overuse of ground water can lower the water table. (20•3)

- The Continental Divide separates two large watershed areas in the United States. The watershed east of the Continental Divide is drained mainly by the Mississippi River system, and the watershed west of the Continental Divide is drained mainly by the Colorado River system. (20•4)
- Lakes and ponds form when water collects in depressions in the earth's surface. (20•5)
- As lakes and ponds age, they gradually become filled in. (20•5)
- The Great Lakes make up the largest region of fresh water in the world. (20•6)

The key terms in this chapter are listed below. Use each term in a sentence that shows the meaning of the term.

acid rain	divide	pond	surplus
aquifer	Great Lakes	river system	water budget
cavern	ground water	stalactite	water table
deficit	lake	stalagmite	

Chapter Review

VOCABULARY

Write the letter of the term that best matches the definition. Not all the terms will be used.

1. A large water-filled depression in the earth's surface
2. An area that separates two watersheds
3. A layer of rock that holds water
4. A record of the precipitation and evaporation for an area
5. The condition that occurs when precipitation is greater than evaporation
6. A river and its tributaries
7. A long calcite structure that hangs from the ceiling of a cavern
8. Water in the zone of saturation
9. A large underground chamber formed by the action of ground water
10. A mixture of rain water and gases from the burning of fossil fuels

a. acid rain
b. aquifer
c. cavern
d. divide
e. ground water
f. lake
g. pond
h. river system
i. stalactite
j. stalagmite
k. surplus
l. water budget
m. water table

CONCEPTS

Choose the number of the term that best matches the letter on the drawing below.

1. aquifer
2. artesian well
3. impermeable rock
4. spring
5. well

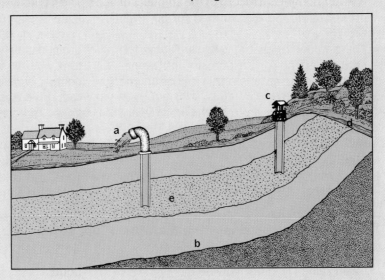

506

Identify each statement as True or False. If a statement is false, replace the underlined term or phrase with a term or phrase that makes the statement true.

6. The source of water for an area's water budget is <u>precipitation</u>.
7. Rocks are least permeable if they have <u>large pores</u>.
8. To provide water, a well must be drilled into the ground until it reaches into an <u>aquifer</u>.
9. Rain water becomes carbonic acid when <u>nitrogen gas</u> enters it.
10. Water drains from the Great Lakes into the <u>Mississippi River</u>.

Answer the following in complete sentences.

11. How can crops be grown in areas where the water budget usually shows a deficit?
12. Describe one condition that might cause a well to go dry.
13. Why can ground water dissolve more limestone than can pure water?
14. Whay are some lakes harmed more by acid rain than by eutrophication?
15. How did glaciers change the drainage of the Great Lakes?

APPLICATION/ CRITICAL THINKING

1. Explain how plant cover on land could increase the supply of ground water.
2. Some detergents are advertised as "low phosphate." How would the use of these detergents affect the eutrophication of lakes?
3. Explain why lakes polluted by acid rain are usually crystal-clear.

EXTENSION

1. Investigate the origin of a civilization that arose along a great river. An example is the Sumerian civilization, which arose along the Tigris and Euphrates rivers in Mesopotamia.
2. Find out how the supply of fresh water is obtained in your area. Does the water come from reservoirs? From wells? Contact a local water company or a municipal water department.

Science in Careers

How is a level house built on sloping ground? Why do some highways run straight for many kilometers, and others wind, bend, and go over hills?

Before a house, highway, or other structure can be built, the shape, or contour, of the land must be measured. Measurements are made by people called surveyors.

Surveyors use a device called a theodolite to measure elevation and distances on land. The measurements can then be used to find the best route for a road or waterway. A surveyor's measurements are used to make sure a house being built is level. The lines that separate properties, counties, and states on maps also come from surveyor's measurements.

Surveyors work outdoors in groups or teams. Courses in mechanical drawing, mathematics, and geography are helpful for surveyors. You will need a high school diploma and will receive on-the-job training.

SURVEYOR

Before structures such as dams, roadways, shopping centers, and office buildings can be built, they must be planned and designed. In addition, these structures must be adapted to the ground on which they are to be built.

Civil engineers plan and design structures and adapt them to the ground. For example, before skyscrapers could be built, civil engineers had to design a type of steel frame that would allow the structures to stand.

Civil engineers must have knowledge of geology and chemistry as well as engineering. They usually work for engineering and construction companies large and small and the government.

To become a civil engineer, you will need a college degree in engineering. Mathematics, computer, and mechanical drawing courses are also important.

CIVIL ENGINEER

People in Science

One goal of meteorologists is to predict weather and climate accurately. United States Navy officer and meteorologist Dr. Florence van Straten has another goal—to control the weather. She has succeeded in developing ways to make rain through cloud seeding.

You may already know something about cloud seeding. In it, particles of dry ice or silver iodide are sent into cold rain clouds. Sometimes, rain results.

Dr. van Straten thought of another way to seed clouds. She knew that clouds contain small water droplets. But usually they are too small and light to fall as rain. She decided to seed clouds with small particles of carbon black. Water in the clouds condenses around the particles. Because the carbon is black, the particles absorb heat, and the water around them evaporates. It then condenses onto other water droplets in the cloud. These grow heavy and fall as rain.

Dr. van Straten was successful because she used her knowledge of physics, chemistry, and meteorology to solve a problem.

Dr. Florence van Straten
METEOROLOGIST

Issues and Technology

Will the Decrease of Tropical Forestland Affect the Earth?

In the time it takes to read this article, over 20 hectares of tropical forestland will be cut down. In a year's time that adds up to a deforested area the size of Pennsylvania. And the destruction doesn't show signs of stopping. People who are watching this situation are worried. There are many important reasons for cutting trees. But loss of the tropical forests could have negative effects scientists are just beginning to understand.

The tropical forests are home to two thirds of the earth's 4.6 million plant and animal species. These forests contain a great many life forms that are not found anywhere else.

In Figure 1, compare the percentage of tropical forests covering the land with the percentage of temperate forests covering the land.

APPLYING CRITICAL THINKING SKILLS

1. What has happened to the amount of tropical forestland and temperate forestland between 1950 and now?

2. Why, would you suppose, has the percentage of land covered by temperate forests remained constant?

3. What factors have caused a decline in the amount of land covered by tropical forests?

Loss of the tropical forests means loss of the habitat for all of its living things. And that could mean their disappearance from the earth forever.

Would this loss be important? Yes, it would be, in terms of what the tropical forests have already given the world. Many foods were first discovered in tropical forests. Such foods are now grown on farms around the world. They include the grains rice and maize, or corn. These are important in the diets of millions of people. Botanists think that tropical forests hold many more undiscovered, edible plants that could one day be cultivated.

Many medicines have also been developed from tropical plants. Forty-five percent of all prescription drugs contain ingredients that originated in tropical forests. This includes the rosy periwinkle,

Figure 1

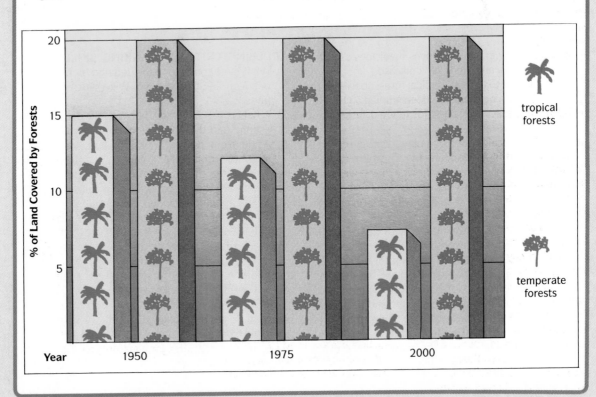

509

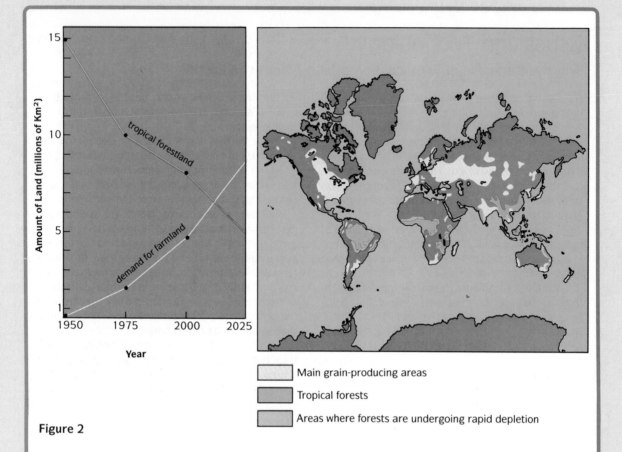

Main grain-producing areas

Tropical forests

Areas where forests are undergoing rapid depletion

Figure 2

which is a flower that produces medicines used to treat leukemia and Hodgkin's disease.

Only one sixth of all tropical forest species that have been discovered have been studied so far. So scientists expect that cures for many diseases can still be discovered.

The tropical forests also play a part in regulating the earth's atmosphere by absorbing carbon dioxide. Too much carbon dioxide in the air could cause the earth to heat up. The trees play a part in the water cycle, and they also help to prevent soil erosion.

The rate of population growth in the areas where these tropical forests are located is high. A larger population causes a demand for more food. This creates a need for more farmland, as shown in Figure 2. The tropical forests are being cut down so that the land can be used for farms and pastures.

Figure 2 is a graph and a map. The graph shows the relationship between deforestation and the demand for farmland, and the map shows earth's main areas of grain production.

APPLYING CRITICAL THINKING SKILLS

1. What has happened to the demand for farmland between 1950 and now? Will this trend continue?
2. What is the relationship between the drop in forestland and the rise in demand for farmland?
3. Aside from demand for farmland, what else might contribute to the depletion of the forest?
4. Where are the main grain-producing areas? Where are the largest areas of tropical forests? What can you conclude from this?

The lushness of the tropical forests suggests that they would make rich farmland. But this is not so. Most of the nutrients of these forests are in plants, not in the soil. The soil is thin and easily overworked. Without its cover of trees, the soil quickly breaks down and erodes.

Crop yields on this land are so poor that farms are abandoned after only a few years. The farmers then push farther into the forests and cut more trees. It takes centuries for a mature tropical forest to grow back.

Tropical forests are also being cut because of the need for wood. Wood is the primary fuel supply for one third of the people on the earth. Supplies are already running short. More than 100 million people do not have enough wood. Tropical forest woods like teak and mahogany are in great demand for making furniture.

Biologists suspect that climate patterns all over the earth would be changed. Trees use up carbon dioxide. So the loss of tropical forests would raise the carbon dioxide level in the atmosphere. When an area of forest is cleared, it is usually burned down. This adds even more carbon dioxide to the air. The oversupply of carbon dioxide in the atmosphere would cause it to hold in more heat. This warming is called the greenhouse effect and would raise world temperatures. The warmer temperatures could melt polar icecaps, causing flooding in coastal cities.

Figure 3 illustrates another result of changes in the amount of carbon dioxide in the atmosphere.

APPLYING CRITICAL THINKING SKILLS

1. According to the map, what factor of climate may be affected by a warmer earth?

2. How could the climate in most of the United States change as a result of more carbon dioxide in the atmosphere?

3. How would much of the grain-producing area of the United States be affected? Would this be a problem? Why or why not?

4. If the moisture patterns of the world are affected as the map suggests, which areas of the earth might become important grain producers?

If the clearing of tropical forests continues at the present rate, they will be gone by the year 2050. There is some replanting going on now. But on the average, just 1 hectare is replanted for every 10 hectares that are cleared.

The problem is a big one. And it has serious consequences for life on the earth. Asking Americans to stop buying mahogany furniture is one thing. Mahogany furniture is not necessary for life. But how is it possible to tell people who need food that forests cannot be cut down to make farmland? And what is to be done about the billions of people who depend on wood from tropical forests to cook? Can these people survive from day to day without using the resources of the tropical forests? But, can the earth survive in the future if the tropical forests disappear?

Figure 3

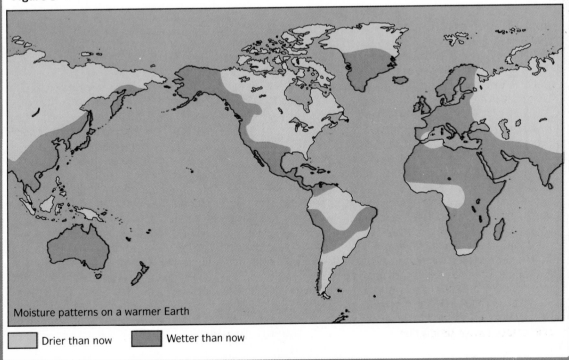

Moisture patterns on a warmer Earth

☐ Drier than now   ▦ Wetter than now

DISCOVERING
THE HUMAN BODY

Science fiction movies sometimes show robots with human form. Often these machines are portrayed as having superhuman abilities. But the human body can do more than can any machine. In this unit you will learn about your bones, muscles, and skin. You will also study the digestive, circulatory, respiratory, and excretory systems.

With training, human muscles can fully develop. ▼

Section of a tooth viewed under an interference microscope. ▼

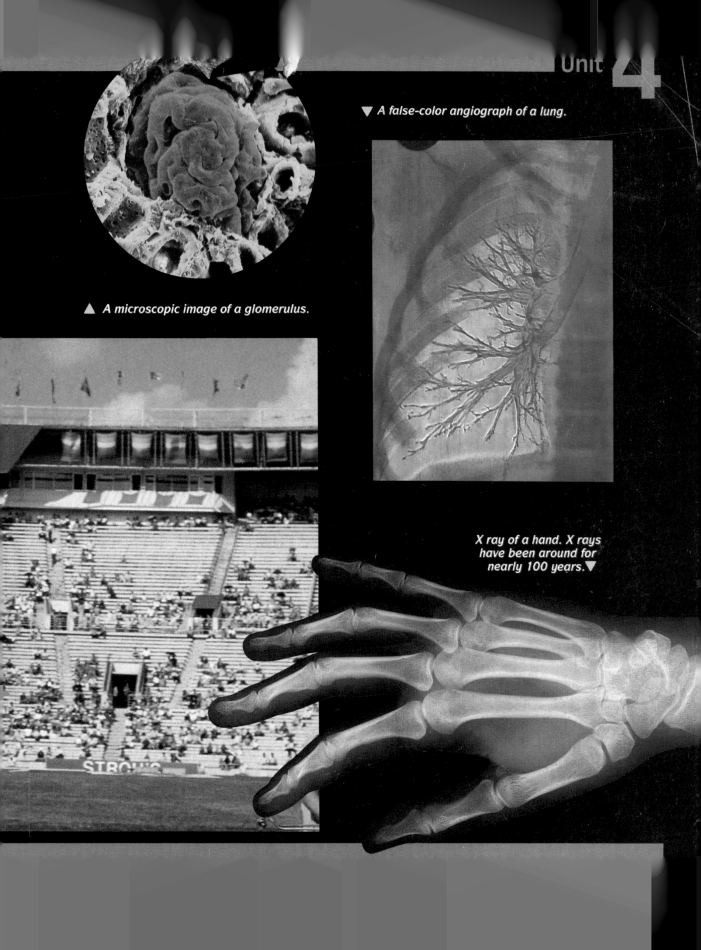

▼ A false-color angiograph of a lung.

▲ A microscopic image of a glomerulus.

X ray of a hand. X rays have been around for nearly 100 years.▼

CHAPTER 21

SUPPORT, MOVEMENT, AND BODY COVERING

*T*his photograph shows human skin enlarged 3500 times. The photograph was taken with a scanning electron microscope. Colors were added to the image so that details would be easier to see. What looks like the entrance to a cave is actually the opening of a pore in the skin. The green spheres are bacteria. One of the functions of the skin is to keep bacteria like these from entering the body.

About 2 m² of skin covers the body's framework of bones and muscles. The skin, the bones, and the muscles of the human body hold the body together and give it a recognizable form.

- *What are the functions of skin?*
- *How do bones and muscles support the body?*

21·1 Organization of the Human Body

After completing this section, you will be able to

- **compare** tissues, organs, and organ systems.
- **describe** the four main kinds of tissues.
- **state** the major organ systems of the body.

The key terms in this section are
connective tissue
epithelial tissue
muscle tissue
nerve tissue
organ
organ system
tissue

The human body is made up of trillions of cells. These cells have different shapes, sizes, and functions. The cells are organized into different types of tissues. A **tissue** is a group of cells that are similar in structure and function. For example, muscle cells make up muscle tissue. The cells of a tissue work together to perform some job.

Just as cells are grouped into tissues, tissues are grouped into organs. An **organ** is a group of two or more different tissues that work together to perform a function. The heart, liver, brain, and eyes are organs.

Organs are arranged into organ systems. An **organ system** is a group of organs that work together to perform one or more functions. The organ systems, their functions, and the major organs of each system are shown in Table 21·1. Which organ systems play a role in movement?

Table 21·1 *Organ Systems: Major Organs and Functions*

Skeletal System	Muscular System	Skin	Digestive System	Respiratory System
Major Organs	**Major Organs**	**Major Organs**	**Major Organs**	**Major Organs**
Bones	Muscles	Skin	Mouth, esophagus, stomach, liver, pancreas, intestines	Lungs, trachea, larynx, bronchi
Functions	**Functions**	**Functions**	**Functions**	**Functions**
Supports, permits movement, protects, stores minerals, produces blood cells	Produces movement of body parts, aids in digestion and circulation	Protects, prevents drying out, removes some wastes, helps to regulate body temperature	Breaks down food (prepares food for absorption into blood)	Exchanges oxygen and carbon dioxide

The organs and systems of the human body contain four basic types of tissues. They are epithelial, muscle, nerve, and connective tissues. Your eyes are made of these tissues. The same four tissues work together in your hand to enable you to lift a pencil off your desk and write your name. Refer to Figure 21·1 on the next page as you read about each type of tissue.

● **Epithelial** (ehp uh THEE lee uhl) **tissue** is made up of sheets of cells that cover and protect both inner surfaces and outer surfaces of the body. The cells of epithelial tissue vary in structure, depending on where they are found. Your skin is made of many layers of flat epithelial cells. The inner surface of the intestines is lined with columnlike epithelial cells. Epithelial tissue also forms glands.

● **Muscle tissue** is made of muscle cells that can contract, or become shorter. Body movement is made possible by the action of muscle tissue. Muscle tissue is found in the muscles that move the body and in the heart, the stomach, and other structures.

Circulatory System	Excretory System	Endocrine System	Nervous System	Reproductive System
Major Organs	**Major Organs**	**Major Organs**	**Major Organs**	**Major Organs**
Heart, blood vessels	Kidneys, lungs, skin	Endocrine glands	Nerves, brain, spinal cord	Ovaries, testes
Functions	**Functions**	**Functions**	**Functions**	**Functions**
Transports materials throughout body	Removes waste products	Regulates chemical activity in body	Receives and transports messages throughout body, coordinates body parts	Produces reproductive cells

- **Nerve tissue** is made of long, branched nerve cells that carry messages throughout the body. Nerve tissue enables you to hear, smell, see, and think, and to control your body.

- **Connective tissue** joins and supports different parts of the body. The body contains many different kinds of connective tissue. Connective tissue may be fluid or solid. Blood, bone, cartilage, and fat are four types of connective tissue. Which of these are solid connective tissue? The different types of connective tissue are made of cells of various shapes and sizes.

Figure 21·1

Four types of tissues: epithelial *(A)*, muscle *(B)*, nerve *(C)*, and connective *(D)*.

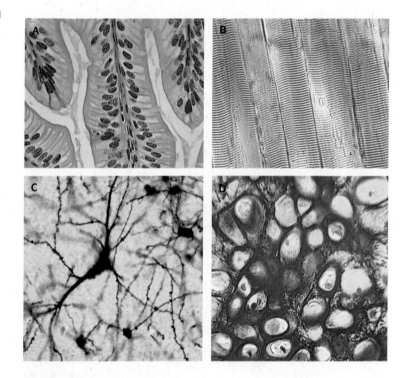

REVIEW

1. How are cells, tissues, organs, and organ systems related to each other?
2. Describe the four types of tissues found in the body.
3. Name three examples of organ systems, and give the functions of each.

CHALLENGE Name every type of tissue that is used in tossing a ball. Explain how you know these types of tissues are needed to perform this task.

21·2 The Skeletal System

FUNCTIONS OF THE SKELETON

Figure 21·2 shows the framework inside the Statue of Liberty. Like the statue, the human body has a framework—a skeleton. The **skeleton** is the framework that supports the body and protects the internal organs. The human skeleton is made up of 206 bones. These bones are organized into a *skeletal system*. The skeletal system is made up of bones, joints, and connective tissue.

The skeleton has several functions. It gives support and the basic shape to the body. Without a skeleton, the body would be a shapeless mass of soft tissues. The skeleton also functions in the movement of the body. The bones of the skeleton are a framework to which muscles are attached. Muscles and bones work together to move the parts of the body. The skeleton also protects the soft organs of the body. For example, part of the skull forms a case that protects the soft tissues of the brain. Bones also store the minerals calcium and phosphorus. These minerals give strength to bones and are used in many other parts of the body.

After completing this section, you will be able to

- **describe** the major functions of the skeleton.
- **identify** major bones in the skeleton.
- **compare** the types of joints in the skeleton.

The key terms in this section are
ball-and-socket joint
gliding joint
hinge joint
joint
pivot joint
skeleton

© Dan Cornish/ESTO

Figure 21·2

The framework inside the Statue of Liberty. How is this framework like a skeleton?

PARTS OF THE SKELETON

Some of the major bones of the skeleton are shown in Figure 21·3. The skull is the part of the skeleton that protects the brain and that forms the face and jaws. The helmet-shaped part of the skull that encloses the brain is the *cranium*.

The *spinal column*, or backbone, is a series of small bones that enclose and protect the spinal cord. The spinal cord is made up of delicate nerve tissue. The 33 small, ringlike bones that form the spinal column are called *vertebrae* (VER tuh bree)(sing., *vertebra*). The spinal column provides the main upright support for the body.

The curved bones attached to the spinal column are the *ribs*. Humans have 12 pairs of ribs. Most of the ribs are joined by connective tissue to the *sternum*, or breastbone. The ribs and the sternum protect the heart and lungs.

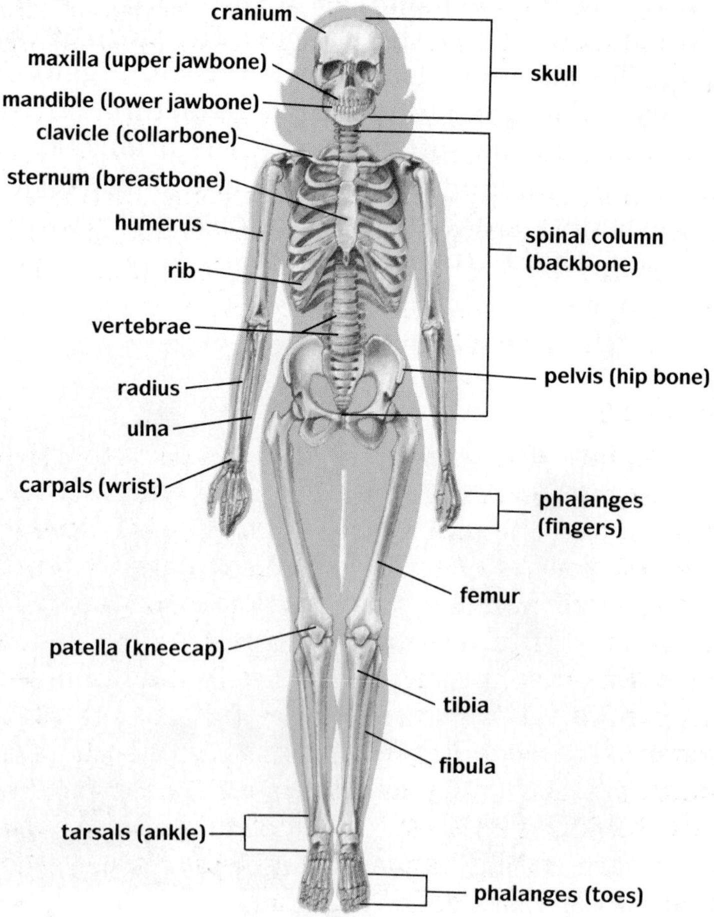

Figure 21·3
The human skeleton.

cranium
maxilla (upper jawbone)
mandible (lower jawbone)
clavicle (collarbone)
sternum (breastbone)
humerus
rib
vertebrae
radius
ulna
carpals (wrist)
patella (kneecap)
tarsals (ankle)
skull
spinal column (backbone)
pelvis (hip bone)
phalanges (fingers)
femur
tibia
fibula
phalanges (toes)

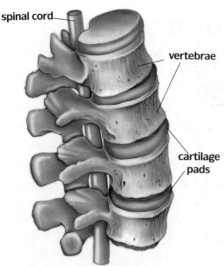

spinal cord

vertebrae

cartilage pads

Figure 21·4
Pads of cartilage between the vertebrae act as shock absorbers in the spinal column.

The bowl-shaped bone that forms the hips is the *pelvis*. The shape of the pelvis enables it to support the internal organs. The pelvis also protects the reproductive organs inside a female's body. The arm bones and leg bones are called long bones because of their length. The long bones of the legs support the pelvis and the weight of the body above it.

The skeleton also contains *cartilage*, a tough, flexible connective tissue. The outer ear and the tip of the nose are supported by this tissue. Cartilage is found wherever two bones meet. It cushions the bones and keeps them from rubbing together. Figure 21·4 shows disks of cartilage between the vertebrae of the spinal column.

JOINTS

A place where two or more bones come together in the skeleton is called a **joint**. The body has three basic types of joints. A joint that allows no movement of bones is a *fixed joint*. Fixed joints are found in the skull and the pelvis. A joint that allows a small amount of movement is a *partially movable joint*. Examples of such joints are found in the spinal column. A joint that allows full movement of bones is a *movable joint*. Examples of movable joints are the knees and the shoulders. Bones at movable joints are held together by ligaments. *Ligaments* are strong bands of connective tissue that hold two or more bones together.

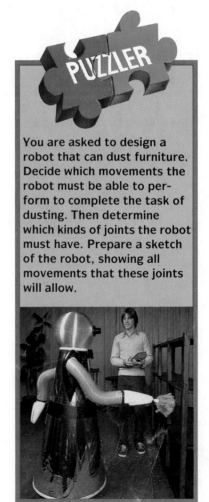

PUZZLER

You are asked to design a robot that can dust furniture. Decide which movements the robot must be able to perform to complete the task of dusting. Then determine which kinds of joints the robot must have. Prepare a sketch of the robot, showing all movements that these joints will allow.

Figure 21·5
Types of joints in the human body.

Figure 21·5 shows the location of some of the joints in the body. A **ball-and-socket joint** is a movable joint that allows movement in many directions. The shoulders and the hips contain ball-and-socket joints. A **hinge joint**, also a movable joint, allows movement in only one direction. Knees and elbows are formed of hinge joints that allow bending.

A **pivot joint** is a movable joint that allows rotating movement from side to side. A pivot joint in the neck is located between the first and second vertebrae. A movable joint that allows gliding movements is called a **gliding joint**. The movement is a simple gliding back and forth or sideways. Such joints are found in the wrists and the ankles.

REVIEW

1. What are the functions of the skeleton?
2. Which bones protect the heart? The brain? The spinal cord?
3. Explain the differences between fixed joints, partially movable joints, and movable joints.

CHALLENGE Suppose a person had a disease in which the bones could not store calcium. What might be the effect on the skeleton?

522

21·3 Structure and Growth of Bones

The living tissue in a bone includes bone cells, blood, blood vessels, nerves, and fat. The nonliving part includes water, protein, and the minerals calcium and phosphorus.

Several types of bones are found in the skeleton. Recall that long bones are found in the arms and legs. The ribs and shoulder blades are flat bones. Irregular bones include the vertebrae and some bones in the skull. Bones all have the same basic structure. Figure 21·6 shows the structure of the upper part of a long bone of the leg.

A bone is covered by a tough outer membrane, which contains many blood vessels. Beneath this membrane is a bony layer, which is hard and strong. It contains living bone cells surrounded by deposits of protein, calcium, and phosphorus. At the ends of the bone, the bony layer contains many small spaces. This type of bone is called spongy bone.

Notice in Figure 21·6 that blood vessels pass through all parts of the bone. Blood brings food and oxygen to the bone cells and carries away wastes. The blood also carries calcium and phosphorus between the bone and other parts of the body.

After completing this section, you will be able to
- **describe** the structure of a long bone.
- **describe** the function of marrow.

The key term in this section is **marrow**

Figure 21·6
The structure of a long bone.

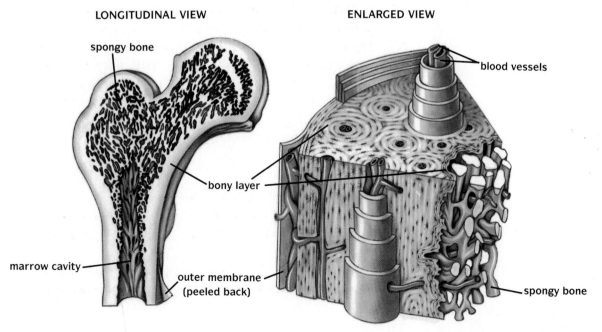

LONGITUDINAL VIEW | ENLARGED VIEW

spongy bone

blood vessels

bony layer

marrow cavity

outer membrane (peeled back)

spongy bone

523

OBJECTIVE
Observe the structure of a long bone.

MATERIALS
uncooked long bone of lamb, cut in half along its length; hand lens

PROCEDURE
A. Examine a long bone of lamb with a hand lens. Look at the outer, uncut surface first. Notice the cartilage covering the ends of the bone.
  1. How does the cartilage function at the joint?

B. Turn the bone over, and examine its internal structure. Most of the bone is composed of the bony layer. Find the area of spongy bone at each end.
C. Locate the marrow.
  2. What color is the marrow?

RESULTS AND CONCLUSIONS
1. Make a sketch of the cut surface of the bone you examined. Label the bony layer, spongy bone, marrow, and cartilage.
2. How does the tissue at each end of the bone differ from the tissue in the middle?

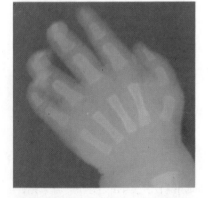

Figure 21·7
X ray of an infant's hand: the white areas show bone; the darker areas show cartilage, which will gradually be replaced by bone.

In the center of the bone is a large space, or cavity, that contains a tissue called marrow. **Marrow** (MAR oh) is a soft tissue in which new blood cells are produced. Marrow is also found in the small spaces of spongy bone. There are two types of marrow. *Red marrow* makes red blood cells. *Yellow marrow* contains much fat and can also produce some red blood cells. In infants, bones contain only red marrow. Beginning at about 5 years of age, the red marrow in some bones is replaced by yellow marrow.

Before birth, the body of a baby contains few hard, rigid bones. Instead the skeleton is made mostly of cartilage. The cartilage is slowly replaced by bones during the early years of life. This occurs as the minerals calcium and phosphorus take the place of cartilage. The minerals, along with protein, fill the spaces between bone cells, making the bones hard and strong.

REVIEW

1. Describe the parts of a long bone.

2. What is the function of bone marrow? How does red marrow differ from yellow marrow?

CHALLENGE Why is it important for infants and children to have foods that contain calcium and phosphorus? What food that infants often eat has a large amount of calcium and phosphorus?

21·4 The Muscular System

In everything you do, you use muscles. When you run, muscles move your arms and legs. When you sit quietly reading a book, eye muscles move your eyes from side to side as you read.

The human body has over 600 different muscles. The *muscular system* is made up of all the muscles in the body that cause movement of body parts. The major muscles of the body and their functions are shown in Figure 21·8. In an adult female, muscles make up about 30 percent of the total body mass. In an adult male, muscles make up about 40 percent of the total body mass.

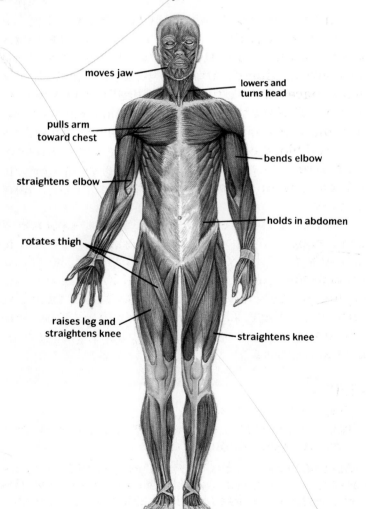

moves jaw

lowers and turns head

pulls arm toward chest

bends elbow

straightens elbow

holds in abdomen

rotates thigh

raises leg and straightens knee

straightens knee

Figure 21·8
Major muscles of the human body and their functions.

GROUPS OF MUSCLES

Muscles can be divided into two major groups: voluntary muscles and involuntary muscles. A **voluntary muscle** is a muscle that is under conscious control. For example, you can control the muscles of your arms and legs when you walk or ride a bicycle. These muscles are voluntary muscles. Figure 21·9 shows some voluntary muscles of the face.

An **involuntary muscle** is a muscle that is not under conscious control. Such a muscle works without your thinking about it. Your heart beats all the time without your ever having to think about it. Heart muscle is an example of involuntary muscle.

Some movements controlled by voluntary muscles are not always under conscious control. The blinking of your eyes is caused by voluntary muscles. When you consciously think about blinking, you can control these muscles. However, at other times you do not consciously control these muscles. You continue to blink when you do not think about it. The muscles that cause blinking are controlled by two sets of nerves. One set of nerves is for voluntary control of the muscles. The other set is for involuntary control.

Figure 21·9

Muscles that cause a smile or a frown. Are these muscles voluntary or involuntary?

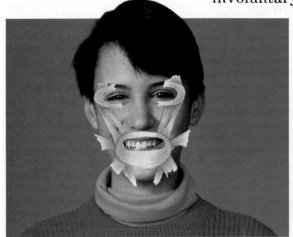
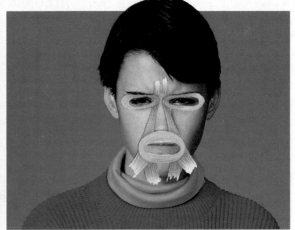

KINDS OF MUSCLE TISSUE

Each muscle is made of one of three kinds of muscle tissue. All three kinds of muscle tissue are made of muscle cells. The three kinds of muscle tissue are shown in Figure 21·10.

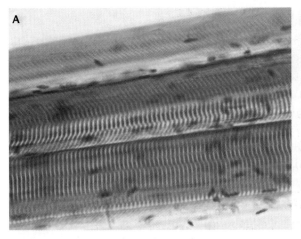
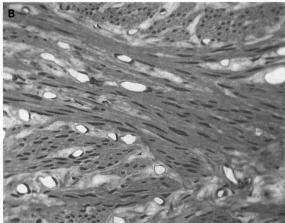

- **Skeletal muscle** is the muscle tissue that is attached to and that moves the skeleton. Skeletal muscle, such as that in your arms and legs, is voluntary muscle and is under conscious control. Skeletal muscle has dark bands or stripes running across the muscle. Locate these stripes in Figure 21·10A.

- **Smooth muscle** is the muscle tissue found in the walls of many organs inside the body. Smooth muscle is involuntary muscle. Organs of the digestive system have smooth muscle in their walls. The walls of many blood vessels also contain smooth muscle. Notice in Figure 21·10B that smooth muscle cells do not have stripes.

- **Cardiac** (KAHR dee ak) **muscle** is the muscle tissue that makes up the heart. In fact, cardiac muscle is found only in the heart. Like smooth muscle, cardiac muscle is involuntary. Like skeletal muscle, cardiac muscle has stripes. In Figure 21·10C you can see that cardiac muscle cells have many light-colored stripes that are separated by darker bands. The cells of cardiac muscle are connected to each other, forming a network.

Figure 21·10
Skeletal muscle *(A)*, smooth muscle *(B)*, and cardiac muscle *(C)*.

kardia (heart)

REVIEW

1. How do voluntary and involuntary muscles differ?
2. How does cardiac muscle compare with smooth muscle? How does cardiac muscle compare with skeletal muscle?

CHALLENGE Identify the problems that might arise if cardiac muscle were voluntary instead of involuntary.

21·5 Body Movement and Disorders

BODY MOVEMENT

Muscle cells are the only cells in the body that can *contract*, or shorten, and *relax*, or lengthen. When a muscle cell relaxes, it returns to its original size. The ability of muscle cells to contract and relax causes movement in the body. Body movements are the results of muscles and bones working together. Bones cannot move by themselves. Only muscles have the ability to cause body movement.

Figure 21·11 shows two of the main muscles of the arm. These muscles are voluntary skeletal muscles. Skeletal muscles are attached to bones by tough bands of connective tissue called *tendons*. Find the tendons in Figure 21·11. Locate the elbow hinge joint and the biceps muscle in the same figure. Notice that a tendon attaches the biceps muscle below the hinge joint.

Skeletal muscles often work in pairs. The biceps and triceps muscles work as a pair to raise and lower the forearm. When the biceps contracts, the elbow bends and the forearm is raised, as shown in Figure 21·11*B*. As the biceps contracts, the triceps relaxes. When the triceps contracts, the forearm is pulled downward and the arm straightens, as shown in Figure 21·11*A*. The biceps relaxes as the triceps contracts. Muscles always move bones by contracting, never by relaxing.

Figure 21·11

Major muscles of the arm when it is extended *(A)* and bent *(B)*. Which muscle contracts when the arm is bent?

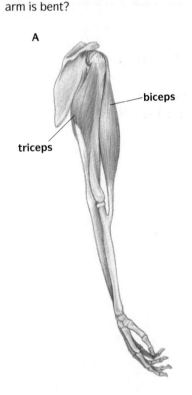

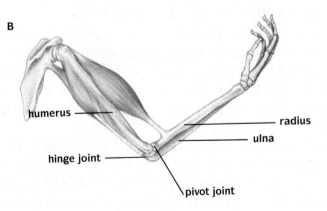

528

OBJECTIVE
Infer how muscles, tendons, joints, and bones work together.

MATERIALS
uncooked chicken wing with skin removed, paper towel

PROCEDURE

A. Place chicken wing on a paper towel.
B. Refer to the drawing to help you locate the muscles, tendons, bones, joints, and cartilage of the chicken wing.
C. Hold the chicken wing at both ends. Slowly bend and straighten the wing several times. Carefully observe the movement of the muscles in the wing.

RESULTS AND CONCLUSIONS

1. Make a drawing of the chicken wing. Label the following parts of the wing: muscles, joint, tendons, bones, and cartilage.

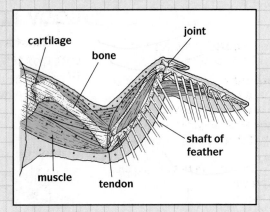

2. Describe the appearance of the tendons.
3. What kind of joint is in the wing?
4. On your drawing of the wing, label which muscles are flexors and which muscles are extensors.
5. Do muscles in a chicken wing work together in pairs to bend and straighten the wing? Make a drawing to explain your answer.

A muscle that causes a joint to bend when the muscle contracts is called a **flexor** (FLEHK suhr). A muscle that causes a joint to straighten when the muscle contracts is called an **extensor** (ehk STEHN-suhr). Look again at Figure 21·11A. Is the biceps muscle a flexor or an extensor?

flectere (bend)

ex- (out)
tendere (stretch)

BONE AND MUSCLE INJURIES

Injuries to bones and muscles occur quite often. A *sprain* is an injury that occurs when a ligament is stretched or torn away from a joint. Recall that ligaments hold bones together at a movable joint. Sprains often result when the bones at a joint are twisted or pulled suddenly.

Sprains are usually treated by applying ice to the injury. The ice reduces swelling and pain. Ice should be used on and off for 24 to 72 hours. Then heat should be applied to speed healing. A joint that is sprained should not be used until the pain is gone.

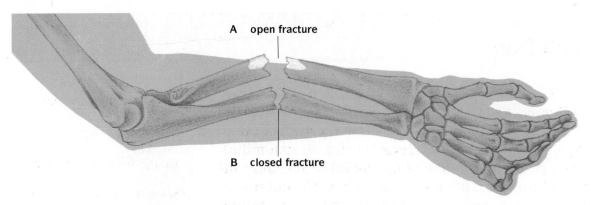

A open fracture

B closed fracture

Figure 21·12
Broken arm bones: open fracture *(top)* and closed fracture *(bottom)*.

A *strain* is an injury that occurs when a tendon or muscle is overstretched. Strains are painful but are less serious than sprains. Treatment of a strain is usually rest and the application of warm compresses to the area.

A *fracture* (FRAK chuhr) is a crack or break in a bone. The most severe type of fracture is an *open fracture*. An open fracture occurs when a broken bone is pushed through the skin. In a *closed fracture* the bone is not pushed through the skin.

When a bone is fractured, a cast is put around the area. The cast prevents the broken ends of the bone from moving and thus allows proper healing. The cast stays on until the fracture is healed, usually after several weeks have passed.

A *cramp* is a painful, involuntary contraction of a muscle. Too much exercise can sometimes cause muscles to cramp. Cramps may also be caused by the failure to warm up before exercising. Rubbing the cramped area can reduce the pain.

A good way to prevent injury to muscles and bones is to wear the right equipment when playing sports. For example, the equipment in Figure 21·13 protects the field hockey player.

Figure 21·13
A field hockey player wearing protective equipment.

REVIEW

1. Describe how the action of muscles allows you to bend your arm and to straighten your arm.
2. What are the differences between a sprain, a strain, and a fracture?

CHALLENGE Which type of fracture causes the greatest danger to the body? Explain why.

21·6 Skin

The skin is the outer covering of the body. Look at Figure 21·14 as you read about the parts of the skin. The skin is made of two main layers. The outer layer of skin is the **epidermis** (ehp uh DER mihs). The epidermis is made of epithelial tissue and contains two kinds of cells. The cells at the outer surface are either dead or dying and are always falling or being rubbed off. These cells contain *keratin*, a protein that waterproofs the skin.

The cells deep inside the epidermis are living. These living cells may contain melanin (MEHL uh-nihn). *Melanin* is a brown pigment that colors the skin. People of different races have different amounts of melanin in their skin. However, all people have melanin in their skin. When skin is exposed to sunlight, extra melanin is made. This darkens, or tans, the skin. Melanin helps to protect the skin from the harmful rays of the sun.

The inner, thicker layer of the skin is the **dermis** (DER mihs). The dermis is made of connective tissue. Most of the structures in the skin are found in the dermis. *Sweat glands* are coiled tubes

After completing this section, you will be able to

- **identify** major structures in the skin.
- **list** the functions of the skin.

The key terms in this section are
dermis
epidermis

derma (skin)

Figure 21·14
Structures in the human skin.

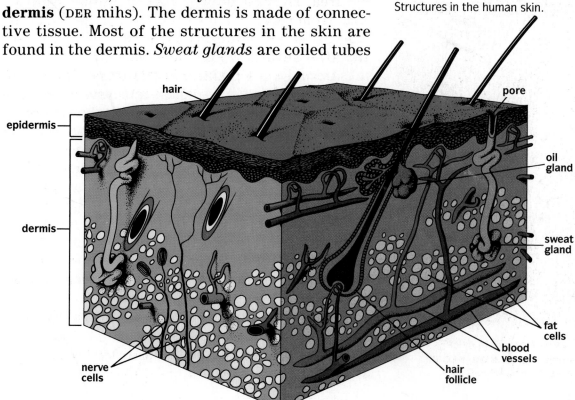

hair

pore

epidermis

oil gland

dermis

sweat gland

fat cells

blood vessels

nerve cells

hair follicle

Each year, about 10,000 people die of severe burns. A burn victim faces two main threats to life: infection and loss of fluids. In a healthy person the skin keeps out disease-causing organisms and keeps in body fluids. A person without a covering of skin lacks this protection.

Many burn victims have had some of their burned skin replaced by skin grafts. These grafts are patches of skin taken from unburned parts of the body. A person with extensive burns, however, does not have enough unburned skin to supply these grafts. Such a person needs another source of skin.

For years, scientists have worked toward making a material that acts like skin. An artificial skin has to have several important qualities. It must be thin and elastic. And it has to allow just the right amount of moisture to enter and leave.

Scientists have made a material that is nearly as good as real skin. From the photograph you can see that the artificial skin looks like moist, elastic paper toweling.

This artificial skin has three main parts—fibers from cowhide, cartilage from sharks, and a rubber called silicone. When joined together in the right way, these substances behave almost like skin. But unlike real skin, artificial skin does not have sweat glands and hair.

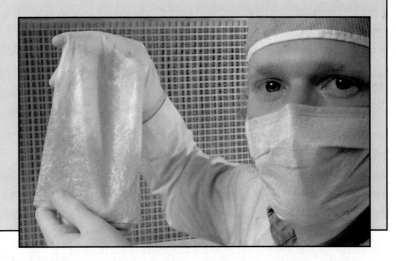

that cool the body by giving off moisture. The openings from the sweat glands to the outside of the skin are called *pores*. Locate a pore and a sweat gland in Figure 21·14. The dermis also contains hair follicles. *Hair follicles* are deep pockets from which hair grows. Oil glands in the dermis are connected to the hair follicles. Oil from these glands keeps the hair and skin soft. The dermis also contains many blood vessels, nerves, and fat cells.

The skin has several functions. The main function of the skin is protection. The skin helps to keep bacteria and other disease-causing organisms from entering the body. The skin protects the internal organs from losing too much water to the air.

Skin also helps to control body temperature. The sweat glands in the skin carry sweat to the surface. Sweat is a liquid that contains water, salt, and some wastes. When the sweat evaporates from the skin, the skin is cooled. There are also nerve cells in the skin that allow you to sense heat, cold, pressure, and pain. These cells also allow you to feel the texture of objects.

REVIEW

1. Describe the two layers of the skin.
2. Describe three structures found in the dermis.
3. How does sweat cool the body?
4. List three functions of the skin.

CHALLENGE During which season of the year would the skin of people in North America produce the most melanin? Why?

CHAPTER SUMMARY

The main ideas in this chapter are listed below. Read these statements before you answer the Chapter Review questions.

- Cells in the human body are organized into tissues, organs, and organ systems. The four main types of tissues are epithelial tissue, muscle tissue, nerve tissue, and connective tissue.(21·1)
- The functions of the skeletal system are to support, move, and protect, and to store minerals the body needs. (21·2)
- There are three main types of joints — fixed joints, partially movable joints, and movable joints. Movable joints include ball-and-socket joints, gliding joints, hinge joints, and pivot joints. (21·2)
- Bones contain both living tissue and nonliving material. Marrow, a soft tissue in which blood cells are produced, is found inside many bones. (21·3)

- The muscular system is made up of muscles that cause the movement of body parts. There are three kinds of muscle tissue. They are skeletal muscle, smooth muscle, and cardiac muscle. (21·4)
- Movement of body parts is often caused by muscles working in pairs. One muscle in the pair contracts while the other relaxes. (21·5)
- Cramps, sprains, strains, and fractures are injuries of muscles and bones. Fractures are breaks in bones, and may be either open or closed. (21·5)
- The functions of the skin include protection against infection and water loss, regulation of temperature, and sensation. (21·6)

The key terms in this chapter are listed below. Use each term in a sentence that shows the meaning of the term.

ball-and-socket joint	extensor	marrow	skeletal muscle
cardiac muscle	flexor	muscle tissue	skeleton
connective tissue	gliding joint	nerve tissue	smooth muscle
dermis	hinge joint	organ	tissue
epidermis	involuntary muscle	organ system	voluntary muscle
epithelial tissue	joint	pivot joint	

Chapter Review

VOCABULARY

Use the key terms from the previous page to complete the following sentences correctly.

1. The part of a skeleton where two or more bones meet is a/an _____ .
2. A/an _____ is a muscle that can be made to contract under conscious control.
3. A/An _____ is a group of two or more tissues that work together to perform some function.
4. The muscle tissue found in the heart is _____ .
5. _____ is the kind of tissue that joins and supports different parts of the body.
6. The _____ is the inner, thick layer of the skin.
7. _____ is the kind of tissue that carries messages throughout the body.
8. _____ is the muscle tissue that is attached to and moves the skeleton.
9. _____ is a soft tissue inside bones that produces blood cells.
10. A muscle that causes a joint to bend is called a/an _____ .

CONCEPTS

Write the correct term for each part of the skin shown in the diagram.

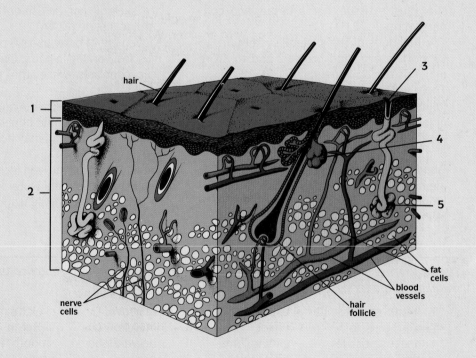

hair

1

2

3

4

5

nerve cells

hair follicle

blood vessels

fat cells

Identify each statement as True or False. If a statement is false, replace the underlined term or phrase with a term or phrase that makes the statement true.

6. A <u>tendon</u> is a strong band of connective tissue that holds two or more bones together.
7. The biceps is an example of <u>voluntary muscle</u>.
8. <u>Melanin</u> is a protein that waterproofs the skin.
9. The shoulder is an example of a <u>hinge joint</u>.
10. Blood cells are produced by the <u>skeletal system</u>.

Answer the following in complete sentences.

11. What are the differences between tissues, organs, and organ systems?
12. Describe the four basic types of tissues found in the body.
13. Describe the functions of the skeleton.
14. Explain how muscles often work in pairs to move the skeleton.
15. Describe the functions of the skin.

APPLICATION/ CRITICAL THINKING

1. Pregnant women are encouraged to eat a diet rich in calcium and phosphorus. Explain why.
2. The thickness of the layer of dead cells in the epidermis varies a great deal from one part of the body to another. Which part of the body do you think has a thick layer of dead cells? Which part has a thin layer? Explain your answers.
3. The cells of cardiac muscle, unlike those of skeletal muscle or smooth muscle, form a branching network. What is the advantage of this structure in cardiac muscle?
4. The casts used to treat fractures in the past were often made of plaster. Today, casts are often made of plastic, fiberglass, or air-filled plastic tubes. Give reasons why the newer casts are better than plaster casts.

EXTENSION

1. Acne is a skin disorder common among teenagers. Find out the cause of acne and how it can be prevented or reduced. Describe different treatments for acne.
2. Find out how artificial joints are made and used. What materials are used to make artificial joints? How long will an artificial joint last?
3. Osteoporosis and rickets are two disorders that affect the skeleton. Find out what causes these disorders and how they can be prevented. Who is most likely to suffer from each of these disorders?

CHAPTER 22

NUTRITION AND DIGESTION

*L*ook at the foods shown in the photograph. Do you eat some of these foods each day? Fruits and vegetables make up one of the groups of foods that you should include in a balanced diet.

You may have been told that eating the right kinds of foods will make you be stronger, grow taller, or have more energy. To some extent this is true. But did you know that eating a balanced diet is important in maintaining good health? A good diet is believed to be an important factor in avoiding high blood pressure, heart disease, and some forms of cancer.

- *Why do people need food?*
- *Do different foods meet different needs of the body?*
- *What happens to food after it enters the body?*

22·1 Carbohydrates, Proteins, and Fats

Food supplies the body with nutrients (NOO-tree uhntz). A **nutrient** is any substance the body needs to live and grow. Some nutrients provide energy. The energy in nutrients is the fuel that allows your body to run, walk, or jump. Energy keeps your heart beating and your brain working. Nutrients also provide material for growth and repair. Some help the body to use other nutrients.

Nutrients are divided into six classes: carbohydrates (kahr boh HĪ drayts), fats, proteins (PROH-teenz), vitamins, minerals, and water. To use nutrients, the body must first get food. Then the food must be broken down. The process by which the body gets and breaks down nutrients is called *nutrition* (noo TRISH uhn).

CARBOHYDRATES

Carbohydrates are nutrients that provide the body with its main source of energy. *Sugars* and *starches* are two kinds of carbohydrates. Sugars are found in fruits, such as apples, peaches, and grapes. Honey and jams contain large amounts of sugars. Starches are found in breads, noodles, and cereals. These foods are all made from grains, such as wheat, corn, rice, and oats. Vegetables such as peas, beets, and potatoes also contain starches.

Figure 22·1

Table sugar and starch are both carbohydrates that are made up of simple sugars.

complex sugar

starch

Key:

= simple sugar

●●●●● = many simple sugar units

There are two types of sugars—simple and complex. Table sugar is a complex sugar. As shown in Figure 22·1, a complex sugar is made of two simple sugars linked together. Based on the figure, how would you describe a starch? In the body, complex sugars and starches are split to form simple sugars. The simple sugars are used as a source of energy.

FATS

Fats are nutrients that provide energy and building material for the body. Gram for gram, fats contain about twice as much energy as do carbohydrates. Fats are also used to build cell membranes. Fats are found in cooking oils, butter, margarine, meat, and nuts. The body not only takes in fats but also makes fats from carbohydrates. Such fats are stored in the body. When the body takes in less food than it needs, it uses the stored fats. Stored fats insulate the body and protect some organs.

ACTIVITY How Can Food Be Tested for Starch?

OBJECTIVE
Identify foods that contain starch.

MATERIALS
lab apron, safety goggles, starch solution, 2 test tubes, test-tube rack, water, iodine solution in dropper bottle, paper towel, food samples, paper cup

PROCEDURE
A. Wear a lab apron and safety goggles.
B. Make a data table with headings like those shown.
C. Add starch solution to a test tube until it is half full. Add water to another test tube until it is half full. Place the test tubes in the test-tube rack.
D. Place five drops of iodine solution in each of the test tubes. Observe the contents of each test tube. **Caution:** Iodine is a stain. Be careful not to spill the iodine or get it on your hands or clothing. If you spill the iodine, tell your teacher at once.
E. Iodine changes from yellow to blue-black in the presence of starch. In the column headed *Food*, list both the starch solution and the water. Complete the table for the results of testing starch and testing water, noting any changes in color.
F. Place pieces of several different foods on a paper towel. If you are testing a liquid, place a small amount in a paper cup. Place one or two drops of iodine solution on each food. Look for a color change in each food. Record the results in your data table.

FOOD	COLOR CHANGE	FOOD HAS STARCH? (YES OR NO)

RESULTS AND CONCLUSIONS
1. Which foods that were tested contain starch?
2. Which foods do not contain starch?

Figure 22·2 shows that fat molecules are made up of smaller molecules called *fatty acids* and *glycerol* (GLIHS uh rohl). Fatty acids and glycerol can be broken down to release energy in cells.

Fats are large molecules that are made up of fatty acids and glycerol.

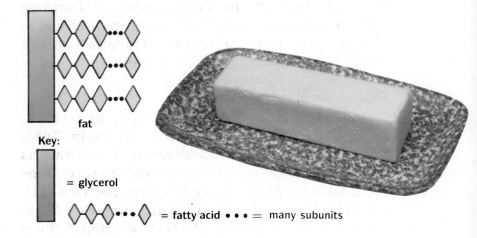

fat

Key:

= glycerol

= fatty acid • • • = many subunits

PROTEINS

Proteins are nutrients that provide the body with material for growth and repair, and that are needed to form enzymes. Recall from Chapter 2 that enzymes control chemical changes in living things. Meat, fish, eggs, milk, and nuts contain proteins.

Proteins are made up of *amino* (uh MEE noh) *acids*. There are about 20 kinds of amino acids that link together in different combinations to form thousands of different proteins. When proteins are used by the body, they are broken down into amino acids. The body then uses these amino acids to form new proteins. Some amino acids can be made in the body. Others cannot be made by the body and must come from foods that contain proteins.

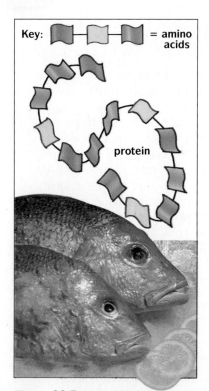

Key: = amino acids

protein

Figure 22·3

Proteins are made up of chains of amino acids.

REVIEW

1. What are nutrients? Why does the body require nutrients?
2. What are the six classes of nutrients needed by the body?
3. What are the functions of carbohydrates, fats, and proteins?
4. Give two examples of foods that contain at least one of each of the following nutrients: sugars, starches, fats, and proteins.

CHALLENGE What might happen to the body if the amino acids that the body cannot make were not in foods?

22·2 Vitamins, Minerals, and Water

Two types of nutrients help the body to function normally and to use other nutrients. These two types of nutrients are vitamins and minerals. Unlike other nutrients, vitamins and minerals are not used by the body as a source of energy.

VITAMINS

A **vitamin** is an organic compound that helps to control the chemical functions of the body. Table 22·1 lists six vitamins and their sources. Vitamins are found in many foods, but no single food contains all the vitamins that the body needs. Eating a variety of foods provides all the vitamins needed. What foods are good sources of the B vitamins? What foods provide vitamin C?

After completing this section, you will be able to

- **give examples** of vitamins, their functions, and their sources.
- **give examples** of minerals, their functions, and their sources.
- **explain** how water is used by the body.

The key terms in this section are
mineral
vitamin

vita (life)

Table 22·1 *Vitamins*

VITAMIN	NEEDED FOR	SOURCES
A	Healthy eyes, hair, and skin	Green and yellow vegetables, fruits, egg yolks, liver, milk, butter
B complex	Obtaining energy from sugar; proper functioning of heart and nerves; healthy skin	Meat, milk, liver, eggs, grains
C	Healthy bones, teeth, and gums; resisting infection	Citrus fruits, tomatoes, potatoes, leafy green vegetables, alfalfa sprouts
D	Healthy bones and teeth	Fortified milk, eggs, tuna, liver; made by the skin in presence of sunlight
E	Healthy cell membranes	Vegetable oils, milk, grains
K	Blood clotting; proper liver functioning	Leafy green vegetables, tomatoes, grains

Only small amounts of each vitamin are needed by the body. When the body takes in more vitamins than it needs, the extra vitamins may leave the body as wastes. However, excess amounts of vitamins A, D, E, and K are stored in the body. Large amounts of them can build up and harm the body if too much is eaten.

When the body does not get enough of a given vitamin, disease may result. Diseases caused by lack of vitamins can be prevented or cured by eating foods rich in the needed vitamins.

MINERALS

A **mineral** is an element that helps the body to function normally and to use other nutrients. Minerals provide material for the growth of bones and teeth and the formation of red blood cells. Minerals are also needed for proper functioning of the circulatory and nervous systems. Some of the minerals needed by the body are listed in Table 22·2. How is iron used by the body?

Table 22·2 *Minerals*

MINERAL	NEEDED FOR	SOURCES
Calcium	Strong bones, teeth, and muscles; blood clotting; nerve function	Milk and milk products, fish, eggs, leafy green vegetables
Phosphorus	Development and growth of bones and teeth; nerve and muscle function	Milk and milk products, beans, meat, whole grains, nuts, broccoli
Potassium	Nerve and muscle function	Bananas, other fruits, meat, vegetables, milk
Sodium	Nerve function; control of amount of water in body	Table salt, most foods
Magnesium	Nerve and muscle function; making proteins	Leafy green vegetables, milk, meat, potatoes, whole grains
Iron	Carrying oxygen in red blood cells	Liver, red meat, egg yolks, nuts, beans, leafy green vegetables
Iodine	Controlling the rate at which energy is used	Fish, shellfish, iodized table salt
Zinc	Healing wounds; making proteins	Meat, eggs, dried beans and peas, milk, green vegetables, eggs, seafood

Table 22·2 also lists some of the foods that contain minerals. Which minerals are found in milk? As with vitamins, no one food contains all the needed minerals. As you can see in Figure 22·4, eating a wide variety of foods provides the body with the minerals needed.

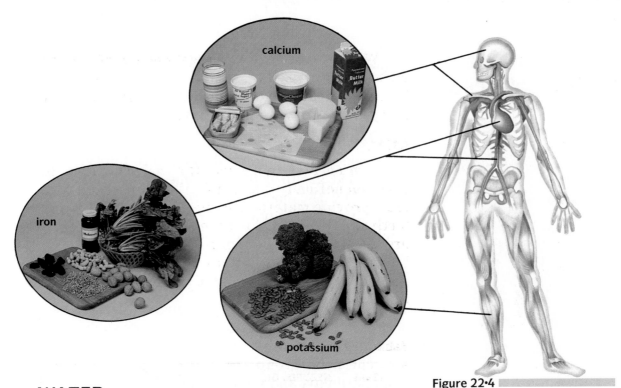

Figure 22·4
Minerals have many uses in the body.

WATER

Water is a nutrient needed for most body functions. It is the nutrient needed in the largest amounts. Figure 22·5 compares the amounts of water and other substances in the body. What percentage of the body's mass is water? Water has many functions in the body. The chemical changes that take place must take place in water. Blood, which is 90 percent water, carries materials throughout the body. Water carries wastes out of the body.

The average adult loses about 2.5 L of water each day. Only about 1.0 L of water is replaced by drinking liquids. The remainder is replaced by eating foods that contain water. Water is found in most foods.

REVIEW

1. Name three vitamins, and give their functions.
2. Name three minerals, and give their functions.
3. What foods are good sources of vitamin C? What foods are good sources of potassium?
4. Describe two functions of water in the body.

CHALLENGE What might be some of the characteristics of a disease that results from a lack of vitamin A?

Figure 22·5
About 70 percent of the body's mass is water.

543

22·3 A Balanced Diet

FOOD GROUPS

Foods are commonly divided into four groups. Each food group contains some of the nutrients needed by the body. By eating foods from each group, you can provide your body with all the nutrients it needs. The four food groups are the *milk group*, the *meat group*, the *fruit and vegetable group*, and the *grain group*.

The milk group provides proteins, minerals, fats, vitamins, and water. Although milk is the best source of nutrients in this group, foods such as yogurt and cheeses also supply many nutrients.

The meat group provides proteins, fats, and some vitamins and minerals. Notice in Figure 22·6 that the meat group contains not only meat, eggs, poultry, and seafood, but also peas and beans. Peas and beans are good sources of proteins, so they are included in the meat group.

The fruit and vegetable group provides the body with carbohydrates, vitamins, minerals, and water. Fruits and vegetables are also good sources

Figure 22·6

The milk group *(left)* and the meat group *(right)*.

544

of fiber, or roughage. **Fiber** is the part of plants that the body cannot digest, or break down. Fiber provides the bulk needed for proper movement of food through the body.

The grain group supplies starches, B vitamins, fiber, and proteins. This group includes many foods that are made from grains. These foods include bread, cereals, crackers, and pastas. What foods from the grain group can you see in Figure 22·7?

Eating the proper amounts of foods from the four food groups provides a *balanced diet*. A balanced diet is a daily intake of foods that supplies the right amounts of nutrients to the body. Look at Figure 22·8. It shows the number of daily servings, from the four food groups, recommended for a balanced diet.

Figure 22·8
The recommended daily servings of the four food groups.

CALORIES

You have probably heard the term *Calorie* (KAL uhr ee) used in discussions of foods. A **Calorie** is a measure of the energy available in a food. Different foods contain different amounts of Calories —that is, they supply different amounts of energy. The package labels on many foods show how many Calories are contained in those foods.

The number of Calories needed per day is different for everyone. In general, teenagers and young adults need the greatest number of Calories. Most males need more energy than do females. People who are very active use more energy than do people who are less active.

If a person takes in the same number of Calories as are used, that person's weight will not change. If a person takes in more Calories than are used, that person will gain weight as the body stores energy in the form of fat.

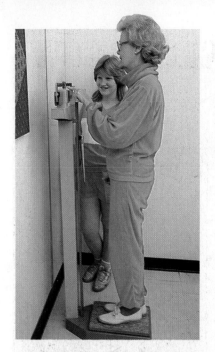

Figure 22·9
A combination of exercise and a good diet can help you maintain a healthy weight.

ACTIVITY   What Nutrition Information Is on Food Labels?

OBJECTIVE
Interpret the nutrition information listed on food labels.

MATERIALS
5 or more food labels from different foods

PROCEDURE
A. Make a data table with headings like those shown.
B. Locate the list of ingredients on several food labels. The ingredients are listed in order from the greatest amount to the smallest amount.
   1. What ingredient is first on each label?
   2. What ingredient is last on each label?
C. Locate the nutrition information on each label. This information should list the ingredients in a single serving. Complete your data table, using the nutrition information listed on each label.

RESULTS AND CONCLUSIONS
1. Of the foods that you studied, which contain proteins?
2. Which food has the most Calories per serving?
3. Which food has the fewest Calories per serving?
4. Which of the foods that you studied contain fats?
5. What information *not* listed in your data table is given on the food labels?
6. How can reading food labels help you plan a balanced diet?

FOOD	SERVING SIZE	CALORIES	PROTEINS	CARBOHYDRATES	FATS	VITAMINS	MINERALS

WARNING: Obesity is hazardous to your health. Will you one day see this type of warning label? Scientists at the National Institutes of Health in Washington, D.C., have studied obesity. They have found that an overweight person is more likely than a person of normal weight to have heart disease, high blood pressure, diabetes, and even some kinds of cancer.

But what is the cause of obesity? It has long been known that eating too much and exercising too little leads to obesity. But scientists have also found that obesity may be linked to characteristics of fat cells in the body.

In an overweight person the fat cells are up to two and a half times as large as the fat cells of an average-weight person. Some scientists believe that fat cells are "programmed" to maintain a given size. That means once these fat cells have grown to a large size, they tend to regain this size quickly. Thus, when an overweight person diets, or takes in small amounts of foods, the fat cells shrink. However, when this person takes in amounts of foods that would be normal for most other people, the fat cells grow to their former large size.

As scientists continue to study fat cells and their role in obesity, the best way to control and avoid obesity is to eat a balanced diet and to exercise regularly.

Obesity (oh BEE suh tee) is a condition in which a person's weight is more than 10 percent above normal for his or her height. Treatment for obesity includes increased exercise and a diet low in Calories. With increased exercise, the body uses more energy. If the person consumes fewer Calories than are used, the body loses weight. Before going on any special diet or exercise program, you should always check with your doctor.

REVIEW

1. Which food groups are a good source of fiber? Which food groups are a good source of proteins?

2. How many daily servings from each of the four food groups are needed to form a balanced diet?

3. How are Calories in food related to body weight?

CHALLENGE Before athletic events, many runners and other athletes eat large amounts of foods from the grain group. Why do athletes eat these foods?

22·4 The Digestive System

STAGES OF DIGESTION

Digestion (duh JEHS chuhn) is the process that breaks food into substances that can be used by cells. Digestion takes place in the *digestive system*, organs that work together to digest food.

There are two stages in the digestive process. *Mechanical digestion* is the process that breaks food into small pieces. Chewing is the first step in mechanical digestion. Mechanical digestion prepares food for *chemical digestion*. Chemical digestion is the process that chemically changes food into simpler substances. Only after food has been broken down by both processes can it be used by cells.

DIGESTIVE ORGANS

Refer to Figure 22·10 as you read about the path of food through the digestive system. Both stages of digestion begin in the mouth. In the mouth, food is

Figure 22·10
The digestive system.

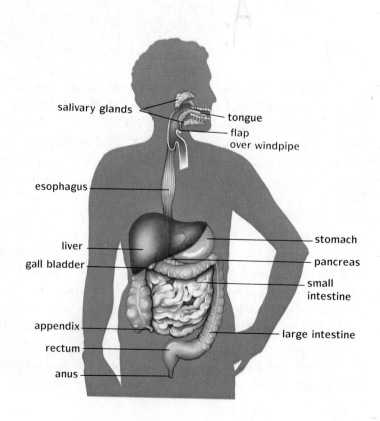

salivary glands
tongue
flap over windpipe
esophagus
liver
stomach
gall bladder
pancreas
small intestine
appendix
rectum
large intestine
anus

548

broken into pieces as it is chewed. The tongue pushes food around the mouth and helps to break the food into smaller pieces. At the same time, the food is mixed with a liquid called *saliva* (suh-LĪ vuh). It contains a substance that begins chemical digestion. Saliva also wets the food, which helps to move food through the digestive system. The tongue pushes food to the back of the mouth, where it is swallowed.

Figure 22·11
The processes of swallowing *(A)* and peristalsis *(B)* move food to the stomach.

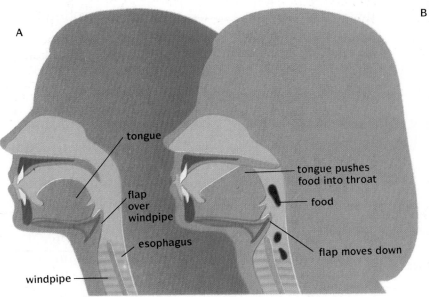

Food moves from the mouth to the esophagus (ee SAHF uh guhs). The **esophagus** is a muscular tube that connects the throat to the stomach. Notice in Figure 22·11*A* that the esophagus lies behind the windpipe. As food is swallowed, a flap of tissue covers the top of the windpipe. This action keeps food out of the windpipe. After food is swallowed, the flap moves up to allow air into the windpipe.

Food is pushed through the esophagus by a squeezing motion of muscles. The squeezing motion that pushes food through the digestive system is called **peristalsis** (pehr uh STAHL sihs). You can compare peristalsis to pushing a marble through a length of rubber tubing. You would need to pinch the tubing to push the marble forward. Figure 22·11*B* shows peristalsis in the esophagus. In relation to the food, where do the muscles contract?

Food moves from the esophagus to the stomach. The **stomach** is a J-shaped, muscular sac that stores food and helps to digest it. Food stays in the stomach for about 4 to 6 hours. The stomach can hold about 1.5 L of food. There are rings of muscles at each end of the stomach that control the flow of food to other parts of the digestive system.

There are three layers of muscles in the wall of the stomach. These muscles cause a churning action in the stomach. This action breaks food into smaller pieces and mixes the food with digestive liquids.

From the stomach, food moves into the small intestine. The **small intestine** is a long, coiled tube in which food is further digested and is absorbed. The small intestine is over 6 m long. It is called the small intestine because it is only about 2.5 cm in diameter. Most chemical digestion of food occurs in the small intestine. This is also where most food is absorbed into the bloodstream. Food takes about 5 to 8 hours to pass through the small intestine.

Food that has not been digested moves to the large intestine. The **large intestine** is a shorter, wider tube that absorbs water from undigested food. Notice in Figure 22·12 that the large intestine looks like an upside-down U surrounding the small

Figure 22·12

The stomach, small intestine, and large intestine *(left)*. How does the structure of the small intestine *(middle)* differ from that of the large intestine *(right)?*

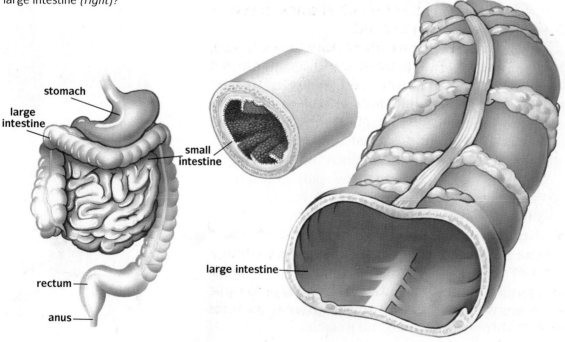

PUZZLER

When astronauts were first sent up in space, scientists wondered how the body would function without gravity. On the ground, in the presence of gravity, food travels down the esophagus to the stomach. It was found that the astronauts had no problems swallowing their food in space. Even if they were upside down, food went through the esophagus to the stomach. Why?

intestine. Food stays in the large intestine for about 8 to 10 hours, but no digestion occurs here. The large intestine is about 1.5 m long and about 6 cm in diameter. Why is it called the large intestine?

At the place where the small intestine joins the large intestine, there is a small pouch called the appendix (uh PEHN dihks). Sometimes the appendix becomes infected and causes pain. This condition is called appendicitis (uh pehn duh SĪ tihs). In severe cases the appendix is removed.

In Figure 22·12, locate the *rectum* (REHK tuhm), the last part of the large intestine. The rectum is a muscular organ that stores solid wastes until they leave the body. Solid wastes, called feces (FEE sees), are the end product of digestion. Feces leave the body through an opening called the *anus* (AY nuhs). The anus is at the lower end of the rectum.

REVIEW

1. What is the function of the digestive system?
2. How do mechanical digestion and chemical digestion differ?
3. List the organs through which food moves as it passes through the digestive system.

CHALLENGE Suggest a reason why water is not absorbed from the digestive system until after all the other digestive processes have been completed.

22·5 Digestion and Absorption

After completing this section, you will be able to

- **describe** the chemical digestion of food.
- **identify** the roles of the salivary glands, pancreas, and liver in digestion.
- **explain** how digested food is distributed to body cells.

The key terms in this section are
digestive enzyme
liver
pancreas
salivary glands
villi

You have learned that mechanical digestion breaks food into small pieces. You have also learned that cells cannot use most nutrients until they are further broken down by chemical digestion. Figure 22·13 shows which stage of digestion occurs in the mouth and in each of the two main digestive organs. Chemical digestion changes food into simpler substances. According to Figure 22·13, what are fats broken down into?

Chemical digestion takes place in the presence of digestive enzymes. A **digestive enzyme** is a substance that chemically breaks down a nutrient. Each digestive organ makes a different set of enzymes. Look again at Figure 22·13. In which organs does chemical digestion break down proteins? In which organs does chemical digestion break down fats? Each enzyme acts on only one type of nutrient. For example, digestive enzymes that act on proteins do not act on fats.

Enzymes are made both in the digestive organs you have learned about and in glands. Glands that produce digestive enzymes are called *digestive glands*. These glands are attached to digestive organs by small tubes, or ducts. Enzymes move through these ducts into the organs in which food is digested.

Figure 22·13

The digestion of carbohydrates, fats, and proteins.

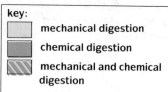

key:
- mechanical digestion
- chemical digestion
- mechanical and chemical digestion

Type of Food	Mouth	Stomach	Small Intestine	End Products
carbohydrates				sugars
proteins				amino acids
fats				fatty acids and glycerol

Recall that mechanical digestion begins in the mouth. With the action of saliva, chemical digestion also begins in the mouth. Saliva contains an enzyme that begins the chemical digestion of starches. Saliva is produced by the **salivary** (SAL uh vehr ee) **glands**. These glands are shown in Figure 22·14. Saliva breaks down starches into sugars. If you chew a cracker for several seconds before swallowing, you may notice a sweet taste. The sweet taste is a result of saliva breaking a starch into a sugar.

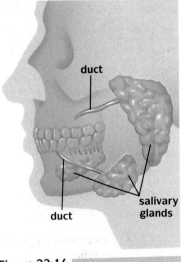

Figure 22·14
The location of the salivary glands.

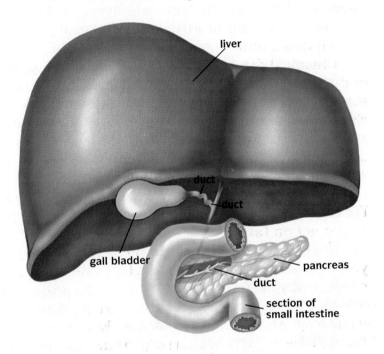

Figure 22·15
The liver, gall bladder, and pancreas.

Chemical digestion continues in the stomach. The stomach makes a liquid called *gastric* (GAS-trihk) *juice*. Gastric juice is a mixture of enzymes and acid that chemically digests food in the stomach. Gastric juice begins the chemical digestion of proteins. As food is churned and mixed with gastric juice in the stomach, the partly digested food is changed to a thick liquid.

This liquid moves into the small intestine. This is where most chemical digestion and most absorption take place. In the small intestine, fats are acted upon by a liquid from the liver. Locate the liver in Figure 22·15. The **liver** is a large, lobed organ that produces *bile*. Bile is a liquid that helps to digest fats. However, bile is not a digestive enzyme. Bile breaks fats into tiny droplets. The droplets of fat are easier for enzymes to digest. Bile is stored in a saclike organ called the *gall bladder*. From the gall bladder, bile moves into the small intestine.

The pancreas (PAN kree uhs) also plays a role in digestion and absorption in the small intestine. The pancreas is found below the stomach. The **pancreas** is a digestive gland that produces pancreatic juice. *Pancreatic juice,* which is also released into the small intestine, is a mixture of several digestive enzymes. The small intestine also makes digestive enzymes. Enzymes made in the wall of the small intestine make up *intestinal juice*. Intestinal juice and pancreatic juice work together. These juices break proteins into amino acids. Intestinal juices also break fats into glycerol and fatty acids, and carbohydrates into simple sugars.

Figure 22·16

Villi in the small intestine, as seen with a scanning electron microscope *(A)*. This close-up of a villus shows the blood vessels in the villus *(B)*.

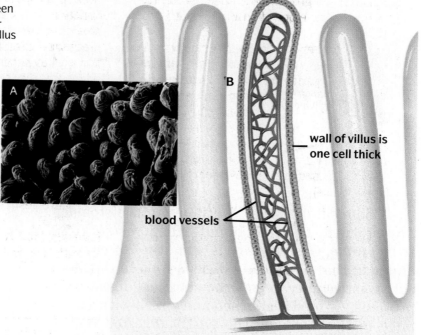

wall of villus is one cell thick

blood vessels

villus (tuft of hair)

After food has been broken down, it is absorbed into the bloodstream. This process takes place in the small intestine. The inner wall of the small intestine is covered with millions of tiny fingerlike structures called **villi** (sing., villus). Look at the villi shown in Figure 22·16. Each villus contains many blood vessels. Nutrients in the small intestine pass through the villi into these blood vessels. The many villi form a large surface through which nutrients are absorbed. Blood carries the nutrients from the villi to cells throughout the body.

REVIEW

1. Describe what happens to fats, proteins, and carbohydrates in the digestive system.
2. Describe the role of the pancreas and the liver in digestion.
3. What happens to food in the small intestine?

CHALLENGE Do you think it is possible for a person to live without a stomach? Explain your answer.

CHAPTER SUMMARY

The main ideas in this chapter are listed below. Read these statements before you answer the Chapter Review questions.

- Nutrients provide the body with energy and material for growth and repair. Some nutrients help the body to use other nutrients. (22·1)
- Carbohydrates provide energy; fats provide energy and building materials; proteins provide material for growth and repair. Proteins are also needed to form enzymes, which control body functions. (22·1)
- Vitamins and minerals are nutrients that help the body to function normally and to use other nutrients. Vitamins and minerals are not be used as a source of energy for the body. (22·2)
- Water is a nutrient needed for chemical changes and most functions in the body. Water makes up the most of the body's mass. (22·2)
- The four food groups are the milk group, the meat group, the fruit and vegetable group, and the grain group. (22·3)

- A balanced diet provides the body with the needed amounts of all nutrients. Eating a variety of foods from the four food groups provides a balanced diet. (22·3)
- Mechanical digestion and chemical digestion work together to break down foods into substances that can be used by cells. (22·4)
- In the digestive system, food moves from the mouth through the esophagus to the stomach and then to the small intestine. Undigested food moves into the large intestine. (22·4)
- Digestive enzymes break down nutrients throughout the digestive system. Most chemical digestion occurs in the small intestine. (22·5)
- Digested food is absorbed into the blood through the wall of the small intestine. (22·5)

The key terms in this chapter are listed below. Use each term in a sentence that shows the meaning of the term.

Calorie	fats	nutrient	small intestine
carbohydrates	fiber	pancreas	stomach
digestion	large intestine	peristalsis	villi
digestive enzyme	liver	proteins	vitamin
esophagus	mineral	salivary glands	

Chapter Review

VOCABULARY

Use the key terms from the previous page to complete the following sentences correctly.

1. The _____ is a long, coiled tube in which food is digested and absorbed.
2. _____ are nutrients that provide the body with its main source of energy.
3. An element that helps the body to function normally and to use other nutrients is a/an _____ .
4. A J-shaped, muscular sac that stores and helps to digest food is the _____ .
5. Any substance that the body needs to live and grow is a/an _____ .
6. The _____ is a large, lobed organ that produces bile.
7. The squeezing motion that pushes food through the digestive system is called _____ .
8. Nutrients that provide the body with material for cell growth and repair, and that control body functions, are called _____ .
9. Fingerlike structures through which food is absorbed in the small intestine are called _____ .
10. The _____ is a short, wide tube in which water is absorbed from undigested food.

CONCEPTS

Write the correct term for each structure shown in the diagram.

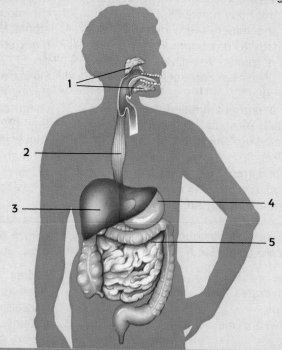

Identify each statement as True or False. If a statement is false, replace the underlined term or phrase with a term or phrase that makes the statement true.

6. Amino acids make up proteins.
7. A nutrient is a measure of the energy available in food.
8. Chewing is the first step in chemical digestion.
9. Gastric juice chemically digests food in the small intestine.
10. Bile is stored in a saclike organ called the gall bladder.

Answer the following questions in complete sentences.

11. List the six kinds of nutrients, and briefly describe how each is used by the body.
12. Identify the four food groups, describe the nutrients provided by each, and give examples of foods from each group.
13. Make a menu for a day's meals to provide the recommended number of servings from the four food groups.
14. How do mechanical digestion and chemical digestion work together to break down food?

APPLICATION/ CRITICAL THINKING

1. Give several examples of healthful snacks that can be part of a balanced diet.
2. How can reading food labels help in planning a balanced diet?
3. Why would a person with a physically active job need a higher intake of food than a person with a less active job?
4. The small intestine is long and coiled, and its inner surface is folded and covered with villi. How is the structure of the small intestine related to its function?
5. Imagine that food was not broken into small pieces by mechanical digestion. How would this situation affect chemical digestion?

EXTENSION

1. Go to the library to research Alexis St. Martin. How did he contribute to the study of digestion?
2. Find out what diseases are caused by too little of the vitamins C, D, and B_1. Report on the symptoms and treatment of each disease.
3. What is cholesterol? Find out how cholesterol functions in the body. Why is it important to limit the intake of cholesterol?

CHAPTER 23

TRANSPORT, RESPIRATION, AND EXCRETION

All of the cells in your body must receive an adequate supply of blood. Blood carries oxygen and nutrients to the cells and carries waste materials away from the cells. The heart is the vital organ that keeps the blood circulating.

This photograph shows valves inside the heart. The long strands that you see are connected to, and are part of, the valve that closes after the blood is pumped through the opening.

- *What body systems transport materials to body tissues?*
- *How does breathing relate to the exchange of gases in cells?*
- *How are waste products removed from the body?*

23·1 Blood

After completing this section, you will be able to

- **describe** the functions of blood and **identify** its parts.
- **explain** the role of red blood cells in carrying oxygen.
- **describe** the functions of white blood cells and platelets.
- **identify** the major blood types and **distinguish** between them.

The key terms in this section are
blood types   **red blood cell**
plasma   **white blood cell**
platelet

FUNCTIONS OF BLOOD

In an adult about one sixteenth of the body weight is blood. Blood flows through tubes called blood vessels. The heart pumps blood through the blood vessels. Together the heart, blood vessels, and blood are known as the *circulatory* (SER kyuh-luh tawr ee) *system*.

Blood has many functions. These functions include carrying materials through the body, helping to keep a constant body temperature, and fighting disease. Carrying materials through the body is the blood's main job. Blood carries oxygen and nutrients to body cells. Wastes from all parts of the body are carried by blood to organs that remove the wastes. Chemical messages are carried from one organ to another by the blood.

COMPOSITION OF BLOOD

Blood includes several types of cells in a large amount of liquid. The liquid portion of the blood is called **plasma**. Figure 23·1 shows blood that has been separated into plasma and cells. Note that more than half of the blood is plasma. Plasma is made of water, nutrients, wastes, proteins, and other substances. Over 90 percent of plasma is composed of water.

Figure 23·1
Blood can be separated into plasma and cells.

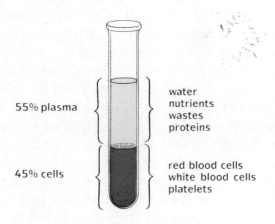

55% plasma — water, nutrients, wastes, proteins

45% cells — red blood cells, white blood cells, platelets

The most numerous cells in the blood are the red blood cells. A **red blood cell** is a blood cell that carries oxygen. Look at the red blood cells in Figure 23·2 (*right*). Notice that they are thinner at the center than at the edges. This shape makes red blood cells flexible and makes it easier for them to exchange gases.

Figure 23·2

Red blood cells and white blood cells as seen through a light microscope *(left)*. Red blood cells as seen through an SEM *(right)*.

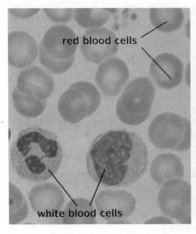

red blood cells

white blood cells

A mature red blood cell lacks a nucleus. The cell consists mainly of a red substance called *hemoglobin* (HEE muh gloh buhn). Hemoglobin is a protein that joins with oxygen and releases oxygen. As blood passes through the lungs, oxygen joins with the hemoglobin in red blood cells. In other parts of the body, the hemoglobin in the red blood cell releases oxygen. The oxygen is used by body cells to release energy from food.

Blood also contains white blood cells. A **white blood cell** is a blood cell that defends the body against disease. White blood cells have nuclei and are larger than red blood cells. White blood cells, shown in Figure 23·3, change shape as they move. Some white cells capture bacteria in much the same way that amoebas get food. Other white cells release chemicals that fight infections.

Blood also contains platelets. A **platelet** is a cell fragment that acts in blood clotting. The clotting of blood is the process that seals cuts in blood vessels. Platelets are formed by bone marrow cells that split into pieces. Follow the steps in Figure 23·4 as you read about the process of clotting on the next page.

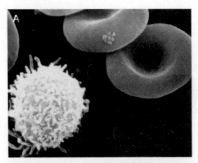
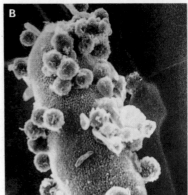

Figure 23·3

An SEM view of a white blood cell among red blood cells *(A)*. Many white blood cells attack a foreign particle *(B)*.

561

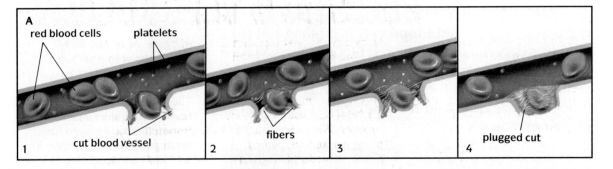

A

red blood cells   platelets

cut blood vessel   1

fibers   2

3

plugged cut   4

1. As blood leaks out of a cut blood vessel, platelets stick to the cut edges.

2. Platelets release chemicals that cause proteins in the plasma to form fibers.

3. The cut is soon filled when a mesh of fibers traps platelets and some red cells.

4. The cut is plugged by a solid mass of platelets, fibers, and red blood cells.

BLOOD TYPES

When a person is seriously injured, a lot of blood may be lost. Lost blood can be replaced with blood from another person. The process by which blood is taken from one person and given to another is called *transfusion*. It is important that a person receives the right type of blood during a transfusion. **Blood types** are groups into which blood is classified based on chemical differences.

The most important blood groups are the ABO blood types. This set includes four blood types known as *A, B, AB,* and *O*. These four types result from substances found on the surface of red blood cells. Type A blood has red cells with substance A on their surface. Type B red cells have substance B on their surface. Both substance A and substance B are found on the surface of type AB red cells. Neither substance is found on type O cells.

Although transfusion has become routine, it must be done with great care. Before transfusion, blood must be tested for the ABO type and for other blood groups. Typing is done by mixing a sample of blood with a testing solution. Figure 23·5 *(top)* shows type A blood being tested. Blood cells have

Figure 23·4

The process of blood clotting *(A)*. Red blood cells caught in a mesh of fibers *(B)*.

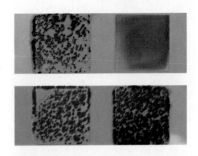

Figure 23·5

Typing blood: type A *(top)* and type AB *(bottom)*.

Often when people are injured or having surgery, they need a blood transfusion. Before receiving a transfusion, a patient's blood type must be matched. But blood of the right type may not be available to be used for the transfusion. To solve this problem, scientists have been studying artificial red blood cells.

One kind of artificial red cell is made by mixing hemoglobin with two types of fats. The fats form a membrane around droplets of hemoglobin. The result is cell-like objects that can carry oxygen. These cell-like objects would match any patient's blood type.

Artificial red cells are smaller than natural red cells. This could make artificial cells useful for patients with blocked blood vessels. Small artificial cells may be able to carry oxygen past blockages.

The membrane of artificial cells is stronger than that of natural red blood cells. This feature may make artificial cells useful in heart surgery. While the heart is being worked on, pumps circulate blood through the body. These pumps put a lot of pressure on the blood cells. Cells with a stronger membrane could better withstand these pressures. The use of artificial red cells could save many lives. Hopefully, the research and testing will soon be over and artificial red blood cells can begin to be used.

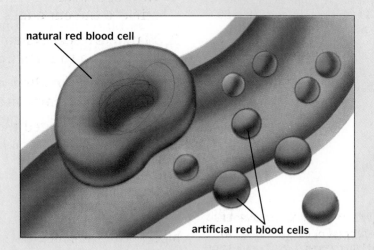

natural red blood cell

artificial red blood cells

clumped together in the solution that tests for substance A. Blood cells have not clumped together in the solution that tests for substance B. Similar clumping takes place in the body if the blood from the transfusion does not match that of the person. If this clumping were to occur, serious illness or death might result.

REVIEW

1. Describe the composition and functions of blood.
2. What is found within red blood cells? What does it do?
3. What are the functions of white blood cells?
4. Describe the process of blood clotting.
5. Why must blood be matched before transfusion?

CHALLENGE There are about a thousand times more red cells than white cells in blood. Relate this difference in number to the functions of each type of cell.

23·2 Blood Vessels and Lymph

TYPES OF BLOOD VESSELS

Recall that blood is pumped through blood vessels to all parts of the body. Blood vessels are the tubes in which the blood travels. There are several kinds of blood vessels. Blood vessels include arteries, capillaries, and veins.

An **artery** (AHR tuhr ee) is a blood vessel that carries blood away from the heart. Arteries have thick, muscular walls, as you can see in Figure 23·6. Blood is pumped out of the heart and into arteries in spurts. Elastic fibers in the walls of arteries allow the arteries to stretch as blood surges through them. The muscle in the walls of arteries controls how much blood can flow through. The blood flowing in an artery is under pressure. The thick, flexible wall of an artery can withstand this pressure.

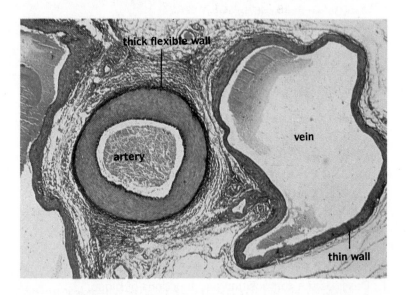

thick flexible wall

vein

artery

thin wall

Figure 23·6
Cross section of an artery and a vein. Why is the wall of the artery so thick?

Two large arteries carry blood out of the heart. These arteries divide into smaller branches away from the heart. The smaller arteries carry blood to the body's organs. Within organs the arteries branch into even smaller blood vessels. The smallest blood vessels are capillaries (KAP uh lehr eez). A **capillary** is a blood vessel whose wall is only one cell thick. Capillaries are only a few micrometers in diameter. As you can see in Figure 23·7, capillaries are so small that blood cells move through in single file.

Notice in Figure 23·8 that a single small artery branches into many capillaries. The capillaries form a network called a *capillary bed*. Much of the work of circulation takes place in the capillary beds. Because the walls of capillaries are thin, many materials can pass through. Oxygen and nutrients move out of the blood into surrounding tissues, where they are used. Carbon dioxide and wastes from tissues pass through capillaries into the blood and are then carried away.

Note in Figure 23·8 that blood flows from capillaries into small veins. A **vein** is a blood vessel that carries blood toward the heart. The walls of veins are much thinner than those of arteries. Look back at Figure 23·6. Compare the walls of the artery and the vein. What might happen if the walls of arteries were as thin as those of veins?

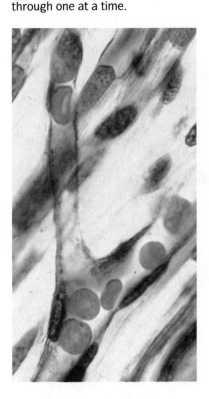

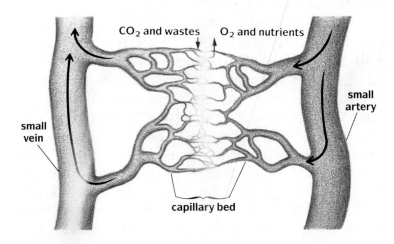

CO₂ and wastes — O₂ and nutrients

small artery

small vein

capillary bed

Small veins join together to form larger veins. Veins from all of the body's organs join into a few large veins that return blood to the heart. Recall that blood is pumped away from the heart with high pressure. However, there is little pressure to move the blood through the veins toward the heart. Thus, veins have valves, flaps of tissue that keep blood flowing toward the heart.

Figure 23·9
The structure of the lymphatic system. Where can you find clusters of lymph nodes?

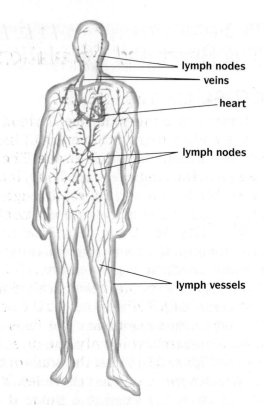

lymph nodes
veins
heart
lymph nodes
lymph vessels

LYMPHATIC SYSTEM

Small amounts of plasma leak out of the capillaries. This liquid is called **lymph**. It surrounds all cells and bathes the tissues. As more and more lymph collects around cells, some of the lymph moves into special vessels. These vessels form the *lymphatic system*. You can see the lymphatic system in Figure 23·9. Lymph is filtered in the structures called *lymph nodes* as shown in Figure 23·9. Cells in these nodes destroy bacteria and other foreign particles. Lymph flows from lymph vessels to two veins in the neck. Thus the liquid lost from blood in the capillaries is returned to the blood by the lymphatic system.

REVIEW

1. Compare the structures of arteries, capillaries, and veins. What is the function of each?
2. What exchanges of materials occur in the capillaries?
3. Where does lymph come from? Where does it go?

CHALLENGE Blockage of a lymphatic vessel causes the surrounding tissue to swell. Explain why.

23·3 The Heart and Circulation

STRUCTURE OF THE HEART

The heart is a pump that keeps blood flowing through the body's many kilometers of blood vessels. Most of the heart is muscle tissue. The heart is the hardest-working muscle in the body. It begins to beat before birth and continues throughout life. Look at Figure 23·10 as you read about the structure of the heart. The heart contains four spaces, or chambers. Each of the two upper chambers of the heart is called an **atrium** (AY tree uhm) (pl., *atria*). Each of the two lower chambers is called a **ventricle** (VEHN truh kuhl). Valves connect the atria with the ventricles. A **valve** is made up of flaps of tissue that allows blood to flow in only one direction.

Notice in Figure 23·10 that the walls of the atria are thinner than those of the ventricles. The atria collect blood from the veins and pump it directly into the ventricles. Compare the walls of the two ventricles. Note that the wall of the left ventricle is thicker than that of the right. The right ventricle pumps blood to the lungs. The muscular left ventricle pumps blood throughout the body.

After completing this section, you will be able to

- **describe** the structure of the heart.
- **trace** the pattern of blood flow through the body.
- **describe** the causes of several disorders of circulation.
- **identify** ways to reduce the chances of developing circulatory disorders.

The key terms in this section are

atrium	valve
pulse	ventricle

atrium (entrance room)

Figure 23·10
The structure of the heart.

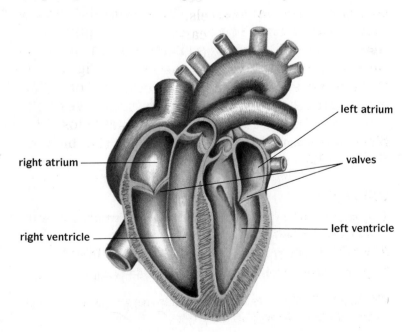

right atrium

right ventricle

left atrium

valves

left ventricle

567

CIRCULATION

In 23·11 *right*, find two blood vessels labeled *vena cava* (VEE nuh KAY vuh) (pl., *venae cavae*). The upper vena cava carries blood from parts of the body that are above the heart. The lower vena cava carries blood from all parts below the heart. The following steps are numbered in Figure 23·11 *(left)*.

1. Blood from the vena cavae flows into the right atrium. This blood has little oxygen. The oxygen was used as the blood flowed through the body.
2. The right atrium pumps the blood through a valve into the right ventricle.
3. The right ventricle pumps blood through a valve into a large artery. This artery goes to the lungs where oxygen is absorbed and carbon dioxide is released.
4. The oxygen-rich blood from the lungs flows through veins to the left atrium.
5. The left atrium pumps the blood through a valve to the left ventricle.
6. The strong left ventricle pumps the blood through a valve into the body's largest artery, the *aorta* (ay AWR tuh). From here the blood moves to all organs except the lungs.

NOTE In Figure 23·11, the right side of the heart is shaded blue. This is to show that the blood has less oxygen. Blood is never blue.

Figure 23·11
Circulation of blood through the heart *(left)*. Main structures of the circulatory system *(right)*.

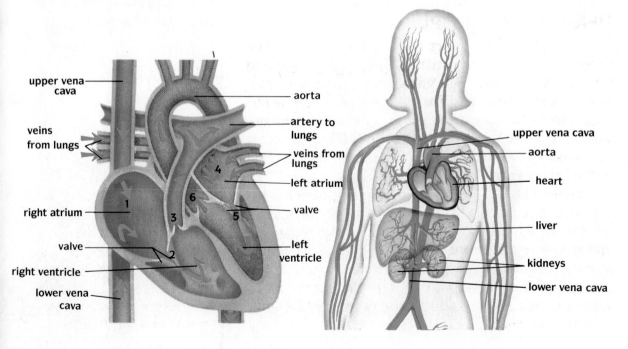

How Does the Pulse Vary?

OBJECTIVES

Determine factors that cause the pulse to change.
Construct a graph to show variations in pulse.

MATERIALS

clock or watch with second hand, graph paper

PROCEDURE

A. Make a data table like the one shown.

RESTING PULSE	PULSE AFTER EXERCISE			
	0 min	2 min	4 min	6 min

B. Work with a partner. Have your partner sit quietly for a few moments.

C. Take your partner's pulse by placing two fingers on the inside of your partner's wrist near the base of the thumb. Move your fingers until you can feel the pulse. Using a clock or watch, count the number of pulse beats in 30 seconds. Multiply the result by 2 to find the number of pulse beats in 1 minute. Record this number as the resting pulse.

D. Have your partner jog in place for 2 minutes and then sit down. Immediately take your partner's pulse as in step **C**. Record the result.

E. Have your partner continue sitting. Take his or her pulse again after 2, 4, and 6 minutes of sitting. Record the results.

RESULTS AND CONCLUSIONS

1. Make a bar graph of your results.
2. Did exercise cause the pulse to increase or decrease? What change occurs in muscles during exercise? How is this change in the muscles related to the change in pulse?
3. Did the pulse return to its resting level after exercise? If so, how long did it take? If not, how much longer do you think it would take?

HEARTBEAT AND PULSE

Not all of the heart muscle contracts at the same time. The atria contract first, pumping blood into the ventricles. The ventricles contract a fraction of a second later. For this reason, each heartbeat can be heard in two parts. The weak contraction of the atria makes one sound. This sound is followed by the stronger sound caused by contraction of the ventricles.

When the left ventricle contracts, blood flows into the arteries and the walls of the arteries are stretched by the pressure. When the ventricle opens, the arteries return to their original sizes. The stretching and relaxing of the arteries can be felt as the **pulse**. The pulse can be felt in places where arteries pass close to the skin. Figure 23·12 shows how to take the pulse.

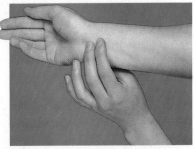

Figure 23·12
A method for taking the pulse.

DISORDERS OF CIRCULATION

Disorders of the circulatory system are one of the main causes of death among Americans. Many of these disorders can be prevented. One of the most common problems of circulation is known as *atherosclerosis* (ath uhr oh skluh ROH sihs). Atherosclerosis is the build-up of fatty materials on the inner walls of arteries. There are several types of fatty materials in these build-ups. One such material is *cholesterol* (kuh LEHS tuh rohl).

Compare the two arteries shown in Figure 23·13. Notice that one artery is partly blocked. Such blockage reduces the flow of blood, and less oxygen reaches the tissues. Tissues cannot live without a supply of oxygen. A *heart attack* is one problem that can result from atherosclerosis. Heart attacks involve death of or damage to part of the heart muscle. If arteries leading to the brain get clogged, a *stroke* may result. Strokes occur when brain cells die from lack of oxygen.

When arteries become clogged, the opening through the arteries becomes smaller. The heart works harder to push the blood through. The pressure of blood in the arteries rises. Abnormally high blood pressure is called *hypertension* (hī puhr-TEHN shuhn). It puts a strain on the heart and can lead to heart disease. Hypertension can be detected by a blood pressure check. This problem is easier to treat if it is found early.

Figure 23·13

Cross section of a normal artery *(A)*. Cross section of an artery affected by atherosclerosis *(B)*. What kind of material has built up on the walls of the artery?

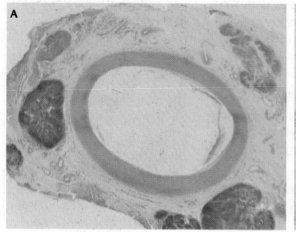

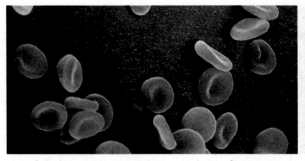
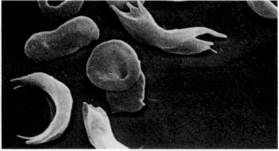

Figure 23·14
Normal red blood cells *(A)*.
Blood cells affected by sickle cell disease *(B)*.

Several factors are thought to cause atherosclerosis and hypertension. These factors include lack of exercise, a diet high in animal fats, and smoking. The chance of developing these disorders is also thought to be inherited. Regular exercise, a balanced diet, and not smoking reduce the chance of developing circulatory disorders.

Some disorders affect the blood cells rather than the blood vessels or heart. *Anemia* (uh NEE-mee uh) is a disorder in which there are too few red blood cells or too little hemoglobin in the blood. In either case, too little oxygen is brought to the body's tissues. Some forms of anemia are caused by poor diet. Other forms are inherited. *Sickle cell disease* is an inherited anemia. Look at the red blood cells in Figure 23·14*B*. How might sickle cell disease have gotten its name? As with other forms of anemia, not enough oxygen gets to the tissues. Transfusions can help in treating people with this disease.

Leukemia (loo KEE mee uh) is a disorder in which many immature white blood cells are produced. These immature cells do not work properly in defending the body against disease.

REVIEW

1. List in order all the structures blood must pass through to get from the right atrium to the aorta.
2. What do heart attacks and strokes have in common?
3. How can the chances of developing circulatory disorders be reduced?

CHALLENGE Sometimes, people with severe atherosclerosis appear to be healthy. Why might they suddenly have a heart attack after heavy exercise?

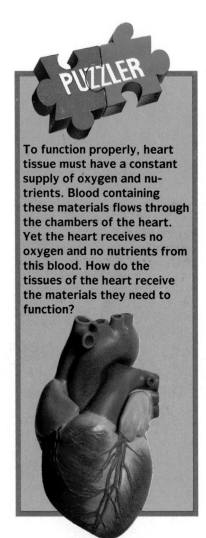

PUZZLER

To function properly, heart tissue must have a constant supply of oxygen and nutrients. Blood containing these materials flows through the chambers of the heart. Yet the heart receives no oxygen and no nutrients from this blood. How do the tissues of the heart receive the materials they need to function?

23·4 The Respiratory System

PARTS OF THE RESPIRATORY SYSTEM

Oxygen is used in all cells in the body to get energy from food. The process of getting energy from food is called *cellular respiration*. Breathing supplies the oxygen used in respiration.

Breathing is the process in which oxygen is taken in from the air and carbon dioxide is given off. The body absorbs oxygen from the air that is taken in when you *inhale*. Carbon dioxide is given off in the air that you *exhale*. The structures used in breathing make up the *respiratory* (REHS puhr uh-tawr ee) *system*.

Refer to Figure 23·16A to trace the path that air takes during breathing. People most often breathe through the nose. Air passing through the nose is warmed, filtered, and moistened to help protect the cells that line the lungs.

From the nose, air enters the *pharynx* (FAR-ihngks). The pharynx is the region behind the nose leading down the throat. At the bottom of the pharynx is the *larynx* (LAR ihngks), or voice box. The larynx contains the vocal cords, which produce the sounds of human speech. A flap of tissue is found at the top of the larynx. When food is swallowed, this flap of tissue moves down to cover the larynx. This action keeps food out of the respiratory system.

Figure 23·15

Respiration in body cells *(A)*. Breathing *(B)*.

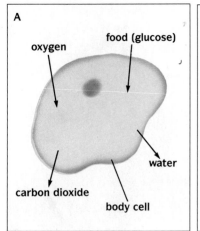

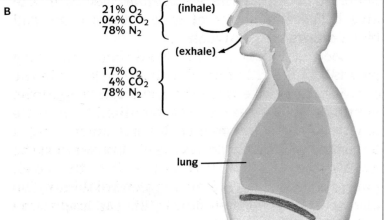

572

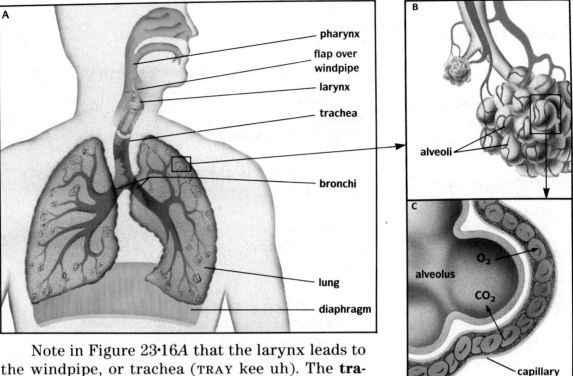

Figure 23·16

The structure of the human respiratory system (A). Enlargement of the alveoli (B). Exchange of gases between an alveolus and a capillary (C).

Note in Figure 23·16A that the larynx leads to the windpipe, or trachea (TRAY kee uh). The **trachea** is a tube that carries air from the larynx to the lungs. The walls of the trachea contain rings of cartilage that keep the air passage open. The trachea divides into two branches in the chest. The two branches of the trachea are called **bronchi** (BRAHNG-kī) (sing., *bronchus*). Each bronchus leads to a lung. Within the lungs the bronchi divide into smaller and smaller branches. The smallest branches end in groups of tiny air sacs called **alveoli** (al VEE uh lī) (sing., *alveolus*). Notice the grapelike cluster of sacs in Figure 23·16B. In these grapelike clusters are the alveoli. The exchange of gases between air and blood occurs in the alveoli.

Look at Figure 23·16C. Note that a capillary passes by the wall of an alveolus. The blood in the capillary has come from the right ventricle of the heart. This blood has much carbon dioxide and little oxygen. The air in the alveolus has much oxygen but little carbon dioxide. As the blood flows past the alveolus, oxygen passes from the air to the blood. Carbon dioxide passes from the blood to the air. The oxygen-rich blood then flows from the lung to the left atrium of the heart.

bronchos (windpipe)

alveus (hollow)

BREATHING

Air in the alveoli is constantly being changed. Inhaling brings in more oxygen. Exhaling carries away carbon dioxide. Inhaling and exhaling require the action of several muscles. The main muscle used in breathing is the diaphragm (DĪ uh fram). The **diaphragm** is a sheet of muscle that forms the lower edge of the chest cavity. Look back at Figure 23·16 to locate the diaphragm. The muscles between the ribs also assist the diaphragm during breathing.

Refer to Figure 23·17 as you read about how breathing occurs. In part *A*, note that before inhaling occurs, the diaphragm curves upward. Now look at part *B*. You can see that the diaphragm contracts and moves downward. The ribs move outward and upward at the same time. These actions increase the size of the chest cavity. Thus, contraction of the diaphragm and rib muscles causes a person to inhale.

In part *C*, notice that the diaphragm moves upward again as it relaxes. The ribs move inward and downward at the same time. The chest cavity is made smaller, pushing air out of the lungs. Relaxation of the diaphragm and rib muscles causes a person to exhale.

When the chest cavity expands, the space in the lungs is larger. This causes the pressure in the lungs to fall. The atmospheric pressure is greater and this causes air to rush into the lungs.

Figure 23·17

Position of the diaphragm before a person inhales *(A)*. Inhaling: diaphragm moves down and chest cavity increases *(B)*. Exhaling: diaphragm moves up and chest cavity decreases *(C)*.

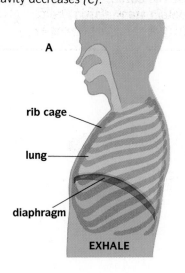

A

rib cage

lung

diaphragm

EXHALE

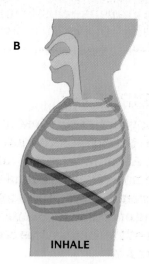

B

INHALE

C

EXHALE

OBJECTIVES

Construct a model of the respiratory system.
Demonstrate how air moves into and out of the lungs.

MATERIALS

sharp scissors, 1-L plastic bottle, small balloon, short length of plastic tubing, masking tape, one-hole rubber stopper, large round balloon, large rubber band

PROCEDURE

A. Use scissors to carefully cut a plastic bottle in half around its center. Use the upper half for this activity.
B. Place the neck of a small balloon over one end of a length of plastic tubing. Use tape to seal the balloon around the tube. Pass the tubing through the neck of the bottle so that the end with the balloon is within the bottle. Pass the free end of the plastic tubing through the hole in a rubber stopper. Push the stopper into the neck of the bottle, as shown.
C. Cut the neck off a large balloon. Discard the neck. Stretch the balloon across the wide bottom opening of the bottle. Secure the balloon with a rubber band.
D. Pull down on the stretched balloon. Observe what happens to the balloon inside the bottle. Release the balloon. Again observe what happens to the balloon inside the bottle.

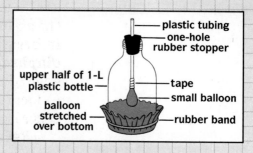

RESULTS AND CONCLUSIONS

1. What happened to the balloon inside the bottle as you pulled down on the stretched balloon? What happened when you released the stretched balloon?
2. Make a table like the one shown. Complete the table to show which parts of the real respiratory system match the parts of the model.

PARTS OF MODEL	RESPIRATORY SYSTEM
Balloon inside bottle	
Plastic tubing	
Bottle	
Stretched balloon	

3. How did the volume of the bottle change when you pulled down on the stretched balloon? What effect did this have on the balloon inside the bottle?
4. The lungs contain many elastic fibers. How do these fibers help you exhale?

DISORDERS OF RESPIRATION

There are several disorders that cause problems in breathing. One of the more common disorders is *asthma* (AZ muh). Asthma is a condition in which the bronchi become narrowed. Asthma may occur as a reaction to foreign particles, such as plant pollen. The narrowing of the bronchi makes it harder to get air in and out of the lungs. This causes the diaphragm to work harder.

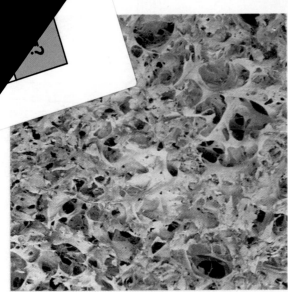
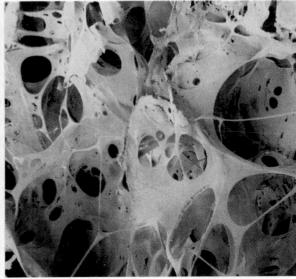

Figure 23·18

Normal lung tissue *(left)* and lung tissue damaged by emphysema *(right)*. Notice that the damaged lung has larger spaces and less living tissue to absorb oxygen.

Emphysema (ehm fuh SEE muh) is a disorder in which the walls of the alveoli are destroyed. In Figure 23·18 you can see the damage caused by this disease. As the walls of the alveoli are destroyed, less oxygen can be absorbed into the blood. A person with emphysema becomes weak and easily tired from the decreased oxygen supply. Smoking is the major cause of emphysema. Some forms of air pollution also help to cause emphysema.

Lung cancer is another respiratory disease where 84 percent is caused by smoking. The lung cancer death rate has been on the rise since 1930, as shown in Figure 23·19. Cancer is a disease in which cells divide in an abnormal way. Cancer cells do not do the job of normal lung cells. Over 40 million people have realized how dangerous smoking can be and have quit smoking.

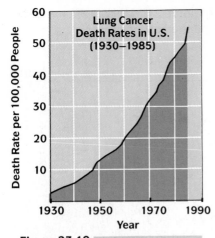

Figure 23·19

The number of people who develop lung cancer has increased in recent years.

REVIEW

1. List in order the structures through which air passes in getting from the nose to the capillaries in the lung.
2. What muscles are used in breathing? How do these muscles cause you to inhale? To exhale?
3. What are two respiratory problems thought to be caused by smoking?

CHALLENGE People with emphysema are unable to do physical exercise. Explain why.

23·5 The Excretory System

Some life processes release waste products in the body. *Excretion* is the process by which wastes are removed from the body. The organs that help in excretion—the lungs, skin, and kidneys—make up the *excretory system*.

Getting energy from food releases carbon dioxide, water, and heat as waste products. The carbon dioxide and some of the water are removed by the lungs. Heat is given off through the skin.

The breakdown of extra proteins in the body forms a waste called *urea*. Urea is a poison and must be removed. Some life processes release salt as a waste product. Salt is not a poison, but it must be excreted to prevent it from building up. Small amounts of urea and salt are excreted by the skin as sweat, but most is excreted by the kidneys. The **kidneys** are the main organs of excretion in humans. Two kidneys lie at the back of the body cavity above the hips. The kidneys form a liquid called *urine*, which contains wastes and water. Locate the kidneys in Figure 23·20. What other organs of excretion are shown?

Each kidney contains about a million microscopic units called *nephrons*. A nephron is a structure in the kidneys that filters blood and forms urine. A nephron is made up of a coiled tube around

After completing this section, you will be able to

- **identify** the sources of wastes that the body produces and the organs that eliminate these wastes.
- **describe** the process by which urine is formed.

The key terms in this section are
bladder   ureters
kidneys   urethra

Figure 23·20
The organs of excretion.

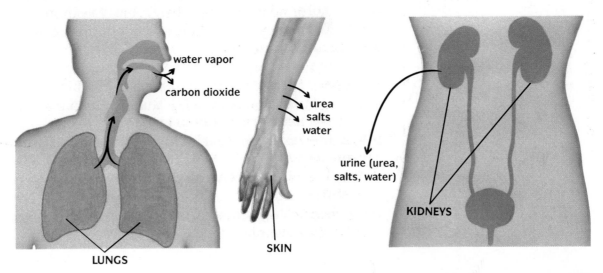

water vapor

carbon dioxide

urea
salts
water

urine (urea, salts, water)

KIDNEYS

SKIN

LUNGS

577

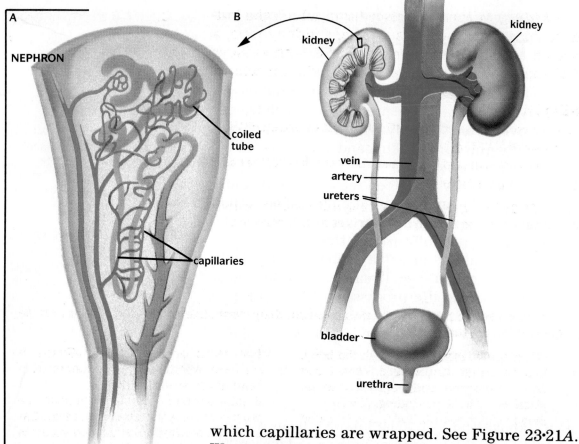

A

NEPHRON

coiled
tube

capillaries

B

kidney

kidney

vein

artery

ureters

bladder

urethra

Figure 23·21

Enlargement of a nephron *(A)*.
Main structures of the excretory
system *(B)*.

which capillaries are wrapped. See Figure 23·21*A*.
Water passes from the blood into the nephrons.
Urea, salt, and wastes are carried along with the
water. Urine forms from these substances within
the nephrons. The urine flows from the nephrons to
a collecting area within the kidney.

The kidneys control the amount of water and
salt in the body. When there is extra water in the
body, more water passes from the blood to the
urine. The same is true for salt. The kidneys can
excrete almost any substance that is in oversupply.
The kidneys not only excrete wastes but also serve
to balance the supply of materials in the blood.

Notice in Figure 23·21*B* that each kidney is
joined to a large artery and a large vein. Notice also
that a tube leads from each kidney. These tubes, the
ureters, carry urine out of the kidneys. The ureters
lead to the bladder. The **bladder** is a saclike organ
that stores urine until it is excreted. Another tube,
the **urethra,** leads out of the bladder and carries
urine out of the body.

Kidney failure is a disorder in which the kidneys do not filter the blood. If one kidney fails, a person can still live normally. But if both kidneys fail, the blood must be filtered by a kidney machine.

REVIEW

1. What processes produce wastes that must be excreted? What are these wastes?
2. Explain how urine is formed, and trace its path out of the body.
3. What is kidney failure?

CHALLENGE During heavy exercise, only half as much blood is in the kidneys as is there when the body is at rest. Explain why.

CHAPTER SUMMARY

The main ideas in this chapter are listed below. Read these statements before you answer the Chapter Review questions.

- Blood carries materials through the body. Red blood cells carry oxygen. White blood cells defend the body against disease. Platelets act in blood clotting. (23•1)
- Blood types include A, B, AB, and O. Blood types must be tested before blood is transfused. (23•1)
- Arteries carry blood away from the heart. Veins carry blood toward the heart. Capillaries allow exchange of materials between blood and tissues. (23•2)
- Extra fluid called lymph is drained from the tissues by the lymphatic system. Lymph is filtered in the lymph nodes. (23•2)
- The heart has two atria and two ventricles. The right side of the heart gets blood from the body and pumps it to the lungs. The left side of the heart gets blood from the lungs and pumps it to the body. (23•3)

- Disorders of circulation include atherosclerosis and hypertension, which can result in heart attack or stroke. (23•3)
- Breathing is part of cellular respiration, the process of using oxygen to get energy. Gas exchange between air and blood occurs in the alveoli of the lungs. The diaphragm and rib muscles act causing air to move into and out of the lungs. (23•4)
- Disorders of the lungs and breathing include asthma, emphysema, and lung cancer. (23•4)
- Wastes released by life processes are excreted by the kidneys, lungs, and skin. Nephrons are tiny structures in each kidney that form urine by filtering wastes from the blood. (23•5)

The key terms in this chapter are listed below. Use each term in a sentence that shows the meaning of the term.

alveoli	capillary	pulse	vein
artery	diaphragm	red blood cell	ventricle
atrium	kidneys	trachea	white blood cell
bladder	lymph	ureters	
blood types	plasma	urethra	
bronchi	platelet	valve	

Chapter Review

VOCABULARY

Use the key terms from this chapter to complete the following sentences correctly.

1. A blood vessel whose wall is only one cell thick
2. A tube that carries air from the larynx toward the lungs
3. The liquid portion of the blood
4. A saclike organ that stores urine until it is excreted
5. A blood vessel that carries blood toward the heart
6. One of the upper chambers of the heart
7. The tube that carries urine out of the body
8. Tiny air sacs in the lungs
9. A sheet of muscle the forms the lower edge of the chest cavity
10. One of the lower chambers of the heart

a. alveoli
b. artery
c. atrium
d. bladder
e. bronchi
f. capillary
g. diaphragm
h. kidneys
i. plasma
j. trachea
k. ureters
l. urethra
m. vein
n. ventricle

CONCEPTS

Write the correct term for each number in the diagram. (1 – 5)

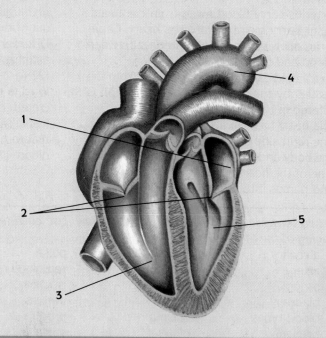

Identify each statement as True or False. If a statement is false, replace the underlined term or phrase with a term or phrase that makes the statement true.

6. It is the <u>hemoglobin</u> in red blood cells that joins with oxygen.
7. A mature <u>white blood cell</u> lacks a nucleus and is smaller than a red blood cell.
8. A liquid called <u>plasma</u> is filtered in the lymph nodes.
9. The diaphragm is a sheet of muscle that moves <u>up</u> as air is inhaled.
10. The <u>capillaries</u> control the amount of water and salt that are found in the body.

Answer the following questions in complete sentences.

11. What kinds of cells and cell fragments are found in the blood? What are their functions?
12. What must be done before blood can be transfused from one person to another?
13. What are the differences between arteries and veins?
14. Explain why there are two parts to the heartbeat.
15. Describe what occurs in the alveoli.
16. Distinguish between urea and urine.

APPLICATION/ CRITICAL THINKING

1. The heart can be thought of as two pumps. What parts of the heart form each of these two pumps? To which parts of the body does each pump direct blood?
2. Some disorders cause abnormal blood clots to form within blood vessels. Such clots are more likely to form within veins than within arteries. Explain why.
3. Explain why the pulse can only be felt in certain places on the body.
4. During quiet breathing the diaphragm and rib muscles work while you inhale and rest while you exhale. During heavy breathing, other muscles help to push air out of the chest as you exhale. What might those other muscles be?

EXTENSION

1. The Heimlich maneuver and cardiopulmonary resuscitation (CPR) are used to revive people who are choking or who have stopped breathing. Find out how to perform these life-saving actions, and find out what each is used for.
2. Smoking is thought to cause several disorders of circulation and respiration. Get information on this topic from the library or from health organizations. Present a report on your findings.

Science in Careers

Have you ever closely examined groceries after you bought them? If so, you may have noticed that meats contain certain amounts of fat. Canned fruits may contain added juice. Dairy products and baked goods have freshness dates. Other food products have lists including Calories and nutrients. It is the job of food laboratory technicians to make sure that food quality is high. They conduct different tests to determine food quality and what nutrients are present.

Food lab technicians also run tests to make certain that foods are free of bacteria and are safe to eat. Tuna fish and other seafoods might contain mercury that was in ocean water. A food lab technician tests these foods to check for mercury.

Some food lab technicians work for the state or federal government. Others work for food companies, restaurant chains, or breweries. Food lab technicians must have a 4-year college degree in food science or microbiology. If you are inter-

FOOD LAB TECHNICIAN

ested in this career, you should take courses in biology and chemistry in high school.

Have you ever seen a respirator? It is a machine that is used to aid people who have breathing problems. It is the job of a respiratory therapist to use the respirator with the patients who have these difficulties. The use of respirators has saved the lives of many people.

Besides using respirators, respiratory therapists also use other breathing equipment. They

test breathing and give therapy. They also teach patients who have respiratory system disorders, such as emphysema and cystic fibrosis, to do breathing exercises. Over time the exercises can help to strengthen a patient's respiratory system.

Respiratory therapists must have a high school diploma and 2 years of additional training. Most respiratory therapists also have special certification. If you are interested in this career, you should take courses in biology and chemistry in high school.

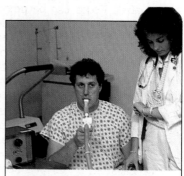

RESPIRATORY THERAPIST

People in Science

Dr. Angella D. Ferguson
MEDICAL DOCTOR

Dr. Angella D. Ferguson is a medical doctor. For many years she has studied the effects of sickle cell disease.

Sickle cell disease usually affects black people. The red blood cells of someone with the disease do not have the usual disk shape. Instead they are shaped like a sickle. These sickle-shaped red blood cells do not carry oxygen well. Also, the disease is a very painful one for the patient.

Dr. Ferguson, along with other scientists, studied how the

disease affects children of different ages. Her studies revealed a pattern in which the symptoms varied with the age of the patient. She also developed treatments that made the symptoms of the disease less severe. These treatments include having the patient exercise, drink large amounts of water, and eat a balanced diet. Although many of her ideas seem simple, Dr. Ferguson's treatment methods have reduced the pain and suffering of many children with sickle cell disease.

Issues and Technology

How Healthy Is Fast Food?

There has been a revolution in the way Americans prepare and eat foods. Fifty years ago, dinner might have been a roast baked in the oven, whole potatoes cooked and mashed by hand, and fresh vegetables. Dessert might have been a homemade pie or cake. All of this food would have taken hours to prepare.

The family today is different from what it was years ago, when people often had hours to spend preparing meals. Today, women and men often work, raise families, and want to have leisure time. They do not want to spend a large part of the day in the kitchen, baking roasts, mashing potatoes, chopping vegetables, and rolling pie crusts.

Modern technology has changed people's eating habits. Foods can be precooked and frozen. They can be dried or freeze-dried. The processed convenience foods served in many homes come already prepared — precooked, powdered, canned, or frozen. Instant mashed potatoes often are used in place of fresh potatoes. Frozen pies are advertised as tasting like homemade pies.

Technology has made it possible for foods to be prepared quickly. Chains of fast-food restaurants make use of technology to serve hot meals to many people very quickly. Each day, one out of every five Americans eats at least one meal at a fast-food restaurant. In 1985, Americans spent $47.5 billion on fast foods. Figure 1 shows how much of this business went to a few national chains of fast-food restaurants. Notice that these numbers do not total $47.5 billion. The remaining amount of money was spent at smaller chains and other restaurants.

Is there anything wrong with this trend? Some people say no. Convenience foods save time, and some are very tasty. Fast foods are thought of as inexpensive. Few restaurants can provide a meal for just a few dollars.

Many fast-food restaurants do serve salads. However, many people do not order them when they go out for fast food.

APPLYING CRITICAL THINKING SKILLS

1. According to Figure 1, what is the most popular kind of fast food?
2. According to Figure 1, what is the least popular kind of fast food?
3. What kinds of fast foods are there which are not included in Figure 1?
4. Suggest reasons why vegetables are not more common in fast-food restaurants.
5. Some fast-food restaurants have salad bars. Do you think this is a good substitute for serving vegetables? Why or why not?
6. Suppose you know someone who eats at fast-food restaurants several times each week. What would you suggest that this person do to improve the balance of his or her diet?

Figure 1

| | Restaurant A (hamburgers) | Restaurant B (hamburgers) | Restaurant C (chicken) | Restaurant D (pizza) |

Critics of fast foods say that these foods do not contain enough fiber from fresh fruits, vegetables, and whole grains. They also do not contain enough vitamin A or C, nor minerals such as calcium. What nutrients are found in the greatest amounts in fast foods? These foods are very high in sugars, starches, fat, and salt.

The high levels of sugars come mostly from soft drinks, milkshakes, pies, and ice cream. Hamburger rolls, french fries, pizza crust, and the coating on fried chicken contain starches. Together these carbohydrates help to make fast foods high-Calorie foods.

Most adults require between 1200 and 2000 Calories a day. A deluxe hamburger has over 600 Calories. A serving of french fries contains about 200 Calories. A milkshake adds another 350 Calories. How many Calories does this add up to? As you can see, one fast-food meal could use up most of a person's Calorie allotment for the day.

Defenders of fast foods point out that these foods do contain protein. They also contain an adequate amount of B vitamins. Calcium is included in the meal if a person has milk or a milkshake instead of a soft drink. Iron is provided if a person chooses

beef or chicken. If people choose wisely, a fast-food meal can be nutritious.

However, choosing a piece of chicken for its protein and iron content also means choosing all the fat the chicken is fried in. Nutrition experts say that fat should make up no more than 35 percent of a person's Calories. But 51 percent of the Calories in an average fast-food meal comes from fats.

Too much fat in the diet can cause such health problems as atherosclerosis. This is a condition in which fatty deposits form on the inside of arteries. This condition keeps blood from flowing normally and can lead to heart attacks.

Fast foods also are high in sodium, a mineral that comes from salt. Too much sodium can contribute to obesity and high blood pressure. Most doctors recommend that people keep sodium intake between 1100 and 3300 mg per day. Figure 2 shows the fat and sodium contents of some fast foods.

APPLYING CRITICAL THINKING SKILLS

1. The body needs between 15 g and 25 g of fat each day. What foods listed have more fat than this? Might this additional fat content cause health problems? Explain your answer.

Figure 2

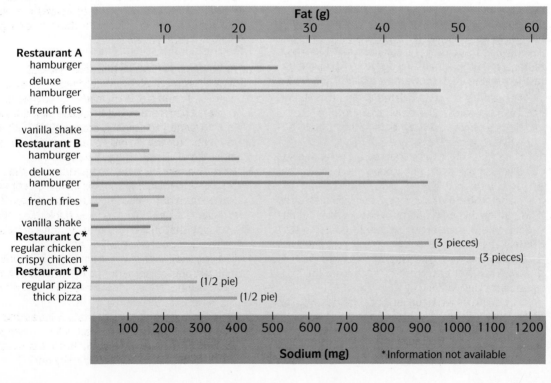

ORANGE DRINK

Nutrition Information Per Serving
Serving Size: 2 Heaping Teaspoons In 4 Fl. Oz. Water
Serving Per Container: 48
Calories 60
Protein 0
Fat 0
Carbohydrate . . . . 15 grams
**Percentage of U.S. Recommended
Daily Allowances (U.S. RDA)**
Vitamin A 20%
Vitamin C 100%
Calcium 6%

Contains Less Than 2% of U.S. RDA Of Protein, Thiamine, Riboflavin, Niacin, And Iron.

INGREDIENTS: SUGAR, CITRIC ACID, DEXTRIN, CALCIUM PHOSPHATE, NATURAL ORANGE FLAVOR, POTASSIUM CITRATE, ASCORBIC ACID (VITAMIN C), VEGETABLE OIL (PARTIALLY HYDROGENATED COTTONSEED OIL AND/OR PARTIALLY HYDROGENATED COCONUT OIL), ARTIFICIAL FLAVOR, XANTHAN GUM, ARTIFICIAL COLOR (FC&C YELLOW #5 AND YELLOW #6) AND VITAMIN A PALMITATE (STABILIZED).

ORANGE JUICE

Nutrition Information Per Serving
Serving Size: 4 Fl. Oz.
Servings Per Container: 16
Calories 55
Protein 1
Fat . . . . less than 1
Carbohydrate . . . . .13 grams
Potassium . . . . .260 mg
**Percentage of U.S. Recommended
Daily Allowances (U.S. RDA)**
Vitamin C 90%
Thiamine 8%

Contains Less Than 2% of the U.S. RDA Of Protein, Vitamin A, Riboflavin, Niacin, Calcium, And Iron.

INGREDIENTS: FRESH ORANGE JUICE

Figure 3

2. Compare the sodium content of the servings of french fries from restaurants A and B. Each restaurant made its own measurements. What difference in how the measurements were made could account for the difference in sodium?
3. A deluxe hamburger usually has twice as much meat as a regular hamburger. It also has about twice the protein and Calories of a regular hamburger. However, the deluxe hamburger has more than twice the fat. Suggest a reason for this difference.
4. The serving of chicken listed is slightly higher in Calories than are the deluxe hamburgers. It also is higher in fat but is lower in carboydrates. Account for these differences.
5. What could be done to decrease the fat and sodium contents of the hamburgers listed? Why, do you think, is this not being done?

One problem with relying heavily on fast foods is that they do not contain as wide a variety of nutrients as a diet that includes fresh foods. To stay healthy the body needs over 40 different nutrients each day. These nutrients include vitamins A, B, C, D, and E, as well as minerals such as calcium, iron, potassium, and iodine.

Both processed convenience foods and fast foods may lack some of these important nutrients. This may be due to the processes used to precook, or dry foods. For example, much of the vitamin C in foods is destroyed during cooking. Vitamins that are lost in processing can be replaced, but vitamins that are normally present in small amounts usually are not replaced.

Another difference between fresh foods and processed foods is that processed foods often contain added chemicals. Figure 3 compares the nutrients in fresh orange juice with those in orange drink made from a powder.

APPLYING CRITICAL THINKING SKILLS

1. Which has more different nutrients—fresh orange juice or orange drink made from a powder?
2. What nutrients are found in greater amounts in fresh orange juice than in orange drink? What nutrients are found in greater amounts in orange drink than in fresh orange juice?
3. Advertisements for the orange drink say that it is fortified with vitamin C. This means vitamin C has been added. What else has been added to the orange drink? Why, do you think, does the company that makes the orange drink not advertise these other ingredients?
4. Notice the difference in the amounts of Calories and carbohydrates in the two drinks. Which has more Calories? Suggest one possible reason for this difference.
5. One serving of orange juice costs twice as much as one serving of orange drink. Why is orange juice more expensive? Do you think it is worth the difference in price? Why or why not?

APPENDIX 1 Taxonomy Tree

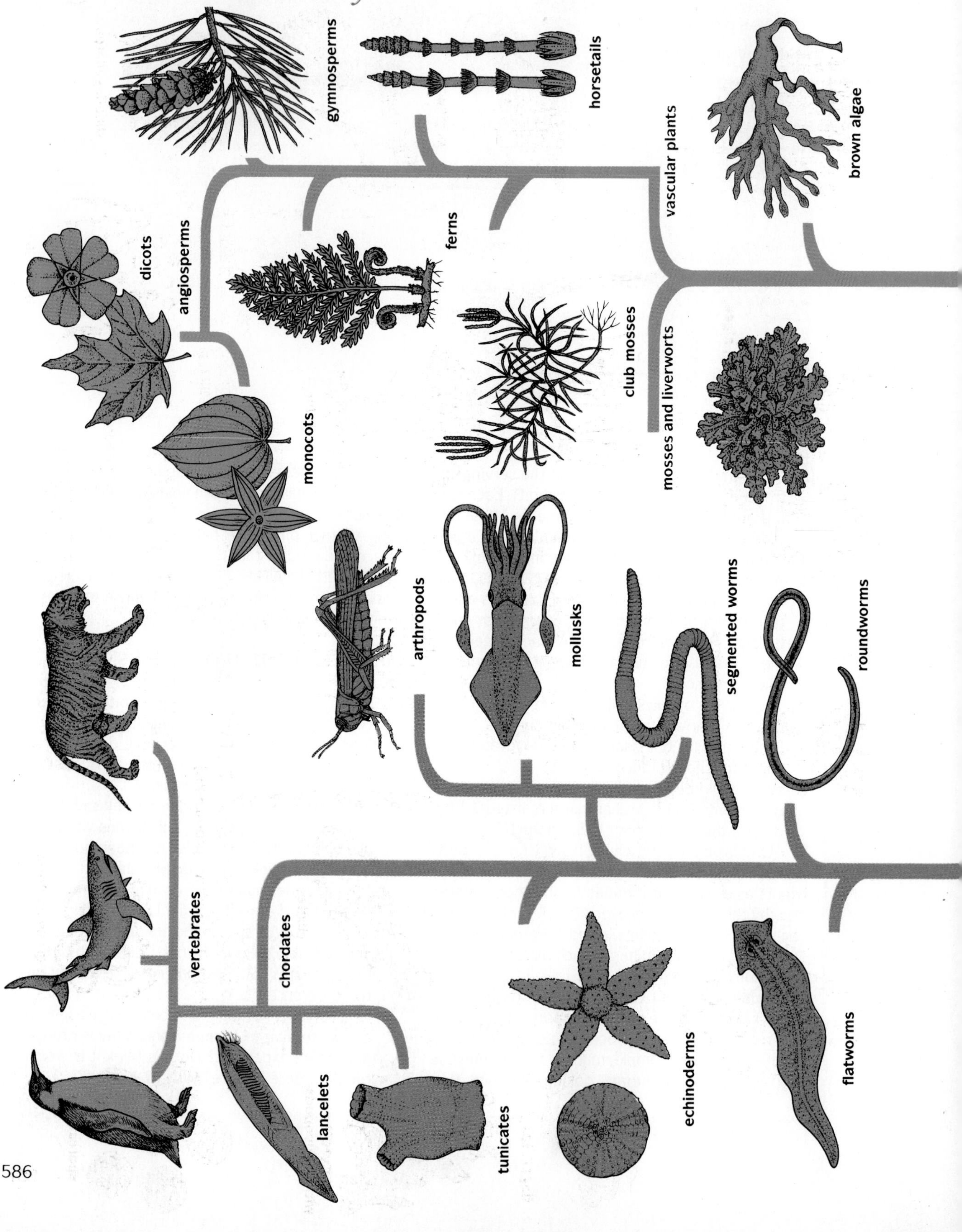
gymnosperms
horsetails
brown algae
vascular plants
ferns
dicots
angiosperms
club mosses
mosses and liverworts
monocots
arthropods
mollusks
segmented worms
roundworms
vertebrates
chordates
flatworms
echinoderms
lancelets
tunicates

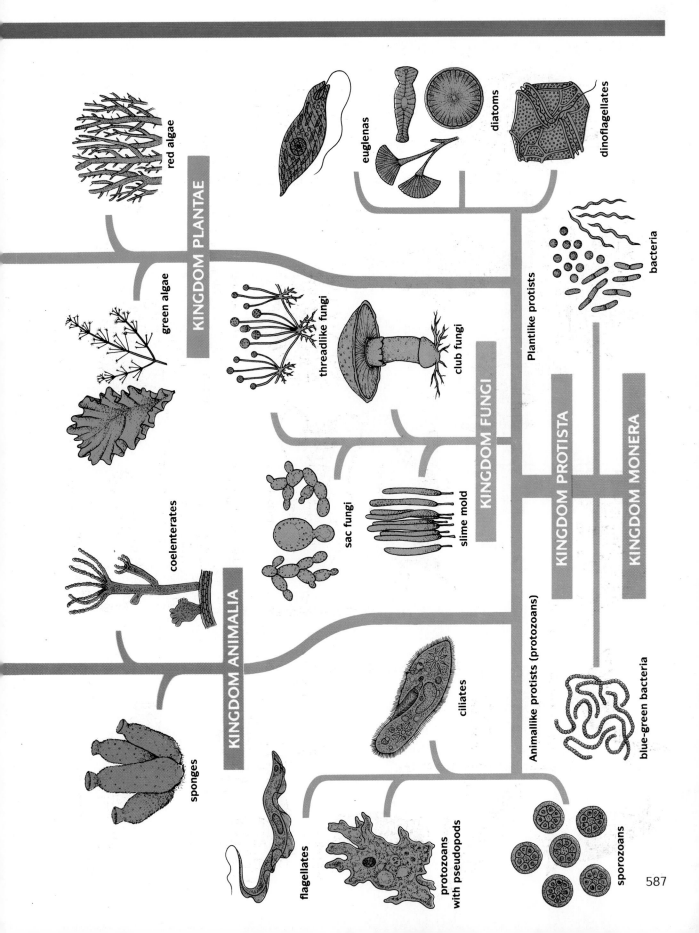

red algae

KINGDOM PLANTAE

green algae

euglenas

diatoms

dinoflagellates

bacteria

threadlike fungi

club fungi

Plantlike protists

KINGDOM FUNGI

KINGDOM PROTISTA

KINGDOM MONERA

coelenterates

sac fungi

slime mold

KINGDOM ANIMALIA

ciliates

Animallike protists (protozoans)

blue-green bacteria

sponges

flagellates

protozoans
with pseudopods

sporozoans

587

APPENDIX 2 *Periodic Table of Elements*

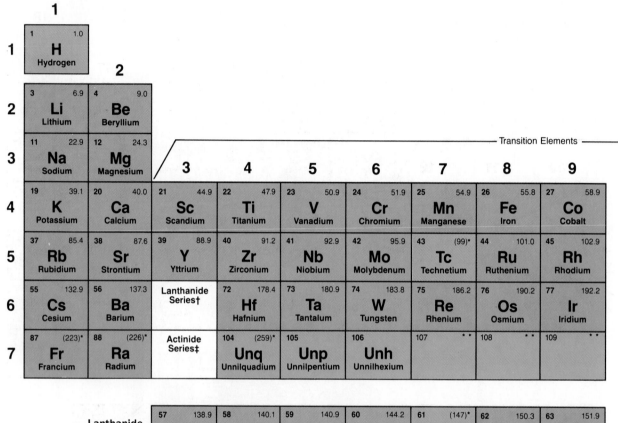

*Atomic masses appearing in parentheses are those of the most stable known isotopes.

These elements occur in nature, and are solids at room temperature (20°C).

These elements occur in nature, and are liquids at room temperature (20°C).

These elements occur in nature, and are gases at room temperature (20°C).

These elements do not occur in nature, and have been produced in laboratories.

18

							2 4.0 **He** Helium

13   **14**   **15**   **16**   **17**

5 10.8 **B** Boron	6 12.0 **C** Carbon	7 14.0 **N** Nitrogen	8 15.9 **O** Oxygen	9 18.9 **F** Fluorine	10 20.1 **Ne** Neon
13 26.9 **Al** Aluminum	14 28.0 **Si** Silicon	15 30.9 **P** Phosphorus	16 32.0 **S** Sulfur	17 35.4 **Cl** Chlorine	18 39.9 **Ar** Argon

10   **11**   **12**

28 58.7 **Ni** Nickel	29 63.5 **Cu** Copper	30 65.3 **Zn** Zinc	31 69.7 **Ga** Gallium	32 72.5 **Ge** Germanium	33 74.9 **As** Arsenic	34 78.9 **Se** Selenium	35 79.9 **Br** Bromine	36 83.8 **Kr** Krypton
46 106.4 **Pd** Palladium	47 107.8 **Ag** Silver	48 112.4 **Cd** Cadmium	49 114.8 **In** Indium	50 118.6 **Sn** Tin	51 121.7 **Sb** Antimony	52 127.6 **Te** Tellurium	53 126.9 **I** Iodine	54 131.3 **Xe** Xenon
78 195.0 **Pt** Platinum	79 196.9 **Au** Gold	80 200.5 **Hg** Mercury	81 204.3 **Tl** Thallium	82 207.1 **Pb** Lead	83 208.9 **Bi** Bismuth	84 (210)* **Po** Polonium	85 (210)* **At** Astatine	86 (222)* **Rn** Radon

64 157.2 **Gd** Gadolinium	65 158.9 **Tb** Terbium	66 162.5 **Dy** Dysprosium	67 164.9 **Ho** Holmium	68 167.2 **Er** Erbium	69 168.9 **Tm** Thulium	70 173.0 **Yb** Ytterbium	71 174.9 **Lu** Lutetium
96 (247)* **Cm** Curium	97 (247)* **Bk** Berkelium	98 (251)* **Cf** Californium	99 (254)* **Es** Einsteinium	100 (257)* **Fm** Fermium	101 (258)* **Md** Mendelevium	102 (255)* **No** Nobelium	103 (256)* **Lr** Lawrencium

* *No names have been given and no mass data is available.

Atomic masses based on C-12 = 12.0000

KEY

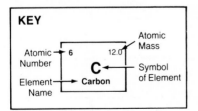

Atomic Number → 6   12.0 ← Atomic Mass
Element Name → **C**   Carbon ← Symbol of Element

APPENDIX 3 *Properties of Minerals*

MINERAL	HARDNESS	FRACTURE OR CLEAVAGE	COLOR	STREAK	CHEMICAL SYMBOL
Metals and non-metals					
gold	2.5–3	none	rich yellow	yellow	Au
silver	2.5–3	none	white	white	Ag
iron	4–5	cubic	steel-gray	gray	Fe
sulfur	2	conchoidal	light yellow	white to yellow	S
graphite	1–2	1 direction	black	black	C
Sulfides					
galena	2.5–2.7	cubic	lead-gray	bluish gray	PbS
sphalerite	3.5–4	4 directions	colorless to yellow-black	yellowish	ZnS
chalcopyrite	3.5–4	none	golden	greenish black	$CuFeS_2$
pyrite	6–6.5	conchoidal	rich yellow	greenish black	FeS_2
Oxides					
cuprite	3.5–4	4 directions	red	red	Cu_2O
corundum	9	conchoidal/uneven	variety of colors	colorless	Al_2O_3
bauxite	1–3	poor	white to red-brown	white to red-brown	$Al(OH)_3$
magnetite	6	none	black	black	Fe_3O_4
Halides					
halite	2.5	cubic	colorless	colorless	NaCl
fluorite	4	4 directions	variety of colors	colorless	CaF_2

MINERAL	HARDNESS	FRACTURE OR CLEAVAGE	COLOR	STREAK	CHEMICAL SYMBOL
Carbonates					
calcite	3	3 directions, not 90°	variety of colors	colorless	$Ca(CO_3)_2$
dolomite	3.5–4	3 directions, not 90°	variety of colors	colorless	$CaMg(CO_3)_2$
Sulfates					
anhydrite	3–3.5	2 directions	colorless, white, gray	colorless	$CaSO_4$
gypsum	2	2 directions	white	white	$CaSO_4 \cdot 2H_2O$
Phosphates					
apatite	5	none	variety of colors	white	$Ca_5(Cl, F)(PO_4)_3$
Silicates					
quartz	7	3 directions	variety of colors	colorless	SiO_2
kaolin	2–2.5	none	white	colorless	$Al_2Si_2O_5(OH)_4$
talc	1	1 direction	white, greenish gray	colorless	$Mg_3Si_4O_{10}(OH)_2$
serpentine	2–5	none	greenish	colorless	$Mg_3Si_2O_5(OH)_4$
chlorite	2–2.5	none	variety of colors	colorless	complex structure
mica (muscovite)	2–2.5	1 direction	white to dark	colorless	complex structure
hornblende	5–6	2 directions	blue-green to black	blue-green to black	complex structure
olivine	6.5–7	conchoidal	green to light gray	white	$(Mg, Fe)_2SiO_4$
feldspar	6	2 directions, 90°	white, pink, yellow	colorless	$KAlSi_3O_8$
topaz	8	3 directions	variety of colors	colorless	complex structure

APPENDIX 4 *Safety*

An important part of your study of science will be working on activities. Most of the activity work you will do is quite safe. Yet some equipment and chemicals can cause you or a classmate injury if you do not handle them properly.

For certain activities, safety symbols are included next to the heading PROCEDURE. These safety symbols alert you to specific hazards in the procedure and to safety measures. Read the following guidelines and safety symbol explanations.

Safety Guidelines

- Prepare for every activity by reading through the entire activity before starting.
- Follow all written directions exactly unless your teacher gives you other directions.
- Make sure your working area is dry and clutter-free.
- Read all labels before using chemicals.
- Work in a careful, organized manner. Do not play or fool around.
- Report all spills, broken glassware, faulty electrical equipment, accidents, or injuries to your teacher immediately.
- Use only tongs, test-tube holders, or hot pads to hold or move hot glassware.
- Do not allow cords from hot plates or electrical equipment to dangle from work tables.
- Do not use any electrical equipment with frayed cords, loose connections, or exposed wires. Do not handle electrical equipment with wet hands.
- Never try to cut a specimen while holding it in your hand.
- Never place unknown plants, berries, seeds, or fruits into your mouth.
- At the end of every activity, clean up your work area, put everything away, and wash your hands.
- Check with your teacher for any additional safety guidelines to follow.

Safety Symbols

 Danger of cuts caused by glassware, scissors, or other possibly sharp laboratory tools.

 A lab apron should be worn to prevent damage to clothes by chemicals, acids, or stains.

 Safety goggles should be worn when there is a possibility of danger to eyes.

 Chemicals can possibly cause noxious fumes; preservatives used on specimens can be an irritant, so proper ventilation is necessary.

 Plants that are studied may have sharp edges or thorns; outdoor work may expose you to plants that can cause an allergic reaction.

 Exhibit care in handling electrical equipment.

 Follow directions when working with chemicals that could be explosive if misused.

 Exhibit caution when working with the Bunsen burner and when handling hot equipment.

 Be careful when using the Bunsen burner and check that the gas outlet is turned off when not in use.

 Substances in an investigation could be poisonous if ingested.

Glossary

abiotic factors   The nonliving things in an environment. *p. 138*

acid rain   A mixture of acid and rain water; a type of pollution formed by a mixture of nitrogen oxides, sulfur dioxide, and rain. *pp. 151, 502*

acoustics (uh KOOS tihks)   The study of sound. *p. 326*

active transport   The use of energy by a cell to move particles across the cell membrane *p. 43*

air mass   A large body of air that has about the same temperature and humidity throughout it. *p. 462*

air pressure   The force caused by the weight of air. *p. 447*

alga (AL guh)   A nonseed plant that lacks roots, stems, and leaves. *p. 86*

alveoli (al VEE uh lī)   Groups of tiny air sacs. *p. 573*

amphibian (am FIHB ee uhn)   A cold-blooded vertebrate that lives in water when young but can live on land as an adult. *p. 117*

amplitude (AM pluh tood)   A measure of the greatest movement of matter from its normal resting position. *p. 311*

anemometer (an uh MAHM uh tuhr)   An instrument that measures wind speed. *p. 450*

angiosperm (AN jee uh sperm)   A seed plant that produces flowers and that forms seeds within a fruit. *p. 98*

aquifer (AK wuh fuhr)   A layer of rock or rock material that holds water. *p. 491*

artery (AHR tuhr ee)   A blood vessel that carries blood away from the heart. *p. 564*

atmosphere (AT muh sfihr)   The layer of air that surrounds the earth; an invisible mixture of gases that surrounds the earth. *pp. 340, 440*

atom   The smallest particle of an element that has the properties of that element. *p. 188*

atomic mass   The mass of an atom in relation to the carbon-12. atom. *p. 194*

atomic mass unit (amu)   One-twelfth the mass of a carbon-12. atom. *p. 194*

atomic number   The number of protons in the nucleus of an atom of an element. *p. 192*

atrium (AY tree uhm)   An upper chamber of the heart. *p. 567*

autumnal equinox (aw TUHM nuhl   EE kwih nahks)   A point in the sky through which the sun passes on the first day of fall in the Northern Hemisphere. *p. 347*

bacteria Monerans that do not contain blue and green pigments. *p. 63*

ball-and-socket joint A movable joint that allows movement in many directions. *p. 522*

barometer An instrument that measures air pressure. *p. 447*

biosphere (BĪ uh sfihr) The zone in which life is found on the earth. *p. 139*

biotic (bī AHT ihk) **factors** The living things in an environment. *p. 138*

bird A warm-blooded vertebrate that has a body covering of feathers. *p. 123*

bladder A saclike organ that stores urine until it is excreted. *p. 578*

blood types Groups into which blood is classified based on chemical differences. *p. 562*

blue-green bacteria Monerans that can make their own food by photosynthesis. *p. 62*

boiling point The temperature at which a liquid boils at sea level. *p. 173*

bony fish A fish that has scales, an endoskeleton made up mostly of bone, and paired fins. *p. 115*

Boyle's law The law stating that the volume of a gas decreases as its pressure increases if the temperature stays the same. *p. 295*

bronchi (BRAHNG kī) The two branches of the trachea. *p. 573*

brown algae Many-celled algae that live in water and that contain both a green pigment and a brown pigment. *p. 88*

budding A form of asexual reproduction in which a new organism forms as an outgrowth of the parent. *p. 76*

buoyant (BOY uhnt) **force** The upward force exerted on an object by a fluid in which the object is placed. *p. 261*

Calorie A measure of the energy available in food. *p. 546*

capillary a blood vessel whose wall is only one cell thick. *p. 564*

carbohydrates (kahr boh HĪ drayts) Organic compounds that are the main source of energy for living things; nutrients that provide the body with its main source of energy. *pp. 34, 538*

cardiac (KAHR dee ak) **muscle** The muscle tissue that makes up the heart. *p. 527*

carnivore (KAHR nuh vawr) A consumer that eats animals. *p. 144*

cartilage fish A fish that has jaws, scales, paired fins, and a skeleton made of cartilage. *p. 114*

cast A fossil that has the same outer shape as the original object. *p. 419*

cavern A large underground chamber formed by the action of ground water. *p. 494*

cell The smallest unit in which all of the life processes are carried on. *p. 32*

cell membrane A structure that controls the flow of materials into and out of a cell. *p. 37*

cell wall A nonliving structure that surrounds a plant cell. *p. 38*

Cenozoic Era The most recent era on the geologic time scale; the era in which mammals dominate. *p. 433*

Charles's law The law stating that the volume of a gas increases as its temperature increases if the pressure stays the same. *p. 296*

chemical bond A force that holds particles of matter together. *p. 219*

chemical change A change that produces one or more kinds of matter that are different from those present before the change. *p. 180*

chemical formula A group of symbols that shows the makeup of a compound. *p. 214*

chemical property The ability of a substance to undergo or resist chemical changes. *p. 182*

chemical symbol A notation of one or more letters that represents an element. *p. 197*

chloroplast (KLAWR uh plast) An organelle in which food is made in a plant cell. *p. 39*

chromosome (KROH muh sohm) A threadlike structure that contains DNA. *p. 49*

chromosphere (KROH muh sfihr) The first layer of the sun's atmosphere. *p. 369*

ciliates (SIHL ee ayts) Protists that move by means of cilia. *p. 72*

classification (klas uh fuh KAY shuhn) The grouping of things according to a system. *p. 56*

cleavage A property that describes how a mineral cleaves, or splits apart, along one or more smooth surfaces. *p. 395*

club moss A small evergreen vascular nonseed plant with tiny, pointed leaves. *p. 94*

coal A solid, black mineral formed from the remains of plants. *p. 405*

cold front A front that forms when a cooler air mass replaces a warmer air mass. *p. 468*

colloid (KAHL oid) A mixture whose properties are between those of a solution and a suspension. *p. 250*

commensalism (kuh MEHN suh lihz uhm) A kind of symbiosis in which one organism is helped and the other is neither helped nor harmed. *p. 148*

community All the organisms living together in an area. *p. 143*

compound A substance that is made up of two or more elements chemically combined; a pure substance made up of two or more elements that are combined chemically. *pp. 164, 212*

compound machine A machine that is made up of two or more simple machines. *p. 277*

compression The part of a compressional wave where the particles of matter are pushed close together. *p. 310*

compressional wave A wave in which particles of matter move back and forth parallel to the direction of the wave. *p. 310*

condensation point The temperature at which a gas condenses, or changes to a liquid. *p. 173*

conduction The transfer of heat by direct contact between particles. *p. 297*

conifer (KOH nuh fuhr) A tree or shrub that bears its seeds in cones. *p. 100*

conjugation (kahn juh GAY shuhn) A form of sexual reproduction in which two cells join and then exchange nuclear material. *p. 73*

connective tissue Tissue that joins and supports different parts of the body. *p. 518*

consumer An organism that eats other organisms. *p. 144*

contour (KAHN tur) **feather** A large feather that gives a bird's body its streamlined shape. *p. 124*

controlled experiment A method for testing hypotheses. *p. 20*

convection The heat transfer that takes place in fluids. *p. 297*

core (sun) The center of the sun. *p. 368*

Coriolis (kawr ee OH lihs) **effect** A change in wind direction caused by the rotation of the earth. *p. 455*

corona The outer layer of the sun's atmosphere. *p. 369*

cotyledon (kaht uh LEE duhn) A food-storing part of a seed. *p. 102*

covalent (koh VAY luhnt) **bond** A bond in which electrons are shared between atoms. *p. 226*

covalent compounds Compounds that contain covalent bonds. *p. 227*

crystal A solid with a regular shape and flat sides. *p. 388*

cyst (sihst) A thick, protective covering formed by a protozoan when conditions are extreme. *p. 72*

cytoplasm (sī tuh plaz uhm) The jellylike material that surrounds the nucleus of a cell. *p. 37*

decibel (dB) The unit used to measure sound intensity. *p. 320*

decomposer (dee kuhm POH suhr) An organism that breaks down the remains of dead plants and animals into simpler substances. *p. 145*

deficit A condition that occurs when the amount of evaporation, or outgo, is greater than the amount of precipitation, or income. *p. 486*

degree Celsius (°C) A unit used for measuring temperature. *p. 19*

density (DEHN suh tee) The mass per unit volume of a substance. *p. 174*

dermis (DER mihs) The inner layer of skin. *p. 531*

diaphragm (DĪ uh fram) The sheet of muscle that forms the lower edge of the chest cavity. *p. 574*

diatom (DĪ uh tahm) A plantlike protist with a glassy cell wall. *p. 70*

dicot (DĪ kaht) An angiosperm with two cotyledons. *p. 103*

diffraction (dih FRAK shuhn) The spreading out of waves past the edge of a barrier. *p. 314*

diffusion (dih FYOO zhuhn) The movement of particles from a crowded area to a less crowded area. *p. 42*

digestion (duh JEHS chuhn) The process that breaks food into substances that can be used by cells. *p. 548*

digestive enzyme A substance that chemically breaks down a nutrient. *p. 552*

dinoflagellate (dī nuh FLAJ uh layt) A plantlike protist that has two flagella. *p. 70*

divide An area of high elevation that separates watersheds. *p. 497*

DNA A nucleic acid that stores all of the information needed for a cell to function. *p. 35*

Doppler effect The change in pitch that occurs when the source of a sound and the listener are moving in relation to each other. *p. 322*

down feather A short, fluffy feather found under the contour feathers, close to the body. *p. 125*

ecology (ee KAHL uh jee) The study of the interactions between living things and their environment. *p. 138*

ecosystem (EE kuh sihs tuhm) An area in which living things interact, exchanging energy and materials. *p. 139*

efficiency A comparison of the amount of work a machine does with the amount of work put into the machine. *p. 272*

effort force The force that is applied to do work. *p. 267*

electron A negatively charged particle in the atom. *p. 189*

element A substance that cannot be changed into simpler substances by ordinary means such as heating, cooling, or crushing. *p. 164*

endangered species A species that is in danger of becoming extinct. *p. 152*

endoplasmic reticulum (ehn doh PLAZ mihk rih TIHK yuh luhm) A network of membranes that runs throughout the cytoplasm. *p. 37*

endoskeleton (ehn doh SKEHL uh tuhn) A skeleton that is inside an animal's body. *p. 111*

energy The ability to do work. *p. 264*

environment (ehn vī ruhn muhnt) All of the living things and nonliving things that affect the life of an organism. *p. 138*

epidermis (ehp uh DER mihs) The outer layer of skin. *p. 531*

epithelial (ehp uh THEE lee uhl) **tissue** Sheets of cells that cover and protect both inner surfaces and outer surfaces of the body. *p. 517*

era A major unit of time based on changes in the earth's crust and on the stages of development in certain life forms. *p. 426*

esophagus (ee SAHF uh guhs) A muscular tube that connects the throat to the stomach. *p. 549*

exosphere (EHK suh sfihr) The last layer of the atmosphere, extending into outer space. *p. 443*

extensor (ehk STEHN suhr) A muscle that causes a joint to straighten when the muscle contracts. *p. 529*

external fertilization The joining of egg and sperm outside the body of the female. *p. 113*

fats Nutrients that provide energy and building material for the body. *p. 539*

fermentation (fer mehn TAY shuhn) The process of releasing energy, alcohol, and carbon dioxide from sugar. *p. 76*

fern A vascular nonseed plant with roots, stems, and leaves. *p. 95*

fiber The part of plants that the body cannot digest, or break down. *p. 545*

fins Winglike structures that a fish uses for balancing and steering when swimming. *p. 113*

fish A cold-blooded vertebrate that lives in water and has gills that are used for breathing. *p. 113*

fission (FIHSH uhn) A process in which bacteria reproduce asexually by splitting into two cells. *p. 65*

flagellates (FLAJ uh layts) Protozoans that use flagella for movement. *p. 71*

flexor (FLEHK suhr) A muscle that causes a joint to bend when the muscle contracts. *p. 529*

food chain The transfer of energy in the form of food from one organism to another. *p. 146*

food web An overlapping of food chains in a community. *p. 146*

force A push or a pull. *p. 256*

formula unit The smallest repeating group of atoms in an ionic compound. *p. 224*

fossils The preserved remains or traces of once-living things that are found in the earth's crust. *p. 417*

fracture A break along an uneven surface of a mineral. *p. 395*

freezing point The temperature at which a liquid freezes. *p. 172*

frequency The number of waves that pass a given point each second. *p. 311*

frond The mature leaf of a fern. *p. 95*

front The boundary between two air masses. *p. 466*

fungus (FUHN guhs)   An organism that lacks chlorophyll, absorbs food, and produces spores. *p. 74*

gas   A state of matter that does not have a definite shape or definite volume. *p. 166*

gem   A mineral that is colorful and that relects much light. *p. 403*

geologic column   A diagram of the sequence of rock layers in an area according to age. *p. 422*

geologic time scale   The division of the earth's history into units of time based on changes in the earth's crust and sudden changes in the forms of life. *p. 426*

gills   Organs (of fish) that absorb oxygen that is dissolved in water. *p. 113*

gliding joint   A movable joint that allows gliding movements. *p. 522*

Great Lakes   The five lakes that make up the largest region of fresh water in the world. *p. 503*

green algae   Simple plants with cells that contain chloroplasts and a rigid cell wall. *p. 86*

greenhouse effect   The warming of the atmosphere due to the absorption of waves of heat energy from the earth. *p. 444*

ground water   The water in the zone of saturation. *p. 489*

group   A vertical column in the Periodic Table, made up of elements that have similar chemical properties. *p. 203*

gymnosperm (JIHM nuh sperm)   A seed plant whose seeds do not form within a fruit. *p. 98*

habitat (HAB uh tat)   The kind of place in which an organism lives. *p. 141*

hardness   The resistance a mineral shows to being scratched. *p. 392*

heat   The total energy of all the particles in a sample of matter. *p. 286*

heat engine   A device that changes the heat energy from burning fuel into mechanical energy. *p. 301*

heat of fusion (FYOO zhuhn)   The amount of heat energy that will change a solid at its melting point to a liquid at the same temperature. *p. 291*

heat of vaporization (vay puhr uh ZAY shuhn)   The amount of heat energy that will change a liquid at its boiling point to a gas at the same temperature. *p. 293*

herbivore (HER buh vawr)   A consumer that eats plants. *p. 144*

heterogeneous (heht uhr uh JEE nee uhs) **mixture**   A mixture whose makeup differs from point to point. *p. 235*

hibernation   The period of inactivity of animals during the winter. *p. 118*

hinge joint   A joint that allows movement in only one direction. *p. 522*

homogeneous (hoh muh JEE nee uhs) **mixture**   A mixture whose makeup is the same throughout. *p. 235*

horsetail   A vascular nonseed plant with hollow stems. *p. 94*

humidity   Water vapor in the air. *p. 462*

hurricane   A large tropical storm that usually develops during late summer near the equator. *p. 478*

hydrosphere (HĪ druh sfihr)   The layer of water that covers the earth. *p. 340*

hyphae (HĪ fee)   The threadlike structures of molds. *p. 75*

hypothesis   An educated guess about the answer to a problem, based on what is already known about a subject. *p. 2*

inclined plane   A simple machine that consists of a sloping surface. *p. 273*

incubation (ihn kyuh BAY shuhn)   The warming of an egg to body temperature over a period of time while the embryo grows. *p. 127*

inner planets   Mercury, Venus, Earth, and Mars—the four planets closest to the sun. *p. 362*

intensity   The loudness of a sound (amplitude of a sound wave). *p. 320*

interference   The effects caused by two or more waves passing through a medium at the same time. *p. 315*

internal fertilization   The joining of egg and sperm cells inside the body of the female. *p. 120*

involuntary muscle   A muscle that is not under conscious control. *p. 526*

ion (Ī ahn)   A charged particle that forms when a neutral atom loses or gains electrons. *p. 219*

ionic bond   A force of attraction between oppositely charged ions. *p. 222*

ionic compound A compound that contains ionic bonds. *p. 223*

isotopes (Ī suh tohps) Atoms of the same element with different numbers of neutrons. *p. 193*

jawless fish Wormlike fish that have no jaws. *p. 114*

jet streams High-speed bands of wind near the top of the troposphere. *p. 456*

joint A place where two or more bones come together in the skeleton. *p. 521*

Jupiter The fifth planet from the sun, and the largest planet in the solar system. *p. 376*

kidneys The main organs of excretion in humans. *p. 577*

kilogram (kg) An SI unit used to measure mass. *p. 17*

kinetic energy Energy of motion. *p. 264*

kinetic theory A theory stating that all matter is made of particles that are in constant motion. *p. 284*

lake A large water-filled depression in the earth's surface. *p. 500*

large intestine A short, wide tube that absorbs water from undigested food. *p. 550*

Law of Conservation of Energy A scientific law stating that energy cannot be created or destroyed but can be changed from one form to another. *p. 266*

lever A rigid bar that moves around a fixed point. *p. 274*

lightning A large electrical discharge that occurs between clouds or between a cloud and the earth. *p. 473*

lipids (LIHP ihdz) Organic compounds that store energy. *p. 34*

liquid A state of matter that has a definite volume but not a definite shape. *p. 166*

liter (L) A unit of volume. *p. 18*

lithosphere (LIHTH uh sfihr) The solid surface of the earth. *p. 340*

liver A large, lobed organ that produces bile. *p. 553*

liverwort (LIHV uhr wert) A small nonvascular plant that grows flat along a surface. *p. 91*

lunar eclipse An event occurring when the moon passes through the shadow of the earth. *p. 352*

luster A physical property that describes how the surface of a mineral reflects light. *p. 394*

lymph Plasma that leaks out of the capillaries and surrounds all cells and bathes the tissues. *p. 566*

mammal A warm-blooded vertebrate that has hair and that feeds milk to its young. *p. 128*

mammary gland A structure in female mammals that secretes milk. *p. 128*

marrow (MAR oh) A soft tissue in which new blood cells are produced. *p. 524*

Mars The fourth planet from the sun. *p. 374*

marsupial (mahr SOO pee uhl) A mammal whose young complete their development in a pouch on the female's body. *p. 129*

mass number The sum of the number of protons and neutrons in an atom. *p. 193*

matter Anything that has mass and takes up space. *p. 164*

mechanical advantage The number of times a machine multiplies an effort force. *p. 271*

melting point The temperature at which a solid becomes a liquid. *p. 172*

Mercury The planet closest to the sun. *p. 372*

mesosphere (MEHS uh sfihr) The third layer of the atmosphere extending from the stratosphere to a height of 80 km. *p. 442*

Mesozoic Era The third large division of geologic time; an era in which dinosaurs were dominant. *p. 432*

metabolism (muh TAB uh lihz uhm) The sum of all the chemical activities that take place in an organism. *p. 29*

metamorphosis (meht uh MAWR fuh sihs) A series of distinct changes in form through which an organism passes as it grows from egg to adult. *p. 118*

meter (m) The SI unit used when measuring length or distance. *p. 17*

migration The seasonal movement of animals from one area to another. *p. 125*

mineral (MIHN uhr uhl) A solid that has a definite makeup and crystalline structure; an element that helps the body function normally and use other nutrients. *pp. 388, 542*

mitochondria (mī tuh KAHN dree uh) Organelles that release energy from food. *p. 37*

mitosis (mī TOH sihs) Cell division in which daughter cells are made that are just like the parent cell. *p. 48*

mixture Two or more substances that can be separated by physical means; a combination of two or more kinds of matter that can be separated by physical means. *pp. 165, 234*

mold A hollow space left in a rock by an object that has dissolved. *p. 419*

molecule The smallest unit of any covalent substance that can exist alone and still show the properties of that substance. *p. 226*

monerans (muh NIHR uhnz) Single-celled organisms that have the simplest cell structure. *p. 62*

monocot (MAHN uh kaht) An angiosperm with one cotyledon. *p. 103*

monotreme (MAHN uh treem) An egg-laying mammal. *p. 129*

moss A small nonvascular plant that often grows in moist areas in woods or near stream banks. *p. 91*

muscle tissue Muscle cells that can contract, or become shorter. *p. 517*

mutualism (MYOO chu uh lihz uhm) A kind of symbiosis in which both organisms benefit. *p. 148*

natural gas A fossil fuel formed by the same processes that form petroleum and made mostly of the gas methane. *p. 405*

natural resource Any material found on the earth and necessary for life or useful to humans. *p. 397*

nebular hypothesis The formation of the solar system from a dust cloud that contracted, or came together. *p. 353*

Neptune The eighth planet from the sun. *p. 378*

nerve tissue Long, branched nerve cells that carry messages throughout the body. *p. 518*

neutron A particle with no charge found in the nucleus of an atom. *p. 189*

niche (nihch) The role of an organism in an ecosystem. *p. 142*

nonrenewable resource A resource that cannot be replaced once it has been used. *p. 398*

nonvascular plants Plants that lack vascular tissue. *p. 85*

nuclear membrane A membrane that surrounds the nucleus and separates it from the rest of the cell. *p. 36*

nucleus (NOO klee uhs) The organelle that controls the activities of a cell; the part of the atom that has most of the mass of the atom and that has a positive charge. *pp. 36, 189*

nutrient Any substance the body needs to live and grow. *p. 538*

occluded (uh KLOO dihd) **front** A front that forms when a cold front "catches up" with a warm front. *p. 469*

omnivore (AHM nuh vawr) A consumer that eats both plants and animals. *p. 145*

ore A mineral deposit in the earth that can be mined for profit. *p. 402*

organ A group of two or more different tissues that work together to perform a function. *p. 516*

organ system A group of organs that work together to perform one or more functions. *p. 516*

organism (AWR guh nihz uhm) A single, complete living thing. *p. 28*

osmosis (ahz MOH sihs) The diffusion of water through a semipermeable membrane. *p. 42*

outer planets Jupiter, Saturn, Uranus (yu RAY nuhs), Neptune, and Pluto. *p. 362*

Paleozoic Era The second era on the geologic time scale; the era in which abundant life forms first appeared. *p. 430*

pancreas A digestive gland that produces pancreatic juice. *p. 554*

parasite (PAR uh sīt) An organism that lives in or on another organism and harms it. *p. 66*

parasitism (PAR uh sī tihz uhm) A form of symbiosis in which one organism is helped and the other is harmed. *p. 149*

period Each horizontal row in the Periodic Table. *p. 206*

periodic law The law stating that the properties of the elements form a pattern if the elements are arranged by increasing atomic number. *p. 202*

Periodic Table A table that has elements arranged in order of increasing atomic number. *p. 202*

peristalsis (pehr uh STAHL sihs) The squeezing motion that pushes food through the digestive system. *p. 549*

petroleum A liquid, also called oil, that forms from the remains of sea life. *p. 404*

phases The different shapes that the moon appears to have. *p. 351*

photosphere (FOH tuh sfihr) The visible surface of the sun. *p. 369*

photosynthesis (foh tuh SIHN thuh sihs) The process by which glucose is made by plants. *p. 46*

physical change A change in which the appearance of matter changes but its chemical properties and makeup remain the same. *p. 179*

physical properties Characteristics of matter that can be studied without changing the makeup of a substance. *p. 168*

pitch How high or low a sound is. *p. 321*

pivot joint A movable joint that allows rotating movement from side to side. *p. 522*

placental (pluh SEHN tuhl) **mammal** A mammal whose young are nourished through a placenta as they grow inside the female's body. *p. 130*

plankton Small organisms that float near the surface of a body of water. *p. 88*

plasma A state of matter that is a hot gas of electrically charged particles; the liquid portion of the blood. *pp. 167, 560*

platelet A cell fragment that acts in blood clotting. *p. 561*

Pluto The ninth planet to be discovered in the solar system, and the smallest planet. *p. 379*

pollution (puh LOO shuhn) The release of unwanted, usually harmful materials into the environment. *p. 150*

pond A small, shallow depression that fills with water. *p. 500*

population A group of organisms of one species that lives in a given area. *p. 143*

potential energy Stored energy. *p. 264*

power The amount of work done in a period of time. *p. 269*

Precambrian (pree KAM bree uhn) **Era** The oldest and longest era on the geologic time scale. *p. 426*

pressure A force acting on a unit area. *pp. 262, 295*

producer An organism that makes its own food. *p. 144*

proteins (PROH teenz) Organic compounds that form the structure and control the function of living things; nutrients that provide the body with material for growth and repair, and that are needed to form enzymes. *pp. 35, 540*

protists (PROH tihsts) Mostly single-celled microscopic organisms that live in water or in moist places. *p. 68*

proton A positively charged particle in the nucleus of an atom. *p. 189*

protoplanets Whirlpools of matter that were the beginning of the bodies of the solar system. *p. 354*

protozoan (proh tuh ZOH uhn) An animallike protist. *p. 71*

pseudopod (SOO duh pahd) A fingerlike extension of the cell, used in moving and feeding. *p. 71*

pulley A machine made up of a rope that turns around a wheel. *p. 275*

pulse The stretching and relaxing of the arteries. *p. 569*

radiant energy Energy that travels in the form of waves. *p. 444*

radiation The transfer of energy by waves. *p. 297*

radiometric dating A process that finds the age of rocks and other objects by measuring the decay of radioactive elements in the rocks and objects. *p. 423*

rarefaction (rair uh FAK shuhn) The part of a compressional wave where particles of matter are spread apart. *p. 310*

red algae Many-celled algae that live in water and that contain green, blue, and red pigments. *p. 89*

red blood cell A blood cell that carries oxygen. *p. 561*

reflection The bouncing back of waves that strike a surface. *p. 313*

refraction (rih FRAK shuhn) The change in direction of a wave as it passes from one medium to another. *p. 314*

relative age The age of something compared with the age of something else. *p. 415*

renewable resource A resource that can be replaced. *p. 398*

reproduction (ree pruh DUHK shuhn) The process by which organisms make others of their kind. *p. 31*

reptile A cold-blooded vertebrate with a dry, scaly skin. *p. 120*

resistance force A force that opposes an effort force. *p. 267*

resonance (REHZ uh nuhns) The response that an object has to vibrations that match its natural frequency. *p. 317*

respiration (rehs puh RAY shuhn) The process of releasing energy from food. *p. 45*

response The reaction of an organism to a stimulus. *p. 30*

revolution The movement of an object along an orbit, or path, around another body. *p. 342*

rhizoid (RĪ zoid) A structure that anchors a moss or liverwort to the soil and that absorbs water and minerals. *p. 91*

rhizome (RĪ zohm) An underground stem of a horsetail or a fern. *p. 95*

ribosomes (RĪ buh sohmz) Organelles that build the proteins needed by a cell. *p. 37*

river system A river and all the tributary streams that flow into it. *p. 497*

rotation The turning of an object on its axis. *p. 342*

salivary (SAL uh vehr ee) **glands** The glands that produce saliva. *p. 553*

satellite Any object that revolves around another object. *p. 380*

saturated solution A solution that contains all the solute that will dissolve at a given temperature. *p. 245*

Saturn The sixth planet from the sun, and the second largest planet. *p. 377*

scales Overlapping, flat plates that cover a fish's body and give protection. *p. 113*

science A method of obtaining knowledge about nature. *p. 1*

scientific name The last two names of an organism—genus and species. *p. 58*

screw An inclined plane that is wound around a cylinder. *p. 274*

seed plant A vascular plant that reproduces by forming seeds. *p. 98*

simple machine A device used to change the size, direction, or speed of a force being used to do work. *p. 271*

skeletal muscle The muscle tissue that is attached to and that moves the skeleton. *p. 527*

skeleton The framework that supports the body and protects the internal organs. *p. 519*

small intestine A long, coiled tube in which food is further digested and is absorbed. *p. 550*

smog A mixture of smoke and fog. *p. 151*

smooth muscle The muscle tissue found in the walls of many organs inside the body. *p. 527*

solar eclipse Event occurring when the earth passes through the moon's shadow. *p. 352*

solar system The sun and the objects that move around it. *p. 362*

solar wind A steady stream of electrically charged particles given off by the sun. *p. 367*

solid A state of matter that has a definite shape and takes up a definite volume. *p. 166*

solubility The amount of solute that will dissolve in a given amount of solvent at a given temperature. *p. 243*

solute The substance present in the smaller amount in a solution. *p. 238*

solution A homogeneous mixture of two or more substances. *p. 238*

solvent The substance that is present in the greater amount in a solution. *p. 238*

space probes Spacecraft sent to study the moon and other planets. *p. 380*

specific gravity The ratio between the density of a substance and the density of water. *p. 177*

specific heat The amount of heat energy needed to raise the temperature of 1.0 g of a substance by 1°C. *p. 286*

sporozoan (spawr uh ZOH uhn) A protozoan that has no means of movement and that sometimes forms spores. *p. 73*

stalactite (stuh LAK tīt) A formation of calcite that extends downward from the roof of a cave. *p. 494*

stalagmite (stuh LAG mīt) A formation of calcite that extends upward from the floor of a cave. *p. 494*

stationary front A front that does not move for a time. *p. 468*

stimulus (STIHM yuh luhs) An event or a condition that causes an organism to react. *p. 30*

stomach A J-shaped, muscular sac that stores food and helps to digest it. *p. 550*

stratosphere (STRAT uh sfihr) The second layer of the atmosphere, extending from the surface of the earth to a height of 50 km. *p. 442*

streak The color of a powder mark made by a mineral as it is rubbed against a porcelain tile. *p. 393*

summer solstice (SAHL stihs) A point in the sky through which the sun passes on the first day of summer in the Northern Hemisphere. *p. 347*

sunspots Dark areas on the surface of the sun. *p. 370*

supersaturated solution A solution that has more dissolved solute than is normal for a given temperature. *p. 246*

surplus A condition that occurs when the amount of precipitation is greater than the amount of evaporation in an area. *p. 486*

suspension A heterogeneous mixture in which particles are temporarily mixed in a liquid. *p. 249*

symbiosis The close relationship between two different kinds of organisms. *p. 78*

technology The use of scientific knowledge to improve the quality of human life. *p. 12*

temperature The measure of the average kinetic energy of the particles in a sample of matter. *p. 284*

theory A hypothesis that has been tested many times and that is supported by evidence. *p. 11*

thermosphere (THER muh sfihr) The fourth layer of the atmosphere extending from the surface of the earth to a height of about 500 km. *p. 443*

thunder The loud crash that accompanies a flash of lightning. *p. 473*

thunderstorm A violent weather system that produces tall clouds, strong winds, heavy rain, lightning, thunder, and sometimes, hail and tornadoes. *p. 471*

time zones The division of the earth into 24 equal segments. *p. 343*

tissue A group of cells that are similar in structure and function. *p. 516*

tornado A small, funnel-shaped whirlwind that spins in a counterclockwise direction around an area of low pressure. *p. 475*

trachea A tube that carries air from the larynx to the lungs. *p. 573*

transverse wave A wave in which particles of matter vibrate up and down at right angles to the direction in which the wave travels. *p. 309*

troposphere (TROH puh sfihr) The first layer of the atmosphere, extending from the surface of the earth to a height of between 7 km and 16 km. *p. 442*

unsaturated solution A solution in which more solute can be dissolved. *p. 246*

Uranus The seventh planet from the sun. *p. 378*

ureter One of the two tubes that carry urine out of the kidneys. *p. 578*

urethra A tube that leads out of the bladder and carries urine out of the body. *p. 578*

vaccine A substance that contains viruses or other disease-causing agents that have been weakened and can no longer cause disease. *p. 61*

vacuoles (VAK yoo ohlz) Fluid-filled sacs in a cell. *p. 37*

valve Flaps of tissue that allow blood to flow in only one direction. *p. 567*

vascular plants Plants that have vascular tissue. *p. 85*

vascular tissue A group of tubelike cells that carries food and water from one part of a plant to another. *p. 84*

vein A blood vessel that carries blood toward the heart. *p. 565*

ventricle (VEHN truh kuhl) Each of the two lower chambers of the heart. *p. 567*

Venus The second planet from the sun. *p. 373*

vernal equinox (VER nuhl   EE kwuh nahks) A point in the sky through which the sun passes on the first day of spring in the Northern Hemisphere. *p. 348*

vertebrate (VER tuh briht) An animal that has a backbone. *p. 110*

villi Millions of tiny fingerlike structures that cover the inner wall of the small intestine. *p. 554*

virus A very small particle made up of nucleic acid with a protein covering, or protein coat. *p. 59*

vitamin An organic compound that helps to control the chemical functions of the body. *p. 541*

voluntary muscle A muscle that is under conscious control. *p. 526*

warm front A front that forms when a warmer air mass replaces a cooler air mass. *p. 467*

water budget A record of the amounts of precipitation and evaporation for an area. *p. 486*

water table The boundary between the zone of aeration and the zone of saturation. *p. 489*

waterspout A tornado that occurs over a body of water. *p. 477*

wavelength The distance from any point on a wave to the same point on the next wave. *p. 311*

weather The condition of the atmosphere in a particular place at a particular time. *p. 462*

wedge A modified inclined plane that has a thick end and a thinner or sharper end. *p. 274*

wheel and axle A simple machine made up of two wheels that turn around a pivot. *p. 276*

white blood cell A blood cell that defends the body against disease. *p. 561*

wind Moving air. *p. 450*

wind vane An instrument that measures the direction of the wind. *p. 451*

winter solstice A point in the sky through which the sun passes on the first day of winter in the Northern Hemisphere. *p. 347*

work The use of a force to move an object through a distance. *p. 267*

Index

A

Abiotic factors, 138
Absolute zero, 286
Acid rain, 151, 502
Acoustics, 325–326
Active transport, 43–44
Adaptation, 120
Adhesion, 170
African sleeping sickness, 71
Agar, 90
Age of Invertebrates, 430
AIDS (Acquired Immune Deficiency Syndrome), 60–61
Air, 399
Air bladder, 116
Air masses, 462–465
Air pollution, 151
Air pressure, 447–449
Air sac, 124
Albumen, 126
Algae, 78, 84, 86–90
Alligators, 121
Alloys, 239
Alveoli, 573
Amino acids, 35, 540
Amoeba, 71–72
Amorphous solid, 166
Amphibians, 117–119
Amplitude, 311
Anaphase, 49
Anemia, 571
Anemometer, 450–451
Angiosperms, 98, 101–104
Animal cells, 36–37
Animallike protists, 71–73
Annuals, 104
Antibiotics, 66
Antibodies, 61
Anus, 551
Aorta, 568
Apollo program, 381
Appendicitis, 551
Appendix, 551
Aqueous solutions, 239
Aquifers, 491
Archimedes' principle, 261–262
Artery, 564
Artesian well, 491
Asexual reproduction, 31
Asteroids, 363

Asthma, 575
Astronomical unit, 339
Atherosclerosis, 570
Atmosphere. *See* Earth's atmosphere.
Atom, 33
    differences among, 192–196
    representation of, 197–206
    structure of 188–191
Atomic mass, 194–195
Atomic mass unit (amu), 194
Atomic number, 192
ATP, 45
Atrium, 567
Autumnal equinox, 347
Axis tilt, 346

B

Bacilli, 64
Bacteria, 63–64
    and disease, 60–61
    growth of, 65–66
    helpful and harmful, 66–67
Balance, double-pan, 17
Balanced diet, 544–547
Balanced forces, 258
Ball-and-socket joint, 522
Barometer, 447
Bases, 50
Behavior, 128–129
Bernoulli's principle, 263
Biceps, 528
Bicycle, 277–278
Biennials, 104
Bile, 553–554
Biosphere, 139–140
Biotic factors, 138
Birds, 123–127
Bladder, 578
Blood, 560
    clotting of, 561–562
    types of, 162–163
    vessels, 564–565
Blue-green bacteria, 62–63
Body. *See* Human body.
Bohr, Niels, 190
Boiling point, 173, 293
Boiling point elevation, 247
Bones, 111, 523–524
Botulism, 66

Boyle's law, 295
Breathing, 572, 574
Brittleness, 171
Bronchi, 573
Brontosaurus, viii–1, 432
Brown algae, 88–89
Budding, 76
Buoyant force, 261

C

Calories, 546–547
Calorimeter, 288
Cambrian Period, 430
Canadian Shield, 428
Cap (mushroom), 77
Capillary, 564–565
Capillary bed, 565
Capsule, 92
Carbohydrates, 34, 538–539
Carbon-14, 424–425
Carboniferous Period, 431
Carbonization, 418
Carbon-12, 424–425
Cardiac muscle, 527
Carnivore, 144
Carrier molecules, 44
Cartilage, 111, 521
Cartilage fish, 114–115
Cast, 419
Caverns, 494–496
Cell membrane, 37, 40–43
Cell theory, 32
Cell wall, 38
Cells, 32
    of animals, 36–37
    division of, 48–49
    energy for, 45–47
    of plants, 38–39
    transport in, 40–45
Cellular respiration, 572
Celsius temperature scale, 19, 285
Cenozoic Era, 429, 433–435
Center of gravity, 260
Centrifuge, 237
Centrioles, 49
Challenger, 382
Change of stage, 172–173, 290–293
Charles's law, 296

Charon, 379
Chemical bond, 219
Chemical change, 180
Chemical digestion, 548, 552–554
Chemical energy, 265
Chemical formulas, 214–215, 223–224
Chemical property, 182
Chemical symbols, 33, 197–199
Chlorella, 87
Chlorophyll, 39
Chloroplasts, 39, 87
Cholesterol, 570
Chondrus, 90
Chordates, 110–111
Chromosomes, 36, 49
Chromosphere, 369
Cilia, 72–73
Ciliates, 72–73
Circulation, 568
Circulatory system, 560
    disorders of, 570–571
Class, 57
Classification, 56–58
Cleavage, 395
Closed fracture, 530
Club mosses, 94
Coal, 405
Cocci, 64
Cohesion, 170
Cold front, 468
Cold-blooded animal, 4–5, 112
Colloids, 250–251
Colony, 62, 86
Colorado River, 498–499
Combined forces, 257–258
Comets, 364–365
Commensalism, 148–149
Community, 143
Compound machines, 277–278
Compounds, 33, 164, 212–213
    covalent, 226–29
    ionic, 219–25
    symbols and formulas for, 214–218
Compression, 310
Compressional wave, 310
Concentrated solution, 243
Condensation point, 173
Conduction, 297, 445
Cones, 98–99
Conifer, 100
Conjugation, 73
Connective tissue, 518
Conservation, 408

Conservation of Energy, Law of, 266
Constructive interference, 315
Consumer, 144
Continental air mass, 464
Continental Divide, 497
Continental polar air mass, 465
Continental tropical air mass, 465
Contour feather, 124
Contraction, 294
Controlled experiment, 20–21
Convection, 297, 445
Convection zone, 368
Cooling systems, 299
Core (sun), 368
Coriolis effect, 455
Corona, 369
Correlation, 422
Corrosion, 182
Cotyledon, 102
Covalent bond, 226
Covalent compounds, 226–229
Cramp, 530
Cranium, 520
Craters, 350
Crescent phase, 351
Crest, 311
Cretaceous Period, 432–433
Crocodiles, 121
Crop, 124
Crystals, 166, 388–390
Cycads, 100–101
Cyst, 72

D

Decibel, 320
Deciduous plant, 99
Decomposer, 145
Deficit, water, 486–487
Deimos, 375
Density, 174–176
Dermis, 531
Desalination, 487
Destructive interference, 315
Devonian Period, 431
Dew point, 466
Diaphragm, 574
Diatom, 70
Dicot, 103
Diesel engine, 302
Diffraction, 313–314
Diffusion, 42

Digestion, 29
    absorption, 552–555
    digestive system, 548–551
Digestive enzyme, 552
Digestive glands, 552
Digestive organs, 548–551
Dilute solution, 243
Dinoflagellate, 70
Dinosaurs, viii–11, 432–433
Distillation, 235, 237
Divide, 497
DNA, 35, 36
    in cell division, 48–49
    role of, 50
Doppler effect, 321–322
Down feather, 125
Ductility, 171

E

Earth
    layers of, 340
    location of, 338–339
    magnetism of, 340–341
    origin of, 353–357
    rotation and revolution of, 342
    seasons of, 346–348
    size and shape of, 339
    time on, 343–345
Earth's atmosphere, 340
    air pressure, 447–449
    composition and structure of, 440–443
    heat transfer in, 444–446
    origin of, 356–357
    wind, 450–457
Earth's history
    fossils, 417–420
    geologic time scale, 426–429
    record of rocks, 414–416
    studying earth's past, 421–425
Earth's resources
    energy, 404–408
    identifying minerals, 392–396
Eclipse, 352
Ecology, 138
Ecosystem, 139–140
Efficiency, 272–273
Effort arm, 274
Effort force, 267
Egg cell, 92
Egg-laying mammals, 129
Eggs, bird, 126–127
Elasticity, 170
Electrical energy, 265
Electrical force, 256

Electron, 189
Electron cloud, 191
Element, 33, 164
Embryo, 126
Emphysema, 576
Endangered species, 152
Endoplasmic reticulum, 37
Endoskeleton, 111
Endospore, 65–66
Energy, 264–266
Energy levels, electron, 195–196
Energy pyramid, 146–147
Energy resources, 404–408
Environment
    biosphere, 138–140
    energy flow in biosphere,
        144–147
    populations and communities,
        141–143
    preservation of, 150–152
    symbiotic relationships in,
        148–149
Enzymes, 35
Eocene Epoch, 434
Epidermis, 531
Epithelial tissue, 517
Epoch, 429
Era, 426
Erie, Lake, 503–505
Esophagus, 549
Euglena, 69
Eutrophication, 501–502
Evergreen plant, 99
Excretion, 30, 577
Excretory system, 577–579
Exosphere, 443
Expansion, 294–295
Extensor, 529
External combustion engine, 301
External fertilization, 113
Extinct species, 152

F

Facies fossils, 421
Family, 57
Fangs, 122
Fats, 539–540
Fatty acids, 540
Feathers, 124–125
Feces, 551
Feldspars, 391
Fermentation, 76
Ferns, 95–97
Fertilization, 92
Fiber, 545

Fiddleheads, 95
Filaments, 86
Film fossils, 418
Fins, 113
First-quarter phase, 351
Fish, 113–116
Fission, 65, 407
Fixed joint, 521
Fixed pulley, 276
Flagella, 64, 70, 71
Flagellates, 71
Flexor, 529
Flood plain, 498
Fluids, forces in, 261–263
Fluorescence, 396
Food chain, 145–146
Food groups, 544–545
Food intake, 28–29
Food web, 146
Force
    center of gravity, 260
    combined forces, 257–258
    in fluids, 261–263
    kinds of, 256–257
    measurement of, 258–259
Formula unit, 224
Fossil fuels, 404–405
Fossils, 6–9, 417–420
Four-stroke engine, 302
Fracture, 395, 530
Freezing point, 172
Freezing point depression, 248
Freon, 299
Frequency, 311–312
Friction, 257
Frond, 95
Fronts, 466–469
Fruit and vegetable group,
    544–545
Fucus, 88
Fulcrum, 274
Full-moon phase, 351
Fungi
    kinds of, 75–77
    relatives of, 77–78
    traits of, 74
Fusion, 366

G

Galaxy, 338
Gall bladder, 554
Gamma rays, 366
Gas, 166
Gastric juice, 553

Gears, 278
Gem, 403
Genus, 57
Geologic column, 422
Geologic time scale, 426–429
Geothermal energy, 407
Geysers, 492
Gibbous phase, 351
Gill cover, 116
Gill slits, 110
Gills (fish), 113
Gills (mushroom), 77
Ginkgoes, 101
Glaciers, 500, 503
Gliding joint, 522
Global winds, 453–456
Glucose, 45, 46
Glycerol, 540
Graduated cylinder, 18
Grain group, 545
Gravitational force, 256
Great Lakes, 503–505
Great Salt Lake, 500
Green algae, 86–88
Greenhouse effect, 444
Ground water, 488–492
    work of, 493–496
Group (Periodic Table), 203
Growth, 28
Gymnosperms, 98, 100–101

H

Habitat, 141
Hair follicles, 532
Half-life, 423
Halite, 390
Halley's comet, 365
Hardness, 392
Hazardous wastes, 151
Heart, 567
Heart attack, 570
Heartbeat, 569
Heat, 286
    expansion and gases, 294–296
Heat energy, 265, 284–289
Heat engines, 301–303
Heat of fusion, 291
Heat of vaporization, 293
Heat transfer, 297–300
Heating systems, 298–299
Hemoglobin, 561
Herbivore, 144
Hertz, 312
Heterogeneous mixture, 235
Hibernation, 118

Highs, 448–449, 469
Hinge joint, 522
Holocene Epoch, 435
Homogeneous mixture, 235
Horsetails, 84, 94–95
Host, 66, 149
Human body
  movement and disorders, 528–530
  bones of, 523–524
  muscular system of, 525–527
  organization of, 516–518
  skeleton, 519–522
  skin of, 531–533
Humidity, 462
Huron, Lake, 503
Hurricanes, 478–481
Hutton, James, 414
Hydroelectric energy, 407
Hydrogen peroxide, 212
Hydrometer, 178
Hydrosphere, 340
Hypertension, 570
Hyphae, 75
Hypothesis, 2, 11

I

Ice Age, 434–435
Imprint, 418–419
Inborn behavior, 128
Incident wave, 313
Inclined planes, 273–274
Incubation, 127
Index fossils, 421–422
Infrared rays, 366
Inner planets, 362, 371–375
Inorganic compounds, 34
Insulation, 300
Intensity, 320
Interference, 315
Internal combustion engine, 301
Internal fertilization, 120
International Date Line, 344
International System of Units (SI), 16–19
Interphase, 48
Intestinal juice, 554
Intrusion, 416
Involuntary muscles, 526
Ionic bonds, 222–223
Ionic compounds, 223–225
Ionosphere, 443
Ions, 219–222
Isobars, 448
Isotopes, 193, 199

J

Jet engine, 303
Jet stream, 456–457, 465
Joints, 521–522
Joule, 268, 287
Jupiter, 376–377
Jurassic Period, 432

K

Karst region, 495
Kelps, 89
Kelvin scale, 286
Keratin, 531
Kidney failure, 579
Kidneys, 577–578
Kilogram, 17
Kinetic energy, 264, 284
Kinetic theory, 284–286

L

Lakes, 500–502
  Great Lakes, 503–505
Lancelet, 111
Land pollution, 151
Landfills, 151
Large intestine, 550–551
Larynx, 572
Last-quarter phase, 351
Lateral line, 116
Lattice, 225
Lawn mower, 277
Lead-206, 424
Learned behavior, 129
Leukemia, 571
Levers, 274–275
Lichen, 78
Life cycle, 28
Life processes, 28–32
Ligaments, 521
Lightning, 473
Light-year, 338
Lipids, 34
Liquid, 166
  properties of, 168–170
Liter, 18
Lithosphere, 340
Litter, 151
Liver, 553
Liverworts, 84, 91
Lizards, 4–5, 122
Local winds, 452–453
Lows, 448–449, 469

Lunar eclipse, 352
Lung cancer, 576
Lungs, 117
Luster, 394
Lymph, 566
Lymph nodes, 566
Lymphatic system, 566

M

Machines. See Compound machines; Simple machines.
Magnetic field, 367
Magnetic force, 257
Magnetism, 396
Magnetosphere, 341
Malaria, 73
Malleability, 170
Mammals, 128–132
Mammary gland, 128
Mare, 350
Mariner, 10, 372
Maritime air mass, 464
Maritime polar air mass, 464–465
Maritime tropical air mass, 464
Marrow, 524
Mars, 374–375
Marsupial, 129
Mass, 17, 164
Mass number, 193–194
Matter, 33, 164–165
  physical and chemical changes in, 179–180, 182
  physical properties of, 168–173
  states of, 166–167
Measurement, 16–19
Meat group, 544
Mechanical advantage, 271–272
Mechanical digestion, 548
Mechanical energy, 265
Mechanical waves, 309–310
Medium, 309
Melanin, 531
Melting point, 172, 291
Mendeleev, Dmitri, 201–202
Mercury, 372
Mesosphere, 442
Mesozoic Era, 429, 432–433
Metabolism, 29
Metallic ores, 402
Metamorphosis, 118
Metaphase, 49
Meteorite, 364
Meteorite impact hypothesis, 433
Meteoroids, 364

Meter, 17
Mica, 390
Michigan, Lake, 503, 505
Migration, 125
Milk group, 544
Milky Way galaxy, 338
Millibar, 447
Mineral deposits, 402
Minerals, 388–391
  identification of, 392–396
Minerals (body), 542
Miocene Epoch, 434
Mississippi River, 497–498
Mitochondria, 37
Mitosis, 48–49
Mixtures, 165
  kinds of, 234–237
  solutions, 238–248
  suspensions and colloids,
    249–251
Models (scientific), 188–191
Mohs scale, 392–393
Mold, 419
Molecule, 33, 226
Molting, 122
Monerans
  bacteria, 63–64
  blue-green bacteria, 62–63
Monocot, 103
Monotreme, 129
Moon
  characteristics of, 349–350
  eclipses of, 352
  phases of, 350–351
Moseley, Henry, 202
Mosses, 84, 91–93
Mouth, 548–549
Movable joint, 521
Movable pulley, 276
Muscle tissue, 517
Muscular system, 525–527
Mushrooms, 77
Musical instruments, 323–324
Mutualism, 148

N

Natural gas, 405
Natural resources, 397–403
Nebula, 353
Nebular hypothesis, 353–355, 371
Negative ions, 221
Nephrons, 577–578
Neptune, 378–379
Nerve cord, 110

Nerve tissue, 518
Neutron, 189
New-moon phase, 351
Newton, 258
Niche, 142
Nitrogen-fixing bacteria, 67
Nodal line, 311
Node, 311
Noise pollution, 326
Nonmetallic ores, 402
Nonrenewable resources, 398,
  401
Nonseed plants, 84–85
  algae, 86–90
  club mosses, horsetails, and
    ferns, 94–97
  mosses and liverworts, 91–93
Nonsilicate minerals, 391
Nonvascular plants, 85
Notochord, 110
Nuclear energy, 266, 407
Nuclear force, 257
Nuclear membrane (cell), 36
Nucleic acids, 35
Nucleus, 36, 189
Numbers pyramid, 147
Nutrient, 538
Nutrition
  balanced diet, 544–547
  carbohydrates, proteins, and
    fats, 538–540
  vitamins, minerals, and water,
    541–543

O

Obesity, 547
Occluded front, 469
Oceans, origin of, 356
Ogallala aquifer, 491
Oligocene Epoch, 434
Omnivore, 145
Ontario, Lake, 503
Open fracture, 530
Order, 57
Ordovician Period, 430
Ore, 402
Organ, 516
Organ system, 516
Organelles, 36–39
Organic compounds, 34–35
Organism, 28
Oscilloscope, 320
Osmosis, 42–43
Outer planets, 362–363, 376–379
Ozone, 366, 442

P

Paleocene Epoch, 434
Paleontologists, 417
Paleozoic Era, 429–431
Pancreas, 554
Pancreatic juice, 554
Paramecium, 73
Parasite, 66, 149
Parasitism, 149
Partially movable joint, 521
Pascal, 262
Pascal's law, 262
Passive transport, 41–43
Pelvis, 521
Penumbra, 352
Perennials, 104
Period, 206
Periodic law, 202
Periodic Table, 201–206
Periods, 429
Peristalsis, 549
Permeability, 488–489
Permeable material, 40
Permian Period, 431
Petrified remains, 417
Petroleum, 404
Pharynx, 572
Phases (moon), 350–351
Phobos, 375
Phosphorescence, 396
Photosphere, 369
Photosynthesis, 46–47, 84
Phylum, 57
Physical change, 179–180
Physical properties, 168–173
Pioneer 11, 378
Pitch, 321
Pivot joint, 522
Placenta, 130
Placental mammals, 130–132
Planets, 362–363
Plankton, 88
Plant cells, 38–39
Plantlike protists, 69–70
Plants
  algae, 86–90
  angiosperms, 98, 101–104
  club mosses, horsetails, and
    ferns, 94–97
  gymnosperms, 100–101
  mosses and liverworts, 91–93
  nonseed, 84–85
  seed, 98–99
Plasma (blood), 560

Plasma (sun), 167, 367
Plastids, 38–39
Platelet, 561
Pleistocene Epoch, 434–435
Pliocene Epoch, 434
Pluto, 379
Polar air mass, 464
Polar easterlies, 456
Pollutant, 150
Pollution, 150–151, 498, 502
Polyatomic ions, 222
Ponds, 500–502
Population, 143
Pores, 532
Porosity, 488
Positive ions, 220
Potential energy, 264
Pouched mammals, 129
Power, 269–270
Precambrian Era, 426, 428–429
Precious stones, 403
Precipitation, 472
Predator, 145
Predicting weather, 470
Pressure, 262, 295
Pressure belts, 453–454
Pressure gradient, 449
Prevailing westerlies, 456
Prey, 145
Producer, 144
Prominence, 370
Prophase, 49
Proteins, 35, 540
Protists
    animallike, 71–73
    plantlike, 69–70
    traits of, 68–69
Protococcus, 86
Proton, 189
Protoplanets, 354
Protostar, 353
Protozoan, 71
Pseudopod, 71
Pulleys, 275–276

Q

Quartz, 390, 391
Quaternary Period, 434–435

R

Radiant energy, 444
Radiation, 297, 444
Radiation zone, 368

Radioactive decay, 423
Radioactive element, 423
Radioactive waste, 407
Radiometric dating, 423–425
Rarefaction, 310
Rectum, 551
Recycling, 408
Red algae, 89–90
Red blood cell, 561
Red marrow, 524
Red tide, 70
Reflected wave, 313
Reflection, 313
Refraction, 314
Relative age, 415
Renewable resources, 398–400
Reproduction, 31
    in bacteria, 65
    in birds, 126–127
    in mosses, 92–93
Reptiles, 120–122
Resistance arm, 274
Resistance force, 267
Resonance, 317–318
Resources. *See* Earth's
    resources.
Respiration, 30, 45
Respiratory system
    breathing, 574
    disorders of, 575–576
    parts of, 572–573
Response, 30
Reverberation, 325
Revolution (earth), 342
Rhizoid, 91
Rhizome, 95
Ribosomes, 37
Ribs, 520
River system, 497
Rivers, 497–499
RNA, 35, 37
Rotation (earth), 342
Runoff, 487

S

St. Lawrence River, 503–504
Salamanders, 119
Saliva, 549, 553
Salivary glands, 553
Salmonella, 67
Satellite, 380
Saturated solutions, 245–246
Saturn, 377–378

Scales, 113
Scavenger, 145
Schrodinger, Erwin, 191
Science, 1–11
    skills of, 16–21
Scientific names, 58
Screw, 274
Sea squirt, 111
Seasons, 347–348
Sedimentary rock, 414–415
Seed plants
    angiosperms, 101–104
    gymnosperms, 100–101
    traits of, 98–99
Semipermeable material, 40–41
Semiprecious stones, 403
Sewage, 150
Sexual reproduction, 31
Shaft, 124
Shell, 126
Shell membrane, 126
Sickle cell disease, 571
Silicate minerals, 390–391
Silurian Period, 431
Simple machines, 271–276
Sinkholes, 493
Skeletal muscle, 527
Skeletal system, 519
Skeleton, 519–522
Skin, 531–533
Slime mold, 77
Small intestine, 550
Smith, William, 422
Smog, 151
Smooth muscle, 527
Snakes, 122
Soil, 400
Soil erosion, 400
Solar collector, 406
Solar eclipse, 352
Solar energy, 406–407
Solar flare, 370
Solar radiation, 366
Solar system, 338
    inner planets, 371–375
    members of, 362–365
    outer planets, 376–379
    space exploration in, 380–383
    sun, 366–370
Solar wind, 367
Solid, 166
    properties of, 170–171
Solubility, 243–245
Solubility curve, 244
Solute, 238

Solutions, 235
  how substances dissolve, 240
  nature of, 238–239
  properties of, 243–248
  rate of solution, 241–242
Solvent, 238
Sonar, 319
Sonic boom, 326
Sound
  acoustics, 325–326
  intensity and pitch, 320–321
  musical instruments, 323–324
  noise pollution, 326
  quality of, 322
  speed of, 318–319
  wave travel, 316–318
  See also Waves.
Sound energy, 265
Source region, 463
Space exploration, 380–383
Space probes, 380–381
Space shuttle, 382
Species, 57
Specific gravity, 176–178, 395
Specific heat, 287
Sperm cell, 92
Spinal column, 520
Spindle, 49
Spirilla, 64
Spirogyra, 87
Spongy bone, 523
Spore, 73, 92, 96
Spore cases, 75
Sporozoan, 73
Sprain, 529
Springs, 492
Stalactite, 496
Stalagmite, 496
Stalk (mushroom), 77
Starches, 34, 538
States of matter, 290–291
Stationary front, 468
Sternum, 520
Stimulus, 30
Stomach, 550
Storm cell, 472
Strain (muscle), 530
Stratosphere, 442
Streak, 393
Strip mining, 405
Stroke, 570
Sublimation, 179
Subscript, 199, 214
Substance, 164
Sucrose, 213
Sugars, 34, 538–539

Summer solstice, 347
Sun, 366–370
Sunspots, 370
Superior, Lake, 503, 505
Superposition, Law of, 415
Supersaturated solutions, 246–247
Surface tension, 169–170
Surplus (water), 486–487
Suspensions, 249
Sweat glands, 531–532
Symbiosis, 78, 148
Synthesis, 29

T

Tadpoles, 118
Tailed amphibians, 119
Tailless amphibians, 117–118
Technology, 12–15
Telophase, 49
Temperature, 19, 284–288
Tendons, 528
Tensile strength, 171
Tertiary Period, 433–435
Theory, 11
Thermosphere, 443
Thunder, 473
Thunderhead, 472
Thunderstorms, 471–474
Tidal energy, 407
Tidal surge, 480
Time, 343–345
Time zones, 343–344
Tissue, 516
Tornado warning, 477
Tornado watch, 477
Tornadoes, 475–477
Tortoises, 121
Trace fossil, 419
Trachea, 573
Trade winds, 456
Transfusion, 562
Transport, 40–44
Transverse wave, 309
Triassic Period, 432
Triceps, 528
Trilobites, 421–422
Tropical air mass, 464
Troposphere, 442
Trough, 311
Turtles, 121
Tyndall effect, 251
Tyrannosaurus, 432

U

Ultrasonic sounds, 321
Ultraviolet rays, 366
Ulva, 86
Umbra, 352
Unbalanced forces, 257
Unchanged remains, 420
Unconformity, 415–416
Uniformitarianism, 414
Unsaturated solutions, 246
Uranium-238, 423–424
Uranus, 378–79
Urea, 577
Ureters, 578
Urethra, 578
Urine, 577

V

Vaccine, 61
Vacuoles, 37
Valve, 567
Van Allen belts, 341
Vane, 124
Vascular plants, 85
Vascular tissue, 84–85
Vein, 565
Vein (rock), 401
Vena cava, 568
Ventricle, 567
Venus, 373
Vernal equinox, 348
Vertebrae, 520
Vertebrates
  amphibians, 117–119
  birds, 123–127
  fish, 113–116
  mammals, 128–132
  reptiles, 120–122
  traits of, 110–112
Viking spacecraft, 375
Villi, 554–555
Viruses, 59
  reproduction of, 60
Viscosity, 168–169
Visible light, 366
Vitamins, 541–542
Volume, 18–19
Voluntary muscles, 526
Volvox, 87
Voyager missions, 381

W

Warm front, 467
Warm-blooded animals, 4–5, 112
Water, 398
  body, 553
  budget, 486–487
  ground, 488–492
  lakes and ponds, 500–502
  rivers, 497–499
  work of ground water, 493–496
Water cycle, 398–99, 486
Water pollution, 150
Water table, 489–490
Watershed, 497
Waterspout, 477
Wavelength, 311

Waves
  behavior of, 313–315
  properties of, 308–312
  See also Sound.
Weak interactions, 257
Weather
  air masses, 462–465
  fronts, 466–470
  hurricanes, 478–481
  thunderstorms, 471–474
  tornadoes, 475–477
Wedge, 274
Weight, 258–259
Wheel and axle, 276
White blood cell, 561
Wildlife protection, 152
Wind, 450–457

Windpipe, 549
Winter solstice, 347–348
Woolly mammoth, 420
Work, 267–268

X

X rays, 366

Y

Yellow marrow, 524

Z

Zone of aeration, 489
Zone of saturation, 489

Credits

Cover: Davis Meltzer

Maps and graphs: JAK Graphics

Activities: Phil Jones

Puzzler: Ernie Albanese

All art by Silver Burdett & Ginn unless otherwise indicated.

Contributing artists Ernie Albanese: 219, 222, 223; Ames and Zak: 85, 92, 95, 96, 103, 124; Michael Adams: 489, 491, 495; Ralph Brillhart: 139 *l.*; Rick Cooley: 15; Mark Hannon: 340, 342, 346, 362, 371, 376, 378, 379, 442, 444, 452, 459; Seward Hung: 19 *m.,b'.*, 59, 188, 258, 262, 273, 274, 275, 311, 315, 322, 325, 328, 364, 366, 447, 520, 522, 525, 526, 528, 530, 531, 534, 543, 574; Susan Johnston: 19 *t.*, 57, 139 *r.*, 147, 338, 339, 341, 343, 344, 345, 347, 349, 367, 368, 399; Philip Jones: 466, 468, 469, 479, 506; George Kelvin: 60, 64 *t.*, 65, 69 *t.*, 166, 169, 224, 226 *m.*, 227, 229, 240, 241, 261, 272, 297, 299, 302, 389, 549, 553 *t.*, 554; Peter Krempasky: 278; Joseph LeMonnier: 244, 263, 422, 423, 424, 462, 493, 545, 576; Richard Loehle: 156, 330, 508, 582; David Meltzer: 2, 3, 4, 6, 7, 10 *t.*, 354, 356, 472, 473; Rebecca Merrilees: 20, 21, 28, 56, 75, 77, 98; Denise Mickalson: 164, 226 *l.*, 312; Jessica Moore: 291; Lisa O'Hanlon: 351, 359, 399 *r.*, 467, 468, 583; Taylor Oughton: viii, 1, 8, 9, 11, 429 *b.*, 430, 431, 432; Alex Pietersen: 332; Tom Powers: 29, 34, 35, 41, 42, 44, 191, 192, 193, 195, 200, 220, 221, 449, 453, 454, 456, 488, 538, 540, 552; Albert Pucci: 154; Stacy Rogers: 397, 405 *b.*, 486, 487; Dolores Santoliquido: 36, 37, 38, 45, 47, 48, 49, 50, 52, 62, 64 *b.*, 69 *b.*, 70, 73, 110, 111, 113, 116, 118, 121, 123, 404, 405, 567, 580; Bill Schmidt: 134, 267, 271, 280; Catherine Twomey: 521, 523, 548, 550, 553 *b.*, 556; Herman Vestal: 125 *t.*; Craig Zuckerman: 516, 517, 562, 563, 565, 566, 568, 572, 573, 577, 578.

All photographs by Silver Burdett & Ginn unless otherwise indicated.

Table of Contents iii: Animals, Animals/© Ralph A. Reinhold. v: The Library of Congress. vi: Alvin Chung/Sygma.

Chapter 1 2: *t.* William E. Ferguson; *b.* Denver Museum of Natural History Archives. 4: IMAGERY. 5: *t.l.* © Roger Tory Peterson/Photo Researchers, Inc.; *t.r.* © Pam Hickman/Valan Photos; *b.* Animals Animals/© Bruce Davidson. 6: British Museum (Natural History); 7: Neg. No. 324393 Photo, R.T. Bird, Courtesy Department of Library Services, American Museum of Natural History. 10: *b.l.* Neg. No. 311399, Courtesy Department of Library Services, American Museum of Natural History; *b.r.* Trans. No. V/C 2419 Courtesy Department of Library Services, American Museum of Natural History. 12: *t.* Richard Gross/The Stock Market of N.Y.; *m.* Courtesy Phillips Fibers Corporation; *b.* Courtesy Burlington Industries. 13: *t.* NASA; *m.l.* © National Oceanic & Atmospheric Assn. (NOAA)/Science Photo Library/Photo Researchers, Inc.; *b.l.* Earth Satellite/Science Photo Library/Photo Researchers, Inc.; *b.r.* Terry Newfarmer/University of Utah. 14: *t.l.* © CNRI/Science Photo Library/Photo Researchers, Inc.; *m.l.* William E. Ferguson; *b.l.* Runk/Schoenberger/Grant Heilman Photography; *b.m.* George H. Harrison/Grant Heilman Photography; *b.r.* Alan Pitcairn/Grant Heilman Photography. 21: *b.l.* © Jon Wilson/Science Photo Library/Photo Researchers, Inc.; *b.m.* E.V. Grave/Phototake; *b.r.* E.R. Degginger.

Unit One Opener 24: *b.l.* Rod Planck/Tom Stack & Associates; *b.r.* Courtesy of Bio-Rad Microscience Division, Cambridge, Mass. 24–25: *t.r.* David Muench/H. Armstrong Roberts; *b.r.* Animals, Animals/© Ralph A. Reinhold.

Chapter 2 26: William E. Ferguson. 30: *t.* Walter Chandoha; *b.l.* © M.I. Walker/Photo Researchers, Inc.; *b.r.* E.R. Degginger. 31: Walter Chandoha. 32: *l.* © Eric Grave/Photo Researchers, Inc. 46: E.R. Degginger. 49–50: © Eric Grave/Photo Researchers, Inc.

Chapter 3 54: Kerry T. Givens/Tom Stack & Associates. 58: *t.* Entheos. Breck P. Kent. 59: *b.l.* © E.H. Cook/Science Photo Library/Photo Researchers, Inc.; *b.m.* © Lee Simon/Science Source/Photo Researchers, Inc. 61: © Science Photo Library. 63: *t.* Phil Degginger; *r.* © Sinclair Stammers/Science Photo Library/Photo Researchers, Inc. 66: *t.l.* Drs. George B. Chapman and Marin Costa/Georgetown University; *t.r.* © Lab of A.M. Siegelman; *b.* Medichrome/The Stock Shop. 67: *l.* © John Walsh/Photo Researchers, Inc. 68: T.E. Adams/Click, Chicago. 70: *t.l.* © Michael Abbey/Photo Researchers, Inc.; *m* © Eric Grave/Photo Researchers, Inc. 71: *t.* Ed Reschke/Peter Arnold, Inc.; *b.l.*, *b.r.* © M. Abbey/Photo Researchers, Inc.; 73: *m.* Manfred Kage/Peter Arnold, Inc. 74: © Biophoto Associates/Photo Researchers, Inc. 75: Taurus Photos. 76: © Dr. Jeremy Burgess/Science Photo Library/Photo Researchers, Inc. 77: *m.*, *b.* E.R. Degginger. 78: *t.l.* W.H. Hodge/Peter Arnold, Inc.; *m.* K.L. Tomkins/Tom Stack & Associates; *r.* Breck P. Kent.

Chapter 4 82: William E. Ferguson. 84: *t.l.* © Farrell Grehan/Photo Researchers, Inc.; *t.m.* Runk/Schoenberger/Grant Heilman Photography; *t.r.* Ken Davis/Tom Stack & Associates; *b.l.* Grant Heilman Photography. 86: *l.* Breck P. Kent; *m.*, inset Runk/Schoenberger/Grant Heilman Photography; *r.* Manfred Kage/Peter Arnold, Inc. 87: *l.* E.R. Degginger. 88: *l.* Phil Degginger; *r.* W.H. Hodge/Peter Arnold, Inc. 89: Tom Smoyer/Harbor Branch Foundation. 90: *t.* Heather Angel/Biophotos; *l.* Martin M. Rotker/Taurus Photos. 91: *l.* John Shaw/Tom Stack & Associates; *r.* Rod Planck/Tom Stack & Associates. 94: Runk/Schoenberger/Grant Heilman Photography. 95: *t.l.* Ed Reschke/Peter Arnold, Inc.; *t.r.* Walter Hodge/Peter Arnold, Inc. 97: Trans. No. K10234(4) Courtesy Department of Library Services, American Museum of Natural History; inset Labs of A.M. Siegelman. 99: E.R. Degginger. 100: *l.* Tom Stack/Tom Stack & Associates; *m.* © Robert Dunne/Photo Researchers, Inc.; *r.* Lysbeth Corsi/Tom Stack & Associates. 101: *t.*, *m.* W.H. Hodge/Peter Arnold, Inc. 102: *l.*, *r.* John Shaw/Tom Stack & Associates; *m.* E.R. Degginger.

Chapter 5 108: Fridmar Damm/Leo deWys, Inc. 110: E.R. Degginger. 111: *t.* © Tom McHugh/Photo Researchers, Inc.; *b.* Heather Angel/Biofotos. 112: *t.l.* © George Porter/Photo Researchers, Inc; *b.m.* © Tom McHugh/Steinhart Aquarium/Photo Researchers, Inc.; *t.r.* © Gregory K. Scott/Photo Researchers, Inc.; *t.r.* © Leonard Lee Rue, III/National Audubon Society/Photo Researchers, Inc. 113: Shostal Associates. 114: *t.l.* Heather Angel/Biofotos; *t.r.* Tom Stack/Tom Stack & Associates; *m.* Doug Wechsler; *b.* Richard Ellis/Photo Researchers, Inc. 115: *t.* Jane Burton/Bruce Coleman; *b.l.*, *b.m.*, *b.r.* E.R. Degginger. 117: © Tom McHugh/Steinhart Aquarium/Photo Researchers, Inc. 118: John J. Gerard. 119: Thomas A. Wiewandt. 120: Alan Blank/Bruce Coleman. 121: *l.* © Russe Kinne/Photo Researchers, Inc.; *r.* Tui A. DeRoy/Bruce Coleman. 122: *t.l.* E.R. Degginger; *t.r.* © Larry Miller/Photo Researchers, Inc.; *b.* Jen and Des Bartlett/Bruce Coleman. 123: *r.* Animals Animals/Oxford Scientific Films/© G.I. Bernard. 126: Warren Garst/Tom Stack & Associates. 127: *t.* John F. O'Connor/PhotoNats.; *b.* Animals Animals/© Margot Conte. 128: *l.* E.R. Degginger; *m.* © Merlin D. Tuttle/Photo Researchers, Inc.; *r.* © William Curtsinger/Photo Researchers, Inc. 129: *t.l.* © Tom McHugh/Taronga-Zoo/Photo Researchers, Inc.; *t.r.* © Tom McHugh/Photo Researchers, Inc. 130: *l.* © Merlin Tuttle/Photo Researchers, Inc. *r.* Gregory K. Scott; *b.r.* Phil Degginger. 131: *t.l.* © Tom McHugh/Photo Researchers, Inc.; *t.r.* © Richard Ellis/Photo Researchers, Inc.; *m.r.* Thomas Kitchin/Valan Photos; *b.l.* Brian Milne/First Light, Toronto. 132: *t.* R.S. Virdee/Grant Heilman Photography; *l.* Gerald Corsi/Tom Stack & Associates; *b.* © Farrell Grehan/Photo Researchers, Inc.

Chapter 6 136: M.P. Kahl/Tom Stack & Associates. 139: John Gerlach/Tom Stack & Associates. 140: Peter Menzel. 142: *l.* Breck P. Kent; *r.* © Kenneth W. Fink/Photo Researchers, Inc.; *r.* © Farrell Grehan/Photo Researchers, Inc. 143: *l.* © Alexander Lowry/Photo Researchers, Inc. 144: *t.l.* Animals Animals/© Patti Murray; *t.r.* G.R. Roberts; *b.l.* Breck P. Kent; *b.r.* IMAGERY. 145: *t.r.* Richard Thom/Tom Stack & Associates; *b.l.* © Yvonne Freund/Photo Researchers, Inc.; *b.m.*, *b.r.* © Stephen Dalton/Photo Researchers, Inc. 148: *b.l.* © Leonard Lee Rue, III/Photo Researchers, Inc.; *b.r.* E.R. Degginger. 149: *t.* Howard Hall/Earth Images; *r.* supplied by Carolina Biological Supply Company. Photographed by William R. West. 150: *b.* Larry Lefever/Grant Heilman Photography; *t.* © Tom McHugh/Photo Researchers, Inc. 151: Jerry Via. 152: *l.* Runk/Schoenberger/Grant Heilman Photography; inset *l.* © James R. Fisher/Photo Researchers, Inc.; inset *r.* Patricia Caulfield/Photo Researchers, Inc.; *r.* © Kenneth W. Fink/Photo Researchers, Inc. 158: Fred Bauendam/Peter Arnold, Inc.

Unit Two Opener 160: *l.* Manfred Kage/Peter Arnold, Inc.; 161: *t.l.* New York Public Library; *t.r.* Thierry Rannou/Gamma-Liaison; *b.* Dr. Gary Settles/Science Photo Library.

Chapter 7 162: © Science Photo Library/Photo Researchers, Inc. 165: *t.l.* Breck P. Kent/Earth Scenes; *t.m.*, *b.r.* Runk/Shoenberger/Grant Heilman Photography. 167: E.R. Degginger. 168: Yoav/Phototake. 169: *t.l.* Alan Blank/Bruce Coleman; *b.* Yoav/Phototake. 170: Doug Handell/The Stock Market of N.Y. 171: *t.l.* Dave Davidson/The Stock Market of N.Y.; *b.l.* Fred Ward/Black Star; *r.* David Barnes/The Stock Market of N.Y. 172: Mike Price/Bruce Coleman. 176: Alan Gurney/The Stock Market of N.Y. 178: *r.* E.R. Degginger. 179: *l.* James Holland/Stock, Boston; *r.* Cary Wolinsky/Stock, Boston. 182: *l.*, *m.* Dan Cornish/ESTO; *r.* Andy Caulfield/The Image Bank.

Chapter 8 186: © Jerry Schad/Photo Researchers, Inc. 189: *l.* Kennedy/TexaStock. 190: Lawrence Berkeley Laboratories. 192: *b.l.*, *b.m.* Yoav/Phototake. 194: Billy Grimes/Leo deWys, Inc. 198: *l.* © George E. Jones, III/Photo Researchers, Inc.; *r.* Dallas and John Heaton/Click, Chicago. 201: Yoav/Phototake. 202: *l.*, *r.* E.R. Degginger. 203: E.R. Degginger/Bruce Coleman; except *b.r.*, Yoav/Phototake.

612